THE INTERNATIONAL CITY MANAGERS' ASSOCIATION

Municipal Management Series

MUNICIPAL POLICE ADMINISTRATION

MUNICIPAL MANAGEMENT SERIES

Edward J. Steenberg

MUNICIPAL
POLICE ADMINISTRATION

Fifth Edition, 1961

*Published for the Institute for Training
in Municipal Administration by*

THE INTERNATIONAL CITY MANAGERS' ASSOCIATION
1313 EAST 60TH STREET
CHICAGO, ILLINOIS

Library of Congress Catalog Card Number 61–7725

PRINTED IN THE UNITED STATES OF AMERICA
LITHOPRINTED BY CUSHING-MALLOY, INC., ANN ARBOR, MICHIGAN
BOUND BY BROCK AND RANKIN, INC., CHICAGO, ILLINOIS

FOREWORD

Municipal Police Administration is one of a series of 10 volumes on municipal administration published by the International City Managers' Association. Each volume is a complete and separate training and reference manual dealing with one field of municipal administration.

The nature and approach of this series can best be explained by a brief review of its origin and development. In 1934 the International City Managers' Association received the first of several special grants from the Spelman Fund of New York for the preparation and administration of in-service training courses for municipal officials at the administrative or management level. This training program has been developed by the Association through its Institute for Training in Municipal Administration.

In its early years the Institute confined its training activities solely to training by the correspondence course method. This, of course, required the preparation of study materials. It was soon discovered that the published texts available were not suitable for the kind of training for which the Institute was established. It was necessary, therefore, for the Institute to prepare its own training texts. By 1941 eight texts had been published, and all eight have been revised several times.

Two new courses and texts were added in 1958 and 1959 to meet special training needs that have developed in recent years. *Supervisory Methods in Municipal Administration* is designed chiefly for on-the-job training of supervisory personnel to work effectively toward organizational goals while serving with understanding in the task of directing employees. *Management Practices for Smaller Cities* is intended for in-service training of mayors, city managers, city clerks, public service directors, and other administrative officials. The volume provides an acquaintance with sound principles and practices of administration in all major municipal activities. *The Technique of Municipal Administration*, now in its fourth edition (1958), is the over-all management manual for chief administrators and department heads in cities of all sizes.

Some of these volumes have been prepared under the direction of a single editor or compiler; others are the product of many contributors. All, however, have drawn heavily on the experience of practical administrators, and all have been subjected to the tempering fire of many critics selected from among outstanding administrators, consultants, and students of municipal administration.

During the first seven years after the Institute was established the texts were made available only in connection with enrollment in its correspondence courses. It soon became apparent, however, that this restrictive policy required modification to meet two new demands. First, there was a demand for these texts for use in connection with group training projects, including both in-service training for public officials and pre-entry schooling provided by colleges and universities. Second, there was an increasingly insistent demand that these texts be made available as reference volumes for public officials and students of local government. Early in 1941 this demand was acknowledged by lifting the ban on the sale of these unique training texts, and they were made available for purchase through the International City Managers' Association.

The two distinguishing features of the volumes in this series are traceable directly to their origin. First, they approach municipal problems from the point of view of top-level administrators — city managers, department heads, and their principal aides. Second, because they were prepared as the basis for training courses, their emphasis is on the "how" rather than the "what" of municipal administration. They are not intended as detailed manuals or as expositions of model systems of administration, but their objective is to help the administrator analyze his duties and responsibilities and to suggest approaches and methods that other administrators have proved by actual experience.

These texts during the past 27 years have established their value both as training manuals and as reference manuals. They are widely used by universities and colleges in courses in municipal administration, particularly at the graduate level. They also are used as the basic texts in group in-service training classes for city hall administrative personnel. Finally, chief administrators and department heads of many local governments use the 10 books in the series as guides in solving local problems.

Orin F. Nolting, *Executive Director*
The International City Managers' Association

Chicago
January, 1961

PREFACE

Urbanization is a fact of life as the United States moves through the second half of the twentieth century. It is a fact which underscores not only a growth of population but also developments in transportation, in communications, and in science. The acceleration of urbanization has had a profound impact on police work. It has demonstrated a need for police agencies to be more adequately prepared to meet problems both of greater magnitude and of greater scope than ever before.

Nowhere is this need felt more keenly than in the preparation of policemen to assume management responsibilities in the line and staff services of police departments. In general, police departments have kept up to date in science and equipment, giving the law breaker no advantage in technology or mobility. Yet it has become clear that police agencies must also be concerned with making good officers out of good policemen. A man with natural attributes of tact, judgment, and ability to appraise men, and trained by experience, can still fall short of being a first-class commanding officer unless he masters and keeps abreast of the techniques and methods of administration -- planning, organization, direction, coordination, reporting, and budgeting. The purpose of this volume is to make available to police officers, especially those who aspire to administrative posts, the best accepted administrative methods applied specifically to police problems.

This volume is the fifth edition of *Municipal Police Administration*. The first edition was issued in 1938, the others in 1943, 1950, and 1954. As was the case with prior editions, special efforts have been made to cover new developments as well as basic principles which another six years of experience show are sound. Thus this book is not only a text — it is a day-to-day working manual.

Because of the lineage that binds all editions of this work, it can be said that this fifth edition reflects the handiwork of many men. Foremost among them were the late Lyman S. Moore, then Assistant Director of the Institute for Training in Municipal Administration, who supervised the preparation of the 1938 edition, and O. W. Wilson, then Professor of Police Administration and Dean of the School of Criminology, University of California, and now Superintendent of Police, Chicago, Illinois, who edited the 1943, 1950, and 1954 editions. Mr. Wilson was assisted as co-editor in the 1943 edition by Theo Hall, then Chief of Police of Wilmette, Illinois. Among the specialists who assisted in the preparation of previous editions were: John D. Holstrom, Franklin M. Kreml, J. A. Lindquist, W. H. Parker, John P. Peper, Donald C. Stone, the late August Vollmer, and Jeter L. Williamson.

The present volume is a complete revision of the fourth edition. The editor is Richard L. Holcomb, Associate Professor and Chief of the Bureau of Police Science, the State University of Iowa. He has been a staff member of the Traffic Institute of Northwestern University; a protection superintendent for Montgomery, Ward and Company, Kansas City, Missouri; and lieutenant and assistant director of the Police Academy for the Kansas City, Missouri, Police Department. He is the author of many publications in the field of police and is book review editor for the *Journal of Criminal Law, Criminology, and Police Science.*

Three chapters in this volume present substantially new or revised material. These are Chapter 6, "Juvenile Delinquency Control," which was rewritten by Mr. Holcomb with considerable assistance from Michael J. Delaney, Captain and Director of Crime Prevention, Chicago Police Department; Chapter 15, "Police Public Relations Programs," a new chapter by Ned L. Wall, Staff Assistant, the International City Managers' Association; and Chapter 16, "Police Administration: The Future," a new chapter prepared by Ray Ashworth, Director of the Field Services Division, International Association of Chiefs of Police.

The following persons reviewed, revised, and rewrote other chapters: Bernard L. Garmire, Chief of Police, Tucson, Arizona, Chapter 2, "Police Organization," and Chapter 3, "Police Management"; Donald E. Nemetz, former Staff Member, Public Administration Service, Chapter 4, "Personnel Management"; Howard W. Hoyt, former Program Director, Law Enforcement Training, School of Police Administration and Public Safety, Michigan State University, Chapter 5, "Training"; Ray Dahl, Deputy Director in Charge of Training, Police Department, Milwaukee, Wisconsin, Chapter 7, "The Patrol Function"; Joseph D. Nicol, Professor, School of Police Administration and Public Safety, Michigan State University, Chapter 8, "Crime Investigation"; Bernard C. Brannon, Chief of Police, Kansas City, Missouri, Chapter 9, "Vice Control"; Bernard R. Caldwell, Director, Traffic Institute of Northwestern University, Chapter 10, "Traffic Supervision"; J. A. Lindquist, Captain, Police Department, Berkeley, California, Chapter 11, "Communications"; Samuel G. Chapman, Assistant Professor, School of Police Administration and Public Safety, Michigan State University, Chapter 12, "Records" (with a review by Herman Goldstein, Executive Assistant to the Superintendent of Police, Chicago); George D. Eastman, Director, the Police-Human Relations Study, School of Police Administration and Public Safety, Michigan State University, Chapter 13, "Other Police Problems"; and S. R. Schrotel, Chief of Police, Cincinnati, Ohio, Chapter 14, "The Police and the Public." Mr. Wall also worked with the editor in preparing Chapters 1, 6, 14, and 16.

The Institute is deeply grateful to these persons for the time and effort they have devoted to this book. Grateful acknowledgement also is made to O. W. Wilson for his wise counsel concerning the content.

Robert L. Brunton and David S. Arnold, respectively Assistant Director and Publications Director of the International City Managers' Association, reviewed the entire manuscript, worked with the editor on content and arrangement, and supervised preparation of copy for the press. The International City Managers' Association is responsible for the final content and arrangement of this book.

Institute for Training in
Municipal Administration

Chicago
January, 1961

TABLE OF CONTENTS

LIST OF FIGURES

LIST OF TABLES

Chapter 1

POLICE ADMINISTRATION: PAST AND PRESENT

Ours is an age of change. In a short space of time ours has become an industrialized and urbanized nation. The man born in 1900 has seen us become a people on wheels and threaten to become a people on wings. Our friend who has lived through all of the 20th century thus far has seen many changes, among them those brought by depression and economic boom, mobilization for war, and, more recently, mobilization for an uneasy peace. He has seen decades take on characteristics epitomized by such labels as "The Roaring Twenties," "The Fabulous Fifties," and (in a hopeful vein) "The Soaring Sixties." Each label carries its implications of attitudes differing from the decade before, and the one following. Transportation, communication, science, and many other aspects of life have undergone radical changes with profound effects on our society. As will be shown later in this volume, these changes have had their impact on police work.

The impact of change on police work is not merely one of magnitude. It is true that between 1950 and 1960 the United States population grew by 18 per cent and the number of housing units by 28 per cent and that this growth brought a natural increase in the number of lawless persons, in the number of crimes, and in the number of officers needed to keep the peace. But as every policeman knows, the scope of police work today is not explained simply by arithmetic. Urbanization has brought more people closer together, multiplying the opportunities for the lawless to operate and their targets for depredations. Changes in our way of living, in some cases, have increased social tensions — the problem of juvenile delinquency a case in point. The introduction and almost universal use of the automobile has created problems of a kind policemen never had to deal with before; it has established a new kind of law violator who cannot be treated with the clear-cut distinctions previously held to separate the "good" people from the "bad" people.

In our study of police administration we need to determine what are the major influences on police work today. We need to know also what the purposes of police work are and how they have been affected by social, scientific, and technological change. We need to know what relationships exist, external and internal, and how they affect police work. Finally, we need to know what goals are valid for police work today and how administrative techniques must be used to achieve those goals. To outline these influences, purposes, relationships, and goals is the purpose of this chapter. By so doing we will obtain a perspective of past developments as well as of major police problems today.

Development of Police Administration

The American police system had its beginnings in England. The colonial and post-Revolution organization of law enforcement was a direct outgrowth of more than nine centuries of development in the British Isles. In the middle of the 19th century, local police organizations again were greatly influenced by the success of Sir Robert Peel's

1

revamping of the London police force in 1829. However, many of the techniques and devices currently used are of recent origin, and the impact of 20th century science and technology is evident.

Historic Background

Late in the ninth century every English freeman was required by King Alfred to pledge (bail or sponsor) for the good behavior of his neighbor in the same group in his community. Freemen who held no land were required to group themselves into "tythings" (10 families to a tything) under a chief tythingman elected from their own group in order to be worth security for their pledge. The chief tythingman was held responsible for raising an alarm called the "hue and cry" when a felon or escaped suspect was known to be at large. A group of 10 tythings with a responsible head was called a "hundred." A "shire" (county) was a group of hundreds under a "shire-reeve," the forerunner of the modern sheriff. The shire-reeve at this time was the supreme judicial and police authority in the county and was in control of the militia. All men went armed; hence the militia was virtually the *posse comitatus,* or ablebodied men, of the county.

Although this early police structure was sound in many respects, it was an emergency organization, and it was not suitable to maintaining continuous order in an urban environment. It was extensive rather than intensive in its operations, yet it did place definite responsibilities on small manageable groups, each with a leader accountable to a head who controlled several such units. In this way definite men were charged with, and held responsible for, certain clearly defined public duties in the interest of a more orderly society.

The Normans in England, 1066-1154, made important use of the institutions set up by the Saxon kings. William the Conqueror centralized authority in the throne by militarizing the civil feudal arrangements of the Saxons. Local courts of the hundreds and shires were placed under control of the King's Court through the appointment of "Vicecomes," traveling or circuit judges who held "Courts of Tourn" at prescribed times and places. Jury trial first began with the assize of Clarendon of Henry II, in 1166. The "jury of presentment" originating at about this time gave rise to our modern grand jury.

"Petty constables" are mentioned by Henry III in a writ in 1252 concerning an established London police force known as the "Watch and Ward." This is the first record of a systematic police patrol. The Watch and Ward was a group of householders appointed in rotation from a roster, and service was compulsory. Paid deputies were allowed to be substituted, but these were carelessly chosen and often themselves criminals.

The Standing Watch System. The compulsory system was replaced in 1263 by the appointment of a "standing watch," or permanent police force, paid for by the city of London. In a few years definite duties were laid upon the watch. The watchmen, or bellmen, carried a lantern and staff. Their superior officer, the constable, carried only a staff. The watchmen reported to their constable for inspection when going off duty. Ruffians harassed these unfortunate officials and plagued their existence in the large cities. The protection afforded by them was so poor that only the most courageous citizens ventured upon the streets after dark on moonless nights, until in 1807 gas lamps were used to light London's streets. Few fundamental changes were made in this inefficient and ineffective system until Peel's police reform.

American Adaptation. The American colonists brought with them the watch and ward system. Parish constables were made responsible for a civilian night watch, and this was supplemented by a military guard. In New York under the Dutch, before the

British occupancy, the police system consisted of a "schout," an official who watched for violations of laws and ordinances, and a rattle watch, so called because the watchmen carried rattles. These were replaced by the constables' watch under the English.

The inadequacies of the night watch became apparent as the 19th century advanced, and the organization by wards and districts showed its obvious weaknesses. Selection of personnel was by political preferment, a further contributing factor to the ineffectiveness of the system and one which hampered efforts to improve police service for many years.

A day police force was first adopted in Boston in 1838, when six men were placed on separate day duty without any connection with the night watch. This arrangement was soon found unworkable, and the forces were consolidated about 1850. No regular uniforms came into general use until about 1855; their use was resisted as un-American and undemocratic. Discipline was well-nigh impossible in the police forces because of the politics with which they were saturated. The police heads were elected in several cities, a practice which retarded the sound development of police organization.

Control by police boards began in the 1850's and spread rapidly in the larger cities. Unsatisfactory exercise of the police power by the cities led to the experiment of state control in New York City, 1857; Baltimore, 1860; St. Louis, Kansas City, and Chicago, 1861; Detroit, 1865; Cleveland, 1866; New Orleans, 1868; Cincinnati, 1877; Indianapolis, 1883; Boston, 1885; Omaha, 1887; and Charleston, 1896. Boston, Baltimore, St. Louis, and a few smaller cities are even now under state control, though elsewhere the hand of the state has been withdrawn.

Changes in 20th Century. A complete change has been made in the nature of police administration during the present century. A principal aspect of this change appears in the adaptation and application of scientific methods and apparatus to the detection of crime and to judicial proof, in improved transportation facilities, in faster and more effective communications, in the improvement of police records, and in the improvement of methods for the selection and training of personnel. While the administrative impact of these changes will be considered later, a brief description of the effects of science, motorization, and improvements in communications will indicate the force with which modern times have struck the police agencies of our communities.

1. Science. Chemistry and physics have been drawn upon heavily and their principles molded to help the policeman at his task of apprehending criminals and establishing their guilt through the collection and preservation of evidence. The greatest contribution of all is the systematic application of the art of fingerprinting, by which personal identity may be surely and demonstrably established. Another contribution to science is the polygraph, which, by recording changes in the subject's blood pressure and respiration, indicates deception. Chemical tests give the police an objective means of determining the state of intoxication of a suspect by measuring the amount of alcohol in the blood. Evidence for court presentation and departmental records may be preserved by photography, and some departments record the actions of suspects on moving pictures and their utterances on sound recording equipment. Television is now being used to disseminate information on wanted persons, for showing prisoners at line-up to district stations, and for jail supervision.

2. Motorization. Auto patrol has enabled fewer men to patrol more territory. Furthermore the automobile gives the policeman a more even chance to cope with the motorized criminal. Mobilization of men and equipment is speeded up greatly by these additions.

3. Communications. Modern police communications, such as radio and teletype,

have supplemented but not displaced the patrol box and recall system. Response to telephoned complaints is now accomplished in mere minutes by combining the radio with motorized transportation. Intercity communication is speeded by police radio systems. Photographs may be transmitted by either wire or radio. Uniform police records systems enable crime and arrest statistics to be collected on a nation-wide basis. Fingerprinting is generally practiced, and identification records are made available through state and national clearing agencies.

What About Police Management?

Police administration has likewise been altered by modern practices, perhaps not as romantic as those developed by scientists, but none the less revolutionary. Procedures, selection, training, and equipment used by most departments represent striking gains over slip-shod methods used just a few years ago.

Advances in technical proficiency have not been paralleled by equal progress in the techniques of managing a police department. It is to this latter phase of police work that the remainder of this volume is devoted. Great effort has been expended toward the improvement of the patrolman and the detective, but too little attention has been given to the development of competent police chiefs or commissioners. Too often it has been assumed that the man who has the longest service or the best record as a policeman may confidently be expected to manage the activities of the department as chief. This is not true, as is evidenced by cases too numerous to mention. Administration of a police department requires not only successful experience as a policeman but also special talent and a number of particular skills that are not acquired in the course of ordinary police training and experience. It is the purpose of this volume, therefore, to approach police problems and to examine different branches of police work from the administrative level.

What Is Administration?

With the foregoing as background we can now describe the nature of police administration as it exists today.

At the beginning of a discussion on administration it is advisable to define the term and explain its components. The term "administration" as hereinafter used means simply the job of the chief of police or any other officer charged with the operation of a department or an identifiable segment within the department. The task of the police administrator can be defined in a number of ways, but for the present purpose his job will be divided into four parts: planning, organization, direction, and external relations. The chief of a department of thousands of men, and the platoon commander in a small department, both constantly use these elements in carrying on their work, whether they realize it or not. The skill with which these principles are applied determines the success or failure of the police administrator. Each of these elements may be analyzed briefly.

Planning

The first concern of a police chief is to plan the work of his department. It may be objected by some that police work is largely emergency in character and does not lend itself to long-term calculation and planning. To a limited extent this is true. The police department deals primarily with personal services rather than with the provision of structural and material things, and personal services by their very nature are more subject to rapid change. Nevertheless, planning is an essential element in police work. No one may predict the exact time, the place, or the particular persons to be involved in any single emergency, but the nature of probable emergencies can be predicted and planned for.

It may be difficult, for example, to anticipate a strike, a race riot, a flood, or a bombing attack, but this does not prevent the formulation of police plans and procedures to be applied should such an emergency occur. In addition, there is planning involved in the distribution of the force for regular and special duty, and also in routing traffic for special occasions. The emergency nature of police work requires a flexible organization which can adapt itself readily to new situations. Foresight and planning are essential for such an organization because there is nothing more inflexible than an organization bound by routine and precedent and unprepared for any situation not previously encountered.

Planning is involved in the construction and layout of police headquarters and in the purchase or construction of police equipment. In a very real sense planning is also involved in the recruitment and training of police officers. The personnel problem is large in any organization, but in a police department, whose chief object is to provide personal services, it is particularly important. The ranking police administrator must have unusual ability to appreciate the qualities necessary for the various positions in his department and to appraise the capacities of his men for different types of work. In a small department the chief administrator also will be the personnel officer, and even in the largest departments the chief must still be the final authority on personnel matters such as the selection and supervision of his highest ranking subordinates.

Budgeting is a distinct phase of planning, for it involves the ability to translate plans, programs, men, and materials into terms of dollars and cents. Furthermore, it is characterized by the concept of balance, of the ability to adjust plans and to distribute personnel and purchases so as to get the maximum result. Each of the several units of the police department naturally conceives itself to be the most important and presses forward with plans for expansion or for improvement. This is a natural and healthy attitude, but someone in the department must decide which division is in greatest need of additional funds, which new program represents the most valuable service to the public at the present time, or how an additional expenditure may be made to satisfy the needs of two or more subordinate units. In a large department a subordinate official may be delegated the task of compiling estimates and requests, but the final decision as to priorities must rest upon the chief administrator.

Planning is a continuous and never-ending task. Unless budget plans are revised each year the revenue needed to carry out various programs will never be anticipated or developed. The planning of personnel demands both long-range plans and a revision each year in terms of accomplishments and new problems, so that the adaptability of the personnel will be sufficient to meet changing conditions. Planning, in one form or another, is the very essence of administration, and the man without foresight is out of place at the head of any administrative unit.

Organization

A good administrator is able to organize men and materials to meet current needs and to establish administrative machinery that will produce satisfactory results with speed, accuracy, and a minimum of friction and waste. In police work coordination means grouping related tasks to assure more effective accomplishment and the establishment of clear-cut channels of communication, authority, and responsibility. One other phase is suggested by John M. Gaus who defines organization as "the relating of efforts and capacities of individuals and groups engaged upon a common task in such a way as to secure the desired objective with the least friction and the most satisfaction to those for whom the task is done and those engaged in the enterprise." The suggestion that there should be satisfaction to "those engaged in the enterprise," as well as to "those for whom the task is done," opens new possibilities for the progressive administrator. The plans and problems of organization will be considered in Chapter 2, while special organizational problems and techniques of organization will receive particular attention in the chapters dealing with the prevention of delinquency, traffic, criminal investigation, vice control, and patrol.

Direction

Important phases of the function of direction are command, coordination, and control. Upon the discharge of this function depends the morale of the department — essential in any police organization. "To command is to issue the orders necessary for the execution of plans, policies and assignments." Command in a police department differs from that in most other city departments, for a police organization is semimilitary in character. Discipline and prompt response to commands are essential particularly in emergency situations. This requires not only a force which has respect for superior authority but also a superior authority capable of commanding. The police administrator must know not only what is to be done but also how much can be expected of his men, for commands that cannot be carried out thwart the administrative organization and destroy the morale of subordinates.

In spite of the necessity for military discipline, it is unwise for a commanding officer to impose upon the subordinate a discipline that requires merely blind obedience and complete dependence upon his superior. The command of a police department necessitates a high degree of leadership in order that subordinates will cooperate as well as obey.

Coordination is an important phase in the function of command. If the police department is to operate as a smooth, well-balanced machine, its several units must be coordinated so that they support and assist each other rather than oppose or overlap. Coordination involves the appraisal of organization and personnel to determine what alterations or adjustments may be necessary to adapt the one to the other. It demands skill in devising procedures to induce cooperation and to eliminate friction. In the final analysis, it rests upon the diplomacy and tact of the police administrator.

Those experienced in police work know that the administration of a police department is particularly susceptible to friction. A bitter rivalry and distrust between the uniformed and detective units, between the traffic division and the patrol unit, or between different shifts or different divisions are a common occurrence. These conflicts not only impair police efficiency, but they also affect morale and are likely to result in the loss of public confidence and respect. The police chief must develop coordination if his administration of the department is to be a success.

Control devices are the tools by which the police administrator is assured that his direction of the department is effective. Among the control devices used are inspections, periodic reports of activities, follow-up procedures, special reports from subordinates, and a rating system.

External Relations

The police chief is the logical person to represent his department in contacts with other city departments, outside law enforcement agencies, and the public. It is impossible for him to delegate this responsibility to subordinates and still act as chief. This does not mean that subordinates will have no outside contacts, but it does mean that the chief must assume the responsibility for all such outside contacts. In addition, the police chief is the focal point of control exercised by the chief administrator (mayor or city manager) of the city over the police department.

The task of creating and maintaining favorable relations between the police department and the public is necessarily an important feature of representation. The chief must be available for direct contacts with the public or with outside agencies. It is his office that represents the department to the citizen who feels that he has been unjustly treated. Because of the nature of police work, subordinates have direct contact with the public also, but the policy for handling these contacts and the final decisions must come from the chief's office alone.

Reporting departmental activities is another feature of external relationships. While it may not be desirable to release some police information, it is necessary to build in the minds of the public a feeling of confidence that information and statistics that are revealed present a true picture of the workings of the department. This can only be accomplished by scrupulous honesty in reporting. Facts must not be withheld merely because they tend to place the department in an unfavorable light. Neither should the department be overpublicized, lest it find itself unable to measure up to the publicity. All external negotiations are a direct responsibility of the police chief, and the discussion and solution of problems must emanate from the chief's office.

Police Administration

It can readily be seen that the basic elements of administration discussed above are common to many kinds of public agencies and private businesses. But there are, in the nature of police work, other elements that affect its administration.

The Purpose of Police. A police department deals for the most part with the actions and behavior of human beings. There are at least four different types of criminal behavior. First, there are the so-called major crimes: felonious homicide, rape, robbery, aggravated assault, burglary, larceny, auto theft, forgery, counterfeiting, embezzlement, fraud, blackmail, arson, and kidnaping. Second, these are offenses against public morals: vice, gambling, liquor, drugs, and offenses against the family. Third, there are offenses which have to do with the maintenance of peace: disorderly conduct, possession of weapons, assault, trespassing, and vagrancy. And finally there are violations of traffic and other regulations not covered by the first three classifications.[1]

But the police department is more than a law-enforcing agency — it has a broader responsibility with regard to the offenses mentioned above. Police activities involve:

1. The Prevention of Criminality. This is one of the newer responsibilities of the police. It is being more and more clearly realized that a constructive approach to the crime problem must go to its very roots — to the factors in community life which create criminal tendencies and lead the criminal to indulge in antisocial behavior. Studies must be made of actual cases to determine the causes that led to delinquency, and on the basis of these facts attempts must be made to eradicate the causes.

2. Repression of Crime. This is a function more firmly embedded in police

---

[1]This classification is adapted from that employed by August Vollmer, *The Police and Modern Society* (Berkeley: University of California Press, 1936).

practice. Adequate patrol plus continuous effort toward eliminating or reducing hazards is stressed as a means of reducing the opportunities for criminal activity.

3. <u>Apprehension of Offenders</u>. Quick apprehension and certain punishment discourage the would-be offender by making the consequences of crime seem less pleasant. In addition to its repressive influence, apprehension enables society to punish offenders; prevents a repetition of their offenses by restraining their movements; and provides an opportunity for their rehabilitation.

4. <u>Recovery of Property</u>. This is an activity intended to reduce the money cost of crime, as well as to restrain those who though not active criminals might benefit from the gains of crime.

5. <u>Regulation of Noncriminal Conduct.</u> Many police activities are concerned only incidentally with criminal behavior. Their main purpose is regulation, and apprehension and punishment of offenders are means of securing obedience. Other methods used to obtain compliance are education of the public in the dangers inherent in the disobedience of regulations; and the use of warnings, either oral or written, which inform the citizen of the violation but do not penalize him. Examples of such activities are the regulation of traffic and the enforcement of minor regulations of sanitation and street use. This type of regulation is time-consuming and drains police energies from those tasks which are more important in the eyes of the public.

<u>Goal of a Police Department</u>. In general, the objective of a police department is to effectively discharge these five purposes. Any of the specific responsibilities of the departments should be evaluated in these terms. It is obvious, however, that without sound management of police activities, without effective utilization of manpower and other resources, without complete and accurate recording of all crimes and the actions taken in dealing with them, the department will not achieve its purposes. In short, there is no effective police department where police administration is ineffective.

The Public and Law Enforcement

The effectiveness of police work depends in large measure on the attitudes of the persons with whom the police department is dealing in any situation. It is necessary to consider some of the major problems which public attitudes present to the police department and the crime situations out of which these problems rise. Some persons, such as the citizen who has had property stolen or a relative murdered, or the business man threatened by a racketeer or asking assistance in the case of labor trouble, are eager to cooperate with the police. Others, such as the citizen patronizing a gambling den or a brothel, are eager to avoid all contact with the police.

A number of factors affect the attitudes of otherwise respectable citizens who run afoul the police at one time or another. These make law enforcement more difficult. Crimes perpetrated by foreign-born against members of their own nationality sometimes are concealed. Such groups may prefer to deal with offenders in their own way rather than to have recourse to a system of justice unfamiliar to them and based on principles foreign to their customs. Human passions, an eagerness for disproportionate rewards, or merely the thrill of the chase lure untold numbers of people into indulging their lust or greed in as many ways as the cunning of human ingenuity can devise. Such are the crimes of prostitution, gambling, confidence games, and other similar offenses. The policeman works with people, and people differ in their attitudes toward law enforcement.

Enforceability of Laws

A number of problems present themselves when the police attempt to enforce laws not generally supported by public opinion. Even where public morals are not concerned, city ordinances often require police to enforce a degree of regulation which is regarded by many citizens as an infringement of their personal liberties. Some municipal ordinances, as well as other laws, have a fatal defect; namely, unless the regulations are reasonable, unless they conform to established practices, their enforcement is next to impossible. Compelling police to enforce unreasonable regulations brings down upon the head of the department as well as the individual policeman the condemnation of the particular group affected and detracts measurably from the assistance that the police might otherwise command.[2] Many outdated and absurd laws on the statute books cannot be enforced, and they make the police look ridiculous should they attempt to enforce them. In some instances they are laws that were necessary for the control of a condition which no longer exists. In other instances, they were ill-conceived regulations designed to apply to a particular happening which was never repeated and hence the law was never needed. In still other instances they represent concessions to small but persistent pressure groups; it was easier or more politic to pass a law than to resist the group fostering it. Regardless of why these laws remain upon the statute books, they are a hindrance to legal progress and emphasize the necessity for periodic and thorough overhauling of all regulatory measures.

Principles To Guide Police in Enforcement. How strict, then, should the police be in the enforcement of regulations? No simple answer can be given, for the degree of enforcement must depend upon the specific city involved and upon the attitudes of citizens as well as police. But a few general principles can be laid down.

First, the source of many difficulties in law enforcement is not in the police department at all, but in the laws which they are expected to enforce. Therefore it is the duty of the police chief, through the chief administrator of the city, to point out the responsibility of the policy-forming agencies in facing the issue squarely.

Second, complete enforcement of all the laws is physically impossible with a limited police force. But if laws are to be selectively enforced, the basis of selection must be laid down by the department, and no departure from it by the individual officer should be tolerated. Only in this way can corruption be prevented from creeping into the department.

Third, in enforcing laws selectively the basis of selection cannot be a personal one. Favoritism in regulation, either for personal or political reasons, will quickly undermine the morale of the force. Above all, no taint of corruption must be allowed to invade the department. This is the basic consideration — that police morale and public confidence must be maintained intact.

Fourth, no police officer should ever authorize an individual or an agency to violate the law.

Police and Politics

The greatest obstacle to efficient local law enforcement today is not weakness of moral character in law enforcement officials. It is the political pressure and interference

---

[2] *Ibid.*, p. 159.

to which our police and prosecuting agencies are so frequently subjected. It is far more common for local law enforcement to break down because of political interference with the police and prosecuting agencies than because of corruption in such agencies. Whenever bad conditions are encountered, and wherever there are conspicuous failures in the enforcement of the law by local agencies, the investigation and inquiry should not end just with the police. More often than not, the police have more zeal for law enforcement than do the people who employ them. It is quite true that sometimes it is the corruption of the chief of police or officers in his department or of a prosecuting attorney that is responsible for the breakdown of law enforcement, clearing the way for organized crime. But more often it is due to someone higher in government or in the political machine who dictates appointments and controls elections.[3]

Partisan Politics and Police Administration. A police department has a definite job to do, and it cannot carry on with any high degree of success when diverted from its goal by the dictates of political preference. Its policy must be consistent, forthright, and impartial, or it will be denied the prestige and wholehearted support of the people whose persons and property it is sworn to safeguard.

Control of the police force is a tremendous asset to a spoils-minded political machine, for the services which such police can render to the machine are legion. Fixing traffic citations has won many a vote and helped many a local campaign fund. Prosecution of minor and serious crimes can sometimes be arranged to suit the convenience of the person charged. By arrangement, an officer may fail to appear against a defendant or may prove a poor witness. Evidence may disappear or an investigation be incompetently performed. These are only a few of the possibilities which politicians have exploited in corrupt police departments.

When the police department is controlled by the "machine," political influence begins with the appointment of the recruit, rallies to save him from discipline or discharge, helps him to secure unearned wages or disability benefits, grants him unusual leaves of absence, secures an unwarranted promotion for him, or gives him a soft job. In countless ways the creeping paralysis of political favoritism spreads and fastens itself upon the force to sap its vitality and destroy its morale for the benefit of the party, at the expense both of the public and of the police force itself.

Politics in the force will gradually undermine the character of rank-and-file policemen. Most of them have families dependent on them for their daily bread. The lives of some of them have been given so long to police work that they would not know where else to turn for employment. Great moral courage is required to withstand the terrific and continuous pressure which can be leveled against them.

Using Police Tools. Politics, however, may not be properly charged with all of the ills of a police department. Discontinuity of leadership, the spoils system, or an already undermined morale may be laid to it. But this does not account for the failure of a department to make the best use of the tools within its grasp. With intelligence and imagination it can successfully combat at the beginning the forces of corruption and destruction of morale. Mismanagement and the lack of initiative in many cities have offered the first opportunity to the encroachment of corrupt practices.

And the police should not be held entirely responsible for political corruption which may characterize the city government as a whole. Almost without exception spoils politics in the police department is a symptom of political ills in the whole of the city government.

---

[3] See State of California, *Final Report of the California Special Crime Study Commission on Organized Crime*, 1953, p. 67.

Too often the remedy for a corrupt police force is thought to be "taking the police out of politics" and placing the department under an independent board or an elected commissioner. This "solution" merely complicates the structure of government, makes it less responsive to public control, and facilitates political maneuvers.

Those who wish to choke off political corruption at its source should aim at reconstruction of the whole city government and make the police responsible to a chief administrator who can be held accountable for the operation of the government, either by the council which appoints him, or by the people who elect him. In this way the police will not suffer unjustly for conforming to practices imposed upon them by their superiors.

On the subject of political interference with local law enforcement, J. Edgar Hoover, director of the Federal Bureau of Investigation, testifying before the Senate Committee on Organized Crime in Interstate Commerce in 1951, said:

> Those who engage in widespread vice activities and rackets could not long survive without their ally — the political renegade. No community in the land is contaminated by rackets and corruption without the assistance of local interests which hold law enforcement in restraint. Law enforcement officers are the people's representatives. They are not persons with unlimited power; they must obey those under whom they hold office. If they are dominated by the criminal-aligned politician, ruthless rackets and vice are inevitable. The law enforcement officials in our nation, for the most part, are honest and anxious to do a good job. Regardless of their personal honesty, however, they are frequently powerless to act. Only aroused and enlightened citizens take the handcuffs off their wrists and place them where they belong, upon the racketeers, criminals, and corrupt politicians.

There can, indeed, be no doubt that the solution to the whole problem lies in the presence of an enlightened, crystallized public opinion brought to bear on local law enforcement and the local administration of criminal justice.

Sources of Public Information

Because healthy public opinion is vital to effective police work, a large part of the policeman's job falls into the category of public relations. It is the police chief's task to see that policemen are properly trained to carry out their public relations function, and to provide controls to make sure they do. Chapters 14 and 15 deal more specifically with public attitudes about police and preparing and carrying out a public relations program. However, some of the recurring problems of supplying the public with information through the mass media may be noted here.

Police and the Press. The press in its search for news has a great stake in the work of the police. Nothing is more vital and fascinating to man's curiosity than the human interest stories uncovered by the police. These are the true stories of the plots, accidents, feuds, successes, and passions of mankind. Criminal offenses occur in all social and economic classes. In their investigation the police lay open the secrets of private lives everywhere for the curious and morbid public to feed upon. These are the dramatic stories which boost circulation.

Americans want this information and feel that they have a right to it. Police censorship of the news is not generally tolerated. The traditional freedom of the press and its characteristic aggressive and competitive policy make it the ideal organ to acquire and transmit this news.

Public Attitude Toward the Police. Of direct interest to the police is the effect of the newspapers and other mass media upon public attitude toward the police. Little is known of how much effect newspapers really have on public attitude, but the newspaperman feels that his task is to exhibit to the public the efficiency or inefficiency of public employees. There are many outstanding examples of reforms that have occurred simply because the press has served well in its role of public watchdog. No one will deny the possibilities for constructive journalism in aiding law enforcement. But if it is to be really helpful the newspaper must sacrifice its desire for sensations to an objective reporting of the facts of local crime.

The police must fight unfair journalism by furnishing to press and public accurate facts as to the real crime condition of the city. Concealment of crime facts by the police is not a legitimate defense against distorted crime news; more is to be gained by keeping and publishing records of such accuracy that they will gain the confidence of the press and the public. Upon examination, the problem of press and police like most other problems, turns out to be no simple question of right or wrong. The press has maintained with a good deal of reason that publication of crime news is instrumental in crime prevention. They point to the awakening of the public to the crime problem. They insist that the press is obligated to report to the public on the efficiency of public officials. They demonstrate the value of the press to the police in publishing information which may lead to the solution of crimes.

On the other hand, the police official can point to serious abuses of the freedom of the press. Sensationalism has a suggestive effect upon potential delinquents, and tends to lower public morale. Unfair advantage has been taken of the police by the creation of fictitious crime waves or charges of inefficiency and corruption. Publication of names of accused persons, and especially juveniles, has made difficult a return to honest life. Premature publication of details about crimes and police movements has aided the escape of criminals. Cooperation between police and press is therefore essential in establishing policies with regard to crime news.

The Police and Organized Crime

Perhaps the most difficult of all police problems is the satisfactory control of prostitution, gambling, liquor, and narcotics. It is made especially difficult by the pressure of one or both of two factors: officials and the public who countenance crime, and a close-knit syndicate which dominates vice operations.

The Vice Problem

The police sometimes have difficulty in learning about the commission of these crimes. Patrons of brothels, gamblers, liquor law violators, and narcotics peddlers avoid any open contact with the police. Anonymous letters, telegrams, and telephone calls — usually from some disgruntled customer — will come in plentifully, but the victim seldom appears in person prepared to give definite information and to sign a complaint upon which effective police action can be taken.

Commercial gambling would be no problem if there were no amateur gamblers. The carnival sharper with his pea-and-shell game could not exist if he had no patrons. Men want to take a chance. No matter how the odds may be stacked against them, they normally prefer to take in silence their gambling losses rather than reveal their mistakes in a report to the police.

The Wide-open City. Some cities deliberately adopt a liberal attitude toward vice and its associated practices. Some are large cities where commerce and industry attract the transient class from the hinterland, who, when their business obligations are discharged, want to have a "good time." The same may be true of a lakeside or seashore city catering to large state or national conventions. In places of this kind the amusement business often assumes great importance, attracting large capital investments and entrenching itself as an influential factor in the city government, sometimes through contributions or a share of the profits. The result is a wide-open town.

In a resort city the profits often have to be made during a brief season of a few weeks. Because of the heavy investments in the equipment of vice and gambling, the strongest possible representations may be made to the city government to have the local police wink at certain violations. This approach failing, an attempt will be made to corrupt individual policemen. Hotel owners will be solicited to add their pressure to ease the enforcement policy. They depend upon the vacationers for their patronage and may be counted upon to support a liberal attitude toward vice and gambling. The police department frequently is unable to withstand such pressure. The individual policeman who resists may be sent to some obscure post where he can see no evil and do no harm.

Influence of Vice on Other Crimes. Prostitution, gambling, liquor, and narcotics evils cannot long exist without giving rise to more serious crimes. In the first place, open vice operations attract criminals and their hangers-on, and where criminals congregate the commission of crime is certain to follow. Organized commercial vice gathers funds into the underworld coffers which may be used to hire expensive legal talent. The success of the leaders against the orderly process of government lends a confidence which may spur an attempt to gain control of legitimate enterprises. This situation creates an unholy union between respectable citizens and commercialized vice, and a vicious circle is thereby instituted. With all the momentum created by such an alliance it is unlikely that police honesty can long remain intact. And in the final analysis the practices of commercialized vice are either crimes in themselves or are but one step removed from actual crime.

Commercial Prostitution. A city cannot have at one and the same time a "wide-open" policy toward prostitution and effective police administration. The policies of segregation and inspection are merely rationalizations which condone a situation that is a crime in itself. In order to administer vice regulations effectively it is necessary that all public and private agencies concerned have a firm policy of repression with regard to such regulation.

The Syndication of Crime and the Mafia[4]

The structure of organized crime today is far different from what it was many years ago. Its power for evil is infinitely greater. The unit of organized crime used to be an individual gang consisting of hoodlums whose activities were obviously predatory. Individual gangs tended to specialize in specific types of criminal activity such as payroll or bank robbery, loft or safe burglary, and pocket picking. These gangs normally confined their activities to particular communities.

New types of criminal gangs emerged during prohibition. The huge profits earned in that era, together with the development of the 20th century transportation and communication, made possible larger and much more powerful gangs covering much greater territory. Organized crime in the last 40 years has taken on new characteristics. The most dangerous criminal gangs today are not specialists in one type of predatory crime,

---

[4] This section is from the *Third Interim Report of the Special Senate Committee to Investigate Crime in Inter-State Commerce* (Washington, D. C.: Government Printing Office, 1951), pp. 144-50.

but engage in many and varied forms of criminality. Criminal groups today are multi-purpose in character, engaging in any racket wherever there is money to be made. The modern gang, moreover, does not rely for its primary source of income on frankly predatory forms of crime such as robbery, burglary, or larceny. Instead the more dangerous criminal elements draw most of their revenues from various forms of gambling, sale and distribution of narcotics, prostitution, business and labor racketeering, and bootlegging into dry areas, among other activities.

The key to successful gang operation is monopoly of illicit enterprises or illegal operations, for monopoly guarantees huge profits. In cities that gangland has organized well, the syndicate or the combination in control of the rackets decides which mobsters are to have what rackets. In cities which have not been well organized, the attempt by one mobster to take over the territory or racket from another mobster inevitably breeds trouble, for modern gangs and criminal syndicates rely on "muscle" and murder to a far greater degree than formerly to eliminate competitors, compel cooperation from reluctant victims, silence informers, and to enforce gangland edicts.

Criminal Organization Like Business Organization. Modern crime syndicate and criminal gangs have copied some of the organizational methods found in modern business. They seek to expand their activities in many different fields and in many different geographic areas, wherever profits may be made. Individual gangsters and gangs in different parts of the country have also frequently worked in close and profitable relationship with each other, particularly in gambling casinos where often members of several gangs participate on a systematic basis. Outside gangs coming into an area often use local hoodlums and local gangs.

It is apparent that the leading figures in organized crime do business with each other. One of the major areas in which leading gangs cooperate is in enforcing each other's edicts, silencing informers, and persuading potential victims through intimidation, violence, and murder. It is obviously far more difficult for local law enforcement officials to detect the work of outside gangsters than the products of their local talent.

Modern gangland operations on any sizable scale cannot be carried on without protection. The gangs have unbelievable cash assets available for this purpose. Much of the money of criminal gangs and syndicates is invested in legitimate enterprises which present special dangers to our economy and our people.

An elusive, shadowy, and sinister organization, the Mafia, has an important part in binding together into a loose association the two major criminal syndicates as well as many minor gangs and individual hoodlums throughout the country. The Mafia originally had high purpose. It was originally one of many secret societies organized in Sicily to free the island of foreign domination. The methods used for securing secrecy of operations — unity of command, intimidation and murder, and the silencing of informers — were adopted by a criminal group that became the Mafia after the Bourbons were driven from Sicily.

This organization grew enormously in Sicily after 1860. Smuggling, cattle stealing, extortion, and shake-downs were its major criminal activities. The administration of justice was openly defied by this organization. Although many arrests were made, law-enforcement agencies found it extremely difficult to break the power of the Mafia. The arrested members of this organization would not talk. Witnesses of various crimes committed by members of the Mafia were intimidated and were afraid to testify. Political influence was used to protect Mafia members charged with crime.

The various drives against the Mafia in Sicily, which were made by Italian Governments from the 1870's down to Mussolini's time, were therefore largely ineffective in destroying the Mafia. However, these drives had the effect of causing large numbers of Mafia members to migrate to the New World, and many of them came to the United States.

As early as the 1880's New Orleans was the focal point of Mafia activity. It overreached itself when it ordered the murder of a popular police officer. A dozen Mafia leaders were arrested, but none were convicted after a trial marred by the intimidation of witnesses and jury fixing. The defendants, however, who had been held in jail on other charges, were lynched by a mob of aroused New Orleans citizens. After these lynchings the power of the Mafia in New Orleans was temporarily broken.

The Mafia became established in other cities besides New Orleans. Moreover, like many other underworld organizations, it grew rich and powerful during prohibition in the sale and distribution of alcoholic beverages. In addition, both during prohibition and since that time, this organization has entered every racket promising easy money. Narcotics, pinball machines, slot machines, gambling in every form and description are some of its major activities.

Many of the individuals suspected of connection with the Mafia operate behind legitimate fronts. The olive oil, cheese, and export businesses are some of the favorite fronts for Mafia operations. They offer a cover, particularly, for narcotics operations. They also help explain interstate and international contacts between persons suspected of Mafia connections.

It is almost inevitable that the Mafia should take an important part in American criminal rackets. Here is a nation-wide organization of outlaws in a sort of oath-bound, blood-cemented brotherhood dedicated to complete defiance of the law. Where personal advantage or interests are concerned, here is a more or less permanently established network, an organized maze of underground conduits, always ready and available when racket enterprise is to be furthered. The organization is such that a member in one part of the country can, with perfect confidence, engage in any sort of illicit business with members in any other section of the country. Most helpful to the Mafia has been the attitude on the part of many law-enforcement officers in connection with its murders. These are sometimes passed over lightly on the theory these cases are just hoodlums killing off one another and that it is not a matter on which to waste police time and energy.

The ruthless elimination of competitors from enterprises which Mafia leaders decide to take over, the ruthless elimination of persons who have weakened in their Mafia loyalties, failed to carry out Mafia orders, or informed against the Mafia, has left a trail of murder from Tampa to San Francisco.

Difficult To Obtain Reliable Evidence. It is difficult to obtain reliable data concerning the extent of Mafia operation, the nature of the Mafia organization, and the way it operates. It is the opinion of experienced police officers and narcotics agents, however, that:

1. There is a nation-wide crime syndicate known as the Mafia whose operations are found in many large cities. It has international ramifications which appear most clearly in connection with the narcotics traffic.

2. Its leaders are usually found in control of the most lucrative rackets in their cities.

3. There are indications of a centralized direction and control of these rackets, but leadership appears to be in a group rather than in a single individual.

4. The Mafia is the cement that helps to bind the Costello-Adonis-Lansky syndicate of New York and the Accardo-Guzik-Fischetti syndicate of Chicago as well as smaller criminals throughout the country. These groups have kept in touch with "Lucky" Luciano since his deportation from this country.

5. The domination of the Mafia is based fundamentally on "muscle" and "murder." The Mafia is a secret conspiracy against law and order that will ruthlessly eliminate anyone who stands in the way of its success in any criminal enterprise in which it is interested. It will destroy anyone who betrays its secrets. It will use any means available — political influence, bribery, intimidation — to defeat any attempt on the part of law enforcement to touch its top figures or to interfere with its operations.

The Mafia today acts closely with many persons who are not of Sicilian descent. Moreover, it must be pointed out most strongly that the Mafia group comprises only a very small fraction of a percentage even of Sicilians. It would be most unfortunate if any inferences were erroneously drawn in any way derogatory to the vast majority of fine law-abiding citizens of Sicilian and Italian extraction.

Infiltration Into Legitimate Business[5]

One of the most perplexing problems in the field of organized crime is that criminals and racketeers are using the profits of organized crime to buy up and operate legitimate enterprises. Men with criminal records who have seen the error of their ways deserve credit for their efforts to earn an honest living by going into some type of legitimate business. Many men sow their "wild oats" in the form of crime in their younger years and then settle down to become decent citizens. This process of rehabilitation of offenders should be encouraged in every possible way. Gangsters and racketeers who continue to pursue their vicious careers and invest the spoils of their illegitimate activity in legitimate enterprise, however, constitute a great danger to our country.

A gangster or racketeer in a legitimate business does not suddenly become respectable. The methods which he used to achieve success in racketeering and gambling enterprises are not easily sloughed off. Thus, evidence was produced before the committee concerning the use of unscrupulous and discriminatory business practices, extortion, bombing, and other forms of violence to eliminate competitors and to compel customers to take articles sold by the mobsters. Monopoly is the key to big money in criminal activity. It is also sought by mobsters when they enter legitimate business. A racketeer who has contempt for the law and who enters legitimate business has no hesitation in engaging in black-market practices. This gives him a considerable advantage over a more timid competitor and is one of the means whereby the racketeer can push such a competitor to the wall.

Gangster infiltration into legitimate business affords the big-time gamblers and racketeers who usually live a life of luxury some way of explaining their source of income to prying income-tax officials. One of the functions of investment into legitimate business enterprise is to provide a source for income which cannot be impeached by the Internal Revenue authorities. Returns from gambling and other illegitimate enterprises are extremely difficult to check. Some of the winnings may be invested in legitimate business

---

[5] *Ibid.*, pp. 170-72, 181.

and taxes may be paid on the income from such business. Taxes on the huge returns from gambling and other illegitimate enterprises have not been paid.

Racketeers Prefer Big-Turnover Businesses. It should be noted, however, that gangsters and racketeers have an affinity for enterprises in which there is a large turn-over and in which problems of accounting and control are difficult. Thus, even when the ill-gotten gains of a racketeer or gangster are invested in a legitimate enterprise there is no assurance that the government will not be defrauded to a considerable degree of its taxes.

There can be little doubt that the public suffers from gangster penetration into legitimate business. It suffers because higher prices must be paid as the result of the monopoly which is often secured and because of unfair trade practices frequently applied. The public suffers because it may have to put up with shoddy and inferior merchandise in fields where gangsters have been able to obtain a monopoly. The tax load of the general public is increased when gangsters and racketeers fail to pay their lawful return on the enterprises in which they are engaged. Finally, the public suffers because the vast resources that gangsters and racketeers control enables them to consolidate their economic and political positions. Money, and particularly ready cash, is power in any community and over and over again instances have been found where racketeers' money has been used to exercise influence with federal, state, and local officials and agencies of government. An official who is beholden to the mob for his election or appointment thinks first of his boss and only secondarily of the people of the community whom he must serve. The money used by hoodlums to buy economic and political control also is used to induce public apathy. Hoodlums, behind the front of their respectable enterprises, contribute enormous sums to hundreds of worthy causes, such contributions tend to fool uninformed people and thus contribute to the relaxation of public vigilance. There is evidence of hoodlum infiltration in approximately 50 areas of business enterprise.

One of the most shocking problems in this connection, and one which constitutes a black page in the history of American industry, is the indisputable evidence of cooperation with major hoodlums on the part of important segments of business enterprise. Finally, hoodlums were found to be holding valuable franchises in the liquor and automobile industries.

Hoodlum penetration of labor unions has decreased steadily over the years. In the 1920's and 1930's hoodlum infiltration into the cleaning and laundry, dairy, the beverage, stage hands, and retail clerks' unions, was on such a large and violent scale that it threatened to disrupt entire industries. Today, however, the hoodlum element has been driven to the wall in all but a few important instances.

Rackets and the Police

A racket has been defined as the activity of a group organized for profit from the sale of goods or services by means of physical violence or an illegitimate use of group pressure. Rackets have so permeated our social institutions as to call forth exercise of equally strong group pressures on the side of democracy and liberty. The success of vice overlords in turning to their own use the functions of government affords them an opportunity to seize control of legitimate business. In this way a dangerous racket may have its origin. First victims are those services, such as laundries, which depend in large part upon the patronage of gangster controlled amusement places. Then follows intimidation of those places of business and services which rely for their existence upon the good will of a large number of establishments. The "muscle-men" come into play, declare themselves "in" on a share of the profits of an enterprise, levy a heavy tribute and promise -- and sometimes deliver -- a virtual monopoly of the business in a restricted area at higher service charges.

When the local police have lost the confidence of the population because of their attitude toward racketeers, an individual tradesman will prefer to donate a reasonable amount as commanded, rather than to risk a bombing, incendiarism, the ruin of his business, or actual physical harm. Rival racketeers are attracted by the profit possibilities and police ineffectiveness. Bloody feuds begin and disorder and unsolved gangland murders increase. A community feeling of insecurity grows apace.

Other Agencies at Work. Clearly beyond the control of the local police, the situations give rise to popular clamor for a special prosecutor and special grand juries. The remedial agencies must have the general confidence of the community; otherwise the necessary information concerning violations will not be divulged by victims whose lives may be endangered by a betrayal of confidence. A considerable amount of money must be made available to the special prosecutor, for he will have to buy much of his evidence. Men do not commonly risk reprisals merely to do their neighbor a good turn.

The federal government has become concerned about the dangers inherent in racketeering, as evidenced by the Federal Anti-Racket Law. Rackets depend on violence — bombings, incendiary fires, smashing of plate glass windows, threats of personal injury — and as such are outside the pale of democracy and law observance. Unfortunately they are not always outside the pale of social tolerance. The division between a racket and a legitimate business is not a line but a shadow. But this shadowy distinction should in no way minimize the revulsion of popular feeling against the out-and-out racket.

The police are on the firing line, but they are helpless without the aid of unified police sentiment, a courageous city government, and a fearless prosecutor. New York City has proved it possible to send to jail racket leaders such as Luciano on charges of racketeering (and not for income tax evasion) by means of an able, honest, fearless, tireless prosecutor who had the full support of the public, the police, the city government, and the courts. All of these elements are necessary in this war on the most vicious form of crime.

Strong Points. Organized crime germinates in the seed-bed of commercialized vice. In the American system of government, the responsibility for enforcing the laws which cover these seed-beds, is primarily the responsibility of local government; that is, municipal and county government. Recent public investigations of organized crime have publicized many of the failures and shortcomings in the administration of local law enforcement. Instances of dishonesty, neglect of duty and incompetence have been revealed necessarily as a part of the general picture of organized crime. It could not be otherwise if the subject is to be treated with candor and frankness. However, the publicity which has been given to these failures has an unfortunate tendency to obscure the fact that local law enforcement as a system is basically strong and in general has been successful.

It is not surprising that the achievements of local government in the way of good law enforcement do not receive publicity comparable to the failures. There is nothing sensational or spectacular or even newsworthy about good government. Good law enforcement means the absence of racketeers, a lack of violence and fear in the community, and a minimum of crime in general. This kind of administration may confer great benefits on the local community, but it doesn't make for news.

There is danger in ignoring the unpublished but general success of our system of local law enforcement, as there is always danger in ignoring any part of the truth. The

fact that in the great majority of our cities and counties, the machinery of local law enforcement works efficiently and effectively proves that, without any radical change in our
system of government, local police and prosecuting systems can be built up and maintained which are independent of political intrigue and are professionally competent to
cope with the most shrewd, skillful, and well-heeled crooks. It proves that our traditional
system of local law enforcement can be made to work and to afford reasonable protection
against the inroads of organized crime. Disgust with the failures and inadequacies of particular local law enforcement officials and impatience with the jurisdictional difficulties
inherent in a decentralized administration of police power should not lead us to abandon
the system which, whatever its deficiencies, has the overwhelming merit of permitting
the ordinary citizen to live in freedom from fear of his own police, a freedom that is all
too rare in the world today.[6]

The Process of Law Enforcement

Local police departments are not, of course, the only police agencies involved in
law enforcement. State and federal agencies are active to detect crimes and apprehend
criminals. Neither are police the only people involved in the law enforcement process.
It is not the policeman's job to punish; other institutions have been created for this purpose.

A Typical Case

The process of law enforcement involves many agencies and offers a wide variety
of possible procedures. The case history of a hypothetical felony will illustrate the various steps that may be involved. This sketch is based on the organization and procedure
in an actual city and therefore may vary somewhat in procedure and in terminology from
that in other jurisdictions. Nevertheless, its essential features have their counterparts
in all sections of the country.

A crime classed by the legislature and the courts as a felony has been committed.
There are several alternatives to arrest. The felony may not be detected; it may not be
reported; or the felon may not be apprehended. Assuming that the felon is apprehended,
he will be arrested by a police officer and a charge placed against him. He will then be
brought before a judge of the municipal court. Here, too, there are many possibilities
of elimination. The municipal court cannot convict or sentence on a felony charge. It
must either bind the case over to the grand jury, reduce the charge to a misdemeanor, or
dismiss the case as unsuitable for further prosecution.

Therefore in the preliminary hearing the felon may be dismissed outright for want
of prosecution or at the request of a prosecuting witness, or the case may be continued
indefinitely. He also has the opportunity to forfeit his bond if it is low or perhaps worthless. If these measures fail, he still has the chance of having the judge sentence him for
a misdemeanor rather than a felony, and even this sentence may be suspended or deferred. The sentence may be either a fine or a term in the workhouse, and in the case of
the latter he may be paroled before his term has expired, or he may escape.

Should he fail to have the advantage of any of these opportunities and be bound over
to the grand jury, he still has reason for hope. It is the duty of the grand jury, with the
advice of the county prosecutor, to determine whether the accused should be indicted.

---

[6]See *Final Report of the California Special Crime Study Commission on Organized Crime*, 1953, p. 67.

The grand jury may ignore his case or it may determine that the evidence does not warrant indictment. If he is indicted, he may have his case *nolle prossed,* he may forfeit his bond, or he may have a plea of guilty to a misdemeanor charge accepted.

The Trial. Should he come to trial he will be arraigned before the court of common pleas and will face prosecution by the county prosecutor, but conviction is by no means certain yet. He may be acquitted, the jury may disagree, or the judge may be persuaded to drop the case upon the motion of the counsel. Again he may be convicted of only a misdemeanor and have the subsequent alternatives described above. Finally, he may be convicted of the felony. His sentence may still be deferred, or it may be suspended, in which case he will be placed under the supervision of a probation officer. Otherwise he will be sent to a penal or correctional institution.

Even at this stage in the process he still has a chance to escape the full penalty imposed upon him. His sentence may be commuted, or he may even be pardoned by the governor, or he may be released on parole before his term is over. Finally, he may escape from prison.

In summing up this review of a felony prosecution the following stages, together with the public official or agency concerned, may be listed:

Detection	Police Department
Arrest	Police Department
Detention or Bail	Clerk of Municipal Court
Prosecution in Preliminary Hearing	Municipal Prosecutor
Preliminary Hearing	Judge of Municipal Court
Detention for Grand Jury	County Jail — Sheriff
Bail	Clerk of Court
Prosecution before Grand Jury	County Prosecutor
Grand Jury	15 members
Detention	County Jail — Sheriff
Bail or Bond	Court of Common Pleas
Prosecution	County Prosecutor
Disposition without Trial	Judge — Court of Common Pleas
Trial by Jury	12 members
Sentence after Conviction	Judge of Common Pleas
Probation	Probation Officers
Execution of Sentence	Penal and Correctional Institutions
Parole	State Board of Clemency
Pardon	Governor

This list shows the many agencies with which police administrators at all levels will be in repeated contact. The next step is to examine in somewhat greater detail the work of the police department and its relations with other agencies, both administrative and judicial.

The Police Department

Primarily, a police department is established to protect life, property, and rights and to preserve order. It is not at all unusual, however, for the police to be burdened with a number of duties for which they have no particular fitness. The police department is often the last resort when something has to be done which is not clearly the duty of some other unit of the government. Among the activities which are only indirectly related to the primary functions of a police department, but which are often given to the police to perform include: licensing, traffic regulation (sometimes extended to include power to designate parking areas, one-way streets, and other matters which are quasi-legislative in their nature), public ambulance service, supervision of paroled convicts, registration of voters and verification of poll lists, neighborhood entertainments, and dog pounds.

In one sense this growth of new functions can be explained by contrasting the "police function," which means the preservation of the peace, with the legal concept known as the "police power." The latter is that inherent power by which a state exercises supervision and control over matters involving the peace, good order, health, morals, and general welfare of the community. Under this broad and vaguely defined power cities pass ordinances relating not only to public peace and order but also to health, morals, public convenience, and general welfare.

The police power may be described as the power to govern men and things within the limits of the state's domain. To a large extent this power is exercised by the states themselves, through criminal and civil codes and general legislation affecting "police power" quite extensively. The city exists as a unit of government by virtue of authority granted to it by the state; hence the exercise of municipal police power is subject to conformance with state statutes. Ordinances providing for the inspection of foods, establishing building codes, and regulating billboards are all embraced in this broad legal concept. Many of the new services undertaken by American cities during the past few decades have their source in the "police power."

Types of Burdensome Ordinances. The difficulties encountered by the police in assuming responsibility for the miscellany of functions outlined above fall into two general categories: those resulting from inspectional activities and those in enforcing nuisance ordinances.

The list of inspectional responsibilities given to police by municipal ordinances are many. While not all cities require all types of inspections by policemen the known list includes investigations prior to issuing various kinds of licenses; inspection of weights and measures; sanitary and health inspection; fire hazard inspection; inspection of pawn shops, dance halls, and amusement places; and the inspection of drug store books, principally to discover the names of persons who are purchasing poison. These can be especially difficult. Unless the policeman proceeds carefully he is likely to not only arouse antagonism of the persons involved, but he may also inadvertently damage their reputations.

Those ordinances dealing specifically with nuisances, such as, for example, the regulatory measures relating to animals, can cause much irritation. Dog laws particularly can arouse people against the policeman. Similarly, antinoise measures, such as those prohibiting playing of pianos after a fixed hour, are burdensome on the individual policeman who must enforce them.

Strain on Police. Many of these ordinances are sound from the points of view of public health and the general well-being of the city. However, the result of placing upon the police the responsibility for enforcing them is often a severe strain. The majority of these new regulations and controls require the exercise of considerable discretion on the part of the enforcing officer. The issue between right and wrong is not so clearly defined as in the case of other criminal laws.

Furthermore there is a difference in public attitude toward the violation. Regulations under the police power, unfortunately, do not always receive sympathetic public support. A man who has violated a traffic ordinance or who has evaded the payment of a license fee does not consider himself a criminal. In fact he is more likely to feel that any punishment imposed upon him is persecution rather than justice, and the police officer is viewed not as a public protector but as an invader of private rights.

The most serious aspect of this attitude is that it soon colors the public reaction to the police officer even when he is enforcing the traditional peace and order. As a consequence the police department is burdened with additional and difficult functions, while at the same time it is being deprived of one of its most essential supports — public opinion.

Another product of the expansion of the use of the police power is that the police officer must have broader and more varied background and training. If he is to be entrusted with discretionary powers in enforcement he must be educated to use his discretion wisely.

Enforcement of these varied ordinances means, also, that the police department has an added responsibility in its public relations program — that of explaining to the public at large and to affected citizens particularly the purpose of the ordinance and exactly what is necessary to comply with it.

Administrative Responsibilities. The solution of this problem is not entirely in the power of the police department. Within the department, however, the problem must be met largely by improving the quality of the personnel. A higher type of recruit, better trained for the varied duties of modern police work, is the primary answer to the new burdens on the police department. And not only will this step result in a better handling of duties imposed under police power regulations; it will also provide a higher type of officer for the performance of the primary functions of the police department — the preservation of peace and order. (Specific suggestions for the improvement of personnel administration in municipal police departments will be considered in Chapter 4.) Both legislative and administrative improvements must be linked if the police department is to be most effective.

Other Local Police Agencies

The municipal police officer will be brought into inevitable contact with sheriffs and coroners when these officers are performing their sworn duties for the county. In addition he may have to deal upon occasion with constables and justices of the peace, the latter sometimes known as squires or magistrates. These official relationships should receive the diligent, understanding attention of all municipal officers.

Sheriff. The sheriff is an elected official whose term is brief, usually two or four years. Because of meager compensation, briefness of term, and the common prohibition against succeeding himself, the sheriff is often forced to supplement his income by following some trade or conducting a small business enterprise.

It is the duty of the sheriff to apprehend criminals. He has full police powers, is custodian of the county jail, and is the server of criminal and civil process. In addition he may be the overseer of highways and bridges, custodian of county funds, tax collector, assessor, or even executioner of persons condemned to death. With few exceptions, time does not permit him to establish any effective police patrol designed to prevent criminal offenses, nor does it allow him to engage in the pursuit of any but the most vicious criminals.

Sometimes the sheriff will have a force of deputies to assist him, mainly as civil process servers. Or he may have a county highway force primarily devoted to traffic problems, especially on weekends and holidays, which also maintains some sort of patrol against crime when not engaged in traffic control.

Under these circumstances the sheriff usually enjoys that prestige and respect as an enforcement officer which his personal competence earns for him. In their dealings with him the municipal police officers may usually manage to serve the best interests of sound law enforcement if they will employ tact, sincerity, and understanding helpfulness.

Constable. Turning to that rural officer, the constable, it is noted that he is mentioned in the constitutions of nearly half the states. The office is elective or appointive — usually the former — and the tenure runs from one to four years. The unit he serves varies widely; it may be a town or township, where these units exist, or a county, a magisterial district, parish, ward, or some other subdivision.

In addition to his responsibility for keeping the peace, the constable is often required to act as a tax collector. Compensation for his official duties is commonly derived solely from fees. At best he is necessarily only a part-time policeman; he can rarely earn enough in fees to sustain him without other employment. Receiving no fees for crime repression or prevention work, it is not to be expected that he will exert himself at such work. The office enjoys no general prestige. The constable is unsupervised, almost always untrained, and is commonly merely a process server.

Coroner. The county coroner, like the sheriff, has an ancient lineage reaching back centuries into early English custom. He is usually elected, though in a few states in the Northeast and South he gains office by appointment. The qualifications are generally simple, consisting of age, residence, citizenship, and an official bond. The term is normally two years but may run to three or four.

Varying somewhat with local laws, the coroner or his deputy investigates the cause and circumstances of all deaths from unknown causes and from such unnatural causes as violence, injury, or criminal means. The coroner may, at his discretion, order autopsies or other scientific procedures. Further, he may subpoena witnesses to appear at an inquest, at which time the facts and events related to the death are recorded. If a crime is suspected by the jury, appropriate criminal proceedings are instituted independently of any other law enforcement agency; thus an accused is brought before a judge.

The medical examiner, similarly subject to variation in local laws, investigates all deaths that occur under the circumstances listed above, and the purposes and goals are the same as those of the coroner.

In a number of states the office of coroner has been abolished and the duties transferred to the justice of the peace, and in a few states, to the prosecutor's office. At least 12 states use medical examiners, either in lieu of or in conjunction with the coroner. Arkansas and Georgia operate a centralized medical examiner office without effect on the coroner system. In Maryland and Virginia local medical examiners are appointed by and are under the supervision of state boards. In Rhode Island, the attorney general may appoint medical examiners. In the large metropolitan areas of Suffolk County (Boston), Massachusetts, and New York City, the coroner has been replaced by an appointed medical examiner with experience in pathology and legal medicine. The system may be used by other counties in these states, but the difficulty in acquiring trained personnel has hampered the growth of the system. Other states that permit counties to use medical examiners are Maine, Michigan, Florida, New Hampshire, New Jersey, and Wisconsin. However, in some of the states (such as New Jersey and Wisconsin) the system may be used by the largest counties only. Connecticut has a unique system in which each town coroner appoints a medical examiner. The coroner must be an attorney and the medical examiner a physician.

Minor differences are to be found between the two systems in the mechanics and administration of the medico-legal investigations. There are three main differences: (1) medical examiner systems require that a physician investigate the scene of death, while coroners usually use trained deputies; (2) the chief medical examiner who directs the activities of his office must be a physician, while coroners who have similar supervisory activities may be laymen; and (3) the medical examiner does not hold inquest proceedings and has no direct authority to bring an accused before a judge; he refers his findings to the district attorney who, in turn, may or may not take action according to his own view or wish.

Coroners in populous jurisdictions generally have a staff of lay investigators who make the "at the scene" investigation into criminal and evidential aspects of the case. These men spend all of their time at this work; most of them make a career of it. As a result, their investigations are generally very patiently and painstakingly done, certainly more so than those made by physicians most of whom consider such investigation secondary to their prime interest and training.

The question arises whether it should be required that all coroners be physicians. Such a requirement would be advisable. A large proportion of the coroner's work, in addition to being supervisory, deals with medical matters. In most jurisdictions, it is best to have a common direction of medical, technical, and investigative personnel in order to integrate their various activities. This could most easily be done by someone trained in the medical sciences. While all "at the scene" investigation need not, and perhaps should not, be made by a physician, the work of the autopsy surgeon, toxicologist, pathologist, and technician is better understood by a physician and thus better integrated into the investigation. For these reasons, the work should be overseen by a coroner who is a physician.[7]

The importance of the coroner in a homicide case is revealed when we consider that he has full charge of the body and may remove it where he will and when he pleases. He may exclude the police and the prosecutor from the premises of the crime and sign an order for the interment or cremation of the corpse. Clashes of jurisdiction between the coroner, on the one hand, and sheriff, constable, prosecutor, and municipal or state police on the other, are possible at many points.

State's Attorney. This officer -- also known as the prosecutor, solicitor, public prosecutor, district attorney, prosecutor of common pleas, county prosecutor, or prosecuting attorney -- is the people's champion of justice in criminal and civil proceedings. Untold power for the betterment or detriment of the public good rests in his hands. The police come in touch with him or his assistants numberless times in the discharge of their official duties. These meetings can be made opportunities for enlightened administration. The state's attorney has the power to breathe life into prosecution in the interest of justice.

In most states the office is elective by counties. The compensation is seldom considerable. Young men of the legal profession commonly contrive to use the office as a training school for themselves and as a means of making contacts helpful in later private practice or as a stepping stone in politics. Some states fix the salary of the prosecuting

---

[7]From Henry W. Turkey, M.D., "Merits of the Present Coroner System," *Journal of American Medical Association,* November 21, 1953, pp. 2, 13, and 18.

attorneys on the basis of county population, with a larger stipend for those who serve the larger population groups.

In counties containing one or more large cities in which municipal courts have been established, the municipal attorney is normally the clearinghouse for cases. He decides whether an affidavit (so-called "short affidavit" or complaint) shall issue. In this way the municipal attorney exercises broad discretionary powers; he may suppress the evidence in many cases which should properly go to trial or he may handle the witnesses in such manner as to cause the state's case to fail in the prosecutor's hand. At these unofficial, off-the-record hearings there is the possibility also that privileges of the office may be misused by minor officials to collect false claims from ignorant victims.

The county prosecutor usually has ample power over the conduct of cases, from the time the crime becomes known, to permit him to establish the necessary controls to insure proper administration. In the case mentioned above, where a municipal attorney intervenes between the police and the county prosecutor, the latter should set up records control devices to provide for adequate written evidence of *nolle prossed* and other cases that are not allowed to go to trial.

The individual policeman is virtually helpless when he sees the facts suppressed by a high official in connection with a serious criminal case. The state's attorney can do something about such a condition. It is his business to see that a prosecution which should be started is actually begun. He should set up a policy for determining whether a case should be dismissed or a bargain made with the defendant's counsel for a plea of guilty on a reduced charge.

Clearly the police, who are usually the first responsible officials to learn of a crime, can be of the greatest assistance to the state's attorney. Their maximum helpfulness will be rendered by thorough investigation. By identifying and locating needed witnesses, protecting them when in danger, and insuring their presence at the trial, the police can perform inestimable service.

An investigation which produces all available physical evidence, as well as the identification and information of principal witnesses, places these valuable tools of justice in the hands of the state's attorney. With the informed investigating officer at his elbow during the trial, the busy prosecutor or his assistant can make effective use of the facts revealed and reported by competent police offices. At such a time, thorough-going investigation stands out in bold contrast to the careless inquiry which relies on meager evidence, confessions, or flimsy damaging statements which may be — and often are — repudiated.

The state's attorney, when truly effective, relies heavily upon police competence and cooperation. This should be accorded him without reserve, so that justice may be realized. As suggested in Chapter 12, the regular index maintained by the police of the proportion of persons arrested who are convicted will inform the police as to (1) the relative efficiency of the police in supplying the prosecutor with evidence which will stand up in court, and (2) the relative success of the prosecution of cases brought in by the police.

Unless the police realize their obligations to the state's attorney, that official will probably maintain a staff of investigative officers and thereby remove the function of investigation from the police. This trend seems to be a dangerous one to the police for, if allowed to continue, it is likely to result in a situation where the police are merely uniformed night watchmen, leaving all investigations for the staff of the state's attorney. If, on the other hand, the police adequately discharge their duties to the prosecutor, and by so doing create a feeling of confidence, this situation probably will not arise.

Probation and Parole Agencies. Probation and parole create certain problems of relationship between the police and those who supervise the conduct of persons who are at liberty under certain restrictions. Probation is the release of a convicted person upon suspension of the sentence so long as he conducts himself in a satisfactory manner. This requires the appointment by the court of probation officers whose duty is to keep in touch with the prisoners placed on probation and to report to the court from time to time regarding them. As the system has developed, more emphasis has been placed upon the duty of the probation officer to act not merely as an inspector, but as a friend of his charges, in advising them, aiding them to secure employment, cautioning them if they appear to be getting into bad company, and, generally, aiding them in their efforts to lead a proper life. Parole is the release of prisoners who have served part of their sentences. Again supervision of the parolee must be maintained.

Both probation and parole are widely used. The use of the probation device in the case of juveniles is more common than in the case of adults. In practice, both probation and parole fall short of their theoretical goals, but their administration in a few jurisdictions is very encouraging. It seems clear that both are here to stay as permanent features of the administration of justice, and police administrators must therefore examine their relationships with probation and parole officers to see that mutual aid and cooperation are achieved.

Probation and parole officers can be of considerable aid to the police. In the first place, by their work of supervision and rehabilitation of persons convicted of crime they are making a definite contribution to the crime prevention program of the city. Probationers and parolees who are cured of their criminal tendencies and made over into law-abiding citizens represent a reduction in crime hazards. Furthermore, the data collected by probation and parole officers are invaluable in the study of the causes of crime, the psychology of the criminal, and the best methods of treatment.

What can the police department do for probation and parole officers? First, the police department should refrain from persecution of probationers and parolees. Although much of the talk about police "hounding" of such individuals has been exaggerated, patrolmen and detectives must understand that nothing is to be gained by treating probationers and parolees in an abusive manner and dogging their footsteps to see that they are guilty of no misconduct. Both probation and parole are attempts to readjust offenders to live normal lives, and any hostility on the part of the police is likely to hinder, rather than help, in this adjustment. This should not be interpreted as meaning that the police should not be on the alert for misbehavior, however.

Probationers and parolees are required to be particularly careful of their behavior, and the police should direct to the attention of probation or parole authorities any suspicious activities. Frequent conferences between the police and probation and parole authorities will make it possible to effect satisfactory clearance of such matters. The police can also assist probation and parole officers by supplying from their records and knowledge any information as to the habits and past record of offenders under such supervision in order that points of danger or weakness can be given special attention.

Judicial Agencies

A proper understanding of the function of judicial agencies at every level at which police and courts come into contact is important to the police administrator.

Justice of the Peace. Another numerically important official with whom the munici-pal police have to deal is the justice of the peace. Like the constable, he has wide consti-tutional status. In three-fourths of the states he is elected. His term is two to seven years, but the short term is common. Candidates come from virtually every known group. The incumbents frequently succeed themselves in office, especially in rural areas.

Compensation of a justice of the peace is commonly by the fee system, although some are paid a small fixed salary. His jurisdiction often extends to civil and criminal action. Civil cases are usually limited to those involving not over $100 to $500. Petty misdemeanors may be tried before him and commitments made in such cases. In serious criminal charges his authority is limited to a determination whether the accused should be held for the action of the grand jury.

A justice of the peace may also hold another elective office and thus exercise legis-lative and administrative powers as well as judicial functions. Commonly untrained, the justice of the peace may find himself embarrassed by his meager knowledge of the law and judicial procedure when a defendant is represented by able counsel. In such a situa-tion a competent police officer can often further the cause of justice, and at the same time, win the cooperation of the justice by timely, tactful suggestions.

Grand Jury. In many states the grand jury is an important cog in the machinery of law enforcement because it must return an indictment against a suspect charged with a felony before he can be tried in court. The grand jury is almost completely under the control of the prosecutor and the courts regarding the cases which it considers, although it may return indictments on the basis of its own knowledge. The relationship of the po-lice to the grand jury is indirect and limited to the evidence the police supply the prose-cutor for use before the grand jury. The grand jury is a cumbersome piece of machinery; to the extent that it clogs the legal process, the police have an interest in it.

Most authorities agree that the grand jury has outlived its usefulness and that it impedes law enforcement without offering any additional protection to those who may be unjustly charged with a crime. While it is desirable that the grand jury be divested of its indictment functions, it still serves a useful purpose as a citizen agency with official status to investigate the administration and enforcement of the law and to make public its findings. In many jurisdictions the grand jury has proved the most effective device for discovering and publicizing abuses by public officials.

Complaints. In those states where the grand jury has been abolished, the filing of information and the issuance of a criminal complaint supplant its previous function. In-deed, in some states, the grand jury can still be called, but the routine criminal business is transacted by the filing of a complaint. Under this procedure, briefly, the complainant appears before the state's attorney and swears or alleges that a certain individual has committed a particular crime. On the basis of this information, a complaint is issued which calls for the defendant to appear before a magistrate. When he appears he is en-titled to a preliminary examination to determine if there are sufficient grounds to hold him for trial on the charge.

If there are sufficient grounds, the court sets the case for trial and allows release on bond. In most cases a police officer is the complainant because he has knowledge of the crime; however, any citizen may cause a complaint to issue if he has knowledge of the guilt of the defendant. This procedure safeguards the rights of the accused, as he is entitled to a hearing, before trial, to determine if there are reasonable grounds for the complaint. The complaint system speeds up criminal action and is less expensive than the grand jury system.

The Courts. Like the grand jury, the courts are of interest to the police primarily because the police are concerned with the disposal of the cases for which they are in the first instance responsible. The important function of the police in presenting evidence in court will be discussed in another chapter. Four aspects of the courts are of special interest to the police, although all four are outside police control.

1. Organization. The tendency of courts in some jurisdictions to break down the judicial function into specialized branches has a direct relation to the principle of crime prevention — that various classes of offenders should receive treatment according to their needs. Thus, the creation of the juvenile court for hearing cases involving offenders below a certain age is of direct aid to the police in their effort to convert juvenile delinquents into useful members of society rather than into hardened criminals. A specialized court makes it possible for the police to bring special cases before judges who are well equipped, by training and experience, to hear them. Examples of such courts are domestic relations, traffic, housing, and morals.

2. Procedure. The police are vitally concerned with the speed with which cases are brought to trial. Overcrowded court calendars which cause months and sometimes years of delay impose great difficulties on the police who must preserve both witnesses and material evidence until the case is tried. The police are also concerned with the attitude of the court toward an officer's testimony, rules of impaneling a jury, change of venue, admission of evidence, grounds for new trial, attitude toward the expert witness and his testimony, rules governing appeals, and many other court procedures. The police administrator's major concern is to be acquainted with these matters and to see that they are brought out in each officer's training.

3. Incorruptibility. Nothing is more demoralizing to an aggressive, able police force than to see air-tight cases lost because of crooked dealings somewhere along the line after indictment and trial machinery has been put in motion. Conversely it is a real stimulus to police morale to know that able presentation of a case by the prosecutor based on adequate evidence secured by the police will not be overcome by corrupt "deals."

4. The Sentence. The discretion that is given to the judge, under the laws of many states, to impose sentence has an important effect on the success of the law enforcement program in preventing crime and rehabilitating offenders. In many cases the court has a choice of penalties and may even be empowered to suspend sentence and place the guilty party on probation. In imposing sentence, the judge takes into consideration the severity of the offense, the provocation, the age of the offender, his previous criminal record, and other factors. His ability to relate the sentence properly both to the offense and to the offender obviously has an effect on the police program. In some states the trial judge sentences the offender for an indeterminate period, and primary responsibility for finally fixing the length of sentence lies with the parole board.

Federal Agencies

Federal governmental agencies — the FBI the most famous — undertake many police activities in enforcing federal laws, often in frequent contact with local law enforcement agencies. Local departments often call upon them for information, and, as will be shown, cooperative machinery between departments is coordinated and facilitated by federal agencies.

Federal Bureau of Investigation. The Federal Bureau of Investigation is the investigative arm of the United States Department of Justice. Founded in 1908, the FBI at present has investigative jurisdiction over more than 160 different violations of federal law.

FBI headquarters are located in Washington, D. C. Here are maintained, in addition to administrative offices, the identification division, the laboratory, and uniform crime reporting facilities. Field division offices are located in major cities. The FBI provides many services to local law enforcement. The principal ones will be discussed briefly.

1. Fingerprints. The identification division was established on July 1, 1924, with a nucleus of 810,188 fingerprints obtained from Leavenworth Penitentiary and the International Association of Chiefs of Police.

These prints are divided into two main files: noncriminal and criminal. Criminal fugitives are identified through fingerprint searches. This is accomplished by placing "stop notices" in the fingerprint files against the fingerprints of persons being sought as fugitives. When information concerning the fugitive's whereabouts is received, it is immediately telegraphed to the interested law enforcement agency. Fingerprint data, in addition, enable the police officer to determine identity and secure arrest records. Fingerprints also serve many humanitarian purposes. Amnesia victims, missing persons, and victims of disasters, such as fire, flood, and crashes, otherwise unidentifiable, may be identified through fingerprints.

2. Laboratory. The FBI laboratory, founded in 1932, is recognized as one of the most outstanding of its kind in the world. Its facilities are available without cost to local law enforcement agencies. Later, if a local case comes to trial, the laboratory will furnish, again free of charge, an examiner to testify as to the scientific examination conducted. In this way a law enforcement agency, regardless of size, can benefit from the latest advances in scientific crime detection.

The laboratory also maintains a number of reference files including, among others, the national fraudulent check file, anonymous letter file, confidence men file, national unidentified ammunition file, tire tread file, and watermark file. Incoming specimens are searched against these files in an effort to make an identification. Virtually every type of scientific examination is conducted in the laboratory: charred paper, indented writing, obliterated writing, typewriting, glass fractures, paint, metallurgical, toolmarks, toxicological, and explosives, among others.

3. National Academy. The FBI also aids local law enforcement through its training facilities. The FBI National Academy, founded in 1935, is designed to train police executives and instructors. National Academy sessions, held twice a year, last for 12 weeks. The first 10 weeks are devoted to required courses, dealing with more than 100 aspects of law enforcement work. Special attention is given to scientific investigative techniques, fingerprinting, crime scene searches, police organization and administration and legal subjects such as constitutional law and the Bill of Rights. The final two weeks are devoted to specialized instruction in a field of the officer's own choosing.

Many police officers, unable to attend the National Academy in Washington, D. C., can receive instruction through local police training schools. In this way training in law enforcement is brought to many thousands of officers in their own departments.

4. Publications. A number of booklets and special publications are issued by the FBI which enable officers to stay abreast of current developments in the law enforcement profession. The *Uniform Crime Reports* bulletin, issued annually, contains crime statistics for the nation based on data submitted voluntarily by law enforcement agencies concerning such matters as offenses known to the police, offenses cleared by arrest, persons found guilty, and the age, sex, and race of arrested persons. These bulletins which are available to the public, provide a yardstick to measure the extent of crime in various localities. The FBI *Law Enforcement Bulletin,* published monthly, provides a medium for

the exchange of ideas in law enforcement. This publication contains articles on crime detection written both by FBI experts and officers from local departments.

5. Investigations. The FBI's investigative responsibilities fall into two main categories: criminal and domestic intelligence. In the early 1930's the Congress passed a number of statutes, often called the Federal Crime Bills, giving the FBI jurisdiction over certain violations. These included, for example, the National Bank Robbery Act, the Federal Extortion Statute, the Federal Kidnapping Statute, and the Unlawful Flight To Avoid Prosecution Statute. The FBI, in cooperation with local law enforcement agencies, immediately waged an intensive war against the criminal world and soon many of the notorious criminals were captured and their gangs broken up.

The FBI's responsibilities in the field of internal security stem from a number of Congressional enactments such as sabotage and espionage statutes, the Smith Act, the Foreign Agents Registration Act, rulings of the attorney general and Presidential directives. In 1939 the President issued a directive placing upon the FBI the responsibility of correlating matters relating to espionage, counterespionage, sabotage, subversive activities, and violations of the neutrality laws. This directive, which was reiterated in 1943 and 1950, called upon local law enforcement officials to furnish promptly information of this type to the FBI.

Other Federal Enforcement Agencies. The FBI is of major importance in the relationships of municipal police to federal agencies primarily because of such activities as the publication of crime statistics, the National Academy, the collection of fingerprints, and the clearing of other crime records on a national basis. As far as investigation activities alone are concerned, municipal police have equally important relationships with such federal agencies as the Alcohol Tax Unit, the Bureau of Narcotics, the Secret Service, and the Post Office.

1. Alcohol Tax Unit. The Alcohol Tax Unit of the Internal Revenue Service is charged with the supervision of the legitimate industry enforcement of the Federal Alcohol Administration Act and related regulations, and investigation, detection, and prevention of willful and fraudulent violations of the internal revenue liquor laws, the National and Federal Firearms Acts, certain parts of the Federal Alcohol Administration Act, and the Liquor Enforcement Act of 1936. The unit encourages state and local officers to handle violations of state liquor or revenue laws which are also minor violations of federal laws and to turn over to the unit for investigation the major cases under state laws which are also major violations of federal laws.

2. Bureau of Narcotics. The Bureau of Narcotics of the Department of the Treasury is responsible for confining traffic in drugs to the amount that is necessary and used for medical and scientific purposes. Its relationship with state and local governments is an important factor in enforcing the Harrison Act. It is not the policy of the federal government to assume the whole burden. It has not attempted, for example, directly to control marihuana, which is domestically produced. The Bureau of Narcotics is required to cooperate with the states in the drafting of legislation for the suppression of narcotics. It is charged with exchanging information with the states on this general subject; at times it assists state and local authorities in the initiation and prosecution of cases before state courts and state licensing boards. To the licensing boards, the Bureau reports the names of licensees who are believed to be drug addicts or who have been convicted of narcotics violations. Such information is used in connection with the revocation or suspension of state licenses to practice a profession or engage in a business involving transactions in narcotic drugs.

3. <u>Secret Service.</u> The Secret Service is the oldest of all federal police agencies, having been established during the Civil War to protect the national currency. This agency has jurisdiction over all cases of counterfeiting of currency and other negotiable instruments of the United States. It also has the duty of safeguarding the person of the President of the United States and his official family. In carrying out its duties, the Secret Service issues information to police agencies regarding the detection of counterfeit money and how to investigate counterfeit cases. This agency will also furnish instructors to local police schools to teach its duties.

4. <u>Post Office.</u> Post Office inspectors have jurisdiction over all acts which involve wrongful use of postal facilities, mail losses, mail depredations, and other offenses arising under the postal laws. Within this limited sphere, their jurisdiction runs the whole gamut of criminality. Continuous cooperation with local police is mutually helpful. Post Office inspectors also assist local investigators in tracing mail.

5. <u>Other Federal Agencies.</u> Municipal police departments have less frequent contacts with a number of agencies including the Coast Guard, the Immigration and Naturalization Service of the Department of Justice, the Intelligence Unit of the Customs Patrol, and agencies of the National Military Establishments such as the Air Force Inspector General, Air Provost Marshal, Office of Special Investigation, Army Provost Marshal General, Office of Naval Intelligence, and the Army Criminal Investigation Division.

State Bureaus of Identification

The FBI, because of its geographical location, cannot serve all states with equal readiness. It cannot engage in certain activities which are desirable within states, and it cannot maintain the intimate contacts with every large and small city and county that are necessary to guide and encourage the effective forces of a whole state toward improved law enforcement.

At least 33 states have some sort of bureau for filing identification data and criminal histories, conducting investigations, carrying on research, training peace officers, coordinating communications, collecting and compiling statistics, or some combination of these functions.

As the FBI continues to expand its identification and training facilities it can be expected that the identification activities of state bureaus will diminish in importance. However, the state bureaus should continue to exercise an important influence in providing training facilities, publication of statistics, and improvement of administrative practice. This present scope of services varies widely, and most could be expanded with considerable benefit to local police authorities.

<u>Ideal Organization.</u> Ideally, a state bureau and local agencies should cooperate along the lines suggested by the "Draft of an Act Creating a State Bureau of Criminal Identification, Investigation, and Statistics" issued by the Committee on Uniform Crime Records of the International Association of Chiefs of Police.

A unit of this kind, under a superintendent trained and experienced in personal identification, investigation, and collection, compilation, and analysis of statistics, is of incalculable service. Continuity of service so essential to productive administration is obtained when the head is appointed by the governor and removable by him only for cause.

The responsibilities of the state bureau should include the receipt, filing, and classification of names, photographs, and fingerprints — as well as other appropriate data —

of persons arrested by the police for other than minor traffic and ordinance violations. An up-to-date record of these offenses committed within the state should be maintained currently.

The state bureau should receive and file information on fugitives from justice, vagrants, narcotic addicts, possessors of stolen goods, and those in illegal possession of burglar's tools, weapons, automobile number defacing tools, money counterfeiting devices, bombs, explosives, and similar articles intended for unlawful purposes. Fingerprints, photographs, and identifying information and articles concerning dead bodies and missing persons should be filed.

Duplicates or copies of reports rendered to the police by pawnshops, secondhand dealers, and traders in weapons should be received and filed by the bureau. Reports of stolen motor vehicles, with their engine and body numbers and descriptions, as well as reported recoveries, should be filed.

Every sheriff, head of a law-enforcement unit, institution superintendent, and coroner should be required by law to submit to the bureau information within such time and in such reasonable form as the superintendent may prescribe. Clerks of courts having original or appellate jurisdiction over indictable offenses should be required to submit information concerning indictments and informations filed in the court, and their disposition. Pleas, convictions, acquittals, probations allowed or refused, and such other dispositions of criminal proceedings in the court should be submitted to, and filed by, the bureau.

Information and Services. The bureau should furnish information concerning the identification and history of any person on file, upon application by the police head of any state or local government unit, the superintendent of any similar state bureau or foreign organization, or the judge or prosecuting attorney of any court in the state in which the subject is being tried. Without formal application the bureau should volunteer information to other units when it discovers that such information may be useful.

The bureau superintendent should organize and maintain a scientific crime detection laboratory and operate and coordinate communication systems. He should aid local peace officers sufficiently in the operation of local identification, investigation, and records systems to insure their satisfactory performance and coordination with the work of his bureau. He should conduct training schools from time to time — or he may cooperate in the conduct of any such schools established by a league of municipalities, police officers' association, or any other proper organization.

Provision should be made in the law to admit any copy of a record, picture, photograph, fingerprint, or paper from the bureau files into evidence in any court of the state in the same manner as the original when certified by the superintendent to be a true copy.

One of the most important functions of a state bureau would be the compilation and publication of criminal statistics based on reports which it receives. Such statistics, uniform in nature and of local significance within the state, would provide local police administrators with a valid factual basis for intelligent administrative action and would be a valuable stimulus to adequate record-keeping in local departments.

In order to require the submission of reports legally required, it might be advisable to provide for removal from office of those peace officers who refuse to so submit. Fine or imprisonment might be needed as a penalty for the falsification or suppression of legally required information.

Police and Legal Procedure

Too often police administrators throw the entire blame for delays and ineffective prosecution of criminal cases on the shoulders of the prosecutors and the courts. Police duties are not finished with apprehension of the criminal. Arrest is merely the first step in the administration of criminal justice. The case must be painstakingly prepared by the police, evidence gathered, witnesses interviewed, statements taken, and all possible facts carefully recorded in preparation for the trial. Even the best prosecutor is not enthusiastic about taking a weak or borderline case into court. The failure to prepare cases properly for court trial helps to defeat the ends of justice in American criminal procedure. Trial delays will decrease in frequency when the police consistently present sound cases to the prosecutor.

Evidence of Defects in Legal Procedure

Experienced police administrators say that the best deterrent to crime is swift and sure, but not necessarily severe, punishment. Criminals and defense counsels know that the surest means to escape punishment is through delay in bringing the case to trial. Man's memory is short and his recollections inaccurate. Witnesses move away from the jurisdiction, die, or forget. Some are susceptible to persuasion. The desire of the victim for justice or revenge fades. He may even have a price or be intimidated. Another evidence of weakness in American judicial procedure is the number of cases that drop out between the time the warrants are served and sentences are executed.

Good cases that are lost through lack of diligence by the prosecutor and because of meaningless legal intricacies in the courtroom are disheartening to the police, and police administrators should carefully examine these weaknesses in our criminal proceedings.

Weaknesses in Legal Procedure

The failure to attend to all the details of preparation for a trial results in wasteful continuances. Absence of witnesses is one reason for delays in the courts. Others are the failure of the state to be ready for trial, procrastination of the defense counsel, threats of change of venue, congested dockets, and unpreparedness of counsel.

Inquiry reveals that at times witnesses are not even subpoenaed, the sheriff's return on the subpoena showing the witnesses "not found." A wrong address is often the reason. Prosecution too often fails to shoulder the responsibility of seeing that court clerks issue subpoenas promptly, with the correct names and addresses, and that the sheriff serve them sufficiently in advance of the trial date. Such careless and dilatory practices, even though without design, operate to defeat effective justice.

The criminal receives further help in many cases from an excessive worship of technicalities of the law. Felons have been released because of insignificant errors in an indictment which could by no stretch of the imagination affect the guilt or innocence of the person charged. In criminal proceedings a man may not be required to take the stand in his own defense. A mistrial may be declared for purely technical legal reasons which exceed the limits of common sense. A judge is hedged in by rules which often serve no useful purpose except to help the criminal. Technicalities frequently appear as the cause for dismissals of appeals without hearing, even though the errors can have no bearing on the facts in the case.

American criminal procedure is in many respects cumbersome and archaic, full of nonessentials and formalities which obstruct the production of the facts in a case. A case should be decided on its merits but sometimes cannot be because of the introduction of technical obstructions. Some of these technicalities have a substantial basis in the protection of the innocent, but many have outworn their usefulness and should be discarded.

Weak Police Administration

The police chief must take a positive stand at every opportunity to insist to the best of his ability that criminal cases be promptly and adequately prosecuted. He should study the particular weaknesses in criminal prosecutions in his locality and discuss them frankly with legislators and members of the legal profession in the hope of improving such practices. But the police administrator cannot afford to be complacent about charging lax enforcement to the vagaries of criminal law procedure. Even in good departments less than 40 per cent of such offenses as auto thefts, burglary, and robbery are cleared by arrest, while in the poorest departments the percentage is much lower. Defects in the machinery of criminal justice can by no stretch of the imagination be held responsible.

Efforts To Simplify Legal Procedures

American legal procedure has many weaknesses, but efforts being made by farseeing administrators and professional groups promise to facilitate criminal proceedings.

The Uniform Arrest Act[8] drafted by Professor Sam B. Warner of the Harvard Law School at the instance of the Interstate Commission on Crime offers a solution to many of the anachronisms in our present law of arrest. This act has already been adopted by the legislatures of several states.

The interstate crime compacts now subscribed to in some form by all states greatly simplify and expedite criminal matters between states.[9] Such procedures as extradition, return of fugitives, arrests and hearings by out-of-state officers are made uniform, and much of the delay and red tape is eliminated.

A model statute has been drafted by the American Bar Association[10] which provides for the creation of a uniform system of inferior courts designed primarily for traffic control. This statute is aimed at removing certain abuses found in some inferior courts.

Cooperation[11]

The importance of cooperation in law enforcement cannot be overemphasized. The rapid expansion of community horizons and the ever widening sphere of individual influence have greatly intensified the necessity for unrestricted cooperation among all agencies charged with the administration of criminal law.

The speed of transportation and its availability to the masses has been an important factor in extending the perimeter of community influences and has contributed greatly to

[8]"The Uniform Arrest Act," by Sam B. Warner, reprinted in *The Virginia Law Review*, January, 1942.

[9]*The Handbook of Interstate Crime Control* (Chicago: Council of State Governments, 1949).

[10]Presented in a report of the National Committee on Traffic Law Enforcement to the National Conference of Judicial Councils at the annual meeting of its section on judicial administration at Indianapolis, 1941. 65pp. Available through the American Bar Association, 1155 East 60th Street, Chicago 37.

[11]This section is used by special permission from Dan L. Kooken, "Police Ethics," *Journal of Criminal Law and Criminology*, July-August, 1947, pp. 180-183, published by the Northwestern University School of Law.

the difficulties of speedy criminal apprehensions. Within the span of a single lifetime we have witnessed the extension of community horizons from the confines of counties to areas of national extent.

Satisfactory progress can be made in the fight to suppress crime if real cooperation is effected among all law enforcement bodies. Cooperation is defined as "association for common benefit." It is obvious then that real cooperation cannot be attained if selfish interests are allowed to enter. True cooperation is teamwork and necessitates full recognition and acceptance of its implications by all the agencies of law enforcement. No agency can claim to be cooperating if it remains only on the receiving end; it must give as well as receive. True cooperation involves a unity of purpose and coordination of effort that is founded upon a sincere desire to heed the common interests of all.

Cooperation is more than promises, it is more than the announcement of programs or plans of coordination, it is more than holding conferences accompanied by back slappings and oratorical pronouncements, and it is more than public pledges and agreements to present a united front. Cooperation is the translation of the principles of good teamwork into definite and continuous action. It is an inescapable fact that the principles that bring about cooperation deal with simple, elemental considerations of harmonious relationships.

The problem of obtaining cooperation in law enforcement is a complex and troublesome task. There is no simple formula or master plan that can be brought to bear upon the situation, nor is there a compulsory authority that can be invoked. Its solution can only be reached by mutual willingness of law enforcement leaders to accept their responsibility in the matter, and to play their part on the team to the limit of their ability.

The greatest bar to achievement in this direction is the petty professional jealousies that permeate the very fabric of law enforcement effort. The blame for this condition primarily rests with the administrators, the heads of enforcement departments, who by compulsion implied in political expediency or by personal design, give first consideration to credit and notoriety. They become so engrossed in accumulating credit and building personal reputations that their departmental policies reflect their attitude, and the policies and concepts of the leaders are in turn definitely reflected in the actions of the rank and file. Jealousies of reputation and bickering over publicity exist not only among law enforcement agencies but are particularly common among members within the same department.

In many police departments the jealousies arising between detectives and members of the uniformed division have become so intense that cooperation has been as effectively blocked as would be the case if an insurmountable wall had been constructed between the two functional divisions. A condition is frequently found in the investigation of singularly important crimes where two or more separate agencies are engaged, and each one will be bending every effort to prevent the other from having access to the facts that it has uncovered. Many examples of lack of cooperation between policemen and between police agencies could be recorded, but they are so commonplace that they need little exposition. The fact that is to be emphasized is that they invariably involve the same motivating factors: namely, desire for credit and publicity.

Cooperation cannot occur among police agencies until their common interests can be fully recognized and appreciated. No one agency of law enforcement, no matter how strong its influence or how sincere its purposes, can alone bring about harmonious cooperation; neither can cooperation be accomplished among many agencies, so long as they are compelled to act independently and without a common objective. Unless there is a common bond and definite organized effort they will not reach common ground, and their efforts no matter how earnest will be at variance by reason of strong individual bias.

Relations with Other Municipal Departments

Today's police department organization must be viewed against the background of the entire city organization. Not only are other city departments performing functions closely related to police work, but police operations are so closely intermeshed with other agencies that not all the real police organization is confined to the police department proper. Some of these relationships are with other governments, typically the independent school board and the health and welfare departments of the county government.

Relations with Auxiliary Services

The auxiliary services are those connected with finance, purchasing, personnel, law, planning, and reporting and public relations.

Finance. Since police work, like all other municipal services, requires money for its performance, it is directly affected by the policies, programs, and procedures of the finance department. The city's general revenue policy and its long-term financial program (if one is in effect) will be a determining factor in drafting the program of the police department. Not only is the finance department the channel through which flow the revenues to support the police department, but it is also the medium of control over expenditures. Through its accounting requirements and expenditure warrants it prescribes the manner in which the funds of the police department can be expended.

Although budgeting is really more of an administrative than a financial function it is treated here as belonging to the finance department. The budget official or office reviews departmental requests in the preparation of the budget document. Transfers of appropriations from one item to another, unanticipated needs, and adjustments to correspond to revenue receipts all clear through the budget office. Finally, the finance department may engage in the collection of cost data pertaining to various municipal services, including the police department, and its findings may be very significant in the planning and administration of police services. When the central agency does not prepare the data in suitable form there is a necessity for police bookkeeping.

Purchasing. Many finance departments include the office of the purchasing agent, but because of the special nature of the purchasing function it is here considered separately. The operation of a police department requires the purchase of a great deal of equipment and supplies such as automobiles, firearms, and communication equipment. Since much of the police equipment is highly specialized, the issue may arise as to whether it should be purchased through the central purchasing office or directly by the police department. If there is a well-established purchasing office under professional direction, this issue should be resolved without serious difficulty, for the purchasing agent will recognize that it is his function to serve the police and all other departments.

Hence he will rely upon the judgment of department officials in the preparation of specifications for specialized equipment, confining his efforts to securing the most favorable terms for the products specified. With respect to standard supplies, such as stationery and typewriters, department heads should appreciate the need for a certain degree of uniformity, and should not insist upon slight but expensive modifications to suit their individual tastes.

The advantages of placing the purchasing function on a central basis, assuming effective administration, may be outlined as follows:

1. Group purchasing leads to lower prices because of the large quantities contracted for or purchased at one time.

2. The adoption of standards for articles used by two or more departments eliminates insignificant variations in articles used for the same purposes and reduces the purchase cost.

3. The use of definite specifications prepared by the purchasing agent facilitates the bidding process, in that vendors are not confused and know exactly what to bid upon.

4. A reduction in the number of purchase orders issued brings marked savings in paper work.

5. The purchasing agent can exercise constant supervision of all vendors, establishing a list of qualified vendors and preventing "fly-by-night" vendors from bidding and causing delays and expense by delivering shoddy merchandise.

6. The central purchasing agency can follow up orders to see that prompt deliveries are made and that goods delivered meet the specifications. This activity serves as the basis for determining which vendors are qualified and which are not.

7. By interviewing all vendors, the purchasing agent saves the time of the busy police chief, who, in the absence of a qualified purchasing agent, spends a lot of time with salesmen whether he is in the market for a purchase or not.

In any city where centralized purchasing has been firmly established, the police department, as well as other units, will be subject to expenditure control by the purchasing office in the form of purchase orders or vouchers. This has already been mentioned in connection with finance, but it is repeated to direct attention to the close relationship between the purchasing office and the police department. Arrangements should be made with the purchasing agent for emergency purchases without strict adherence to normal purchasing procedures.

Personnel. Since 85 per cent of the expenditures of the police department are for personal services, it is apparent that the department has many significant relations with the central personnel agency of the city. In recruiting, training, promoting, disciplining, dismissing, or retiring its employees the department must come in contact with the personnel office. The personnel problems of a police department are presented in Chapter 4.

Legal. To the extent that the city's legal department is concerned with the prosecution of cases in court, its relationships are obvious and need not receive further comment here. In addition, the city attorney provides legal advice to city officials and represents the city in suits brought by or against it. In both of these functions the police department has an interest. In the enforcement of ordinances and laws the police often need the assistance of a legal advisor, and such assistance is particularly valuable in emergency situations when the police department must take drastic action. Many damage claims against the city may arise out of the actions or the negligence of police officers, and here again the police department and the legal office must establish a close working relationship. In some cities the city attorney's office also includes a legal aid bureau or a public defender, and where such services are provided they are clearly related to the work of the police department.

Planning. Most cities have official city plan commissions, and there also may be some office or officer chiefly responsible for city planning activities. One aspect of a planning program which directly affects police administration is the layout of streets and parkways in relation to automobile traffic. A well-planned system of streets and highways designed for expansion as well as for present needs is the best guarantee of adequate traffic control. Conversely, in most cities with acute traffic problems the fault is largely a lack of planning. The planning and location of public buildings, including civic and neighborhood centers, are of concern to the police department, since police headquarters and station houses will be included in such plans, as well as facilities for other departments with which the police have frequent contact.

Another phase of planning that is of extreme importance to the police is the prevention, control, or correction of slum and delinquency areas. Because of shifts in population and economic groups to different sections of the city, or because of poor planning of the city's land use, or for similar reasons, most cities of any size in this country have one or more "blighted areas" or slum sections. It is well known to anyone familiar with crime and delinquency prevention that such areas produce particularly difficult police problems. Delinquent youths, reared in squalor and taught by more seasoned offenders, soon graduate into the ranks of hardened criminals. The cure for such problems is much more than can be provided by a planning agency, to be sure, but this does not minimize the importance of physical factors that are within the scope of sound planning. By careful planning and zoning much can be done to avoid the development of "blighted areas."

Reporting and Public Relations. Reporting may be divided roughly into two classes — administrative and public reports. Administrative reports include those made to the mayor or city manager, to the finance department, and to other city departments. Closely related are reports made to the city council as a whole or to council committees. All such reports provide basic data for the formulation and administration of municipal policies. It is clear that the nature of the reports required and the use to which they are put will have a distinct bearing on the police department itself.

Reports to the public include annual municipal reports, special publications, newspaper releases, "open house" at the city hall, and radio and TV broadcasts. Many of the general reports will include information concerning the police; hence it is important that the reporting agency and the police department work together in order that the public be given a clear and accurate picture of police services.

Such public reports are an important part of the police department's public relations activities. However, they are by no means the only public relations activity. As will be shown in Chapter 14, public support of police work stems principally from a knowledge of police work, agreement with the objectives of law enforcement, and respect for those trusted with enforcement. Public relations, planned or unplanned, permeate every departmental undertaking. As with other administrative functions, public relations must be planned. Chapter 15 deals with the establishment of a police public relations program.

However, there are two public relations activities that frequently bring the police department into contact with other offices of the city government. In some cities all press releases (except current police incidents) are cleared through one office, which is usually that of the city manager or mayor, and this of course accentuates the need for a close and sympathetic relationship between this office and the police department. Another important phase of public reporting is handling citizen complaints. A number of progressive cities have set up central information and complaint bureaus. Complaints filed at this central office are not only received courteously but are carefully referred to the proper department for investigation and follow-up. Such a procedure has great possibilities in the improvement of the city's public relations, and it scarcely needs to be pointed out that the police department, as well as other city offices, will be directly affected by the operations of a system of this type. This does not mean, of course, that citizens would come to this central bureau to report crimes or to file complaints against other persons, but they might prefer to enter elsewhere than at the police headquarters a complaint concerning police service or a police officer. The centralization of reporting activities does not relieve the police department itself of its responsibility for public reporting and maintaining satisfactory relations with the public.

Relations with Line Departments

The other line departments with which police departments come into frequent contact are fire, public works, health, welfare, parks and recreation, schools, and utilities.

Fire. A close relationship exists between the police and fire departments. The most obvious instances of contact between the police and fire forces are for fire calls. Every call demands cooperation from the police department — special traffic rights for fire trucks, men to handle the crowds which follow the apparatus, and perhaps police investigation into the cause of the fire in cases of suspected arson. In some cities the number of arson investigations is so great that a special man is assigned from the detective division to work with the fire department. Two more instances which may be cited of police aid to the fire department are the enforcement of fire prevention ordinances and the investigation of false alarms.

The police and fire departments need to cooperate in the case of major disasters, but even in less serious public disorders the fire department may be of aid to the police department. For example, if ordinary means fail in dispersing an unruly mob, a stream of water from a fire hose is very effective. Finally, interdepartmental cooperation is needed in the use of communication systems. In a number of cities the fire chief and sometimes other fire department officers have their cars equipped with police radio. In smaller cities there may be a joint switchboard to receive both fire and police calls.

Public Works. One of the most common activities of the public works department is construction, maintenance, and repair of city streets. Just as the proper planning of streets is related to the congestion of traffic, so their construction and repair also affect the flow of traffic at any given time. Construction and repairs undertaken without regard to their effect on normal channels of traffic may lead to serious problems for the traffic details of the police department. In cities subject to heavy seasonal snowfall the snow removal activities of the public works department will of course have a distinct bearing on traffic control. Street lighting, another public works function, also has its bearing on police problems, not only with respect to traffic accidents and control but also to felonies on the streets in the "tough" parts of the city.

The public works department plays an important role in major disasters when there is an obvious need for cooperation with the police. The control of motor equipment may prove another point of contact between the two departments in cities where there is a central garage or motor equipment pool. The nature of the demand for police cars will probably make it necessary for the police department to have its motor equipment under its own control, but special pieces of equipment (motor trucks and repair cars) may be borrowed from the central garage.

The police, in turn, may be of service to the public works department. In the course of their rounds, patrolmen may discover street light outages, defects in pavements or in utility lines, or damaged or missing manhole covers, and these should be reported promptly to the public works department.

Health. To a certain extent the work of the city or county health department is legislative in nature, since regulations are issued which have the validity of law. Although the health department may have its own inspectors, many of the regulations imposed, as well as health ordinances passed by the city council, place a burden of enforcement upon police officers. This demands close cooperation between the two departments for effective enforcement.

Welfare. The significance of delinquency areas and the problem of crime prevention have already been noted, and the department of welfare, usually an agency of the county government, is naturally a vital factor in their correction and treatment. Dealing as it does with those who have suffered most in our economic system and with those whose need may be desperate, it is clear that the welfare department can prove a valuable ally of the police department in preventing crime, both juvenile and adult. Social work is concerned not only with financial relief but also with correcting the physical and mental handicaps of persons in need. Psychiatric and medical social workers are being added to the staffs of progressive welfare agencies throughout the country in an effort to rehabilitate as well as to relieve the destitute.

These positive, rehabilitating activities are of particular importance to police departments, for the correction of physical or mental ailments in many cases means transforming an irresponsible or delinquent person into a self-supporting, self-respecting citizen. The treatment of underprivileged children, which may even involve taking them away from parents who are either unable or unfit to give them proper care, is a phase of social work especially significant in crime prevention.

Parks and Recreation. To the extent that parks and playgrounds provide innocent amusement for youths who are potential delinquents, they must be considered as elements in the crime prevention movement. Much has been done in recent years to organize community centers with recreation and athletic programs in an attempt to turn the attention of neighborhood gangs into healthful channels. On the other hand, parks place certain additional burdens on the police department. Parks large enough for roads may require special traffic police on Sundays and holidays, and all parks are likely to need special patrolling at night, since they are frequently the scenes of crimes or misdemeanors.

Parks offer a convenient opportunity for the congregation and operation of certain antisocial types of personalities. The opportunity for mutual clearing of information between the police and park departments regarding problem persons should not be overlooked. Parks which serve as places for outdoor public assemblies may prove to be the center of public demonstrations or riots. For all of these reasons the police will find frequent occasion to contact the park and recreation department in order that these common problems may receive united attention.

Schools. One of the most common demands upon police departments is for special officers to guard school children against traffic accidents. Closely related is the growth of junior traffic patrols consisting of schoolboys. This traffic problem is sufficient to establish the need for a sympathetic relationship between the schools and the police, but there are additional reasons. The friendly protection provided by the police officer at the school crossing is one of the police department's most valuable assets, for, more than any amount of writing or speaking, it creates a friendly feeling toward the police officer, an attitude which is not only gratifying but essential to the best police administration.

Public education plans conducted by the police frequently include lectures or demonstrations for school children. This has been notably true in accident prevention campaigns. In turn, the manner in which schools exercise their responsibility for safety training, social training, and citizenship training has an obvious effect on police activity.

Utilities. In cities where transportation facilities are publicly owned, the police department may find opportunities for frequent contact with them. Street cars and buses create special traffic problems which must be met by cooperation between the police and the utilities. In cases of large crowds in attendance at parades and athletic contests special services or schedules may need to be devised by the utilities in order to help the police handle the acute traffic situation. Emergency repair trucks operated by the utilities in turn require special privileges from the police in order to avoid transportation delays.

Other utilities, such as light and water, have fewer contacts with the police department, but they are not entirely unrelated. The police department may need the cooperation of the power and light utility in the installation of communications equipment; the water department may cause traffic detours by its installation and repairs of water mains; and both utilities are of course important elements in the disaster preparedness plan. So far the assumption has been that these utilities are municipally owned, but the relationships and need for cooperation will be materially the same if they are privately owned and operated. Some private utilities, as well as other private corporations, will have special agents and investigators whose activities will have a relationship to police work.

Summary

This chapter has attempted to summarize the administrative problems facing the police administrator and to indicate the tools he has available to deal with them. The rest of this book elaborates on the points made here.

An attempt has been made also to provide a framework for administrative operations, in terms of public attitudes toward policemen and criminality, inherited practices such as political selection of policemen, the rise of organized crime on a nation-wide basis, the influences of other police agencies and the judicial system, and the relationships with other agencies and departments of local government. Because these too cannot be separated from the administrative stream of government, they will again appear or be implied in the remainder of this volume.

The development of police administration has by no means reached a standstill. Because police work involves the entire public and because we live in an era of change, new problems arise and old ones take new form. Chapter 16 will examine some of these problems that increasingly will receive the attention of those in government both within and outside the police department who are responsible for effective police enforcement and the safety of the public at large.

Chapter 2

POLICE ORGANIZATION

A very small community where the hazards to life and property are few may have only one policeman. Obviously there is no problem of organization in such a force; one man attends to all police needs. But in the police department where scores, hundreds, or thousands of men are employed, effective organization is essential.

Organization should not be merely a long word used to describe a police institution which may long since have been outmoded; rather it ought to suggest that a proper grouping of activities and designation of responsibility are necessary if the police department is to carry out its functions effectively. Any specific plan of structural organization should be retained only so long as it facilitates the purposes for which a police department is established. There is nothing either sacred or omnipotent about a form of organization as such. It is only the skeleton upon which the department depends for mechanical convenience. Organization of itself does not think, has no initiative, and cannot respond to a situation. The effective work is accomplished by the members of the organization working under the supervision of responsible administrators, and it is only facilitated by sound skeletal framework.

Before police organization is discussed, however, it is important to survey the relationships between the department and the citizens it serves. This relationship should be of the closest possible sort. Nearness of the administrator to the people served is some assurance against faulty police administration. The problem centers around the nature of the control to be exercised over the police by the representatives of the people.

Forms of Control

Bruce Smith makes an excellent summary of both the essential problem and some of the alternate forms of control:

The search for some means for keeping police operations within the bounds of constitutional rights and guaranties, and of preventing them from becoming unduly repressive, probably is inspired in part by the age-old popular fear and distrust of armed force. Professional military and police forces both came into existence in response to the need for defensive measures, to be executed by trained specialists who are armed with extraordinary powers to act with vigor and decision. Both have therefore been the subject of concern, lest they override not only private rights of long standing, but also the established processes of civil government. One device for controlling military power is to place its general regulation and control in the hands of a nonprofessional administrator who is displaced with sufficient frequency to prevent eventual domination by the technically skilled military caste. Something akin to this device has been used also in regulating the police function. Professional police administrators have been subordinated at times to the daily supervision of legislative committees, administrative boards, and lay directing heads, who, no matter what their general competence might be, could make no pretense at specialized skill in police management. [1]

---

[1] Bruce Smith, *Police Systems in the United States* (New York: Harper and Brothers, 2nd rev. ed., 1960), p. 183. The paragraphs which follow, through the section on "Commission Government Charters," are abstracted from pp. 183-87 of this book.

Early Forms

Popular election was the earliest of the various expedients, the sheriff and constable being the only police officers during the early colonial period. With the rise of cities, however, separately organized night and day watches appeared, and at this point the practice of appointment began to make substantial headway. The power of appointment, together with the general duty of controlling and directing police affairs, was often lodged in a standing committee of the city council. Appointments to police office, whether high or low, were made in strict accord with partisan interest and were often for limited terms. The usual characteristics of the legislative scene — representation of special interests, responsiveness to temporary change in popular opinion, rotation in office, and so on — had so unfavorable an effect upon police administration that while direct legislative control was ascendant, little or no progress in police methods could be made.

Administrative Boards

The next major change in the form of control occurred during the middle 19th century. It lodged supervision in administrative boards, sometimes ex officio in their composition, sometimes specially appointed. Such departures were hailed at the time as impressive reforms in police management and ushered in a period of experimentation in multiple control which still exercises a certain influence upon American police forces. The new boards were of great variety. Judges, mayors, city councilmen, and private citizens were propelled into the technical direction of police affairs. Almost invariably such service was of a part-time character. Often it was not only inexpert, but meddlesome. None of the various types of boards, whether designated unpartisan, bipartisan, or nonpartisan, seems ever to have risen above party and partisanship. Both police management and police protection continued to flounder in political uncertainty, intrigue, partisanship, and corruption.

Meanwhile mounting urban populations threatened the legislative control which had been exercised by landed proprietors; police corruption rode high on this rising tide of urban domination. State legislatures, still predominately rural, struck and struck swiftly. In practically every great city, and in many smaller places, local control of police was swept away by statute, and police administrators appointed by state authorities were substituted.

State Control

There was some justification for state control, not only because abuses had developed under local control but also because, since the laws the local police enforced were state laws, the state appeared to have a duty to assure adequate and equal enforcement. The scheme met with little success, however. For one thing, the theory of state control of the police functions was not uniformly applied. It was primarily directed at the larger cities by legislatures which sought continuance of rural domination of urban affairs. Moreover, since the cities thus singled out were generally of a differing political inclination from that which prevailed in the rural districts, the police officials designated by the state were almost inevitably not in political harmony with the majority of the people whom they were charged to protect. Furthermore, although rural standards of private conduct differ materially from those prevailing in the larger cities, an effort was made to impose them on the cities.

Collisions between the municipal authorities and those managing the police force on behalf of the state were common. Police costs rose because the police boards were not even indirectly responsible to the local taxpaying publics they served. Nor, with few exceptions, did the quality of police service improve. In city after city the unsuccessful experiment was abandoned, and the local forces were returned to local control. Very few city police departments are under state control today.

Commission Government Charters

The next major change in police control occurred in the first decade of this century with the enactment of commission government for many cities. The outstanding feature is the combination of both executive and legislative powers in a small commission directly elected by popular vote. Quite aside from any basic shortcomings of this scheme as a form of local government stands the fact that the member of the commission who is designated as commissioner of public safety is charged with the management not only of the police force but also of the fire-fighting force as well, with building regulations, and occasionally also health and welfare, thrown in. Thus amateur supervision by a popularly elected, transient police administrator is complicated by the demands of other important municipal services.

The police forces which have enjoyed even a moderate success under such control devices are so few that it may be asserted that the future of police development does not lie in this direction. Indeed, the entire commission-government plan has gone into a decline during recent years, many of the cities which adopted it either turning to the council-manager form or reverting to the older mayor-council system.

Unified Administrative Leadership

After trial of these forms of popular control it is interesting to note that the police in most cities and states, and all of the federal police agencies, are directed by appointed administrators rather than by elected heads or administrative boards. The appointment of town and village constables is becoming increasingly common, and the sheriff remains the sole type of law-enforcement officer who characteristically enjoys elective status. Thus, although there is yet no absolute uniformity of practice, the trend is too clear to permit real doubt as to the ultimate result. American police administrators seem destined to be appointed by general executive officers and to exercise their proper powers free from the indecision and confusion which go hand in hand with multiple control.

General Principles of Organization

A police force is organized for the purpose of facilitating the attainment of its objectives. Organization is the arrangement of persons with a common purpose in a manner to enable the performance by specified individuals of related tasks grouped for the purpose of assignment, and the establishment of areas of responsibility with clear-cut channels of communication and authority.

It is difficult to generalize about organization and to isolate principles that are applicable to all organizations at all times. Organizations are made up of persons, not things, and no realistic approach to organization problems can ignore this fact. It does not follow, however, that each police department is confronted by such unusual problems as to make impossible the application of certain principles that have been found applicable in other organizations. Out of the experiences of hundreds of administrators in all forms of endeavor there appear to be at least six principles that are generally applicable:

1. The work should be apportioned among the various individuals and units according to some logical plan.

2. Lines of authority and responsibility should be made as definite and direct as possible.

3. There is a limit to the number of subordinates who can be effectively supervised by one officer, and this limit seldom should be exceeded.

4. There should be "unity of command" throughout the organization.

5. Responsibility cannot be placed without delegating commensurate authority, and authority should not be delegated without holding the user to account for the use he makes of it.

6. The efforts of the organizational units and of their component members must be coordinated so that all will be directed harmoniously toward the accomplishment of the police purpose, the components thus coordinated enabling the organization to function as a well-integrated unit.

The paramount purpose of organization is to promote efficiency. There may be times when certain conditions seem to block usage of a principle of organization, and nonconforming steps must be taken to expedite routine business. For example, a doddering captain, living in the past, may be "locked" in as head of a division because of civil service rules or political power. Through necessity a subordinate may gradually take over and for all practical purposes become the leader of the division. The blockade has to be overcome or the division will founder, but this type of thing is not conducive to the most efficient operation.

These principles do not by any means comprise the whole of the science and art of administrative organization. Neither are they ready-made rules that can be pieced together by any novice and made to apply to any organization problem. If intelligently applied, however, they provide the answers — or at least clues to the answers — of a surprisingly large share of the questions relating to organization that arise in municipal police departments. The application of these principles to police organization is discussed in the sections that follow.

Division of Work[2]

In any department where there is more than one officer, the problem arises of dividing the work among them. The manner and extent of the division of work influences organization structure, operating procedures, and extent of specialization in the department. In organizing a police force, therefore, the division of work deserves first and careful attention. If the division is to be wisely made, police tasks must be analyzed and consideration given to the bases on which the division will be made.

Bases for Division of Work

The need for dividing work among members of the force is recognized by everyone, but the bases on which to divide it are not as clear. There are at least five factors on which the division of work in an organization may be based — purpose, process or method,

---

[2]See Chapter 2, "Organization as to Type of Duty, Time, and Place," in O. W. Wilson, *Police Administration* (New York: McGraw-Hill Book Company, 1950).

clientele, time, and area. In any organization two or more of these factors may be applied at the same time, for no single base is the best for all purposes. The first three of these factors will be considered first.

1. <u>Purpose.</u> Probably the most common method of dividing work is to unite into one unit all activities directed toward a certain objective. The police department itself is segregated from other city departments because it fulfills a specific purpose — i.e., the protection of life and property, the apprehension of criminals, and the maintenance of public order. Similarly, the internal organization of the department is divided into units with a common objective. Even in the smallest departments, some officers may be assigned to criminal investigation work and others to traffic duty. As the department becomes larger separate units may be created to maintain records, to deal with juvenile delinquency, or to cope with organized vice. The number of purpose units generally increases with the size of the department.

2. <u>Process or Method.</u> The second basis for division of work is process or method. A process unit is organized according to the method of work, all similar processes being in the same unit. A common police example is motorized patrol, which is separate from the remainder of the department principally because it uses a separate tool or method, regardless of its purpose. In a large department all clerical personnel may be organized into one unit because of the common method of work. Organization by process is well adapted to the creation of occupational standards and pride in the work. This is true because if all personnel doing a similar type of work are united in a single unit, promotion can be channelized, standards of work drawn up, and comparative results more easily measured.

3. <u>Clientele.</u> Work may also be divided according to the clientele served or worked with. This means that certain activities may be grouped together because they are directed toward a certain group or class of persons. For example, the juvenile division is primarily concerned with juveniles; the traffic division with motorists and pedestrians; the vice division with gamblers, prostitutes, and narcotic addicts and peddlers; the jail staff with prisoners.

Analysis of Police Work

Before considering the necessity of dividing police duties according to the time and area, it is advisable to consider the division of tasks on the basis of the three factors just mentioned — i.e., purpose, method, and clientele. Analysis of police tasks will assist in their wise and logical division into related groups for assignment to members of the force grouped into organizational units for their performance. For this purpose, police tasks may be classified as primary, secondary, and administrative.

<u>Primary Police Duties.</u> Police departments are created for the purpose of performing certain tasks. These are called primary tasks, and the divisions of a department created for their performance are called line or operating divisions. The primary police duties may be classified as follows: to patrol the streets; to regulate traffic; to investigate crimes; to suppress vice; to control juvenile delinquency. The first category (patrol) is based on a process. This is an important distinction, as will be seen later, because the process of patrol is intended to accomplish the other primary tasks. The other categories are based on purpose (and in consequence to some extent on clientele).

All tasks that do not fall in the category of line are administrative because it is management's responsibility to support and supply the line. However, to simplify division of function, management responsibilities shall be divided into two categories: secondary, or auxiliary police tasks, and administrative police tasks.

Secondary Police Tasks. Police departments are not created primarily to perform the secondary police tasks; these duties are performed because they aid in the accomplishment of the primary tasks. The secondary tasks are also sometimes called auxiliary duties or services. They include records, communications, jail, and maintenance of property and equipment. Division of the secondary police tasks is based on process, and the process is usually department-wide. This means that the service (or process) may be used or participated in by any or all of the line divisions.

Administrative Police Tasks. Administrative police tasks relate to the management and administration of the department and as such are more especially the responsibility of the chief. The police department, like any other organization, must be financed; tasks relating to budgetary matters must be performed. The department must be staffed; tasks relating to the management of personnel must be performed. Public relations require attention to other tasks. Police operations must be planned, and controls must be provided to assure the accomplishment of the plan. The processes of planning and controlling necessitate the accumulation of facts from research and intelligence.

Dangers of Overspecialization

It is not necessary to create a separate unit in every force to perform each of the primary, secondary, and administrative tasks. The extent to which this is done will determine the degree of specialization. Some specialization is essential for effective operation, however, and greater specialization is needed in a large force than in a small one.

Specialization has disadvantages that deserve attention. Specialization creates difficult problems of integration and coordination; it divides the department into separate forces that sometimes operate independently of each other. Sometimes the independence is so great that they function antagonistically and at cross purposes. The department is then no longer motivated by a common purpose; frictions arise; there is strong and hostile competition for staff, facilities, and equipment. Specialization also sometimes leads to neglect of police duties; specialists are prone to ignore work that is the primary responsibility of some other unit, and citizens are sometimes shunted from one specialist to another in search of service.

Because of these serious consequences, specialization should be held to the minimum consistent with effective operations. In order to comprehend more readily the need for specialization, it is necessary to understand four fundamental processes that function in an organization. It will then be apparent that the extent of specialization may be sharply restricted, to avoid the disadvantages, without interfering with effective operation.

Processes of Operation

Four processes are at work in the organization: planning, doing, controlling, and evaluating. They must operate to accomplish any one of the primary police tasks. For example, traffic control must be planned; the plans must be placed in operation; controls must operate to assure their satisfactory accomplishment; and then the accomplishments must be evaluated.

The doing process requires line personnel to carry the plan into operation. The planning, controlling, and evaluating processes, however, are not necessarily performed by line officers. As previously noted, they are an administrative responsibility. As such they may be performed by staff officers (those who have no direct control over the line or operating personnel).

Although there may be specialization in one or more of these processes, it is not essential that there be specialization in all. The need for specialization occurs in planning and controlling before it does in execution. In a relatively small department, for example, planning traffic operations and controlling the execution of the plans may be the task of an officer who may have no personnel to execute his plans; the patrol division would then carry them into operation. The dangers in overspecialization are not found in planning and controlling; they invariably arise from the unwise and unnecessary assignment of operating personnel to a restricted special field.

Specialization in planning and control is essential for effective operations. It must be provided if the department objectives are to be attained. The error arises in concluding that, because there is need for specialization in planning and controlling, there is equal need for special operating personnel. The police chief should avoid unnecessary specialization at the level of execution. Police tasks should be performed as far as possible by the members of the patrol division. The best rule is to assign to the patrol division all police tasks that do not interfere with regular patrol duties and that patrolmen are able to perform substantially as well as specialized personnel.

Organization in the Small City

While problems of police organization are less complex in the small department, there is still need for a logical division of labor and equal need for protecting the chief from too much detail work. In a department of 10 men, for example, it is not possible to establish specialized divisions; however, the auxiliary functions must be performed, and certain tasks requiring skill or training need to be done. Too often in departments of this size the chief acts as records officer, detective, vice squad, fingerprint expert, and photographer. There are two paramount disadvantages inherent in this situation. First, too much of the chief's actual working time is taken up in detail and routine work, and he is not able to devote enough of his time to the larger problems of planning, administration, and public relations. Second, by assuming all the specialized functions himself, initiative of subordinates is stifled.

The small city organization problem is partially solved by developing the talents of the officers through training and experience and apportioning the work fairly among them. No officer should be a full-time specialist, but each should perform some specialized duty in addition to his routine tasks. The need for careful selection and adequate and continuous training becomes even more important in the small department because the lack of equipment and scarcity of expert personnel demand maximum resourcefulness from all. As an example, one desk officer may keep all records and serve as a follow-up officer, while another may classify and file fingerprints. Other officers may specialize in traffic accident investigation, criminal investigation, vice control, and so on. This plan of organization not only frees the chief from routine duties, but it also increases the enthusiastic interest of all officers and the quality of the services they render.

Numerical Strength

How many policemen does a city need, and how is this number calculated? If cost were not a factor, it might be possible to provide enough policemen so that virtually all accidents, crimes, and misdemeanors could be prevented by the mere presence of the police. At the same time there would be a point of diminishing returns where the cost of police service would exceed the cost of the lawlessness it was intended to prevent. It is this point which police administrators and budget makers are constantly trying to find.

The chief of police ordinarily is the best qualified man in the community to say whether he has enough policemen. His position will be fortified by crime statistics and by the respect which citizens and the press accord the police force. But to support a request for more manpower he must be prepared to show that his present force is working at peak efficiency and that an increased manpower will reduce crime rates.

There is some relationship between the number of police employed by a city and the amount of crime in that city, but it is not a simple, direct relationship. Industrial cities with large mixed populations generally have more crime and require more police protection than homogeneous residential communities, yet each may support the same size of police department. While the police in the established residential city can devote more time to preventive work and services to residents, those in the heterogeneous community must devote all their energies to reducing the substantial number of crimes that are committed and to preventing violence and excesses.

In 1941, average (median) police manpower ranged from 1.09 employees per 1,000 population in cities of 10,000 to 25,000 population to 2.23 in cities over 500,000. In 1954, after some post-war fluctuations, these averages ranged from 1.35 to 2.37. By 1959 they had again increased to a range at the median of 1.65 to 2.78 (see Table 1.)[3] These median figures indicate the consensus of American cities regarding police requirements and their ability to pay for them, but the wide range in figures for each population group, shown in Table 1, suggests caution in applying them literally to the police situation in a specific community.

Table 1

Number of Police Employees per 1,000 Population in Cities over 10,000

Population Group	No. of Cities Reporting	Lowest	Lower Quartile	Median	Upper Quartile	Highest
Over 500,000	18	1.29	2.25	2.78	3.07	3.81
250,000 to 500,000 . . .	20	1.18	1.73	1.98	2.09	3.46
100,000 to 250,000 . . .	65	1.30	1.58	1.92	2.19	3.77
50,000 to 100,000	128	0.99	1.45	1.73	2.02	3.45
25,000 to 50,000	268	0.11	1.37	1.68	2.01	5.78
10,000 to 25,000	484	0.45	1.36	1.65	2.08	6.20

Source: *The Municipal Year Book, 1960* (Chicago: International City Managers' Association, 1960), p. 394.

There are many criteria on which to base an estimate of the required numerical strength: area, population, topography, and geographical peculiarities of the municipality. On one or more sides may be a lake, ocean, or river. The size of the lake, the width of the river, composition of the marine traffic, and presence of docks and warehouses will be of importance to the police. On one border may be a large or small city. Location of

[3] *The Municipal Year Book, 1941, 1954,* and *1960* (Chicago: International City Managers' Association).

schools, churches, and hospitals and their demands for traffic supervision and regulation enter heavily into the problem of numerical strength. Number and direction of streets as well as typical uses and types of paving are important. The nature of the vehicular street traffic bears weight in determining police needs.

These facts reflect physical conditions which in the main are subject to fairly definite control. The problems they present are predictable to a considerable degree, and plans can be formulated to meet them. Some of the most deeply disturbing police problems, however, do not lend themselves to such an approximation. These are the more serious crime questions arising out of community social structure. Pool rooms, bowling alleys, saloons, and certain clubs may demand frequent observation and regulation. Some meeting places are potential places of violence, requiring careful attention.

There are certain types of crime which the police are powerless to prevent. Most murders and suicides are of this class, as are many cases of aggravated assault, rape, and manslaughter. Crimes within a family can rarely be prevented by any sort of police action, no matter how numerous the police might be, for the police cannot supervise private home life. Thus actions and predispositions which might lead to crime are generally not visible to the police, and even if they are — as in family quarrels — the police are often without jurisdiction until the crime is committed.

Some crime arises out of insanity and lesser mental disorders. Numerous sex crimes are in this category. Murder may be committed by the insane, and arson is often the product of a disordered intellect. A person of abnormal mentality may remain peaceful for years and then suddenly and without apparent provocation commit some heinous crime.

A municipality depending almost exclusively upon the heavy industries for its livelihood may attract a class of people whose frequently boisterous use of leisure time presents trying problems of police control. The clash of race cultures and national habits and customs sometimes breeds serious social problems.

Nationality, composition of the population, and its pursuits, then, may present serious problems to the police. The age distribution of the citizenry also bears weight in the analysis, for the incidence of crime is greater among certain age groups. Even the proportion of males to females in the population and the prevalence of married and single persons affects the difficulties of police control.

Distribution of Manpower

On what basis should the numerical distribution of men among the various divisions be determined? This question cannot be answered by any formula.

Will the addition of two men to the juvenile division, for example, secure better results in protecting life and property than the addition of two men to the traffic division? The answer depends largely on (1) the present size of the two divisions, and (2) the past accomplishment of each as shown by the statistics. The police department in a city of 100,000 population that engages in no juvenile crime control activities but has a traffic squad of 25 officers is overbalanced in its distribution of men between these activities. It is unlikely that no juvenile problem exists and quite possible that traffic personnel are performing activities that might better be left to other agencies. Community agencies and courts should be consulted and police records analyzed to determine the extent of the juvenile problem and the degree to which the traffic squad is engaged in nonpolice duties.

This appraisal will either justify the existing emphasis or point up the type of change that is desirable for well-balanced police service.

This example is reasonably simple. The problem becomes more complex when a chief has to consider the need for more personnel in all divisions under his command. There is no arbitrary method of evaluating the comparative social loss of one case of juvenile delinquency, one death due to a traffic accident, one adult case of larceny, one murder, and one apprehended felon with insufficient evidence to convict. And yet these are the subjective, qualitative comparisons that a chief must make in balancing competing demands on the manpower of the department. No chief ever has completely adequate manpower; he must do the best he can with the resources at his command. If he is aware of his problems, he will keep in mind continuously the problem of effective distribution of personnel among various activities, and he will realize that what may be effective distribution for one set of conditions at one time may cease to be effective as conditions change.

The final answer to the problem of distributing the personnel of the department among the various divisions must come from the chief himself. The results of his attempts to meet this problem will be reflected in the records of the department's accomplishments. The alert administrator remembers that this is a dynamic, ever-changing problem that is never completely solved because the very nature of police work is constantly changing.

Organization According to Function, Time, and Place

The division of work up to this point has been on the basis of its nature (purpose, process, or clientele). The grouping of the members of the force to perform work thus divided is called functional organization. Police service, however, must be provided throughout the 24 hours of the day and in every part of the territorial jurisdiction. Related tasks (grouped according to their nature) must therefore be further divided according to the hour and the geographical area of performance. The members of the force grouped according to the nature of their work must, therefore, be further divided into shifts and among territorial districts or beats.

Organization as to Time

Since the police department operates on a 24-hour basis, its work must be divided according to the time of day. Most police departments operate on a three-shift basis. The shifts are sometimes called platoons and sometimes watches.

Twenty-four hour service is not provided by all branches of police service; the need for continuous service is greater in some than in others. Patrol must be provided at all hours. The extent to which the other line divisions will operate beyond an eight-hour tour of duty will be determined by the extent of specialization, i.e., by the extent to which tasks in the special field are performed exclusively by the specialist in contrast to their performance by the patrol division. Some of the auxiliary services should likewise be provided on a 24-hour basis, e.g., communications, records, and jail services. The need for more than eight-hour service from the line divisions will be discussed in the chapters devoted to each of them.

Since the patrol force must provide 24-hour service, decisions must be made as to the number and most desirable hours of the shifts, and the proportion of manpower to be assigned to each. Variations in the hourly need for patrol service, as measured by the records of the department in terms of calls for police service, arrests, and accidents, clearly establish that the nature and amount of work to be done is not the same on each of the three shifts. The patrol force should be distributed among the shifts, therefore, in proportion to the need for service.

The shifts must be so organized that maximum manpower is available during the hours of greatest need and yet is not held on duty during hours when the need is substantially less. Some departments find such wide variations in the hourly need for police service as to justify a fourth shift, overlapping two of the basic shifts. The time distribution of the patrol force is discussed at greater length in Chapter 7.

Territorial Organization[4]

The inclusion of "area" as a factor in police organization gives rise to two problems: (1) establishing substations or division stations, which applies only to the larger departments; and (2) organizing patrol beats. The second is more properly a patrol problem and will be discussed in Chapter 7.

The operation of district police stations has clear disadvantages. They are expensive in terms of site, building, furnishings and equipment, operating personnel, services, and maintenance. Knotty administrative and organizational problems accompany the decentralization of police operations. The complexity of decentralized operations may result in loosened controls and diminished effectiveness. The disadvantages are so great as to justify avoiding decentralization as long as possible.

District stations meet two needs that in very large cities may be sufficiently pressing to justify their creation in spite of their disadvantages: they provide a convenience to citizens who may wish to call at a police station for some service, and they save police time by reducing the distance between the location of their duties and their station. Analysis reveals, however, that citizens transact most of their police business by telephone. Checks made of citizens who call in person at district stations for police service in cities where such stations are provided indicate that the number is surprisingly small. District stations can rarely be justified on the basis of public convenience; they are justified principally on the ground that they facilitate police operations.

District stations save police time by reducing the distance officers must travel to and from their beats. The need for this travel arises when officers report on and off duty and when they return to their station with prisoners, evidence, found persons and property, and to prepare reports.

Careful study should be made of the time so spent that might be saved by decentralizing operations to district stations. Such studies frequently reveal that the time saved is not equal in money value to the cost of building and operating a district station. They also frequently prove the advisability of discontinuing or consolidating presently operated district stations.

Centralized operations are not only more economical than services provided through district stations, but they also eliminate administrative and organizational problems and thus simplify the administrative tasks, tighten control, and assure more effective operations.

The decision to establish district stations as a means of decentralizing activities

---

[4]See Wilson, *op. cit.*, Chapter 18, "District Stations."

should not be undertaken without considerable study and reflection. No line can be drawn in terms of population or geographical area as to when police departments should establish district stations. Motor transportation and radio and telephone communication have facilitated tremendously the assembling and dispatching of men and receiving of complaints. At least three cities of more than 250,000 population and 55 square miles in area now provide all police services from one central headquarters. None but the largest cities will be able to justify district stations.

The above discussion should suggest to many cities the possibility of discontinuing stations which were established 20, 30, or 40 years ago, in the days of horse-drawn vehicles, foot patrol, and word-of-mouth communication. This discontinuance of unnecessary district stations will result not only in financial savings, but in increased men for outside duty.

Decentralization of Other Police Activities. When detectives, traffic men, and other specialists are assigned to district stations important questions of control are raised. The district station generally is commanded by a captain who is responsible to a superior in the patrol division for patrol operations in that area. Are the detectives assigned to that district to work under the supervision of the commanding officer of the district, thus tending to create within the district a complete police unit by itself, or are the detectives to continue under the supervision of superiors in the investigation division at headquarters? Should each district commander have detailed to him a number of traffic officers in proportion to his needs, to work directly under his supervision, as he would have were he the chief of police of a city the size of the district, or should the traffic officers work directly under the control of the central traffic division? Similar questions will arise with regard to records and communications, vice control, and juvenile crime control.

The answer to these questions usually is that where these men are on permanent assignment in any one functional division their work will be subject to the general supervision and review of a superior officer in that functional division at headquarters. In other words, specialized officers detailed to a district will report to the district commander as the immediate source of command, and will be subject to his review in matters of routine supervision, while the central division at headquarters is responsible for the successful functioning of the specialized process and is not concerned with its detail. For example, a detective working out of a district station will be under the immediate supervision of the district commander as to punctuality, sick leave, and discipline, and his assignments and reports will clear through the district commander. The headquarters detective division is responsible ultimately for the appraisal of investigations and in important cases may take complete charge.

This type of organizational relationship seems to be the most sound from the point of view of administration of the department. However, the above type of relationship is an aggravated case of the problem of functional supervision cutting across the direct lines of authority. Bruce Smith explains the dangers:

But when specialized headquarters officers exercise actual power to direct local operations under any given set of conditions, the chain of command is weakened, administrative responsibility is destroyed, and the morale of the force is soon impaired by the effect of conflicting orders and directions. Much of the fear of specialization springs from this type of situation; from a profound distrust of some of the uses to which specialized techniques may be put, rather than from any failure of specialization as an essential feature of the organization process.[5]

[5]Op. cit., pp. 250-51.

In summarizing the problem of territorial division of activities, three basic rules seem to be apparent:

1. Territorial division of personnel, other than the patrol division, should not be made until the size of the city and complexity of the problem justify it.

2. When this division is justified in a large city, commanding officers to supervise the specialists may be assigned to each district station so that the organization of the other units of the department parallels that of the patrol division, but is distinct from it.

3. If such a command group cannot be provided, then the specialized personnel should be assigned directly to the district captain who should direct their efforts as though he were a police chief. Functional supervision under this plan would be maintained by the headquarters staff, but the latter should exercise no direct control over district personnel. Staff or functional supervision is described later.

Delineation of Responsibility

The discussion up to this point has been restricted to the grouping of the members of the force for the purpose of performing police tasks according to their nature and the time and place of their performance. The organization of the force based on this logical division of tasks is the application of the first of the organizational principles listed earlier in the chapter.

The force can be best organized by arranging the members in a pyramid-like structure of responsibility and authority made up of the functional, time, and place units. Each part of the pyramid is responsible for, and has authority over, some portion of the work of the department. The chief is at the top of the pyramid, and immediately under him are the division heads; under these are bureau heads, and so on, until each officer is represented in the pattern. When cooperation is needed between any two officers in the department, the problem may be referred upward in the pyramid to an officer, superior to both, who can deal with it.

The most common type of police organization is this purpose or function pyramid, with a specialized unit established to perform each of the primary functions of the department, i.e., patrol, traffic, detective, vice, and juvenile. These units are the line or operating units, and their work is expedited by organizing one or more service units to perform the auxiliary functions. Typical of the auxiliary functions are records, communications, maintenance of building and equipment, and property management. In a police department serving a city of 100,000 population the administrator may need to establish only one auxiliary unit and combine in it records and communications, personnel and property management, and the maintenance functions. In the largest departments a separate unit may be established for each of these.

Attention will now be given to the application of the remaining principles. The second principle states that lines of authority and responsibility should be made as definite and direct as possible.

The division of the force in the manner described into functional, time, and place units provides its skeleton form. The precise nature of the organization, however, will be determined by more exact definitions of the duties of the organizational units and of their component members. These definitions correlate responsibility and authority and clarify the organization structure by delineating lines of authority and channels of communication. Responsibility is then unmistakably placed.

The importance of clear and precise definitions of duties and of lines of authority cannot be overemphasized. Every member of the force should know where he fits into the organization pattern, to whom he is responsible, who is responsible to him, and his exact duties and responsibilities. This knowledge is made available to the members through an organization chart, department regulations, and duty manuals. One of the important administrative duties is to provide this information to all members of the force and to make certain that all understand the duties and relationships. Otherwise the force cannot operate as a well-integrated unit.

Lines of authority should be clearly defined but not so rigid that the chief becomes inaccessible to everyone but his closest subordinates. For example, any member of the force should be free to communicate suggestions for improvement of procedures directly to the chief, who should consider carefully all such suggestions and return them to the originator with a notation as to their disposition. Such an approach will have a far-reaching effect on the morale of the force, will often lead to improvements in organization and procedure, and will aid in discovering natural leaders among subordinate officers who might otherwise go unnoticed.

Span of Control

The third principle is that there is a limit to the number of subordinates who can be effectively supervised by one officer and that this limit should not be exceeded. When there are too many organizational units whose heads report directly to the chief of police, the chief becomes engrossed in detail and is unable to deal effectively with the various services. This applies also to assistant chiefs and captains; the size of any office unit or field force should not be greater than can be adequately supervised.

For example, at one time the commissioner of the Chicago police department supervised 19 separate officers or units, some of them physically remote from his office. It was impossible for him to discharge his duties properly by giving their work any sort of intimate supervision because the days were not long enough to confer with each unit head. The net effect of this arrangement was that most of these officers and units got no supervision whatever.[6]

To fill the police chief's day with a round of routine repetitious duties of minor significance is to destroy the value of his office. His job is to see to the fulfillment of the larger purpose for which the department was created. He should not interest himself primarily in the detailed functioning of a single unit but in matters which affect his whole department. The chief also must give attention to the relationship of the police and the press; to public reaction to the police role in a major crime; or to the conduct of his men in handling an emergency. He should be alert to detect faulty structural organization in the department, asking himself whether the work is properly distributed among the various divisions and searching for evidences of poorly adjusted administrative machinery.

Over how many men can a chief executive exercise effective control? How many different channels of activity can he coordinate effectively? There are obviously limitations of some kind, but the experts cannot agree on just where the limits should be placed. Some say that no executive should attempt to supervise more than five persons. Others say seven, others up to 12, and some still higher. Some military men say three. For the most responsible type of civil administration, the consensus seems to favor from three to 12 subordinates. It would be easy to make the dogmatic assertion that a particular number is exactly correct, but the simple fact is that the appropriate number in one case

---

[6]Citizens' Police Committee, *Chicago Police Problems* (Chicago: University of Chicago Press, 1931), p. 12.

might be twice that in another. Something depends on the individual capacities of the executive. Much depends on how much diversification of functions is represented by the subordinates, and how urgent the functions are, and how high a premium must be placed on speed.[7]

It is impossible to estimate accurately the maximum number of subordinates that one superior can adequately control. The number varies according to the type of work being done, the capacity of the administrator, the ability of subordinates, and other factors. In many departments the span of control has been increased through the years because when the department began a new activity, a bureau would be established with the head reporting directly to the chief. When the chief is a "one-man gang" and seeks to supervise personally every minor activity of the department, his office becomes a bottleneck which hampers the operation of the entire department. The police department should be organized so that its head exercises direct supervision over perhaps only six or seven divisional commanders. Even then he should leave the responsibility for details to subordinates and confine himself to larger problems of administration. With the more important of these division heads he will confer daily.

The problem of arriving at a workable span of control may be approached from two directions. First, the number of subordinates reporting directly to the police chief should be kept at the lowest possible figure that will permit effective control. Related activities should be grouped into divisions so he need supervise directly only one subordinate for each major function or group of activities.

In the larger cities, and even in some smaller cities, it may be found that, after every reasonable grouping of related activities has been made, there are still more men reporting to the chief than one man can effectively supervise. This problem may be reduced to a limited extent by procedural improvements. Thus, better devised administrative reports and measurements help to conserve the time of the chief in reviewing the work of his subordinates. The most effective means, however, is to provide the administrator with assistants to help him with his managerial duties. For example, in relatively large departments, it may be desirable to reduce the chief's span of control by grouping the main divisions under assistant or deputy chiefs. When this is done, there is advantage in grouping divisions with related tasks. In a very large city there may be justification for the appointment of three assistant chiefs, one in charge of operations (the line divisions), another in charge of the auxiliary services, and the third in charge of administrative tasks.

In some departments there may be need for two assistant chiefs for operations, one in charge of police operations decentralized among many district stations, and the other in charge of the special line divisions operating out of headquarters. In smaller departments, two assistant chiefs may be adequate: one in charge of operations and the other of services and administrative tasks, although some of the latter tasks may be left under the direct control of the chief with his two assistant chiefs directing the remaining. Administrative tasks that the chief should relinquish last to an assistant chief are those of planning and controlling.

The authority of the assistant chiefs of police is ordinarily restricted to their pyramid of responsibility. In departments where the span of control imposed on the chief is not great, and where other conditions do not seem to warrant the appointment of an assistant chief of police, the administrative burdens of the chief may be lessened by the appointment of an administrative assistant whose responsibilities would be wider and more varied than those of assistants who perform such administrative tasks as personnel

---

[7]Roy F. Henderson, "Organization," *Personnel Bulletin*, July, 1940, p. 4.

management. Such assistants, it must be emphasized, should share the work but not the authority of the chief. In other words, their job is to help the chief perform the managerial functions which he cannot afford to delegate. They may assist the chief in arriving at decisions, and they can transmit and apply his orders, but managerial assistants cannot make decisions or give orders on their own authority without violating the principle of unity of command. They can, however, take over some of the work load of the chief so that he can devote more time to the problems of coordination.

In addition to being difficult to administer, an excessively large span of control sets up problems that progress with the adding of each additional unit of the span. Each person who must report to the chief must also communicate with each of the other units. The more of these relationships that exist the greater becomes the problem of coordination.

Unity of Command

The principle of unity of command (the fourth principle) is that an employee should be under the direct control of one and only one immediate supervisor. This principle also dictates that an operation requiring the action of two or more policemen must be under the direct control of only one immediate superior officer. Sometimes this principle works at cross-purposes as when officers from different units (and consequently under the direct control of different immediate superiors) must engage in an operation which should be under the control of only one man.

Even in the above situation, the principle must be adhered to for a policeman given conflicting orders by several superiors becomes confused, inefficient, and irresponsible. The orders are seldom harmonious because they are usually directed at different objectives.

The significance of this principle in the process of coordination and organization must not be lost sight of. In building an organization structure it is often tempting to set up more than one boss for a man who is doing work which has more than one relationship. The rigid adherence to the principle of unity of command may have its absurdities; these are, however, unimportant in comparison with the certainty of confusion, inefficiency, and irresponsibility which arise from the violation of the principle.[8]

Authority and Responsibility

The fifth principle, that authority should be commensurate with responsibility, is frequently violated in practice. The most common violation is to grant an official insufficient authority to perform tasks for which he is held responsible. Perhaps the greatest offender in this respect is the executive who is unwilling to delegate any authority and who insists on by-passing his principal subordinates by making detailed decisions on matters within the subordinates' realm of responsibility. For example, the executive who encourages or permits low-ranking employees to come directly to him with every question or grievance creates an intolerable situation for his subofficers who are held responsible for the management of their units while denied authority to direct and discipline their subordinates. Likewise officers who are responsible for specified functions, such as records, maintenance of vehicles, crime investigations, and so on, should have suitable voice in the formulation of procedures designed to guide all members in carrying

[8]Luther Gulick and L. Urwick, editors, *Papers on the Science of Administration* (New York: Institute of Public Administration, 1937), p. 9.

out these processes, authority to initiate action against nonconformists, and assurance that suitable action will be taken in case of noncompliance with procedural regulations.

A corollary to the principle that responsibility cannot be placed without the delegation of commensurate authority is that when authority is delegated to a person he must be held accountable for the use he makes of it. The process of control (holding a person to account) is dependent on a knowledge of what he did. This information is made available by some form of inspection. Control, therefore, is implemented by inspection.

Integration and Coordination[9]

The division of the force into functional, time, and place units creates some serious problems of coordination that must be solved if the organization is to serve its purpose. The frictions and cross-purposes that result when organizational units are created to accomplish a part of the total police task tend to prevent the harmonious coordination of the efforts of all toward the attainment of the total police objective. The sixth principle states that the organizational units must be integrated in such a manner as to provide a well-articulated organization, all of the members of which move without interfering with the smooth operation of the others. When the force functions effectively as a unit, it is well organized.

Desirable integration of the component organizational units is dependent on something more than mere organization structure. Relationships and procedures must also be established which will assure attention to the organization principles that have been discussed. In a sense, the problems of coordination and integration grow out of the application of these organization principles. The division of the work among a number of units tempts a violation of the span of control of the administrator. In order to eliminate the excessive red tape due to the formal up-and-down line of authority, the administrator is prone to have every division, bureau, and unit supervisor report directly to him.

The tendency to exceed the span of control is further stimulated by the reluctance of many executives to delegate authority. This failure constitutes a violation of the principle that responsibility cannot be placed unless commensurate authority is delegated. As the number of organizational units is increased, it also becomes increasingly difficult to hold accountable those to whom authority is delegated.

Increasing the number of units also increases the temptation to violate unity of command. For example, on the one hand there may be a superior officer in command of an operation that requires the participation of a number of specialists who are not members of his functional unit and yet who must be commanded by him; and on the other hand a patrolman may at the same time perform regular patrol duties, traffic duties, and other specialized work, but he cannot be responsible to one supervisor for his patrol job, to another for his traffic work, and so on, if unity of command is to be held inviolate. The undue delay required to obtain cooperation between the various units of the department through formal channels of control wastes time, creates friction between units, and further encourages violation of the principle of unity of command by cutting across the lines of control.

The more complex the organization and the more highly specialized the division of work, the greater is the need for coordinating authority and machinery at the top. In small, relatively simple organizations there may be enough personal contacts among all

---

[9]See Wilson, *op. cit.*, Chapter X, "Organization for Command."

of the personnel so that each understands where his task fits into the whole program, and the head of the organization can personally adjust any disputes or misunderstandings relating to jurisdiction, objectives, and procedures. In larger and more complex organizations, there is a tendency for each subordinate unit to become so engrossed in its own segment of the program that it loses sight of the objectives of the organization as a whole. This "compartmentalization" produces interoffice jealousies, misunderstanding, and friction.

Friction is particularly likely to arise between units that have been established on different bases of specialization. For example, a process division, such as the patrol division that is called on to perform all police tasks, may clash with a purpose agency, such as detective division, regarding jurisdiction over the investigation of crimes. The benefits of such specialization need to be weighed against the accompanying disadvantages of confusion and friction, and if the former are deemed to outweight the latter, the specialization of assignments should be accompanied by steps to strengthen the coordinating authority and machinery at the top of the organization.

Inter-Unit Relationships

The basic purpose of organization should not be lost sight of in its operation. Its purpose is to channel the efforts of its members in such a manner as to facilitate the attainment of its objectives. The principles that guide its construction and that aid in the establishment of sound relationships between the component units are all intended to make it a more effectively functioning organism.

Relationships between and among departmental units are established by departmental order. They may be portrayed by chart and defined in detail in general orders, regulations, and duty manuals. The orders establishing relationships should be designed to attain two objectives: (1) the elimination of action-hampering, time-consuming, friction-producing relationships and the substitution of relationships that facilitate operations by making them as free and easy as possible, and (2) the assurance that the relationships established do not violate an organizational principle.

Relationships should be created that permit adjustment to changed conditions and situations. Such flexibility in relationships may be obtained by (1) defining conditions and situations that automatically cause a shift in the line of command, and (2) creating relationships that for all ordinary, routine operations make unnecessary the strict adherence to formal up-and-down channels of supervision and control.

Automatic Change in Line of Authority

Under ordinary conditions and in routine operations, individual members of a pyramid of authority are under the direct control of the head of that pyramid; no other superior should give direct orders to these subordinate officers. Thus is the principle of unity of command applied. There are conditions and situations, however, that require another superior to give direct orders to these subordinates if the purpose of the organization is not to be jeopardized. Action must sometimes be taken immediately. Delay incident to following channels of command would defeat the purpose of organization. Regulations should define these situations and conditions and should provide for adjustments in the line of command so that immediate action may be taken.

The conditions that justify such shift in the line of command in order that immediate action be taken are: (1) emergency operations that may necessitate the combined action of two or more organizational units, and (2) proposed actions by units or individuals that might jeopardize the purpose or reputation of the department. Regulations that provide for such shifts in the line of command and the action of superior officers in accordance therewith are not in violation of the principle of unity of command. The regulations are necessary to hold the principle inviolate and at the same time permit the necessary immediate action.

Functional Supervision

Supervision of associates by a superior is the process of overseeing their performance in the accomplishment of their tasks. The superior is provided with authority to order the immediate correction of any derelictions that he may discover.

Supervision is so essential to effective operation as to justify the rule that every individual at the level of execution should be under the direct supervision of a superior. While the superior cannot keep all subordinates in his actual presence at all times, he should be constantly available to assist them, and he should make frequent and irregular checks on their performance.

The patrol division invariably provides 24-hour service. Some of the other units in the organization do not do so. Some of the special branches of service may have a need for such a limited number of members on duty at night as not to justify the assignment of a supervisor to direct their activities. These men then work without direct personal supervision, although some other provision is usually made for their control.

Department regulations, to meet this need, should create a relationship that may be called a staff or functional supervision in which the supervisor is responsible for some degree of supervision although it does not have assigned to him the complete, in person, control of the subordinate.

The distinguishing feature of staff supervision is that it is an advisory relationship, outside the regular hierarchy of command and responsibility, in which a supervisor may review the work of another employee who is responsible to another superior officer but who is, under particular circumstances, engaged in work falling within the jurisdiction of the staff supervisor. For example, the platoon commander of the patrol division may be given staff supervision over subordinate officers from other divisions who are on duty at hours when their superiors are not. This supervision would be restricted to attention to duty, promptness in reporting, compliance with department regulations, and so on; it would not relate to the detailed performance of their special tasks. This is a supervision of the man rather than the task.

Staff supervision also is needed when a subordinate is engaged in technical or semi-technical tasks that may be beyond the competence of his immediate superior. A specialist should then be charged with a staff supervision of his task. A special investigator charged with the search of crime scenes for physical evidence may employ equipment and techniques that are beyond the experience and training of his immediate superior. A laboratory staff member should make a staff supervision of his operations. This is supervision of the task rather than the man.

Indifference or lack of sympathy of superior officers toward tasks that their subordinates are charged with performing also makes desirable a staff supervision by the unit responsible for the operation. A traffic enforcement plan developed by the traffic division but to be accomplished by the patrol division is an example.

Staff supervision is provided by an officer who is acting in a staff capacity; he does not have direct control of the subordinate. The staff supervisor does not have the authority to make an immediate correction of a dereliction. He may discuss the matter with the subordinate and point out mistakes and suggest improvements, but he lacks authority to take disciplinary action or to give a command except under the previously mentioned conditions when the purpose or reputation of the department are in jeopardy. The staff supervisor, instead, must report his findings through designated channels for action. When tactfully administered, staff supervision is nearly as effective as direct command. Its success is dependent on the personalities involved and on the spirit of the members of the organization.

So long as these relationships and the channels to be followed are defined by departmental regulations, staff supervision is not a violation of the principle of unity of command. Much of the friction and misunderstanding that arises from staff supervision results from a failure of the members to understand its true nature. Those who undertake staff supervision must remember that they are not authorized to enforce policies and regulations but can only inform, suggest, or assist. Most of the difficulties that arise can be avoided if the chief holds regular staff meetings to explain the relationships and discuss the problems of division heads as they arise.

Maintenance of Control [10]

Another problem to be met by administrators of large police organizations is that of maintaining full control, while at the same time reducing the span of executive attention to a workable minimum. Theoretically it is sufficient to divide the force into a total of five to seven primary support and line units, headed by deputies serving also as a general staff or council. However, this plan often results in the formation of practically independent organizations which block the vertical flow of communication so vital to control. Consequently, instead of aggressively leading, the chief finds himself cast in an increasingly impotent role in department affairs. The answer to this problem is not to abandon the principles of organization but rather to retain control of key activities. These are internal discipline, intelligence, public relations, vice control, and planning.

The most efficient method of handling these control functions appears to consist in giving to the field forces the line authority to accomplish the tasks, while checking and balancing their efforts through administrative divisions with both staff and line authority. Thus, for example, vice control is directly accomplished by patrol and detective forces with an administrative vice division coordinating their efforts, spot checking their effectiveness and integrity, and reporting to the chief the volume and direction of vice activities throughout the city. These staff services can be combined into a primary departmental unit, commanded by an administrative deputy.

Well-established principles of administration should guide the chief of police in all but the most unusual cases. Yet certain problems peculiar to large city police organizations do not respond readily to broad generalizations. The first of these that the department head is likely to meet is the question of an assistant chief. This position is usually created in the hope of reducing the administrative work burden. It is reasoned that an assistant chief can handle routine matters, act as a "buffer," and digest and condense information directed upwards.

There is no greater fallacy in police administration. The true assistants of the chief are his council of deputies. If these commanders are not functioning, little is gained

[10]W. H. Parker, "The Police Challenge in Our Great Cities," *The Annals of the American Academy of Political and Social Science*, January, 1954, pp. 8, 9.

by creating an intermediate position which obscures this fact. At best, an assistant chief accomplishes tasks that are properly the duties of an executive officer or adjutant; at worst, he isolates the chief from the department, takes over policy decisions without which the department head cannot be chief-in-fact, and becomes a sort of "grand vizier" to which all ranks must bow in order to have their requests granted.

The chief cannot share his ultimate responsibilities. If his work burden exceeds human limits, the answer will be found in organizational and administrative failures.

Integrated Police and Fire Services

The foregoing discussion of police organization applies to an agency that is responsible only for the functions described earlier in this chapter in the section on "Analysis of Police Work." A few cities, however, have assigned responsibility for preventing and fighting fires to a single organic unit that also accomplishes the police task. When both police and fire duties are performed by the same personnel the agency is known as an "integrated" department of public safety.

Some 60 cities in the United States and Canada have had experience with some degree of fire-police integration. In a few of these cities it has been abandoned.[11]

Degrees of Integration

In many cities it is unwise to use an explosive term like "integration." Most cities prefer to use such terms as "coordinated fire-police service" or "cooperative fire-police patrol." Regardless of name, integration in practice has taken three general forms, ranging from a completely unified department of public safety to partial organization for combined services.

Complete Integration. Under complete integration the public safety department eliminates the separate departments of police and fire. The personnel in the public safety department are known as public safety officers who are capable equally of performing police and fire duties. All public safety officers normally serve on police patrol and are responsible for normal police activities, fire prevention and inspection, and all fire calls. Specialization is kept to a minimum, although there will be need for certain technicians, investigation officers, fire apparatus operators, and others. The public safety department is headed by a director whose primary responsibility is to coordinate all police-fire activities.

A variation of complete integration has been undertaken in Winston-Salem, North Carolina, and in Danville, Virginia. In both cities the police and fire departments are separate, but a fire-police patrol has been established for an assigned area of the city. Within this patrol area the services are completely integrated.

Partial Integration. Here the public safety department combines the operation of the police and fire departments but retains them as separate organizations. All officers are trained in both police and fire service, but there are separate divisions of police and fire, and personnel are assigned to each. A director of public safety heads the department

---

[11] The basic references on fire-police integration are the two books by Charles S. James entitled *A Frontier of Municipal Safety* and *Police and Fire Integration in the Small City*. Both books are based on detailed surveys and include charts, tables, record forms, suggested work schedules, ordinances, and other reference materials. Both books were published in 1955 by Public Administration Service, Chicago.

and acts as coordinator between the two services. The public safety officers assigned to the police division are primarily patrolmen who will assist and cooperate in fire fighting. The public safety officers who are primarily firemen will be assigned as standby personnel to man the fire apparatus. The number of such personnel will be kept to a minimum for additional manpower will be secured from public safety officers assigned to police patrol.

An Integrated Department with a Volunteer Fire Department. The third type of organization is generally found in small communities which never had an organized fire department. In these cities the police force has always handled some of the fire function, supplemented by a volunteer fire department or by other city employees acting as call firemen. The police force is trained to fight fires and to operate fire equipment.

Reasons for Integration

Mounting costs of local government, coupled with the steady trend toward shorter work weeks for police and fire employees, and increased demands for police service give a degree of urgency to the search for suitable methods of keeping public safety costs within funds available. Some municipal leaders visualize the integrated department as serving the needs of the community better, regardless of cost. Unless the organization can meet the test of better service it is not likely to survive solely as an economy measure alone.

The key to successful operation of any police or fire department is prevention. Patrol service is overwhelmingly the largest single police activity and it exists to prevent police incidents. Fire prevention is universally accepted as the primary mission of fire departments. It is exactly here, in the field of prevention, that the opportunities for improving public safety through integration are greatest.

In carrying out joint police and fire prevention work, the public safety officer can probably attain maximum effectiveness in prevention with minimum inconvenience to the citizens whom he serves. A patrolman visits more premises than any other public employee. In so doing he can promote public understanding and eliminate hazards of all kinds before they give rise to incidents. The community obviously profits by using him as its eyes and ears in all undertakings that are within his capabilities and area of responsibility.

The ideal organization of an integrated department of public safety can hardly be defined on the basis of the limited experience now available. The essentials may, however, be pointed out. First, generalization of duties should be carried to an extreme only with respect to patrol officers, whose basic tasks will be to prevent both crimes and fires and to take decisive action when either occurs. Second, there must be adequate specialization and staff facilities so that operations in any field of public safety will be based upon experience that has been carefully analyzed and plans that have been developed by persons with extensive knowledge of their particular fields. Third, there must be provision for utilizing specialists wherever emergency situations present problems that are likely to be beyond the knowledge or skill of the general public safety officer.

In an integrated public safety organization, fires, as considered from an operational point of view, constitute one additional kind of emergency that confronts public safety organizations. Fires probably are the most dangerous of all emergencies short of outright disasters, and a city must be organized and equipped to prevent them or to extinguish them when they do occur. Such provision does not necessarily exclude the possibility of assembling crews to fight fires in the same way that coordinated police effort is achieved in case of major robberies, riots, or other incidents requiring the concentration of relatively large numbers of men.

Specialized equipment is of course needed for fire fighting, but it can be dispatched in an integrated department in the same way as at present. Further, it may be necessary to employ full-time firemen in an integrated department in certain places or perhaps at certain times when the fire risk and need for their services demand it.

Firemen often spend less than 1 per cent of their time in fighting fires. It would seem advisable therefore to plan the effective use of the remainder of their time. Neither the men nor the city profit from long periods of inactivity. Firemen can be more productively employed on a normal shift basis as public safety officers engaged primarily in prevention but immediately available to combat fires.

To provide service without either neglecting or overemphasizing any element of the work is the basic problem of integrated public safety operations, but that problem is administrative rather than technical in nature. As such, its solution depends in large measure upon the capabilities and personality of the chief and his superiors. This is also the case in separate departments, however. It is well known that at times certain parts of the total police or fire program have been woefully neglected and others magnified out of all proportion when a city or department administrator has been unwilling or unable to give proper balance to all his responsibilities.

Combined police and fire operations pose no really new problems in municipal administration. A capable administrator, armed with sufficient facts and guided by sound advice, can give his community adequate service under almost any organization. He may find a possibility of better service offered by integrated public safety organization, as exemplified by the experience of the cities which have tried them.

Other Organization Problems

The police force is called upon, on occasion, to perform tasks beyond those listed among the primary duties of the department in the first part of this chapter. Included among these tasks are those arising from a number of emergency situations, such as strikes, riots, war duties, racial tension, and the investigation of subversive activities. Modification in the organization of the force to meet these special needs is discussed in Chapter 13.

Examples of Police Organization

The principles of organization discussed above are somewhat theoretical. The terms, "purpose," "process," "organizational pyramid," and others referred to in this chapter are no doubt strange to the ears of the police administrator. A discussion of types of police organization in several American cities may serve to illustrate some of the principles.

In analyzing the structure of police organizations, the reason for organizing a force — to facilitate attainment of its objectives — should be borne in mind. So long as the organization structure aids accomplishment of the police purpose, it is sound; when it impedes provision of a superior service to the public, it is defective.

Distinction also should be made between services to the public (line operations) and services to the line divisions serving the public (auxiliary services). Finally, those tasks which are to be performed by auxiliary or service divisions must be distinguished from those to be performed by an administrative force even though both are the peculiar responsibility of the chief of police.

In studying the police organizations described in this chapter, variations in the use of terms describing the various organic units should be noted. For example, the Los Angeles department, contrary to the others described, divides a bureau into divisions.

Los Angeles

The organization and functions of the Los Angeles police department are shown in Figure 1. (Los Angeles has a 1960 population of 2,448,018 and a land area of 458 square miles.) Attention is called to the inclusion of the auxiliary services in the technical services bureau and administrative tasks in two bureaus, personnel and training and bureau of administration.

The traffic bureau has its own traffic services division responsible for analyzing traffic statistics, planning traffic and crowd control at major public events, preparing safety information for the public, and training police officers in traffic procedures. The other line bureaus of the department have similar tasks performed for them by the bureau of administration and the personnel and training bureau.

Detroit

Figure 2 shows the organization of the Detroit police department (1960 population of 1,672,574 and land area of 140 square miles.)

The research and planning bureau performs the following tasks: (1) analyzes statistical reports on crime trends and makes pertinent recommendations; (2) studies and analyzes present police requirements and advises on standard measurements of police service; (3) conducts surveys for the establishment of precinct boundaries, patrol areas, and precinct stations; (4) compiles all special, general, and notation orders that have been issued by the department; (5) edits and revises rules, regulations, and procedures; and (6) edits monthly, annual, and special reports.

Statistical and analytical services are provided with punched card equipment by both the personnel records bureau in the personnel director's office, which is designed to provide auxiliary services, and by the accident prevention bureau, a line unit of the traffic division.

Kansas City, Missouri

Figure 3 shows the organization of the police department in Kansas City, Missouri (1960 population of 468,325 and land area of 130 square miles.) The Kansas City police organization groups line operations, auxiliary services, and administrative tasks into four major divisions.

Financial administration is the responsibility of the business manager who reports directly to the board of police commissioners. This department is one of the few major forces under state control. The governor appoints four police commissioners who in turn appoint the chief and through him exercise full control over the department. The

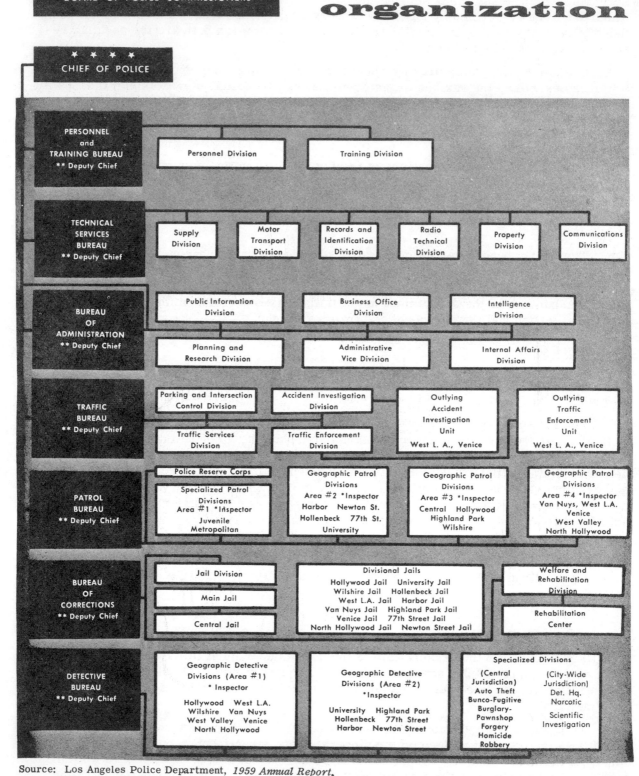

Source: Los Angeles Police Department, *1959 Annual Report*.

Figure 1 — Los Angeles Police Department

functions

★ ★ PERSONNEL AND TRAINING BUREAU

From the first investigation of a recruit's character and background to the final process of retirement, this Bureau guides the career of the individual police officer. The Personnel Division handles details involving injuries, deaths, resignations, retirements and transfers. The Training Division conducts both recruit and in-service training and maintains facilities for physical conditioning and off-duty recreation. The complement of the Bureau is 142 officers (3.1% of Department strength), augmented by 31 civilian personnel.

★ ★ TECHNICAL SERVICES BUREAU

This Bureau furnishes and maintains basic services necessary to all police activity. The typical police action involves a radio message received and transmitted by the Communications Division over equipment serviced by the Radio Technical Division. Required transportation is maintained by the Motor Transport Division. Supplies are stored and distributed by the Supply Division. Evidence is booked with Property Division and reports are processed by the Records and identification Division. The complement of the Bureau is 146 officers (3.2% of the Department strength), augmented by 624 civilian personnel.

★ ★ BUREAU OF ADMINISTRATION

Designed to assist the Chief in Departmental administration, this Bureau performs staff functions necessary for planning, directing, co-ordinating, and controlling police activity. It maintains internal discipline, provides the Chief with units to combat vice and organized crime, and maintains a command post when the Office of the Chief is closed. The complement of the Bureau is 164 officers (3.6% of Department strength), augmented by 94 civilian personnel.

★ ★ TRAFFIC BUREAU

Traffic control is the task of the second largest Bureau of the Department. The Parking and Intersection Control Division mans intersections and enforces parking laws. The Traffic Enforcement Division enforces the rules of the Road. The Accident Investigation Division furnishes collision reports necessary for analysis by the Traffic Services Division, which also conducts public education programs. The complement of the Bureau is 698 officers (15.2% of Department strength), augmented by 35 civilian personnel.

★ ★ PATROL BUREAU

Performing the traditional and basic police task, the Patrol Bureau is the largest subdivision of the Department. Its broad duties consist of crime prevention, juvenile delinquency control, crime repression by means of 24-hour uniformed patrol, protection of life and property and providing advice, information, and assistance to the public. The complement of the Bureau is 2,383 officers (51.8% of Department strength), augmented by 504 civilian personnel of which 263 are Crossing Guards.

★ ★ BUREAU OF CORRECTIONS

Secure, but humane, custody of imprisoned law violators is the basic task of the Department's largest service bureau. The Jail Division maintains the Main Jail, and the Central Jail and exercises advisory supervision over the twelve geographic jails. The Welfare and Rehabilitation Division maintains the Rehabilitation Center near Saugus, together with other services calculated to benefit prisoners mentally and morally. The complement of the Bureau is 362 officers (7.8% of Department strength, augmented by 136 civilian personnel, including 37 correctional officers.

★ ★ DETECTIVE BUREAU

The primary functions of this Bureau are the investigation of crimes, recovery of property, and the identification and apprehension of offenders. It is divided into specialized divisions located in the Police Building and divisions located at the geographic police stations. The Scientific Investigation Division maintains a criminalistics laboratory considered one of the finest in the nation. The complement of the Bureau is 681 officers (14.8% of Department strength), augmented by 56 civilian personnel.

★ Five additional officers (.1% of Department strength) include the Chief and his office staff. Twenty-one officers (.4% of Department strength) and 30 civilian personnel are assigned to the office of the Police Commission.

Figure 1 – Los Angeles Police Department (continued)

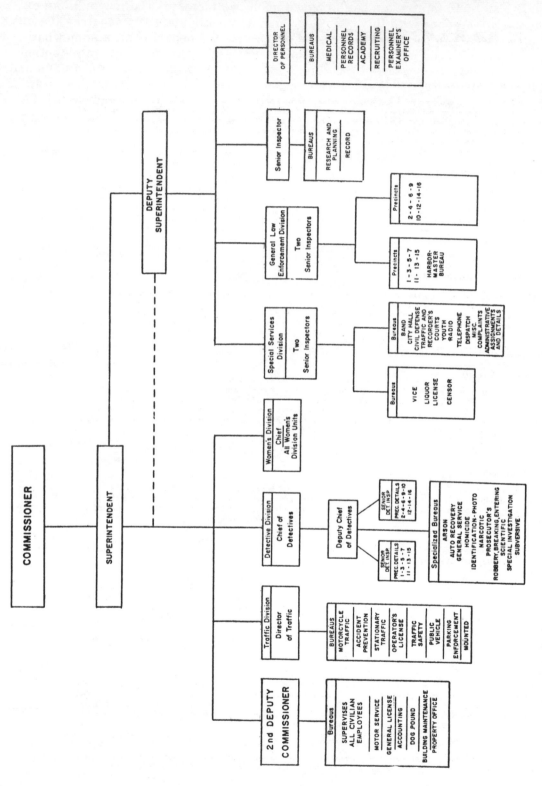

Figure 2 – Detroit Police Department

Note: Since this chart was prepared in December, 1958, precincts 3 and 9 in the general law enforcement division have been closed and the area assigned to adjoining precincts. In addition to savings in maintenance, this has eliminated salaries for 10 lieutenants and 26 sergeants.

only control the city administration has is based upon two factors: The mayor is an ex officio member of the board with full voting powers; and while state law requires the city to appropriate one-fifth of the general revenue to operate the department, a somewhat larger amount is needed, so some control is thus exercised. This form of state control is a direct result of the operations of the notorious Pendergast Machine in the 1920's and 1930's. Drastic action was necessary to reform the department, and state control was instituted in 1939. Except for a short period of time, this system has operated well, but this is largely due to the appointment of high caliber police commissioners and their selection of outstanding chiefs of police, rather from any inherent merit in the plan. Since the entire operation of the force, including salary ranges, is dependent upon legislative action, this is a very cumbersome system with no advantage over city control, and with the major defect that it is not directly responsive to the citizens who are paying for and receiving the benefits of the operation.

Berkeley, California

The organization structure of the Berkeley police department (1960 population of 108,539, and land area of 10 square miles), shown in Figure 4, includes an administrative unit and four divisions: personnel and training, patrol, detective, and services.

The Administrative Unit. This consists of the office of the chief of police and a staff lieutenant who serves as administrative assistant. Its major functions are to undertake long-range departmental planning and set future objectives; develop rules, regulations, and procedures; inspect and promote personnel; prepare departmental reports; and undertake similar activities in the over-all direction of the department.

Personnel and Training Division. This division is administered by a lieutenant who is responsible directly to the chief. Its main assignments relate to personnel records and reports and in-service training. The division also is responsible for police reserves.

Personnel work includes maintenance and control of attendance records, investigation and disposition of citizen complaints regarding actions of police officers, assistance to the city personnel director in recruitment and promotion of police officers, investigation of employee conduct that is contrary to departmental policy, and control of attendance and leave records.

Training activities, both recruit and in-service training, include compilation of training materials, maintenance of the police library, and liaison with other police agencies.

Police reserves are supervised by a sergeant who is directly responsible to the personnel and training lieutenant. When reserves are assigned to police duty, supervision is provided by the commanding officer of the division to which assigned. The police reserve program includes recruitment and training of civilian volunteers who assist regular policemen in time of disaster or when the need for police service exceeds that available from the regular force.

The warden service is supervised by a chief warden who holds the rank of sergeant and who is directly responsible to the chief of police. This also is an organization of civilian volunteers with representatives in every city block. The major responsibilities are for civil defense and disaster. Responsibility of the warden service includes selection, training, and supervision of civilian members; instruction on civil defense regulations; maintenance of records and preparation of reports; and related activities.

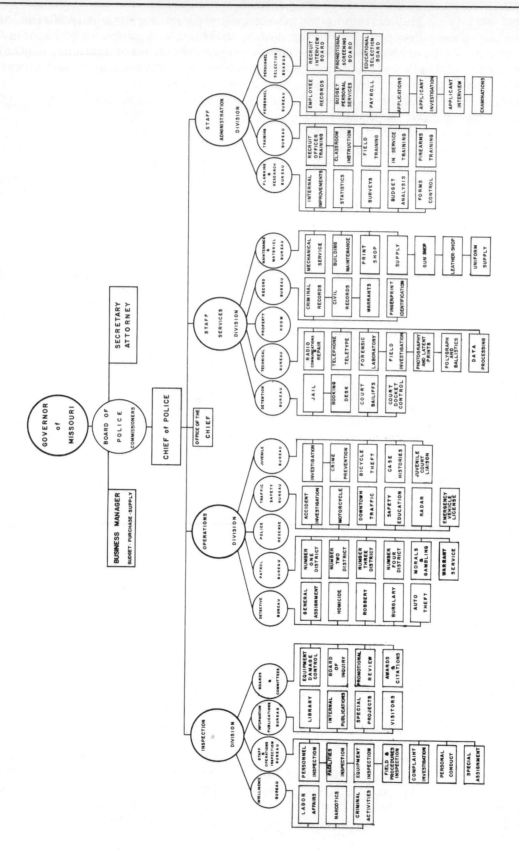

Figure 3 — Kansas City, Missouri, Police Department

Patrol Division. This division contains the police patrol force, traffic bureau, warrant bureau, and the animal pound. The division is directed by a captain who reports to the chief. Major patrol activities include regular police patrol, investigations, control of public meetings, receiving and handling citizen complaints, and observation and investigation of suspicious persons or situations.

The traffic bureau is responsible for automobile traffic and parking enforcement; investigation of traffic accidents and hazards; preparation of maps, charts, and reports; training and supervision of junior traffic police; working with the city traffic engineer in developing plans for solution of traffic problems; and similar activities.

The warrant bureau serves arrest warrants and criminal subpoenas. The animal pound is administered by a civilian pound master who is responsible also for picking up stray and unlicensed dogs.

Detective Division. The inspectors bureau handles routine and special investigations

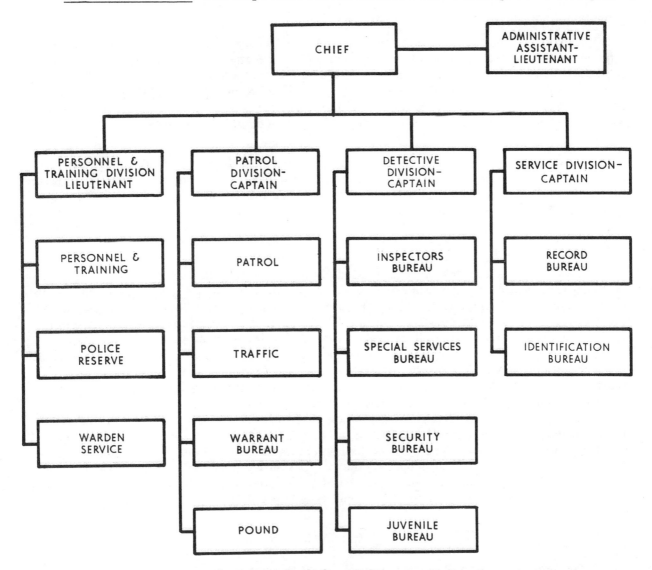

Figure 4 — Organization of Berkeley, California, Police Department

for known and suspected felonies and interrogates arrested persons. The special services bureau works for the control of gambling, prostitution, and other forms of vice and enforces regulations on the sale of alcoholic beverages. The security bureau investigates matters relating to national security and maintains liaison with other governmental agencies, including the Federal Bureau of Investigation and intelligence units of the armed forces. The juvenile bureau works on all cases involving juveniles whether or not an arrest is made. The bureau maintains cooperative and referral relationships with welfare agencies, health agencies, and the courts.

Service Division. The record bureau is charged with maintenance and administration of the jail, police records and departmental files, maintenance of police buildings, emergency ambulance service, and follow-up on police cases. The identification bureau handles fingerprinting, photography, fingerprint identification and photographic files, and laboratory and other technical services.

Pasadena and Kalamazoo

Pasadena, California, had a 1960 population of 115,000 and has a land area of 23 square miles. Kalamazoo, Michigan, is a city of 24 square miles with 81,375 inhabitants in 1960. Organization charts of their police departments are shown in Figures 5 and 6. In these departments, as in Berkeley's, no specific units have been created to perform administrative tasks, but an examination of the functions of the several offices and divisions reveals that provision has been made for performance of these tasks.

The Pasadena department is characterized by absence of specialization in traffic control except within the three uniform division platoons. In contrast, the Kalamazoo department has a traffic division commanded by a captain. The Service Division in Kalamazoo is newly formed and follows sound administrative practice by combining the various units that serve the field force.

Summary

All of these examples of organization plans are from cities with at least 100 officers on the force. However, the same principles of organization will apply to even the smallest departments. The organization plan for Kalamazoo shows quite clearly the work that a police organization must do. The job is there, even if it is so minor as to require only the part-time service of one officer. For example, a force of 25 men may not have a traffic division, but it may have a sergeant who spends part of his time in a staff capacity analyzing and filing records, pinning up the spot map, and assisting the chief in solving traffic problems and developing policy. The rest of his time would be spent in a patrol car investigating accidents, making traffic arrests, patrolling on the look-out for any violation of any law, and checking suspicious persons and performing all of the other basic police duties. Similarly, the detective division may be only one or two officers working in plain clothes. The point to be remembered is that these duties must be performed, and to be performed properly, the responsibility must be assigned, along with sufficient authority to do the job. There can be specialization only on a part-time basis on a small force. The rest of the time must be spent doing the basic police functions.

Conclusion

The police function should be administered through a regular city department headed by a police chief directly responsible to the chief administrator of the city. A separate or

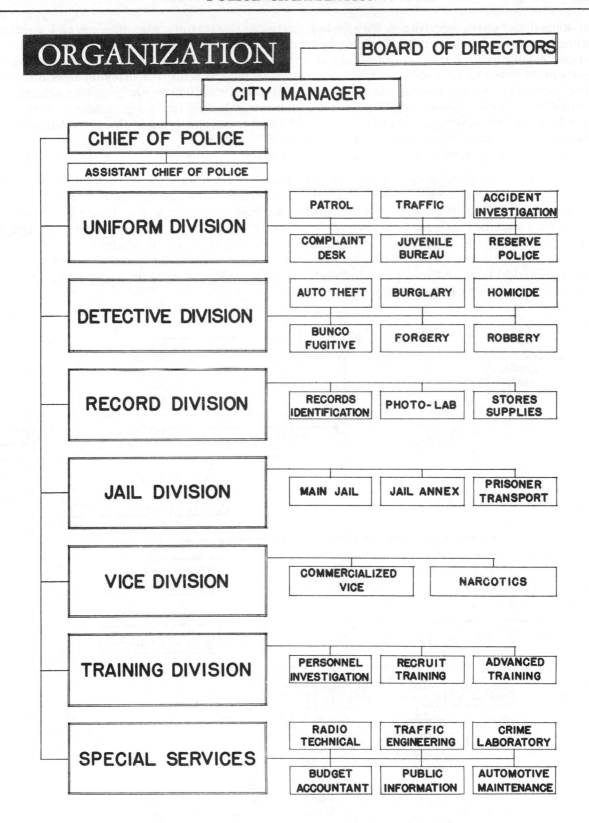

Figure 5 — Pasadena, California, Police Department

independent board, however it may be set up, is not desirable. Appointment of the police chief should be made by the chief administrator of the city, mayor or city manager, rather than by a separate board or commission or by the city council. The appointing authority should not have to pick local residents when making appointments. Appointment should be for indefinite tenure, but the chief should not be so entrenched in his post that official discipline or popular dissatisfaction cannot reach him effectively. Long tenure is desirable if not forced by statute or arbitrary rules. Brief terms can impede the growth and development and delay needed improvements in the department. Appointment should carry with it absolute, unqualified command and accountability.

Police work and police manpower are readily divisible into five different patterns of organization — purpose, methods employed, persons for whom or against whom activities are conducted, time at which the work is carried on, and place at which it is performed. Each of these plays a part in the work assignments of individual officers and of departmental units. They are supplementary rather than mutually exclusive. For example, an officer detailed to prevent or clear up juvenile crimes (purpose), interviews minors and others (method and clientele), on the day shift (time), throughout the city (area) in carrying out his assignment.

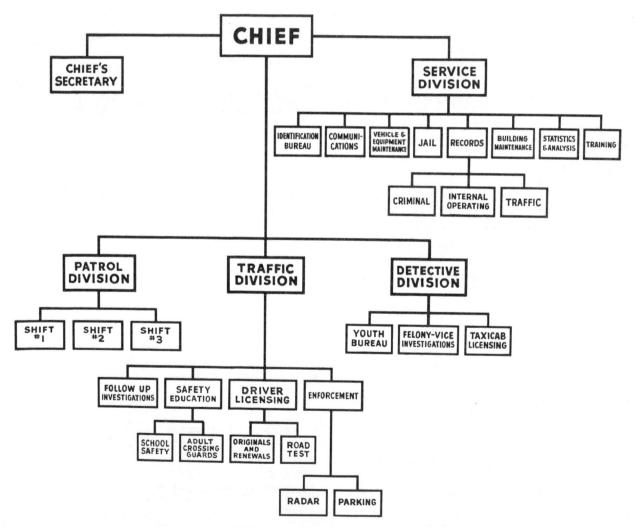

Figure 6 — Kalamazoo, Michigan, Police Department

Organizations that function effectively can usually be found following several rules for administrative organization that have been proved in practice to be desirable. Among them are these: (1) No supervisor should be responsible for more subordinates than he can effectively control at one time. The number varies with the complexity of tasks being supervised, but in police work possibly ranges between five and 12. (2) No employee should have more than one supervisor, and supervisory relationships should be clear at all times. (Exceptions which arise out of specialized phases of police work should be covered thoroughly in administrative rules.) (3) Every officer should be given enough authority to accomplish the work for which he is responsible, and he should be held to account for his performance and for use of his authority.

Organization in the police department should be as simple as the size and functions of the department permit. The chief should maintain direct contact with his division heads and should permit only as many levels of supervision as are required to obtain effective operation and to maintain a workable span of control. When the detail in his office becomes more than he can handle alone, he should appoint one or more aids or assistants rather than establish an extra level of authority. Aides may function in planning, inspection, or personnel in the name of the chief but with no command authority of their own.

Public safety functions have long been conceived broadly as embracing both police protection and fire protection, or more specifically, crime prevention and fire prevention. These preventive and suppressive activities have been integrated into single public safety departments in a number of cities in the United States and Canada with the same personnel performing both police and fire duties. The purposes of integration are to provide better over-all community protection, fuller use of available manpower, and more varied and interesting work for individual officers.

Organization of police departments varies from city to city and depends on available personnel, quality of supervision, and nature of community problems. Large city operations provide opportunity for specialization, while small city police work requires individual officers to be generalists, well-versed in all phases of police activity. Organization charts of selected cities may suggest useful changes in local organization but they should never be adopted literally. Organization should remain fluid, being modified whenever necessary to meet changing circumstances in the community and in the composition of the police force.

Chapter 3

POLICE MANAGEMENT

This chapter will deal entirely with administration, which can be defined as the control and direction of the people and things of an organization to achieve group objectives. In America the primary police objectives are to support and maintain the legally elected or appointed public officials in maintaining democracy in government, and to protect the constitutional rights, lives, and property of all persons. The basic police duties involved are patrol, investigation, and enforcement — with their myriad subtasks and procedures. These are the basic functions that go to make up operational work, or as they are sometimes called, line operations. All other tasks are administrative or auxiliary in nature.

The chief of police alone must be responsible for the proper management of his department, and he usually is given administrative authority commensurate with his position and responsibility. He may delegate some of this authority to other members of the department, and he may hold them responsible for the reasonable and proper use of this authority; but he can never delegate the end responsibility. It is his alone.

It is in this area of administration that American police find their greatest need. The police field has untold numbers of expert policemen — men who can patrol, investigate, and enforce with the greatest degree of understanding and proficiency, but there is a lack of men who can satisfactorily control and direct these policemen toward the organizational objectives.

As for the police administrators themselves, they may be either lay persons drawn from civil life, or they may be professional persons drawn from police ranks. In the former case, when the lay administrator serves only a limited term of office, the results, while not always downright bad, are seldom really good. The blame, experience seems to indicate, rests more upon shortness of tenure than upon technical inexperience; notable successes have been made by well-qualified lay administrators who were able to remain in office long enough to consolidate the hard-won gains of their leadership.

Either type of police administrator, lay or professional, has his peculiar advantages and disadvantages. The police administrator drawn directly from civil life is more closely in touch with public attitudes, more sensitive to popular needs, and therefore better adapted to the purposes and requirements of popular control. He is also more likely to have enjoyed the advantages of broad interests and wide experience than is the man risen from the ranks, who has been subjected throughout his career to the narrowing effects of official routine. In addition, the lay administrator does not assume the responsibilities of general command with the kind of burdens which long and friendly association in the ranks sometimes imposes on the newly elevated police official. On the other hand, men from private enterprise may have a different set of standards and philosophies from those compatible with public service.

Before a man can become a good administrator in any field, he must believe so strongly in what he is doing that these beliefs become second nature to him. Even though a lay administrator can learn the police problems he will have great difficulty in changing his philosophies and standards. In private business the gauge or standard used to determine success or failure is the dollar. If an enterprise is successful, it makes money; if not, it is a failure. Such standards seldom apply to the public service. There are only guides by which an administrator may measure his success or failure, and these guides are vacillating in nature. Sometimes they are nothing more than the whim of a newspaper editor.

This is a truism that is difficult for even trained police administrators to digest. Police administration is an art for which there is no ideal pattern — there are no black or white answers. There are only general principles by which the administrator can guide himself; and sometimes he will seem to violate principles but will not actually be doing so if a more efficient organization is developed.

One philosophy a businessman must overcome before he can be a successful public administrator is that of preferential treatment. It is a common and accepted practice of business people to give gifts and special services to selected customers or potential customers and in turn to receive like treatment from a wooing seller or other business contact. The success or failure of private enterprise sometimes hinges on these practices. These practices are untenable in a police administration. A police chief and ranking executives in a police department must believe and practice the basic tenet of equal treatment for all; and this philosophy must seep down and permeate the whole organization.

The police administrator drawn from the ranks has the important advantage of knowledge of police techniques — a knowledge which can be acquired only by experience. He has this information at hand from the moment of his appointment and can therefore move swiftly and certainly toward his objectives. The administrator who has not risen from the ranks is, of course, in a more difficult position. At best he can merely select a few trusted advisors within the force and rely upon them in forming his personal judgments. This is far from the perfect method, though it often seems to work fairly well and may be less of a handicap as time goes on and the administrator becomes better acquainted with the tools with which he is working.

The administrator who has come up from the ranks has another point in his favor. Professional training inculcates respect for certain professional ethical standards which in turn play a part in developing the growing code that, however vague and uncertain its present outlines, holds great promise for the future. Prominent in this code is the determination on the part of certain police leaders to avoid participation in political activities, to leave the formulation of public policies to the elected representatives of the people, and to confine themselves to the meticulous execution of such policies as are clearly defined and accepted.

It is because of these basic differences that police departments must look into their own ranks for administrators and to take the necessary steps to prepare promising men for the top posts of the future.

Major Administrative Functions

The police administrator must concern himself with at least 10 management functions which for ease of remembering can be associated with the word POST-BECPIRD. Each letter is the initial of a management function as follows:

Planning
Organization (the subject of Chapter 2)
Staffing
Training

Budgeting
Equipment
Coordination
Public Information
Reporting
Directing

Obviously this is a formidable array, and any administrator finding himself at the head of a police department will need help to successfully perform these functions. Some of the people whose primary duty it is to help the chief do these things are part of what is known as staff. The following paragraphs will clarify the distinctions between staff and line. The balance of this chapter then will discuss the management functions listed above (except for "Organization" which is the subject of Chapter 2).

Staff and Line

The word staff as it will be used in this chapter does not mean employees who do personal things such as servants or secretaries who are generally referred to as "personal staff." Nor will it necessarily mean "a body of persons associated" as when all command officers are referred to as "the command staff."

Staff as it will be used here means those people or tasks which are administrative. It is not entirely accurate, but for ease of orientation the words staff and administration throughout this discussion may be considered synonomous. A staff man is a person who is performing any of the functions that are the responsibility of administration. Any of the 10 previously listed functions are staff functions.

As was indicated earlier, those tasks that are not administrative, staff, or auxiliary in nature are line operations. For the purpose of this discussion line shall mean those functions for which the organization exists. A police department exists to patrol, investigate, and enforce; therefore officers involved in those functions are line officers. A service division is itself an organization which exists to provide auxiliary service to the line organizations; therefore, it is a staff function on the departmental level.

The people in the service division who are performing those tasks for which that organization exists, although the division is staff to the department, are line to the division. It is entirely possible that the officer in charge of the service division will have a person assigned to do his planning or other management tasks within the division. This person then is staff to the division commander.

Service, personnel, training, and other administrative divisions and sections which are pictured in an organizational chart on the same level as line operations are generally called special staff. The personnel assigned to the Chief's office may be called general or executive staff or technical staff.

General staff performs all of its administrative functions on a departmental plane. It may plan the departmental budget or other top-level tasks. In progressive departments some of these tasks may be assigned to a planning unit or section which may or may not be relegated to the category of special staff depending upon the administrative thinking of the chief.

Technical staff generally would be a technician who develops plans for the line personnel to execute, such as a traffic expert who outlines a selective enforcement program for the patrol division to put into operation.

Staff personnel generally have no operational command authority over line personnel, but they may have authority over the procedures employed by line personnel; that is, they may dictate how a thing should be done, and then it becomes the responsibility of the line commanders to see that it is done in that manner. This is called functional authority.

It is not uncommon to find individuals who spend a portion of their time on the line and the remainder of their time performing as staff. This is almost always true on a small force. For example, a sergeant may spend 10 per cent of his time in planning the accident investigation and traffic enforcement program and the remaining 90 per cent in the line function of accident investigation and patrol. Sometimes the differences between line and staff become so vague that they are almost indistinguishable.

Planning

Planning may be considered the heart of administration. Without it the objectives of any organization cannot be achieved effectively and efficiently. Planning precedes and accompanies the twin tasks of operation and management. Failure to plan invariably results in the resources of the department not being used to their best advantage.

Planning is the process of developing a method, procedure, or arrangement of parts intended to facilitate the achievement of a defined objective. There are five basic steps in planning:

1. The need for the plan must be discovered.

2. A statement of the objective must be formulated.

3. Relevant data must be gathered and analyzed.

4. The details of the plan must be developed.

5. Concurrences must be obtained from organizational units (both within and outside the department) whose operations may be affected by the proposed plan.

In addition to being considered basic, planning is all encompassing. Like cream in coffee, planning permeates and diffuses through every facet of the organization to the degree that its whole flavor, color, and consistency changes in direct proportion to the amount added. Every member of a police department plans, and almost everything that is done has been planned. Some plans are exceedingly formal, others are completely informal, and many fall somewhere between. Some plans take long periods of time to develop; others may take but seconds. Some take years to execute; others are acted upon and forgotten in minutes.

A patrolman on the beat observes a hazard on a busy street, he plans his course of action, executes his plan, and is on his way in no time. This is an example of a completely informal operational plan which was developed in seconds and acted upon in an equally short span of time. At the same time another member of the department may be planning for a new police building; while still another is planning how to sell the idea to the public: these are administrative plans.

The need for the plan must be discovered. This step is often, and properly so, completed in a few minutes as a result of experiences being discussed in a staff meeting. Other times the need may not be as apparent, and a more complicated procedure may be desirable. There are many ways to complete this step: a chief may wish to do it himself at his leisure; he may wish to direct his "staff of commanders" to think about the problem for further discussion and decision at a subsequent commanders meeting; or he may assign it to a staff member as a staff study.

Completed Staff Work

It must be kept in mind by all staff men that the administrator is a busy man or he would be making the study himself; and for this reason he should not be burdened with excessive amounts of written material. Everything presented to the chief should be distilled down to distinct, concise, and clear statements. To do this the staff man must know the chief's philosophies and ways of thinking. This places the responsibility on the chief to spend enough time with his staff men to promote a reasonable consensus or he will not get what he wants from his subordinates. Figure 7 provides a checklist both for the chief and his planners.

The U. S. Army is well known for its staff structure. Some administrative leaders are of the opinion that the army has one of the finest administrative systems in the world. It is for this reason that the Army's "staff study" format will be used as an example in this chapter (see Figure 8).

It is to be noted that all of the information asked for in Figure 8 is presented on the first and perhaps the second page of the completed staff study. Lengthy reports, exhibits, and other information are attached and numbered as annexes. This provides the reader with easy reference to supporting data. Figure 9 is an example of the face sheet of a completed staff study. The recommendation clearly points out to the chief, according to step 1 of the planning process, that a need does exist.

The next step (a statement of the objective must be formulated) is for the chief to decide whether or not he wants to act on the recommendation. If he does, he must then direct that the recommended General Order be prepared. This order then becomes a "statement of the objective" which completes step 2.

The staff man must then concern himself with step 3 (relevant data must be gathered and analyzed) which might require a great deal of research, or the information may already be available in the annexes attached to the staff study. At any rate it is obvious that the plan can go no further until all relevant data have been gathered and analyzed. Some data might be assembled with little effort even on the part of an inexperienced man; but analysis of the data, if done correctly, is vital and often cannot be satisfactorily completed except by members of the department who have wide experience and understanding.

For completion of step 4, "the details of the plan must be developed." The answers to the questions who will do what, where, when, why, and how must be clearly outlined.

Step 5 requires that "concurrences must be obtained from other units —." A plan cannot be executed if a blockade exists in any other unit or department. There must be assurance that there are no such blockades before execution is attempted. When this is done, the plan is complete, and the chief need only sign the order. The implementation of this, a departmental plan, automatically brings into being the necessity of other less formal plans within the divisions, sections, and units of the department.

After the plan has been executed and controls have provided for proper supervision, it then falls to the planner again to evaluate the plan to determine if the desired result was accomplished.

COMPLETED STAFF WORK

HOW TO DO IT

Study of a problem and presentation of its solution in such form that only approval or disapproval of the complete action is required.

1. Work out all details completely.

2. Consult other staff officers.

3. Study, write, restudy, rewrite.

4. Present a single, coordinated proposed action. Do not equivocate.

5. Do not present long memoranda or explanations. Correct solutions are usually recognizable.

6. Advise the Chief what to do. Do not ask him.

If you were the chief would YOU sign the paper you have prepared and thus stake your professional reputation on its being right? If not, take it back and work it over; it is not yet completed staff work.

HOW TO GET IT

Assignment of a problem and a request for a solution in such a way that complete staff work is readily possible.

1. Know the problem.

2. Make one individual responsible to you for the solution.

3. State the problem to him clearly, precisely; explain reasons, background; limit the area to be studied.

4. Give the individual the advantage of your knowledge and experience in this problem.

5. Set a time limit; or request assignee to estimate completion date.

6. Assure him that you are available for discussion as work progresses.

If you were the subordinate would YOU consider the guidance, given at the time the assignment is made and as the directed work progresses, to be adequate for readily completed staff work? Adequate guidance eliminates wasted effort, makes for completed staff work.

Figure 7 – Staff Work Checklist

Source: *Army Information Digest*, January, 1953.

FORM AND CONTENT OF A COMPLETED STAFF STUDY

File No. _____

Department
Division
Date

SUBJECT: Sufficient information for identification.
A key statement from Paragraph #1 is usually sufficient.

1. PROBLEM. Concise statement of the problem in form of a mission or objective. Frequently noted as an argument or statement of fact rather than as a problem, which is in error. A single subject is correct.

2. ASSUMPTIONS. Any assumptions necessary for a logical discussion of the problem which cannot be accepted and considered as facts. Omit this paragraph if not needed. Frequently confused with facts.

3. FACTS BEARING ON THE PROBLEM. Essential facts, in logical sequence, which must be considered. Facts must be undeniable and pertinent.

4. DISCUSSION. A careful analysis of the essential facts and assumptions, presenting considerations, pro and con, to arrive logically at sound conclusions. Keep discussion brief. They must be pertinent, objective, and adequately support the conclusions.

5. CONCLUSIONS. Statement of the results derived from a reasoned judgment of the effects and implications of the essential facts. Do not include alternate lines of action.

6. ACTION RECOMMENDED. Complete, concise and clear-cut statement of action recommended presented in such form that all remaining for the chief to do is indicate his approval or disapproval.

_____
Initiating Staff Officer

ANNEXES: List those accompanying the study.

CONCURRENCES: Each staff officer concerned indicates his concurrence by name, rank, and official position title.

NONCONCURRENCES: Each officer concerned indicates his nonconcurrences by name, rank, and official position title. Reasons for nonconcurrence stated briefly on separate memorandum attached as additional annex.

CONSIDERATION OF NONCONCURRENCES: The author of the staff study states the result of his consideration of any nonconcurrences. If his consideration shows that the nonconcurrence cannot be supported, the reasons therefore will be stated. The author will sign or initial this consideration of nonconcurrence.

ANNEXES ADDED: (List the annexes containing nonconcurrences)

ACTION BY APPROVING AUTHORITY: (Heading not necessary)

Date

Approved (Disapproved), including (excluding) exceptions.

_____
Signature

Source: Adapted from Form 16, *Staff Officers' Field Manual* (FM 101-5), United States Department of the Army.

Figure 8 — Outline for Staff Study

Police Department
Administrative Division
Date

File No. _____

SUBJECT: Uniform Allowance for Blank Police Department.

1. PROBLEM - To recommend for or against adoption of a uniform allowance for the
   Uniformed Force.

2. ASSUMPTIONS - A uniformly well-dressed police force is a necessary part of a
   sound public relations program. Present method of uniform replacement
   is unsatisfactory.

3. FACTS BEARING ON PROBLEM - Timely replacement of uniforms is desirable.
   Three methods of replacement are used in the police field.
   a. Replacement by personnel individually.
   b. Department provides uniforms.   } See Annex 1
   c. Department provides allowance for replacement.

4. DISCUSSION
   a. Uniformed personnel constantly engaged in a public relations program.
      Their appearance provides background for their public relations activity.
   b. Inspection records indicate deficiencies exist. (Annex 2)
   c. Line commanders believe present method of personal replacement is
      inadequate. Staff inspections and discussions with uniformed personnel
      corroborate this conclusion. (Annexes 3 & 4)
   d. Replacement by Department undesirable as it reduces personal pride in
      uniforms and eliminates incentive for proper care of uniforms.
   e. Replacement by means of a uniform allowance is best method to meet
      departmental needs.

5. CONCLUSIONS - That a yearly allowance of $110.00 providing for purchase of one
   jacket, one pair trousers, one cap, two shirts, and two neckties annually be
   adopted. (Annex 5)

6. ACTION RECOMMENDED
   a. That department adopt a yearly uniform allowance of $110.00.
   b. That General Order so providing be signed and issued.

_____
Initiating Staff Officer

ANNEXES: 1. Survey of replacement methods in use.
         2. Departmental inspection records.
         3. Line commanders' concurrences.
         4. Results of staff inspections.
         5. Experience in uniform wear and results of University tests of materials
            used.

NONCURRENCES: None

ACTION BY APPROVING AUTHORITY: General Order establishing Uniform Allowance.

Source: Adapted through the courtesy of the Traffic Institute of Northwestern University.

Figure 9 — Sample of Completed Staff Study

Types of Plans

Three broad types of plans may categorize all administrative planning: goal, single use, and standing plans.

Goal Plans. These outline ways to realize the end objective. The Law Enforcement Code of Ethics is a policy statement which indicates a goal. Plans to realize this goal would include raising standards of recruitment, training, techniques, and so on.

Programming is also part of goal planning. The chief of a rapidly expanding community may want to establish a substation but finds that due to accelerated promotions and "crash" growth he has no corps of supervisors experienced enough to move out from the watchful eye of headquarters. He would then of necessity develop a plan to realize the goal of developing dependable supervisors.

Standing Plans. These provide for questions and problems that are arising constantly and for which the same answer can always be given — for example: the "mugging and printing" of suspects arrested. The chief must plan for the answer to the question of who shall be fingerprinted and photographed. This then becomes a standing plan — the answer will always be the same.

Single-Use Plans. These provide answers to foreseeable problems that must be dealt with such as special parades or a visit from the President. Once the incident is over the plan is of very little value except as a guide for a similar future incident.

Classification of Plans

These three broad types of plans may be broken down into more specific classifications to cover various areas of police responsibility. O. W. Wilson, although he admits they are controversial, has named five classifications.[1] They are Management, Operational, Procedural, Tactical, and Extradepartmental.

Limitations on Completed Staff Work. The precise and formalized procedures for completed staff work outlined in Figures 7, 8, and 9 are not suitable for all police management problems unless some modifications are made. Some of the more difficult problems do not lend themselves to a clear-cut, yes-or-no answer because of policy ramifications affecting other city departments, the city council, the general public, and even other governmental jurisdictions in the area. The concept of completed staff work should be flexible enough so that alternative lines of action can be suggested in areas of judgment and political sensitivity.

A completed staff study, for example, may show convincingly to the police chief that salary increases of a specific amount are needed for members of the department. This will not necessarily, however, convince the chief administrator or the city council. These officials must consider the total impact on the city budget and the salary relationships with all other departments in the city service. They also must give consideration to salary relationships with other governmental jurisdictions in the area. This is an area of judgment and policy formulation where an answer is not easily and simply found. On the other hand, the police chief can quite properly recommend that salary increases be granted for the department and point out the consequences if the increases are not made (the likelihood of difficulty in recruiting good men and the loss of good men already on the force, for example).

---

[1] O. W. Wilson, *Police Planning* (Springfield, Illinois: Charles C Thomas Company, 2nd ed., 1957), Chapter 1.

Completed staff work has its greatest value, for all problems, in forcing the staff officer to tackle a problem systematically, step by step. He is forced to think through each step and complete it before beginning the next step. He must have his reasons and his explanations, and they must be documented. The staff officer must do his research thoroughly and consider all relevant factors that can be anticipated.

Management Plans. These relate to equipping, staffing, and preparing the department to do the job, rather than to its actual operation as an organized force. They include the organization plan (with definitions of the duties of the component units), the budget, and procedures for accounting, purchasing, and personnel management (recruitment, training, rating, selection for promotion, discipline, and welfare).

Operational Plans. The work programs of the line divisions are operational plans. The work to be done to accomplish the purposes of patrol, crime investigation, traffic, etc., must be analyzed from the point of view of the nature, time, and place of the component tasks and measured in terms of man-power and equipment requirements. Men and equipment must be assigned to each branch of service; specific objectives must be defined and methods of action developed for their achievement. Some procedures relating specifically to the accomplishment of these objectives also will be planned.

Procedural Plans. These include every procedure that has been outlined and officially adopted as the standard method of action to be followed by all members of the department under specified circumstances. These plans constitute the "Standard Operating Procedures" of the department. Procedural plans include such things as reporting regulations; record division operations; dispatching procedures; and procedures to be followed in stopping, questioning, searching, handcuffing, and transporting persons.

Tactical Plans. These plans are restricted to methods of action to be taken at a designated location and under specific situations. Action that is to be taken in the event of a jail emergency or when a report is received that a robbery is in progress at a specified location, such as at the First National Bank, are examples of tactical plans.

Extradepartmental Plans. These include those plans that require action or assistance from persons or agencies outside the police department, or that relate to some form of community organization.

It can easily be seen that of the four basic processes at work in an organization — Planning, Doing, Controlling, and Evaluating — planning is the foundation of all success. Progressive cities have found it essential to create planning units within their departments to satisfy this administrative need.

Planning Unit [2]

The planning process includes research. Facts in a wide variety of forms must be discovered; they must be compiled in an orderly, systematic fashion; and they must be critically analyzed to discover the need and to develop the details of the proposal. Research includes seeking principles that may be applied in the improvement of police service. For example, measuring devices are needed to appraise the demand for service in every field of police activity. While the need may be estimated proportionately, its absolute measurement in terms of man-power requirements also is desirable. Thus measures of the accomplishment of each organic unit and of its individual members should be devised. Research also includes evaluation of the effectiveness of present

[2] O. W. Wilson, *A Memorandum on the Need for a Planning Unit in the Detroit Police Department* (Detroit: Citizens Research Council of Michigan, 1952), p. 12.

procedures. As examples: Are procedures for appointment and promotion invariably selecting the best man for the job? Can present patrol procedures be made more effective? The above points are intended to show that research is an integral part of the planning process, not something distinct and apart from planning.

In the light of the foregoing considerations, the relationship of the planning unit to other organic elements of the department should be established so that the planning unit has primary responsibility for:

1. Developing plans that are department-wide in scope.

2. Supervising (in a staff sense) the planning activities of all other units and analyzing periodically all departmental plans and procedures.

3. Discovering unusual needs for police services by maintaining a continuing analysis of the crime situation.

A secondary or advisory responsibility exists with regard to planning done by the individual operating divisions for their own concern. The extent of the responsibility in this area will be determined largely by:

1. The ability of the operating division to accomplish its planning duties unassisted.

2. The extent to which assistance may be desired.

3. The failure of an operating division to prepare essential plans, a situation which it is the planning unit's responsibility to discover and report.

The success of the planning unit will depend greatly on the qualifications of its staff members. They should have imagination, good judgment, initiative, persuasiveness, and knowledge of the principles of police administration. They must be personable and able to work well with people since a part of their task will consist of gaining concurrences on the solution of a specific problem or the acceptance of a point of view.

Staffing

Staffing is the third area of concern requiring attention of the chief of police and has to do with filling positions in the department with the most competent people. Staffing is treated in detail in Chapter 4, "Personnel Management."

The modern police chief must recognize that the demands on him and his force to perform on an increasingly higher and higher plane each day cannot be met unless each member of the department is of high quality.

Fundamentally a chief puts two principles to work when filling out the table of organization for his department. First, he may define the job and then look for a man with the ability to fill the job. Second, he may evaluate his man and then look for a job within the organization that the man can fill.

In either case the chief must set the highest possible standards and then staunchly resist the degrading of standards even if it becomes necessary to continue short handed. Progressive administrators would rather have a few top quality men than many mediocre men on the premise that good men will produce more and higher quality work.

Professionalization of police service is in the minds of many people. Toward this end, there are some interesting attempts to raise the stature of the police officer in the eyes of the public, as well as to raise the quality of the man who becomes a police officer.

Street intersection control, marking tires, and enforcing parking meter violations are looked upon by many as tasks that can be performed by anyone with minimum training. The performance of these tasks by police officers has, in the opinion of some administrators, lowered the police status in the minds of the public to a degree that professionalization is not possible as long as it continues.

This has been overcome to some extent with the employment of "assistant police officers" in the form of "meter maids" and school crossing guards. (There are also many arguments against the use of "meter maids.") Some have carried the idea a step further in their planning for the distant future and envision the day when the tasks of door shaking and similar simple but time consuming chores will be performed by "assistant police officers."

Some departments have employed "cadets" to perform as "assistant police officers" and as working trainees. Basically cadets are young men who qualify as police officer candidates in every respect except age (and perhaps size, if they are still growing.) There is no single method in use that can be identified as "the" cadet system — each city employs cadets according to the end product desired.

Generally a cadet is a high school graduate who has shown interest in becoming a police officer. He is employed by the department to work as clerical help or in other positions during part of his working time and then to receive training during the remainder of the time. When he receives adequate training and reaches the required age (usually 21) he is sworn in as a police officer and is ready to go to work with no further basic training necessary. Experience has indicated that the advantages of a cadet system outweigh the disadvantages.

Manpower Requirements

A chief must consider the number of men he will need to adequately police the city, but no sound standard has been developed to guide the administrator. An arbitrary figure of two police personnel per 1,000 population has been set by some as an adequate manpower need. Others do not accept this and are attempting to develop definite figures based on time studies of the different tasks, incidents, and functions in which police are ordinarily involved. This approach becomes vague since it is nearly impossible, for example, to place a crime prevention value on patrol manhours, even though it is only a matter of keeping track of time to estimate the average manhours expended on the investigation of a larceny. Even this becomes indefinite when considering the fact that a larceny investigation is seldom a nonstop process. Often a larceny investigation and similar investigations are sandwiched in between others, and it is difficult to determine where work on a particular incident begins and ends.

Training

A chief of police must assume full responsibility for training all personnel in the department. He must begin training an officer the moment the man takes his oath of office, and he must continue the training until the man leaves the department regardless of tenure or rank. Training is treated thoroughly in Chapter 5.

Generally speaking, police training in the past has been directed almost entirely toward the operational level, but there are at least two other areas of police activity which need much more attention. The first has to do with the philosophy of police — Why police? What is the source of police authority? What is the police product? Too many men have served their police career without knowing why they existed as police, thinking that their product only was arrests and cases cleared. They did not know that a healthy, growing, violence-free community was their concern and end product.

Second, many officers have gone through their years of police service not knowing to which branch of the government family they belonged or even that they were part of an over-all government. Nor did they truly know what their authority was and how it was to be used.

Generally speaking administration courses (such as the material in this book) have not had the emphasis they should have early enough in a man's career. It is in the field of administration that the police service must begin to train doubly hard. The sooner this subject can be effectively introduced into a police officer's career the greater will be the dividends accruing to his department and to the citizens served.

If the police service hopes to attain professional status these two areas of training, as well as operational techniques, must be given added attention.

Budgeting

A police department is supported by a legislative (city council) appropriation. The appropriation enables the chief to obtain the men, equipment, and other facilities needed to accomplish the police purpose; success is clearly dependent on an appropriation that will assure resources adequate to meet anticipated needs.

The need for monetary appropriation is apparent. Not so well understood is the manner in which sound budgetary requests should be prepared and the importance of substantiating the requests with facts. Municipalities rarely if ever have an amount of money equal to the sum of the appropriation requests from all departments. Keen competition among all city departments for budget appropriations is therefore inevitable. The department that justifies its request with the soundest arguments and the most indisputable factual evidence of need is the one most likely to obtain its desired appropriation.

City councilmen, however qualified to judge police needs, appreciate being given facts on which to base their budgetary decisions. Without facts, their decisions cannot be uniformly sound, and appropriations are likely to be based on sentiment influenced by personal relations of the individual with the police and by community pressures. Without facts, the chief administrator and the council are inclined to be unsympathetic toward appropriation requests, and the police budget is then almost certain to suffer even between the frequent periods of budget stringency. It is important, therefore, to present substantiating facts in support of each budget-request item.

Budget Planning Versus Budget Execution

An examination of the distinction between budget planning and budget execution will explain why matters relating to the budget may be dealt with by quite separate administrative units. The budget is an instrument which records work programs in terms of appropriations needed to place them into effect. It is prepared through a process of planning: the services to be rendered and the projects to be undertaken are outlined with estimates of expenditures needed to carry out the work program. Decisions must be made therefore as to what the department proposes to do in the ensuing year. Estimates must be made of man-power, equipment, space, utility, supply, and other requirements needed to carry out the proposals. These must be translated into their anticipated money cost. This represents the budget request.

The budget also is a control device to assure that expenditures are made in accordance with the purposes for which the appropriations were made and that they do not exceed the amount appropriated. The budget is a management tool intended to assure that work programs are carried out as planned. Administrative control is thereby simplified and made effective.

Budget execution is the administrative task of controlling the expenditure of appropriations so as to carry out the plans recorded in the budget. Allotments to subaccounts in greater detail than in the appropriation document are sometimes necessary. Expenditures must be controlled by a system which assures that requisitions are issued and expenditures made only in accordance with the conditions of the appropriations and that accounts are encumbered as requisitions are issued or expenditures made in order to assure that expenditures do not exceed total appropriations.

Provision must also be made for the transfer of funds from one account or subaccount to another. Such transfers represent a change in the detail of the original plan, a change often occasioned by unanticipated events or conditions. The level at which authority is granted to make decisions relating to the transfer of funds establishes the location of an important budgetary control. Practice varies from city to city and also according to the nature of the account. For example, transfer of funds from the salary account to some other account requires city council approval in most cities; in some the decision-making power is vested in the city manager or other administrative head of the government. This authority usually is not vested in the chief of police although he may be given power to transfer funds from one subaccount to another.

Budget control, for the reasons indicated above, is an essential management tool for the administrative head of a city. For the same reason, it is also an important management tool for the chief of police. Budgetary control obviously becomes more vital to effective management as the size of the department increases.

The value of the budget as a management tool is not restricted, however, to its use as a control device in budget execution. Wise budget planning forces a review and justification of current programs and should require participation of operating personnel down to the smallest organic unit in the departmental structure. Not only should operating personnel participate, but they should understand the relationship of budgeting to well-planned police operations; they should accept the necessity of reviewing and justifying both their present and proposed use of departmental resources. The concept of performance budgeting proves useful in placing greater emphasis on a definite program of work and objectives than on the perpetuation of traditional services, the need for which is too seldom reviewed.

The Budget Request

The forms on which money requests are recorded usually are prescribed by the city finance director to correspond to the accounts and subaccounts maintained in his office. The finance director in some cities prepares blank forms on which city departments submit their budget requests. The form may have separate columns to show for each line item: (1) the appropriation for the current fiscal year, (2) the department request, and (3) the recommendation of the official, such as the city manager, who presents the budget proposal to the city council for action.

Past expenditures *by themselves* should not be considered as sole justification for a current request even for such recurrent items as utilities, telephone, gasoline and oil, repairs, and other supplies the need for which remains nearly constant from one year to the next. The appropriating authority, however, as well as the recommending authority, is invariably interested in comparing past with proposed expenditures, especially those for nonrecurrent items. Since this comparison reveals changes in program, the data should be incorporated in the budget-request document.

The basic budget-request document is nothing more than columns of figures recording anticipated needs in dollar terms on an item-by-item basis. The extent to which the document has the several accounts itemized will be determined by local accounting practices. This basic document records department work programs. Since the record is in terms of dollars it must be translated into proposed action if the appropriating authority is to understand why each item is requested. In so doing, the request for each item must be justified.

Budget-Request Justifications. Sheets containing the explanation of and justification for each item should be attached to the basic budget-request document. The planning and research division plays an important part in this. Since this division will have participated in analyzing department needs in reaching money-request decisions, it will have facts at hand to support the proposals.

Justifications should be made a part of the budget-request to facilitate understanding of the information included. If a nonrecurrent item is a replacement, facts should be presented to show conclusively the need for and wisdom of the replacement. The fact that the item to be replaced is worn out may be substantiated by its age, repair costs, its impaired usefulness, its unreliability, the waste of costly man-hours resulting from being in bad order, and, in the case of vehicles, their mileage.

If the nonrecurrent item is an addition, the need for it must be demonstrated. This may be done by showing that its use will save man-hours, extend police service, and increase the effectiveness of operations. Mere statements to this effect, however, are not adequate; facts must be marshaled to prove each contention.

Recurrent items, the need for which remains substantially unchanged from one year to the next, may be justified in most instances by reference to past expenditures. When increases are requested, however, they must be justified. For example, if the vehicle fleet is to be increased by 5 per cent, a 5 per cent increase in the items for gasoline, oil, tires, batteries, and repairs is justified. (The 5 per cent increase in the number of vehicles must have been justified, however, in the manner indicated in the paragraph above.)

Since the salary account is by far the largest single item in the police budget, careful study should be made of manpower use in order to justify the present complement as well as any increase in strength that may be requested. The need for each present and proposed assignment should be proved; analysis may reveal that some tasks are not essential or that their purpose can be achieved in some less expensive way.

Time studies of the performance of essential tasks will assist in demonstrating the need for much manpower. This is especially true of clerical jobs as well as of tasks that occupy a substantial part or the full time of a man, such as checking overtime parking and intersection and cross-walk assignments. While the determination of the optimum case load of detectives must await research, the case load does provide evidence of manpower requirements in this branch of service.

Since more than half the force in most cities is assigned to patrol, special attention should be given to substantiating the need for patrol manpower. Because requested additions to the department are usually intended to strengthen a patrol force depleted by assignments to other branches of the service, the need for these assignments must be substantiated in making a case for an increase in the strength of patrol.

Some patrol tasks may be measured in terms of the man-hours required for their performance. This applies to the time spent in dealing with incidents and in security and other inspections. Between 50 and 60 per cent of patrol time, however, is spent in routine preventive patrol. The number of man-hours that are justified for this routine patrol is not easily established. A study of patrol-time use in a number of departments may reveal that those using the most efficient methods of patrol provide substantially the same number of man-hours of routine patrol for each incident that the patrol is intended to prevent. This discovery may serve as the base for a more accurate measure of the absolute patrol manpower requirements than is presently available.

Patrol manpower needs may be justified in two ways:

1. Calculations may be made of man-hours needed to deal with incidents and to make essential security and other inspections plus man-hours that should be devoted to a preventive patrol on the basis of the number of preventable incidents multiplied by the man-hours that should be devoted to the prevention of each. The number of man-hours that should be devoted to the prevention of each incident must at present be an empirical decision somewhat similar to the decision as to the number of security checks of business establishments that should be made each night. When a number of departments have measured their own practices, the number of hours used by superior departments may then be applied in partial justification of the local request.

2. Comparisons may be made of manpower strength of the local department and of forces in comparable communities. While such comparisons do not provide absolute proof of local needs, they may indicate whether the local force is greatly undermanned as compared to others having similar police problems.

Requests for salary increases must also be justified. Comparisons with the salaries of other police departments, studies of cost-of-living indexes, and analysis of pay increases in nonpolice jobs and comparisons of these increases with police salary increases in recent years will sometimes provide facts to substantiate the requests.

Budgeting Techniques

Budgeting forces an administrator to plan whether he likes it or not. Some chiefs of police require each division commander to submit a proposed budget for the division. These proposals then are reviewed by the chief, added to or subtracted from to make them more realistic, and then interpolated into the whole budget.

Budgeting is a greatly misunderstood function. Too often it is thought of as a once-a-year project that causes a lot of extra work. This may be true of the annual document called a budget, but budgeting is a constant and daily task. Actually, it is practiced by almost all members of an organization at one time or another without their realizing it.

When a division commander, in a speech, tells the PTA that the police department needs additional manpower to combat juvenile delinquency, he, in a broad sense, is budgeting. He is soliciting public support which he hopes will be translated into dollars through the city council's response to public demand. When a patrolman, at 3:00 a.m. in a dark alley, remarks to his partner that they could perform their task better if the spot lights were replaced, he is talking budget. He should do more than talk — he should advise his chief in writing through the chain of command that the replacement is needed and give good arguments as to why it is needed. In keeping with this philosophy, supervisors may be required to keep personal running files of budgetary needs. As a need comes to mind, the supervisor notes it in his budget file. When the budget proposals are to be made, he then includes those items in his request.

Proposals of the various units need not be submitted on an official form, but specific instructions regarding continuity and format should be issued. Figure 10 is a good example of typical instructions issued to unit commanders for guidance in compiling their estimates.

If the fiscal year begins on July 1, the chief of police must submit his official budget requests to his supervisor sometime within the first six months of the year — often in March. Figure 11 is a typical example of an official budget request.

The supplies, equipment, and facilities available to a police officer not only provide the wherewithal that allows for quality work, but also have a definite effect on individual and departmental morale, as well as developing or making positive impressions in the minds of the citizens.

Equipment

Supplies, equipment, and facilities are tools of the profession which the chief must make every effort to provide in adequate quality and quantity. The expenditures allowed for supplies, equipment, and facilities from paper clips to police buildings are generally rigidly controlled by budget limitations so police personnel and administrators must make the best possible use of equipment and maintain equipment and facilities in the most attractive and efficient condition.

In addition to providing equipment and facilities, the chief also must establish controls to assure proper purchase and use. Before equipment is ordered or purchased it must be determined that the need exists; that the equipment is exactly what is needed and that it is the most economical. The tendency to buy what is not needed should be closely watched for and stopped when it exists.

One strong argument often overlooked in making requests for equipment is that the police force is open and operating 168 hours a week or over four times the usual 40-hour week. As a result, things wear out four times as fast. Laymen often overlook this point and feel that the police are unduly hard on desks, typewriters, and other equipment. It is hard for them to see why a desk that will last 40 years in the city treasurer's office lasts only 10 years in the police department

Physical Layout of Headquarters [3]

Location. Police headquarters is the center of administration of the department. To it come messages and reports from the entire area of jurisdiction and from it go the

---

[3] For a detailed discussion of principles in designing or remodeling police headquarters, see O. W. Wilson, *Police Administration* (New York: McGraw-Hill Book Company, 1950), Chapter 16, "The Police Building."

CITY OF TUCSON

Captain John Breglia
Captain Wm. Ross
To __Captain Paul H. Bohardt_____   From_____Bernard L. Garmire, Chief of Police

Subject_____1960-61 Budget requests_____Date__12-14-59_____

In preparing your budget requests for 1960-61 for your particular division, please submit requests in the following order:

1. Personal Services - Personnel
2. M & O of Cars and Cycles
3. Administrative and Records
4. Officer's Supplies
5. Investigations
6. Uniform Allowance
7. Utilities and Communications
8. Training
9. Travel (Administrative budget only)
10. Medical Services (Service Division budget only)
11. Furniture & Equipment
12. Mobile Equipment

1. __PERSONNEL__ - Please indicate present personnel and their assigned duties and any additional personnel requested and where they would be assigned provided they were authorized.

Example:	Present	Proposed	Additional
Captain	1	1	0
Sergeant	3	4	1
Patrolmen	16	24	8
Clerical	3	4	1

2. __M & O* OF CARS AND CYCLES__ - List all mobile equipment assigned to your division at the present time showing average mileage per month. List additional equipment requested separately.

Mileage costs:	Patrol Cars and Investigation Cars	.065/mile
	Chief's car	.045/mile
	Panel Delivery.	.045/mile
	Pick-up trucks	.045/mile
	Solos and 3-Wheelers	.020/mile

Example:
PRESENT EQUIPMENT:
30 Patrol Sedans (Marked) — average 140,400 miles per month —
    1,684,800 miles per year @.065 per mile $109,512.00

ADDITIONAL EQUIPMENT REQUESTED:
  5 Sedans —   average 56,160 miles per year per car —
    280,800 miles per year @.065 per mile 18,252.00

Total . . . $127,764.00

*(Maintenance and Operation)

Figure 10 — Budget Instructions, Tucson, Arizona

3. ADMINISTRATIVE AND RECORDS:

Stationery and office supplies will be shown in the Service Division Budget. Included in this item — printed forms, cards, folders, ribbons, etc.

Maintenance and Repair of equipment — this should cover maintenance and repair to all typewriters, audograph equipment, furniture, cameras, guns, etc. Present equipment and additional equipment listed separately.

Bicycle Registration forms, licenses, seals; drunkometer supplies, breathalyzer supplies, I. D. and Photo supplies will be requested in the Service Division Budget only.

First Aid kits and first aid supplies — blankets for cars.

4. OFFICER'S SUPPLIES:

Ammunition supplies for reloading; targets, backs and tapes; full load ammunition is to be requested in the TRAINING BUDGET (Administrative).
Gas supplies should also be shown in the Training Budget requests.
Batteries, bulbs, fuses.
Measuring Tapes, crash helmets, traffic control gloves, raincoats, safety belts, yawara sticks, gas masks, etc.
Police Accessories such as handcuffs, handcuff cases, cartridge holders, belts, holsters, badges, traffic book holders, belt keepers, daily record books, flashlights, whistles, keys, shoulder patches, whistle chains, etc. should also be indicated under this heading. Please indicate separate count for replacement (normal wear, tear and loss) supplies and accessories needed for additional personnel.
Lts. & Captains Bars — Sergeant chevrons.
Cool cushions.

5. INVESTIGATIONS:

Laboratory and scientific analysis.
Monies expended for securing information through paid informants and securing evidence buys.

6. UNIFORM ALLOWANCE

7. UTILITIES AND COMMUNICATIONS:

Telephone, telegraph and teletype costs will be budgeted by the Service Division; however, if additional telephone equipment is desired by any division please so indicate in your budget.

Radio Maintenance: Present Equipment
                    Additional Equipment   — Monthly charge per unit, $12.00.

Installation of radio equipment in additional equipment requested — $12.50/unit.
Maintenance of motorcycle battery chargers, radar speed meter and chart supplies, motorola power megaphones (2) and one battery megaphone, movie camera audio system, intercom between desk, radio and jail.

Figure 10 -- Budget Instructions, Tucson, Arizona (continued)

7. UTILITIES & COMMUNICATIONS continued:

   Installation and transfer of radio equipment to _____ vehicles
   $25.00 per vehicle. THIS APPLIES WHEN VEHICLES ARE REPLACED.

8. TRAINING - This will appear in the Administrative Budget, but each division should
   list any desired training for any of their personnel.

9. TRAVEL - This account is primarily for the Chief of Police and should appear in the
   Administrative Budget.

10. MEDICAL SERVICES - This is for medical care of prisoners and examination of police
    personnel and will appear in the SERVICE DIVISION BUDGET.

11. FURNITURE AND EQUIPMENT - Any files, desks, chairs, typewriters, audograph equipment,
    adding machines, typewriter stands, tables, spot maps, cameras and accessories,
    sirens-beacon ray lights — (for new equipment), radio equipment for additional
    requested mobile equipment, etc.

    IN OTHER WORDS ANY FIXED ASSET SHOULD BE INCLUDED UNDER THIS
    ACCOUNT.

12. MOBILE EQUIPMENT

    Additional cars or cycles desired - (Please show any vehicles to be traded by
    number).

    Under this item please indicate car distribution - Example:

UNIFORM DIVISION	Current Equipment	Additional Requested	Total
Sedans	30	6	36

    23 Beat Cars
     6 Sergeant Cars
     1 Lt.
     1 Division Commander
     5 Spares (to be used when other cars are being serviced or repaired.)

    36 Total

                                        [S] Bernard L. Garmire
                                             Chief of Police

Figure 10 — Budget Instructions, Tucson, Arizona (continued)

1B-2

CITY OF TUCSON
PROPOSED EXPENDITURES

Function: PUBLIC SAFETY   Department: POLICE

Fiscal Budget   Fund: GENERAL   Division: PATROL

Requested By: CAPTAIN JOHN BREGLIA (Division Head)   Approved: BERNARD L. GARMIRE (Department Head)   Date: FEBRUARY 15, 1960

ESTIMATE -A-
SUMMARY OF EXPENDITURES

Activity No. 2A2

1. Account	2. Classification	3. Position Quota				4. Last Year	5. Current Year				6. Next Year	
		Current Budget	Current Actual	Request	Allowed	a. Actual Expenditures	a. Actual 8 Months	b. Estimated 4 Months	c. Estimated Total	d. Current Budget	a. Budget Request	b. Manager's Recommendation
2A2-10	**PERSONAL SERVICES**											
	CAPTAIN	1	1	1						7,088	8,263	
	LIEUTENANTS	5	5	5						30,150	33,127	
	SERGEANTS	22	19	22						110,780	122,460	
	PATROLMEN	134	131	130						509,895	585,014	
	CLERK STENO I	0	0	1						-0-	3,096	
	OVERTIME & HOLIDAY COMPENSATION	x	x	x						20,104	28,000	
	TOTAL	162	156	159		386,159	327,829	344,921	672,750	678,017	779,960	
	NON-PERSONAL EXPENSES											
-21	M&O of Vehicles					66,969	53,835	60,000	113,835	117,838	78,853	
-22	Office Supplies & Miscellaneous					1,000	175	125	300	300	357	
-23	Officer's Supplies					6,771	2,803	10,750	13,553	13,553	8,439	
-26	Utilities & Communications					4,000	2,605	4,948	7,553	7,553	6,334	
-27	Travel					-0-	-0-	-0-	-0-	-0-	-0-	
-29	Other					-0-	-0-	-0-	-0-	-0-	28,440	
	TOTAL					78,740	59,418	75,823	135,241	139,244	122,423	
	CAPITAL OUTLAY											
-30	Furniture and Equipment					9,332	445	11,265	11,710	11,710	13,213	
-31	Mobile Equipment					47,417	-0-	8,635	8,635	8,635	2,500	
	TOTAL					56,749	445	19,900	20,345	20,345	15,713	
	GRAND TOTAL					521,648	387,692	440,644	828,336	837,606	918,096	

Figure 11 — Budget Justification, Tucson, Arizona

CITY OF TUCSON
PROPOSED EXPENDITURES
Fiscal Budget

ESTIMATE -C-
EXPENSES and
CAPITAL IMPROVEMENTS

Function _____ PUBLIC SAFETY _____ Department _____ POLICE
Fund _____ GENERAL _____ Division _____ PATROL
Requested By _____ CAPTAIN JOHN BREGLIA _____ Approved _____ BERNARD L. GARMIRE _____ Date _____

Activity No. 2A2
FEBRUARY 15, 1960

Account	EXPLANATION OF REQUIREMENTS State reasons for additional personnel, if any, detail estimated expenses and capital improvements requested.	Requested	Recommended
2A2-10	PERSONAL SERVICES - SALARIES		

PROMOTION OF 3 PATROLMEN TO RANK OF SERGEANT

At the present time, it is in the area of supervision that the division is short handed. Because of the extreme low level of experience in the Patrol Division, it is very important that adequate supervision be provided. By the addition of 3 Sergeants to the present 19 assigned to the division, we will be providing a minimum supervisorial coverage for the proposed number of patrolmen - 130. This will enable us to put 4 Sergeants in the field on each shift.

CLERK STENO I

The Patrol Division is the largest in the department and as such experiences a commensurate administrative problem. This requires the keeping of many records, the compiling of statistics, intra and inter-divisional communications and other administrative tasks. At the present time, the Captain of the Patrol Division does all of his own clerical work as well as much of the division clerical work. This robs him of most of his time - time which should be spent in organizing, re-organizing, co-ordinating, and supervising the division. The assignment of one Clerk Steno I would relieve the Captain of these menial chores which would result in a more efficient operation of the entire division.

NOTE:

Reduction in Patrolmen strength is justified by employment of 19 civilian Communications Specialists as requested in Service Division Budget.
Ref: SERVICE DIVISION BUDGET 2A4

Figure 11 – Budget Justification, Tucson, Arizona (continued)

commands for direction and control of the whole force. Its physical location should be as close as possible to the center of operations. This point is not necessarily at the geographic, population, or business center of the municipality but may be removed from one or more of these by a considerable distance. The working center of police activities, as determined by research, is the desirable spot for headquarters.

If the growth of the city is causing a steady movement of this central point, this movement should be taken into account in locating the building. Once located, the head-quarters station cannot shortly be removed to another point without an unreasonable outlay of public funds.

Design of Police Buildings. It is not easy to design a good police building. There are many major problems to consider and innumerable minor decisions to be made. Few architects have had experience in designing a police building, and the problem is further complicated by a limited budget, the characteristics of the site, and many other factors. When a new building is to be built or there is to be major remodeling of the old structure, the chief should make it one of his major duties to work closely on both the planning and the construction. If the chief's duties are such that he will not have suffi-cient time available, this duty should be assigned to a commanding officer who can live with the project from start to finish. In turn commanding officers should consult with men in their command to get their ideas about space needed and internal arrangements. The man who is actually doing the job will have many ideas as to what can be done to im-prove the layout.

Before Los Angeles started on the design of a new police building, several com-manding officers and an architect visited a number of large cities with new police build-ings and went through them room by room, talking to the officers using the space and finding out what they liked, what they didn't like, and how the building could be improved. As a result they were able to embody many good ideas of design and construction and to avoid mistakes.

One common complaint of architects is that it is difficult to secure police coopera-tion, that the police give them only vague ideas about what they want, or none at all. One reason for this is easy to see. Most police have been working in such inadequate quar-ters for so long that any sort of new building looks fine to them. When they see on the plans that the detective division is going to be expanded from a chief of detective's office and a squad room to a whole suite of offices, they think their problem is solved. But they fail to give the careful consideration needed to work out a truly usable design. Any-one who has ever built his own house knows the many problems that such a relatively un-complicated structure presents. The proper design and construction of a good police building is of such importance to the operation of the force that the job must not be left only to other city officials and the architect.

Principles of Police Building Design. Because local situations vary so much, it is not possible to develop a standard set of plans that will apply to even two cities of the same size, let alone cities of varying size. The final design will depend on organization of the force, site, money available, the inclusion of other functions such as the court in the same building, and many other factors. However there are a number of principles and suggestions for design that can be applied to any police building. They are discussed next and the design of a new police and court building in Kalamazoo, Michigan is shown in Figure 12 as an illustration of the application of sound principles.

1. Group the units that are closely related. For example, all of the operating di-visions of the Kalamazoo department make constant use of the record room, so it is cen-trally located.

2. Place units that have considerable public contact, such as traffic, for easy public access. Immediately upon entering the building a visitor should see a police employee. On many forces, this will be the desk officer. In the largest forces, it may be a civilian receptionist who will direct him to the proper location.

3. Some activities might well be located outside the police building because of convenience, to reduce the noise factor, or because they can be housed at lower cost for site and construction. Such activities as vehicle and radio service and repair, street painters, signs and signal maintenance, and similar work could well be located in a service building and need not be adjacent to headquarters. It may be desirable to have training located where space is available for an outside range and athletic fields. This may be immediately adjacent to headquarters, as in Houston, Texas, or at some distance, as in Los Angeles.

4. There must be room for growth. The new building will be in use for many, many years, and there will be new police functions now undreamed of. For example, when many present buildings were constructed, the traffic division did not exist. This room for growth may be planned in a number of ways. Kansas City, Missouri, included an entire unfinished floor in the building. This was a low cost way of allowing for future expansion. Within five years this space was in full use as a police academy. Other ways to allow for growth are to put in footings and plan the building so that additional stories can be added or plan for expansion along one or more sides of the building. (A one- or two-story building with sufficient land for horizontal expansion is the most economical structure for all but the largest cities.)

5. The public should have only limited access to the building with entrance to areas used for police business controlled. This is easy to do in the small department by a gate in the counter at one public entrance. In the large building there must be considerable planning and this principle may apply only to units of the force with the public circulating through many of the halls.

6. A separate rear or side entrance should be provided to allow officers, witnesses, and prisoners to come in and out without being generally observed.

7. Prisoners should be secure from the time of entrance and should not be observed by the public. Many police stations were designed so that prisoners had to be brought in through the front door. Many drunken and cursing bums have been booked while standing next to a lady paying an overparking ticket. In a small station the prisoner may come directly from a secure back door into a hall with only the cells, a booking cell, and facilities for fingerprinting and photographing. In a large building there may be a drive-in space for cars with electrically operated doors, an elevator not used by the public and designed to hold prisoners, and a much more complex design. Somewhere in this design, even in the case of the smallest forces, there should be small lockers where the officers can leave their sidearms while they enter the booking cell to search a prisoner or to go into the jail area.

8. There should be specific facilities for booking prisoners. In a small force this may be a holding cell of solid construction with a heavily shuttered window opening into the desk sergeant's office. In the larger forces, this may be a larger area. The small booking cell has many uses. The prisoner is entirely secure, he can be thoroughly searched, and he can be held without being put in jail if the officers bringing him in must leave on an emergency call. He can be held there to make phone calls, and, with the proper window and grill, this can be used as a visiting cell. In a large station, the entire area will be secure with a direct elevator to the jail. One major department has two types of cells for temporary holding in the booking area; one is a large, standard jail

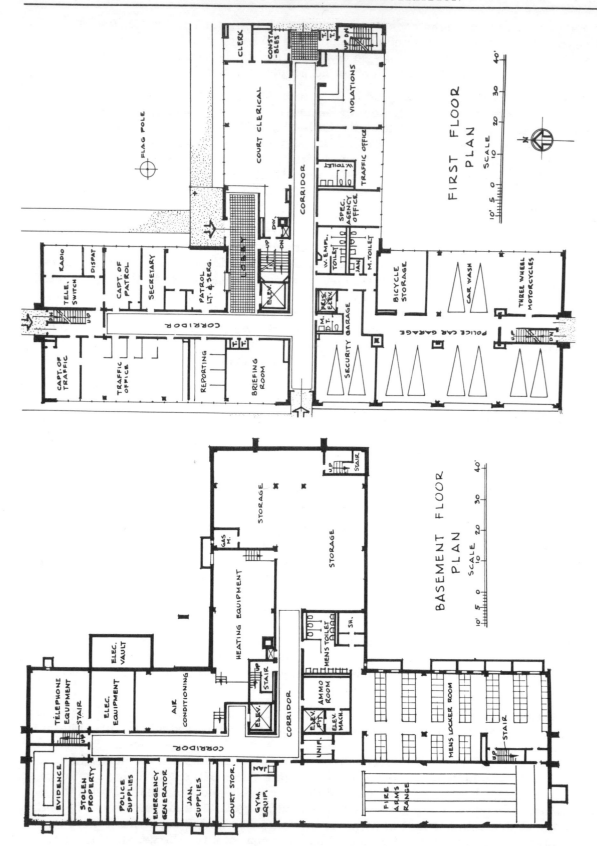

Figure 12 – Police and Court Building, Kalamazoo, Michigan

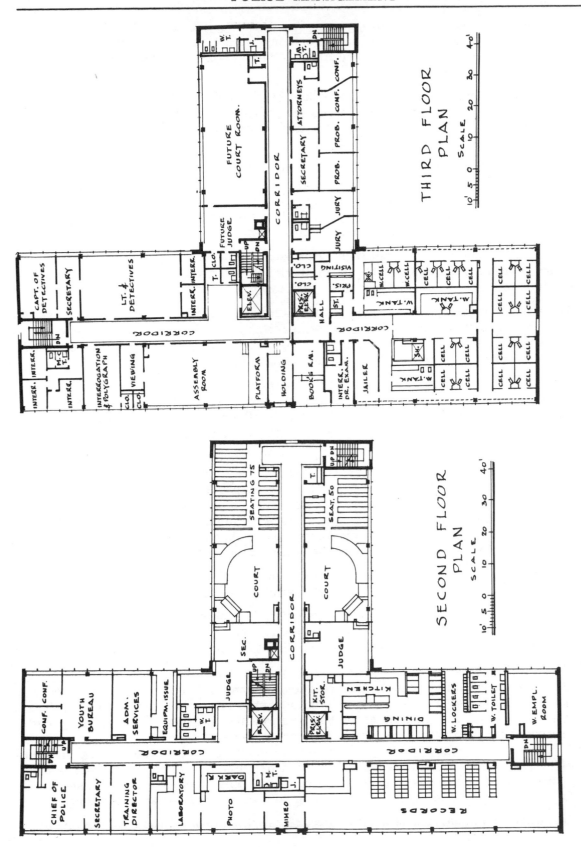

Figure 12 – Police and Court Building, Kalamazoo, Michigan (continued)

cell, the other could pass for a waiting room in a doctor's office. The standard cell is used to hold drunks, vagrants, or prisoners causing a disturbance, the other for prisoners who will not cause trouble and are likely to be released on bond in a short time. Both cells are equally secure.

9. Several kinds of storage areas should be provided, including storage conveniently located for evidence; property storage for prisoners' property and for lost, found, and recovered articles; perhaps an area for such bulky things as bicycles; and space for departmental supplies and equipment.

10. Special-purpose rooms with limited use should be avoided. Some forces, for example, have a show-up room that can be used only a few minutes a day because it is improperly ventilated and designed. Other forces have combined the show-up room with the squad room, or a room has been lighted, ventilated, and furnished so that it can be used also as a class room and a general meeting room.

11. Lighting should be carefully planned because the building will be in use 24 hours a day. Areas with considerable paper work should be very well lighted. This avoids fatigue and eye-strain and increases efficiency.

12. Air conditioning is no longer in the luxury classification. The building can be much more efficiently constructed if it is not necessary to have air shafts and excessive window space as an essential part of the plan. Air conditioning also will give improved ventilation and will definitely increase employee morale.

13. The police building gets continuous use so it should be well built. It is false economy to cut costs in many parts of the construction. Materials should be selected for durability and low maintenance costs. Since much of the building is never vacant, the cleaning people should be able to come in and clean with a minimum of interference.

14. Intercommunication should be a part of the original design. The telephone company should be consulted in planning trunk lines, the switchboard, extensions, tie lines, and other features of a modern system. The telephone system may be supplemented by direct intercom equipment. In large buildings pneumatic tubes may be needed to transmit police records from point to point. One or more remote radio control points may be needed. For example, some very large forces have a disaster control unit equipped with facilities to talk directly to the police cars.

15. A conference room is useful in all but small departments. The room also can be used for training classes, examinations, and similar purposes.

16. Adequate training facilities are essential. As mentioned earlier, these might be in a separate building. These should include classrooms, a library, offices, a range, and, if possible, a gymnasium. It might be possible to combine the gymnasium and range facilities.

17. There should be adequate facilities for the comfort and convenience of the personnel, including well lighted and ventilated locker rooms and lounge space. Police officers spend a great deal of time at the building waiting to testify in court, being held in reserve, and for many other reasons. They should be able to do this without hanging around the rest of the station, giving the public the impression they are loafing, or interfering with the officers who are working. Some departments have dormitory space to accommodate visiting officers in to pick up prisoners, police who are taking a short break from a long investigation, or police being held in reserve for an emergency.

18. Radio communications must be secure. It should not be possible for one or

more men to gain access to the dispatchers or radio equipment and paralyze the entire police operation. In departments where this is a separate function, not another duty for a desk officer, the equipment and dispatchers should be behind a steel door with this the only means of entrance.

19. Unless there is no possible chance for a power failure, the police headquarters should have an auxiliary source of electrical power that will furnish enough current to operate the radio equipment and lights at key points in the building.

20. Interrogation rooms are needed. A majority of cases depend upon interrogation more than any other single police method for their solution. It is not possible to do the best job of interrogation except in a suitable room. While the interrogation rooms should be adjacent to the detective division, they should not be regarded as the detectives' exclusive property but should be available to other divisions. In most circumstances, the juvenile unit should have its own interrogations facilities.

21. Ample space should be provided for police vehicles and cars of personnel and visitors. If there is no garage space for cars unloading prisoners, shift changes, and so on, there should be a carport so that occupants will not be exposed to the weather.

22. In larger cities a press room is convenient for newsmen assigned to the police beat.

23. Larger departments may provide office space for officers from other agencies making local investigations. This space may be used by officers from other city departments, and state or federal agencies. This sort of cooperation is essential to good law enforcement.

24. Proper construction of a jail will vary depending on local conditions, laws, and policies. The National Jail Association can recommend qualified jail architects for this phase of the planning.

This listing of points is by no means complete, but it does suggest what a major undertaking designing a new police building is. Remodeling an old building can be even more difficult because of the restrictions resulting from the original plan and construction of the building. In any case the cost of proper planning will be more than repaid with increased efficiency, durability, attractiveness, and low operating and maintenance costs.

Management of Police Property

Economy demands that a periodic or perpetual inventory be made of all police property. Necessary supplies or equipment should not be allowed to become exhausted. A regular accounting is advisable as well to detect leaks; experience teaches that certain articles have a way of disappearing from a police station. A check-up search will bring the problem to the surface at an early date and afford an opportunity to stop the petty thievery which, in time, might amount to large sums. Adequate records control is the essence of police property management.

Management Personnel. This control should be in the hands of a man who can say "no," who will honestly carry out his duties, and who will not grant a special favor to prevent the loss of a friend. He must regard the public budget as a thing to use properly rather than abuse.

In many departments the control of police property is assigned to some officer who has suffered an accident or illness, a practice which is based on the assumption that property management is a task that can be performed by anybody available. Although the sympathy is understandable, the light regard for the importance of property management is an unfounded and costly attitude. Lax control of property can result in large financial losses, which means that the total appropriation available for police services is not being used to best advantage. Furthermore, it is not true that property management requires no special skill.

Management of property and equipment represents a responsibility of the police which they are unsuited by training and experience to discharge efficiently. The conventional police approach does not ordinarily yield satisfactory results when dealing with problems not concerned with professional police duties. The problems of a manager of police properties have much in common with similar problems encountered in commerce and industry. These include details concerning the maintenance of buildings and equipment, of depreciation, the procedure of control records, financial arrangements, and the minutiae of related matters. Familiarity with the terminology of the business world and experience in its practices are necessary qualifications.

This practical contact with commercial customs cannot readily be obtained in a police department. Perhaps there are individuals on the force who have all of the required talents, but they prove difficult to find and in any case can be more usefully employed at patrol or other active police duty. Moreover, civilians may usually be employed at a similar scale to do the same or better work.

Functions of Property Management. The work of police property management may be classified under five major heads: (1) purchase of equipment and supplies, (2) custody and issue of supplies, (3) custody of recovered property and evidence, (4) maintenance of plant, and (5) servicing and storage of automotive equipment. In some cities police also are responsible for maintenance of traffic signs and signals.

1. Purchase of Equipment and Supplies. Sound purchasing practice demands much more than honesty and familiarity with the items to be purchased. It also requires a knowledge of markets, evaluation of bids, ability to prepare specifications, and testing of purchases to insure that specifications have been met. With the possible exception of departments in the largest cities, few police departments have, or can afford to have, departmental purchasing offices which meet the highest standards of facilities and personnel. For this reason the question may be raised as to what extent the purchases of a police department should be handled by the central purchasing office of the city, providing such an agency exists.

The volume of purchases made by such an office plus the highly trained personnel which it can afford make possible considerable economies. The principal argument against such a practice is that police equipment and supplies are so technical and so highly specialized that the police department is the only agency qualified to purchase them. To a certain extent this is true, but even this fact loses its significance if the central purchasing office recognizes the special needs of the police department by depending on the department for the preparation of specifications. Furthermore many of the supplies of the police department — gasoline, office furniture, and stationery — are also required by other departments.

The answer to this problem will probably be determined by the competence and the attitude of the central purchasing office in any given city, but police administrators should be alert to capitalize on any opportunities for obtaining expert assistance in purchasing. Even in the event that purchasing remains a departmental function, the best methods and practices of general city purchasing should be observed and copied. [4]

Although it is not possible to go into detail regarding purchasing methods and procedure, a brief sketch of the "paper work" involved in the purchasing process usually is represented by four types of documents: (1) a requisition, often supplemented by names of bidders or proposal forms; (2) purchase orders; (3) advice of receipt of goods, often including inspection or testing reports; and (4) vendors' invoices. Generally at least, three departments have an interest in each of these papers, and it is therefore the general rule to have them prepared in triplicate. The departments which need copies for filing or for making entries thereon are (1) the using department, (2) the purchasing office, and (3) the finance office.

The requisition originates in the using department, the purchase order in the purchasing office, the advice of receipt in the using department, and the invoice in the supplying firm. A voucher covering these documents and summarizing the whole series of steps involved in the transaction, including the accounting entries and the fiscal approval for final payment, is usually prepared either in the purchasing or finance office. In a well-devised set-up it is provided that purchase orders cannot be accepted as valid offers or orders unless countersigned by the finance officer as to adequacy of funds and unencumbered appropriation or allotment credits.

This orderly procedure should be strictly enforced and a rule adopted that no purchases shall be made by anyone except the purchasing agent unless authorized by him. There are times when emergency purchases must be made in the field. It is recommended that the purchasing agent should approve such orders by telephone; if he is not available, the order should be confirmed in writing by the next mail or other delivery. It is essential that these emergency purchases be controlled and held to a minimum if the full benefits of group purchasing are to be obtained, for it is on these noncompetitive purchases that the vendors stand to make the greatest margin of profit.

It is assumed, of course, that the purchasing office will set up standards and specifications, take advantage of all opportunities to secure discounts for prompt cash payment, investigate the qualifications of bidders, depend upon competitive bidding wherever possible, and utilize all available community facilities for testing the quality of materials and supplies delivered. These are essential elements in sound purchasing.

2. Custody and Issuance of Supplies. The principal point here is the need for adequate storage facilities and for complete and accurate records. The warehouses and storage facilities utilized in many otherwise well-run departments are not only inadequate but unsafe. Dilapidated frame buildings, themselves fire hazards, are used to store ammunition, gasoline, and other combustible or perishable supplies. Such conditions not only endanger the public directly but indirectly as well, for the loss of the materials and equipment stored there might seriously interrupt police activities.

With regard to supply records the main objectives are to prevent loss, to provide information concerning the amount of equipment and supplies on hand and their location, and to prevent embarrassing shortages. Card files containing information regarding every piece of equipment and every item of supplies should be maintained. All articles of police property which can be so marked should have a serial number or the name of

---

[4] See Russell Forbes, *Purchasing for Small Cities* (Chicago: Public Administration Service, 1951), 23pp. See also publications of the National Institute of Governmental Purchasing and books and pamphlets dealing with various aspects of purchasing listed annually in the finance section of *The Municipal Year Book*.

the department or both. Firearms normally bear serial numbers. Official badges and shields usually have a number prominently displayed for the convenience of citizens in identifying an officer. Automobiles, motorcycles, and bicycles should display a permanently stenciled number for easy identification.

Issues of durable department property for permanent or temporary use should be charged to the officer receiving it, noting the serial number or other mark and the condition. Property which wears out in use may be replaced only upon presentation of the worn-out articles. With proper records the average life of various articles in different branches of the service will become known and serve as a useful guide in preparing the annual budget and as a control device.

Good property management of course requires that regular (at least annual) inventories be made. Periodic inspections of property in use and in stock will furnish an appraisal of needs. Reports of findings and recommendations to commanding officers can be utilized to establish effective cooperation between line officers and the property manager. Significant savings may result from a timely suggestion which is translated into action.

3. Custody of Recovered Property. Every police department builds up a considerable volume of lost or stolen property which has been recovered and is awaiting identification by the lawful owner. In addition items of property are held in custody for prisoners and other persons. Such property demands particular care since it is held in trust. The property manager may properly be entrusted with the care of a large proportion of such property, provided careful records are kept. Items held as evidence or small items which will soon be returned to their owners may be kept at headquarters to make them easily accessible. If adequate storage facilities are provided there, these items may immediately be entrusted to the property manager. If, on the other hand, all storage and warehouse facilities are located at some distance from headquarters, only those items not claimed after a period of time (e.g., 30 days) may be transferred from headquarters to the warehouse or storage quarters. Some property held in custody may be sold at auction after a period of time, and the custodian of the property will either handle the sale or make arrangements with auctioneers for such sales.

4. Maintenance of Plant. Police buildings should be kept in good condition at all times. This requires the services of carpenters, plumbers, and electricians as well as janitors. In some large departments a separate maintenance staff is maintained, but in most cases it will prove more advantageous and economical to have such work performed under the supervision of the general city department of building construction and maintenance. Again it should be emphasized that such work is best performed by civilians rather than by officers incapacitated for active police duty.

5. Servicing and Storage of Motor Equipment. The large number of police automobiles, motorcycles, and other motor equipment creates a special problem of property management, especially since police cars are in such constant use and must be in first-class condition.

Again we encounter the issue of departmental versus centralized control. Many cities maintain central storage and repair service for city-owned vehicles, or at least for public works motor equipment, and the question arises as to whether police vehicles should be included under this central control. Economies in purchases, in labor, and in storage facilities can undoubtedly be effected by centralization. On the other hand, police executives often feel that the energency nature of police service and the special character of police vehicles demand departmental control. The answer probably will depend on circumstances in a given city. If a good central agency is available, it should be used; if not, it may be necessary to compromise between extreme departmentalization and complete centralization.

In a very large city, where the large number of police vehicles permits the economies of large-scale operation, considerable independence may be justified. Even so, some services may well be centralized. Purchases of cars, of gasoline, and of parts may well be combined with those of the central municipal garage for the sake of economies of large-scale buying. Special repair equipment may be used jointly by police and other city departments. Furthermore, district garages and storage facilities maintained by the central garage, if conveniently located, may be used by district police stations as well.

Small and medium-sized cities may profit from even greater centralization. In small cities where only one police station is needed, it may be that a central garage can handle all storage and repairs. In cities somewhat larger, small repairs may be handled by department employees and heavy repairs by the central garage. In either case it may be well to have departmental mechanics operating under the general supervision of the central garage. In some cities the fire and police departments have been able to pool some of their repair services.

Whatever arrangement is made, certain services and controls must be provided. Periodic inspections (on a mileage basis) of all motor equipment should be made. Accurate and complete service records should be maintained for each vehicle, showing mileage; gasoline, oil, and grease consumed; repairs made; and any other items of operating expense. Such vehicle records not only assist the garage superintendent in his monthly inspections, but they also provide the basis for comparative cost analyses of different types and makes of motor equipment. They are also useful in determining the relative economies of buying new equipment or repairing old (see Figure 13).

A word might also be said at this point about policy with regard to the replacement of old equipment. Police work requires an exceptionally high quality of performance from motor equipment. Police vehicles must be able to compete with high-powered cars operated by criminals, and the public prestige of the department demands that they also be presentable in appearance. Furthermore, the constant use of police vehicles prohibits the operation of equipment in frequent need of repairs. Nevertheless there is a tendency on the part of some police officials to assume that these conditions obviate the need for economy in purchase and replacement. Vehicles which are not of most recent design are replaced with scant regard for considerations of economy. A careful study of actual police needs will reveal that not all vehicles need be high-powered and that a policy of systematic replacement and transfer may produce equal results with lower costs. A planned program of equipment replacement can provide the department with some new equipment each year without the expense of an entire new fleet of cars. Furthermore, more careful attention to the inspection of vehicles and the maintenance of cost records will not only increase their useful life but will provide comparative data which will make possible more effective and economical purchases in the future. Special attention in purchasing should be given to the disposition of equipment to be replaced. Calculation of trade-in offers of different bidders may show a discrepancy between gross and net cost of new equipment. It may also appear after investigation that greater economies can be effected by disposing of old vehicles at public sale or by transferring them to other city departments whose needs do not require such exacting performance.

6. Signs, Signals, and Markings. Many police departments are assigned the task of maintaining traffic signs and signals and markings and have a maintenance staff for

this duty. Manufactured traffic signs can be purchased, of a uniform nature, without the necessity of manufacturing them locally. Before any new installation of a sign, signal, or street marking, a careful survey should be made to warrant such action.[5] Signs should be inspected periodically and repaired, repainted, or replaced as necessary. In selecting materials for painting street signs, parking lanes, and other uses, care should be exercised to obtain high-type materials that will stand up under outdoor conditions.[6] Frequently when parking meters are installed, the duty of maintaining this equipment is delegated to the police department. This is a specialized maintenance function and should be supervised by competent mechanics. The procedures for handling such maintenance work and records for its control depend on local circumstances.

Organization for Property Management. The principal functions of police property control and management have been discussed briefly, and some possible procedures for assigning these duties have been suggested. In conclusion, this function may be divided into two types of duties — custody of property and maintenance of property. The logical place in the police organization for the custody of property seems to be the records unit. This duty should be assigned to one officer, who is often titled the property clerk. His duties would include the custody of found, recovered, and prisoners' property, and, when there is no police laboratory, evidence. By this procedure, responsibility can be fixed, and a foolproof system of handling property can be maintained. In a large department the property clerk may have a staff of assistants. In any event, this custodial duty should be assigned to the records division for the following reasons: (1) it is of a service nature, and not specifically related to any line activity, and (2) it is largely straight record-keeping work.

The place of the property maintenance function in the organization of the department is not so readily discernible. In a large department, all maintenance tasks of the department may be gathered together into one unit. Some departments have even organized a maintenance division. This procedure has all the advantages of specialization in that competent, trained personnel may be assigned to this work and an orderly system of repairing and servicing police equipment may be instituted. In smaller departments the above system may not be feasible. Frequently, the maintenance tasks are divided among various units. For example, the service and repair of autos may be assigned to the patrol division; the maintenance of motorcycles to the traffic division; maintenance of the radio system to the communications unit; and so forth. The organization of property and equipment maintenance will depend on local conditions and the size of the force. Whatever the organization, the criterion of property maintenance is the efficiency of the services performed.

Coordination

The art and skill of coordination is a talent needed by any leader of a large group of men. Without coordination and control an organization will develop as many identities and goals as there are subdivisions of the whole.

A chief of police is responsible for keeping his department on the track as a single

---

[5] Bureau of Public Roads, *Manual on Uniform Traffic Control Devices for Streets and Highways* (Washington, D.C.: Government Printing Office, 1948), 223pp. Revisions adopted 1953-54.
[6] See *Traffic Engineering Handbook* (New York: Institute of Traffic Engineers and National Conservation Bureau, 2nd ed., 1950), 520pp. See also *Manual of Traffic Engineering Studies* (New York: Association of Casualty and Surety Companies, 1953), 278pp.

INDIVIDUAL EQUIPMENT RECORD

1. Equipment No.
2. Motor No.   Serial No.
3. Make
4. Type
5. Capacity

6. Date Purchased   19
7. Original Cost . . . . $
8. Value Start of this Year . $
9. Estimated Salvage Value . $
10. Remaining Depreciation . $

For Year Ending
11. Estimated Depreciation This Year . $
12. Estimated Hours or Miles This Year
13. Depreciation Rate per $\frac{Hour}{Mile}$ . . . . . $

MONTH (1)	GASOLINE (2)		OIL (3)		TIRES & SUPPLIES (4)	REPAIR LABOR (5)		REPAIR PARTS (6)	OUTSIDE REPAIRS (7)	OVER-HEAD (8)	TOTAL DIRECT EXPENSE (9)	DEPRECIA-TION (10)	TOTAL COST (11)	MILEAGE FIRST OF MONTH (12)	MILES RUN (13)	COST PER MILE (14)	HOURS RUN (15)	COST PER HOUR (16)	MILES PER GAL. (17)	RENTALS EARNED (Credits) (18)
	Gals.	Amt.	Qts.	Amt.		Hrs.	Amt.													
TOTALS																				

INSTRUCTIONS: Use separate sheet for each passenger car, transportation, construction, or other piece of city equipment. The entries at the top are made once each year from an inventory and depreciation schedule. At the close of each month postings are made to columns 2 to 6 from a monthly summary of equipment expense. Column 7 is posted from the invoices for outside repairs. Column 10 figures are obtained by multiplying the hours or miles run by the hourly or mileage depreciation rate listed at the top of the record. Overhead includes insurance, salaries of garage employees that cannot be distributed to individual pieces of equipment, fuel, power, small tools, etc. The entries for columns 12 and 15 are obtained from the equipment operators' daily reports. Column 18 refers to the rentals earned or charges made to the cost accounts for the use of the equipment.

Figure 13 — Individual Equipment Record

Source: Public Administration Service.

unit toward set objectives. It is not a product that just happens; coordination requires planning and evaluation and probably is the major management function in which personality plays a large role. Leadership ability of an administrator is reflected in almost direct proportion to the amount of teamwork evident in the organization.

Each division in a department, at first glance, might appear to have different end goals; this is not so. Without coordination, control, teamwork, and leadership, each division will develop separate end goals to such an extent that they may be identified as separate departments.

An administrator must be aware of the personality differences of his ranking commanders, and he must align these personalities in relationship to one another in assignments which generate the least friction and promote the most efficiency. Further the chief must make each commander aware of the other's problems and limitations — then he must motivate each toward a desire to cooperate with one another. This goal is best brought about by frequent meetings of the group to discuss each of their problems. Frequent informal meetings should also be encouraged. It is more natural for a man to cooperate with another whom he knows and understands than with one he does not know.

The same concept holds true for all members of the department. Subcommanders, supervisors, and the patrolmen should be encouraged to get together with their problems as often as possible — both formally and informally. If the meetings do not come about naturally, it may become necessary for the administrator to schedule meetings. Generally coordination and cooperation are fostered by going further and further down into the ranks to place responsibility — the greater the responsibility of a man the greater will be his feeling of belonging.

Control is an integral part of coordination. Control provides for satisfactory performance and uniformity in goals, functions, and tasks through statistical analyses, reports, and inspection.

Coordination and control are sometimes the assigned functions of a designated staff officer. Great care should be exercised in choosing a man for such an assignment; if not, more harm than good may result. He should be one who knows how the chief thinks and what he wants; he should have a thorough knowledge of the department and police work; and he must be respected by all with whom he works.

Control by Inspection

Control is effected through application of the principle that a person to whom authority is granted shall be held to account by the superior who made the delegation. Authority is delegated by some form of command (usually in the form of an assignment) because responsibility cannot be placed (i.e., an order given to do something) without the delegation of authority needed to carry out the order. Superiors who give orders, therefore, have a responsibility to see that the orders are carried out as assigned.

Persons to whom authority is delegated cannot be held accountable until the consequences of their use of authority have been ascertained. These results are appraised by inspection. The principle of accountability, therefore, must be implemented by inspection.

Inspection is the process of obtaining facts relating to persons, things, conditions, and actions by observation, inquiry, examination, and analysis. Facts thus discovered reveal needs. They provide an appraisal of the adequacy and suitability of staff, equipment, and all procedures relating to preparation for a task and its accomplishment.

Facts thus obtained also reveal conditions in the community relating to persons and things that may indicate other needs. Police hazards, criminal activities, and the attitude of the public toward the police, are also discovered.

Inspection is of two kinds: (1) a staff inspection made by someone who lacks direct control over the subject of the inspection; and (2) an authoritative inspection made by those in direct command. Inspection is a major duty of the immediate supervisor of officers at the level of execution; it enables him to hold his subordinates to account. This task of immediate supervision is relatively simple. As the hierarchy of command is ascended, however, the difficulty of holding subordinates accountable becomes increasingly difficult for a number of reasons.

1. The scope of responsibility becomes broader because usually the height of the apex of the pyramid in the hierarchy determines its area of responsibility. As the scope is increased, proportionately less time is available for inspections. Lack of time prevents those in command from making detailed, continuous inspection of all persons, things, conditions, and acts that fall within their pyramids of responsibility.

2. The nature of the work at the upper levels changes from one of execution to other forms, such as planning and direction, which are usually not so readily appraised. Often the evaluation of work at the lowest level is the final objective, the upper level work being merely auxiliary to it and having no excuse for being except to facilitate accomplishment at the level of execution.

3. In contrast to the relative ease with which orders descend the line of command, facts relating to the fulfillment of the orders ascend the channels slowly, laboriously, and sometimes not at all.

While the immediate supervisor spends much of his time in holding his associates to account, those at higher levels must resort to sampling inspections to ascertain facts on which to base an appraisal of the work of their subordinates. Spot audits may be made from time to time to test whether the requirements of satisfactory supervision and control have been met. While such checks should always be continued, the chief needs inspectional assistance to assure the discovery of facts needed in holding subordinates accountable and in strengthening weaknesses.

Assistance to the command group should be provided in the form of staff inspections carried out by line as well as service officers and, in larger departments, by one or more staff officers designated for this purpose and called inspectors. The duty of the inspector is to assist the chief in the performance of his administrative task of control. The inspector should have no direct authority over the members of the force but should operate exclusively as a staff officer.

The inspector should prepare procedures and report forms for both staff and authoritative inspections. He should provide staff supervision of their operations and should stimulate the inspectional process throughout the organization. Control is thereby effected.

The distinction between authoritative and staff inspections should be understood. Authoritative inspections are made by those in command who have authority to require an immediate correction to comply with department regulations whereas staff inspections are made by staff officers (or by line officers acting in a staff capacity) who lack such authority in their own right and can only call attention to deficiencies they discover.

The chief should require all supervisors to make regular periodic authoritative inspections. In order to assure himself that all is well, the chief must, in addition, make some inspections himself. Lack of time will usually prevent the chief, especially in a fairly large department, from performing this essential act of control. He must then have a department inspector to assist him in the performance of these important tasks.

The police inspector is a staff officer who should not have authority in his own right to correct unsatisfactory conditions. While many corrections will be voluntarily made when deficiencies are called to the attention of operating personnel, it will be necessary for the inspector to report some situations either to commanding officers or to the chief for corrective action.

The inspector must be circumspect in his relations with both commanding officers and subordinates in order to avoid friction. His findings and any resultant suggestions or requests made to subordinates should be reported punctiliously to the commanding officer with further suggestions. Care must be used in making suggestions and requests, especially to subordinates, to avoid creating an impression that they are commands.

The police inspector will spend most of his time in personal inspections of persons, operations, and conditions regarding which he can in no other way receive reliable information. It is in the inspection of these less tangible things that he will render the greatest service to the chief.

The appointment of a department inspector should not lessen the need for authoritative inspections by command officers; instead, the inspector should be required to stimulate the inspectional process throughout the entire department by systems of inspections and reports by operating personnel. The purpose and nature of inspection and the duties of the police inspector are outlined below.

Purpose and Nature of Inspection.[7] The purpose is to promote effectiveness and economy by the inspection of

Persons
Things
Procedures
Results

in order to reveal

Conditions
Situations
Actions

that adversely influence the success of police operations because of weaknesses and failures in

Personnel
Material
Procedures

which indicate a need for modified or additional

Organization
Regulation
Procedure
Equipment

[7] For a detailed discussion of this subject, see section on "Inspection by the Chief" in O. W. Wilson, *Police Administration*, 1950, pp. 66-74, from which this outline was taken by permission of McGraw-Hill Book Company, Inc., New York.

Headquarters facilities
Manpower
Training
Direction
Leadership

The nature of inspection is accomplished by interviews with

Members of the force
Persons involved in police incidents
The general public

and analysis of

Inspection reports
Police records
Police statistics
Police procedures

and observation of condition of

Police quarters
Jail
Public places
Equipment
Personnel

in order to ascertain whether:

1. Department morale is satisfactory.
2. Morale-destroying influences are at work.
3. The attitudes, actions, reactions, and accomplishments of members of the force are satisfactory.
4. Training, direction, and supervision are satisfactory.
5. Rules governing the care of the body are complied with.
6. The integrity of all members is above reproach.
7. The moral standards of the members are satisfactory.
8. Regulations concerning the maintenance and use of equipment and property are complied with.
9. Equipment and property require repair or replacement.
10. Impaired condition of equipment and property has resulted from improper use or inadequate maintenance.
11. Equipment and space are adequate.
12. Departmental procedures are suitable.
13. Departmental procedures are being followed.
14. Operations are carried out as planned.
15. Departmental resources are used to best advantage.
16. Organization units are operating satisfactorily.
17. Any part of the police job is being neglected.
18. Community conditions affecting operations against crime and vice are satisfactory.
19. Public reaction to department policies, methods, and officials is satisfactory.
20. Persons and incidents are satisfactorily dealt with.

Duties of the Police Inspector. As an agent of the chief of police, the police inspector will:

1. Conduct open inspection of personnel, material, procedures, and results of police operations.

2. Correct without reference to the chief such unsatisfactory conditions as he is able to remedy.

3. Inform the chief on
   a. Action taken by the inspector.
   b. Action desired of the chief.

4. Promote and stimulate supervision on the part of operating personnel by
   a. Devising well-conceived inspection reports for their use that will require a positive statement that a condition is satisfactory or unsatisfactory.
   b. Instructing supervisory personnel in
      (1) The use of inspection reports.
      (2) The nature of authoritative and staff inspections.
   c. Spot checking on inspection reports.

5. Inspect and effect correction of conditions reported unsatisfactory.

6. Maintain satisfactory relationships with subordinate and commanding officers.

7. Focus his attention on task of appraising such intangibles as public relations, conditions in the community affecting police operations, and the morale of the men.

Intelligence

Whereas inspections are made openly, certain information needed by the chief, if he is to discharge his obligations effectively, must be obtained somewhat covertly. This information relates to the integrity of the force and to conditions in the community that may be conducive to the development of organized crime. Since commercialized vice is the seedbed of most organized crime, close attention also must be given to operations in this field of criminal activity; surveillance must also be kept on the activities of known and suspected gangsters and racketeers.

Both tasks may be the responsibility of one organic unit although in very large departments they may be assigned to separate units. For example, the Los Angeles department leaves principal responsibility for assuring the integrity of the force to the internal affairs division while the intelligence division devotes its attention to gangsters, racketeers, organized crime, and commercialized vice that operate in spite of the efforts of district commanders and the vice division (see Figure 1 in Chapter 2).

The value of an intelligence division to the chief of a large department is best appreciated through a few comments on the intelligence division of the Los Angeles department. The intelligence division is responsible for gathering information on and investigating all phases of organized crime including individuals who, by their previous associations or suspected endeavors, constitute a potential hazard to society. Special attention is given to vice operators and racketeers in labor, business, or bunco.

The primary purpose of this division is to gather information; it is not an enforcement unit. Very few arrests are made; instead, information is given to an enforcement arm of the department which effects the arrest and conducts subsequent investigation and court proceedings. Officers of the intelligence division cooperate and are at times loaned to complete the investigation. The objective is obtained when an activity is broken up and effectiveness is considerably increased by the intelligence division officers not being identified with such operation. The division works closely with other law enforcement agencies — local, state, and federal. It is not confined to geographical boundaries in its investigations.

Success in obtaining information on organized crime is dependent on officers who are particularly well adapted to obtaining and maintaining sources of information. Fraternization by intelligence division members with underworld characters is not tolerated, and departmental regulations prohibit any officer from accepting for his personal use any gratuities or rewards. All such contributions must be turned over to the city retirement fund.

Officers usually work in pairs, and each team is assigned to coverage on a group of known hoodlums. These officers are further responsible for maintaining the individual dossier file on each of the assigned characters. All officers are required to be on the alert for other individuals whose past histories indicate a lack of legitimate enterprise. One team of officers devotes full time to background checking, i.e., credit reports, bank information, utilities, and others, in a constant attempt to establish association between known characters or infiltration of known hoodlums into legitimate business.

Investigations of police personnel are not ordinarily undertaken by this division; instances wherein police personnel are suspected of being allied with hoodlums are taken up with the division of internal affairs and subsequent investigation may be handled by either or both divisions.

Records and Files. The intelligence division maintains its own filing system. All files therein are the property of the chief of police and are not considered official police records subject to subpoena under the provisions of Section 1886.5, Code of Civil Procedure of the state of California. The files are not open to perusal by members of the department except with the approval of the intelligence division commander. His refusal can be countermanded only by the chief of police.

The files are cross-indexed with the general criminal files of the department, however, and all officers are encouraged to consult the intelligence division whenever they are interested in a person identified in its files. Assistance to an officer seeking information in an investigation is provided by the division desk officer who ascertains the nature of the information desired, makes a file search, and reports the results to the officer.

Members of the division are required to make written reports on all information and observations so that officers 10 years hence may have the benefit of past activities and operations of these individuals. A code, confidential between the reporting officer and the commander, is used to identify sources of information.

An alphabetical master card is maintained on all persons who have been brought to attention. For this file, a 5 x 8 inch card is used which contains space for name, physical description, photograph, various police numbers, addresses, phone, description and license of car, location, friendly activities, and associates. The back of the card is used for posting department report numbers in which the subject's name is mentioned.

In addition to dossier files on the more prominent hoodlums, reports are filed by subject matter and a second copy is filed chronologically. The following 3 x 5 size files are kept:

1. A building file where credit reports have been obtained on businesses suspected of being connected in organized crime.

2. An address file which gives the known addresses of all subjects.

3. A telephone number file of all individuals and businesses.

4. An automobile file containing license number and description of the cars operated by those persons of interest to this division.

5. An alphabetical file maintained on registered bookmakers.

One further operation is the subscription to a news clipping service of some 20 metropolitan newspapers throughout the United States. News items are distributed to the specialized units such as robbery, burglary, and narcotics. Items on racketeers and prominent hoodlums are indexed and filed in the intelligence division.

The only formal report to the chief of police is a weekly progress report which summarizes briefly the week's work.

Public Information

Probably no facet of police management is more important or more neglected than public information. Neglect of this area by the administrator has resulted in many of the present-day misconceptions of the police and their function within the American way of life. The able chief, or his staff representative who has the chore of keeping the public informed, faces a formidable task. Certainly to gain any goal is impossible without the cooperation of the people the police serve. This subject is important. It will be discussed more fully in Chapters 14 and 15.

Reporting

The process of reporting as it will be referred to in this chapter is not necessarily limited to the making and keeping of police records, although those functions are included. The subject of police records is thoroughly treated in Chapter 12.

Administrative reporting fundamentally is the communication of information necessary for the efficient management of the organization. Many police administrators look upon public information duties as part of the reporting function; whereas others do not. Some like to keep the two separate; looking upon public information as being more selective, dramatic, and promotional in character while administrative reporting transmits all information in its most naked state, whether good news or bad.

Communication is one of the most talked about subjects among administrators. Human relations enthusiasts, personnel management people, and industrial psychologists turn quickly to the subject of communications when discussing morale and the efficiency of workers of all ranks. It is generally agreed that the greater the understanding between the chief and all other members of the department the greater will be the efficiency of the organization.

A chief must recognize this and then see that communication of information and understanding is provided *up* the chain of command as well as down. The downward flow of information generally is far more efficient than the flow upward; one of a chief's greatest problems is getting objective reports of what the feeling is among the men and of what is actually occurring on the operational line. It is the chief's responsibility to get this information. He must plan for it, and he must work at it.

Some information will flow upward through routine crime reports; some will come up through inspection reports and other required administrative communications. The best results will be realized when all personnel recognize that they and the department will benefit most by the transmitting of all necessary information upward to the chief. This makes training necessary, but most of all it requires that the chief acquire for

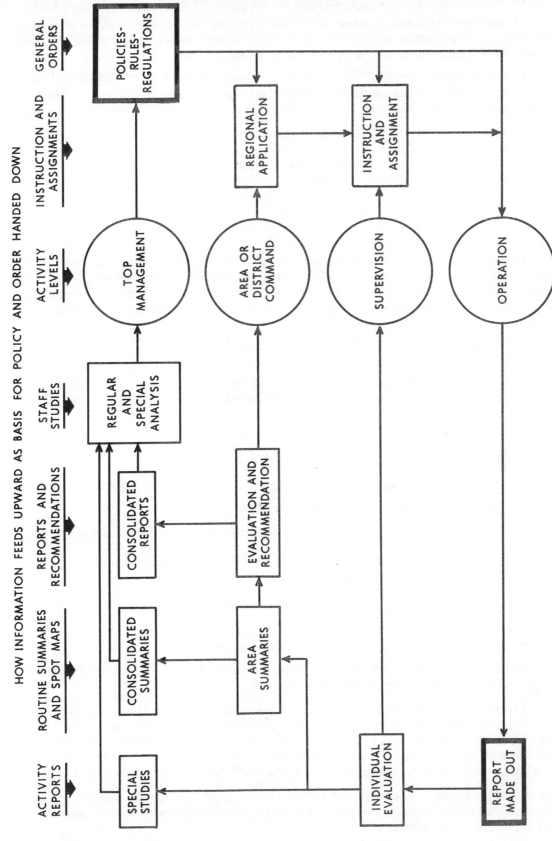

TRAFFIC INSTITUTE, NORTHWESTERN UNIVERSITY
TRAFFIC RECORDS

HOW INFORMATION FEEDS UPWARD AS BASIS FOR POLICY AND ORDER HANDED DOWN

GENERAL ORDERS

INSTRUCTION AND ASSIGNMENTS

ACTIVITY LEVELS

STAFF STUDIES

REPORTS AND RECOMMENDATIONS

ROUTINE SUMMARIES AND SPOT MAPS

ACTIVITY REPORTS

POLICIES-RULES-REGULATIONS

REGIONAL APPLICATION

INSTRUCTION AND ASSIGNMENT

TOP MANAGEMENT

AREA OR DISTRICT COMMAND

SUPERVISION

OPERATION

REGULAR AND SPECIAL ANALYSIS

CONSOLIDATED REPORTS

EVALUATION AND RECOMMENDATION

CONSOLIDATED SUMMARIES

AREA SUMMARIES

SPECIAL STUDIES

INDIVIDUAL EVALUATION

REPORT MADE OUT

Figure 14 — Processing Information

himself a reputation for understanding and fair play. If the men doubt the chief's integrity and impartiality, he will experience difficulty in getting information to flow upward. The chief also is likely to fall victim to those members of the department who, motivated by many selfish reasons, are eager to carry tales.

Routine reports probably provide the greatest single source of information upon which down-flowing administrative communications are based. Figure 14 portrays a typical processing of information as it flows upwards and then down.

In addition to providing for intradepartmental communications a chief of police must establish open and friendly lines between the police department and other departments and agencies as well as with the chief administrative officer. It is a chief's duty to keep the city officials fully informed of all department activities.

Directing

Directing is the final step in administration — that is, telling and showing what is to be done. It is the responsibility of the chief to establish a comprehensive and understandable system of directives in his department. A directive may be defined as an instruction or order issued to a subordinate or group of subordinates. Included are policy statements, general and special orders, training bulletins, standard operating procedures, and rules and regulations. A directive may be given orally or in writing, but this section is concerned only with written administrative directives.

Written rules and regulations are necessary in any police organization. They provide the guides for the administration of the department. In addition to rules and regulations there must be other forms of directives.

Directives generally serve the following purposes:

1. Prevent haphazard, "all-directional" courses of action.

2. Form basic foundation for operational and administrative functions.

3. Provide officers with guides for action.

4. Promote good morale by telling each officer what is expected of him.

5. Establish communications lines — up, down, and across.

6. Establish the organization structure.

7. Provide certain legal requirements and protection for officers and/or employees.

8. Establish authority and responsibility at all levels in the department.

In addition to rules and regulations some chiefs define administrative directives for the guidance of their personnel, for example:

Policy Statement: A groad outline of the organization, objectives, plans, principles, or course of action. It generally requires interpretation, and any action within its boundaries is acceptable. The Law Enforcement Code of Ethics is a policy statement that has been adopted by many departments. A department member can find the answer to any question he may have regarding required conduct within the framework of this policy.

General Order: A permanent order that includes the whole department or unit of the department and is effective until rescinded — for example an order establishing an intelligence unit is a general order.

Special Order: An order affecting the department or units of the department. It is of a temporary nature and often expires upon execution of the order. For example, an order providing for parade assignments.

Standard Operating Procedure or SOP: A directive that outlines a particular procedure step by step. For example, a booking procedure.

Rule: A directive which sets down specific minor requirements. For example, an order prohibiting officers reading newspapers at the complaint desk.

Here are a few basic rules to follow when compiling directives:

1. Be sure the problem to be solved is clearly defined.

2. Determine the key factors required — what, who, where, when, how, and why. Often the success or failure of a directive depends upon an understanding of "why." If possible the reasons for a directive should be included in its text.

3. It must contribute to making policy or policies effective.

4. It must maintain uniformity of action.

5. It must be reasonable to the recipient.

6. It must be complete.

7. It must be understandable.

The issuance of directives is not enough. Whenever possible every person who is affected should get a copy. Each written directive should be identified by title, number, and date of origin. Directives should be indexed when the volume is large.

Summary

The success of any undertaking is dependent largely on the quality of its leadership. No organization can rise to a higher level than its head, and this is especially true in police service. This chapter has undertaken to outline the way in which the performance of management tasks may be assured by the chief of police. His success is almost entirely dependent on the effectiveness of his administration of personnel; his ingenuity in providing adequate resources — men and tools for them to work with; his ability to provide acceptable official and public relations and information; and finally, his skill in planning operations and directing and controlling the efforts of his force. The measure of his leadership ability, therefore, will be in terms of the performance of these important management tasks.

Chapter 4

PERSONNEL MANAGEMENT

At the risk of oversimplification, it can be said that the purpose of personnel management is to attract and retain the highest possible quality of employee. Certain systems, procedures, and techniques have been developed which give greater promise of achieving this objective than the earlier and more traditional approaches to personnel administration. "Merit" has remained the touchstone of modern public personnel systems, while "civil service" has taken on the connotation of protection for the mediocre. But regardless of terms used, an acceptable police personnel program must be firmly grounded in the concept that qualifications for and performance in the job shall be the decisive factors in fixing and administering personnel policies.

The following functions are essential in a comprehensive personnel program designed to establish and maintain a superior police force:

1. A duties classification of positions — a grouping of positions into classes sufficiently similar so that the same descriptive title may be given, the same qualifications and tests of fitness may be used to recruit qualified employees, and the same rates of pay may be applied.

2. The preparation and administration of a compensation plan that provides for attractive and equitable salaries and for salary advancement based on satisfactory performance of duties.

3. The recruitment and selection of employees on a competitive merit basis for entrance into the service.

4. An intensive program of in-service training to equip the new recruit with specific skills and to insure the continuing development of all officers on the force.[1]

5. A program for promotion based on demonstrated merit.

6. An equitable system of evaluating job performance.

7. The regulation of conditions of service, such as vacations, sick leave, transfers, hours of work, and attendance.

8. An effective program of employee relations.

9. The provision of effective machinery for maintaining discipline in the department, which should include recognition for outstanding performance as well as punishment for improper conduct.

10. An actuarially sound retirement system that permits the employees to look forward to retirement with full assurance of economic security in their old age.

---

[1] Training is considered sufficiently important in the police field to warrant a whole chapter in this volume. See Chapter 5.

Police Department-Central Personnel Agency Relations

The first thing the police must consider in developing a personnel system is the relationship of such a system to whatever personnel program exists for the city service as a whole.

Police Personnel Problems Not Unique

Some police officials consider police work so different from other types of public employment as to require completely separate and different handling of personnel programs and activities. The differences are in degree, not kind. For example, municipal utilities must maintain continuous, uninterrupted service; health and welfare personnel deal directly with citizens under conditions of stress; street maintenance workers are exposed to the elements; the repair and maintenance of power lines is a highly hazardous occupation; and every municipal department has its own peak loads which require overtime on occasion.

Modern public personnel administration is required to deal with a large variety of employments and services and to adjust its basic techniques and methods to meet the special conditions which prevail in each type of work. Police officials should not be reluctant to invite or accept the assistance and services provided by the central personnel program where one exists and is functioning with reasonable effectiveness. The sorting out of responsibilities for personnel management between the police department and the central personnel office is important, but not too difficult.

Where There Is a Central Personnel Agency

The smallest cities seldom have a central personnel agency and may not even have any one person with part-time responsibility for personnel matters. However, as the size of the city increases, specialized personnel functions will of necessity begin to appear: first as a part of the duties of an individual, then as a full-time job, and finally as an organization with skilled technicians and administrators.

A properly staffed central personnel agency of any size can provide valuable assistance not only in the functions of recruitment, classification, wage determination, and maintenance of personnel records, but also in furnishing guidance in the fields of human relations, training, employee motivation, and discipline. The extent to which this assistance is or is not effective depends largely on the police chief. Unwarranted hostility on the part of the chief toward the central personnel agency or unfounded resentment against "interference" in police affairs is as harmful to proper personnel administration as is the central personnel agency oriented only toward developing its own program without a concept of service to other city departments.

In the subsequent discussion it is assumed that an adequate central personnel agency exists. Where such an agency does not exist, or when its personnel are less than competent, the recommendations of this chapter will need to be modified accordingly. The following discussion will outline a comprehensive police personnel program, the successful administration of which depends upon the availability of staff personnel who possess certain qualifications and skills. If such skills are available in the central personnel agency, the police chief should make full use of them; if such is not the case, then they must be provided from within the police department.

Division of Functions

All line departments of the city, including the police department, should perform as many of the personnel functions as they are competent to perform. Ideally, the central personnel agency should so thoroughly indoctrinate the line departments in sound personnel administration that there would remain for the personnel department only the functions of insuring uniformity of standards and principles, advising on new techniques and developments, performing specialized tasks such as test construction, and rendering special assistance on request.

Certain functions by their nature may be performed more economically and with desirable uniformity when administered centrally; for example, recruitment and selection up to a point. A classification plan can obviously be administered more uniformly by a central agency than by each department attempting to establish and maintain its individual plan.

On the other hand certain personnel functions, in addition to the day-to-day problems of personnel administration, properly are the responsibility of the police department. Training is one. But the personnel department should be prepared to advise, assist, and give guidance in the development of that program when so requested by the police department. Assignment and discipline of personnel is another, though there may be general rules for all departments within limits of which the police department must also work.

Even where local law or administrative policy clearly delineates the personnel functions to be performed by the central personnel agency and by the line departments, the farsighted police chief will solicit the assistance of the central personnel agency in the performance of those functions for which he is responsible, and he should be assured of willing cooperation from the central agency in such instances.

Even where the best of cooperation and teamwork exists, differences of opinion will arise between the central agency and the police chief. Proper organization requires that both the police chief and the personnel officer be responsible to the chief administrator (city manager or mayor); thus isolated differences of opinion which cannot be ironed out by intelligent cooperation between the police chief and the personnel director can be taken to the chief administrator for decision.

Below are set forth the functions which ordinarily would be assigned to the central personnel agency and to the police chief.

Functions Normally Performed by a Central Personnel Agency

Preparation and administration of the position classification plan
Preparation and administration of the pay plan
Recruiting and examining (with substantial participation by the police department)
Formulation of rules regulating leaves of absence and vacations
Formulation of rules for administration of service ratings
Formulation of rules governing personnel actions
Maintenance of certain personnel records
Facilitating establishment and operation of health and welfare plans

Personnel Functions Normally Performed by the Police Department

Selection of new personnel from eligible lists
Recommending salary step increases
Rating of employees' job performance
Assignment and reassignment of police personnel
Maintenance of certain personnel records
Assignment of hours of duty and dates of vacation
Approval, consistent with rules, of leaves of absence with pay
Establishing and conducting training programs
Employee motivation and morale
Maintenance of desirable working environment
Disciplinary and commendatory actions
Formulation of rules governing conduct of police personnel

Even in cities with a central personnel agency the police department will need to have its own full- or part-time departmental personnel officer and supporting staff. Training alone may require the full time of several individuals. In all cities the power to appoint, discipline, and discharge should rest with the police chief under authority and responsibility delegated by the mayor or city manager. The chief administrator should not be expected or required to give attention to routine appointments, assignments, or disciplinary actions other than those affecting his immediate associates and department heads, nor should the central personnel department be concerned with these primarily administrative activities except to make certain they are in line with over-all policy. But the chief administrator should be consulted or briefed whenever disciplinary action may ultimately require more than routine handling, or when civil service commissions become involved in appeals from disciplinary actions.

The fear is sometimes expressed that an administrator, given conclusive authority to hire and fire, may abuse this power. This is conceivable, although the probability is not great, for every administrator is responsible to some higher authority for the efficiency and morale of his unit and should be at least as aware of the need for fairness and equity in personnel matters as would be any appellate group.

Some jurisdictions have sought to minimize the danger of abuse of disciplinary and discharge authority by the chief administrator or his associates through the creation of advisory personnel boards which hear appeals initiated by disciplined or discharged employees. These boards are advisory only; their findings are not binding on the chief administrator, but because a hearing throws the spotlight of publicity on discipline and discharge actions its effect is to encourage the department head and chief administrator to act wisely in such matters.

In police departments of suitable size a full-time personnel officer should serve as the chief point of contact between the central personnel agency and the police department. All departmental personnel actions should funnel through his office, whether the central personnel agency is involved or not, and a harmonious working relationship should exist between the departmental personnel officer and the central personnel agency.

In the smaller cities, where central personnel agencies rarely exist, the entire responsibility for personnel administration may fall back on the line department. Then the police chief must work out his own personnel system or delegate this responsibility on a part-time basis to a subordinate officer. In such cases, the department can obtain assistance from the special advisory services of the International City Managers' Association, the Public Personnel Association, state police agencies, state leagues of municipalities, neighboring cities, or other outside sources.

Independent Programs for Police Personnel

Critical police situations, particularly in large cities and metropolitan areas, have led to the adoption of unusual measures in seeking to effect reform. Most commonly these arise from a loss of public confidence in the competence or integrity of the individual members of the police force, and thus the personnel program ranks high in the list of areas requiring reform. A ready, and perhaps too easy, answer is found in the establishment of a police personnel system which is completely independent of that for "ordinary" municipal employees. Only most unusual circumstances should justify resort to this extreme measure, such as the complete inability or disinclination of the existing central agency to cope with the problem or the existence of unwholesome political influences which cannot be otherwise dealt with. Just as a physical separation rarely resolves a family problem, this separation of policemen from all other municipal employees is apt to create more problems than it solves.

The establishment of separate systems of personnel administration on a departmental or independent basis should be avoided. Functioning independently of the local governing body or chief executive, there is a tendency for such boards to encroach on the authority of the chief administrator and at times to work counter to local policies adopted by the city council. The personnel problem is substantially similar in all departments and can be handled best on a central staff basis without according privileged status to special groups, whether police or any other.

Position Classification

When a service to be performed requires the efforts of more than one person, the need for some sort of duties classification arises. Positions are classified in two ways, on the basis of the *kind* and the *level* of the duties and responsibilities. For example, a position in the records unit will differ in kind from that of a foot patrolman, whereas the position of sergeant differs from that of lieutenant primarily on the basis of level. A position-classification plan, when properly established and kept current, gives a relatively complete and reliable picture of the services performed. It involves (1) ascertaining and recording the duties of each position; (2) grouping positions in classes on the basis of duties performed, responsibilities carried, authority exercised, and qualifications required; (3) assigning short descriptive titles to various classes and writing specifications which describe each class in terms of minimum qualifications, general duties, typical tasks, and lines of promotion; (4) allocating individual positions to the appropriate classes; and (5) maintaining the plan on a current basis.

Current maintenance of the position-classification plan is essential to its effective use. Changes in individual positions and in position classes must be recorded and acted upon if the plan is to be meaningful. A classification plan established 10 or even five years ago, and to which no amendments have been made, would today be completely unreliable.

A position-classification plan can be a valuable resource for the police administrator. It provides a comprehensive analysis of the work done in the department;

facilitates organization studies, planning, and work programming; is an aid in budget administration and in manpower control; encourages similar and equitable treatment of positions and employees in work assignment, personnel selection, promotion, training, efficiency ratings, and retirement system administration; and can be a decisive factor in establishing and maintaining good morale.

Use in the Police Service

The content of individual positions and classes is in the first instance determined by the department head or chief executive through the assignment of duties. The broadest possible classes are generally desirable; highly specialized or narrow classes should be avoided wherever possible. The police service does not present an unusual classification problem, nor should it receive special treatment. The principle that class descriptions should be descriptive and not restrictive is perhaps particularly pertinent to the police and fire services, but is nonetheless valid in other areas of the government service. To the extent that this principle is observed in practice, the police administrator has flexibility in assignments. It should be possible, for example, to assign an employee hired as a "Police Patrolman" to traffic duty, crime prevention, records and identification, or general patrol duty at the same rate of pay, provided the classification plan properly reflects this use of positions and employees. If such assignments are customarily made and the classification plan does not reflect them, then the plan should be modified accordingly.

Classification procedures may seem intricate for use in a small city, but the fewer the employees the less complicated is the process. Even in the smallest cities, where each employee necessarily performs a large number of varied and changing tasks, a formal classification plan is desirable. The chief administrator of the city (city manager or mayor) may have an intimate personal acquaintance with each employee and his duties, yet his knowledge should not be substituted for the written classification plan which will serve as a guide to department heads and all other employees in matters of qualification, assignment, and pay.

The classification plan will become obsolete and decreasingly valuable for personnel and other functions unless department heads cooperate in notifying the personnel agency of permanent changes in the duties given to employees which might warrant reclassification of positions, modification of classes, or other action. The competent police chief will not view position classification as an administrative hindrance and "red tape," if it is operated as an aid to management as well as a control mechanism.

Salary Administration

Historically a single pay rate often prevailed for each police rank. This plan was attractive to new entrants, who were offered as much pay immediately as was allowed an experienced man. Thus it facilitated recruiting. The few departments which still use the flat-rate system of pay may carry a competitive advantage in obtaining more mature recruits, if these are wanted, for flat rate pay is often higher than the minimum rate of ranged pay scales. On the whole, however, this scheme has been no more satisfactory when applied to police patrolmen than it has been in other municipal employments and has been largely discarded.

In a more discriminating plan the patrolman may be paid a fairly low rate on joining the force, possibly for the first six or 12 months, with annual increases — most commonly of approximately 5 per cent each — for four or five years. Some departments require a patrolman to attain a certain grade on periodic service ratings to be eligible for pay increases within his salary range. More common but not necessarily preferred practice is to grant raises automatically on completion of each year of service till the maximum is reached. Additional "longevity" pay increases may be granted at longer intervals after the top salary for the class has been reached, similar to the practice in the armed forces; there has been expanded use of this technique in recent years, though its desirability has not been clearly demonstrated.

Each step in a pay range is intended to serve as a reward for experience and recognition of increased value to the police service. In addition, the salary range should serve as an inducement for experienced policemen to remain in service, since their normal increases help them to keep pace with family obligations that also tend to increase with time. Similarly there is good justification for using pay ranges rather than a single rate for sergeant, lieutenant, captain and other ranks. In many of the instances in which a flat rate is used instead of a range, the justification has been made on the grounds of avoiding pushing the top salaries too high for city council acceptance, disregarding the technical soundness of the device. Many city and state police forces provide salary ranges through all ranks to and including that of chief or commissioner, and several large forces have found it convenient to leave the pay of captains and higher ranks flexible, the rate for an individual being dependent upon the type of duties he performs.

The Desirability of a Wide Pay Range

Little uniformity exists among police departments as to the width of pay ranges. In major cities with a modern pay plan for patrolman, a common range is 25 to 30 per cent of the minimum pay. Since comparatively few policemen can expect to rise above the rank of patrolman, there is some justification for broadening the range to 50 per cent or more through the addition of longevity increases awarded less frequently than annual increases. Since a sergeant's expectation of becoming a lieutenant is comparatively good, a pay range of 25 to 30 per cent is sufficient. For similar reasons, the range in pay for the higher ranks may be somewhat narrower — 20 to 25 per cent.

It is a general rule in industry that a supervisor should be paid at least 15 per cent more than the highest paid to any person supervised by him. In most cities using pay ranges, the maximum pay for patrolmen is lower than the minimum pay for sergeants, the maximum pay for sergeants is lower than the minimum pay for lieutenants, and the maximum pay for lieutenants is lower than the minimum pay for captains. Police officers generally favor this common pay scheme in which the young supervisor is paid more than even a senior subordinate. Policemen contend that the hierarchy of command will be confused if a senior patrolman is paid more than the young or less experienced sergeants, or if senior sergeants are paid more than a young or less experienced lieutenant. The military services which have many problems similar to a police agency, have on the other hand, freely accepted the practice of overlapping pay ranges.

Though police tradition is against overlapping the pay range of the several ranks, progressive police administrators recognize its value to the service. If the broad pay ranges now so generally recognized as being advantageous to the police are adopted, and the traditional lack of pay range overlap is also adhered to, the maximum pay of a lieutenant would have to be at least twice the minimum pay for patrolmen. Pay rates for captains, assistant chiefs, and chiefs then would be so high as to be unacceptable to city councils and state legislatures. An artificial restriction of entrance salaries would be the inevitable result.

Salary Standardization

The position-classification plan program provides a sound basis for an equitable compensation program. The grouping of all positions involving approximately equal work into one class permits the establishment of a single salary range for that class. This is an important step towards the compensation plan objective of equal pay for equal work. However, a position-classification plan and a salary plan are distinct in basis and purpose. A pay plan is a logical arrangement or scaling of the pay for various classes of work, based on difficulty and responsibility, as defined in the position-classification plan. It includes a code of formal rules governing installation, amendment, and administration.

The following factors generally have had a direct bearing on the establishment and amendment of governmental pay plans:

1. Prevailing wages for comparable work paid by governmental jurisdictions in the area.

2. Prevailing wages for comparable work paid by private industry in the same labor market or area.

3. Relative benefits of public and private employment other than direct wages.

4. Changes in cost of living, usually as evidenced by changes in the Consumer Price Index of the U. S. Bureau of Labor Statistics.

5. The inter-relationships between classes, i.e., the salary differentials that should exist between different types and levels of work.

6. Relative ease or difficulty in recruiting qualified employees.

7. The financial position and resultant general pay policy of the city as determined by the city council.

These factors will have varying weights from city to city. Two factors having considerable influence in many municipalities in recent years have been (1) the industry-wide and craft-wide wage agreements made periodically in private industry, and (2) the pressure brought to bear by organized municipal employees, particularly when focused on the need for a general increase in the pay level of the jurisdiction.

Employees should be able to voice their opinions during the preparation of a pay plan, but the danger of establishing pay rates based on individual pleading is great and should be constantly guarded against. As is pointed out in a later section of this chapter, policemen commonly belong to national or local organizations either of police personnel exclusively or as members of or affiliated with other employee groups. More and more these organizations are insisting on being heard on salary matters and are in some cases engaging in extensive survey and research work directed toward improving salaries. Pressures are mounting for more formalized negotiation and bargaining, and several cities in the past few years have accepted the concept of formal arbitration on various personnel matters, including salaries. This trend may or may not be in the public interest, but it is a very real problem facing officials charged with determining the salary policies of a city.

Special attention must be given to the establishment and maintenance of proper salary relationships among all classes in a given municipal service in order to prevent the salary ranges for any one group of classes from pulling ahead of or falling behind in any general changes in the pay plan. However, changes in pay relationships between classes may be justified by labor market conditions; for example, a severe shortage of radio technicians in the area may require a city to increase the salary offered for such personnel well above that offered for other types of work normally considered comparable.

A matter to be considered in setting pay ranges for police classes is whether personal equipment is furnished to officers. Practices vary widely, with some cities requiring policemen to buy almost all their own equipment, while other cities furnish part or all of it. Whether uniforms and equipment are furnished must be considered when comparing local salaries to those of other police forces. The policy here may make a difference of $300 or more at the time of original employment and as much as $150 a year for men already on the force. The policy of furnishing uniforms must also be considered when comparing police to nonpolice salaries. Police uniforms cost more, depreciate faster, and require more cleaning and upkeep than usual business or working clothes. In addition, there is special equipment which must be purchased, such as the pistol, handcuffs, and holster.

There is also the question of a clothing allowance for police detectives who do not usually work in uniform. Four major arguments in favor of giving such law enforcement personnel the same allowance as men regularly in uniform are advanced. First, they must have a gun, holster, and cuffs even when in plain clothes. Second, their clothing is subject to more than normal wear and tear because of scuffles with prisoners, going into dirty areas, and working in all sorts of weather to make arrests, searches, or investigations. Third, they are often required to, and should, have a complete uniform in case of disasters or riots when they may be transferred temporarily to uniformed duty. Fourth, a clothing allowance is the simplest way to compute pay differentials between similar jobs where a uniform is usually worn and jobs where plain clothes are usually worn.

The often-found provision that all positions and employees in the same class shall receive pay within the limits of the pay range is a step toward accomplishing equal pay for equal work, but a perplexing question is still unanswered: how to compensate equitably employees hired in the same class at the same salary step who render vastly different quantities of work? Some attempts, such as limiting the top class salary steps to employees with superior efficiency ratings have been made. These attempts generally appear to be less than workable, principally because of employee nonacceptance.

Special Police Problems in Salary Administration

Certain salary problems occur in police departments that either do not occur in other city departments or are more pronounced in the police service because of the type of operation.

Cities have a number of policies for compensating policemen for overtime work. These vary from no set policy at all to the Texas state law that requires payment at time and one-half for any time in excess of the regular work week. Policies may vary on the basis of the reason for the overtime. The three usual classifications of reasons for police overtime are court appearances, training, and duty.

There seems to be more policy established in the classification of court appearances. This will vary from no announced policy but with practice of allowing the individual commanding officers to give compensatory time off, to well established written policies. Most departments with a written policy compensate on the basis of equal time off. Usually the time off is at the discretion of the individual commanding officer. Some departments allow only one-half of the time off, but others, particularly the largest cities, allow court time plus travel time. Some cities allow men on the dog watch (usually midnight to 8:00 a.m.) to go off duty at 5:00 a.m. before a court appearance in order to get some rest and to clean up and allow men on the 4:00 p.m. to midnight watch to delay reporting for work until 6:00 p.m.

Compensation for overtime spent attending training sessions varies widely, but the tendency is to grant only limited overtime credit or none at all on the basis that the man being trained also gains. Overtime as a result of regular duty usually is compensated for by allowing time off; some departments have added this to sick leave accumulation. Some allow men to accumulate overtime and add it to their regular vacation period, or to carry a day or two until their next regular day off. These devices are all satisfactory provided that the police command has final authority to make certain that a full operating force is available.

Another police compensation problem where policy must be made is relative to the acceptance of witness fees by officers. This is generally prohibited, often by law, since in many cases officers have made considerable amounts by collecting the witness fees for appearance in many minor cases and because it allows the officer to personally gain from making an arrest. However, there are certain reasonable exceptions. Some policies allow an officer to collect the witness fee if he testifies when not on duty; others allow the witness fee in a civil case and if the officer is not on duty.

Policies relative to officers working at other employment on their time off are essential. Such policies vary widely. Ideally no police officer should work on his time off except under very special circumstances and then not on a regular basis. However, some cities have found themselves so far behind in competition with private industry that they have relaxed or discarded their rules in order that the police can earn a reasonable living. Practices vary where there is a regulation. Some departments allow any kind of work for any length of time; some allow only specified types of employment and do not, for example, allow officers to work as bartenders or cab drivers.

Some allow only limited employment that must be related directly to police work. This system has some merit. Under it officers may work on their own time on jobs often given to the department as an undesirable regular duty, such as funeral escorts, traffic handling at special events, supervision of public dance halls, or policing at athletic events. The department may even act as an employment agency for this type of duty since it has definite benefits to both the officers and the force. However, care must be taken in establishing such policies, particularly where the officer is allowed to wear his regular police uniform.

Pay differentials between shifts are common in industry but are seldom used in police work. Few officers, if given a choice, would turn down the day shift, but the feeling seems to be that advancement to more desirable shifts is a reward for time spent on the force. It is questionable whether hope of such a change in working hours is sufficient compensation, and this question should be carefully examined.

One special problem of salary administration in the police service is that of providing extra pay for the performance of particular types of duty such as plain clothes, traffic investigation and education, identification, laboratory, motorcycle, and many others. This practice has become so widespread in some departments as to provide extra pay for nearly everyone except the regular patrol officer, who is the only one really doing a well-rounded police job. Perhaps thought should be given to rewarding the policeman who does not become a narrow specialist. It is preferred practice not to grant extra compensation for performance of the above-type duties, just as it is to avoid undue specialization in police work. Elimination of such extra pay will promote a more flexible and better balanced police force. However, if it appears that the specialized duties require a considerable increase in ability, training, or responsibility, the classification of this position should be reviewed to see if an increase in rank, rather than a special salary scale, is justified.

Several types of police work may be considered borderline in this regard, particularly in large departments, the work of the detective being the best example. Three approaches are taken: (1) a separate class of positions with a separate salary range; (2) administrative assignment to detective work with extra pay; and (3) assignment to plain clothes duties without a pay differential. Large departments may use all three methods, and small forces most commonly rely on the third alternative.

The development of position-classification and pay plans calls for techniques which require the services of trained personnel technicians. If there is no personnel agency in the municipal government, or if the existing agency is not qualified to undertake the development of such plans, then the chief administrator should procure assistance from the public personnel agency of a nearby jurisdiction or engage an outside consulting organization to do the work.

The Recruitment Process

The selection of competent personnel is vital to the operation of an effective police department. Personnel must be selected, retained, and promoted on the basis of their capacity and demonstrated ability to perform the duties and responsibilities with which they are charged. Such a system is commonly termed a merit system.

For many years the personnel movement in government had crystallized around tenure as the basic feature of the merit system. In recent years, with the realization that tenure without careful selection simply "freezes" incompetents into public jobs, emphasis has shifted from tenure to careful original selection of personnel. And now pressure is being exerted to re-examine the whole concept of tenure with a view to making it easier to discharge public employees who are incompetent or ineffective. A counter-pressure also is developing through the growth in size and effectiveness of employee organizations which too often protect the incompetent.

Although generally effective techniques are available for the selection of police recruits, there is urgent need for the development of reasonably economical methods of determining whether or not police candidates have sufficient emotional stability to withstand the weathering which occurs in police work.[2]

The first step in recruiting, and the one which should receive greatest emphasis, is that of attracting well-qualified applicants. The best selection devices available are of little value if the recruiting efforts have failed to attract candidates of high caliber. Widespread publicity directed at the particular element of the population which it is hoped will be attracted to the examination is the best method of seeking outstanding applicants. However, in order to direct publicity into the most effective channels, it is necessary to know what type of candidate to look for. In police work, as in any other type of employment, it is necessary to analyze the duties and responsibilities of the class of positions for which applicants are being sought to determine what qualifications are needed. What kind of man will make the best policeman? This is by no means an easy question to answer, particularly since the answer must be realistic rather than utopian.

---

[2] An excellent publication on the selection of police personnel, published by Public Personnel Association, 1313 East 60 Street, Chicago 37, is *How To Recruit and Select Policemen and Firemen*, by Robert W. and Barbara Coppock. 1958. It is an operating how-to-do-it manual containing detailed forms, procedures, and records.

Qualifications for Police Work

The central personnel agency should work closely with the police administrator and the departmental personnel officer, if there is one, in determining desirable qualifications for police work. In this way the knowledge of the police department can be combined with the specialized knowledge of the central personnel agency regarding human aptitudes and abilities, and testing techniques, to select employees who have a high probability of success on the job.

Intelligence. The modern policeman is required to deal with complex legal concepts and often is involved in community problems which require considerable insight and the ability to adapt to widely different circumstances. He must be able, both as a recruit and later as a supervisory officer, to absorb readily the constantly expanding volume of material with which a policeman must be familiar. No one is quite sure what intelligence is. One of the experts in the field defines it as the thing intelligence tests measure. However, if a well standardized adult intelligence test is used, the applicants who will have trouble keeping up with the rest of the class in recruit school can be eliminated. It is not possible to set an IQ or a percentile rating that would hold for every intelligence test or every department. One of the best, the Army General Classification Test, was standardized on hundreds of thousands of subjects. A number of cities in one state use the 75th percentile on this test as passing, as an example. In any case, the police recruit must be of above average intelligence. How far above is determined in part by the local labor market and experience with a well-standardized test.

Education. At present many cities require applicants for police work to have a high school education. Additional cities would adopt this requirement were it not for charter provisions which prohibit a formal educational standard. An educational requirement is not essential in that the personnel agency can so construct its written examination as to measure the actual academic achievement of the candidates, and with greater accuracy than a mere count of the number of years of formal education or possession of a diploma. There is every reason to believe that the educational requirements will gradually be raised. More and more universities and colleges are offering courses in police work. More and more students are staying in school beyond high school. It is difficult for most municipal police forces to attract a man who has spent more than the average time getting an education. Salaries are not competitive; men the police want can get better paying jobs in business and industry.

Experience. Only under exceptional circumstances is there justification for requiring experience of applicants for entrance level police positions. The police chief of a small city which has urgent problems and no training facilities might find it advisable to require previous police experience or experience somewhat related to police work; but in those cities in which training is given to police recruits previous police experience may actually prove undesirable.

Personality. Few types of employment in the public service place as many stresses and strains on personality as does police work. Police operations run the gamut of the social community from dealing with the most sordid crime to helping the kindergarten child across the street.

No single personality type, or more properly no single pattern of personality traits, can be singled out as the more desirable for police work. What is wanted is a well-adjusted personality, free of extreme or marked traits. The crusader for justice is as unfitted for police work as the angel of mercy. Where there is internal conflict, or where there is a deep-seated neurosis or emotional immaturity, the individual tends to expend the greater part of his energies in fighting his own problems rather than those of the police department. Moreover, such an individual has a harmful effect on his co-workers and on the morale of the force.

Perhaps the most difficult problem in the selection of policemen is to determine whether an individual has sufficient emotional stability. General practice in the selection of policemen is to use an interview board to pass on the acceptability of each candidate's personality trait pattern. This method has been fairly effective. Another method is to supplement the written tests of intelligence and knowledge with written personality tests. These are satisfactory only in the hands of a highly qualified examiner. Their use by an untrained person is dangerous. Discovering candidates with deep-seated emotional instability or personality conflicts cannot always be done by an interview board or a simple paper and pencil test. Increasing use is being made of the screening psychiatric examination — one-half to one hour per candidate — to uncover personality defects.

Physical Attributes. To have a high probability of success as a policeman a candidate should meet the following standards:

1. Physical condition should be excellent. Policemen need not be singled out from other municipal employees so far as general health is concerned, but the special requirements of their work — keen observations, endurance, and good public appearance — justify certain special physical qualifications. Decision as to the state of health of a given applicant should rest with a competent physician.

2. Physical agility and strength equal at least to the average amount possessed by high school seniors should be required. It is obvious that police work frequently requires good physical coordination, speed of movement, and strength. Because all of these are susceptible to relatively rapid deterioration in the individual, it is suggested that where so-called physical agility tests are administered to determine the physical fitness of applicants these tests be considered qualifying only, and no preference in selection be given to those who exceed the minimum qualifying standards. If the police chief of the small city finds it not practicable to give such tests, he should ask the examining physician to get some measure of the candidate's physical index.

3. Height requirements for police candidates have a psychological rather than a medical basis. Apparently taller men have a more imposing appearance which in turn makes it necessary for them to resort to force less often. The most common minimum height requirement is 5 feet, 9 inches with some cities accepting candidates down to 5 feet, 7 inches. There is very little general agreement as to maximum acceptable height. The mortality rate among men of extreme height is significantly greater than among those of average height or slightly taller. In addition, unusually tall men are difficult to uniform, have trouble getting in and out of automobiles, and may be poorly coordinated.

4. The most generally accepted practice is to require a minimum weight of 150 pounds and to permit a candidate to qualify whose weight is in proportion to his height as indicated by height-weight tables which have been established by insurance companies, the United States Army, and others. This practice is most feasible in the largest cities in which thousands of applicants must be examined. While the use of such tables is convenient administratively, it does not rule out the possibility that applicants will qualify whose physiques are not satisfactory. Other departments should establish a general standard that weight be proportionate to height and require the examining physician to make the determination subject to the veto of the police chief or the central personnel agency, according to the provisions of local law or rules.

Character and Reputation. A policeman's character and reputation should be of the highest order. A police chief cannot afford to appoint to his force an applicant whose reputation is questionable, or one whose character is such as to cast doubt on his future actions. The policeman must have a reputation for moderation in his mode of living and in his use of intoxicating beverages.

It is the practice of some jurisdictions to disqualify any candidate who has ever been involved in offenses other than minor traffic violations. Other jurisdictions exclude offenses committed as a juvenile, although this can be a dangerous practice. A growing number of cities review the case of each applicant who has an arrest record and accept or disqualify the man on the basis of the facts in the case. The last method is certainly the most socially acceptable and, if done with care, the one most likely to produce the best results. It is doubtful if a single offense of a less serious nature should disqualify an otherwise outstanding candidate, particularly when committed as a juvenile.

In addition to the above qualifications the question of age should be considered. Because of the desirability of recruiting young men into the police service with a view to training and keeping them for the maximum period of service, because promotion in most police systems is restricted to those within the system, and to reduce the cost of the pension plan, age requirements should be kept low. The tendency generally has been to reduce both minimum and maximum age limits so that at present many municipal police systems use a minimum age limit of 21 years, and few accept candidates over 35 years of age. Except in the presence of a tight labor market, the recommended age limits are 21 through 28 years. Some municipalities permit candidates aged 20 to compete but do not consider them for appointments until they reach their 21st birthday. Departments may well consider waiving age requirements for patrolmen properly trained in other departments in order to allow greater mobility within the profession and to broaden the base of available recruits. It is fairly common practice to increase the maximum age limit somewhat for veterans; this practice can be justified during immediate post-war periods but not as a permanent arrangement.

The opinion is often voiced that police work requires older men because they must be mature. Maturity is not a function of age alone. Younger men generally are more adaptable and learn more quickly with less effort, and police discipline and training can instill in them the habits and attitudes which maturity alone will not bring. A force with a relatively low average age will probably have more drive and energy and better esprit de corps than one comprised of older members. In a force which recruits young men before they have established themselves in another vocation the turnover rate probably will be lower, since younger men without training in other fields are less likely to be enticed into private industry.

Attracting Qualified Candidates

When the central personnel agency and representatives of the police department have decided upon the qualifications to be required, the next step is to attract the maximum number of qualified candidates. Generally the publicity media to be used depend on the kind of applicants desired. Publicity should be directed to all places which might be expected to yield competent applicants. Recruitment efforts should not be restricted to the legal boundaries of the city unless local law requires it. Every effort should be made to achieve the elimination of such restrictive provisions because they deprive the city of the services of competent men and constitute an obstacle to eventual professionalization. On the other hand, care should be taken not to go further afield than is necessary. Candidates rarely will be willing to incur sizable expense simply for the privilege of competing with strong competition for entrance level police jobs. If competition is expected to be light and residence is waived, it is possible to give at least the screening tests in other communities.

The amount of effort devoted to recruitment should relate to the estimated number of employees needed, the anticipated difficulty of the examination, and an estimate of the condition of the labor market. Following is a list of media through which police examinations can be effectively publicized:

Examination Announcements. Care should be taken to make the announcement as attractive and as easily read as possible. It should present information about duties, salary, promotional opportunities, working conditions, qualification requirements, and the general nature of the examination. An example of such an announcement is shown in Figure 15.

These announcements should be posted in such locations as YMCA's, state employment offices, colleges and universities — particularly those offering specialization in criminology — veterans' organizations, recreation centers, barber shops, and military installations. In addition, announcements should be sent to those individuals who have asked to be placed on a mailing list or who have filed applications previously.

Radio, Television, and Theaters. Radio and television stations usually will cooperate by making brief spot announcements or arranging for the police to put on a "job caster" type of program. Most theater managers will show brief film trailers that can be prepared at low cost.

The Press. Newspapers, including throwaways and shopping news, will publish stories of pending police examinations. Paid advertising can be justified if there is reason to believe that a sufficient number of well-qualified men will not otherwise compete. It is being used with increasing frequency. Both classified ads in the "Help wanted" section and display ads have been used. In addition, there may be a requirement to publish a legal announcement of the examination. If the form is not specified, this legal announcement can be an effective advertisement rather than an uninteresting compliance with the law placed in a part of the paper few people read.

Billboards. A small billboard displaying suitably designed posters placed in theaters and other lobbies and on the sidewalk in front of public buildings also can be effective. Local advertisers will sometimes provide space on large billboards for recruitment notices. Some departments display posters on the back of police cars.

Direct Contact. In selecting devices for notifying potential candidates of job opportunities, attention should be given to the value of "word-of-mouth" publicity — public comment which may come to the attention of interested persons who have not been reached directly by advertising. Particular effort should be made to encourage members of the force to talk to likely applicants. Research has shown that this direct contact by members of the force is one of the most effective ways of bringing in high quality applicants. Patrol officers will notice a likely looking young fellow working in a filling station, or he may be a neighbor. They are in the best possible position to tell him of the advantages and disadvantages of joining the force.

The Selection Process

The purpose of the selection process is to secure those candidates who have the highest potential for developing into good policemen. The process involves two basic functions: the first is to eliminate unqualified applicants; the second is to rank the remaining candidates in order of their qualification.

The selection process is largely one of eliminating unqualified candidates.

THE CITY OF BERKELEY
Berkeley, California

announces continuous open competitive examinations for

BERKELEY POLICE DEPARTMENT

PATROLMAN $517-570
PATROLMAN-CLERK $530-584

Qualified and ambitious young men are invited to apply for positions offering an
opportunity for a life-time career in an outstanding police department. Recruits
receive excellent training in all phases of police work, including beat patrol,
criminal investigation, records, traffic and related activities. Working
conditions are excellent and include paid vacations, sick leave, membership in a
retirement system, and promotion from the ranks through examinations.

PATROLMAN duties include beat and traffic patrol, investigation of crimes and
offenses, performance of a wide variety of emergency services, and crime
prevention activity.

PATROLMAN-CLERK duties include work in records, identification, dispatching activities, jail supervision, and emergency operation of ambulance and patrol vehicles.

HOW TO QUALIFY: File an application with the Personnel Department if you meet the
following requirements:
    Are between the ages of 20 and 29 by the final date of filing application
    Have successfully completed the equivalent of 2 years (60 semester hours
       or 90 quarter hours) in an accredited college or university
    Have a valid Motor Vehicle Operator's License and a good driving record
    Are at least 5'9" in height, without shoes, and have proportionate weight
    Are in good general health and physical condition, including uncorrected vision
       of at least 20/40 in both eyes correctable to 20/20; good color vision
    Have a personal history above reproach
    Patrolman-Clerks must also be able to type at least 35 net words per minute
                QUALIFIED CANDIDATES MAY FILE FOR BOTH POSITIONS

Candidates must earn a score of 70% or better on each part of the examination,
which consists of: Mental aptitude test -------- Qualifying
                    Physical agility test ------- Qualifying
                    Written test ---------------- 60%
                    Personal interview ---------- 40%

SUCCESSFUL CANDIDATES who earn a final grade of 70% or better will have their
names entered on an open-continuous employment list from which appointments are
made. Persons selected for appointment must pass a medical examination by a City
physician prior to appointment. A loyalty oath is administered, and a background
investigation completed before appointment. No candidate will be appointed until
he has reached his 21st birthday, and no candidate will be appointed who has
                        reached his 30th birthday.

APPLICATIONS MAY BE OBTAINED BY WRITING THE PERSONNEL DEPARTMENT, CITY HALL, IN
             BERKELEY, OR BY CALLING THORNWALL 1-0200 IN BERKELEY
        BERKELEY RESIDENCE IS NOT REQUIRED TO QUALIFY FOR THIS POSITION
     UNITED STATES CITIZENSHIP IS REQUIRED TO QUALIFY FOR THIS POSITION

                                                           10-20-60

Figure 15 — Examination Announcement

Normally in the selection of entrance level policemen it will consist of: application, fingerprint check, written examination, physical agility tests, personal interview, medical examination, character investigation, and the probationary period. The exact order of these steps may vary. The best rule is to put the low-cost steps first so that the minimum number of applicants will remain for the more expensive processing.

At the same time applicants are being eliminated, those remaining are accumulating a score that will place them in order so that the best men will be appointed first. It is not possible to be so accurate that the best candidate will always be first and the least acceptable last, but such a listing is obviously desirable, often required by law, and is approximately accurate. In order to make such a list, some of the steps in the process must be scored, others cannot.

1. Application. This cannot be scored. The applicant will either have or not have the basic qualifications of age, residence (if required), citizenship, and education. The possible exception is education where the equivalent of formal education may be allowed either as shown by testing or experience in certain skilled areas.

2. Fingerprint Check. This also includes a check on the file for police records where prints were not taken. Scoring is not possible. Each case where offenses are so minor that there is a question must be considered on its merits.

3. Written Examination. A score is often used here. In the case of written intelligence tests, however, it is not possible to say whether or not a man in the top percentile will be a better officer than a man in the middle of the passing group. (As a matter of fact, it is always a good plan to carefully check the applicants with exceptionally high intelligence test scores. They often have difficulty in adjustment to many kinds of routine work.) If possible, the written intelligence test should be only qualifying or disqualifying. If it must enter into a final score, the raw scores can rarely be used directly but must be reduced to percentiles and the final score based on percentile rank. If a reliable and valid examination has been devised, and there are few such, it can well enter into the scoring.

4. Physical Agility. This check should be only qualifying. This ability can be easily increased with training.

5. Personal Interview. Properly done, this will be one of the soundest evaluations of an applicant and should carry considerable weight in the final score. It may be that the character investigation should precede the personal interview since the interview board may also make the final decision based on the facts uncovered by the character investigation. The board also will have an opportunity to question the applicant relative to material discovered in the investigation and to hear his explanations.

6. Medical Examination. This is only qualifying or disqualifying. The only exception would be correctable conditions such as under- or overweight, temporary illness, or conditions that the examining physician states could be totally corrected by treatment or an operation. In such a case the applicant could be conditionally passed.

7. Background or Character Investigation. This is not scored, but it is the most important qualifying standard of all. Integrity, moral fitness, and adaptability to all kinds of people are indispensable attributes of the good policeman.

8. Probationary Period. While this is an essential part of the selection procedure it cannot be scored well and of course comes after the need for listing qualified applicants.

It is apparent that only two of the steps, the written examination and the interview result in a score. Various departments have given various weights to these two scores. A usual weighting is 60 per cent to the written and 40 per cent to the interview. With a high quality interview board, however, this proportion could be 50-50 or even reversed.

The selection process begins with the review of applications and the disqualification of those applicants who do not meet the requirements as stated in the examination announcement. (Some applicants who obviously do not qualify may not be given application forms.) In the same manner, each candidate who fails to meet the required minimum standards in each succeeding part of the selection process is eliminated from further competition, until only those candidates meeting all the requirements are left. These are ranked according to their relative qualifications as determined by the rating or score on the graded portions of the examination.

Each of the above eight steps is designed to screen the candidates for those qualifications which job analysis has shown are essential. The application form is used to eliminate candidates who do not meet age, residence, citizenship, height, weight, education or experience requirements and as a basis for a background investigation. The fingerprint record is taken to insure that the candidate has an acceptably clear record. The written test generally is used to insure that successful candidates have the required minimum aptitudes, knowledge, and abilities necessary for proper performance. The physical agility test, if properly constructed, will afford a measure of muscular coordination, strength, and speed of movement. The function of the personal interview is to determine whether the candidate's pattern of personality traits is suitable for police work. The medical examination establishes that the candidate is in good health and is free from obvious defects that would disable or reduce efficiency. The purpose of the character or background investigation is to determine the candidate's reputation and character among the people with whom he has worked and lived and to ascertain if his habits and attitudes make him a good prospect for police work. It can also be used to verify impressions obtained in the oral interview. Experience in large cities with well developed selection methods has shown that about only one man in 20 who comes in and asks for an application is finally appointed to the force. This does not mean that all are rejected. About 30 per cent withdraw of their own volition during the process because they have secured another job, are concerned with failing the selection procedure, or for some other reason. The probationary period is the last and most exacting element in the entire selection process. It refers to that period of time after appointment when the new recruit is on trial and can be fired without cause. It obviously is the most valid and practical test of the man's qualification to do the job. Unfortunately it is often the most neglected phase of the process.

Applications and Testing

Individuals who apply for police work should be required to submit applications according to a standard format which should be as simple as possible consistent with the information needed. All candidates who do not meet the basic age, height-weight, education and citizenship requirements should be rejected at this point. Height and weight measurements should be taken at the time the person submits his application if there is any doubt of his meeting the standards. Those whose applications are accepted should be notified by mail of the time and place to appear for the written examination.

Figures 16 and 17 illustrate application forms. Figure 16 is a short preliminary application form and asks only for enough information to determine if the applicant meets basic requirements. A short form is used because the written examination will eliminate about half of the applicants. In addition, a certain number will not return their applications or appear for the examination. This saves them the time required to fill out the longer form. The applicants who have the basic qualifications and pass the written examination then fill out the long application form (Figure 17). This form was devised as a basis for later interview and investigation of the applicants. Another variation of this form has a section for use of the personnel division at the bottom of the first page. This section is used to record each of the steps of the selection procedure so that the application also serves as the record of the selection procedure.

Fingerprinting. Fingerprinting practice varies widely. Some cities require applicants to be "printed" at the time of filing applications; others fingerprint only those candidates who are successful in those parts of the examination which precede the personal interview; still others fingerprint only those candidates who are successful in the entire examination. The first method gives ample time for a record check before the eligible list is established and for this reason is preferred.

Written Tests. Written tests generally are the most economical and effective means of determining if candidates possess the required aptitudes, abilities, and knowledge. The orthodox written examination for policemen may include an intelligence or general mental ability test, a memory test, and perhaps a general information or reading comprehension test.

1. Intelligence Tests. The testing of candidates' intelligence has already been discussed. Scores should be considered only as qualifying or failing and not be made a weighted part of the examination for rating or ranking candidates.

A number of different kinds of intelligence tests are available commercially. Those that have certain advantages over the others are: (1) Otis Self-Administering Test of Mental Ability Higher Examination, (2) Ohio State University Psychological Test, and (3) The Army General Classification Test — Civilian Edition. The final selection of the test should be made by a qualified person who should administer, score, and interpret the test. These tests are carefully standardized and must not be handled haphazardly.

2. Memory Tests. Many public service examinations include a test for the special ability of memory. The test is usually called "keenness of observation" and consists of having the candidates study a picture of a crime scene or an accident for a given period of time. Later they are required to answer questions based on the picture from memory. Memory, as a special ability, does not correlate highly with general intelligence. A memory test based on a crime scene or an accident scene has the advantage over a symbol memory test in appearing to be more directly related to police work and will correlate more highly with intelligence because of its verbal content. An alternate form, which has proved quite reliable, includes pictures and biographic sketches of several "criminals" to be studied for a measured period of time following which the candidate must answer a number of questions related to what he has just seen. Construction and use of such a test is a job for an expert.

3. General Information Test. As the name implies this test is used to get a measure of the candidate's information on a wide variety of subjects. It is based on the assumption that a candidate who is well informed will make a better policeman, other factors being equal, than one who is not.

The usefulness of this test will depend on how well the questions sample the many fields of knowledge which it covers. A well-constructed general information test will correlate highly with intelligence. Such a test sometimes eliminates the individual who, even though he has adequate intelligence, has not applied it as effectively as others in acquiring knowledge or developing judgment. Such tests are not widely used.

IOWA STANDARD   Work Desired_____
PRELIMINARY APPLICATION   Second Choice_____
                                 Third Choice_____

1. Name (print)_____Sex_____

2. Present
    address_____City_____State_____

3. How long at   Own or
    this address_____Phone_____Neighbors_____
                                    Place of birth:
4   Date of birth_____ City_____State_____

          Height
5. Age_____(Without shoes)_____Weight_____

6. Single, married, widowed, divorced or separated?_____

7. Name of last or present employer_____

    _____

    How long did you work there? From_____to _____
                                        (month) (year) (month)   (year)
    Salary or wages_____

    Your position and nature of duties_____

    _____

    Reason for leaving_____

    _____

8. Were you ever in the U.S. armed forces?_____Branch of service_____

    _____Length of service_____

9. Have you ever drawn a disability pension or compensation or otherwise been
    reimbursed for an illness or injury?_____If "yes," explain._____

    _____

    _____

10. Do you know of anything that might possibly disqualify you for appointment to,
    or prevent the full discharge of, the duties of the position for which you are
    applying?_____. If answer is "yes," explain on a separate sheet.

    Date_____Signed _____

Figure 16 — Preliminary Application Form

IOWA STANDARD APPLICATION

Use typewriter or ink. Applications not properly filled out will not be accepted. You will be judged in part on the neatness and completeness of this application. Read the application through once before starting.

Work Desired _____

Second Choice _____

Third Choice _____

1. Name (print)_____ Sex_____ Date_____
   Last   First   Middle

2. Present address_____ City_____ State_____

3. How long at this address_____ Phone_____ Own or Neighbors_____

4. Addresses for the past ten years. (Do not include present address -- Place most recent address first and work back.)

Street and Number	City and State	From Month and Year	To Month and Year

5. Would you be willing to take a lie detector test over the statements made in this application?_____

6. Date of birth_____ Place of birth: City_____ State_____

7. Are you a citizen of the United States of America?_____ If naturalized, give all details (date of final papers, country of birth, date and port of entry, etc.) on a separate sheet.

8. Age_____ Height (without shoes)_____ Weight_____ Race (check) White____ Negro____ Other____

9. Single, married, widowed, divorced or separated?_____
   If under more than one classification, show both.
   If divorced or separated, give wife's or husband's present name and address_____

10. If married, how long?_____ How many people are completely dependent upon you for support?_____
    Partially?_____

11. Is your wife or husband now employed?_____ By whom?_____

12. Is any member of your family in poor health?_____

13. Do you have any relatives living in a foreign country?_____

This form was devised by and may be obtained from the Institute of Public Affairs, State University of Iowa, Iowa City

Figure 17 — Final Application Form

14.

	Place of Birth	Age
Father's Name		
Mother's Maiden Name		
Wife's maiden name or husband's name		

15. What income do you have at present, in addition to your regular salary or wages?_____

16. Have you ever drawn a disability pension or compensation or otherwise been reimbursed for an illness or injury?_____ If "yes", explain on a separate sheet.

17. How much time have you lost from work during the last five years due to illness or injury?_____

18. Have you ever been refused life insurance?_____

19. How much life insurance do you carry?_____ Who is your beneficiary? Name_____

Address_____ Relationship to you:_____

20. What charge or time payment accounts do you now have?

Name of Firm	Address	Type of Merchandise

21. Do you rent, own your own home, or live with relatives?_____

22. Do you own a car?_____ Make_____ Year_____ Amount owed on it_____

23. Do you own your own furniture?_____ Amount owed on it_____

24. Have you ever been sued or had your wages garnisheed?_____ If answer is "yes", explain on a separate sheet.

25. Have your creditors treated you fairly?_____

26. Were you ever in the U. S. Army, Navy, Marine Corps or any other military organization?_____ If answer is "yes", give date of enlistment, discharge, type of discharge, ranks held and whether or not you saw active duty.

27. Were you ever court martialed, or subject to other disciplinary action?_____

28. Are you a member, or have you ever been associated with, any Bund, Communist group, or any group or organization advocating the overthrow of the United States government by force?_____ If answer is "yes", explain on a separate sheet.

29. Do you use any intoxicating liquor?_____ Moderately?_____ In excess?_____

30. Have you ever been arrested FOR ANY REASON (including traffic arrests or tickets)? If answer is "yes", give date and city of arrest, reason for arrest and disposition of case.

31. Were you ever involved in a traffic accident while you were driving?_____ (If so, describe the circumstances briefly on a separate sheet, and tell what settlement was made, whether any charges were filed, etc.)

32. Has your driver's license ever been revoked or suspended?_____ If "yes", explain on a separate sheet.

33. What are your hobbies?_____

Figure 17 — Final Application Form (continued)

34. List any skilled trades you may know, and state the extent of your experience in each:_____

_____

_____

35. Education:

Name of School	Location (City and State)	From Mo. & Yr.	To Mo. & Yr.	Highest Grade Completed
Grade School				
Grammar or Junior High				
High School				

Were you graduated from high school?_____

Name of College or University	Location (City and State)	From Mo. & Yr.	To Mo. & Yr.	Years Completed

Did you graduate?_____   Major and Minors_____

Other education, including additional Colleges or Universities, night schools, trade schools, correspondence courses, etc.

Name of School	Location (City and State)	From Mo. & Yr.	To Mo. & Yr.	Part or Full-time

Type of training:_____

Name of School	Location (City and State)	From Mo. & Yr.	To Mo. & Yr.	Part or Full-time

Type of training:_____

36. References: Give the names of three responsible persons, other than relatives or former employers, who know you well enough to give information about you.

Name	Address	Occupation	How Long Acquainted

37. Are any of your relatives now employed by the governmental unit that gave you this application?_____

(If "yes", tell who, in what department, etc.)_____

_____

_____

38. Do you know of anything that might possibly disqualify you for appointment to, or prevent the full discharge of the duties of, the positions for which you are applying?_____ If answer is "yes", explain on a separate sheet.

39. You may indicate in the space below and on additional blank sheets, if necessary, such experience, training or ability that you believe will qualify you for the position for which this application is filed. Describe fully positions you have held which required executive ability, the exercise of authority or the ability to lead others.

_____

_____

_____

_____

Figure 17 — Final Application Form (continued)

40. Employment: Start with the place where you are now employed or where you were last employed and give a complete record of all employment since you first started to work. Include service in the armed forces. Show all periods of unemployment. If former employers are now out of business, state this fact. If you were in business for yourself, give nature, location, and names of two clients. Be accurate. You must account for all of your time.

Company Name and Address	From		To		Total time in Months	Salary or Wages	Your Position and Nature of Duties	Reason for Leaving
	Month	Year	Month	Year				
Last or Present Employer Address								
Previous Employer Address								
Previous Employer Address								
Previous Employer Address								
Previous Employer Address								
Previous Employer Address								

If you do not have sufficient space to give your complete employment record, attach an additional sheet and continue as above.

Paste in this space an individual photograph of yourself, not in a group, that was taken within the last two years. Write your name in ink on the back of the photograph.

It will not be necessary to furnish a photograph if the person issuing applications has initialed on this line: _____

I hereby certify that there are no willful misrepresentations in, or falsifications of, the above statements and answers to questions. I am aware that should investigation disclose such misrepresentation or falsifications, my application will be rejected and I will be disqualified from applying in the future for any position with this governmental agency. I also authorize my former employers to give any information regarding my employment, together with any information they may have regarding me whether or not it is on their records. I hereby release them and their company for any damage whatsoever for issuing same.

Date _____   Signed _____

Witness _____

Figure 17 – Final Application Form (continued)

4. Combined Test. All of the attributes measured by the three specialized tests can be measured in a combined type of test. An excellent one having the added advantage of appearing to be particularly pertinent to police work — which it is — has been developed by the Public Personnel Association (1313 East 60 Street, Chicago 37) and is available, at modest cost, to public agencies. A number of cities with able personnel technicians have developed their own examinations along these same lines.

The Physical Agility Test. The physical agility test is designed to eliminate candidates who at the time of the test do not have the required coordination, strength, and speed of movement. The test contained in Figure 18 is effective in weeding out those whose physical agility is not adequate. Only rarely will a candidate who is markedly overweight be able to qualify.

In setting standards for a physical agility test it must be borne in mind that while requiring candidates to scale a six-foot wall is a good test, requiring them to scale a 12-foot wall is not necessarily twice as good a test. Excessively high physical agility standards tend to overemphasize the importance of muscles in police work.

Thorough treatment is given this subject in a publication of the Public Personnel Association entitled *Physical Condition Tests in the Selection of Public Employees*,[3] based largely on techniques developed by the state of New Jersey and city of Philadelphia services.

The Personal Interview. The purpose of the personal interview is to determine if the candidate's personality is suitable for police work. Although the personality characteristics of a policeman are extremely important, their precise measurement is not possible. The personal interview is a less reliable measure, statistically, than the written test and, being less objective, is more subject to criticism. For these reasons it generally is given less weight than the written test in the total examination.

The oral interview may also be used to explain to the applicant just what the work of a police officer is like. Many applicants believe that this is a glamorous job with the only duty being to ride around in a police car. Certain members of the interview board may tell him the facts of life about police work. His reactions are worth noting, and in some cases the applicant will withdraw. If this step is not a part of the interview, it should be inserted in the procedure at about this time, before the selection process goes any further.

Some of the more progressive departments extend this procedure to include the applicant's wife. A commanding officer may make an appointment, go to the home and explain just what the police job really is to both the applicant and his wife. The bad features of the job get a full share of attention; such things as working nights, Sundays, and holidays; the hazards; being subject to call; and all other unpleasant things are fully explained, along with such advantages as the retirement system and opportunities for advancement. Some departments have a leaflet addressed to the wife telling her just what it will be like to have her husband on the force. This is a good plan. While some good applicants will be lost, it is much better to lose them at this stage than after the city has spent considerable money in selection and training.

The make-up of the interview board varies. Some cities prefer to use persons not connected with the police department. In such case the board may consist of police officials of other jurisdictions or it may include outside police officials and responsible local citizens, such as representatives of the local bar association, school officials, or

---

[3] By Forbes E. McCann and others (Chicago: Public Personnel Association, 1958), 55pp.

PHYSICAL AGILITY TEST

The physical agility test consists of four parts:

1. <u>Broad jump</u>: Candidate must make a standing broad jump of at least 7 feet to qualify. He shall toe the marker at the broad jump pit and take off from a standing position.

2. <u>Chin-up</u>: Candidate must complete 7 chin-ups to qualify. At the chinning bar, he shall jump and catch the bar with fingers facing either way. Bring chin to the top of the bar each time. Between chin-ups, he must drop to the full extension of both arms. There is no time limit but once the bar is grasped, it cannot be released.

3. <u>Sit-up</u>: Candidate must complete thirty sit-ups to qualify. He shall lie on his back with both legs fully extended, arms at sides, and raise to a full sitting position with the heels of both feet remaining on the floor. The body shall be lowered in the same manner. Head and shoulders must touch the floor on each return.

4. <u>Obstacle course</u>: Candidate must complete the 180 yard course outlined below within 48 seconds to qualify. He shall start on the command, run to the right outside the line, hurdle or jump the two 30" barriers, crawl under the 20" bar, repeat the outside course a second time, weave up and back through the 4 equally spaced chairs twice and finish at the starting point.

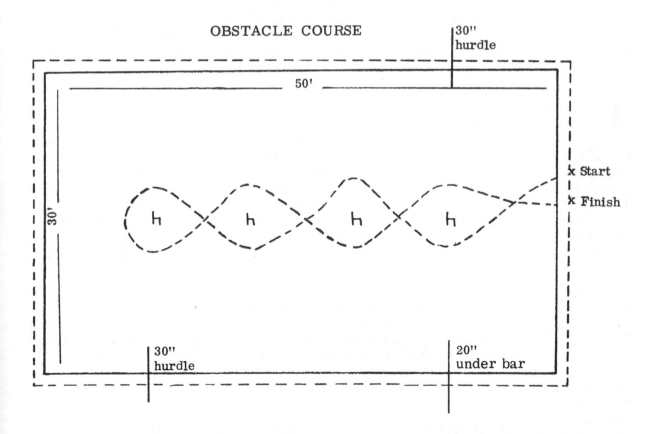

Figure 18 — Physical Agility Test, Berkeley, California

personnel specialists. Other jurisdictions use their own police staff officers on the board or have at least one or more such representatives on the board, or a combination of types of interviewers may be used.

While local conditions should play a considerable part in determining the composition of the interview board, it is recommended generally that the board have not more than one departmental representative and that other members be selected from other police departments and from able and respected citizens in the community. Such a board represents a better cross section of opinion. For the purpose of statistical reliability a five-man board is to be preferred to a lesser number. Where large numbers of candidates are to be examined and economy is an important factor, a three-member board may be acceptable.

In any event, the board should be carefully instructed prior to the interviews both as to its purpose and the method of rating. It is desirable that the police chief, if he is not sitting as a member of the board, spend some time with the board to explain the operation and problems of the department. Sample questions designed to bring out personality factors should be made available to the board for study and use as the members see fit. Throughout the interview the board should be concerned with creating a friendly atmosphere in which the candidate does most of the talking. In this way the candidate's personality is most likely to be revealed.

For interviews in which candidates for the class of police patrolman are being interviewed, a time allowance of not less than 20 minutes is recommended. For supervisory police positions a minimum of 30 minutes should be allowed. The board should be furnished with the candidate's application forms but should not know the score each candidate earned on the written tests. Such information does not assist in the evaluation of personality and tends to bias board members in favor of candidates with better written scores.

Opinions differ as to whether over-all or integrative ratings are more valid than those of the analytical method. In the former no attempt is made to rate the candidates on a series of specific traits, each candidate being given an over-all rating. In the analytical method the board members are required to rate each candidate on each of a series of traits, and the final rating is an average of the individual ratings or is the sum of total of the ratings on the individual traits. Figure 19 is a typical interview form which combines features of both methods, i.e., the interviewer is told to use the form as a guide in reaching his over-all rating. In view of the essential subjectivity of the interview technique, efforts to make the rating appear too precise are best avoided. Each board member should be asked for his over-all rating of the total person rather than the arithmetic average of a group of subjective judgments.

The personal interview technique has its faults. Most of its shortcomings arise because of the lack of training on the part of the interviewers. Despite its faults the interview technique is superior to other existing methods. Very large police departments faced with selecting 500 or more patrolmen at one time commonly do not include an oral interview in the selection process. Thought has been given to substituting the written personality-type test, but it cannot replace the face-to-face interview. It would be preferable to use several boards both to speed up the process and to avoid imposing unduly on the time or interviewers.

The Medical Examination. For economy reasons the medical examination should not be administered until the eligible list or the list from which selection will be made has been established, at which time those candidates to be considered for appointment should be examined. In view of the time, effort, and expense involved in training new

Personnel Department   <u>ORAL BOARD RATING SHEET</u>   City of Berkeley

Candidate's Name _____   Date _____

	Weak	Average	Good	Out-standing

Title of Examination _____

1. APPEARANCE, MANNER, BEARING: Will they help or hinder him in this job; in conferences and interviews; in contacts with civic and citizen groups, the public and other government officials?

2. ABILITY TO PRESENT IDEAS: Is it adequate for this job? Does he have the ability to express himself in a logical, convincing, persuasive manner? Or does he ramble, get confused, talk vaguely, become verbose?

3. SOCIAL ADAPTABILITY: Will he be at ease, friendly, confident, tactful, and adaptable in dealing with public officials, civic and business leaders, co-workers, and others? Or would he tend to be submissive, overbearing, or impatient under trying conditions?

4. ALERTNESS: Does he grasp ideas quickly, and do his responses indicate that he would quickly understand the problems in this job? Or does he appear to be slow to understand, and would grasp only the more obvious points?

5. JUDGMENT: Will he separate important from unimportant; consider all facts before arriving at a decision; know when to act; when to acquire more information before action; know what situations justify departure from policy? Would you trust his judgment in this job?

6. TRAINING: How pertinent is his academic training? Is it sufficient for this job? Was it obtained in academically outstanding schools?

7. ADEQUACY OF EXPERIENCE: Does his experience fit him for the duties of this position; give him a broad, extensive, adequate background?

8. INITIATIVE, DRIVE AND INTEREST: Does he exhibit positive interest to sustain him in his work; believe in this type of work; carry the conversation adequately and ask questions when necessary; show energy and ambition?

PERCENTAGE RATING GUIDE:

OVERALL PERCENTAGE RATING: _____

Weak	Average		Good	Outstanding
65	70	80	90	100

_____
Rater's Signature

Additional comments:

Figure 19 — Oral Rating Form, Berkeley, California

policemen, and the costly effect of sickness or enforced early retirement of a policeman, it is essential that each candidate be given a thorough examination. The condition of heart, lungs, eyesight, ears, feet, muscular ability, joints, genitals, circulatory system, kidney, skin, nerves, and teeth should be searchingly examined. The X-ray, electro-cardiogram, and laboratory tests should be used. A police department might do well to question (but not necessarily abandon) a rule that requires natural teeth, all fingers, or 20/20 uncorrected vision. Medical standards might well be established or reviewed by a panel of physicians or surgeons to assist in establishing qualifications that are suitable locally.

Medical examinations should be supplemented by neurological, psychiatric, and laboratory tests, when these are indicated, to eliminate candidates who are emotionally or temperamentally unstable, psychotic, or suffering from organic or functional disorders. Careful attention should be given to visual acuity. Color perception should be carefully tested but only with a highly reliable and practical method.

Psychiatric and Psychological Examinations. It has already been suggested that police work by its very nature exposes the individual to unusual stresses and strains, requiring of him a high degree of emotional stability and freedom from strong prejudice or extreme attitudes. Lack of these qualities should disqualify a person from becoming a policeman, for it will not be possible to rely on his judgment in time of crisis. Only recently have some municipalities incorporated a mental or psychiatric examination in the selection process for policemen.

The argument that psychiatric examinations are too expensive is not well founded. The elimination of one emotionally unstable candidate is sufficiently important to dictate that psychiatric examinations be used whenever circumstances suggest the need for them. It should be noted, however, that psychiatric examination frequently merely corroborates the findings of a careful character and background investigation and the ratings developed during the probationary period.

Character and Background Investigation. Investigations into the background and character of candidates is probably the most important step in the selection process. Emotionally unfit, poorly adjusted, dishonest, or otherwise unqualified applicants will be discovered by this technique. The request for character references has been standard practice for some time, and certain municipalities even go through the unrewarding exercise of a form letter contact with the references given. It is also widespread practice to fingerprint applicants and have a routine check made. This is not enough of a look into the background of police candidates.

This is a task the police are well equipped to do. No person should be appointed without a thorough investigation of his character and background going well beyond a routine check on fingerprint or police records. An able police investigator should, using the application form as a basis, check the neighborhood where the man now lives and where he has lived for at least the last 10 years. He should talk to his landlords, owners of neighborhood stores, and the people who lived on each side, across the street, and above or below him in an apartment house. A careful credit check should be made. The files of the credit bureau will often give much information beyond his credit rating. School teachers should be interviewed. If the applicant has been divorced, hunt up his ex-wife. She may be biased, but she will have a lot to say. In checking employment talk to not only the top man or the personnel division but also to his immediate supervisor and the people he worked with. The extent of this investigation is only limited by the time available and the ingenuity of the investigator. A good investigator will discover, and support, facts that will eliminate many applicants. Again, this will cost money, but not nearly as much as it would if an unfit applicant were hired. Rejection should not be restricted solely to past convictions on felonies and offenses involving moral turpitude. When the past actions of an individual raise doubt as to his qualification for police service, the doubt should always be resolved in favor of the department, not in favor of the candidate. This may at first glance appear unfair, but the public interest and welfare demand the highest personal integrity in policemen.

Personal history investigations and oral interviews tend to support each other. For this reason when a candidate falls below an acceptable standard on either of these tests, the other should be evaluated more critically.

In recent years there has been a rapid growth in the use of the polygraph (lie detector) in screening job applicants for positions in which honesty is a critical factor. Some police departments have begun such screening of patrolmen candidates, using the personnel history record submitted by the candidate as the source document.

Probation Period

Most departments have a probationary period. During this time the recruit may be summarily dismissed without a hearing. On appointment he enters the recruit training school, then is assigned to duty with an older officer. The probationary period is the most important part of the selection system. The testing and investigation up to now have only selected men who are likely to make good police officers. The real test is what the man now does working as an officer. The recruit school with experienced police officers serving as instructors provides an opportunity for some sort of an evaluation. Some cities also handle the probationary period quite effectively by selecting a number of experienced officers and training them in how to instruct and evaluate recruits. A recruit is assigned to work with each of these older officers for a month; at the end of the month he is assigned to another older officer and so on until the end of his probationary period. At the end of each month the older officer and the sergeant, lieutenant, and captain each rate the recruit. As a result, the probationary period is both an excellent training and selection device. Experience in one city has shown that 15 per cent of the recruits are dropped during the probationary period because of some defect discovered by the men he is working with.

During the period of field instruction, situations and assignments should be devised, if they do not arise in the daily work, that will test personal characteristics only partially measured in the formal selection process. For instance, performance on the job is the only way the recruit can demonstrate how much moral and physical courage he possesses, how well he can apply his knowledges and abilities to real problems, his emotional stability, and how his personality holds up under the stresses of police work.

The probation period is only six months in many departments, although this is too short a period of time to give adequate opportunity for appraising the police probationer. In six months, half of which may be spent in the training school, the recruit may not yet be oriented to his new work. He may have an inherent weakness that will not appear during this short period. Or he may be temperamentally unfit for certain types of duty that occur only occasionally. Furthermore, his stamina and sustained interest in police work are difficult to appraise during the first six months while he is under the stimulus of novel and unaccustomed duties. For these reasons it is recommended that the probationary period be not less than one year.

Promotion

One of the strong attractions police service holds for the young man is a career with opportunity to rise through the ranks. The chances for promotion are, however, only about one in five in the smaller cities and as low as one in 10 in large cities. It follows therefore that competition for promotion will generally be intense. Police administrators should make every effort to see that promotion policies and procedures are established to select the best qualified men, that they are fair, allow for the widest possible competition, and are based on the most valid and realistic selection devices available.

Promotion is essentially the movement of an employee from a position in one class, for example patrolman, to a position in another class, involving more responsibility and a higher rate of pay, such as sergeant. A mere change in duties, as reassignment from traffic duty to beat patrol, or an increase in salary within the same salary range, are not properly designated as promotions.

To be fully effective, promotional policies and procedures must accomplish two things:

1. Select for promotion those officers who are best suited for increased responsibilities.

2. Convince the mass of unsuccessful competitors that selection for promotion is based on pertinent, objective, and fair methods, free from personal bias.

It is certain that the morale and effectiveness of some of the unsuccessful competitors will suffer, at least for a time, but wise policies can do much to hold this to a minimum. The police chief or his personnel officer will do well to talk frankly to those unsuccessful candidates who are openly disturbed and those who will always lack the basic qualifications for promotion should be told so. It is far better to lose such men than to persuade them that they might be more fortunate next time. A certain amount of turnover, particularly in the policeman rank, is healthy — provided it is not always the superior men who are leaving.

Problems of Promotion Policy

Some of the difficulties encountered in formulating a sound promotion policy are discussed below:

1. Promotion is limited to about 8 to 20 per cent of all employees who enter at the bottom of the scale. A few will be promoted from in the service, but the majority will remain at the bottom grade and their advancement will be limited to within-the-range salary increases.

2. Specifying the classes from which promotions may be made can be difficult. Although promotion should be open to all qualified officers in the department, local law may require the promotional opportunity be limited to officers in the next lower rank or class. However, when this is not required, any qualified officer should have the opportunity of taking the examination. There are two reasons for this. In the smaller cities this is essential to get a large enough group to allow adequate choice. Second, the better men in the lower ranks should be allowed to advance in line with their ability and not be held back by an artificial barrier. Even in the very largest cities where many men are in each rank, these same principles apply.

3. There is conflict of opinion regarding the weight to be given for length of service — seniority — in the selection of men for promotion. Because of the semimilitary

nature of police department organization there has been a tendency to rely heavily on seniority as the determining factor in promotion. As our military services have learned, this practice has a deadening effect on employees who have a capacity for more rapid advancement than their seniority would warrant. At the same time it tends to elevate into the supervisory level men who have no particular qualifications other than years of service.

4. In filling the higher posts in the department there are differences of opinion, and practice, concerning the relative value of making promotions entirely from within the department or opening the top positions to competition by qualified nonresidents. The elimination of local residence requirements with open competition for the top positions, especially the job of chief of police, will undoubtedly result in an over-all improvement of police services in the country. Strong opposition often develops from within the police force and from the groups advocating "local jobs for local boys," but the trend is definitely in the direction of the broader base.

5. There are differences over the extent to which employees should be allowed a voice in formulating promotional policies and determining examination content, without jeopardizing departmental discipline or security of the test procedure. The members of the force should be informed of promotional policies and of proposed changes therein, and should be allowed to make comments and proposals, but to go beyond this is to invite trouble.

Competitive Promotion Procedure

The time interval between promotional tests depends on the number of eligibles and the frequency with which vacancies in higher ranks occur. The usual period is two to three years. It may also be set by law. It is desirable to keep eligible lists short by maintaining high standards, so that most eligibles will be appointed during the life of the list.

As in original selection, the techniques used should be based on the content of the jobs to which promotion will be made. Specific selection devices and degree of formality should have a close relationship to the size of the department, the existing personnel system, and local precedents. Various combinations are possible. The least formal and usually the least reliable method, is a simple review by the chief in a small department of the past performance and potential leadership growth of officers in his department. A much more formalized process is used in most departments, including written tests, personal interviews, efficiency or service ratings, and seniority. As a prerequisite for promotion, some departments require a minimum number of years of police experience, or a minimum number of years of experience in the next lower class, or a combination of both. Absolute restrictions which prevent the early advancement of officers who excel in leadership qualities are undesirable if they extend beyond a reasonable period.

Written tests, personal interviews and the probationary period generally should be used in essentially the same manner as in the original selection process. If there are not regular physical examinations for all members of the department, such an examination should be included in the procedure to make certain that the officer has the physical condition to handle the job. However, in contrast to written tests used in original selection, the promotional written tests should emphasize measurement of the candidates' factual knowledge regarding police work rather than aptitudes for learning police work. The importance of written tests in promotional examinations is somewhat less than in the original selection of patrolmen. The oral interview becomes more significant in the selection of higher officers where supervisory and leadership talents are so important.

Efficiency or service ratings may be used in either or both of two ways (1) as a screening device where an employee must obtain a rating of at least "satisfactory" before being permitted to compete in promotional examinations, and (2) as an integral and weighted portion of the examination.

Seniority as such should not be a weighted factor in promotional examinations. Length of service figures indirectly in both the written tests of knowledge and in service ratings which evaluate leadership and administrative potential. The individual with long service has had opportunity to see and do more than his colleague with less service, and if he has profited from this experience this will be reflected in his knowledge and judgment as measured in sound written and oral examinations. He also should have had more occasion to demonstrate his initiative and to develop his judgment and capacity to supervise. Adding seniority as a separate factor only cancels out the preference that should be given for demonstrated knowledge, initiative, and judgment.

Giving recognition to seniority is fairly common. Some people favor the practice because of the ease of applying it, and local pressure may require the police department to go along with the practice. Where such is the case, seniority credit should not exceed 5 per cent of the candidates' written examination score, and this credit should not be added unless he has passed a qualifying score. Thus qualified men can achieve preference over equally qualified men with less experience, but marginal candidates will not be aided.

Selection of the Police Chief

Should the police chief be selected by a promotional examination under civil service requirements or appointed by the chief administrator of the city according to his own standards? The nature of the chief's duties are such that he may properly be selected by formal examination, regardless of whether he will be under civil service or serve at the pleasure of the chief administrator.

If the position is not placed under civil service, the police chief should be appointed by the chief administrator, not by the city council. If the chief administrator does not select the police chief by examination he should follow a careful selection process which would be the equivalent of a competitive examination. He may properly set his own standards, within charter and statutory limits, and discover by interview, review of experience, educational record, and character investigation, which candidate most nearly meets those standards.

The trend in the selection of police chiefs is appointment by the chief administrator — the mayor or the city manager. The chief administrator generally, and rightly, insists that he cannot be expected to get results unless he is given a free hand in the selection of department heads. He knows his organization, has clearly in mind what he expects to accomplish, and has a wide acquaintance or means of contact with persons capable of filling the position. The central personnel officer or agency can of course be of considerable help to him in his selection process. The chief administrator of the city is frequently under pressure to appoint persons who have no particular qualifications for the position of police chief of the city; and it is important to good police services that such pressures be resisted.

Consideration of Nonresidents. It is highly desirable that out-of-town persons be considered. An outsider often can deal with a difficult disciplinary situation better than one who has grown up in the department.[4] He will have a fresh view and approach not attained by a local man. It is true that ambition and industry on the part of department personnel is promoted by the assurance that the highest award of the service — promotion to the position of chief — is attainable by any man qualified for and deserving of the position. This is in agreement with the career service system, under which new recruits are brought in at the bottom, and top positions are filled by promotion from among those in the service. But carrying the career concept to its logical conclusion, it follows that the best qualified man be selected, regardless of resistence or any other factor not directly related to the requirements of the job. To open police chief positions to intercity competition will not restrict the opportunities to advancement for good police officers within the department. In fact, it will enlarge the opportunity and at the same time raise the level of competence of the whole police service. Yet perhaps no hard-and-fast rule should be adopted. The chief administrator, who appoints the police chief, should decide in each case whether it is to the advantage of the service to open the promotion test to qualified applicants from the outside or to limit the test to those in the department.

Rating Employee Performance

Should cities use a formalized system for rating policemen on the basis of their job performance? Actually, supervising officers are continually rating their subordinates, making judgments as to their working relationships, the quality and quantity of their work, and their dependability. Such judgments are ratings — whether formal or informal, whether written or unwritten. When the question is viewed this way the problem is not whether to rate employees but how to rate them. Should employees be rated in an informal manner without definitely prescribed and uniform standards? Or should they be rated in a systematic way, under an established procedure, against uniform standards?

A number of questions should be answered before the decision is made as to the type of rating system, if any, to be adopted. Is the working environment one that will be receptive to the installation of a rating system? Has such a system been tried before? What happened to it? Does the city have the facilities and staff skills necessary to build and operate a workable service rating system? What is expected of the system? Has there been pressure from the employees to establish such a system? Are the supervisory personnel capable of becoming trained raters? Will the probable benefits override the additional work and the conflicts that arise as a result of adopting a formal service rating system?

Basic to the establishment of formal ratings is the determination of their uses. When the primary approach is to force supervisors to consciously evaluate subordinates, there is a good chance that a formal rating system will succeed. However, when the number of uses is large or when any one use generates considerable employee resistance, the adverse results of utilizing formal ratings may fail to justify their continuation. With varying degrees of success, formal ratings have been used at various times for one or more of these purposes:

---

[4] Among the cities that have selected chiefs of police from outside the city are Chicago, Illinois; Burbank, Compton, Monterey, Pasadena, San Diego, San Mateo, and San Pablo, California; South Bend, Indiana; Houston, Texas; Tucson, Arizona; Hutchinson, Kansas; Highland Park, Wilmette, and Winnetka, Illinois; Flint, Kalamazoo, and Saginaw, Michigan; Eau Claire and Two Rivers, Wisconsin; Greensboro, North Carolina; and many others. This trend seems to be growing. See the article by Bernard L. Garmire, chief of police, Tucson, Arizona, on "Appointment of Outside Police Chiefs," in *Public Management*, August, 1960, pp. 170-75.

as an aid in the development of training programs

as an aid in awarding salary advancements within a salary range

as screening and selection devices for promotions

as a basis for layoffs or reductions in force

as substantiation for disciplinary action or discharge

as an aid to management in evaluating the work of supervisors

as a guide in assigning work to employees

as an aid to evaluating employees' strengths and weaknesses

to stimulate employees by acknowledging their strengths and pointing out their weaknesses

to give employees a relatively objective and complete picture of their work performance.

Use of service ratings as one factor in promotions is probably the most common application, and police chiefs would do well to limit the use of ratings to this single purpose until ratings are firmly established and accepted. Other uses will develop naturally over a period of time as the need is recognized. One of the common, and controversial, uses of the performance rating is in granting or withholding within-range salary increases. Unusual pressures are placed on the rating official to give everyone a "satisfactory" rating, and these pressures are effective in most cases. It is best not to use the rating as the only or major determining factor for salary increases.

The duties of positions vary from class to class, from one occupational group to another, and from service to service. It follows that the work factors to be rated should be closely related to the duties of the job classes to which employees are assigned. An example of one service rating form, used to evaluate promotion potential, is shown in Figure 20. The number of factors should be based on the duties of the jobs and should be carefully described on the form in a manner understandable to those making the ratings. The number of factors usually varies from four to 10. Generally, the simpler rating methods are to be preferred.

There are a number of types of ratings forms such as the graphic rating scale, checklist rating form, and the man-to-man rating form. The Ohio State Highway Patrol has developed a comprehensive rating system which is easily the most unusual and interesting one to appear in recent years. Any police department facing the question of whether to adopt or discard a performance rating plan would do well to review the Ohio system.[5]

The Ohio State Highway Patrol used standard types of rating scales for many years. The Patrol recognized the weaknesses of these scales. A rater could place a man anywhere on the scale he wished to; even the best raters had some degree of bias; and the scales they were using placed 95 per cent of the men at the top of the distribution. The Patrol then started a carefully controlled study to devise an effective method and, as a result of considerable effort, developed the Diagnostic Forced-Choice Personnel Evaluation procedure. As they describe it, "The rater is presented a block of four statements which look to be equally nice things to say about a person. However, only two of these

---

[5]*Diagnostic Forced-Choice Personnel Evaluation, Patrolman Performance Report,* copyrighted by Ohio State Highway Patrol, Columbus.

PERSONNEL DEPARTMENT   CITY OF **BERKELEY**

PROMOTIONAL SERVICE RATING

POLICE DEPARTMENT
EMPLOYEE'S NAME _____ FOR RANK OF _____ DATE _____

Indicate Ratings by " ✓ " Marks

SERVICE FACTORS	IMPROVEMENT REQUIRED	SATISFACTORY WITH MINOR FAULTS	SATISFACTORY	SUPERIOR	OUTSTANDING
1. **PERSONALITY** - Does he have the poise, appearance, personality, sense of humor which he must have to stimulate confidence in the public, subordinates and superiors? Does he have objectionable habits or characteristics which are a major annoyance or source of irritation to others?					
2. **TEMPERAMENT** - Does he habitually exercise self-control? Does he become excited under stress? Does he take criticism well? Does he rapidly adjust well to people and situations? Is he usually firm yet fair and impartial?					
3. **INTEREST** - Has he shown sustained interest in police work? Has he sought to improve himself? Does his interest show on the job? Does he show interest in all phases of his job? Does he subordinate police work to outside interests?					
4. **QUANTITY OF WORK — INDUSTRY** - Is he industrious? Does he always do a full day's work? Does he do his share? Does he organize his time well? Does he waste time? Is he easily diverted into non-productive activity?					
5. **QUALITY OF WORK — PERFORMANCE** - Is he thorough? Accurate? Effective? Does he exercise imagination? Initiative, Does he perform well in all phases of his work? Or emphasize those he likes in detriment to others? Does he cooperate fully?					
6. **EXPRESSION** - Does he express himself clearly and concisely? Are his oral and written explanations understandable? Is his language acceptable?					
7. **JUDGMENT** - Do you have confidence in his judgment? In your absence would you worry about his decisions? Is he flexible? Adaptable? Does he generally show "common sense?"					
8. **DEPENDABILITY** - Is he reliable? Does he require less than average supervision? Are his reports factual and accurate?					
9. **LOYALTY** - Does he adhere to departmental aims and ideals? Does he show pride in his work? Does he support his superiors? Does he carry out departmental policies?					
10. **KNOWLEDGE OF HIS JOB** - Does he exhibit good job knowledge? Has he demonstrated that he can learn and apply techniques and procedures? Does his performance indicate that he will learn and practice techniques and procedures in the promotional job?					
11. **LEADERSHIP** - Does he have the capacity to direct, control and influence others? Has he demonstrated leadership in his daily relations with other officers? Does he contribute to good morale? Will he be able to handle complicated personnel matters in an effective and satisfactory manner?					

Figure 20 — Promotional Service Rating Form, Berkeley, California

phrases are related to effective performance. The rater is asked to choose the two phrases that he considers to be descriptive of the ratee." This is a sample block:

a. Has a good standing with
other local departments.

b. Helps younger patrolmen
with violators.

c. Keeps his head in emergencies.

d. Always trying to learn
something.

The advantages of the forced-choice technique rest upon the use of phrases which describe specific bits of behaviour and upon the inability of the rater to detect those phrases that are actually related to successful performance. Actually then, the forced-choice procedure separates the reporting of an individual's behaviour from the evaluation of that behaviour. The rater is not asked to say how much of a certain characteristic or behaviour an individual possesses nor whether it is good or bad to have this trait. He only has to indicate which of several phrases is most typical of the rates. Since the rater cannot tell or perhaps cannot realize that there is a difference in the discriminating value between the phrases, he is forced to make an honest choice of the phrases that best describe the individual.

This rating system was worked out with the most advanced personnel and statistical techniques. How well this was done is best illustrated by several statistical results. In the first place, the resulting scores give an almost perfect normal distribution instead of crowding all of the men up to the top end like most rating systems do. Some of the men rank high, some low, with the majority on either side of average. Second, there was a high correlation between the ratings made in 1958 and those made in 1959. The officers were rated just about like they had been the year before. Third, and more important, there was a very high correlation between the ratings of men who had been transferred and were thus rated by two different commanders. This shows a very high degree of reliability. The value of this system is well illustrated by a comparison made by the Ohio State Highway Patrol.

Diagnostic Forced-Choice Personnel Evaluation	Former Rating Scale
1. High relationship to "buddy ratings."	1. No relationship to "buddy ratings."
2. Bell-shaped curve of scores.	2. Pile up at high end of scale.
3. No relationship between score and seniority.	3. Older men get higher score.
4. No difference between the average score of districts.	4. Great difference between the average score of districts; some grade high, some grade low.
5. Rater cannot let personalities influence score.	5. Rater can influence score.
6. Men from different sections of state can be compared.	6. Men cannot be compared from different parts of the state.
7. Score does not suffer because of transfer to new post.	7. Score suffers because of transfer to new post.

This rating system has only one apparent weakness. Since the rating officer does not know just how his rating of the individual will score, he cannot use this form to discuss points that require improvement with the ratee. This has been taken care of by adding a Performance Report Summary to the forced-choice forms. This Summary is a well worked out rating scale following the usual patterns so that it can serve as a basis for discussion of an officer's rating. However, the score on this rating is used only for that purpose, although administrative copies are kept, and the ratee receives a copy.

One caution should be expressed. This technique requires the services of a professional psychologist with more than usual ability. The procedure can be developed only after most careful study and analysis. While highly reliable for the Ohio State Highway Patrol, the identical forms might not apply equally well for a municipal police department. It might be necessary to construct a similar system using the same principles developed here.

In addition to the rating of patrolmen, the Patrol has developed similar systems for line supervisors, command level supervisors, radio men, and drivers license examiners.

Each employee should be rated by his immediate supervisor; thus normally a patrolman will be rated by a sergeant. If the employee has had more than one supervisor in the rating period, they should independently rate him and then confer to produce a joint rating. The ratings should be reviewed by commanding officers and the police chief to insure application of uniform standards.

The most important step in rating is instruction of the raters. Supervising officers should have the purpose and the means of rating thoroughly explained to them, preferably at the time of each rating period, by the departmental or central personnel officer. Understanding and support can generally be achieved through staff conferences in which officers are encouraged to ask questions, express doubts, and agree on the basic requirements before making their ratings. They should be dissuaded from looking on ratings as nothing more than a piece of required paper work, for a poorly administered system is worse than no system at all.

Frequency of ratings varies, the general standard being once a year with all employees rated at approximately the same time. Employees serving a probationary period should be rated more frequently with the results used for counseling. Rating supervisors should be indoctrinated with the facts that informal rating of employees is a continuous process and that formal ratings are made periodically to obtain a relatively objective record of those informal ratings.

If employees are convinced that formal ratings are fair, useful, and sensibly utilized, their acceptance can be established and maintained. An aid to acceptance is to remove the mystery by explaining such points as purpose, uses, methods, and limitations of the formal rating. Another aid to acceptance is the full and frank discussion of each rating between the rating officer and the employee rated, which should take place immediately after the rating has been made and reviewed.

It should be remembered that there is a point of diminishing returns beyond which the effort expended is not justified by the results obtained. The primary purpose of a police department is to provide police service to the public. Formal ratings are justified if they contribute appreciably to this through achieving greater effectiveness of personnel. If ratings consistently take up too much of the supervisors' time or adversely affect morale, their continued use may be difficult to justify in all but the very largest departments. In large departments, however, the urgent need for recording information on the performance of several thousand employees may constitute sufficient justification. It is almost axiomatic that the need for formality and system grows in direct proportion to the size of the organization.

Conditions of Employment

"Conditions of employment" is a sort of catch-all phrase covering a broad area in personnel management, ranging from relatively objective matters, such as leaves and hours of work, to such intangibles as job satisfaction and prestige. For this discussion conditions of employment are the nonsalary factors of the total work environment. Working conditions are, of course, an important factor in the attraction and retention of able personnel and in the quality and quantity of work or services performed.

Physical Conditions

For police employees working inside, light, heat, ventilation, noise control, and furniture and equipment are of great concern. For those working outside, the equipment provided, such as transportation and communications, is of most importance. Generally the more satisfactory the physical conditions, the easier it is to maintain high levels of work output.

Hours of Work

Police must provide 24 hours per day of active service. For this reason most police departments use the three-platoon system, with patrolmen working from 8:00 a.m. to 4:00 p.m.; 4:00 p.m. to midnight; and midnight to 8:00 a.m. It is generally considered better practice to assign officers permanently to a given platoon, rather than to rotate their duty hours from month to month. Methods of determining hours of work and the use of officers is more fully discussed in Chapter 7.

Hours of work per week generally range from 40 to 48, with a definite movement toward the 40-hour week. The smaller departments are more apt to retain longer working hours; most large departments are now on a 40-hour week.[6]

Leaves of Absence

Leaves of absence generally fall into six categories: (1) sick leave; (2) vacation; (3) leave with pay, other than sick leave or vacation; (4) leave without pay; (5) injury or workmen's compensation leave; and (6) military leave. It is essential to make regular provisions for all leaves of absence, in line with those of other city departments, to publish such regulations in central personnel or departmental rules, and to administer the leave program uniformly and fairly. Employees have the right to know in advance under what conditions leaves are granted, and lost time can be avoided by proper planning. The six types of leaves listed above will be considered in order.

1. Sick Leave. The purpose of sick leave is to permit employees to recuperate from illness or disability and to prevent sick employees from spreading illness. Sick leave should be accumulated systematically, as for example, at the rate of one day for each calendar month of service. Leave should be granted with full pay for the duration of any illness to the extent of time earned and accumulated. Sometimes sick leave is

---

[6]See the section on "Police Department Statistics" in the current *Municipal Year Book*.

granted for serious illness or death in an employee's immediate family. Many cities grant a special leave of one to three days for death in the immediate family which is not charged against regular sick leave. Policies on leave for serious illness in the immediate family are not so clearly drawn because of the difficulty in defining what constitutes "serious illness."

Many departments allow members to accumulate unused sick leave from year to year to protect the employee against loss of income during serious illnesses which last for several weeks or months. Such accumulation may be up to 60, 90, 120, or more days. Some departments allow unlimited accumulation. There is a strong argument for this policy. Sick leave is a part of the officer's compensation, and it is unfair to take away accumulated time from an officer who has used very little of his sick leave as contrasted to officers who use it as fast as it accumulates. This is actually a form of savings, and it is questionable to penalize an officer who has been frugal in accumulating for a long illness that is more likely to occur as he grows older. On termination of employment there is generally no settlement for accrued sick leave.

Department heads should have authority to approve sick leave and should insist on firm supervision to prevent abuses. A police department's sick leave usage should not average more than that of other city departments nor in general more than five to six days per year per employee. A higher rate is sufficient justification for a study of sicknesses, sick leave, and supervision in the department. Several methods are employed to prevent malingering, including (1) requirement of a physician's certificate as to the nature and duration of the illness, (2) home visits by a city nurse or physician to verify the illness, and (3) home visit by a sergeant or other officer to establish the fact that the man at least is at home. These may or may not be done routinely; some departments apply such a provedure only for illness of two or more days and some only in cases where the supervisor has reason to suspect malingering.

2. Vacation or Annual Leave. Vacation leave is intended to allow employees to refresh themselves physically and mentally. Such leave should be with full pay and should be accumulated systematically. The most general vacation allowance is two weeks per year, although a few cities allow three weeks, and a sizeable number grant additional vacation time after 10 or 15 years of service. Provisions controlling vacation leave should be as flexible as local conditions permit in such matters as split vacations, accumulation of vacation leave credits, and months during which vacation can be taken. The police chief should have authority to specify the timing of vacations so that the department continues to provide uninterrupted services.

3. Leave with Pay. The purpose of paid leaves of absence for other than sickness, family death, or vacation, is to permit employees to improve themselves professionally and thereby become better employees. Such leave properly can be authorized for meetings, professional conferences, institutes, and short training courses, or to carry out such assignments as assisting other jurisdictions in problems requiring the help of an "outsider." Detailed rules governing such leave should be avoided, each case should be handled on its merits, and approval should be granted by the police chief only on recommendation of the employee's commanding officer.

4. Leave without Pay. Voluntary leave without pay occurs at the request of the policeman for such reasons as illness extending beyond the maximum permissible sick leave, temporary outside work which will equip him to render more valuable service to the city, extended absence for special training, and similar cases where there is little or no justification for paying the employee his wages while absent.

Furloughs made necessary due to lack of funds, staff reduction, or similar reasons should be treated as layoffs, and re-employment lists and mandatory re-employment should be used.

5. Injury or Compensation Leave. Practice varies widely in granting leave to employees injured in the line of duty, ranging from leave without pay (where the employee is entitled only to workmen's compensation insurance benefits) to the guarantee that the employee receive the equivalent of full salary as long as the service-connected injury exists. The jursidiction should pay at least part of the salary of an employee injured in line of duty, in conjunction with workmen's compensation. Injuries not incurred in line of duty should be treated the same as an illness with sick leave authorized to the extent of accumulation followed by leave without pay. Some jurisdictions make the distinction that injuries arising from the misconduct of the employee, for example, fighting in a bar, will not carry sick leave. Some police pension or retirement plans incorporate provisions for disability compensation for both on- and off-the-job injuries and illnesses.

6. Military Leave. Military leave commonly is of two types: (1) short periods of training — two weeks annually — for reserve personnel, and (2) active military service in time of war or mobilization. The first is granted by most jurisdictions, some with pay and some without pay and may be controlled by law. The second is of course without pay, but it carries such rights as re-employment at the same or higher rank, no loss of time for retirement, and the like. The two- or three-hour weekly evening meetings of National Guard or reserve units may present a problem. In small departments, this can be worked out informally, but on larger forces a written policy should be developed.

Health and Welfare Activities

Whether official or informal, city- or employee-sponsored, health and welfare activities are a part of employment conditions contributing to the prestige of the service, job satisfaction, and work output. Some of the more common activities are: group insurance, including medical and health insurance; credit unions; cooperative safety-training programs; employee periodicals; and recreational facilities and programs. Local conditions should determine the scope of health and welfare activities, and police chiefs should encourage those programs that contribute to the morale and effectiveness of the force.

Here as in other phases of personnel management, the best development occurs where the chief administrator, the police chief, and the personnel administrator work closely to develop a program balanced with other city departments. In the larger cities this cooperative effort is not likely to be as close or as essential as in smaller cities. Regardless of the size of the city, however, it is desirable to allow employees to participate in the development of programs that concern them. The extent to which they take part will help determine the extent to which health and welfare activities contribute positively to their efficiency. Many departments have a police welfare, burial, or similar association financed by police sponsorship of dances, circuses, or similar devices. While such groups are of long standing, there are many objections because their methods of raising funds are often not compatible with high police standards. This subject is discussed later in this chapter and in Chapter 14.

Retirement Provisions

Retirement provisions are of unusual importance, particularly in the police and fire services where intercity movements are much more strictly limited than in other types of work, and where movement between private industry and government service is almost nonexistent. The purposes of retirement systems are discussed later in this chapter.

Employee Relations

Conditions of employment discussed above, to the extent they are a concern of management and need to be administered, are a part of the functional area of personnel management commonly termed "employee relations." The paragraphs that follow are addressed to the problem of and the need for maintaining desirable "relations" between the manager and the managed. To have good employee relations means essentially that management and employees understand each other, are reasonably satisfied with their working relationships, and are working toward group goals. To fail in this means that communication has broken down, that management does not comprehend the needs or desires of its employees, or that employees misinterpret the intent and purposes of management. Defined actively, employee relations are the steps that management takes to fathom the physical and psychological requirements of employees and the means it uses to achieve employee acceptance of its policies and recommendations.

A police department has the same problems of employee relations as any other department in city government or as any business or industry: the extent to which employees should be allowed or encouraged to participate in management decisions affecting personnel or technical police matters; the type of employee organizations to be permitted in the department and the extent of recognition to be accorded them; and the means of informing employees of departmental policies, regulations, and matters of general interest and concern.

Joint Participation in Decision-Making

As early as 1933 it was apparent from experiments in industry that employee morale and productivity were dependent on the types of relationships in effect between employer and employee.[7] This early research at the Hawthorne plant of the Western Electric Company demonstrated the importance of treating workers as individuals and helping them to resolve their personal as well as employment problems to achieve maximum satisfaction and output. These studies were the forerunner of additional research in industrial psychology and communications that has continued to show that employees do more and better work when treated as associates rather than as subordinates.[8] Employee participation in various phases of the management process has therefore passed out of the experimental stage and is being actively applied both in industry and in government, through on-the-job training in administration, bargaining with employee organizations, suggestion programs, and the like.

Police departments can take advantage of these devices. Administrative training along lines discussed in Chapter 5 is highly desirable. Training officers have a choice between straight classroom lectures in which supervisors are told what is expected of

[7]Elton Mayo, *Human Problems of an Industrial Civilization* (New York: The Macmillan Company, 1933). See also Edwin E. Ghisilli and Clarence W. Brown, *Personnel and Industrial Psychology* (New York: McGraw-Hill Book Co., 1948), Chapter 16, particularly page 447: " ... The conclusion drawn from the Hawthorne experiment, that the relationship between the employee and the management is more important in the productivity and happiness of the worker than any other factor, has been corroborated."

[8]F. J. Roethlisberger and Wm. J. Dickson, *Management and the Worker* (Cambridge: Harvard University Press, 1939); Daniel Katz, Nathan Maccoby, and Nancy C. Morse, *Productivity, Supervision, and Morale in an Office Situation* (Ann Arbor: University of Michigan Press, 1950); Lester Coch and John R. P. French, Jr. "Overcoming Resistance to Change," *Human Relations*, August, 1948, pp. 512-32.

them and how to handle problems they meet, and conference-type discussions in which the supervisors contribute their own ideas suggesting alternate ways of coping with a problem. With the first "autocratic" method, the chief makes all the decisions unassisted. With the second "democratic" method, he may make the final determination, but he is frequently assisted in arriving at his conclusion by the contributions of other officers. The democratic method normally results in better understanding and acceptance of management decisions, although the autocratic method may be more readily accepted in an old-line department where the chief knows his business and men are accustomed to accepting orders without question.

Employee councils consider and advise management on matters of personnel policy. They cannot decide policy merely by presenting their recommendations; however, where the council deliberates responsibly and is broadly representative, its recommendations are likely to carry considerable weight. A typical employee council is one in Wichita, Kansas, where the 21 members are elected from each major department of the city government. An employee serves as chairman and the city personnel director as executive secretary. Department and division heads are not eligible for election. Functions of the council are: (1) to investigate matters pertaining to the general welfare of employees and make recommendations thereon; (2) upon request, to advise any appointing authority (department head) concerning personnel problems; (3) to consider personnel problems and policies submitted by the personnel director; (4) to elect a representative to the personnel advisory board; and (5) individually, to assist employees in obtaining prompt settlement of grievances. The council meets regularly or at the call of its chairman and individual members serve as the nucleus of departmental grievance committees.

In some cities this type of employee organization is sometimes a management device to discourage unionization among employees, and as such, may carry the stigma of paternalism. However, it has potential for constructive relationships between management and employee groups and can well be encouraged and utilized on this basis.

It is perhaps appropriate at this point — recognizing this to be the age of togetherness — to note that this type of group participation in administrative decision should in no way dilute the authority of the administrator to act, to ignore advice from others as he chooses, or to lessen his responsibility for the consequences of his actions.

Recognizing Employee Organizations[9]

An important consideration in employee relations is the type of employee organization to be accorded recognition. In police departments this question has special ramifications based on the nature of the work and the legal and social factors that arise from certain kinds of affiliations.

As a rule, city officials, including the police chief, can and do recognize responsible local groups where they exist, deal with them openly and willingly, and encourage their formation when interest is expressed by the men. Negotiating with an employee organization can be expected to have these advantages: (1) to provide the men with an orderly, impersonal means of expressing their desires and dissatisfactions; (2) to forestall efforts to go over the heads of local officials to the state legislature for special benefits which, thus imposed, seldom provide the necessary means of financing; (3) to

[9]See Emma Schweppe, *The Firemen's and Patrolmen's Unions in the City of New York* (New York: King's Crown Press, 1948), Chapter 1, "Unions in City Public Safety Departments," pp. 1-40; Audrey L. Davies, "The History and Legality of Police Unions," *GRA Reporter*, July-August, 1953, pp. 40-47; Don L. Kooken and Loren D. Ayres, "Police Unions and the Public Safety," *The Annals*, January, 1954, pp. 152-58; *Police Unions* (Washington, D.C.: International Association of Chiefs of Police, 1958).

give administrative officials opportunity to educate employees, or their representatives, regarding management problems and thus build employee appreciation of the reasons why requests cannot always be granted.

Fraternal Groups. Fraternal and benevolent associations have existed in the police service since before the beginning of the century. There are many local and state groups, some of which are affiliated for professional, educational and legislative purposes. Local organizations of this kind have two main objectives — to obtain better working conditions and salaries for police officers, and to provide a social outlet for officers with similar interests. The social aspect is frequently accompanied by educational and benevolent objectives including financial provision for families of officers who are disabled or die.

Historically police associations have banded together to lobby actively at the state level for benefits they were unable to achieve locally, and many continue to work this way. While local officials will find this tendency disconcerting, the best means of meeting it are to show good faith in dealing with employees on matters affecting their welfare and to maintain effective relations with the legislature so as to discourage the enactment of legislation granting special benefits to the police group contrary to the community interests and discriminating against other employee groups. Such state legislation does violence to home rule concepts and is to be discouraged.

One unprofessional characteristic of some local police associations is the tendency to engage in political activity for or against city councilmen while claiming the immunity from discharge or discipline that is provided by civil service. The public interest and the good of the service require that this practice be prohibited, though it may take considerable education to convince officers with political leanings that the ban does not curtail their political rights. Its wisdom and legality are well established, however, and federal and state civil service laws generally carry such a prohibition. The *Model City Charter* has an appropriate statement for cities.[10]

Solicitation of financial support from merchants and other citizens is another fairly common police association practice that should be discouraged. This may take the form of tickets to annual picnics and other events, or simply donations for such purposes as pensions or widows' and orphans' funds. The practice is well-established and accepted in some communities, but wherever it exists it creates or perpetuates an unhealthy relationship between citizens and police officers. This has become a major problem in some cities where as many as a half-dozen "associations" of police officers exist, side by side, each seeking public support through ticket sales, advertising in association publications, or outright requests for donations. Too often the contributions carrying an implied immunity from punishment for minor infractions of the law. The issuance of identity cards and decals for automobile windows by these groups must be prohibited whenever possible.

Fraternal Order of Police. This is a national organization with locals in many cities that has objectives generally similar to those of independent police associations; but the FOP uses and encourages some other activities that are open to serious question. Membership has been banned in a number of cities on grounds of incompatibility with the public interest, and the prohibition has been upheld by the courts.[11]

---

[10] *Model City Charter* (New York: National Municipal League, 1941), p. 55.

[11] For example, *State Lodge of Michigan, Fraternal Order of Police* v. *Detroit*, 318 Mich. 182, 27 NW (2nd) 612 (1947), and *Fraternal Order of Police* v. *Lansing Board of Police and Fire Commissioners*, 306 Mich. 68, 10 NW (2nd) 310, 321 US 784 (1943).

Two activities of the organization that are contrary to good public policy and police procedure are (1) soliciting advertising from local merchants and business establishments, and (2) issuing associate membership and vehicle courtesy cards to citizens in no way connected with police work. Solicitation of advertising places a police officer in the position of taking favors from people who conduct businesses, such as taverns and pool halls, under the supervision of the police department. Since the officer may ultimately be in the position of enforcing the law on these same people, the tendency is to compromise the department and weaken enforcement machinery.

Regarding car emblems furnished to associate members of the Fraternal Order of Police, the Michigan Supreme Court stated, "One would be naive, indeed, to assume that such automobile emblem did not carry with it the intimation of special privileges to associate members. This of itself is enough to require the determination that existence of plaintiff organizations within the law enforcement body of a municipality is contrary to public policy." [12]

Legal decisions of this kind have apparently not seriously impeded the continued growth of the Fraternal Order of Police in a substantial number of cities, and any police administrator may ultimately have to face the question of recognition or prohibition. A reasonable middle ground would appear to be that of recognizing the organization on matters relating to the personal welfare and working conditions of the police force while discouraging or prohibiting activities, such as those described above, that are distinctly contrary to the public interest.

National Labor Unions. Denial of police membership in labor unions has a long history and strong legal and philosophical backing. Police unionization was just beginning to get off the ground in 1919, after the American Federation of Labor had changed its policy, in effect since 1897, of refusing to charter police organizations, when a strike by the Boston police department suddenly and dramatically brought the issue to a head, resulting in the dismissal of 1,100 striking Boston policemen and such a wave of public and official revulsion that the union movement for policemen has not yet recovered. Locals which had been chartered by the AFL were forced to withdraw, and it was not until 1937 — 20 years later — that another police local was chartered. Following World War II, efforts of national labor unions to organize police officers increased slightly but only with very limited success. It is fairly common practice, however, for members of police departments to join city-wide employee associations or unions, some of which have national affiliations.

Two principal grounds for banning police unions affiliated nationally are (1) unilateral identification of the police force with a single section of the social structure, namely labor, and (2) the power to strike. The philosophical and legal background for outright prohibition is contained in statements by Governor Calvin Coolidge of Massachusetts and President Woodrow Wilson at the time of the Boston police strike; President Franklin Roosevelt in a letter to the National Federation of Federal Employees at its 20th Jubilee Convention in 1937; and court decisions in New York, Michigan, and Mississippi. [13]

The more recent trend is the growth of the AFL-CIO affiliate, the American Federation of State, County, and Municipal Employees, which opens its membership to all employees regardless of "craft." It is quite common for police personnel to comprise the dominant group within a local of this union. From the standpoint of the public interest,

---

[12] *Ibid.* at p. 80.
[13] See Charles S. Rhyne, *Labor Unions and Municipal Employee Law* (Washington, D. C.: National Institute of Municipal Law Officers, 1946).

this form of organization is probably preferable to the "craft-type" police union. The *Municipal Year Book* for 1960 indicates that locals of this organization are found in about one-third of the cities over 10,000 population.

It is highly essential for police officers to maintain impartiality in serving all elements of the population. This is one element in professionalization. When the right to join or organize an employee union is prohibited, a clear responsibility is placed upon municipal officials to conduct a personnel program constructive enough to offset the need to organize for influence or pressure.

Means of Communication

Where employee organizations are functioning under effective and responsible leadership, negotiation on matters affecting their welfare provides an effective means of two-way communication between management and employees. It gives employees a channel for expressing their needs, desires, and complaints, and it gives administrators the chance to discuss larger issues of departmental policy that require department-wide understanding and acceptance. When these conferences are successful, they can sometimes be extended into areas other than those of immediate interest, with the employee group constituting a sounding board for new administrative plans. At present, however, it is perhaps more common for a police chief and the representatives of a local police association to deal at arm's length, neither side quite able or willing to completely trust the other. In such cases, it is extremely important for the chief to be honest, open, and fair, for only in this way can he expect ultimately to win the confidence of employees.

It should be remembered that communication is a two-way exchange, it being as important for the chief to know what his men are thinking as for them to know what is on his mind. A normal channel is by word of mouth, and down through the supervisory structure. Thus it is essential that supervisory personnel enjoy the respect of their associates — officers who are honest, competent, and fair; men to whom employees will talk in confidence knowing they will not be betrayed; and officers who, at the same time, will demand the best of their men and remain loyal to departmental objectives. Consistently advancing the best qualified men to supervisory ranks is one way to win and hold employee confidence.

Employee manuals are another effective communications device. Most police departments have administrative and procedural rules. These should be written clearly and published attractively in convenient form so that each man can have a personal copy. Good examples of this type of duty manual are those of Oak Park, Illinois; Portland, Maine; University City, Missouri; Phoenix, Arizona; Salem, Oregon; and Greensboro, North Carolina. Many departments also function under personnel rules administered by a central department of the city government. These rules are sometimes published formally as in Oxnard, California, and Pontiac, Michigan, while in other cities they are published in an informal, folksy style to give the gist of privileges and responsibilities without the legal language. Representative manuals of this kind can be found in Wichita, Kansas; Cincinnati, Ohio; and Winnetka, Illinois.

A number of cities publish newsletters or house organs carrying information of general interest about official activities. These may be confined exclusively to municipal business or they may include vital statistics and personal items about individuals in various city departments. In the latter case, one or more people in each department serve as reporters. Newsletters may be supplemented occasionally by special bulletins on a single topic of major importance, in order to furnish each employee full information in convenient form. Large police departments may find it worth while to have their own house organs in lieu of or supplementing one of city-wide coverage — the training bulletin of the Los Angeles department comes close to this.

In addition to negotiating with employee representatives on a more or less regular basis the police chief may call departmental meetings from time to time to lay the groundwork for a new undertaking, to explain a proposed change in policy, or to give employees the opportunity to express themselves on personnel or departmental operations. The roll-call training period described in the next chapter provides a convenient occasion for this kind of communication.

Employee suggestion systems can be productive, or they can be the subject of ridicule. Their success depends in large part on the manner of their administration. Clear and definite recognition must be provided for each man who submits a workable idea, and there must be provision for putting useful suggestions into operation. Financial incentives, representing a percentage of first-year savings by the new idea, frequently are recommended to recognize individual contributions. There is no objection to this practice, but ideally employees should submit their suggestions spontaneously without thought of concrete rewards.

The problem of communications within an organization has attracted the attention of a number of academicians and practitioners in the field of public administration. Concepts of the "informal" organization and lateral communications, alias the grapevine, have been developed and explored. Police administration in the larger departments would profit from exploring some of the recent literature on this subject.

Discipline

The modern police chief strives to enlist the interest, intelligence, enthusiasm, and loyalty of the employees associated with him. He seeks to recruit promising new employees, provides for their training, and supplies them with manuals telling what to do and why the rule has been adopted. He tries to have acceptable conditions of work, and he provides an orderly way in which employee representatives can discuss such matters with him and present grievances. He develops ways in which distinctive service can be given recognition so that employees will know that meritorious service will be recognized and the prestige of public service in the community will be enhanced. He appreciates that in the public service far more is achieved by the administrator who is a leader than by the administrator who is a driver. Thus he seeks to secure good order and work results through the intelligent cooperation of employees. These are the positive aspects of discipline.

The police chief at times will fall short of the ideal, partly because of his own limitations and the imperfections of existing personnel methods, and partly because of human frailties in the personnel under his direction. When his positive methods fail, he must resort to the negative approach of disciplinary actions.

The problem of discipline is common to all departments of government. In the police service it is similar to that found in all other government functions, except that the relative importance of discipline is greater because of the special requirements of trust imposed by the mission of protecting the public and the frequent opportunities for misbehavior.

The Nature of Discipline

Discipline may be regarded from the two standpoints — the positive approach based on developing an *esprit de corps,* and the negative approach through the threat or application of punishment. Both stem from accepted definitions of the word "discipline," and both are commonly associated with organizations of the command type such as police departments and military units.

A well-disciplined police force with high morale is based on mutual respect between officers and men and on understanding and acceptance of rules for administration. The normal requirement is for reasonable rules, sensibly, firmly, and evenly enforced. Mary Parker Follett, an authority on business administration, identified order-giving as "the law of the situation," under which one receiving an order is impelled to follow it because he understands its need and purpose just as well as the one who gives it. *Esprit de corps* or discipline in a police force may depend as much on the efforts of commanding officers to develop a code of rules based on the law of the situation as it does upon their insistence that whatever rules are in force be obeyed. Employees need not agree with a regulation — although this is desirable — to comply, but they should understand it.

In its alternative sense, discipline originally meant training, but a punitive concept has grown up around the word because of the need to enforce obedience in the training process. During the earlier history in American police departments, the punitive aspect of discipline had primary emphasis, on the basis that commanding officers knew what they were doing and men had no right to question their orders. In business and government, in the military forces, and in police departments, this concept is giving way to the more constructive idea of discipline as training or retraining. Included in this concept is the notion that when disciplinary action becomes necessary, the supervisor shares responsibility with the offender for a breach of regulations — he has not applied "the law of the situation." This notion has a certain limited validity, for it is the responsibility of supervisors to enforce obedience and of subordinates to obey, regardless of their personal inclinations and even though both sides may personally dislike the regulation being enforced.

Purposes of Disciplinary Action

Disciplinary procedure may have several ends in view. The primary aim is to bring about a change in the attitude and action of the individual officer whose work has not been in conformance with department standards, so that he performs as he should. A second aim is to dissuade other potential offenders from similar derelictions. A third is to inform the public that compliance is uniformly insisted upon from all members of the force. The first objective is thus to train or retrain the individual and to establish or heighten his effectiveness; the second, to improve and preserve the morale of the group; and the third, to raise and maintain the prestige of the department.

Administering Discipline

In order to accomplish these purposes, disciplinary action must be taken quickly, positively, and justly. The two principal deterrents to dereliction are swiftness and certainty of action. Delay or awkwardness in handling a case only aggravates the problem and tends to encourage contempt for the disciplinary process or for individual officers who neglect their responsibilities. Severity is of minor importance in comparison.

Various forms of disciplinary action are open to supervisors, ranging from mild or strong oral reprimands, through transfers, fines, and suspensions, to outright dismissal. An oral reprimand is the broadest and most flexible disciplinary act. It is a warning procedure rather than a punitive one. It can be used more than once on the same individual with widely varying degrees of emphasis and meaning, while preserving his dignity and spirit. In its mildest form, the reprimand may be a cooperative effort to determine the cause of a breach of discipline and to work out a remedy for it. For example, it is frequently found that employee lapses are due to conditions outside the job — serious illness at home, financial worries, or mental depression — which the employee often can be helped to surmount by the understanding guidance of his supervisors. In a more serious form, reprimand carries implication of stronger action to follow if an employee persists in his error. Such further discipline is invariably punitive in its intent, being used as a more forceful reminder after counseling and explanation have failed to bring about the necessary improvement.

In all cases except a minor reprimand given on the spot, it is wise to write up a memorandum of the incident covering the following points: (1) the situation calling for the interview with the employee; (2) specific reasons for the interview; (3) summary of employee's statement or explanation; (4) summary of supervisor's statement; and (5) mutual understanding of what employee and supervisor will do to improve performance or prevent a recurrence with an understanding of future disciplinary action if the employee fails to correct. Such a memorandum thus shows all of the facts of the case, including the fact that the employee now knows just what is expected of him. It is a good idea for the employee to read this memorandum and sign a brief statement that he has. It is a good plan in certain cases to set a follow-up time when the employee's performance is again reviewed to see if the corrections have been made. If they have, a second memorandum is made showing this, and again the employee sees it and knows it will be in his file showing that his performance has improved. This system of memorandums is essential if there is to be a fair and effective plan for handling disciplinary matters.

Possibly the most widely used form of discipline in small departments is the extra duty assignment, since it is always possible to utilize additional manpower. Assignment of an officer to extra duty two or three hours a day for definite periods generally has a lasting effect on him and his fellows since it confronts them each day during the disciplinary period. As an alternate, extra duty may be combined with suspension and an officer allowed to work several of his days off, in lieu of a suspension without pay. This penalizes the officer through the loss of cherished time off but not through his pay check.

Disciplinary infractions serious enough to warrant suspension without pay suggest the possibility that an officer may be unfit to continue long in service. It would be unusual to permit an officer to remain on a police force after committing a second offense of sufficient gravity to call for suspension. If departmental rules are generally accepted, suspension of a chronic offender not only sets him apart from the group, but it also imposes a financial burden on his family and reduces the effective strength of the police force. Should the necessity for discipline reach this stage, that in the interests of the man and the department, the officer should think seriously of obtaining employment in another field.

Police officials in American cities are rather frequently impeded in prompt and effective administration of disciplinary action by police commission or trial board forms of organization in which the disciplinary function is largely removed from the hands of the chief. In the most extreme form a chief must prefer charges before the trial board for even the most minor infractions unless the man waives his right to "trial" and accepts the proposed disciplinary action. In other cases, officers are entitled to appeal to the courts from disciplinary actions ordered or taken by the administrator or administrative body. Based on general statutes permitting review by the courts of administrative actions adversely affecting an individual, courts have sometimes interpreted such statutes as permitting a second-guessing on all types of administrative decisions.

While there is an employee as well as an administrative interest in the matter of job security, it should not be made as difficult to administer discipline as it is to convict persons of felonies. Such hide-bound procedures can benefit only the individual who is determined to place his personal advantage above the department and the public. Such restrictions are of no value to the public, to the department, or even to the overwhelming majority of police officers whose ethical and moral values impel them to accept merited discipline when it is administered fairly.

Despite legal barriers, many police officials and police commissions or trial boards have achieved a *modus vivendi* which strikes a balance between complete administrative efficiency and the complete protection of the individual against disciplinary action. To continue improving the situation, civil service or trial boards on the one hand need to become more alert to the fact that no person has a right to employment in the same sense as he has a right to security in his person, and that no useful purpose is served by half-hearted discipline. Ultimately it should be feasible to shift the balance of authority from the board toward the executive by changing applicable legal provisions.

Police officials on the other hand need to build public and employee confidence by demonstrating complete fairness and impartiality of their disciplinary actions and by preparing a complete documentary record for each case to be reviewed by a civil service board or by the courts. It is not sufficient to affirm that a man's attitude has been poor and that he has had frequent conflicts with his commanding officer; it is essential to show by records the extent to which his work has fallen below an acceptable standard and to present written memoranda of the conferences in which his deficiencies have been pointed out.

This is particularly true in the preparation of cases for dismissal. Frequency of dismissal from the public service is not high, and its significance therefore can be rather easily exaggerated. But where dismissal becomes necessary, the administrator must be able to demonstrate that the individual was given every opportunity to correct his errors and that it is in the departmental and the public interest to require his separation. Loss of a dismissal case suggests either an administrative error in evaluating its seriousness or inadequate preparation and presentation of the case. Culpability in citizen boards, or their desire to give an employee another chance, cannot stand the light of publicity when a case has been prepared well in a community that expects good government.

A department head must take and hold the initiative in dismissing an incompetent. While he may hesitate to expose himself to a prolonged battle with an employee before a civil service commission, his reluctance can perhaps be cured by a realization of the harm to his staff, to the individual employee, and to the public which results from continuing an employee in a post for which he is not and cannot be fitted. To ease the situation, an employee may be directed toward other employment for which he is better suited. He may also be given opportunity to resign rather than suffer the unfavorable publicity and record of discharge proceedings. All but a few people recognize and accept the soundness of such an offer. It is especially important for the administrator to stand his ground against the few who do not; but if his case is weak he will do better to yield quietly until he is in a stronger position.

A middle ground between the unlimited dismissal power of the administrator and the "protective" appeal board is the advisory lay board to which the employee can appeal from certain types of actions and be given a public hearing, followed by an advisory opinion from the board to the administrator. This approach is gaining increased acceptance and deserves consideration. In some jurisdictions the employee's right of appeal is limited to those instances in which religious, racial, or political discrimination or favoritism is changed. Subjecting an administrative decision to this type of advisory review and publicity is highly effective in requiring an official not only to substantiate his case thoroughly and carefully, but also to make his disciplinary action reasonable and justifiable. At the same time, by lodging final authority in administrative officials, it insures that the interests of a single employee are not placed above those of the city organization or the public by a lay group.

Major disciplinary action, including discharge of a policeman from the force, should stimulate a searching inquiry into the methods of recruitment, training, and administration. Something is wrong somewhere. An investigation should be made as to how the person was first selected and how a similar selection can be avoided in the future. Removals are costly to the municipality. The training which has been given the policeman is thrown to the winds as far as the force is concerned; his dependents suffer; and his own sense of personal well-being may be undermined. The usefulness of the discharged member to the community at large may be lessened as a result of emotional and psychological upset.

Retirement

Retirement planning is a fairly recent development in personnel administration. Despite their recency, retirement systems are now widely accepted as an integral part of good personnel practice in both industry and government. The importance of old age security to city employees was first recognized in 1857 when a pension system was established for New York City police. Some of the earliest pension plans were set up exclusively for the benefit of police or firemen and financed with inadequate reserves. Many of these have failed, or they have been absorbed by city-wide or state systems with financial reserves set up on an actuarial basis to assure solvency. Nonactuarial pension plans that are still in existence can be expected ultimately to fail or to impose an unreasonable burden on the financial capacity of a community.

Advantages of Retirement

The strong movement for retirement benefits which arose at the time of the depression of the 1930's had several substantial objectives. One was to reduce the expense of public welfare administration by providing an actuarial fund for support of the aged instead of current outlay as they became unemployed. Another was to remove the aged from employment rolls but with an independent income capable of sustaining them on a reasonable basis. The latter purpose was two-fold: (1) to bring about retirement of elderly people before their efficiency was significantly impaired, and (2) to provide increased promotional opportunities for younger people. This phase of retirement programming has been virtually superseded by other considerations.

To the employee in government a retirement system provides these advantages: (1) forced savings, generally at interest compounded annually, which are matched or more than matched by the employer; (2) assured income in case of early forced retirement due to disability; (3) family benefits in case of premature death; and (4) opportunity to retire with, frequently, a considerable part of his useful life still ahead of him. This last advantage enables an employee to begin early in his life to plan for retirement, although it is offset to a certain extent by the provision in most retirement plans requiring him to retire at a fixed age regardless of his health or occupational efficiency. One additional benefit may be noted for cities that have adopted federal social security (Old Age and Survivors Insurance), namely the transferability of benefits between cities or even to other occupations. Where cities have merged their local plans with social security there may also be more liberal benefits.

From the side of government, retirement systems may be expected to: (1) decrease the cost of the unfit employee by retiring him on a jointly accumulated pension instead of retaining him on a wholly government-contributed salary; (2) improve the morale of the active employees by increasing their chances of promotion, and securing them against the vicissitudes of sickness, disability, and old age; and (3) attract and retain in the public service men who, realizing the importance of old-age security, would otherwise seek the assurance of governmentally enforced pensions in private employment. To these must be added the advantage that, as an employee accumulates an equity in the retirement plan, he incurs a positive incentive to remain employed in the same jurisdiction. The city retains the advantage of his experience, can exercise discipline more effectively, and has a corresponding responsibility to provide for the training and advancement of these permanent employees.

Certain disadvantages of permanent retirement systems also should be noted: (1) once older employees are cleared out of the service by an enforced retirement age and their positions are filled by younger employees, the initial advantage of increased promotional opportunities is not as great; (2) a service which provides no mobility — where retirement benefits cannot be transferred from city to city or to other types of employment — tends to stultify and become ingrown; (3) enforced retirement at a specified age without regard to other factors may result in important manpower losses to an employing agency and in creation of other equally serious social problems. There is a considerable body of informed opinion and some research indicating that a compulsory retirement age is not the answer to this phase of the old age question.[14]

Responsibility for Economic Risks

The need for providing employees with reasonable protection against certain insurable contingencies, such as old age, death, and disability, is now widely accepted in both government and industry. Security eliminates to a great extent the worries which hamper the best efforts of employees. A sound retirement system also enables an employer to maintain standards of working efficiency by separating elderly and disabled employees from the service with humane provision for their needs. This last factor may be of particular significance in police and fire departments, where advanced age and physical disability have a greater adverse effect on working ability than in some other municipal occupations. Policemen are required to protect lives and property and to employ such means as the situation demands to carry out this responsibility. When they are disabled or killed in the discharge of duty, the community has a correlative responsibility to provide financial assistance during disability or to care for the families of those whose injuries are fatal. The pension fund can and should be set up to include both contingencies.

At the same time individuals, whether policemen or others, have a responsibility to provide for their own financial security. A contributory retirement plan set up on an

---

[14] See for example, J. Howard Wyner, "Toward More Flexible Retirement Policies," *Personnel*, March, 1954, p. 386.

actuarial basis — in which employee and employer both contribute and the appropriations are budgeted for future requirements — is therefore strongly preferred. As previously indicated, policemen and firemen have traditionally preferred to maintain separate retirement systems for themselves alone. This is unwise, not only because it frequently saddles a community with a financial burden it cannot afford, but also because the soundness of the retirement system depends in great part on a large and diversified membership to spread the risk.

Administrative Problems of Retirement Management

Management of a retirement fund sometimes is vested in the personnel agency, sometimes in a finance officer, but more often in a board on which both the employer and the employees are represented.

Sources of Revenue. Municipal retirement systems are supported from two major sources: employee contributions and city contributions. The city contribution is normally recognized as a general fund expense, although some plans are financed in part through dedicated revenues such as license fees and municipal court costs and such other sources as special financial rewards to policemen and firemen, and the like. Irregular funds from these latter sources are inadequate and do little to support a sound pension system. Solvency of a retirement fund depends on annual contributions sufficient to meet future demands as estimated by an actuarial survey, and these contributions (or premiums) should be made a regular part of the annual budget.

Actuarial Basis. The pension fund should be established on an actuarial basis of estimated future annual payments to retirants for at least 10 years ahead. If available funds and contributions do not meet the anticipated ordinary risks and do not provide a surplus against the possibility of unpredictable calls for annuities, the retirement is not a sound one.

Under a retirement system operated on an actuarial reserve basis, current taxes provide sufficient funds to meet current payments to all employees on the retirement list, plus an additional amount (which is invested in interest-bearing securities) for future payments when the system has attained its full retired membership. This may not occur for 20 or more years in the case of a new system, and it is the misleading factor that has resulted in insolvency for many nonactuarial pension schemes. Under the type of retirement scheme known as the cash disbursement system, current taxpayers pay current benefits only. New members join the retired list each year, and they may continue on the rolls for a considerable period; therefore the amount of current benefits increases substantially until a balance is reached between those who retire and those who leave the system through death. There is no reserve to earn interest, and municipal revenues cannot expand indefinitely; therefore, cash disbursement systems almost always lead to insolvency as do disguised cash systems that provide inadequate reserves against the time when maximum demands are made on the system.

A retirement system may be said to be on a sound actuarial basis when a competent actuary has estimated the future cost or proposed benefits and when contributions plus earnings on investments will provide sufficient funds to pay all fixed benefits. Systems with less than 300 employees should endeavor to join a state retirement system for municipal employees, or merge with federal social security. It is now possible in a few states for police officers to be covered by social security.

Contributions. Contributions to the fund are normally made by the employee and the municipality. A common method for joint contributions is the so-called "50-50" basis, with equal amounts paid by the employees and the employing municipality, excluding the portion required for prior service and for certain collateral benefits. Membership is compulsory. Interest is added to the individual's periodic contributions at regular intervals, and this, with the principal, is generally returned to a member who is separated from the service. In some systems, employee contributions are not returned after a certain period of membership but remain invested until death or eligible retirement age when they are paid back in a reduced retirement allowance. In others, he may receive only his contribution, plus interest upon separation. Although arguments have been advanced in favor of supporting retirement systems wholly out of government contributions or wholly out of employee contributions, reciprocal benefits accrue to both parties and the fairest method seems to be the "jointly contributory" system whereby the government and the employees each contribute a fair proportion.

Eligibility. Eligibility for retirement may be based on age or on the number of years of service, but probably is most often based on a combination of both. Ideally, a retirement system would provide retirement on the basis of age, years of service, and physical and mental condition of employees as related to the duties of given position classes. Attainment of this ideal is still in the future. Age limits for voluntary retirement range from 45 up. Compulsory retirement age limits range from 50 to 72. Years of service required before retirement range from 20 to 30 years. Police and fire pensions, patterned so often after military service plans, are often more liberal than need be. It would seem reasonable to require at least 25 years of service and age 55 for retirement without reduced benefits.

Age, rather than length of service, is the important factor to be considered in fixing the time of retirement. A fixed age, while eliminating many who should be retired, will also separate a few who are fully competent to carry on for a few years. For this reason some systems set an optional retirement age at 60 and make retirement compulsory at 70; either the city or the employee may exercise the option when the employee reaches 60 and at any time thereafter until the mandatory age is reached. Whether compulsory retirement ages are appropriate may be open to question. In the police service where physical demands on the employee are frequently greater than in other branches of the municipal service, the retirement age for those on active patrol duty may need to be lower than for detectives or supervisory officers.

In determining appropriate retirement age there is some conflict between efficiency requirements, which tend to push the age down, and the desire to avoid excessive retirement expenditures, which tend to push the age up. Some systems permit retirement after 20 years of service, an extremely costly provision, and in some cities it is not uncommon to find an employee in his late forties or early fifties drawing a pension from the fire or police department and holding a full-time job in some other department. This is indefensible, and no employee should be permitted to receive a pension while employed in some other capacity by the city. Nor, it may be said, should he be encouraged by an over-liberal pension plan to retire from his normal occupation in the prime of life.

Amount of Pension. Municipalities commonly allow pension payments which together with employee annuities equal one-third to one-half of the average pay for the three to five years preceding retirement. England and Wales, with a well-matured pension system, allow one-half pay after 25 years of service, increasing in equal increments each year thereafter until a maximum of two-thirds is reached after 30 years. This seems a fair plan, if the municipality can afford to take the initial financial steps to provide it. Such a plan should reap a harvest, over a period of years, in improved service.

   In addition to provisions for members grown old in service there should be financial arrangements for the several classes of disabilities occurring in such a service unit. Chief among the disabilities is that incurred while in performance of duty. This class has been discussed in the section on conditions of employment. It is sometimes possible to retrain these men and absorb them into the active payroll. When this is done, their pay scale should be commensurate with the job to which they are assigned, and in accordance with the established pay plan. There are reasonable limits within which human sympathy can be counted upon to make allowances for disparities between compensation and services. While memories are fresh this adjustment may be easy, but time erases the generosity of compassion, and incoming employees may look askance at a fellow employee, even though disabled in service, who is compensated out of proportion to his duties. Such apparent injustices are magnified by opportunities for daily comparisons, and the morale of the entire unit may suffer.[15]

---

[15] For a more extended discussion of retirement plan administration, see *Municipal Personnel Administration* (Chicago: International City Managers' Association, 6th ed., 1960), pp. 214-27.

Chaper 5

TRAINING

Police work today is approaching the status of a profession. While it may be some years before this objective is achieved, the educational preparation and on-the-job training of police officers will materially contribute to it. This chapter is devoted to discussion of post-induction and in-service training of police officers, a basic essential for every police department and for every officer.

General Considerations

Why Training?

In a police department a large number of men work individually and often independently to accomplish the police mission. On occasion — as in disasters, community disturbances, or special investigations — these men must work as a unified team. Further, some phases of police work have become highly specialized, requiring intensive application to attain expertness. The need to develop proficiency in each of the many phases of police work, as well as in the capacity to lead and command men, is clear, but few officers can do this unaided.

Organized training is the means by which officers individually are given the knowledges and skills they require for self-reliant patrol; the police team is afforded sufficient practice in combined operations to insure effective coordination in emergencies; specialists who devote their time to scientific crime detection obtain the technical qualifications they require; and command personnel extend their knowledge of human relations, organization, and administration.

Individual Officers and the Police Team. When recruits are selected so as to insure their intelligence, emotional stability, physical fitness, and integrity, they bring to the job considerable native ability but little knowledge or experience in police work. In a short time they must be prepared to operate alone on the street under a variety of conditions that call for knowledge of laws and ordinances, legal procedures, police practice, and human relations. As they progress they must not only acquire more of the same kind of knowledge but also should develop some specialized understanding of investigative techniques and scientific crime detection. This will enable them to conduct initial investigations and to preserve vital evidence for the specialists in fingerprinting, firearms identification, photography, chemical analysis, physics, and microscopy who follow them on difficult cases. Some of these same officers will become specialists themselves, while others will prepare for command positions. Departmental training, instruction by state and federal law enforcement officers, specialized schools or short-term institutes, and university police administration programs all contribute to the development of the individual officer and fit him for integration into the police team.

175

A police force of individuals working independently can be only partly effective. There must be thorough operational integration, not only in raids, disasters, or manhunts but also in routine functions such as use and care of vehicles, selective enforcement, traffic regulation, or vice control. While police officers operate alone most of the time, they must be sufficiently familiar with the techniques that make a working unit out of the force. His understanding of the mission of each element of the department, of the operating procedures, and of full use of the various channels of communication all contribute to smooth operation. This must be accompanied by sufficient experience to develop proficiency. Training on the job provides the theory and practice necessary to mold a heterogeneous group into a unified, effective force that commands public respect.

Changes in Police Work. In the past 25 years changes have taken place in the employee relations, public relations, and technology of police work as well as in educational preparation for police careers. This has been a continuous process in the entire social structure, and neither additional changes nor their effects are likely to lessen in the next 25 years. Communications, equipment, supervision, and tactics require modification to meet changing conditions, and they become increasingly complex. Therefore experienced officers must be briefed on new developments that will enable them to do their work better and more easily. Recruits must be given thorough grounding in the police function and their relationship to it in order to be equipped for the job. Men do not stay trained. Even if they do not forget what they have learned it is continually made obsolete by improved technology and social changes, and frequent renewal is required to keep it current and useful.

Obstacles to Police Training

Continuous active training of police officers in any department may be impeded by inertia. Inertia takes form in claims of lack of facilities, money, time, or know-how. Yet each of these, appraised coolly, has little substance and more often than not is the rationalization for more subtle resistance.

Every police department has a squad room or an office that can be shifted into training use for part of the day. Chairs, a table, blackboard, and chalk are standard equipment everywhere and can be easily moved from place to place. Schoolrooms can very often be used without cost or for a nominal charge, and projection equipment may also be available at schools. Thus adequate facilities can be obtained with little effort.

Shortage of funds is a common and convenient argument, yet training need not cost anything except the time of the personnel involved and an incidental outlay for textbooks, some of which can even be borrowed from public libraries. (But any city that proposes to conduct extensive training can devote about as much money as it desires to training aids, equipment, and instructors.) Federal funds are available through state boards of vocational education for defraying some of the costs of regular training programs for police officers. The state department of education also has advisers and technicians to assist in preparing and presenting training material. Since this training assistance and some of the costs are financed from federal and state taxes already collected, cities should take advantage of it.

Finding time for the collective training of police officers is one of the difficulties because police are on duty around the clock, and every day of the week is a day off for part of the police force. Therefore, lectures have to be repeated on different days and at different times of the day in order to provide training for all of the force. Some of the time-saving techniques for training that are in use are: providing roll-call training for

15 minutes at the beginning of each shift, requiring training on off-duty time as a regular condition of employment, and scheduling training courses when police activity is the lightest so as to be able to bring in the largest number of men without impairing the efficiency of the department.

The problem of developing men capable of instructing others, of "training the trainers," is another valid training objective. The capacity to teach, and training in how to teach, should be a requirement for every sergeant, since instruction is one of his main day-to-day jobs.

There are many sources available to police officials for outside assistance in securing instructors and developing programs. Among these are police academies of larger cities, universities and special institutes operating in many states, the FBI, the local school system, and state departments of vocational education which conduct instructor training as a regular part of their vocational education curriculum. Thus the means exist for developing local officers to carry on continuous training programs and for using outside personnel to supplement instructors already in the department.

Another obstacle often to be surmounted by the training conscious police chief is that of convincing the city council that training is a necessity, not a luxury. Examples can be used which illustrate that errors made by untrained police officers have often cost the community many times more than would be the cost of training the police. Police administrators should set as their goal for training 1 per cent of their total annual budget.

Much of the spade work of promoting training for police officers has already been done. This is apparent by the existence of many state and local training programs developed by state police forces, police associations, higher educational institutions, boards of vocational education, police courses offered by colleges and universities, and increased enrollments in correspondence courses. The major need now is for local police departments to overcome their own inertia, adopt and expand the training that will raise the standard of law enforcement in local communities, and thus help to elevate police work to a professional status.

Standards in Police Training

The recommendations of a conference of experienced law enforcement officers held under the joint auspices of the Federal Bureau of Investigation and the United States Office of Education are still pertinent to this discussion of training: [1]

1. The major portion of a training program should be functional. This means that the controlling purpose of the program should be to bring about improvement in the performance of the duties of law enforcement officers. When a program is functional in character, it is directed toward:

    a. Providing information needed in the performance of duty, or in meeting responsibilities.
    b. Developing ability to perform duties.
    c. Developing and maintaining high morale. [2]
    d. Developing ability to think clearly and to exercise sound judgment in the performance of duties.

---

[1] Conference Report, *Standards in Police Training* (Washington, D.C.: United States Department of Justice, Federal Bureau of Investigation, 1939), 93pp.
[2] High morale is indicated when cooperation and loyalty prevail and when the members of the organization take pride in their work and in the organization to which they belong.

2. All training programs operated by law enforcement agencies should limit their enrollment to law enforcement officers.

3. Training courses should be set up in prescribed units of instruction arranged on a time schedule.

4. Practical recruit training subsequent to employment should be provided. No organization is too small either to maintain such training or to participate in a joint program serving several small departments.

5. Instructors of police training should be qualified in at least four particulars, as follows:

a. Knowledge of the job based upon successful experience.
b. Sufficient general education to meet instructional demands.
c. Ability to apply good training methods in instructional work.
d. Such personal characteristics as are important for instructors.

6. Working conditions affecting the training program should be sufficiently favorable to make it possible to do a satisfactory job. Some of the more important conditions, which can be varied widely to meet local conditions, include:

a. Time schedules: time of day, length of periods.
b. Frequency of class meetings.
c. Classroom facilities.
d. Equipment and supplies.
e. Requirements concerning attendance.

In 1949 a special committee of the International Association of Chiefs of Police made three specific recommendations regarding the training of recruit and regular policemen[3] which are also still basically sound, although many jurisdictions have raised these requirements:

1. For recruits, a minimum of four weeks of training between appointment and assignment.

2. For regular officers, a refresher course each year, a minimum of 48 hours.

3. Training of all sergeants as instructors so that patrolmen will receive some instruction each day at roll call and on their posts.

Some progress toward standardization of police training has been brought about by national, state, and regional schools and college curricula. In the last 25 years the FBI National Academy has trained 3,800 officers of city police departments who are expected to conduct local training programs. Regional or state programs, such as the Southern Police Institute at the University of Louisville; basic and advanced short courses and specialized courses, such as at Michigan State University; and peace officers' training schools such as at the University of Kansas, also graduate several hundred officers in both command and subordinate positions each year. While local training courses must be adapted to fit local conditions, when one or more officers in a community attends a national or regional school the effect is to broaden and raise the local conception of training.

Several states, by statute, have set up minimum standards for police, whereby every new officer must satisfactorily complete an approved recruit training course

---

[3] "Police Education and Training Report," *Police Chiefs' News*, January, 1949, p. 6.

within a certain period of time and meet other minimum standards before he can be permanently employed. These standards are drawn up by a council composed of representative law enforcement officials. This is another step toward professionalizing the police services.

Training Needs

There are six principal phases of police training: (1) induction training of recruits; (2) continuation training of recruits throughout their probationary period; (3) refresher and advanced training of experienced police officers, including presentation of new methods in such areas as traffic control, juvenile delinquency, and investigation; (4) training of command officers in supervision, departmental objectives, and administration; (5) pre- and post-employment university training; and (6) specialist training such as identification, juvenile work, criminal investigation, interrogation techniques, and traffic administration.

Each division of police service and all ranks of officers should be included in the training program. Specific aspects of training for these groups are discussed in this chapter.

Vocational Education Assistance

Federal vocational education acts were passed in 1917 and broadened in 1946 and 1958 in recognition of the need for promotion and encouragement of organized training for employees in government and industry. Under these acts annual appropriations are allocated for salaries and traveling expenses of teachers, supervisors, and directors of public service training. The funds appropriated are allocated to states and territories on the basis of their nonfarm populations and are available to states and local communities on a matching basis for use in local, regional, and state training programs.

The appropriation is not earmarked for specific courses, and its use is determined entirely by the educational authorities in vocational education (specifically trade and industrial education or public service training). The funds must be used for less-than-college-grade training. A city or a police department interested in a particular field of training must request the instructional and financial aid it desires. Ordinarily, vocational education funds are administered by local public school boards. Availability of the federal appropriations has proved a stimulus to police training, and cities should request assistance whenever they feel they can utilize it. Contacts for assistance should be made with one of the following: (1) the local vocational education director or supervisor of trade and industrial education (superintendent of schools if neither exists), (2) the state supervisor of trade and industrial education, or (3) the state director of vocational education.

Federal and state funds are available through state boards of vocational education for defraying some of the costs of regular training programs for police officers. The state departments of education also have advisers and consultants to assist in preparing and presenting training material. Cities should take advantage of every opportunity to utilize available resources.

The most recent vocational education legislation embodied in the National Defense Education Act of 1958 provides for the support of *highly skilled technicians*. In order to qualify for training in these occupations, it is incumbent that the training be for technicians who will be (1) highly skilled, (2) in recognized occupations requiring scientific knowledge, and (3) in fields necessary for the national defense. Substantiation must be made by surveys and occupational analyses.

The California Plan. The California plan for police training conducted by the state department of education has been in operation since 1931 and is probably the oldest police officers' training program operating with vocational education funds. It is organized so that all law enforcement agencies within the state may participate. These include members of local police departments, district attorneys, sheriffs, special agents of private corporations, and agents of federal and state law enforcement agencies. The plan also provides for pre-employment training of men and women who plan to enter the public service in some branch of law enforcement work.

The purpose of the California plan is to provide an organized training program for all law enforcement officers, including the fundamentals of police work for recruits and advanced work for experienced officers. It is conducted by the bureau of trade and industrial education of the state department of education. The state supervisor of peace officers' training is appointed primarily on the basis of his police experience — a minimum of seven years — and he must also possess a class "A" vocational education teaching credential. To assist the supervisor in formulating effective training programs based on local needs, there is a state-wide advisory committee made up of technicians in the field and representatives of governmental and professional organizations.

The bureau provides technical and financial aid to public officials and educational institutions in six areas of police training: (1) departmental training schools for individual agencies such as police departments and school districts; (2) zone training schools for cooperative training among several law enforcement agencies in a county or other geographical area; (3) pre-employment educational programs in cooperation with junior colleges, state colleges, and other institutions of higher learning; (4) an annual two-week "technical institute" for full-time law enforcement officers in cooperation with the FBI; (5) training of peace officers as instructors for departmental and zone training schools; and (6) training of supervisory officers in conference leadership.[4]

The California Plan is an effective program. Other states have the same theoretical potential and would do well to follow this example.

Types of Training Programs

Four principal types of training programs for law enforcement officers can be identified from the material in this chapter: (1) local programs, (2) zone schools, (3) institutes or short courses, and (4) extended college and university training in police administration, criminology, and specialized police fields. Each of these has advantages for particular training situations, but closer analysis will reveal specific benefits and shortcomings with each type of organization.

Local Training Programs

Local training programs have many advantages. They are best suited to meet local training needs and build *esprit de corps;* they maintain local control over scope and

---

[4]Police officers may obtain a list of reference materials developed by experienced peace officers and used for instructional purposes in the California Peace Officers' Training Program from the State Supervisor of Peace Officers' Training, 1014 Ninth Street, Sacramento 14.

objectives of training; they involve no travel cost while providing opportunity to study at home; they stimulate favorable publicity for the department; they provide opportunity for free discussion of problems; they offer opportunity to clear up misunderstandings; and they encourage mutual understanding and respect among participants.

Apparent disadvantages of local training programs are the difficulty in small agencies of finding suitable instructors with time to develop training programs and possible limitation of outside contacts and thinking — a tendency to become "ingrown." Local training should be the assigned responsibility of a member of the force. This might be the chief in a small force. The departmental personnel officer or a specially designated training supervisor on up to a ranking officer with a considerable staff should supervise training in the largest departments.

Larger police agencies operate continuous police training programs. Many provide three months of continuous full-time training to their recruits before they are assigned to regular duty. Facilities of such departments are often made available to members of near-by smaller forces. Medium-sized and smaller cities also may operate part-time schools or combine their own staff with instructors from other law enforcement agencies (municipal, state, and federal) to train recruits.

Zone Schools

These are set up to serve a county or other geographical area embracing several law enforcement agencies, promote uniformity of law enforcement work, and facilitate cooperation among neighboring communities in communications and operations. Zone schools may have permanent staffs partially financed by state vocational training funds or other agencies, or they may convene only periodically, using instructors from the several participating departments or other sources.

Disadvantages of zone schools from the standpoint of any local community are that travel distance and cost may interfere with attendance and prevent continuous use of facilities and instructors, and material covered must be more general in scope thus perhaps not meeting specific local needs.

Institute or Short Courses

Institute or short courses are from a few days to several weeks' duration, conducted at a central location, and many serve an entire state or multistate region. They range from general basic or recruit training to specialized courses, such as command officer training, investigators' courses, or courses in traffic records. The advantages are better instructors, personal contact among other officers from many departments, and improved facilities. The police officers, being away from their normal responsibilities and worries, can be regimented into an environment that will provide the maximum learning with the most lasting benefit in the shortest period of time.

The disadvantages are that the departments are without the services of the student officers; there is the expense of travel and tuition; and fewer officers can benefit from such training.

College and University Training

Several colleges and universities provide extended training in police and related fields as described in a subsequent section of this chapter. Such training ranges from one quarter (11 or 12 weeks) to an academic program of four years or more. (These and many other colleges and universities also participate extensively in local programs, zone schools, and institutes and short courses.) In general, the same advantages and disadvantages apply as in institutes or short courses.

Basic Recruit Training

Before a police recruit can perform the simplest police task he must have assimilated a wide field of knowledge. Most other occupations are so different from police work that the average recruit will have no background or experience even remotely comparable to it. When a police recruit completes the entrance examinations and qualifies for a position on the force, he is eager to complete his training, take his place on the street, and leave his "rookie" days as rapidly as possible. How, then, is he to receive this training so that he can qualify as a full-fledged policeman?

Constructive Induction

Veteran members of the force should be prepared to receive the recruit constructively. They should assist him at every opportunity and refrain from undue criticism. Mild "hazing" can be expected in forces with high morale, and it contributes to a recruit's adjustment. If experienced policemen are slow to accept a rookie as an equal until he has proved himself, a certain amount of this reserve is justified. But hazing should not be allowed to get out of hand, nor should a recruit be belittled or made to appear ridiculous before the public. Supervising officers should maintain a clear distinction between the antics of accepting a rookie into the police brotherhood and the steps required to assure his qualifications as a law enforcement officer. If he makes a mistake, he should be corrected in private. In this way he is made to understand that police work is a dignified and serious business.

Much of the training the recruit must master is dry and uninteresting in its raw form. Laws, ordinances, regulations, and rules of evidence should be presented in easy stages. Their purpose and value should be explained and, when possible, related to the recruit's background and experience. It is unnecessary and undesirable to start beginners with long hours in the classroom, subjecting them to continuous lectures and requiring them to memorize long passages of written material. Methods of presentation ought to be diversified, with motion pictures, field trips, first aid, discussion, and pupil participation encouraged and mixed with lectures. There should be frequent examinations over the material covered. This tests both the recruit and the instructors and impresses the recruit with the need to seriously apply himself.

Qualified Instructors

Instructors both in the classroom and in the field should be given training in their task and should be able to salt their lectures with interesting examples, personal experiences, and field examples. The training school day should be divided into lecture and discussion or question sessions, gymnasium periods, and a tour of actually patrolling a district in company with an older officer. This latter method of training, traditional in police work, should be carefully planned and executed. Some departments develop manuals to remind instructors of their obligations to the recruit and to outline the field training program.

For example, in general patrol work the instructor must explain each situation that arises during the course of the patrol. If there is opportunity, he must handle each situation in the presence of the recruit, and if possible enable the recruit to handle a similar situation himself. This method has brought excellent results and is highly recommended because it provides the instructor with a checklist for training the recruit and a means of recording his progress in specific instances. In these departments, all field instructors are brought together for frequent conferences during the training period to discuss programs of the recruits and to receive information on methods of instruction. The average recruit will enjoy his field training more than the classroom variety, and when the two are integrated so he can see the fruits of his classroom training in actual field experience, a well-rounded training program will be achieved.

Police officials cannot give too much attention to recruit training, for it is during the first days or weeks in the department that the recruit forms attitudes and opinions of the service that may influence him for years and perhaps even during his entire working life.

Content of Recruit Training

In planning a recruit training course, care must be exercised to select the subjects that will contribute most to the development of the men in the time available. If the course is not carefully planned from the recruit point of view, relatively unimportant subjects may be overemphasized and important ones neglected. The topics discussed below might be considered a minimum in a police recruit training course. They appear in the course outlines of several schools and can be expanded or compressed to fit the amount of time that can be devoted to a basic training course.

These subjects are discussed in order of importance according to the amount of time devoted to them in the basic peace officers' training course of the California State Department of Education.[5] The course was developed by a selected group of law enforcement officials. The program consists of 180 hours in fundamental police subjects (see Figure 21) and is given two or three times a year to city and other police officers in California. Recruits from Berkeley, for example, attend the school following appointment but before assignment to regular duty. The city pays their salaries, travel expenses, and board and room while in attendance.

First Aid. Qualified and competent Red Cross instructors are available in every community, so the Red Cross training can be omitted from centralized, and more expensive recruit schools, thus lessening the number of hours of the total course or providing these hours for more technical subjects.

Police Procedures. These deal with the most common police duties. A number of these procedures are mentioned below:

1. Investigation Principles. Patrolmen make the initial investigations of accidents and crimes, since they are generally the first to arrive and have primary responsibility for conditions on their beats. Recruits must be given some understanding of the habits and methods of criminals, methods of investigation, and what evidence to look for and what to save for the specialists.

---

[5] *Report of Conference for the Development of a Peace Officer Training Curriculum* (Sacramento: California State Department of Education, 1948), 39pp. The report contains, besides the suggested curriculum, a description of each course.

SUBJECT	HOURS
Public Relations	6
Introduction and Miscellaneous Subjects	3
Notebooks — Note Taking (School and Field)	5
Race Relations	2
Firearms	12
Self Defense	12
Court Appearance and Conduct	2
Care and Use of Departmental Equipment	1
Crowd Control: Civil Disturbances and Riot Control	4
First Aid	18
Patrol Procedures and Observations	8
Fundamentals of Penal Code and Related Laws	10
Report Writing, *Modus Operandi* Report	8
Juvenile Procedure	4
Transportation of Prisoners and Insane Persons	1
Mechanics of Arrest	6
Searches and Seizures	2
Law of Arrest	4
Rules of Evidence	6
Value of Scientific Aid	4
Police Procedures	18
Principles of Investigation	12
Traffic	12
Interviews and Interrogation	8
Fundamentals of Civil Process	8
Powers and Duties of the Sheriff	4
Total Hours	180

Figure 21 — Basic Peace Officers' Training Course,
California State Department of Education

2. Traffic. A recruit must be made aware that traffic occupies a great share of time and skill of any patrolman. He must become skillful in point traffic control for crowds or special events, investigating accidents, the importance of enforcement of both moving and parking violations, the correct and tactful approach to the traffic violator, and how to recognize a traffic hazard on his beat and how to report it.

3. Patrol and Observation. Most of the police force spends most of its time on patrol. During this time officers develop the confidence of citizens as they render such services as checking businesses, vacant homes, and responding to complaints. They develop their powers of observation, detecting and interrogating suspicious persons in cars and on foot.

4. Interviews and Interrogation. Officers may have to question regular residents and strangers on their beats, and they may be called upon to interrogate suspects who are not disposed to talk. Each situation requires a different approach, and recruits should be given general rules to follow in each type of case.

5. Crowd Control. Fires, picket lines, accidents, and public events, as well as riots and other disturbances, attract large groups of people who must be dispersed or restrained. Recruits should learn the procedures for individual as well as combined operations in maintaining order among such groups, and they should understand the civil rights relating to free speech and public assembly.

6. Mechanics of Arrest. An arrest potentially is a hazardous procedure. An officer must learn habitually to use methods that will effect the arrest with the greatest possible safety. Individuals have certain rights of person and property which police officers are obligated to observe. Rookies should learn early in their careers what these rights are and how to treat cooperative as well as disorderly individuals.

7. Report Writing. Clear, accurate reporting is the backbone of any police department. Correct report writing is a skill that can be developed with training and practice. Since officers will always have to write reports, the art of preparing reports correctly must be developed early in police service.

8. Juveniles. Recruits should learn the nature and extent of the juvenile problem in their community and be familiar with methods of juvenile crime prevention.

9. Court Appearance and Conduct. This topic includes court procedures, conduct on the witness stand, methods of questioning used by attorneys, and the proper way to present testimony.

10. Transportation of Prisoners and Mentally Ill Persons. Officers should know the recommended procedures for preventing violence or escape when prisoners or mentally ill people are being transported.

Weapons. Because use of the revolver is seldom required, and then only in crises, recruits should be thoroughly schooled first, in when to use it, then in how to use and maintain it. Sufficient pistol firing should be required to establish automatic reflexes in firing technique and to establish good safety habits. Revolver practice should include the FBI Practical Pistol course which simulates actual field conditions or similar practical training. New officers also should become familiar with other weapons in the police arsenal — rifle, riot gun, gas gun and grenades, and machine gun.

Self Defense. Judo or jujitsu is a highly practical means of self defense without weapons that makes use of an opponent's strength and weight to disable and control him. In the recruit school judo may be combined with boxing, wrestling, calisthenics, and close order drill to increase physical fitness and defensive ability. A second aim of calisthenics and drill is to teach discipline and unity of action.

Laws and Ordinances. Knowing the laws and ordinances to the patrolman is as basic as mathematics to the engineer. He should become familiar enough with the law so that he will know where and how to find answers when his recruit training is over.

Legal and Judicial Procedures. Recruits should be given sufficient background in the operation of courts and in the legal basis of their own activities to make effective arrests. Subjects which should be covered include rules of evidence, the law of arrest, the law of searches and seizures, powers and duties of police officers, and criminal procedure.

Public Relations. Most police contacts are with the ordinary citizen who reports a crime, seeks assistance or information, or who has committed a minor violation. Proper relationship with these people is essential to a successful police operation. The recruit must learn that he represents both the police department and the city government to the many people who notice him because of his uniform. He must learn how to act and dress so as to create maximum respect.

Scientific Aids. Basic training of recruits should include some understanding of scientific aids to crime detection — fingerprinting, ballistics, photography, chemical analysis, physics, and microscopy. This will help the officer to recognize, protect, and preserve evidence discovered in preliminary investigation.

Use and Care of Equipment. Morale in police departments, as in military units, generally is reflected by the care given to uniforms, personal equipment, and vehicles. A high standard of personal appearance should be inculcated in recruits from their first day. Emphasis should be placed on safe and proper operation of police cars. Many departments now include a course in how to drive as safe and carefully as possible on emergency runs.

Sociology and Criminology. Well-rounded police work includes some conception of the causes and cures for social tension and criminality. Recruits may bring to their new occupation long-standing prejudices regarding nationality, racial, and religious groups. Misconceptions and prejudices should be replaced with general factual data. Training should be given on the social composition of the community, areas and causes of probable tension, constructive and degenerative forces at work in the community, areas of specific types of frequent crimes, and ways to identify harmful social conditions.

Geography, Rules, Local Organization. Knowledge of local geography is essential. Basic information for recruits should include location of state and county trunklines, street names and the numbering system, location of prominent landmarks and buildings, and location of natural barriers with their relation to the street pattern.

Departmental rules include personnel regulations, such as vacation and sick leave; rules of personal conduct, such as appearance and reporting for duty; and operating procedures in various kinds of routine and emergency situations, such as auto and foot patrol, checking business houses or vacant homes, stopping suspicious cars, and establishing blockades. Combined operations that are used infrequently should be practiced from time to time to assure efficiency when needed.

Police recruits should gain some conception of the command structure and the functions of each unit or division of the force. They should learn the general functions and operations of other city departments. They should know the relations of the police department to other branches of the city government so as to feel at home in the family of city government.

Other Training. The purpose of the police academy or basic training school is to give recruits enough of an over-all view of police work to fit them for regular duty under guidance of an experienced officer and to provide a basis for further learning on the job. Some police officials may wish to add subjects other than those described here that will further contribute to the effectiveness of rookie officers, such as public speaking, record keeping, or jail procedure.

Recruit Training as Part of the Selection Process

The recruit school provides the most favorable time and conditions for instructing rookies in basic concepts and procedures of police work. It also gives commanding officers and the personnel agency significant opportunity to corroborate selection procedures and to determine the possible future worth of each recruit. The close and continuous surveillance that is possible in a recruit school will ordinarily never again be duplicated. Each instructor who observes an officer for any considerable period of time should carefully rate his performance both in the classroom and in the field and attempt to evaluate his probable future potential in the police service. Temperament and personality should be noted and compared with results in the selection tests. If discrepancies appear they should be investigated quickly and closely in order to confirm the man's fitness to continue in the service, as well as the reliability of the tests used.

Intelligence and alertness as exhibited during the training period should also be compared with the entrance tests. Negative signs will suggest either that improper testing methods have been used -- which will be unlikely if standardized tests were employed -- or that the individual is lazy or has some other character fault which prevents him from doing his best work. The recruit school should uncover the occasional employment hazard who slips through in the initial selection process. The police officer on probation and in recruit school is on better behavior and is making more effort than he will after his appointment is confirmed. If certain characteristics are noticeable during this period, one might expect them to be even more evident later. Therefore, clear-cut cases should be washed out immediately, while those that are doubtful can be extended into the probationary period when the officer goes on full-time duty.

If a man is not eliminated during the recruit school or the remainder of his probationary period, the department, in effect, acknowledges that it has done all it can to test him and has found him suitable for permanent membership on the force. Since it is properly more difficult for officers to be removed from the force after they have completed their probationary period satisfactorily, police officials should use the training and probationary period stringently to cull out those rookie officers who do not show promise of being a credit to the department. When in doubt always resolve in favor of the city. Additional material on the probationary period as a part of the selection process appears in Chapter 4.

New York and California Programs

Discussion of basic recruit training would not be complete without mention of the programs authorized in 1960 by the state legislatures in New York and California. Both programs are intended to promote the basic training of municipal police officers by establishing minimum courses of instruction for recruits and making other provisions for in-service training.

The eight-member Municipal Police Training Council was created in New York to combine minimum standards of police training and to make recommendations to the governor concerning police training schools. A second provision of the law calls for satisfactory completion of the prescribed training course and certification as a prerequisite for permanent appointment as a police officer of any county, city, town, village, or police district in the state of New York.

The Council may recommend to the governor rules and regulations with respect to such matters as approval of municipal police training schools; minimum courses of study, attendance requirements, equipment and facilities at approved schools; minimum qualifications for instructors; and requirements for minimum basic training and advanced in-service training programs.

The executive director, to be appointed by the governor, has the responsibility to certify instructors, approve schools, and certify police officers who have successfully completed basic training. He also is responsible for making studies and surveys regarding municipal training schools; cooperating with schools in the development of advanced in-service training; cooperating with colleges, universities, and institutes for development of courses in police science and administration; and cooperating with other state agencies in police training.

California created in the department of justice a Commission on Peace Officer Standards and Training, consisting of nine members appointed by the governor. The Commission is required to establish standards for recruitment and training of local peace officers. A peace officer training fund was created in the state treasury supported by assessments equal to 5 per cent of fines and forfeitures other than for vehicle code violations. The Commission is authorized to allocate to counties and cities, which have made application, the money needed to pay one-half of the salary paid to peace officers while they participate in training programs approved by the Commission.

Advanced In-Service Training

When a rookie graduates from his basic training course, whether it has been given locally in the department or at a zone training center, he will have the bare essentials for starting his service on a regular assignment. The recruit school should create an appetite with the recruit for more study. Properly, his training should continue under the guidance of a veteran officer and he may continue to attend training classes. Experienced officers also should be given advanced or refresher training from time to time to keep them mentally active and aware of current developments in the field and to qualify them for promotion.

Continued Training for Recruits

Training of recruits should be extended beyond the recruit school to provide systematic broadening of the background of each man and to assure that questions and problems arising on his tour of duty are answered to his satisfaction. Officers who have attended a centralized basic course, such as those in Michigan or California, may be given intensive supplemental training when they return to their own department; or, as after completion of a departmental training course, they may be assigned directly to field work. This duty assignment is customarily the midnight to 8:00 a.m. shift — least desirable from the standpoint of veteran officers, lightest in work load, and out of the public eye.

One example of a continuation training program for recruits can be taken from Berkeley, California. Here, men who have completed their basic training at the centralized school report to a training sergeant on the midnight to 8:00 a.m. shift, receiving full-time on-the-job training for one month, principally in local subjects — regulations, history and organization of the department, and city ordinances -- but also some supplemental work in first aid and typing.

Pasadena, California, also places responsibility for further training on the patrol sergeant during duty hours and provides him with a recruit training manual. This lists all of the procedures a patrolman must perform before he is considered a finished product. The manual contains three columns for checkmarks by the supervisor — one to indicate he has explained a procedure to the recruit, a second to show he has demonstrated it, the third to verify that the patrolman himself has shown mastery of the assignment.

The recruit keeps the manual in his possession for reference and study during the training program.

After a rookie is oriented to departmental operations and the work on his beat, formal training may be further reduced. Thus Glendale, California, substitutes weekly conferences for daily classes during the initial period of application of the principles and information learned in the recruit school. With the help of a qualified instructor, these new patrolmen discuss the problems they have encountered in their daily work or which are presented by supervising officers.

Continued Training for Experienced Officers

Specific training for experienced patrolmen keeps them mentally active, apprises them of new developments in the police field and in their local departments, and prepares for promotion those who are qualified. Changes in police work evolve from changing social patterns and technology. Crowded urban conditions encourage development of criminality and make criminals harder to discover. Such social conditions, and criminal adoption of scientific advances, have required ingenuity and adaptation by the police. Each gives occasion for retraining police officers.

There are other reasons besides changing social patterns and technology for periodic briefing of veteran officers. One is to keep the men informed of the composite crime picture in their community and conscious of their over-all effectiveness. Another is to maintain selective enforcement — emphasis on eradication of particular crimes or misdemeanors that are causing the most trouble in the community or that are impairing the departmental record and prestige.

Briefing on new ordinances and laws also provides occasion for departmental training sessions. Not only must the purpose and effect of new regulations be spelled out and understood, but a progressive plan of enforcement must be adopted. Recent federal and state court decisions and what they mean to the operating police officer must be examined as soon as possible, and the department policy in light of the new decisions must be carefully explained.

An occasional session can profitably be devoted to discussion of new problems facing the police and of complaints received from the public, means of correcting them, and progress made since the last session. This kind of clinic presumes careful records and frequency tabulations of complaints as well as careful follow-up and reporting procedures when requests are received and disposed of.

Police officers who have been in the habit of getting together frequently to keep abreast of local conditions and effective tactics should respond more effectively to minor or major crises than if they had not been accustomed to collective thinking and action. They will more enthusiastically support departmental policies if they feel they have had a hand in developing them through these periodic meetings.

Roll Call Training. A technique of providing continuous departmental training was inaugurated in the Los Angeles Police Department in the fall of 1948 in the form of a roll call training procedure utilizing printed material to facilitate instruction.[6] It was first handled through a short discussion period at roll call time. Later the plan was extended to all divisions, and the roll call period was lengthened to allow an uninterrupted training period of 15 minutes each day.

---

[6] W. A. Worton, *Roll Call Training* (Los Angeles: Police Department, 1949), 6pp. Los Angeles Police Department, *Daily Training Bulletin*, Volumes I and II (Springfield, Illinois: Charles C Thomas, Publisher, 1954 and 1958).

Since field supervisors were too occupied with their regular duties to spend the time necessary for research in preparing teaching material, a field unit of the training division was created to do this work. This unit conducted a survey in which over 20 per cent of the officers of the department suggested subjects they thought should be covered. This means of curriculum selection was considered a most important aspect of the roll call program.

Roll call training was carried on seven days a week, the first five days devoted to teaching, discussing, and reviewing material prepared by the field training unit. These lessons consisted of information on topics suggested in the survey and on other problems confronting the officers. Two days a week were reserved for special review of previous lessons or to the discussion of divisional problems.

To supplement the instruction given during the roll call period, a two-page "Daily Training Bulletin" was issued each time new material was taught. The bulletins were illustrated with cartoons to aid in presentation of the material (see Figure 22), numbered consecutively, and punched to fit a standard notebook.

Information in the training bulletins often was not available from any published source, so the Los Angeles Police Department developed some of the material from conferences and interviews among officers and supervisors. For example, a series of bulletins on how policemen could improve their chances of apprehending an armed robber originated from a conference of men who had been successful in this phase of work. More than 250 sergeants and lieutenants in the department were trained in the techniques of teaching, and these officers conducted the daily training sessions.

The practicality of this type of training is indicated by the subjects covered in the first 100 bulletins. The titles of nearly all started with the words "How to" and dealt with such subjects as use of the field telephone, developing a good oddity file, care of automotive equipment, making a burglary report, determining intoxication, controlling civil disturbances, and testifying effectively in court.

Since the original roll call training procedure was developed by the Los Angeles department, many other police departments have now developed their own roll call training plans with some variations. Some are on a weekly basis.

Suggested Advanced Curriculum. The same group representing the California department of education that developed the recruit training program described above also commended an intermediate curriculum for continuation training of police officers with the subjects listed below. Some of the topics are new while others carry forward subjects introduced in the recruit course:

Police Tactics
Patrol Procedures
Police Procedures
Civil Cases Reported as Criminal Offenses
Techniques of Investigation
Penal Code and Related Criminal Laws
Juvenile Control
Note Taking (field)
First Aid
Typing
Raids
Road Blocks and Covering Plans

Photography
Public Speaking
Departmental Rules and Regulations
Reading for Self-Improvement
Mental Illness (psychiatry)
Law of Evidence
Collection, Preservation, Identification
    and Storage of Evidence
Criminal Laboratory and Scientific Aids
Interrogation
Crime Prevention and Repression
    (not juvenile)

Self Defense and Offense Techniques
Firearms, Gas and Explosives
Race Relations and Minority Groups
Subversive Activities
Civil Process and Procedure
Municipal Organization
Installation and Use of Recording Devices
Surveillance
Federal and Military Agencies
Crowd Control
Civil Disturbance Control
Mutual Aid
Laws of Arrest
Court Procedure and Conduct
Techniques and Mechanics of Arrest
Search and Seizure
Identification
Description of Persons
Description of Property

Communications
Records
Report Writing
Departmental Orders
Extradition
Supervisory Officer Training
Public Relations
Jails, Detention and Custodial Care
Classification of Prisoners
Care and Use of Departmental Equipment
Traffic Enforcement
Traffic Division Organization
Traffic Accident Investigation
Sources of Police Information and
　Confidential Informants
Vice
Statements and Confessions
Undercover Investigations

Some departments provide special training for veteran officers only occasionally. The Detroit Police Academy, for example, schedules courses only when a special need arises. Other departments run continuous programs for a good part of the year. In Berkeley police training is conducted through the evening trade school and runs concurrently with the school year. The program is supervised by the state department of education, and instructors are paid from vocational education funds.

Employee training is a function of the central personnel office in Berkeley, but for police courses the personnel director is assisted by a training advisory committee of five members of the police department of various ranks and a school system representative. The committee suggests courses to be offered, recommends instructors, decides what courses should be given, and determines which members should attend. Courses are given weekly in two-hour sessions, and each session is repeated three times on different days and at different hours and thus gives everyone in the department three opportunities each week to attend. Mandatory attendance varies according to the course content and training needs of individual officers. Those attending classes do so on off-duty time and are credited with one hour of recoverable overtime for each two hours in class. Courses are selected from those in the suggested curriculum listed above.

Departmental Library. No department should overlook the training possibilities of a departmental library. A modest appropriation will suffice to establish an up-to-date collection of fundamental police books. A selected bibliography of basic literature in the police field, published by the International Association of Chiefs of Police, is a useful guide to establishing a library.[7] While some of the more frequently used books must be kept available for reference purposes, a local department should have no difficulty in working out a loan system for reading and study in off-duty hours.

Books selected for the library should be classified by major subjects and a classified list should be furnished to all members of the force, with periodic revisions. In

---

[7] Also see Bibliography in this book for selected references. For a more detailed list of standard references in the police field and for new books and pamphlets issued each year see the police section in the current *Municipal Year Book*.

Daily Training Bulletin

LOS ANGELES POLICE DEPARTMENT
VOLUME II, BULLETIN 1   **FIELD TRAINING UNIT**

W. A. WORTON, CHIEF OF POLICE
Friday, January 13, 1950

HOW TO CONDUCT FIELD INTERROGATIONS--PEDESTRIANS--I

Officers who obtain good results from field interrogations are successful because they have developed a suspicious nature, are keenly observant, and are attentive to apparently insignificant details. Recently, an alert officer, by his perception and quick analysis of circumstances, was able to effect the arrest of a long-sought burglar because of a field interrogation. The officer observed a man walking along the sidewalk at a late hour, carrying a bag of groceries. The fact that all the grocery stores in the neighborhood had been closed for a considerable time aroused the officer's suspicion. A careful interrogation resulted in an admission by the suspect that he had committed a series of burglaries. He had averted suspicion by habitually carrying a bag of groceries at night when prowling. Although this ruse had deceived officers on many occasions, one officer by his attention to detail had observed that something was out of place and by thorough investigation was able to make the arrest.

DETERMINING WHOM TO INTERROGATE: There is no hard and fast rule which will determine when a field interrogation should be made. The decision to interrogate a person must be based upon the circumstances of each individual case. Generally, the circumstances will involve *time, place, appearance and actions of a person*. When one or more of these elements appears to be out of the ordinary, it may indicate that an interrogation should be made.

An officer cannot expect that every interrogation will lead to an immediate arrest. Investigations of seemingly identical sets of conditions will not always produce the same result. However, it is worthwhile to consider some examples of circumstances under which arrests have been made as a result of field interrogations.

Source: Reprinted by special permission of the Los Angeles Police Department. Copyright, 1950, by the City of Los Angeles Police Department.

Figure 22 — Example of Roll Call Training Bulletin

These examples are general "suspicion-arousers" and should not be considered as being the only circumstances under which field interrogations should be made. However, alertness to such indications coupled with a knowledge of criminal operations should enable an officer to make more satisfactory "shakedowns."

UNUSUAL DRESS OR APPEARANCE: Persons who do not "fit" the surroundings are good subjects for interrogation. For example, shabbily dressed persons in a wealthy neighborhood, persons wearing sneakers at night, persons wearing a combination of new and old clothing, or persons wearing or carrying unseasonal clothing should usually be investigated.

UNUSUAL OR SUSPICIOUS ACTIONS: An officer should be alert for individuals whose actions appear unusual. He should be suspicious of persons who are carrying large bundles, suitcases, barracks bags, tool boxes, etc., at a time when such activity would not be usual. A person who seems unreasonably nervous upon meeting an officer or one who turns onto a side street or who crosses to the opposite side of the street as the officer approaches might be a good subject for interrogation. If a man is observed following a woman, the need for questioning might be indicated. Others who may warrant investigation are persons who feign intoxication, those who move rapidly from between buildings or from alleys and then slacken their pace or attempt to blend with a crowd upon reaching a busy street, and persons who dispose of objects as an officer approaches. Even if the object appears to be only an empty cigarette package, it should be investigated.

SUSPICIOUS GROUPS: An officer should be alert for groups that disperse as he approaches, as those who leave a group hurriedly may do so to divert attention from one who stands his ground and who may have something in his possession that he wishes to conceal from the officer.

LOITERERS: Loitering in itself is not unusual, but when coupled with other circumstances may often indicate that an interrogation should be made. Persons who loiter in darkened doorways, persons loitering on dark streets near parked automobiles, in the vicinity of calls, about business houses near closing time, in and about transportation centers, or around locations where crimes have recently been committed should be interrogated. Persons who loiter in or around banks, check cashing establishments, or "hangouts" of known criminals and perverts should also be investigated.

FOLLOWING SUSPICIOUS PERSONS: It may often be desirable to follow a person whose actions arouse suspicion. For example, one who appears to be walking aimlessly through parking lots may be an auto thief. He will often walk through several lots before choosing an automobile to steal. In such cases, a premature interrogation may only succeed in forcing the suspect to operate in another area, while by following him and waiting until he performs an overt act or actually attempts to steal a car, officers may have a much better opportunity to effect an arrest.

(Prepared from material obtained in a conference on October 6, 1949, attended by Lt. S. L. Posner, Central Division; Lt. J. W. Powers, Robbery Division; Sgt. H. E. Donlan, Central Division; Sgt. O. H. Tucker, Accident Investigation Division; Sgt. M.V. Duncan, Administrative Vice Division; Sgt. M. H. Ricks, University Division; Ofcr. W. R. Danheiser, Wilshire Division; Ofcr. M. L. Schwartz, Central Division; and Ofcr. F. M. Snedeker, Newton Street Division.)

Figure 22 — Roll Call Training Bulletin (continued)

addition, a record of loans placed in each man's personnel folder will build up his record, encourage outside reading, and enable the personnel officer to spot promotional material and men with special interests. Such a library also offers opportunity for continuation training of commanding officers as well as those in the ranks.

One police department runs a regular reading course for supervisory officers, a device that other departments might follow with profit. The procedure provides for each new officer to read one book a month for a year and to write a review of each book. A two-hour session each month gives the men a chance to discuss application of the principles they have read to problems in the department. For the second year the requirement is one book a quarter, and periodic assignments are made each year thereafter. Some of the suggested books included in this program are in the field of industrial management and deal with problems of leadership, supervision, and applied psychology.

Another means for making the best use of available literature is to clip magazine or journal articles, classify them, and assign them to the proper ranking officers for use in training their subordinates. Best use of a departmental library requires that one person be made responsible for authorizing book purchases, making reading assignments, and stimulating interest. The departmental personnel officer or training officer is the logical man for this task, but in small departments any commander can be detailed.

Specialized In-Service Training

Sooner or later as officers develop experience some will demonstrate interest and aptitude for a special phase of police work. They will have been aided in making this progress by the basic and secondary training they have received and by the attention and guidance of supervising officers. Those who demonstrate special aptitude should be encouraged and aided to take advanced training. This may be either in specialties, such as traffic, juvenile control, or laboratory techniques, or in supervision and administration.

Police Specialties

Only a few agencies offer extensive specialized work for policemen. Attendance at these schools is selective and men commonly go on scholarships or fellowships. Another group of institutions offers short-term courses. These usually require payment of modest tuition or registration fees.

Traffic. The Northwestern University Traffic Institute in Evanston, Illinois, offers a number of unit courses and one extensive advanced course for police traffic officers.[8] The advanced course, covering a full academic year, is for officers capable of planning and executing sound traffic control programs. Candidates for this course are selected competitively and each attends the Institute on a fellowship or scholarship. The nine-month program is divided into four sections: nonpolice highway transportation agencies and problems; functions of traffic police; management of police services; and general education, including writing, speech, and social science courses. As a final step, each officer visits a police department similar in size and other characteristics to his own for a one-week investigation of its traffic operation. He then returns to the school and spends a week in preparing a report and recommendations from the observations he has made. This report is used only for education of the officer and is not made available to the department visited.

---

[8] *Program and Objectives* (Evanston, Illinois: Northwestern University Traffic Institute, 1960), 12pp.

Unit courses of one to five weeks' duration are held at the Traffic Institute throughout the academic year. There are no academic prerequisites and no screening of registrants. Most of these courses are designed primarily for supervisory and command officers who have specific responsibilities in subject areas. The training is aimed at methods to improve these operations through better supervision, training, and use of management guides. Typical subjects include accident investigation, law enforcement, traffic direction and control, chemical tests for intoxication, traffic law, supervision of police personnel, personnel management, training methods and programs, police traffic records, and introduction to police management.

The Traffic Institute also cooperates with local or regional law enforcement agencies and educational institutions in providing a limited number of traffic training courses at departmental schools or cooperating universities.

Through the cooperation of local civic and support groups, a limited number of grants-in-aid are available for some of the unit and regional courses. Information on these can be had by writing the Director, The Traffic Institute, Evanston, Illinois.

Juvenile Delinquency Control. The Delinquency Control Institute was established by the University of Southern California to provide specialized training for law enforcement officers in understanding and working with youth. This school is discussed in some detail in Chapter 6.

Other Training Areas. Institutes of one to four weeks are held in various parts of the country for officers interested in some special field of police activity.

As an example, the School of Police Administration and Public Safety of Michigan State University in East Lansing offers 14 to 20 short courses, some repeated once or twice a year, in such fields as Police Juvenile Officers' Training Course, Criminal Investigation Course, Traffic Law Enforcement Course, Command Officers Training Course, and Fundamentals of Traffic Engineering (for those who have the traffic engineering responsibilities in the cities that do not have graduate traffic engineers). A seminar for law enforcement administrators also is conducted once or twice a year depending on the demand of the police chiefs and sheriffs associations. The School also sponsors an annual national institute on police-community relations, attended by top police officials and community leaders from throughout the nation, where the problems that cause tensions and police incidents are discussed.

The Southern Police Institute of the University of Louisville, the Traffic Institute of Northwestern University, the Traffic Safety Institute of Purdue University, and the Police Training Center at the University of Indiana are a few of the other institutions that sponsor short courses in advanced training for police.

Supervisory Training

Supervisory and administrative officers, like recruits and regular patrolmen, will do their jobs better if they are trained. Awareness of this is mounting, and the evidence supports those who have pioneered in insisting on the worth of training leaders and commanders — the International Association of Chiefs of Police, the FBI through its National Academy, the International City Managers' Association, some colleges and universities, and police administrators like August Vollmer and O. W. Wilson.

It is well established that training, to be successful, must begin at the top. In police service this maxim implies both that commanding officers must accept the principle of training for the men they command and that they must themselves be prepared intellectually and temperamentally to fulfill the responsibilities of their positions. Administrative police work demands not only the highest technical competence but also a thorough appreciation of personnel psychology, personnel management, and administration. Officers who consider that training and personal development are for other men will ultimately find themselves crowded by the ambition of those under them and oppressed by the demands of the situation around and above them. The results are personal frustration and personal and departmental mediocrity — for men as well as officers.

Opportunities for administrative training exist in only a few agencies, but in these the training is of such quality as to establish a high standard for the entire police profession. These agencies for administrative training will be discussed in the section below. The number of officers they can train in any reasonable time is slight in comparison with the potential, so that expansion and multiplication of facilities like them should have high priority among police officials and educators.

The Federal Bureau of Investigation offers its full resources for the training of law enforcement personnel through its National Academy. Two sessions of the National Academy, comprised of approximately 60 men each, are held annually; each session lasts 12 weeks. A candidate to the National Academy must be nominated by the head of his department; where the prospective candidate is a head of the department, he must be nominated by his superior. The nominating official gives careful consideration as to which of his men will be best able to grasp a tremendous amount of information in a short period of time and be able to impart what he has learned to his fellow officers. No more than one man from a single agency may attend a specific session, since the aim of the National Academy is to provide trained administrators and instructors for the largest possible number of police departments. No tuition is charged.

The curriculum of the Academy is continually adapted to meet changing needs of law enforcement. Some of the subjects included are police organization and administration, police records, investigating methods and techniques, scientific aids in crime detection, traffic control, uses of photography in law enforcement, and independent research in law enforcement and teaching techniques. In addition, all candidates take rugged physical training including disarming tactics, and they must qualify on the FBI weapons course. Emphasis is given to command and administrative aspects of police work. The Police Academy was started in 1935, and during the next 25 years the FBI National Academy graduated more than 3,800 officers, each equipped to pass on to his fellow officers the valuable knowledge and training gained through 12 weeks of concentrated hard work.

National Academy graduates continue close relationships with each other and with the FBI, through the FBI National Academy Associates, and its regional chapters throughout the United States. In addition, the *National Academy Newsletter,* distributed bimonthly to the members of the National Academy Associates, keeps them informed of the progress and experiences of other graduates.

Municipal Police Administration. The International City Managers' Association has offered an in-service training course based on this textbook since 1938. The course is open to individuals by correspondence and to groups on a conference method plan of round-table discussion. In both cases the participants answer prepared questions which require applying the text material to analysis and evaluation of local operating conditions, problems, and procedures.

Answers to these lesson questions are prepared in written form and submitted for review and comment by an instructor who is himself an active police official. With groups, the report represents a composite of the group thinking developed by discussion. A typical group consists of 12 to 15 police officers who meet once every week for a two-hour session under the guidance of a local discussion leader. Training usually is given on city time, and enrollment and textbook costs are borne by the city. Enrollees who complete the course are awarded certificates as evidence of satisfactory performance.

In one recent year, police officers from 17 cities in 14 states enrolled in groups in the police administration course with an average attendance of 14 members per group. Four of these cities were under 15,000 population. Group on-the-job training offers several advantages to local police departments. The one most frequently cited by officials themselves is the satisfaction of those who participate in being permitted freewheeling discussion and criticism of methods described in the text and practiced in their own departments. Formal changes in rules, organization, or operating methods result from about one out of seven of these group training courses, and improvements in morale, supervision, and divisional or interdepartmental cooperation are frequently mentioned by officers who complete the course.

Southern Police Institute. The Southern Police Institute, University of Louisville, is an advanced training school for law enforcement officers. It was established in 1951 to meet the need for higher and more comprehensive training than that available within local departments.

The Institute is financed by the Ford Foundation, the city and University of Louisville, and other eastern and southern foundations. Its regular (long) course is given twice a year, in the spring and in the fall. This term lasts for 12 weeks and covers 420 hours of instruction. Enrollment is limited to 30 specially selected law enforcement officers. Preference is given to applicants holding commanding, supervisory, and administrative positions within their departments. All officers attend on tuition scholarships. Graduates who meet University of Louisville qualifications receive 12 semester hours of credit from the University.

In the three-month period between the fall and spring terms, the Institute presents a program of mid-winter seminars. Four two-week seminars are offered annually in January, February, and March. Subjects of major importance in law enforcement are covered. Thirty officers are accepted for each seminar.

Training is directed along practical lines and includes the latest methods in crime detection and prevention. Major emphasis is given to police organization and administration, traffic control and engineering, psychology, and psychiatry. Socio-economic studies and police ethics are also included, and the Institute is pioneering in special techniques for handling disorders and tensions resulting from disagreements between various racial, social, and economic groups.

The Michigan Plan. The Michigan Plan developed out of the four-year undergraduate police administration course offered at Michigan State University and the need for training city police officers. Besides the basic and juvenile courses mentioned earlier, the school now offers a one-week command officers' training course twice a year and a one-week administrators' traffic course annually. The command officers' course deals primarily with human relations and supervision in such areas as personnel selection, factors affecting morale and behavior, maintaining discipline and foundations of leadership, but it also includes material on police history and general organization, field supervision, and use of statistical records.

The Traffic Highway Safety Center at Michigan State University assists in traffic courses which deal with traffic management, safety education and public support development, accident investigation, and related subjects. Out-state personnel as well as members of local police agencies may participate in any of the Michigan courses in a limited number.

Other Supervisory Training. Cities that have any doubt about their own adequacy to prepare and administer training programs for supervising police officers can safely and profitably look outside their own organizations for assistance. Local high schools and colleges frequently have considerable civic interest as well as personnel capable of preparing adequate training programs. Ogden, Utah, presented its initial program in Municipal Police Administration in cooperation with the local college and the state board for vocational education, and this original administration course quickly grew into several others.

The Detroit Police Academy has developed special supervisory training courses for sergeants and lieutenants, and the New York Police Academy regularly conducts an officers' training school to which members of smaller departments may be admitted in limited number.

Police officials can profitably use staff meetings as a means of training, for not all training need be formal. The city managers of several cities, among them East Lansing, Michigan, and Eau Claire, Wisconsin, have used a booklet published by the International City Managers' Association that deals with management economies as the basis for departmental staff conferences.[9] These cities not only used the booklet for administrative discussions, but made the checklist the basis for departmental action in programming administrative improvements.

These suggestions for outside aid should be considered as examples, rather than limits. Any police official who recognizes the need, which is great, for having a corps of sharply trained, alert field supervisors can undoubtedly obtain first-rate assistance close at hand if he does not already have it within his own organization.

University Training for Police Officers

In the past two decades the number of universities and colleges that offer organized programs of study in some aspect of criminology has reached substantial proportions. Some of the programs are designed primarily for the undergraduate student who is preparing himself for service in some field of criminal justice. Others are in-service training programs, restricted to regular employees of law enforcement agencies. The tendency of all of them is to raise police work from the level of an occupation with primary emphasis on physical and enforcement aspects to that of a profession concerned with social forces, human motivation, and crime prevention.

College level training in police administration combines the specialties of police work with broad liberal arts training. In varying degree, depending on a particular institution's interpretation of its educational mission, it relates the solution of law enforcement problems to social and cultural considerations.

Probably the first course designed for police training in a large university in this country was offered at the University of California summer session at Berkeley in 1916.

---

[9] *Checklist on How To Improve Municipal Services* (Chicago: International City Managers' Association, 1958), 62pp. The police section of this booklet has 78 questions on administration, personnel, operational and equipment phases of police work and another 50 on transportation, several of which apply to the police department.

The first organized undergraduate program of training for prospective policemen was offered at San Jose State College in 1931. Michigan State University introduced a somewhat similar program in 1934.

Nearly all of the programs require basic educational preparation equivalent to two years of liberal arts — introductory courses in sociology, political science, psychology, economics, English, public speaking, physiology, basic science, statistics, military science, and physical education. Courses that relate specifically to the field of criminology are given in some colleges during the last two undergraduate years while others spread them throughout all four undergraduate years.

Pre-Service Training

The curriculum at Michigan State University may be considered representative of universities offering pre-service education for men and women desiring careers in law enforcement work. It has six fields of specialization.

1. The Law Enforcement Administration Program is designed for those students who desire a general, well-rounded background preparatory to career service in law enforcement agencies. Upon graduation they may seek employment with local, state, and federal law enforcement agencies. Beginning employment will ordinarily start in the lower echelons.

2. The Police Science-Criminalistics courses are for students who wish to go into laboratory and scientific crime detection work. The core of this program is similar to that of a chemistry major, thereby providing the student with an opportunity to acquire a second degree in chemistry upon completion of certain additional courses, or to continue his studies in the graduate level in one of the several forensic science specialized areas. Graduates are eligible to apply for positions in scientific crime detection laboratories at the federal, state, and local levels. The graduate can assume a position of minor responsibility in a police science laboratory without difficulty.

3. The Prevention and Control of Delinquency and Crime studies are designed for those who will follow a program emphasizing social science and social work. This program is followed by specific courses providing the information and training necessary to plan, organize, and administer prevention programs. Graduates seek career opportunities with police departments, local community organizations, state youth commissions, and public and private agencies concerned with delinquency prevention and control.

4. The Correctional Administration Area students specialize in probation, parole, and institutional programming. Specific training in administration, counseling, and education is provided. They may seek career opportunities in probation and parole systems and in public and private institutional work at the federal, state, and local levels.

5. The Program of Highway Traffic Administration is designed for those students who plan on entering governmental service at the state or local level in activities related to the management of the motor vehicle transportation system. This would include police service, driver licensing, and motor vehicle administration, and the work of safety commissions or work in safety councils or in associations whose objectives include greater efficiency in motor vehicle transportation.

6. The Industrial Security Administration program includes an orientation in law enforcement with a major emphasis on industrial and commercial perspective. The studies are similar to the law enforcement administration majors, but courses stress, describe, and evaluate the objectives, functions, and activities of security and protection

programs as carried on by private agencies. Graduates may seek employment with a wide range of private organizations, such as insurance companies, banks, retail merchandising enterprises, industrial plants, and transportation agencies.

The Michigan State University plan provides a 20-week field service training program for the first two terms of the student's senior year. In this field work, the students move about among several municipal departments, the state police, other state agencies, the sheriff's office, an industrial plant, courts, and federal agencies. Those specializing in the correctional field spend time in penal institutions and in parole and probation offices. The highway traffic administration field work takes students to safety councils, safety commissions, and highway engineering departments. They file daily and weekly reports that are graded and recorded by the School.

The final term of the senior year is spent on campus taking a seminar type course designed to correlate field training experience with the theoretical material in the curriculum. In addition, the student writes a research report on some phase of law enforcement work.

Michigan State University also offers graduate studies in each of the six areas. Candidates continue more intensive studies in their fields together with research, experimentation, consultation, conferences, and institutes. They work closely with the organizations that operate criminal justice programs.

Most universities already offer a wide variety of courses useful to prospective police officers — courses in government, law, English, psychology, sociology, and the physical sciences. A rearrangement of existing courses, with the addition of a few specialized police courses, often will suffice to create an adequate curriculum of police training. Only one qualified instructor with police experience usually needs to be added to the instructional staff at the start.

Admission Requirements. The admission requirements vary from no restrictions at the University of California (beyond general admission to the university) to requirements comparable to those for appointment to police departments using progressive selection methods.

For example, applicants for the police curriculum at the State College of Washington, in addition to general admission requirements, must possess certain basic qualifications for police service, including robust health, mental balance, and the intelligence and aptitude required for success as a police officer. At the time of admission they must pass a comprehensive entrance examination with a superior score. This battery of tests is the equivalent of police entrance examinations in the strictest American police departments.

In addition, a rigid character investigation is made of all applicants, and each year of the four-year professional training program may be considered as part of a screening process. A student may be disqualified at any time for further study in the police major if he fails to meet the standards of scholarship and performance prescribed by the department. Each applicant admitted to the police curriculum must present to the head of the department a letter of recommendation from the chief of police in his home town.

In-Service Training

Advanced in-service law enforcement training such as that at the University of Southern California holds great promise for ultimate professionalization of the police service. The University offers four kinds of educational programs in police administration, and each of the four stresses previous law enforcement experience.

1. Bachelor of science degree with law enforcement as the field of concentration, requiring a two-year liberal arts background, and combining three additional groups of courses of equal weight — police science and administration, public administration, and social science electives. This course is similar to those described under Pre-Service Training but has an in-service emphasis.

2. Graduate programs leading to master of science and doctor's degrees in public administration, with emphasis on personal and professional maturity, administrative ability, and demonstrated capacity for original thinking and research in the law enforcement field. A considerable emphasis is placed on preparing graduate students for teaching and research in universities and colleges.

3. Certificates in public administration with law enforcement as the major field — a two-year course for mature police officers who do not have the educational background to become degree candidates.

4. Selected courses for police officers who do not care about the degree programs but desire specialized work in various phases of police technique and procedure. Courses are open to any officer regularly employed who desires to take college work without pursuing a formal program. The courses are the same as those offered in the degree and certificate curricula.

This four-point program takes up where basic recruit and advanced vocational training leave off, by integrating a cultural and broadly social education with the vocational elements in law enforcement work.[10] It replaces mandatory attendance with voluntary self-development, but the program has made such advances into the police community of southern California as virtually to require every officer who desires advancement to prepare himself by means of one of the programs offered.

In any college educational program, graduate and upper-division undergraduate work generally requires considerable independent research and thought, as well as verbal expression, both oral and written. Advanced research into the methods and philosophy of law enforcement and crime prevention, particularly at the graduate level, as at USC, presents opportunities for applying the disciplines of the physical and social sciences to the suppression of antisocial behavior represented by delinquency, criminality, and vice. This program represents a significant advance on the way to police professionalization.

Coordination of Training and Service

There is need for further coordination of university training programs and the law enforcement services for which the students are being prepared for several reasons: (1) universities should provide the kind of training that will best fit potential officers for useful police careers; (2) police (or probation, parole, and correctional) agencies provide a realistic field "laboratory" in which students can test their academic training; (3) agencies can utilize the talents of student interns and will benefit from placement of graduates who have some knowledge of agency operations; (4) graduates and agencies may have trouble finding each other unless there is close placement liaison between agencies and schools.

Close coordination has been effected in some of the universities. For example, a distinguishing feature of the Michigan State University program is its field training offering balance between theory and practice and enabling the student to compare his knowledge to the actual operation.

---

[10] See Donal E. J. MacNamara, "Higher Police Training at the University Level," *Journal of Criminal Law and Criminology*, January-February, 1950, pp. 657-65.

Training Methods

Perhaps nothing contributes more to a police training school than permanence and continuity. A staff that devotes its energies continuously to the development of curriculum, acquisition of material and equipment, improvement of training techniques and subject matter, and enlistment of expert instructors will ordinarily reap benefits for the department far in excess of its cost. Even the smallest nucleus of a permanent staff is important to maintain if the police budget and the size of the force will permit.

Qualifications of Instructors

After permanence, which permits systematic preparation for the school, the qualifications of instructors must be considered. They must have a good knowledge of their subject or they cannot teach it adequately. They will need teaching technique in order to do the job effectively. Personality and character will be important factors in their success — extroversion to give students the sense of vitality many academic subjects otherwise lack, self-discipline and industry to set a good example, good humor, and intellectual honesty. A permanent staff and visiting instructors should complement each other. Not every lecturer need be dry, nor a first-rate humorist; nor does every drill instructor need be a martinet. But all should appreciate their topic and have some effective way to put it across.

The California State Department of Education has set an example for other states in providing instructors and instructors' schools for local departments and regions. All instructors have teaching certificates, and the instructors' schools are limited to training in techniques of instruction rather than in subject matter. Other states have potentially similar, but less extensive programs, and some are frankly waiting for urging by cities before attempting to organize extensive local training. Vocational education funds, as previously mentioned, can be used for both instructor training and the preparation of teaching materials through local school boards or a state agency.

Laws and ordinances are particularly difficult to teach, requiring a nice balance between understanding and rote memory. Law is the "crystallized, enforceable, social morality" of a people and should be perceived as such rather than as arbitrary rules for harassment or regulations to be broken or evaded with impunity. Instructors should be skillful in imparting this concept as well as in analyzing specific ordinances and giving them vitality with examples of everyday enforcement.

A procedure manual with rules and regulations can serve both as a training aid for instructors and students and as a guide to the new policeman in carrying out his work. However, a manual cannot describe the minutiae of the policeman's approach to situations, since no two incidents will ever be identical. The logic and principles of action can be developed in the training program, giving the officer a foundation for exercising his own reason and good judgment.

Instructors should plan lectures, discussions, and written examinations carefully. Blackboard illustrations, demonstrations, slides, visual cast projections, and films to supplement lectures should be employed whenever they can be of practical value in the teaching scheme. Actual objects should be used as examples whenever feasible. In their absence models may be substituted.

Training Films

Motion picture films are excellent training devices, provided they are used as aids rather than as ends in themselves. The drama, plus visual and audio presentation, heightens perception and understanding. No training film should ever be shown in classes unless the instructor has reviewed and outlined it first, noting significant points to bring to the attention of the students. Each showing should be preceded by a briefing so that the students will be alerted to observe important points. After the movie, a short discussion or quiz should be held to re-emphasize the key ideas.

A number of films have been made for specific police training; still others, while not designed for this purpose, make suitable training aids. Army training films can be obtained from the film libraries of Army installations, and other films are available through commercial or state university film rental libraries. A number of law enforcement agencies have made films for training their own personnel.

Dramatic Teaching Devices

Every useful teaching device may be profitably brought into play. Appeal may be made through the eye, ear, touch, taste, and smell. The art of dramatic surprise may be employed to lend emphasis to desirable situations and to aid retention. No practical aid to the teaching art should be ignored. The FBI National Academy, for example, has been extremely successful in simulating actual crime situations where students can practice investigation techniques. The student group may enter a disordered room where a "crime" has just been committed and find a freshly murdered dummy on the floor. A "rogue's den" is set up to resemble a hideout for kidnappers or bank robbers. A special model of a country estate gives the students practice in maneuvering a force to prevent the escape of a criminal. Such devices lend reality to instruction and test the capacity of the students to absorb and apply the teaching.

Four-Step Teaching Process

Some value may be attached to the four-step process of teaching which has been accepted as standard in the field of vocational education. These four steps are (1) preparation — being sure that the student's mind is ready to receive information; (2) presentation — giving the student the new knowledge or demonstrating the new operation; (3) application — giving the student an opportunity to apply his newly gained knowledge; (4) the test — checking the ability of the student to perform the operation or to apply the knowledge in a new situation. Another summary of the teaching process in lighter vein is the preacher's description of his sermons in which he said, "I tell 'em what I'm going to tell 'em, then I tell 'em, and I wind up by tellin' 'em what I told 'em."

The conference procedure is also a valid teaching device which is particularly appropriate for weekly departmental meetings. Thought-provoking questions and typical cases may be used in the group to analyze basic problems; the experience and thought of each member of the group will be brought to bear on the problem.

The most successful instructor is not the one who puts the greatest number of questions. The highest values will come from stimulating the student to learn. An instructor will demand discipline and promptness in attendance; he himself must set the example. He must be patient and display a genuine interest in his students.

All of the energy that goes into these training programs will be of far-reaching benefit to the police service and to the public. It should improve the prestige of the police in public esteem. Public approval should itself react favorably to stimulate the self-respect of the service.

Chapter 6

JUVENILES

Perhaps no police responsibility has eluded precise definition for so long a time as that involved in work with juveniles. It has been extremely difficult to draw a line to mark the limit of proper police action in this field. On the one hand, students of police administration are generally hostile to the pressures that result in expansion of police work into other than traditional functions, not only in juvenile work but in all phases of police activity. At the other extreme are people with a social service point of view who see in the nature of police work an opportunity for effective rehabilitative action by policemen, an opportunity that a social service agency cannot have.

The moderate position, lying somewhere between these extremes, has never been fully articulated with precision, largely because of the difficulty in defining how and under what conditions these divergent positions can be brought closely together (if not completely reconciled) to permit the use of police experience and opportunities without undue disruption of normal police functions. This is a continuing police problem, one that is best viewed within the context of the broad background of ideas and philosophies which affect police work with juveniles. The first part of this chapter deals with this background. The remaining sections deal with organization and administration of juvenile units.

The "Juvenile Problem"

The "juvenile problem" has received considerable attention in recent years. The "problem," of course, extends well beyond the police sphere of activity and is the concern of many professional people in education, recreation, and social work. Much has been written and said, but as to the scope of the problem there is little agreement. "Overwhelming" say those persons alarmed by what the youngsters do; "about what it has always been" say others who tend to downgrade the significance of antisocial and criminal activities of young people. There is as little agreement on the roots of the problem and its solution.

It is not entirely possible to separate the police sphere of work with juveniles from other spheres. Yet there is a tendency to equate the "juvenile problem" with juvenile lawlessness with which the police are directly concerned. A number of experienced officers, the Delinquency Control Institute at the University of Southern California, and the Children's Bureau of the U. S. Department of Health, Education, and Welfare, have made definite progress in developing sound organizational, administrative, and operational techniques for police units working with juveniles. This section leans heavily upon their work.[1]

---

[1] Reported in U. S. Children's Bureau, *Police Services for Juveniles* (Washington, D. C.: Government Printing Office, 1954).

The definition of a juvenile varies from state to state. It also varies from city to city within those states that have only loosely limited local discretion on this point. A survey made as part of an American Municipal Association study in 1957 indicates the breadth of the term "juvenile."[2]

A total of 141 cities over 50,000 reported the upper age limit of the juvenile classification. In only two (New York and Little Rock) were all youths of less than "legal" (21 years) age subject to classification as juveniles. In all of the rest of the cities, the range was between 15 and 18 years, broken down as follows: 15 years, 12 cities; 16 years, 30 cities; 17 years, 64 cities; and 18 years, 33 cities.

Usually the age limits apply equally to boys and girls, but in 17 cities the maximum age for classification of girls as juveniles was one or two years higher than for boys. Among other factors shown to influence classification of a young person as a juvenile was whether he or she is still attending school.

Extent of the Problem

No one knows for certain just how much juvenile delinquency has increased. It apparently has, and at first glance the statistics look pretty dark. For example, in 1959 (for the 11th consecutive year) cases disposed of by juvenile courts increased. Table 2 shows the increase in crime in the under-21 age group for a five-year period. However, while all of these data are accurately tabulated by the reporting agency, there are many factors that seriously affect the validity of what these figures seem to show.

Population Growth. In the first place, the number of persons under 21 has increased disproportionately in the past 10 years. The only other group with a higher-than-average increase in number are the older people, but they have gone into a natural decline in their criminal activities, probably because of age. So a part of this increase can be attributed to a higher proportion of juveniles in the population. In any case, these data reported by the FBI are the best available. The FBI has limited itself to carefully defined crimes and is using a reporting method that has been well developed over a period of time.

Terminology. When data are reported from some other sources and for offenses other than the major crimes shown above, great care must be taken in their interpretation.

Table 2

Per Cent of Total Crimes Committed by Persons
Under 21 Years of Age

Classification	1953	1958
All offenses	14.7	19.7
Criminal homicide	12.2	14.9
Robbery	36.4	43.4
Burglary	63.2	65.0
Larceny	51.2	60.9
Auto theft	69.8	79.3

Source: Federal Bureau of Investigation, *Uniform Crime Reports*.

---

[2] J. L. Levin. *How Cities Control Juvenile Delinquency.* (Chicago: American Municipal Association, 1957). Table 1, pp. 6-9.

Even more care must be taken if two cities are to be compared. The true picture is rarely seen because of many sources of error.

One major difficulty is a difference in terminology. Just who is a delinquent? Must he have committed a crime or is it enough that he was "incorrigible," a term that covers almost everything a child might do? Are neglected children (where the parents are at fault) reported in some part of the total mass? Except for the FBI crime reports of major offenses, juvenile delinquency reporting has a long way to go.

Effects of Social Change. There are many other sources of distortion. Many a child, along with his parents, has been moving into urban areas. He no longer lives in the small town where an offended neighbor took him home by the ear and that was the last of that. The urban neighbor calls the police, and we have another tally mark on our chart.

A major factor that results in a marked apparent increase is more vigorous police activity. Many police juvenile units have been established, older ones have been reorganized, and training has increased. As a result, the police do a more careful job of reporting. Beat officers now call for the juvenile unit instead of scaring the kid and sending him home. The public, realizing that the police are doing a better job, now calls them when something happens. And we add whole rows of tally marks.

Other changes have resulted in a true increase. Contacts, and along with them chances to get in trouble, have increased. The anonymity of the city allows children to at least try to do things they could not do in a community where everyone knew them. The small town policeman who knew every kid in town has been replaced by a much more efficient but distant policeman who hardly sees them as he drives by in his squad car, until they get into trouble. One of the reasons the family moved into town was so that the mother could get a job. Even if she doesn't work, the father spends an extra hour or so getting to and from his job so that his time spent with his family is less. All of these factors combine, and the juveniles on the borderline get into trouble.

Another major factor is economic. There has been a high rate of employment generally, and many juveniles can get good jobs, and with them a sort of independence that is not always good. With their money they can buy an automobile. Even if they can't find a job or don't need to, they still may get a car. Again their contacts increase; again they become even more anonymous as they get into new neighborhoods and new towns. A whole new group of ways of getting into trouble with the police have opened up for them. Many of them will act even less mature than the average adult driver, and down to the station they go. The temptation to get gas, or tires, accessories, or a new battery proves to be too great, and they steal. We have one more tally mark.

Conclusions. Even if we are not sure of the significance of our figures, one fact remains. This field of juvenile delinquency, however defined, is a major police problem, but a problem that can be adequately controlled by the application of sound police methods. The importance of police attention to juvenile delinquents is underscored by the other general conclusions that can be drawn about the problem and its relationship to police work.

First, nearly all serious adult criminals have been juvenile offenders, although some may not have been apprehended as juvenile offenders.

Second, the number of crimes committed by youths, based on police crime statistics, is much greater than the proportion of youths in the entire population.

Third, more than 70 per cent of juvenile court cases originate with the police.

Juveniles Are Not Adults

Perhaps the most important principle underlying the approach of police, prosecuting authorities, and the judiciary toward juvenile delinquency is the acceptance of the fact that juveniles are not adults. It is a principle that must be kept in mind when attempting to define the scope of police activity in the field.

Abilities Vary. Most adults can and do accept responsibility for essential self-discipline, voluntarily controlling their natural instincts and inclinations which generally motivate unlawful conduct. The law recognizes that all individuals do not possess identical ability to discipline themselves voluntarily. This has led to special provisions for dealing with violators who are mentally incompetent or subject to compulsions beyond their control. Similar reasoning is applied to juveniles — they are not considered sufficiently mature to meet and to be judged by adult standards of responsibility for conduct.

As commonly used, the word "juvenile" connotes a state of immaturity or incomplete development. As used here, it refers to children and adolescents accorded a special status under the law. Thus, cases involving misconduct by people within this age group are treated in a manner substantially different from that applied to adult offenders.

State Responsibility. Although most states permit juveniles to be tried as adults, unlawful conduct by juveniles is generally termed delinquency and is dealt with in a special juvenile court. Trial in such a court may be termed an acceptance of special responsibility by the state, rather than as a legally guaranteed right of the juvenile. In most cases, trial in juvenile court may be withheld by the prosecuting or judicial authority and action which may lead to a grand jury indictment must be taken. It is possible for two youths of identical age to be tried for similar offenses in different courts, using different methods, within the same jurisdiction.

The juvenile court processes are not considered to involve legal jeopardy and are not rigidly circumscribed by essential observance of the individual's legal rights, as are criminal court procedures. The major difference may be defined as a marked change in focus; the juvenile court being concerned with benefiting and protecting society, with due regard to the individual's legal rights.

It is to be regretted deeply that this special status and its implications are not more fully understood, accepted, and implemented by all persons concerned with the proper character development of children. This same special status and its implications may be recognized in the vast variety of public health, safety, education, labor, and welfare laws and services specifically designed to benefit and protect our children and youth. Many of these beneficient laws deny to children rights and privileges guaranteed by the Constitution to adults, thus clearly establishing their dependent status under the law.

The Task of Other Agencies. Police and others concerned with the cause and correction of attitudes conducive to delinquent behavior frequently are in conflict. The difficulties arise because police responsibility must be focused on the individual as a violator, while other professional effort seeks to focus on the violator as an individual who is in need of special help to become a self-disciplining member of society. When taken together, both of these will be seen as interrelated efforts toward a common objective.

The matter of cooperation becomes important when workers with street corner gangs and other "hard-to-reach" groups acquire knowledge of a committed or contemplated crime. Generally, no legal status of confidentialness exists in these cases. It may be noted, however, that by tradition and custom there is recognized a considerable degree of latitude in dealing with minor violations by adults and that this latitude is extended when juveniles are involved. In the interest of assuring cooperative effort toward the objective, the police and other professions can and should establish standards for permissive action in connection with knowledge of unlawful conduct.

It must be emphasized that police concern with violations, as distinct from concern with violators, is an essential, inescapable responsibility. No violation of the law will be capriciously ignored by the competent police officer.

A Major Question. There is a tendency to oversimplify the relationship between environment and causation in delinquent behavior. Frequently, those finding a record of deficiencies in home, neighborhood, or associates come up with a cure that looks simple. For example, if the boy comes from a neighborhood where his status is likely to be rated on how many crimes he can commit without getting caught, then the answer is to put him in a better neighborhood. Unfortunately, the answers are not as easy as they first appear, nor do they work by themselves.

Yet despite the difficult problems that arise, it is possible to rehabilitate many juveniles. For one thing the causes are apparent, if not crystal clear; for another, the juvenile is less set in his ways than an adult offender. Finally, the law permits rehabilitation efforts not possible in attempts to reform adults. Police see all of these possibilities and how they would apply to youngsters they come into contact with. The temptation to try to put the possibilities into practice is great. Besides it's a good way to get personal satisfaction and publicity. Most people like kids. As a result, a picture of a policeman with a group of predelinquent baseball players gathered around him goes over big in the newspaper — even though the story on another page complains that the department is undermanned. The big question is: "How deeply should police become involved?"

A national emphasis on prevention of crime, particularly among young people, has important implications when attempts are made to answer this question. Primarily it focuses attention upon organization, criteria for staffing and training, span of supervisory command, and the relationship of the police department to the community. Particularly in regard to the latter, preventive programs require a high order of teamwork which involves public and private agencies serving the economic, social, recreational, religious, educational, medical, and psychological needs not only of the individual youth, but of the family. It requires a common acceptance and understanding of the principles and techniques of youth service and the integral value and relationship of each type of public and private agency to the other.

The Police Position

The police function has been defined as the protection of the life, property, and rights of all people and the preservation of order. We must constantly review this definition and apply it strictly, say many policemen. We must always remember that the police are oriented toward the protection of the victim; that decisions involving assistance to the victim as against helping the offender must be resolved in favor of the victim. Other public and private agencies are concerned with the offender, and the police must not decide to usurp their responsibilities. Such decisions often occur in juvenile work.

This distinction is most difficult to hold to because juveniles present a much different problem from the adult offender. Society recognized this long ago, and the resulting philosophy is now a part of our social structure. It is often charged that modern methods coddle young offenders and are of no value. These charges are valid if police fail to properly use the methods as a result of a lack of ability, knowledge, or facilities. But it has been proven, time and time again, that a complete, well operated program gives excellent results.

The police administrator must constantly be on guard to see that he does not become too deeply engrossed in social work even though he himself wants to do something personal for some of the unfortunate kids he sees every day. If juveniles agencies are inadequate, or if the personnel of these agencies are a little lazy, it is all too easy for the police to find they are developing a comprehensive program far outside the area of primary police functions. When there is no adequate community program for juveniles, it is most difficult for a police administrator to say that he will not allow the department to develop such a program. But he must come to this decision. If he does not, or if he allows such a program as a stop-gap measure until the community can get organized, he will find the program will be always with him. Why should the agencies whose duty it is to establish a program act when the police are already doing a good job? The two activities where the police have particularly overextended themselves are recreation and voluntary supervision. These activities occur so frequently that each will be discussed in some detail.

Police Juvenile Recreation Programs. Police organize, direct, and sponsor many sorts of recreational activity: boys clubs, Boy Scout troops, athletic leagues, firearms training classes, junior police, and so on. They may be elaborate programs financed by money collected from local businessmen by police officers; they may be weak, the sponsoring groups meeting for a few times and then losing their original drive.

The American Municipal Association survey mentioned earlier noticed "one unmistakable trend" among the reporting cities. This is the police entry into the recreation field, particularly by means of police athletic leagues and related athletic programs. Supervised "hot rod" clubs and municipal "drag strips" also have attracted the attention of people (including police) who hope to divert youthful interests into healthy channels. It should be noted, however, that automobile safety groups have strongly condemned drag strips.

It must be stressed that the basic philosophy of recreation as a device to reduce juvenile delinquency is open to serious question. The Children's Bureau says, "Research indicates that providing additional recreation facilities in an area usually does not bring about significant change in the volume of juvenile delinquency. ... Recreation won't solve the deep-seated problems which beset delinquent or pre-delinquent youngsters who need individualized guidance and treatment, nor is it supposed to." This must not be taken to mean that recreation programs for everyone are not a good thing, but rather that they are of not much help to reducing juvenile delinquency. They certainly are of even less help if they are not a part of a well-rounded, skillfully developed program giving individual guidance.

This is not easy for many people to believe. It seems obvious that if a child is kept busy playing baseball or doing bead work, he will not have time to get into trouble. There is also a vague feeling that the child will be so appreciative of the program and so admire the fine men and women directing it that, out of sheer gratitude he will not get into trouble. This may be true of most children, but not delinquents. The very reason that they are classified as "delinquent" is because they don't conform, that their interests are different.

This discussion does not mean that the police should totally disregard recreational programs. If such programs are lacking or inadequate, the police can very well point out the problem and give limited advice to the people establishing and later directing such a program. Neither does this discussion mean that interested police officers should not participate in such programs while not on duty. If they have an interest in these things, it is an entirely worthwhile activity.

Police Voluntary Supervision. Police voluntary supervision may be defined as "any supervision given by police officers to a juvenile after an offense has been committed."[3] Here again there is considerable disagreement as to the role of the police. One of the first points of difference goes back again to the fundamental duties of the police. In spending considerable time serving the offender, can the police best fulfill their obligation to the victim? One argument in favor of voluntary supervision is based on the belief that such supervision does prevent crime by preventing occurrence. If this argument is to be accepted, the police then must consider extending their activities to include all offenders and all rehabilitative methods. This is obviously impractical.

Most other arguments in favor of supervision are based upon one or both of the following: The police should do the job because no other agency is available; if such an agency is available, the police can do a better job because of their original and close association with the problem. Neither argument is sound. As with recreation programs, the solution is to develop agencies to perform these important functions. While the police should call attention to the need and advise in the establishment, their duty clearly ends here. Moreover, such police supervision is often extralegal and rarely voluntary on the part of the juvenile.

One phase of this problem, first-contact supervision, does require consideration as a matter of policy. A number of police contacts with children are for minor offenses involving a child who has had no prior contact with police. It is not at all unusual for the beat officer, in minor cases, to explain to the child what he has done wrong, the possible consequences of repeating this behavior, and then to release him or take him home and turn him over to a parent with a similar explanation. Even here a record should be made both to give a true picture of police activity and to use in case of a second offense. There are advantages to this procedure. From the standpoint of the department a great deal of time is saved, and if the officer has exercised good judgment, there often is no repetition. From the standpoint of the child and the parent, this fast, simple handling of the case has a good effect, a favorable attitude is developed toward the police by both the child and the parent. The major fault with this system is that it is an easy thing to do. Unless supervision is alert, many cases that should have a more complete handling are written off. The policy should be carefully spelled out both in training and in the police manual.

Relationship with Other Agencies

In practice, the above view is extremely difficult to hold to, simply because there is a real need for police cooperation with other agencies. The problem is to determine the degree of cooperation which will bring the maximum results for the efforts expended. Police resources and manpower should not be dispersed to the detriment of the department's ability to perform its primary functions. It is true that such dispersion, resulting from community pressures dumping new and additional functions onto the police, is a prime problem. Yet, it may be possible to spell out areas in which the police department (usually in the person of the chief or a top staff man) can and should be active with no damage to the work of the department. It is clear that many police departments are not making the most of their opportunities for cooperating with and influencing the activities of private and public welfare, recreation, and similar agencies.

Community Planning Groups. These groups generally comprise representatives

---

[3]Arthur L. Peterson and Gertrude Hengerer, *Voluntary Police Supervision for Juvenile Offenders* (Los Angeles: Delinquency Control Institute, 1948).

from public and private agencies in the community, often extending their representation beyond the city's boundaries. They carry various names such as "community council," "council of social agencies," and "health and welfare council." The police department should be represented where such an agency exists and should help to start one where there is none. Such membership gives the police an opportunity to see the entire picture of services to the community, to bring their services to the attention of other agencies and to the public, and to learn what resources the department can call upon for assistance when needed.

In particular the police department can supply to such a council information on: the delinquency rate, focal points of crime and delinquency, and areas lacking family and children services. The department can also bring its problems to the council, such as the inadequacy of detention or shelter care facilities, need for new laws or law revision, need for additional personnel to serve juveniles, and, perhaps most important, the need to develop ways to inform the public of laws and their purposes.

General Contacts. The most important public agencies with which the police department comes into contact were listed in Chapter 1. In addition, the department (and especially its juvenile officers) should maintain a close and continuing relationship with private agencies which come into contact with the same people the police deal with. Whether private or public, the agency's relations with the department can be improved by a few fundamental arrangements.

1. Representatives of the department and agency should plan jointly how the two agencies can work together to serve juveniles and their parents. This should be a continuous arrangement so that adjustments may be made when necessary. Agreements should be placed in writing.

2. The department and agency should exchange speakers so that staff members of one may understand how the other operates.

3. The police should invite speakers from the social casework field and from recreation work to appear before conferences of law enforcement agencies. If there is an opportunity to reciprocate, police representatives should do so.

Some agencies require further elaboration on the type of contacts and agreements which should be reached.

Juvenile Court and the Probation Department. Among the matters calling for meeting and agreement by the police and the juvenile court are:

1. Each should understand the other's administrative policies and procedures. Legal provisions controlling functions and program should be thoroughly explained.

2. The specific functions of each should be carefully defined. Particular attention should be given to the extent of police investigation and the type of report to be submitted to the probation department.

3. Definite policies governing detention and shelter care should be worked out, covering both delinquent and neglected children.

4. An arrangement should be worked out so that policemen do not need to attend juvenile court hearings to testify unless the facts in the case are disputed.

5. A method should be worked out for the juvenile court to inform the police about the final disposition of cases initiated by the police.

Casework Agencies. Three areas of police contacts with casework agencies need clarification:

1. Definite agreement should be reached as to the types of cases that the police are to refer to the treatment agency.

2. Methods of referral should be agreed upon.

3. Police officers should become well acquainted with the agency's intake workers. Mutual understanding between those individuals who must work together will make it easier for the police to get minor questions and problems settled.

Schools. The schools and the police department frequently have occasion to work together in the case of juveniles who are in need of special types of help from community agencies. Policies should be jointly formulated that:

1. Define the role of the police in relation to truants, clarifying the relationship between attendance officers and police officers.

2. Specify the violations of law within the school building that school officials will report to the police for investigation.

3. Specify procedures that an officer will follow in taking a child into custody at school or in interviewing a youngster in school.

4. Establish police responsibility for the protection of children from adults loitering around school grounds with unlawful intent.

5. Specify the extent to which school records will be made available to police officers and police records available to school personnel.

6. Set forth police responsibility for regulation of juvenile traffic to and from school and for aiding in traffic safety education.

7. Provide for police services in handling large crowds at athletic meets and social functions.

Recreation and Other Group Work Agencies. Agreement should be sought on:

1. The type of cases to be referred to the leisure-time agency.

2. The use of the leisure time agency's facility for police interviewing purposes.

3. Arrangements for the police officer to visit the leisure-time agency as a friend interested in observing its constructive activities.

4. The procedures that an officer will follow in taking a child into custody at a recreational agency or in interviewing a child at a recreation agency.

5. Law violations that take place on agency property that will be reported to the police for investigation.

Health Agencies. To insure proper use of health facilities:

1. Officers should be thoroughly familiar with the intake policies of both public and private hospitals and out-patient clinics.

2. Agreement should be worked out regarding the use of hospital and health agency records by the police.

Business and Civic Groups. There are many such organizations in most communities. The department should:

1. Take the initiative in providing speakers to appear at their meetings.

2. Obtain members of the police department to serve as special advisory consultants within the organizations and point up some of the needs of the community.

3. Invite members of the various groups to visit police headquarters.

4. Provide written information, such as annual reports, to keep these groups abreast of current police juvenile activities.

State Agencies. Police departments need to develop good working relationships with appropriate state agencies, particularly those concerned with:

1. Licensing business establishments.

2. Licensing foster homes and institutions for children.

3. Institutional care of emotionally disturbed and mentally retarded children.

Conclusion. Policemen should not attempt juvenile case work. Everyone, including most social workers, agrees on this point. However, failure of top police administrators to become involved with other community agencies in the prevention of delinquency will inevitably result in a big gap in the mobilization of community resources in the field.

Organization for Juvenile Work

While there is some question as to just what duties the police should assume in relation to juveniles, there is agreement that certain things are a police function. These are: the prevention of juvenile offenses and offenses against juveniles through patrol with its related methods; the investigation of cases involving juvenile offenders; and the investigation of cases where the juvenile is a victim. The best job of performing these functions cannot be done until proper organization has been developed.

Specialization

The pros and cons of specialization are discussed at several points in this book, and again we must consider them. The basic reason for specialization is to do a better job. Because of major differences in the police handling of juveniles and adult offenders, some degree of specialization is advisable except in the smallest forces. Table 3 shows the number of communities with juvenile specialists in cities of various population sizes and the extent of specialization. Table 3 clearly indicates that the larger cities tend to have special units.

Place of the Juvenile Unit. Even in the case of a six- or eight-man force, there will usually be an officer with an interest in juveniles and a resulting ability to work with them. Specialization may begin with such an officer spending a part of his time handling the department's juvenile cases with the remainder spent in his usual duties.

The force does not have to be very large until the full time of an officer can be spent with juveniles. It is not yet necessary to form a juvenile division, but this officer may now report to the chief instead of to a shift commander, he will probably work in plain clothes, and his hours may be varied so that he can best use his time. The next step up is to assign an additional man to this duty, and we now have a juvenile unit with one of them in command.

Since a force of this size will also have a detective bureau, the question arises,

Table 3

Extent of Juvenile Specialization, by Population Groups

| Population | Jurisdictions Responding | | | Basis of Assignment | | |
| | | With Juvenile Specialists | | | | |
	Total	Number	Per Cent	Part-time Only	Full-time with Part-time*	Full-time Only*
500,000 and more	20	20	100	--	2	18
100,000 to 500,000	54	48	89	1	6	41
25,000 to 100,000	173	112	64	23	11	78
10,000 to 25,000	172	70	41	34	11	25
Under 10,000	192	53	28	29	2	22
Total	611	303	50	87	32	184

Source: U. S. Children's Bureau, *Police Services for Juveniles,* pp. 67 and 69.

*One or more full-time officers

who should the juvenile unit now report to? The people who have worked most in this field believe the bureau should report directly to the chief rather than to the chief of detectives. This is always true when any new unit is started; the commander wants to report directly to the chief. This being true, the history of police organizations during a period of increasing specializations has been one of concentration of special units reporting directly to the chief. However, there comes a point in any growing organization where this practice creates a span of control that no chief can manage adequately. When this point is reached, the most obvious and practical place to put the juvenile unit, since all of its duties are of an investigative nature, is under the chief of detectives.

Organization should not be restricted by hard and fast rules, however. Because cases often originate with the patrol division (and juvenile patrol is an important feature of the work), principles would not be violated if the unit were placed there. There is even a successful juvenile unit under traffic because of the many contacts juveniles do have with traffic officers. This is not generally recommended, and the handling of juvenile traffic offenders will be discussed later.

The arguments for placing the juvenile unit under the chief cannot be lightly dismissed. This is particularly true when the unit is just getting started. This unit does have many contacts with the patrol, detective, and traffic divisions. While most of their methods follow usual police practices, the attitude — the point of view — of policemen working with juveniles should be different. While the same sorts of things are done, they are often done in a slightly different but significant way. After the organization has been perfected, policies established, and the rest of the force has learned to apply the basic techniques of working with juveniles, the unit can be moved to the detective division.

Size of the Juvenile Unit. The number of personnel assigned will vary from city to city. One very rough rule is that the unit should be 5 per cent of the force. Much depends on the effectiveness of the total force and the type of community duties assigned (for example, all missing persons including juveniles may be under the detective bureau). It is usually difficult for a new unit to get personnel, but if experience shows it is overstaffed or the duties decreased by increased skilled participation by other divisions of the force, it is equally difficult to reduce personnel. Sound planning and adequate review of effectiveness in relation to manpower and duties is the key to proper staffing.

As the size of the juvenile unit increases, some plan of organization will need to be developed. Specialists will become even more specialized in the largest cities, there will be breakdowns by time of day, and even by area. The same principles of organization that apply to the entire force also apply here.

Selection

The policemen in the juvenile unit will almost invariably be drawn from the force. This simplifies the problem of selection. The commander of the bureau (and he should have a major role here) will have the entrance exams, background investigations, training records, ratings, and personnel files to assist him. He will be able to talk to a number of officers who can give him a good evaluation of men he is considering. He can have a likely prospect assigned on a temporary basis so that he can size him up.

What Should He Look For? First, a juvenile officer should be a good all-around policeman. Because of the variety of work he will do, he should know patrol, traffic, and investigation methods. Varied experience will give him a wide acquaintance with the men of the force, many citizens, and various areas of the city.

He should have better than average personality and appearance. Juveniles are impressionable and are responsive to these factors. He will need to be able to talk easily and fluently. Juveniles are one of the most difficult groups to interrogate. Since many of the cases are minor, it often takes a lot more talking to get information from witnesses than it does in serious offenses. The juvenile officer should be mature. This does not mean that he must be old, but he should not be accepted by the juveniles as "one of the gang." He should have more than the average education so that he can see the many facets in his work and be able to keep abreast of new developments.

Most important, he should want to work in the division. Assigning an officer who has no interest in juveniles is a waste of time. He will not give the same effort or show the understanding of a man who wants the assignment. A good commanding officer will constantly note the patrolmen who show interest and ability in this area. Many of them will come to him and ask about the possibilities of assignment to this unit. Others will be spotted by the good work they are doing with juveniles where they make the original contact. Application of these selection methods will insure good personnel for the unit.

Policewomen

This topic could have been discussed in several other sections of this book, but most policewomen are attached to a juvenile unit so their relation to a police force will be discussed here.

Sources and Performance. Women have been used as police officers for many years. Some of them did outstanding jobs in many types of police service, but in many cases they were relegated (often through no fault of their own) to duty as matrons, clerks, or social workers employed by the police force. In the past 20 years the status of the policewoman has improved. Now there are many able women in positions of responsibility. Much of this increase in status is due to the policewomen themselves. They showed the quality of work they could do, increased their own ability through training in the department or at colleges and universities, and formed professional organizations.

One major problem is the difficulty of hiring competent women. Many women are married and not interested in other employment; the minimum entrance age is usually high enough to ensure maturity; and a lot of them just do not want the job. This means that the recruitment campaign will usually take a different approach than in the case of hiring policemen. Instead of using a shot-gun approach with widespread publicity, it is usually more productive to look in the places where qualified and interested candidates will be found.

One possible source is the placement agency of a college. Girls who have graduated in sociology or a related field may be interested in and become good policewomen. On the other hand, turnover with the younger college graduates is quite high. Successful police-women have had many types of prior employment: a number of them have been teachers, nurses, reporters, clerks, stenographers (don't overlook women presently employed by the department), and personnel workers. Social workers with limited experience also have been successful. However, caution should be given in selecting an older social worker because she may be changing jobs because of inability to be promoted. As with policemen, one of the best sources is eligible women whom members of the force encourage to apply.

Qualifications. Many of the qualifications will be the same as for policemen. In a few cases, a higher educational standard is required. There are no generally agreed on standards of physical size, but high standards of physical condition and health are usually required. The minimum age is usually higher, generally at least 25. The maximum age may be raised proportionately.

Selection. The same principles used in the selection of policemen will apply here, with minor modifications. The physical ability test will be modified, and the make-up of the interview board should include one or more women. As with the policemen, their work during the probationary period should be carefully reviewed.

Training of Policewomen. Policewomen should be given the same basic training as policemen. This may take a little doing in the hand-to-hand combat class, but in a short time the instructor will realize that he is the one who needs the care and consideration.

Specialized Training for Juvenile Officers

The training methods discussed in Chapter 5 apply here. One of the problems will be that since this is a specialized group, it will ordinarily be quite small and it may not be possible to set up a formal training program at the local level. The largest departments of course will be able to offer considerable in-service training. Even if it is not possible to develop a local, formal school, there can be considerable effective informal training. Officers also may receive outside training.

Man-to-Man Training. The only method of police training a few years ago was to assign a recruit to an older officer to "break in" and then hope that he learned more good police practices than bad. In some cases this worked. A conscientious older officer can do an excellent job of teaching by example and brief, informal instruction as the team goes about its duties.

This system is greatly improved if a little planning is done, and in a specialized division, this is a sound training device. One of the ways to improve this informal training is to list the many techniques that the new officer must learn, as for example, dance hall checks, juvenile traffic arrests, and theater checks. Then after each entry have three columns headed: Explained — Demonstrated — Performed. Such a list may run to a considerable length. As time is available, the older officer explains the method of checking a dance hall and checks the column headed "Explained." When the opportunity presents, he demonstrates how to do it and checks "Demonstrated." Finally, when he thinks the younger officer can do it properly, he checks "Performed." This is a highly practical method used by a number of departments, even where there are excellent police academies. There is no substitute for actual demonstration and experience.

External Training. When the department is too small to offer specialized formal training there are still a number of ways to get the job done. There may be a local college or university offering courses in the sociology or psychology departments that would be of value to a juvenile officer. The department might pay his tuition and allow him the time off to attend. A nearby large city will usually be highly cooperative in admitting officers to training courses.

A number of universities offer short courses in juvenile work. Among them are the State College of Washington, several of the California schools, Michigan State, the University of Indiana, and the Southern Police Institute. By far the most extensive and well established program is offered by the Delinquency Control Institute of the University of Southern California. This program began in 1946. Two 12-week courses are offered each year, starting in September and March. Both men and women approved by their department are accepted with no age limitation. Each week is made up of four days of class instruction and one day of field trips where organizations and institutions, whose programs are closely related to the material discussed in that week, are visited. Trips include visits to police departments in cities of 25,000 to 2,000,000 population, a sheriff's office, detention homes, juvenile courts, and a mental health center. Students have attended from most of the states and from many foreign countries. Some unusual features about this educational program: (1) it offers scholarships to officers from law enforcement agencies anywhere in the world; (2) it is a unique, specialized training program on a university level that aims to meet the educational needs of police-juvenile officers; (3) 12 units of college credit are granted to students satisfactorily completing the program; (4) a well-balanced program is provided through 10 different courses taught by experienced police officers, various experts, and university professors; (5) officers are granted leaves of absence, with full pay in most cases; (6) the only expenses involved are living expenses, travel costs, and a small sum for text books; and (7) classroom sessions are conducted in an informal manner to encourage maximum student participation.

Training of Other Policemen. One important training area is in-service training of present personnel not assigned to the juvenile unit. Since all line personnel including command officers have almost daily contact with juveniles, they should be given training in the methods of best working with them. Certain staff personnel should also receive as much of this training as their duties in relation to juveniles requires.

This training program will not be as intensive or specialized as that given officers assigned to the juvenile unit. It can be given in the form of roll-call training, a series of classes meeting at weekly intervals, or a school of several days length depending upon department policies. Instructors can be from the juvenile unit, the court, other agencies working with juveniles, local attorneys, teachers or counselors from the local school system, and experts from other law-enforcement agencies. The subjects to be covered can include the causes of delinquency, programs dealing with delinquency, community agencies involved, and the relation of the police to the total program as well as specific police subjects, including operation of the juvenile unit, departmental regulations and policies regarding juveniles, state laws and city ordinances, questioning juveniles, and similar subjects.

This in-service training is essential if the program is to develop properly. The whole department must know just how the unit works. When men on the force see a planned, well organized, and developed program aimed directly at an area where they have been having trouble, they will much more readily support it than if they know nothing about it.

Housing the Juvenile Unit

Space is almost always at a premium around a police station. It is often difficult to find a location for the newer units. The usual procedure is to give the juvenile unit a left-over office, a vacated storage room, or some such place. The unit attempts to operate an effective program with the personnel crowded into one room, usually including parents and miscellaneous people waiting to see one of the juvenile officers. Such inadequate housing materially affects the efficiency of the program and costs more, through reduced efficiency, than proper housing. This is a difficult point to sell to the city council. Many councils seem to think a police station is adequate if everyone can get in out of the rain.

Principal Needs. Because there are so many different sizes of juvenile units and because their functions will vary somewhat, it is not possible to give a model floor plan for the unit. However, there are certain principles that will apply to all units and can serve as a guide, even though it is not possible to achieve an ideal situation.

The unit should be so located in the police building that it is not difficult to find. Many of the people visiting it will be coming in voluntarily rather than with a police escort. If possible, visitors should be able to avoid contact with adult prisoners or large numbers of the public. Many people, even visiting voluntarily, are not happy about the contact with the police and would like a minimum of public attention. There should also be a back entrance. This allows witnesses, prisoners, and officers to enter or leave without being generally observed and is sometimes very important.

Even a one-man juvenile unit needs at least two rooms: a general office and an interrogation room. While many successful interrogations have occurred under adverse circumstances, many have failed because of some distraction that would be avoided in an interrogation room.

The interrogation room should be equipped with a one-way mirror and a microphone. This has many values; an important one is allowing a secretary or another officer to monitor interrogations of girls by a policeman and so avoid possible charges of his misconduct. If the interrogation room has no window, as in the newer air conditioned buildings, or if the window is secure, it can be used for brief detention and so avoid placing the subject in a cell or other form of security.

As soon as the unit grows, an additional office will be needed. While this will basically be for the officer in command, it can serve as a second interrogation room and for interviews with parents, complainants, and other persons. This will allow the outer office to be used as a reception and waiting room, record room, squad room for the remaining personnel, and many other functions.

The juvenile offices should avoid a formal, institutional appearance. A child should not feel that this is the first step to prison when he comes through the door. This is not easy to achieve with city-issued furniture, but it can be greatly improved with attention to such things as the use of cheerful colors in painting and a few pictures other than an outside view of the city hall on the wall.

Detention Facilities. Policies related to detention of juveniles will be discussed later in this chapter. Detention of juveniles is usually controlled by state law, and it may be that the police are not allowed to detain juveniles except for very short periods. If the police do hold juveniles, certain principles should be followed in the construction of such facilities. The first is to completely segregate juveniles from older prisoners. Not even the same entrance to the detention facilities should be used. Second, the facilities should be entirely secure without a jail look. This has been done in many good juvenile detention facilities and in mental hospitals. It is not necessary to use bars to get security. Special screens, certain types of windows, and solid doors with "bullet proof" glass may be used. Again, colors need not be the standard jail grey or tan. There should be shower facilities and, if the children are to be held any time, laundry facilities. A limited number of books and magazines should be available and radio and television if possible. There is no thought of pampering the prisoner; rather this is an attempt to make the break from the usual environment a little less noticeable, an attempt to avoid developing the feeling in the child that he is now in jail with a criminal record. These few additions to the usual jail equipment and furnishings will not convince the juvenile that he isn't locked up, but they will help him feel that he has not severed all connections with normal society and make future treatment a little easier.

Police Juvenile Operations

The basic functions of a juvenile unit can be outlined as:

1. Discovery of:
    1. Delinquent behavior.
    2. Potential delinquents.
    3. Conditions causing delinquency.

2. Investigation of:
    1. Cases of juvenile delinquency.
    2. Cases where a juvenile is involved with an adult as an accessory or a victim.

3. Protection of juveniles:
    1. Referral of neglected children, finding runaways, acting against amusement centers operating in violation of law, and so on.

4. Final disposition of the case:
    1. Ranges from referral to a social welfare agency up to prosecution for murder.

Each of these functions is important. Each must get full attention if the unit is to do the job. There is too much of a tendency, for example, to consider that the juvenile unit has only the function of investigation, that the officers can sit around and wait until a child commits a crime before they go into action. Such a concept violates every principle of sound police work. Each function will be discussed separately.

Discovery

There are many ways of discovering juvenile delinquency. A number of cases will originate as a complaint; patrols and alert officers will detect other cases.

Complaints. The number of complaints made will show a marked increase when the public discovers that the juvenile unit is an active, effective division of the force and that when they do report something, it will be given fast, intelligent action. Like other complaints to the police, many will have no basis, many will be frivilous, or from a typical "crank." All of these must be investigated for several reasons. First, you never know until you do investigate what has actually occurred. You may find that when a lady who has called in every week for months on end and said the kids are killing each other in the alley calls in for the four hundredth time, she is finally right, and a juvenile homicide has occurred. Most of these complainants are good, sincere citizens who want to help. They should always be thanked for the information and, although it takes a special effort, should be told the result of the call, even if it is only that the children throwing rocks at the street light were gone when the patrol car arrived.

Tips. Other information will come from sources who are friends of the juvenile officers, or at least want to look like friends. An effective officer constantly gets tips from all sorts of people: cab drivers, waitresses, bartenders, bellhops, and theater door-men. A good juvenile officer will constantly be receiving information on wanted juveniles, learning what the talk is about the latest burglary, who is bragging at the all-night lunch counter that he passed a bad check, and where a girl who looks like a runaway from a small town is staying. Not all of these tips will bear fruit, but to keep getting them each informant must be treated as if the information were important.

Patrol. A primary source for the discovery of juvenile offenses and offenders is patrol, both routine patrol by the entire police force and more specialized patrol by the juvenile unit. It must always be remembered that the formation of the juvenile unit, or any other specialized unit, does not relieve any member of the force from taking proper police action. The largest juvenile divisions have a specialized patrol unit in their plan of organization, but even in the one-man bureau, this one man should not sit around wait-ing for the phone to ring. Patrol is the very basis of crime prevention and a good part of the time available must be spent on this function.

Patrol and inspection by the juvenile officers use the same basic patrol methods as the rest of the force. The only difference is that the juvenile officers concentrate in those areas where young people are most likely to get into trouble. Such patrol is effective not only in discovering offenses and offenders but also in preventing offenses. Children who are only potential offenders see and appreciate good police coverage.

Juvenile officers on patrol are on the lookout for many things. They try to spot known criminals associating with juveniles. The danger is obvious: an older thief will try to get a young one to take all of the risk and only a small part of the gain while the "mastermind" sits safely by. Officers watch carefully for youngsters who have been drinking. This may be delinquent behavior in itself, but more important it may lead to much more serious acts. Similarly, any possible use of narcotics is carefully watched for. While relatively few in the younger ages have advanced to heroin or another of the needle drugs, they may be smoking marihuana, chewing inhalers, or using one of the many brightly colored capsules that may or may not give them the lift they are looking for.

Gambling by juveniles is a danger sign as well as an offense. Most young gamblers do not do very well, and it is an easy step to get their money back through a stick-up or a burglary.

A good juvenile officer will always pay particular attention to automobiles. Auto theft is a leading juvenile crime. True, most of the thefts are for joy rides and the car is soon abandoned, but some cars are wrecked while driving around and some are used in committing another crime. While the entire car may not be the target, the gasoline, tires, battery, hub caps, or other accessories may be.

The juvenile officer will be looking for runaways and lost or neglected children. As it gets later at night and the crowds reduce, all juveniles, especially the younger ones and those who are not actually loitering but seem to have no apparent idea of where they are going, should be checked. This is an invaluable source of information to a juvenile unit. Juveniles in areas where they don't fit should be watched. They may be in the wholesale district late at night to break open parking meters; poorly dressed ones may be out in the country club section because they have just broken in one of the houses. These field interrogations should be recorded just as in adult cases.

All police must carefully watch any known sexual deviate associating with juveniles. Maybe the man has "been away" and released as cured, but the cure may not stand up to the temptations not found in a mental hospital.

Problem Areas. Special attention should be given to areas where trouble has been known to occur such as parks frequented by gangs and corners that seem to be hangouts. Patrol officers know who is usually found there, and they get the feel of the area so they can often spot trouble in advance. Dance halls, theaters, penny arcades, and pool halls should get more than the usual share of attention because trouble often starts in these establishments.

It is a good thing to know the make-up of gangs, who runs around with whom, and the leaders. Many crimes have been solved because an alert police officer remembered a group being together earlier in the evening and made up of just the sort of talent needed to pull a certain type of crime. Taverns known to sell to juveniles require special attention. If the license was not taken away after the first offense, the owners will usually try it again. Such a tavern is often a hang-out for many types of characters that either victimize juveniles or use them as accessories.

Bus and railroad stations, cheap hotels, and all-night restaurants should be checked. Potential delinquents often hang out in such places, and these places also are good spots to check for runaways.

The police cannot be in all of these places all of the time so they should make friends with people who work where juveniles are found. A good share of these people want to do the right thing and will be very helpful in pointing out trouble makers or possible runaways. Every juvenile officer should have a wide acquaintance with a variety of people. The officer is the eyes and ears of the department, and these people are extensions of his eyes and ears.

A great deal of information will be gathered by an alert officer, much more than can be recorded. However, there will be some things that are so important that they must be recorded and some things that will result in the start of an investigation. What should be recorded and how it should be done will be discussed in the section on juvenile records.

Juvenile Investigations

All of the rules for making sound investigations apply to the juvenile area as well as to any other. Because society has accepted an increased responsibility for juvenile offenders, these investigations are often more thorough. While the police cannot accept the responsibility for rehabilitating offenders, they can properly furnish more facts and more of the juvenile's background than might be needed to sustain a conviction in the case of an adult offender.

Investigations in juvenile cases often are more difficult than for adult offenses. Juveniles are often very difficult to interrogate. Emotion, maladjustment, and varying degrees of mental illness seem to play a greater part with the juvenile. Many juvenile offenses involve a group, and not always the same group in each offense. The juvenile being questioned in a petty larceny may admit that he did it with Joe, Fred, Bill, and Suzie, and that the night before he was along when Joe cashed a bad check and that he got part of the money but Fred wrote it out and Bill signed it and some kid whom he doesn't know but is a good friend of Henry told them how to do it. Then the juvenile officer finds that the suspect has made a few mistakes as to who he was with each night and one of the kids has an ironclad alibi. So the officer ends up, after starting a minor investigation, with a whole series of other investigations and a long list of names to sort out as to who was involved, who was there and knew what was going on, and who just happened to come by after it was all over. This can all be sorted out, but it takes a thorough, patient, and able investigator to do the job.

In making juvenile investigations care must be taken to see that excessive time is not used in making background investigations that are not needed to satisfy the police function but are wanted by an agency concerned with the juvenile after the police have completed their work. There will be many requests from individuals and organizations to furnish case histories of not only the offender but also of his parents, brothers and sisters, and even aunts, uncles, and grandparents. Of course the police can do a good job on such investigations, and it is hard to refuse a sincere social worker with an effective but understaffed program. But a definite policy must be established in line with the primary duties of the police.

Relationship of the Juvenile and Detective Divisions. The juvenile unit may be a part of the detective division, but in any case relationships between detectives and the juvenile officers must be based on known and understood policy. Both will be making investigations, and in some areas there will be questions as to who is responsible. It is essential that the two groups work in close harmony, the detectives using the special skills of the juvenile officer for such things as questioning a juvenile and the juvenile officer making full use of the varied abilities of the detectives.

Certain cases generally are assigned originally to the juvenile unit:

1. Where the offender is known or believed to be a juvenile.
2. Bicycle theft.
3. Desertion, neglect, and abuse of children.
4. Sale of obscene material to juveniles.
5. Offenses on school property.
6. Missing children.

Department policy and experience will doubtless add other classifications to this list.

From time to time there will be a rapid solution to a case and an immediate arrest. It may be that the juvenile unit discovers an adult and a juvenile who have just pulled a burglary and arrested both within a few minutes. There should be no hard feelings because the detectives were not invited to participate in the arrest. The same illustration could be reversed with the detectives making the arrest. In either case, however, an additional copy of the report should be sent to the other unit so that they will be fully informed. All police officers welcome a well operated juvenile unit because not too many of them like to make the necessarily detailed investigations and to write all of the resulting reports.

Protection of Juveniles. This is the third basic function in relation to juveniles. The same police work that discovers juvenile offenders will also discover juveniles who need protection and situations harmful to juveniles. The police almost routinely find young children, inadequately clothed and hungry, wandering the streets at all hours;

receive complaints of neglect and abuse of juveniles; and receive calls that the mother and father are in a tavern and the children are locked up in the apartment with nothing to eat. Neighborhood candy stores may be supplementing their income with punch boards, and school children will be gambling with their lunch money, or even stealing to continue trying their luck.

Some of these situations involve crimes, and the police are well equipped to handle this aspect of the case. Other situations require some form of assistance to the juvenile. Shelter, food, and clothing may be needed immediately. A program may need to be developed to insure the future security of the child. What is done will depend upon the community resources available. A welfare agency may give immediate assistance in the form of shelter and food, while the court may handle the case of the delinquent father who has failed to provide for his family. A family counselor may try to work out a long-range solution, and some of the children may receive medical assistance or special schooling from still other agencies. The responsibility of the police is to discover the situations where assistance is needed, take action if a law is broken, and see that the cases are referred to the appropriate community agencies: churches, schools, the public welfare department, private welfare agencies, boys clubs, and public health clinics, among others.

In many communities, however, such agencies may be limited in number and resources and thus may be ineffective. What do the police do then? The planning should be done well in advance. The police administrator must call attention to the lack of proper facilities or to the inadequacy of present services. Officially they can do little more. However, an able police administrator can accomplish a great deal in performing these functions. If the people of the community like and trust him, they will readily accept his word that help is needed, and this is the first step. He can participate in the establishment of agencies. This is a good idea because he will be in a position to see that the police are not saddled with welfare duties.

Even where there are a number of adequately financed assistance agencies, practical problems arise. Some of these agencies operate on the basis of a closely defined program with many rules and regulations and subscribe strongly to the 40-hour week. Unfortunately, many of the cases where children need assistance do not arise during regular working hours. It often seems that the neighbors wait until dark before calling the police about a family that needs food and coal. It is of little help to be told that a caseworker will visit the family the following day. While it is fully realized that these services must be handled systematically, the immediate problem is still there.

The problem is finally solved in any of several ways. Many welfare workers do not recognize regular office hours and are available whenever the need arises. A few agencies, and the Salvation Army is one, give help first and then ask questions. In some cases the police have found that the immediate solution is to phone a grocer with a kind heart and tell him about it. This, of course, is a solution, but not the best one, although that food looks awfully good to a hungry child who is little concerned with lines of authority and responsibility. Another solution is to have a small fund available in the police department for such immediate assistance. The source of this money is usually from donations and from many sources. This seems like a good idea, but there is a very real danger. This again is not a police function, but again the police will do a good job. Phonies who need a little food or gas to get to the next town because they spent their last dollar for a bottle are less likely to go to the police for help. Policemen live on limited budgets themselves, and they know how to get the last pickle out of the food dollar. The major danger is that the police seem like such a good agency to perform these relief services that they are likely to suddenly find that they have a full-time welfare service with the police station as a community center.

Disposition of Cases. All cases that come to police attention must finally be disposed of, through court action, through finding that the case was unfounded, or for other reasons. There are many ways to the final disposition of juvenile cases. Disposition of a case may not mean closing the case because the police usually have a continuing responsibility. These dispositions may be classified as follows:

1. Brought before juvenile court. This action is usually in the form of a petition. Procedures vary from state to state.

2. Brought before the regular court using the same procedures as with an adult. This may occur in traffic cases or in serious offenses. Again, the practice varies.

3. Referral to other agencies. This will occur when the case should be investigated further and the juvenile needs guidance or rehabilitation.

4. Transferred to another unit of the police department upon discovery that the subject is an adult. Some subjects may conceal their true age in an attempt to receive treatment as a juvenile.

5. Transferred to another agency. Investigation may show that the juvenile is already under the jurisdiction of another agency such as the probation department or another law enforcement agency that is in a better position to handle the case.

6. Action suspended. In many cases the parents and the juvenile can achieve a satisfactory solution without assistance.

7. Charge dropped on basis of insufficient evidence. This does not mean that the juvenile is forever cleared; later developments may result in additional evidence.

8. Exonerated. Evidence is developed that clearly proves the juvenile is not involved.

It is apparent that there are more ways of disposing of a juvenile case than that of an adult offender. In order to keep the records clear and to avoid errors, the juvenile unit should have the responsibility to assign the disposition to the case. If this is not done there will be variances that make it difficult to secure an accurate statistical picture.

Typical Organizations

A close look at the practice in large, medium, and small-sized cities will indicate some of the alternatives open to administrators responsible for juvenile unit operations. The Chicago, Illinois, youth division is the model for the large city; Peoria, Illinois, the medium-sized city; while the small city presentation represents a composite view.

Large City Youth Division

A deputy superintendent, reporting to the superintendent of police, heads the Chicago youth division. His assigned duties, in addition to the routine matters of personnel and organization, specifically include continuous contact with the Family Court (juvenile court), schools, Youth Commission, and social service agencies. The staff includes an adjutant and a secretary. The adjutant aids in administration and planning. The complement of the division is approximately 300 officers.

Organization and Duties. Immediate operations of the division are under a director, assisted by a shift officer (lieutenant). Sergeants are assigned to headquarters, to training duties, and to immediate supervision of district and mobile patrol operations on a 24-hour basis. Each of the city's 38 police districts is assigned one to four youth officers on the day and evening shifts. The number of assignees depends on delinquency experience and other considerations. In addition, the districts are grouped into six police areas on a geographical basis; each area has a regular assignment of two squad cars and four youth officers.

Youth squad crews work three shifts and provide immediate investigation and handling of children, either as offenders or victims. (Follow-up of routine cases and the supervised adjustments are performed by the district youth officers.) Their main functions are to patrol and inspect. Frequent visits are made to schools and other public places, bowling alleys, dance halls, skating rinks, roadside stands, taverns, and similar locations that tend to serve as meeting places for young people. Drinking, loitering, group car riders, and gang activities are a paramount inspectional duty for youth squads on patrol. While prevention of delinquency is emphasized, the youth squads take cognizance of all types of law violations, regardless of the age of the offender.

Group control squads are special mobile units manned by youth officers equipped to deal with all types of gang activities, usually in the high crime rate areas. Three officers are assigned to these cars and they operate on a selective time, location, and volume basis. The use of police trained in juvenile work is an important factor in a successful operation of this kind. Their knowledge, understanding, and experience with young people equips them better to cope with the hostile individual or group.

Youth worker programs are sponsored by agencies volunteering group control services outside of the conventional in-building types of programs. The majority of known active and fighting gangs are provided workers by the larger agencies such as the Y.M.C.A., boys clubs, and youth centers in Chicago, with a sprinkling of group workers from agencies confined to a neighborhood.

Juvenile Investigations. When an act of delinquency or neglect is brought to the attention of a youth officer, he immediately initiates investigative police action. It is the responsibility of the youth officer to ascertain the facts of juvenile cases. When the investigation is completed, he determines the most favorable disposition: i.e., admonition of the child and/or parents; referral to a community agency; voluntary supervision; place in custody of the parents with orderly referral to the juvenile detention home.

Juvenile Detention. The Arthur J. Audy Home for Children is an institution for the temporary custodial care of delinquent, dependent, truant, and mentally defective children that come to the attention of various Cook County authorities. Delinquent and dependent children make up the majority of cases referred to the Home by the family court, the police, or child-caring agency of Cook County. A child placed in the intake department of the Home cannot be released without the approval of the judge of the Family Court of Cook County.

A preliminary hearing is conducted in the intake department of the Audy Home each afternoon, except Saturday, by a referee appointed by the judge of the Family Court. It is the duty of the referee to pass upon the case of each child registered in the intake department within the previous 24 hours and determine in each instance, whether the child will be released to the parent or guardian or appear at a hearing before the Court the next morning, where a circuit court judge will rule on detention of the child.

Missing Juveniles. The district youth officer makes a daily inspection of missing returnees and juveniles still reported as missing. A card of a missing juvenile, with pertinent information, is filed at the police district of residence and at youth headquarters.

The duplicate card is retained at the district station until the missing child has been located, when it is sent to central records with complete data on the child.

Juvenile Traffic Violators. When a juvenile is arrested for a minor traffic violation and there is no indication of delinquency, the arrest is processed through the regular traffic branch of the courts. When delinquency is indicated, the juvenile is handled by a youth officer.

Specialized Bureaus. Cooperation is efficiently effected with districts and the detective bureau and its specialized units. Summarily dispatching credible information eliminates conflict and duplication of police performance, particularly as it applies to murder, robbery, burglary, narcotics, and other areas of special services.

Youth Bureau Forms and Reports. The records of juvenile offenders are maintained at the central headquarters of the youth bureau services division. Summary cards convey any prior contact the juvenile had with the police, from an insignificant warning to the commission of a felonious crime. Said records are actively maintained through minor years (17 through 20 years of age) after which they are forwarded to central records for microfilming. The over-age file serves a purpose in the investigation and control of groups coming to the attention of the police. Frequently the over-age, as well as the "known gangs" file, is a ready reference for investigators, especially in cases involving age groups ranging from 15 to the adult age of all years. Judicious reference to such records has resulted in several clear-ups. The index has proved an invaluable reference to other units and divisions of the police on special occasions. Other records include:

1. Adult Arrest Cards. Prepared when an adult is arrested with a juvenile, either as victim or accomplice.

2. History of Minors. The record and a brief narrative of male violators of 17 years through 20 years of age who have been arrested by the police. These are arrestees whose cases are arraigned in a special branch of the municipal court (Boy's Court). It is based on an interview conducted by a youth officer.

3. Nicknames. Identifications are invaluable as a means of recognizing youthful violators that otherwise remain as unknowns to the police. Such titles are characteristically accurate. Accomplices and victims remember nicknames they have heard at the scene of a crime.

4. Curfew Warning Notices. Prepared when juveniles violate the curfew ordinance. A warning notice is personally served on the parent or guardian, usually when the child is released at the district station. A second notice of violation provides cause for arrest and court hearing.

5. Missing Juvenile Card. A history of the juvenile or runaway along with all available information about the child's disappearance. This activity supplements the function of the missing persons bureau.

6. School, Store, Amusement, and Business Reports. Must be submitted on such facilities and establishments after an inspection of the premises and interview with neighboring interests.

7. Group History (Gang) Cards. Completed by youth officers for each known group, whether athletic, social, or fighting gang. Information about the group and their interests is most essential in determining the need for organizing a control force to curtail group conflicts.

8. Stop Orders. Attached to the records of adults and youngsters who are wanted as violators, missing, runaways, and escapees.

Youth Bureau in Medium-Sized City

Headed by a director appointed by the chief of police, the Peoria Youth Bureau includes 12 men. It has the advantage of adequate and modern facilities.

Functions of the Youth Bureau. The Peoria Youth Bureau has two main objectives: to prevent youth from getting into trouble and to help those youths already in trouble. In the field of crime prevention the youth staff analyzes factors conducive to deviant behavior. Its youth officers study trouble spots and tension areas and plan suitable programs for alleviating conditions peculiar to such areas. The bureau anticipates potential flare-ups by posting a staff member at all teen-age functions including school affairs, athletic events, class meetings, and special celebrations marking Halloween and other special occasions. Close surveillance is kept at places physically associated with youth such as pool halls, corner drug stores, ice cream parlors, drive-in theatres, dance halls, and, in some instances, taverns and roadhouses. Considerable attention is focused on blighted areas of the city.

The Staff at Work. In 1958 bureau staff travelled 65,000 miles in its youth program. The lecture group spoke before 150 organizations, schools, churches, and youth assemblies. In its field activities the bureau visited 1,500 businesses and 2,100 homes and interviewed 624 youths brought to central headquarters for interviewing and processing.

The bureau functions on many sources of information. The first source is its members, who by vigilance and observation obtain invaluable data for the many programs in effect. The second source is an informed public. Lastly, schools, churches, and many other agencies throughout the city cooperate fully in the interests of youth itself.

First Contact with Youth. Great care is exercised in the handling of youth by staff members. Youth officers are trained in these matters, especially in the treatment of first offenders. In some instances a youth is released immediately after an interview. Sometimes a youth is released without an interview and contacted at a later date when he is alone and free from tension and distraction of his associates. When a youth officer is assured that a youth is in more serious trouble he is brought to headquarters for further interrogation. In interviewing, the youngster is assured that his interests are first and foremost; that the youth officer is duty-bound to help a boy or girl in trouble.

Needs of Youth and Community Resources. Sometimes the social and physical needs of youth becomes quite obvious to a staff member when interviewing one of the less fortunate. A subject lacking one or more of the essentials of a healthy existence, must be corrected before other therapy is attempted. Many a child is delinquent because he is hungry, unclean, unwanted, and ragged. Peoria is fortunate in having at its call excellent community resources. Some of the more important agencies are the Elks, Moose, Red Cross, Catholic and Protestant welfare groups, and others.

In a Small City

The fallacy that the small community has no juvenile problem has been exploded. While it is true that the big city presents an aggravated delinquency situation, most of the component factors -- improper home conditions, economic want, physical handicaps, and psychological maladjustments -- are to be found in most communities, regardless of size.

In fact, the small community may have some features particularly leading to delinquency. For example, the absence or lack of variety in entertainment and recreational activities may result in gangs of high school boys and girls devising unwholesome forms of amusement. Small cities often lack other community resources such as a child guidance clinic, a visiting teacher or school psychologist, or staff for juvenile court and probation.

Assignment of Responsibility. If the need for delinquency prevention work in small cities is granted, how can such work be adapted to the limited personnel and funds at the disposal of the police department? In the small city each member of the police force is frequently required to perform a variety of duties, since neither the volume of work nor the size of the force will permit specialization. In some of the smaller cities and villages, the chief, even when he is adequately staffed, assumes direct responsibility for the more difficult juvenile cases. He personally participates because of the importance of properly handling them. Further, he has gained the respect and cooperation of the community as a whole and particularly of the parents of the children involved.

The recommended form of specialization which can be suggested is the employment of a policewoman to serve as a juvenile officer and to handle cases involving women. By adding this one specialized person to the force, a good beginning is made on a delinquency prevention program while the department also provides itself with the much needed services of a policewoman for cases involving adults.

Special Assignments. If it is not possible to employ a policewoman full time for this work, it may be found practicable to work out a cooperative plan with the local school system by which a part of the salary of a juvenile officer is paid by the police and part by the school. In return, the juvenile officer would serve the school as part-time truant officer and also act as a police juvenile officer.

If such a plan is not possible, the least that can be done is to train a member of the force who is most adept at handling children and to assign him to any delinquency problem which may arise. To a certain extent, this practice can be applied to advantage in larger departments, for there are some men without any special training who are naturally liked and respected by children. Training programs for juvenile officers are available in many states today, and in the smaller departments the chief is usually the first member to be in attendance.

Coordination of Community Agencies. One other aspect of organization which should receive attention is the coordination of police activity with other community agencies. No city that is large enough to have a police department is too small to have churches, schools, Boy and Girl Scout troops, and relief agencies. These should be coordinated along the same lines as the more numerous agencies in a larger city.

Activities. As for delinquency prevention activities in the small city, careful review of the more elaborate big-city programs outlined earlier will reveal that many of them can be applied in a small community. Investigation of home environment, direction of interests of delinquents into constructive channels, organization of athletic teams and hobby clubs — all of these and many other activities can be easily applied in a small community. Other activities, such as investigations of dance halls, bowling alleys, and skating rinks, should, of course, be assumed by a police department in any city regardless of size.

The first step is to recognize the nature of delinquency problems and to accept the need for a prevention program. Next should follow a study of the organization and activities of juvenile divisions in larger cities. If these steps are taken, a little initiative and ingenuity will suggest a number of profitable activities which can be undertaken by the smaller city police department.

Questions of Juvenile Policy

Many policies must be established for the proper operation of the juvenile unit. Some of the most troublesome will be discussed.

Fingerprinting and Identification Photos

This topic has had considerable discussion in the juvenile field, centering around the rules that should be adopted governing fingerprinting juveniles and the disposition of those prints. Many people, but few police officers, are opposed to fingerprinting juveniles except in extreme cases. It is interesting that a number of these same arguments were heard at the start of this century in opposition to fingerprinting adult offenders.

Before a policy is established, state law and rules of local juvenile court should be considered. It may be that the policies have already been well defined.

Arguments Against. Opposition to fingerprinting juveniles is based on several arguments: (1) a stigma is attached to fingerprinting that will effect both the attitude of the juvenile and the attitude of people in relation to him; (2) this practice is contrary to the principles of the juvenile court since it treats him as a criminal; (3) the juvenile may consider himself as a "tough guy" and look upon being printed as a mark of distinction; and (4) the most telling argument is that the fingerprint card may come to light years later and have an adverse effect on his obtaining employment or getting a security clearance. The fourth point actually is an argument for the proper control of police records, rather than a reason against taking prints.

Arguments For. The arguments in favor of fingerprinting are substantial. First, it is the best method of identification. Fingerprinting is so generally used now, because it is a positive method of identification, that the criminal stigma is lacking. It is certainly no worse for the police to take fingerprints than it is to ask for name, age, place of birth, and many other questions.

The second argument also advanced is that fingerprints are a good form of protection in many circumstances. If a single clear print of the offender is found at a crime scene, and a suspect is brought in and his prints do not match, he is eliminated with the highest degree of certainty. They are also of great value in cases of injury-producing unconsciousness and amnesia. Finally, many police officers believe that the mere fact that a juvenile's prints are on file has definite preventive value. The juvenile knows how helpful prints are to the police and so is afraid to take chances.

I.D. Photographs. The same general types of argument apply to identification photographs of juveniles, but there is not as much controversy.

Policy Points. The following points are recommended as a basis for a police policy in fingerprinting juveniles. These are not all in agreement with views held by many non-police experts, and they do not contain their usual recommendation that the courts set the policy.

It is believed, unless there are legislative restrictions, that use of fingerprints is clearly a police function and that fingerprints should be taken of juveniles: (1) when he is a suspect in or has admitted a felony; (2) when he has a long history of delinquent activity and is likely to repeat; and (3) when prints are specifically needed for identification, for example, to match with prints known to be the offender; when the child is a victim of amnesia, or unable to identify himself because of illness or injury; or when the child is an offender or a runaway and refuses to identify himself.

Juvenile Arrest Policy

The law is quite clear in every jurisdiction as to what constitutes an arrest. Some groups working with juveniles, however, are opposed to the term "arrest." The Standard Juvenile Court Acts says about this, "When any child found violating any law or ordinance, or whose surroundings are such as to endanger his welfare, is taken into custody, such taking into custody shall not be termed an arrest."

This will be a little hard for most police officers to understand because the taking into custody to answer for a violation of a law or ordinance is universally termed an arrest. From a practical standpoint what actually happens is that the juvenile is arrested. Calling it "taking into custody" isn't going to change anything very much, but it will cause a lot of confusion in police reporting. If the police officer made a mistake in his "taking into custody," the child's attorney would be quick to consider such action under the law of false arrest.

In an effort to reduce this confusion, the Southern California Juvenile Officers Association and the Research Committee of the Delinquency Control Institute have been working on a set of uniform terms to be applied to juveniles handled by the police. Three definitions have been developed concerning arrest.

Juveniles Arrested and Detained. Juveniles arrested and detained shall mean those cases of juveniles who have been arrested pursuant to the laws of arrest as contained in the state code and juveniles incarcerated in juvenile hall or in some other suitable place that has been designated by the juvenile authority. (This category does not include those juveniles who are held temporarily in office or station pending release to parents or guardians.)

Juveniles Arrested and Released. Juveniles arrested and released shall mean an arrest was made pursuant to the laws of arrest, and when a juvenile is released by the arresting agency to his parents, guardians, or other responsible person without placing him in juvenile hall or other place designated by the juvenile court, after processing the arrest and prior to the completion of the investigation of the case.

Traffic Arrests. A traffic arrest is consummated when a citation is issued to the juvenile offender. If the juvenile is to be detained because of the seriousness of the offense or other circumstances then the same procedure will be adhered to as in the first category, "Juveniles Arrested and Detained."

This discussion has pointed up, if nothing else, that there is considerable differences in the terms that may be used in relation to juvenile arrests or whatever else they may be called. Two points are clear. The department should develop its own definitions in line with practice in their area. Second, in reporting to the Uniform Crime Reports system of the FBI, the department should use their definitions and follow their forms exactly, no matter what local practice may be, so that data will be comparable to those reported by other agencies.

Uniform and Marked Cars. It is almost universal practice for juvenile officers to work in plain clothes and to use unmarked cars. Much of their work is investigative in nature and a uniform may be a liability. Also the effect on the juvenile and his family of having a uniformed police officer talk to him at home, at the playground, or at school should be considered. This may have a poor effect, lead to unwarranted unfavorable attitudes toward the child, and start him on a definitely negative attitude toward the police. The day has not yet arrived when people think of the police officer only as a guardian of the peace engaged in constructive work.

There will be situations when the officer must be in uniform in a marked car. Many of the first contacts with juveniles will be by the uniformed patrol. There will be times when even the juvenile officers should be in uniform, as for example some inspectional duties, so that they can be readily recognized and will carry more authority. In the small force without a specialized unit, many investigations will be made by uniformed officers. As a result, it is not practical to set hard and fast rules. But as a general principle, as many contacts with juveniles as possible should be made by officers in plainclothes and driving unmarked cars.

Other Policy Problems

Two other policy problems are subjects of considerable, and often heated, debate in relation to police work with juveniles: reporting information about juvenile delinquents, and detention following arrest.

Release of Juveniles Names and Photographs to News Media. There has been considerable discussion of this topic, and policies vary widely. Some states provide by legislation that the names and photographs of juvenile offenders may not be used in news stories. The decision in *Kozler* v. *N. Y. Telephone Company, 108 Atl. (N.J.) 375,* has upheld such a provision. Many news services voluntarily have established a policy of not printing names of juveniles.

On the other extreme is the view that the public is entitled to know what is happening and that the press should have no restrictions. However, it is generally held that except in certain special circumstances the release of names is in direct conflict with the whole concept of the treatment of the juvenile offender and that great damage may be done to any program of rehabilitation. It is also believed that it is unfair to have a juvenile record follow a person through life. This is entirely sound, but there are limited circumstances where juveniles might be identified in news stories. Such circumstances are in cases of very serious crimes or where the name, description, and photograph might help in the apprehension of a highly dangerous juvenile.

Similar policies should also be developed relative to the release of the names of juvenile victims of adult acts. This is particularly important if the crime against the juvenile is one where there may be considerable psychological involvement, as in the case of sex crimes. It is sound policy not to release the names of juvenile victims of sex offenders since this would make their recovery from the resulting psychological trauma increasingly difficult.

If the policy is not controlled by law, the police administrator, the judge of the juvenile court, and key juvenile agency heads should meet with the various press services and work out a definite policy. Almost all news services are entirely reasonable in relation to this problem but would like to have sound, written policies developed to act as a guide as to just what they can and cannot print.

Detention During Investigation. Few investigations are completed on the spot. It is often necessary to hold a juvenile until considerable investigation has been made. Again, there may be a very specific state law regulating such detention. If the law does not spell out a complete policy, it will be necessary for the police department and the juvenile court to develop such a policy.

The juvenile should never be put in detention just for punishment, nor should he be held only so the officers can investigate the case at their convenience. The sound reasons for detention are:

1. To allow for completion of the investigation with all reasonable dispatch.

2. If the child is so incorrigible as to be beyond the control of his parents, the parents cannot be located, or where there is good reason to believe that they will not accept the responsibility.

3. Where the child has no home because of abandonment or similar circumstances.

4. Where the child has a previous bad record. Just what constitutes a "bad record" must be defined so that he will not be placed in detention because he may have incurred the enmity of an officer.

When a child is placed in detention, the parents must be notified and, if the school is in session, school authorities. Some states have a law requiring immediate notification of the parents as soon as the child is taken into custody. This requirement rarely interferes with police work except in those cases where the parents might be a part of the child's criminal activity. In such cases the parents would soon be under arrest themselves, and such notification would not be necessary.

The place of detention has been discussed previously. However, what about holding the child for short periods at the police station? This is often highly desirable for the investigation may be progressing so fast that it would be highly inconvenient to go back and forth to the juvenile home or some other approved detention facility in order to question the juvenile further and confront him with witnesses or accomplices. Here a policy should be established in conjunction with the juvenile court. Most judges will realize that such detention is often necessary for a proper investigation.

How long should such a detention last? Again the law may answer this question. The period may be as short as two hours. Some people believe it should be as long as 48 hours. It is not possible to set a definite time limit. In the case of adult offenders charged with violations of state laws, no court has said just how long they may be held before a charge is filed, because there is too much variation among individual cases. From a police standpoint a good policy would be that the juvenile might be held by the police in proper facilities until the juvenile court judge is available and can be informed of the facts. He then can decide where and for how long the juvenile can be held, taking into consideration the facts of each individual case. The final policy should be agreed upon by the police and the juvenile court and put into writing.

Forms Required. Many of the forms used in a well developed police record system apply equally well for juveniles. There is rarely need for a separate juvenile arrest form although many agencies do use such a form. Their reason for doing this is because it is important in juvenile cases to have certain additional information about the family, school, and the disposition of the case. However, this additional information can always be obtained on the investigation form except in the minor cases where an immediate disposition is made without additional investigation. In such minor cases, the additional information is rarely needed, so there is no sound reason to have a special juvenile arrest form.

Except for the limited additional information mentioned above, a juvenile investigation form is little different from the standard form. However, for convenience, it is desirable to have a juvenile investigation form so that the basic data can be most easily recorded. It is a good idea to have this form in a color different from the adult form so as to facilitate record handling.

A question of policy arises in the use of a social history form by the police. Some agencies who receive a juvenile form from the police would like to have a long record disclosing many social factors about previous history and present status. Their reason for this is that it will save them an hour or two getting all of this data from the child. A policy should be established here. The records made by the police should be entirely adequate for them to perform their function, but no more. If part or all of the data requested by the agency are of demonstrated value to the police, they will have already recorded it and, if there is no reason of policy to the contrary, the agency can be furnished with a copy. The police should not make records, however, only for the convenience of someone else.

The juvenile unit duties are enough different from other units of the department that a different daily activity report form may be needed. If it is not possible to use the same form as used by another unit, or if minor additions would not make it usable by more than one unit, an additional form should be devised.

Juvenile Records

The same principles and methods of records operation that are discussed in Chapter 12 apply to juvenile records. A few additional forms or variations in forms used with adults will be needed, but the systems are basically the same and all records should be the responsibility of a central records unit. This does not mean that the juvenile unit does not retain copies of certain records, or receive copies from other divisions that are needed in their day-to-day operations. Care must be taken to see that in their enthusiasm the juvenile officers do not establish an independent record system. The only exception would be the occurrence of a highly restrictive law, advocated by nonpolice agencies concerned with juveniles, that might prohibit the combining of juvenile and adult records in the same system. Even if there is the more frequently found type of law that limits disclosure of juvenile record information, this is no reason why juvenile records cannot be properly maintained in a central system.

Records Systems and Policies

The reasons for a juvenile record system are very much the same as for the entire police record system:

1. Assist in the investigation of cases.

2. Help lay programs that will reduce the problem by locating problem areas and circumstances related to delinquency.

3. Evaluate the effectiveness of the operation and allow administrative planning and control.

4. Evaluate individual officers.

5. Assist in the disposition of cases in juvenile court, through referral to an agency or by other approved methods.

Filing of Juvenile Records. Unless there is a provision of the law to the contrary, juvenile records should be filed with all police records, using the same methods of filing and indexing. One additional control file may be of value, a family file. Juvenile problems tend to run in certain families, so a single file on the background of the family and the police contacts with it may save considerable trouble when a member of that family appears in police circles. While it would be possible to assemble all of this information from the files on the various members of the family, it may prove time-saving to develop this file. A nickname or monicker file is of considerable value with juveniles since many of their acquaintances are on the basis of nicknames. If the department has a nickname file already, there is no reason why the juveniles cannot be included in it. If not, this is a good file to develop.

The juvenile unit may try to get an independent record system, either entirely apart from the regular record system or as a complete duplication of the system. Unless this is required by law, it should not be permitted. This same difficulty has appeared over the years with all specialized units of the police, and in each case, in spite of the many arguments that have been advanced, it has always proven that the close central control of records is essential.

Access to Juvenile Records. Again the law may define who has access to juvenile records. If it does not, the department must establish a policy because there may be many sorts of agencies that would like to come down to the station and rummage through the records. The various units of the police department, of course, should have access, following the same procedures as for other records. Access by agencies with an acceptable program of working with juveniles should also be allowed, with certain limitations. The exact policies will depend upon the local situation. Some official agencies may be allowed the same access as the police have; others should be limited to securing records through the assistance of a juvenile officer. Some with stated high purposes may not have access at all, depending upon how well their stated and realized objectives coincide.

Chapter 7

THE PATROL FUNCTION

Much of the important work which police departments are called upon to perform is of an emergency nature. Some elements of these emergencies, however, are conditions that can be observed and recorded and sometimes eliminated or altered by routine police operations. These day-to-day duties of lessening the likelihood of incidents that require police attention, and of dealing with those that arise, fall upon the patrol force.

The patrol force is the backbone of the police department. It is its largest unit. Distributed throughout the area of the municipality, it is in continual contact with the citizens of the community. These men are the eyes and ears of the police administrator. Plans and tactics devised by these administrators for the solution of police problems depend heavily on the information gathered and reported by the uniformed force.

The work of the patrol force includes all police functions. Therefore, the more effective the patrol division, the less need there is for the other, more specialized, operating divisions. Because it is impossible for the patrol force to be 100 per cent effective in all police functions, the other operating divisions are necessary only to the extent that the patrol division falls short of this ideal. Therefore any efforts made to improve or strengthen the other divisions at the expense of the patrol division will result in a vicious circle, for the weakening of patrol only increases the burden on the special units.

Because of their proximity to the place of occurrence, and because of the speedy response of radio-equipped cars, one or more members of the patrol division usually arrive first at the scene of a crime or disaster. The measures adopted to apprehend violators, preserve evidence, or give relief are most telling when promptly instituted. Hence the work of the patrolmen is of far-reaching importance, and the quality of service rendered by the whole department is largely dependent upon their competence.

Seen on all occasions and in all places on the streets of the community, the patrolmen are the public symbols of the department. Their conduct and the nature of their services impress citizens with the degree of worth of their police guardians. The patrolman who performs in a slovenly or ineffective manner may impair the standing of the whole force in the eyes of the community. A few instances of gross misconduct can easily bring the entire force into disrepute. Much time and earnest work are required to build an enviable reputation, but a few brief moments of error may destroy it.

The manner of selecting, training, directing, and disciplining policemen will determine the effectiveness and affect the prestige of the patrol force. Capabilities of personnel will in great part either limit or aid the police commander in his efforts to carry out a plan.

Objectives and Activities of the Patrol Force

Principal duties of the patrol force are: to prevent violations of laws and ordinances;

to suppress disturbances; to arrest offenders; and to give aid, relief, and information to all citizens as circumstances require. These responsibilities are accomplished by active patrol on the streets in all areas and particularly those areas where crimes frequently occur. An active patrol force is the municipality's open guarantee of orderly government carried out, if possible, by persuasion; if necessary, by force.

Objectives

The functions of the police department were discussed in Chapter 2, but it may be well to give particular consideration at the beginning of this chapter to the objectives as they apply to the patrol division.

Prevention of Crime. A well turned-out officer, on foot or in a clean, conspicuously marked car, represents a deterrent force that helps prevent crime before it starts. A patrolman observes conditions which are conducive to crime, such as unattended property, and observes suspicious persons. He follows up with inquiry, which further contributes to crime prevention.

Enforcement of Laws. A patrolman must know his duties and responsibilities and also know the law. He frequently is called on to make on-the-spot investigations and take appropriate enforcement action.

Protection of Life and Property. Citizens depend upon the patrol officer to protect them and their property from crimes and disasters by ridding the area of criminals and requiring safe practices, especially relating to traffic.

Preservation of Peace. A large portion of the patrolman's time is spent in handling drunk and disorderly persons, crimes of violence, possession of firearms, trespassing, vagrancy, and related offenses.

Apprehension of Criminals. Since a patrolman makes many arrests on the spot and without warning, he must know the techniques and mechanics of arrest for his own protection and for that of the public.

These objectives cover a wide scope, and the operative methods or procedures applied by patrolmen in their achievement are marked by an even greater variety and range.

Activities

Police patrol activities may, in turn, be discussed at length under 10 general headings: (1) patrol and observation, (2) control of public gatherings, (3) miscellaneous field services, (4) answering calls, (5) disposing of complaints, (6) investigation on patrol, (7) collection and preservation of evidence, (8) arrest of offenders, (9) preparation of reports, and (10) testifying in court.

Patrol and Observation. Patrol diminishes the potential offender's belief in the existence of an opportunity to violate the law successfully. The patrolman must be constantly alert, while moving about his beat, for conditions and things which may facilitate or promote the commission of crimes and other incidents that require police service.

Observation is the function that most completely describes the patrolman's job; most other duties depend on what he observes. The extent and accuracy of his observation influence his ability to discover insecure premises, unwholesome conditions, questionable characters, and other police hazards. His power to observe also enables him to report offenses, to detect offenders, to know the habits of people living on his beat, to be familiar with the residential and commercial districts that are the most frequent scenes of crime, and to size up the social environment and influences which must be controlled if crime is to be prevented. His power of observation assists the patrolman to perform effectively his first and most important task — to prevent law violations. It also makes him useful to the chief and his command group and to the officers assigned to the specialized divisions. The patrolman thus serves as the eyes and ears of the department. His function of observation not only makes him the focal point of police operation and administration but also permits him to aid other city departments.

Control of Public Gatherings. The patrolman is frequently assigned to public meetings and assemblies. He may be sent to a regularly scheduled meeting, to maintain order and to quell disturbances. Or he may be called upon to handle a spontaneous gathering of citizens at a fire, accident scene, or similar incident. Usually the patrolman is concerned only with maintaining order and preventing violence. Sometimes, however, the assembly must be dispersed either because it is obstructing traffic or because it is trespassing unlawfully on private property. Then great tact is required to avoid an open clash between the police and citizens. In all such cases the patrolman must keep in mind that free speech and peaceful assembly are important constitutional rights which should not be denied unless there is open violation of law.

Miscellaneous Field Services. The patrolman performs a wide variety of public services while on duty. Some services are provided to citizens who telephone to headquarters or approach the officer on the street for assistance. Many, however, are initiated by the officer himself on observing a situation that requires his attention.

Since the patrolman's primary duty is to prevent crime, his first attention should be given to the security of persons and property on his beat. For this reason he inspects business establishments that are likely to attract burglars or other thieves. When he discovers points vulnerable to attack, he must persuade the proprietor to strengthen the physical security of his premises and his operating procedures so the hazard will be lessened. The patrolman also checks the security of commercial establishments after closing hours and of homes left temporarily vacant. His presence in areas of greatest hazard, made known by frequent and conspicuous patrol, lessens the opportunity for criminal attack.

In addition to duties that contribute directly to crime prevention and law enforcement, the patrolman has other responsibilities, such as caring for persons who are injured, sick, or lost; caring for or destroying injured, vicious, or strayed animals; referring sick or destitute persons to welfare agencies; and so on. Probably the most time-consuming activity of patrolmen is the enforcement of miscellaneous minor regulations.

As previously indicated, many of the patrolman's duties are of assistance to other city departments. These might include discovering and reporting fires and fire hazards, leaking water mains, open manholes, pavement and sidewalk defects, street light outages, failures to obtain licenses and permits, illegal posting of signs and other advertisements, and improper storage, display, or handling of foodstuffs, garbage, or trash.

Duties of the patrolman in connection with vice and juvenile delinquency control will vary according to the size of the department and the nature of its organization and operating procedures. The best administrative practice is to assign to the patrolmen on their beats only the duties that do not interfere with their essential patrol activities and that are not performed substantially better by the specialists.

Answering Calls. The patrolman is dispatched to every conceivable type of emergency, including suicides, illnesses, childbirth, fires, explosions, and catastrophes. He must be able to render first aid and other assistance and to know what is required in the particular situation. When sent to the scene of a crime, he should arrest the perpetrator or pursue him if apprehension seems likely, take care of injured persons, safeguard physical evidence, and recover stolen property. He is also called upon to render a wide variety of services that have no relationships to crime or criminals yet may protect life and property.

Disposing of Minor Complaints. The patrolman is called upon to settle a variety of complaints that are noncriminal in character or that involve minor violations. The more friendly the patrolman is with the people on his beat (and the number of his friends is one measure of his value as a patrolman), the more likely they are to come to him for advice and help when they are in trouble. They often expect him to take action in cases that are not criminal in nature. He will be appealed to in neighborhood and family quarrels, in unethical but not criminal business details, in cases which are grounds for civil but not criminal action in court. Cases of this type are potential stimuli to criminal acts, and the patrolman should make every effort to adjust and settle such disputes peacefully, by persuasion and explanation of the laws or regulations involved. When he lacks authority to act, he must explain the limits of his jurisdiction to the parties concerned and refer the persons involved to the proper agencies or individuals.

The patrolman also receives many complaints regarding other services rendered by the city, such as garbage and refuse collection, street repairs, and planting and care of street trees. He must respond to these complaints courteously and refer them immediately to the proper city department in accordance with department policy.

Investigation on Patrol. The patrolman makes many investigations. Some relate to the complaints mentioned above; others grow out of the observation by the patrolman of conditions or situations on his beat that require his attention. Investigations include gathering evidence on vice activities on his beat; investigating door-to-door canvassers, beggars, and other suspicious persons; checking vehicles with defaced or no license plates; or stopping automobiles driven in a suspicious manner.

Whenever the investigation can be made on the spot, the patrolman should do so. For example, if investigation of a suspicious character reveals that he is wanted, the officer should take him to headquarters at once. In many instances, however, circumstances make it desirable to summon help.

A patrolman should also make the preliminary investigation of crimes that are committed on his beat. The preliminary investigation is defined and other investigative tasks that patrolmen should perform for detectives are discussed in Chapter 8. The patrolman also has a responsibility to detect and investigate vice, juvenile, traffic, and similar situations on his beat. He should complete minor investigations and report major cases to the special divisions concerned when necessary. Effective investigation and clearance of cases by patrolmen conserves time and reduces the number of specialists required. When competent patrolmen perform and all branches of the department are coordinated, the force works as a unit, and a superior quality of police service is provided.

Collection and Preservation of Physical Evidence. Evidence which might be tampered with, removed, or destroyed must be preserved as nearly as possible in the condition in which it was found. The volume of evidence destroyed by the carelessness of policemen in many departments is appalling. The ability of the patrolman to recognize what constitutes good evidence and how to safeguard it is a basic factor in the prosecution of offenders. The whole structure of the administration of justice depends in no small part on the patrolman's effectiveness in preserving evidence.

Arrest of Offenders. Arrest is a primary patrol duty. When the first officer arrives, the trail of the criminal may be "hot," and immediate pursuit is the logical move. He is constantly on the alert for wanted persons. He is frequently called upon to make arrests by warrant. In order to carry out this function, he must be well trained in the strategy of arrest where resistance or escape is likely.

In addition to the arrest of criminals, patrolmen must dispose of hundreds of less serious violators. Some of these may require physical arrest and transportation to headquarters for booking; many will be disposed of more conveniently and economically by citation. Minor violators may receive only a warning.

Preparation of Reports. If the patrolman's observation and investigation activities are to be most productive, they must be documented and supported by complete and carefully prepared reports. Throughout this volume the value of accurate and up-to-date records and statistical information as the basis for the entire police operation is stressed. Since the patrolman is the primary contact man of the department it is up to him to provide the bulk of the raw data from which adequate records can be prepared.

Testifying in Court. Patrolmen are often witnesses in criminal cases. Sometimes the patrolman is the only witness to the commission of a crime, or he may have secured important evidence such as dying declarations or confessions. The patrolman's testimony naturally carries great weight with the jury, hence it must be presented effectively.

Types of Patrol

The most common and best known form of patrol the world over is that performed on foot and in uniform. Its development in England as the principal device to be used in the prevention of crimes and disorders may be traced to action taken by Henry Fielding as a Bow Street Magistrate in London in 1763. He created an organized police force of deputy constables: the Bow Street Runners to investigate crimes and apprehend criminals for prosecution in the Bow Street Court, and the Bow Street Patrols engaged in foot and horse patrol to prevent the criminal depredations and disorders then rampant. The Bow Street Runners were intended to repress criminal activities by apprehending and prosecuting the criminal, the patrols to prevent the criminal act in the first instance.

The demonstrated success of these patrols gave rise to Sir Robert Peel's Metropolitan Police Act of 1829. The Peel Act created a single uniformed force of professional police to provide a patrol of the entire jurisdiction by day as well as by night. Its primary task was to prevent crime and disorder. The criminal investigation division of the Metropolitan Police was not created until many years later.

Since the creation of the London Metropolitan Police, almost every organized community in the civilized world has employed uniformed patrol (civilian in contrast to military) to protect the lives and property of its citizens. Adaptations of this device have consisted principally in the provision of some more suitable mode of transportation for the patrolman and a variation in the number of men patrolling together on a beat.

Horse Patrol

Horses are rarely used by police in the United States. Policemen mounted on horses provide a most colorful patrol, and they look well on parade. Thus cities sometimes continue their use largely for these sentimental reasons in spite of a cost far in excess of the value received.

Bicycle Patrol

The simple and silent bicycle is inexpensive and has decided advantages in places where the climate and conditions permit its use. They are very nearly noiseless and can be ridden where no auto could go and where the resultant noise of such a vehicle or of a motorcycle would destroy the element of surprise. Such areas as parks and playgrounds may be so patrolled with obvious advantages. The development of lightweight, transistorized police radio has stimulated a new interest in this form of patrol.

Motorcycle Patrol

Motorcycles, both two-wheel and three-wheel, are often used in parking and traffic control and, to a lesser extent, for general patrol. The two-wheel motorcycles have lost ground to both cars and three-wheel motorcycles in recent years. While from 1949 to 1956 the number of patrol cars in cities over 100,000 increased by 36 per cent and the number of three-wheel motorcycles increased by 121 per cent, the number of two-wheel motorcycles increased by only 6 per cent.[1]

While two-wheel motorcycles are popular for traffic enforcement, parade, and escort duty, the motorcycle officer is frequently in a special class for both prestige and pay. The pay is often earned because accidents are frequent and serious as demonstrated by insurance rates. Proper supervision is difficult, radio equipment is hard to maintain, and these machines can be used only in good weather thus limiting their operations to use less than 50 per cent of the year in many parts of the United States.

The three-wheel motorcycle is considerably safer at low speeds and less wearing on the officer. It has great utility in traffic patrol in congested areas, in enforcement of parking regulations, and in escort duty. It has been used for general patrol in certain cities. Some cities are now using the American-made compact cars on an experimental basis to replace some three-wheel motorcycles because the cars have the advantage of protecting the officer and equipment from the weather, are safer, and allow prisoners to be transported.

Careful records should be kept of the relative costs of operating motorcycles and cars. Time lost by accidents should also be included in the cost, but even if this is not done, the actual cost of motorcycle operation closely approaches that of an automobile. When time lost because of accidents is included, the cost is usually much greater. The use of motorcycles should be very carefully considered to make certain that they can do the job well enough to offset this increased cost and hazard. It should be noted here that the danger to personnel has been reduced somewhat by requiring the officers to wear a specially designed helmet. If motorcycles are used, such helmets should be furnished with specific regulations as to fitting and wearing them properly.

Automobile Patrol

Auto patrol is the standard in police departments throughout the country. The automobile gets the patrolman over the streets and through the alleys quickly so that large areas can be covered, protects him from the elements, provides protection in traffic or in a gun battle, gives him equipment comparable to the criminal or traffic violator he sometimes must pursue, and enables several officers or prisoners to be transported at one time.

---

[1] *The Municipal Year Book* (Chicago: International City Managers' Association, 1950 and 1957).

An auto patrolman should not ride continuously in his car; he should stop occasionally to patrol an area on foot. This supplemental foot patrol is especially desirable where doors should be tried and windows inspected in small clusters of retail stores found in residential districts. Foot patrol should also be interspersed with driving in areas where complaints and violations frequently originate. Occasional foot patrol enables the officer to become acquainted with the people on his beat and with conditions that deserve his attention. His value as the eyes and ears of the department is thus enhanced.

Special care must be taken to preserve contact with headquarters during periods of foot patrol. When two-way radio is used, the patrolman can notify headquarters before he leaves the car and immediately on his return, or he may increase the loud-speaker volume so that he can hear it through an open car window from some distance and thus return as soon as he hears a broadcast. By the use of a call selector, the dispatcher may cause the horn to blow or a light to burn on the top of any selected police auto, thus permitting the driver greater freedom in patrolling at a distance from his car.

Foot versus Auto Patrol. A growing number of police administrators believe that foot patrol should be replaced by automobile patrol except in areas where the full time of the patrolman is devoted to inspectional duties. In the largest cities, some foot patrol will continue to be necessary to expeditiously check the security of business establishments and to perform other inspectional tasks. In most cities, however, analysis of the need for foot patrol will show that nearly all can be replaced by auto patrol with greater efficiency and economy in operation.

The greater area that can be patrolled, the ability of auto patrolmen to overtake offenders in automobiles, the speed with which officers can respond to emergency calls without impairing their physical and mental powers by physical exhaustion, are obvious advantages gained by mounting patrolmen in cars. The auto protects the patrolman from inclement weather and permits him to carry extra clothing, a first aid kit, fire extinguisher, a riot gun, and other equipment. The auto can transport other officers as well as prisoners. The automobile is an all-weather machine, in contrast to the motorcycle. By means of two-way radio the officer is in constant communication with headquarters.

There are certain disadvantages to auto patrol. They arise from loss of contact between the officer and the people on his beat. He may not have close contact with people who are in a position to assist when help is needed; it is not as easy to develop sources of information from juveniles, cab drivers, and other sources; he may not be as well informed about the habits and "hang-outs" of criminals; and it may be more difficult to perform inspectional duties. In general, public relations are more difficult because of this loss of contact.

Many of these disadvantages are compensated, however, if officers are indoctrinated in the proper use of the patrol car. The patrolman should learn that it is simply a piece of equipment used to help him do a better job of patrol. If foot patrol is most effective in a certain area, he should get out of the car and patrol on foot, returning to the car to go to another point for foot patrol or to cover areas where the auto is more effective.

Motor and foot patrols are not mutually exclusive in all cases, for the same area may be covered by both. Even in those areas where foot patrol is deemed necessary, it may be well to supplement this coverage by including the area within the beat of a radio-equipped patrol car in order that constant contact with headquarters may be maintained. The patrol sergeant supervising foot patrolmen should cover his rounds by car, thus increasing his opportunities to observe and to supplement foot patrol with the more flexible and responsive patrol car.

One-Man versus Two-Man Car Patrol. When automobiles were first introduced into police work they were merely an auxiliary to foot patrol. The auto squad was held in reserve to answer direct calls from headquarters in emergency cases which frequently occasioned sending two or more men at once. The practice of assigning more than one officer to a car developed from this auto squad plan, and the tradition of two men in patrol cars has persisted in a small proportion of cities (see Table 4). In 90 per cent of the cities over 10,000 population, however, one-man patrol is used exclusively or in conjunction with two-man patrol (Table 4).

Under all ordinary patrol conditions one-man car patrol should be adequate, in the same way that a one-man foot patrol is adequate under ordinary conditions. Improved police communications and speed of response both make the single officer in a car more effective than his earlier counterpart on foot and provide him with quicker, more effective support when he calls for it. Single patrolmen operating alone in cars are more efficient than pairs, for two reasons:

1. Let us assume that the city has available 10 men for patrol duty during a particular shift. If the men operate in pairs, the city is divided into five patrol areas. If they operate singly, the city can be divided into 10 districts, each only half as large. Twice the patrol service is thus provided; a police car gives twice as much attention to the district; a given police hazard can be inspected or passed during a tour of duty twice as many times as it would if there were only half as many units, and the distance to travel on support missions is effectively reduced.

2. An officer patrolling alone must give first attention to police duties. There are no distractions other than those he is obligated to notice on his beat, and he is completely self dependent for his own safety and welfare. It has been demonstrated that an officer patrolling by himself in a car is actually safer than when accompanied by a brother officer. The presence of a second officer appears to discourage reasonable caution, either because of pride that prevents the second officer from observing danger or because of failure to take suitable precautions lest the companion interpret caution as cowardice. When an officer is alone in a patrol car he knows that he has no one else to rely upon in the event of trouble. Consequently he is cautious in stepping into dangerous situations and is better prepared to take care of unexpected emergencies.

When officers are placed alone in automobiles, they must be trained in the proper technique of stopping suspicious cars in order to minimize the danger to themselves. It is also advisable to have the police cars equipped with floodlights to illuminate the interior of the car being stopped and to prevent occupants from easily seeing what the officer is doing.

An effective way of assisting the lone officer and providing the dispatcher with important information consists of having each officer radio the dispatcher of the location, license number, make, and any unusual characteristics of the vehicle he is about to approach. The benefits of such a procedure are twofold, reminding the officer of the gravity of his position and allowing tight control by the commanding officer. Once such a procedure is adopted it should be incorporated in the manual of procedures, and compliance by all personnel should be mandatory.

When officers operate singly in patrol cars it is also essential that dispatching procedures be developed to assure that a sufficient force is sent on each call to accomplish the police purpose and to lessen the hazard to the officers. An example of dispatching procedures to be used when a call is received that a criminal is in operation is found in a later section of this chapter.

Table 4

Manning of Police Patrol Cars in Cities Over 10,000: 1959

Population Group	Number of Cities Reporting Motorized Patrol	Two-Man Patrol Cars Only		One-Man and Two-Man Patrol Cars		One-Man Patrol Cars Only	
		Number	Per Cent	Number	Per Cent	Number	Per Cent
Cities over 500,000 ...	18	6	33.3	11	61.1	1	5.6
250,000 to 500,000	20	1	5.0	16	80.0	3	15.0
100,000 to 250,000	65	11	16.9	48	73.8	6	9.3
50,000 to 100,000	125	21	16.8	89	71.2	15	23.0
25,000 to 50,000......	266	27	10.2	167	62.8	72	37.0
10,000 to 25,000......	483	34	7.0	293	60.7	156	32.3
All cities over 10,000 ..	977	100	10.2	624	63.9	253	25.9

Source: *The Municipal Year Book, 1960*, p. 396.

Conspicuous Patrol Car. Most police departments mark their police cars by signs and letters on the sides and rear and frequently by distinctive color combinations. The effect of this practice is good. Not only are potential violators warned of the presence of police, but all citizens who observe them have a feeling of confidence inspired by the knowledge that their guardians are on duty.

The desirability of having a patrolman in uniform is universally recognized, and all of the reasons for doing so apply equally to uniforming his car. The practice increases public consciousness of police service. It also increases the preventative value of patrol by making apparent the presence of the police. The deterrent value on the potential traffic violator is strong, and it is equally effective in the case of the criminal. Distinctively marked police cars minimize the chances of a citizen's mistaking the identity of a police car and refusing to stop when directed to, or using nonrecognition as an excuse in the event he tries to outrun the police. A conspicuous and distinctive vehicle serves as a constant reminder to the police officer that he is on responsible public business requiring exemplary behavior and close and continuous attention to duty. In addition, the patrol sergeant's job of supervision is made easier when patrolmen operate in conspicuously marked cars.

British Patrol Experiments[2]

The British, traditionally sound in police philosophy, have also demonstrated an enviable audacity in their approach to more productive patrol methods. A full generation ago a highly decentralized system for distributing and supervising patrols was developed. This plan has literally swept the British Isles during the past 20 years, thus demonstrating a commendable willingness to meet new problems with new methods.

A further departure is "team policing" employed in Aberdeen and in the borough of Salford, each with a population around 180,000. Designed to achieve a better integration of communications and motor equipment and more varied duties for uniformed constables,

[2] See Stanley R. Schrotel, "Changing Patrol Methods," *The Annals*, January, 1954, pp. 51-53.

team policing in these communities has produced a greater element of surprise in patrol coverage, a more adequate response in emergencies, and an increasing interest in patrol among the rank and file.

In Aberdeen

Aberdeen abolished fixed beats worked by single constables and has substituted much larger patrol areas worked by a team of constables under a sergeant. Each team has been given a police car, which the sergeant uses to move his men from one part of the patrol area to another. Constables are encouraged to follow up any incidents themselves, without calling on specialists to help except in cases of real difficulty. The main features of the system are its mobility and the fact that constables act as a team rather than as individuals. The results in Aberdeen have been good. A substantial saving in manpower has been effected, and the number of arrests has increased.

The Salford Plan

Salford retains the idea of a team of constables operating from a police car but provides greater flexibility than the Aberdeen plan. The city is divided into police districts, but the patrol areas in each district are kept flexible. Rough boundaries are laid down for beats during each of the three tours of duty to assure that there are enough on duty when and where they are most likely to be needed. Boundaries of beats are changed three times a day to accommodate to changing needs, but the officer in charge of each district also exercises wide powers to change the beats whenever circumstances make it necessary. A beat bordering the docks, for example, may be made much smaller during a dock strike, with its abnormal possibilities of trouble, than would be necessary during normal working conditions.

In the Salford plan, a police team consists of nine constables with a sergeant in charge. A police car fitted with radio serves each team. Before each team starts its eight-hour tour of duty the district commander and the sergeant review the work that is likely to arise. They consider the recent incidence and location of crimes and street accidents, complaints from the public of general nuisances, any property requiring special protection, and similar matters. The sergeant then draws up a list of "operations" for each man. Two or three may be detailed for point duty, others will be given particular streets to patrol, and the chances are that one man will be kept with the sergeant and the driver in the car, which also will be used for patrol duties. The whole team is told what to look for and what sort of incidents are likely to occur. The car serves the dual purpose of a mobile police station and a quick means of moving the constables about from one area to another.

As in the traditional beat system, the constable remains individually responsible for a definite area or duty. The chief difference from more familiar systems is that the beat is changed immediately to fit any situation. Particularly notable is the fact that the interest and keenness of the patrolmen are greatly increased. The monotony of patrolling the same area week after week, waiting for something to turn up, is broken, and the constable accordingly gains more experience in a shorter time than is possible under orthodox systems. Improvement in morale has been a salient feature.

On the basis of limited experience thus far, the proportion of indictable offenses cleared by arrest has risen one-third. Patrols make nearly twice as many arrests as they did before the system was introduced, and the number of incidents reported has increased by nearly 50 per cent. With such a record of achievement, team policing appears destined for wider adoption in Great Britain, and results there have been watched with keen interest here.

Patrol Strength

No exact formula for determining adequate patrol strength exists, although there have been attempts to devise such a formula. An estimate was made for Chicago many years ago on the basis of the following data collected for each police district in the city:[3]

1. Number, name, and boundaries
2. Topographical peculiarities
3. Total area
4. Areas protected by park police
5. Population
6. Density of population
7. Use areas
   (1) Residential mileage
   (2) Commercial mileage
   (3) Industrial mileage
   (4) Mileage of open spaces and sparsely populated areas
8. Juvenile delinquency rate
9. Crime rates
   (1) Burglary
   (2) Robbery
   (3) All other
10. High risk areas (central business district, stockyards, etc.)
11. Patrol barriers (viaducts, railroads, etc.)

By using different patrol scales for residential, commercial, and industrial mileage, arbitrarily weighing districts on the basis of crime rates and delinquency, allowing for supplementary park police, and increasing patrol strength during night hours because of a high crime rate and reduced visibility, it was possible to estimate roughly the number of patrolmen needed. On the basis of this analysis it was proposed that the patrol force be increased from 4,874 to 13,096.[4] The addition of more than 8,000 men at an annual cost of more than $10 million was both politically and financially impractical, but the exercise in determining optimum staffing based on definite, observed factors was useful and a good illustration for other departments.

Since the Chicago study, a number of cities have improved the method used, and with the development of machine analysis of statistical data have been able to make more inclusive studies. Los Angeles is presently doing advanced research on manpower requirements, but at this time there is no simple, easy way to determine patrol strength. However, a good police administrator will be able to develop estimates that are certainly more accurate than pulling a figure out of a hat or only comparing his city with those of similar size. Such careful estimates do give the police chief, the chief administrator of the city, the legislative body, and the public some idea of how far below numerical adequacy the present force is. They also give a legitimate basis for balancing the need for additional patrolmen against other budgetary needs when additional funds are available.

The amount and kind of crime current in the community will be the principal factors

---

[3] See Citizens' Police Committee of Chicago, *Chicago Police Problems* (Chicago: University of Chicago Press, 1931), pp. 258-59.
[4] *Ibid.*, pp. 258-69.

in determining how many policemen are required. Place of occurrence and time of commission also have weight in the decision. The book of experience itself must be consulted for this basic material. A competent determination of required numerical strength rests heavily upon accurate and adequate police records. From no other source is this information completely available.

In any estimate of required patrol strength, careful account should be taken of the actual drain on the patrol force for purposes other than basic patrol. In most municipalities street traffic regulation makes heavy demands upon the police personnel. Cross-traffic must be regulated to relieve congestion and tangles, and parking laws must be enforced. School children must be protected four times daily at numerous street crossings on school days. Schoolboy patrols or auxiliary police in many cities are utilized to relieve regular policemen of these duties, but they too must be supervised and trained in their duties by policemen.

In the larger cities there may be further heavy drains for special details. In Chicago, for example, it was found that there were 62 special details which accounted for a daily average service loss of about 200 men. Some of these details were to other law enforcement agencies such as the state's attorney, the election commission, and the criminal court. Others were to private groups and individuals such as the civic opera, the ball parks, the automobile show, and various newspapers.[5]

Other public departments should not expect to tap the police force continuously. If these departments require permanently assigned police, the cost should be included in their own budgets and the police department should be augmented by the number of men involved; or else these departments should engage their own guards and watchmen officers. Police must be responsible for patrolling streets and controlling traffic wherever large crowds gather, as at a ball game, but they should not be expected to police the interior of the ball park unless the city is fully compensated for their services.

Distribution of Patrol Force[6]

Until recent years the practice in organizing the work in almost all police departments has been to distribute the patrol force evenly among three eight-hour shifts and to assign the officers to beats of equal area. This method of distribution evidences either ignorance of hourly and geographical fluctuations in the police load or indifference to the increase in efficiency that results from distributing the force on the basis of need. When beats of equal area or shifts of equal strength are established independently of variations in need for police service, some are likely to require several times more police work than others.

Use of the police car for patrol service did not change the problem of distribution except to expand patrol to cover the entire city. At first, the cities were divided into districts of equal area. When the number of patrol cars was very limited, this procedure sometimes resulted in fairly equitable divisions, especially in smaller cities whose expansion had been relatively even in all directions. In such cities the four districts formed by the intersection of the main streets constituted patrol districts. These were often

---

[5] *Ibid.*, pp. 254-55.

[6] A step-by-step procedure for distribution of police patrol is found in O. W. Wilson, *Police Administration* (New York: McGraw-Hill Book Company, 1950), appendix; see also, by same author, *Police Planning* (Springfield, Illinois: Charles C Thomas, Publisher, 1952), pp. 84-97.

similar in area and police hazards, although perhaps just as often they were dissimilar and it took considerable experience to recognize the fact.

As the number of patrol cars increased, inequalities in the police load in districts of equal area became apparent to some police chiefs and they attempted to equalize loads by varying the size of the districts. At first they relied entirely on their impressions of the distribution of offenses to estimate the need for police service in various sections of the community. When the unreliability of these estimates became apparent, a few developed pin maps to show the location of offenses. This step was the beginning of a statistical method for determining patrol distribution needs. Use of census tract maps and crime, traffic accident, misdemeanor, and complaint data properly plotted are today's measuring devices for distribution of patrol force.

The first phase of the problem of distribution relates to chronological assignment of the force throughout the day on the basis of hourly need for police service. The second phase involves division of the total area into beats, each patrolled by one man or one car with the size determined by relative need for police service. If the city is very large and has police substations, the first step would be to divide the force among the stations because the need for police service on the basis of time would probably vary from substation to substation. Further divisions by time and beat area could then be made.

Data Required[7]

The type of patrol used and the speed with which beats are to be covered are fundamental in the plan. Once these decisions have been made, and a given number of officers is assigned for patrol duty, the task of distributing the force according to need for police service begins.

The first step in distribution is to determine if there are certain areas where conditions justify maintenance of foot patrol. Foot patrol may be necessary in major business districts and areas where occurrences requiring police actions are frequent. Examples are districts in which large numbers of people congregate, recreational centers, and districts in which honkytonks and cheap dives predominate. The layout of the foot beat is relatively simple, involving a determination of the man-hours needed to cover the distances involved and to meet police hazards predominating in the area. The balance of the patrol force should be motorized and assigned to the various districts into which the area of the city is divided.

Data for measuring the proportionate need for police service come largely from the records of the department since past experience and operations are the best criteria for estimating future needs. For distribution of patrol forces, it is sufficient to classify the incidents which result from police hazards as Part I crimes, Part II offenses, accidents, miscellaneous complaints, and arrests. These constitute the major areas of active police work with which the patrol force must constantly be concerned.

The need for patrol service results from police hazards, situations, or conditions which promote incidents that make some police work necessary. Events which call for an arrest, the recovery of stolen or lost property, or the investigation of a complaint or accident develop from police hazards, and the actions necessary to dispose of them are termed "called-for services."

In addition to the called-for services, the patrol force is expected to perform other

---

[7] See O. W. Wilson, *Police Administration, op. cit.,* appendix.

functions devoted to preventing incidents by minimizing or eliminating hazards. While many police hazards are too intangible to isolate and measure, the amount of police time necessary to minimize others may be fairly accurately determined. Stores present a special burglary hazard at night when employees are absent; therefore store doors, windows, and safes are inspected by the police in order to minimize this hazard. Recreation centers and retail liquor establishments are inspected to overcome other special hazards.

The need for inspectional services varies throughout the day and is a factor to be considered in distributing the force among the several shifts. Services of this character can be measured in terms of the man-hours spent in performing them. While some hazards can be isolated and measured in terms of time spent in minimizing them, others cannot be so measured because of their intangible character. The amount of time needed for meeting intangible hazards need not be known, however, to affect an equitable distribution of the patrol force. This is true because the administrator knows the manpower he has available for patrol service, and therefore he needs only to distribute his force in proportion to the frequency and seriousness of the incidents.

Determination of Shift Hours[8]

The selection of hours for the various shifts of the patrol division is an important problem for the administrator because each shift should have a force adequate to meet the need for those hours. This may be assured by assigning to each shift a force in proportion to the load. Thus if 40 per cent of the daily need for patrol service occurs on one shift, 40 per cent of the patrol force should be assigned to it. Shift periods also should be scheduled, as nearly as practicable, to provide minimum hourly deviations from their average hourly load. Even when the force detailed to one shift is sufficient to meet the average hourly need, it may not be used to full advantage during hours of less than average need, while during the hours of more than average need its quality of service will be impaired.

In order to determine hourly manpower requirements, called-for and inspectional services should be tabulated on an hourly basis and reduced to common percentages so that the hours of the day can be compared regarding the need for police services. This can be done for a full year or on the basis of representative samples for every day of the week in each season of the year. Usually the patrol force is divided into three shifts, consisting of a day shift, an afternoon and early evening shift, and a late shift. The peak load for police service commonly comes during the early evening hours. Some departments have instituted an overlapping fourth shift during the hours of this peak load working, for example, from 6:00 p.m. to 2:00 a.m.

Types of Beat Organizations

There are two schools of thought regarding the proper basis for beat organization. The first holds that beat layouts should be based on the amount of time spent in performing police services, thus necessitating reduction of all primary beat activities to a time basis. The second school holds that beat layouts should be determined by location and frequency of crimes or offenses, both actual and potential. A third and somewhat different approach, which is yet to be applied, would make beat assignments so as to bring about the greatest possible reduction in the aggregate volume of crime for the city.

This third method differs from the second in that, instead of assigning a patrol force

[8] See O. W. Wilson, *Police Records* (Chicago: Public Administration Service, 1942), pp. 237-39.

in strict proportion to the location and frequency of crime, larger forces would be detailed to the few areas of greatest hazard to bring about substantial reduction of actual and potential crime in these areas, with only sufficient details in other sections to hold conditions substantially level. The idea corresponds with selective enforcement in the traffic field although it may be more difficult to plan and carry out successfully and possibly has not been tried for this reason.

In good practice, both the time and the hazard basis can be combined to achieve effective distribution of patrol forces. The time survey determines what hours during the day occasion greatest police activity (and these may be different on Saturday than on Monday or Tuesday) thereby establishing the proportion of men needed on each shift. The hazard survey determines the areas of greatest need for police services, thereby showing where the men should be placed.

Time Basis. An illustration of the first or time approach is a study made in Cincinnati.[9] This survey was undertaken to decide accurately the amount of work that a patrolman could efficiently perform in an eight-hour shift. It was concerned only with foot patrol assignments. The following findings were made before the beat survey was actually undertaken:

1. Most of the beats were too large to permit efficient patrol.

2. Conditions had so changed since the beats were last laid out that there was no uniformity in the amount of activity required to police them.

3. Police districts or precincts should follow "natural" boundaries but should as nearly as possible contain uniform social and business conditions and should require approximately the same level of police service. There was considerable variation among police districts in these respects.

4. Police beats and districts did not conform to census tracts which had been adopted by other city departments and private agencies as the basis of their record systems. Thus no comparison was possible between police statistics and data on fire, health, and social welfare. Not only would comparable police statistics be of value to other social agencies, but the police would benefit by being able to use other social statistics in crime prevention.

The survey then proceeded to make a time study of the beat on the basis of a unit time computed for each type of police activity — auto accidents; Part I arrests; checking low-hazard, medium-hazard, and high-hazard stores; walking the beat; closing inspections; and so on. For each block covered by the survey the number of arrests and investigations made and the number of services rendered were secured from the records. Combining these data with the time-study, the number of minutes required for the effective patrol of each block was computed. The next task was to combine blocks into beats with due regard to the following factors:

1. Beats should not overlap census tracts.

2. Beats should be shaped rectangularly so that the patrolman could be located quickly by persons simply traversing the central street of the beat.

3. Beats should be laid out so that call boxes could be reached quickly and conveniently.

---

[9] Cincinnati Regional Crime Committee, *Cincinnati Police Beat Survey* (Chicago: American Public Welfare Association, 1936).

Much time and patient work were needed to satisfy these requirements. Then beats were combined into new districts with nearly uniform activity loads and nearly uniform social conditions and following "natural" boundary lines. As a result of this survey, which was concerned primarily with the "Basin" area of Cincinnati (an area with a vast amount of crime) it was recommended that 111 men be added to the force for the effective patrol of this area. Thus the survey shed light both on the proper layout of beats and on the adequacy of the force.[10]

In some cases it may not be practical to have beat boundaries follow census tracts. For example, a beat may have a natural boundary formed by a high cliff with only one or two routes from the base to the top of the cliff making it almost impossible for the patrolman to adequately cover both the upper and the lower area. In other cases, a census tract boundary may run along a diagonal railroad track. This puts a burden on the radio dispatchers when they try to determine which beat a call for the police falls into on the basis of the street number given since the boundary of the beat would be at a different number for each intersecting street. However, where practical, it is of value to follow census tract lines.

The Cincinnati beat survey is a concrete example of a practical approach to the perplexing problem of beat layout, but it does not represent the sole approach to the problem. It assumes, for example, that the frequency of crime and the amount of crime hazard in a particular area remain fairly constant. Where this assumption does not hold true, it may be more effective to distribute patrolmen in proportion to hazards rather than according to time spent on police activities. A study of time spent in police activities does not consider, for example, the effectiveness of these activities in achieving police objectives.

To say that a patrolman averages 30 minutes in checking store entrances does not indicate the effect of spending more or less time in this activity nor the number of store burglaries in the area. This suggests a somewhat broader approach which starts with the assumption that beats should be laid out so as to minimize crime. To make a distribution on this basis involves a knowledge of how and to what extent various police practices affect crime rates, and today this is known only in a very general way. However, an analysis of crime rates before and after beat redistribution will suggest changes in the formula and thus lead to progressive refinement of the beat organization method.

"Door Shaking." For many years some police departments have followed the practice of trying each door of places of business, or "door shaking." Most departments have dropped this practice for a number of reasons. First, it is not effective. A very small percentage of doors are found unlocked, such a small percentage that it would not be worth while for a burglar to try all of the doors he would need to in order to find one open. Second, it is time consuming and requires time that can be more effectively used to prevent burglaries. If an officer is to shake doors, he must be on foot, moving quite slowly and making a certain amount of noise. If he is to get all of the doors on his beat checked, he will need to move in a systematic manner for long periods of time, allowing a criminal to set up a schedule of his activities. Another reason that it consumes so much time occurs when a door is found unlocked. Then the officer must call the responsible person and wait until he arrives so that the premises can be secured. All too often, the worst offenders when it comes to leaving a door unlocked are the slowest to arrive, and the officer thus may be tied up for an hour or more. Third, because of the excessive time required by this duty, the police may not be able to give adequate coverage to other areas and will spend far too much of their time in the business area.

---

[10] Several complicating aspects of the study have not been discussed in this brief, general description.

This opposition to door shaking does not mean that business places should not be checked very carefully. They should get full patrol coverage, but this can be done as effectively and more rapidly if the officer does not go up to each door and shake it, but rather observes the entire area, including the door, for lack of security or evidence of breaking and entering. In some areas this will need to be done on foot either by a foot patrolman or an officer who parks his car while he goes on foot patrol.

The practice of rattling individual doors has led to some other requests for service by businessmen. In some cities the police turn off and on lights in display windows, raise or lower awnings, and in a few exceptional cases, even fire the furnace. These, of course are out of line with police responsibilities, but once started these services are difficult to get rid of. If a department is shaking doors, the chief should meet with businessmen and explain why he is discontinuing the practice and how this will allow the department to give them more effective protection through more efficient and much more frequent coverage. At the same time he can tell them how they can assist the police by doing such things to improve their security as lighting the interior, putting the safe where it can be seen from the outside, and bolting it down so it cannot be carried off.

Hazard Basis.[11] There are more calls for service and greater need of routine police activities in some sections of the city than in others. In certain sections crime and accident rates are high and many arrests are made. In some sections more stores require attention, or more recreational centers need inspection and regulation, and there is greater flow of traffic. More routine time must be spent on patrol in these sections than in others.

To apportion the force equally to areas of the same size will not distribute manpower effectively. Each section of the community should be assured police service in proportion to its needs. Such a policy will provide an indisputable answer to pressure groups, political or otherwise, who may wish to concentrate a disporportionate amount of patrol service in a particular section of the city. Reasons of economy and efficiency also dictate the distribution of the force in proportion to need. Furthermore, proper geographical distribution should be made in fairness to the public and to the individual police officers. Each beat, that is, should have substantially the same work load as all the others, although it may be considerably different in size.

The number of patrolmen required for each shift is determined by the chronological tabulation of called-for and inspectional services described earlier. This also determines the number of beats on each shift, since one man (or two where they patrol in pairs) ordinarily constitutes a beat.

Under the hazard basis of beat layout, size and location of each beat is based on geographical distribution of: (1) called-for service and routine patrol as measured by Part I crimes, Part II offenses, miscellaneous complaints, accidents, and booked arrests; (2) inspectional services as measured by the number of stores to be checked and the number of beer parlors, dance halls, rooming houses, and other places presenting easily identifiable police hazards; and (3) area.

The application of these factors in determining the size of each patrol district is a trial-and-error process. The small districts into which the city must be arbitrarily divided in order to gather data on the distribution of incidents should be combined experimentally until an approximately equal amount of each of these factors and their component parts fall into each patrol area or beat. Four considerations, however, somewhat limit

---

[11] See O. W. Wilson, *Police Administration*, op. cit., appendix.

the determination of the area to be included in each beat. In the first place, natural boundaries, such as rivers and main thoroughfares, should be used wherever possible. Second, the social character of the beat should be as uniform as possible. Third, it may be impossible in some cases to set up areas with an equal number of each of the factors; in these cases a deficiency of a certain number of occurrences of one of the factors must be made up by using an excess of occurrences of another of the factors. Fourth, some areas containing considerable undeveloped land or large, little used parks may require a beat simply on the basis of time required to answer an emergency call for police service, even though the need for police service may not compare with the average. In no section of the city should the citizens have to wait an excessive time for emergency service.

Other Considerations in Distributing the Patrol Force

Distribution of the force in point of time can be determined from the records of the department plus special studies. Beats can be laid out geographically so that an approximately equal amount of police service is needed on each. Under the theory of selective distribution of the patrol force the patrolmen must be concentrated at the time, as well as in the area, of greatest police hazards.

Time of occurrence and types of violations on the beat will help determine the number of patrolmen and kind of patrol required. No single factor is the deciding element in arranging for patrol requirements. All important influences which affect the problem must be weighed in the balance if lives and property are to be protected to the maximum extent with the available manpower.

The need for frequent revision and adjustment of assignments should be emphasized. At least once a year the assignments should be re-examined in the light of records and statistics to determine that both the time and the area of greatest crime are properly reflected in the distribution of the patrol force.

Supplementary Patrol. A number of cities supplement the patrolmen assigned to fixed districts or beats with a small tactical unit or mobile force. This is ordinarily a small force of picked men with the number and ranks of the commanding officers determined by its size. The group may vary from one or two men on a small force to 100 or more on large forces. The group is motorized and assigned on the basis of where and when police problems are occurring as determined by research. They may work in one section of the city for a week from 7:00 p.m. to 3:00 a.m. because of burglaries occurring in that area and at that time. Then for a few days, they may be assigned to enforce certain traffic laws in an area determined by an analysis of accident records. If there is no specific problem, they may be scattered over a considerable area of the city, then suddenly pulled together as a unit to search for a murder suspect. This tactical unit, when properly used, is a good way to fit the force available to the problem. While the day-to-day requests for police service, the arrests, and investigations can be forecast with some degree of accuracy, there will always be constant exceptions to this pattern. Here is where the tactical force fits in.

There are variations on this plan. One is "saturation" patrol. In saturation patrol a large number of officers will be put into an area and that area will be very closely policed with a resultant and very definite drop in criminal activity. This method has been used for a short time in some cities as a demonstration of just what can be accomplished with sufficient police officers and it allows the administrator to say, "This is what I can do if I have the manpower." A major point that must be considered is that this is too easy an answer. There is too much of a tendency for some police administrators to say in relation to any police problem "Give me 10 more or 100 more or 1,000 more men and I can do the job" without first trying to improve the efficiency of their operations. When requests for additional manpower are not met, they have an easy answer to criticism, namely, "The city won't give me the men to do the job." This does not mean that when a police department is operating at full efficiency, it will not do a better job with additional personnel, but rather that the use of more manpower is not the only way to solve police problems. Saturation patrol does have an entirely legitimate use to demonstrate what increased patrol coverage will do in reducing the crime rate, but in addition, a few cities use this on a regular basis. The patrol force in a section of the city may be suddenly doubled or tripled in size with no announcement and no explanation given by the police. Then in a few days, another area will get the same treatment. The criminals know what is going on, but they do not know where this tremendous increase in patrol will be next, and they are afraid to plan a job anywhere. This system has the effect of keeping the criminal group off balance, with increased police activity as unpredictable as criminal activity. Actually, there will be considerable planning in the use of this force, and many times it will be assigned just as the tactical force is, to work on specific problems.

Fixed Versus Rotating Platoon

Hours of work are an important consideration for the patrolman. Most cities employ a three-platoon or three-shift basis for the patrol force, with patrolmen working from 8:00 a.m. to 4:00 p.m., 4:00 p.m. to midnight, and midnight to 8:00 a.m., or a variation based on chronological distribution of service requirements or on community custom. In a department with district stations it is a sound practice to change shifts at staggered times so as not to have the entire force involved in a shift change at the same time. For example, Station 1 might change shifts at 3:45 p.m., Station 2 at 4:00 p.m., and Station 3 at 4:15 p.m. The first platoon in any case, is the dogwatch or early morning shift; the second platoon is the day shift; and the third platoon is the evening shift.

Rotating shift assignments from month to month is a common but undesirable practice. From a personal standpoint, some men find it difficult to adapt their eating and sleeping habits to changing requirements, where the shifts are rotated monthly. Their health may suffer as a result. From a departmental standpoint the detailed knowledge of beats that is required for effective police work can be acquired best when the shifts are fairly stable.

Some of the disadvantages of the rotating system can be corrected by the ladder platoon system under which relatively permanent shifts are assigned, with opportunity for advancement to a different platoon based on merit and seniority. Experience has proved that continuous assignment to the dogwatch can be made without impairing the health or morale of the patrolman, so long as opportunity for advancement is held before him.

The system of starting the recruit on the dogwatch, then as he gains seniority promoting him to the evening shift, with the most experienced officers on the day shift, has these advantages: (1) policemen and their families can plan their home life and recreation on a long-time basis; (2) physical ailments due to irregular sleeping and eating habits can be reduced; (3) a better opportunity is offered for the training of recruits; (4) the dogwatch can be used for disciplinary purposes; (5) the lower ranking watches can be used as stopping places for less promising material; (6) the dogwatch affords an opportunity to test and study recruits' moral and physical courage, patience, initiative, and so forth;

and (7) police work differs during hours of the day and night, so this plan provides further specialization.

Supervision of Patrol Force

Every municipal police department will be organized in a chain of responsibility which originates in the patrolman, carrying through sergeant, lieutenant, and captain, to the police chief. The departments of considerable size will divide their areas of responsible jurisdiction into police districts or precincts.[12] Each district will normally be commanded by a captain who is chargeable for the control of crime and all other matters of police jurisdiction in his district. He may report directly to the chief of police or through such intermediate officers as the organization requires for effective supervisory control. The district captain will be assisted by lieutenants — one or more for each platoon or shift who in turn exercise direct control over the sergeants. Sergeants form the first line of supervision in controlling the activities of patrolmen assigned to beats in the several areas in which police service is provided. Any weak point in this chain of responsibility and command will reflect itself in the quality of work performed. Sergeants, being the first line supervisors, play a particularly significant role.

Role of the Sergeant

The patrol beat is the area for which a patrolman is made responsible. Several — perhaps six — of these beats may be placed under a patrol sergeant whose responsibility it is to see that the patrolmen perform their duties in a faithful and effective manner. The number depends on the type of patrol because officers are more difficult to locate on some types of patrol than on others. Supervision is most difficult when patrolmen are motorized; a larger number may be supervised when they are on foot, and a still larger number when they are on fixed post in a relatively small area. The patrol sergeant constantly visits his men, sees that reports are properly prepared, checks on follow-up cases, notes the way in which they go about their duties, and instructs them in the responsibilities of their office. The sergeant is expected to get the work out of his men. That is his job. If he expects anything less than full and honest performance from them he is negligent in his own duty.

On the patrol sergeant rests the success or failure of the patrol force. Slothful or ineffective sergeants depress the standards of performance of the men under their supervision. Likewise, alive, alert, and competent sergeants lead their men into better ways and set the pace for their patrolmen so that the task is never too easy but always a challenge calling for more and better work.

It is customary in most municipalities for the patrol force to go on duty in platoons at a designated hour which is the same for all members of the platoon. The men report at the stationhouse where they are prepared for inspection by their sergeants. The lieutenant on duty during that tour calls the roll, reads the orders, and instructs the men on any points of information pertaining to their duties. He inspects the men's clothing and equipment.

Following inspection, the patrolmen are dispersed to their several beats, where patrol duties begin. The patrol sergeants now take over direct responsibility and see that

---

[12] See section on "Territorial Organization" in Chapter 2, for discussion of the criteria determining the need for districts.

patrolmen carry out their assignments satisfactorily. Supervision of the patrol sergeants is effected by irregular inspections by the lieutenant and by his review of reports from the sergeant and patrolman.

The patrol sergeant has opportunity to conceal many facts in the administration of personnel. His integrity must be unquestioned and his reports complete and accurate. He holds a key position in the shaping of department morale. Selection for such a post should be invariably for merit.

Effective supervision is essential as a control device if the men at the top who are responsible for broad administrative policies are to know what patrolmen on the beat are doing. Channels of authority must be clear for the flow of authority from top to bottom and for the flow of information from bottom to top. To a large extent the effectiveness of supervision depends on the presence in supervisory officers of those qualities of leadership which have already been discussed, and on the degree to which the objectives of the department are interpreted and made clear to every member of the force, superior and subordinate officers alike. This last duty is a primary responsibility of the chief.

Police Tactics

A detailed discussion of police tactics has no place in this volume, which is devoted to principles and procedures of police administration. However, the police administrator should know how tactics are developed because he is responsible for training his men in anticipation of emergency action and for seeing that every man knows his function in situations which recur frequently. These tactics should be incorporated in a manual which is available to all members of the force for sustained study. A situation which every police force must face frequently is the procedure to be followed when a criminal is reported to be in operation. A formal statement of tactics to be used in such a situation has been prepared by the Wichita police department and is reproduced here both as an example and because it illustrates the relationship between the patrol force and other police divisions and officers. [13]

Procedure When Criminal is in Operation

(Example — criminal in a building; car being stripped; peeping tom; etc.)

Note: In the absence of a superior officer, the beat officer shall be considered the ranking officer unless otherwise designated.

Flashlight Code: One short flash — "Here I am." Three short flashes — "Come here at once."

A. Radio Dispatcher

1. On receipt of information, keep the complainant on the telephone when possible, while dispatching officers to the scene, in order to obtain additional information and descriptions which may be broadcast before the officers arrive.

2. Dispatch the beat officer, the special investigator, the patrol sergeant, and one other officer to the scene.

---

[13] *Police Tactics* was prepared by the superior officers of the Wichita police department and reproduced in the Wichita Police Department and in the manual of instruction of several annual Kansas police schools, first conducted by the Kansas League of Municipalities and later by the Kansas State Board for Vocational Education.

3. Officers from adjoining beats will also be dispatched if their assistance seems necessary, in which case assign one to each quadrant, assigning the nearest to each. Unless it is known that the criminal has escaped, instruct them to surround the premises first and to search their quadrants when it is found that the criminal has escaped.

4. When officers call back for further instructions, send them back to their beats if there are no other instructions. Officers will not discontinue assignment until instructed to do so.

5. When desirable, dispatch officers to strategic locations where criminals may pass in making getaway.

6. If it be a serious crime involving the necessity of calling out off-duty officers, have PBX operator notify commanding officers or superior officers of platoons to be called out with instructions for them to notify their subordinates. In the event the PBX operator cannot reach commanding or superior officers, telephone the officers of that squad. In the event there is no PBX operator on duty, call the jailer to fill the position of PBX operator.

B. Officers. (Officers sent to the scene where criminal is operating should remember that the purpose is to capture the criminal.)

1. Approach quickly and quietly, but observe all persons you pass while approaching the scene; write down license number of cars if possible. In your haste to get there you may pass up the criminal on his way out. Shut off motor and lights and coast to within three or four doors of location or just around the corner. Remove the ignition key. Flashlights must not be used until the building is properly surrounded.

2. The first officer at the scene will cover the avenue of easiest and most likely escape, which will usually be the rear, standing concealed at one corner where two sides of the building are visible. He will indicate his position on arrival of second officer by one short flash.

3. The second officer will ascertain the post of the first officer and will then cover the opposite (diagonal) corner.

4. On arrival of the third and fourth officers, the ranking officer will take charge. If it be deemed necessary to obtain further help, he will post officers as above and then proceed to effect entrance. If it be a residence, he will go to the front door and ring bell or knock, giving the criminal a chance to run out the back entrance into the arms of the officers there. If no reply, he will enter through some unfastened opening. If it be a store, he will determine the best course to pursue at that time.

5. During the search of the building in which the criminal is supposed to be located, keep flashlight away from body when using it. To go through a door, open the door about an inch, then with flashlight and gun ready, give door a quick shove with foot with sufficient force to strike against the wall in order to detect if anyone is hiding behind it. Step back and listen before entering the room. If a noise is heard, crouch near the floor without using flashlight. Close each room door after searching to prevent the criminal entering and hiding in a room already searched.

C. Duties at a Scene of a Crime. (Note: The scene of a crime is the area within the immediate vicinity in which evidence might be found.)

1. Rank

    (At Scene of Crime)   (Away from Scene of Crime)

1. Captain of Detectives	Instructions	Usual line of authority in
2. Detective Assigned	through ranking	Patrol Division
3. Capt. of Patrol Div.	officer	
4. Lieut. of Patrol Div.		
5. Sergeant of Squad		
6. Beat Officer		
7. First Officer there		

2. Duties at the Scene of a Crime
   a. Duties of the ranking officer at the scene of the crime
      1. Get a brief outline of the situation from the officer in charge, determining if information for broadcast has been sent in and what assignments have been made.
      2. Place officers dispatched to the scene of the crime at points to aid in handling the public. They are responsible for keeping the scene intact until all necessary photographs, sketches, and investigations have been made.
      3. In assault cases assign an officer to accompany the victim to the hospital to obtain statements or other evidence.
      4. Supervise the special investigator and beat officer in their investigation.
      5. Obtain any other information necessary and determine that the investigation is complete.
      6. Assign extra officers at points or quadrants away from the scene of the crime. Do not permit curious officers to stand around scene. Give them assignments or return them to their beats.
   b. Duties of beat officer (or first officer at scene)
      1. Take details of the crime: (a) In case a persons-wanted notice is to be issued, get the best description available and immediately call the station before proceeding with other details; (b) obtain the names and addresses of the major parties and witnesses; (c) question the major parties and witnesses, taking their statements and any concrete information they may have on the case.
      2. Perform the duties of the ranking officer until he arrives.
      3. Call the attention of the special investigator to any evidence before it is touched or altered in order that it may be photographed or a diagram made thereof.
   c. Duties of the special investigator
      1. Obtain all physical evidence.
      2. Photograph all physical evidence found by himself or any other person.
      3. Take measurements, etc., to be used in drawing charts or diagrams of the scene and surroundings.
      4. Make charts and diagrams.
      5. Aid the beat officer in working the details of the case into a proper and presentable form: (a) compare notes on witness's statements with those made on the position of physical evidence; (b) when making out reports, work in the preliminary details so that the information will not have to be rechecked by the detectives who handle the case.
   d. Duties of all officers on the case
      1. Obtain all available information.
      2. Help work out details of the case so as to make the best case possible.

3. Keep the scene intact until the special investigator has completed his job.

D. Officers sent to search quadrant will:

1. Proceed immediately on the quadrant designated toward the scene of the crime.

2. Approach to within a distance from the scene of the crime that a man might walk on foot (one block per minute) or drive in a car if it is known that he has a car, during the elapsed time, but not closer than one block, questioning any likely suspects that you may meet on the way, except when instructed to go directly to the scene.

3. From this point, work out, covering the quadrant thoroughly.

4. Question everyone possible. Too much activity is impossible. If the suspect questioned be a law-abiding citizen, the contact is valuable because (a) he may have observed something of importance; (b) he will look for something of value and report the matter if he sees it; (c) he will have a greater appreciation of the service being rendered.

5. When a suspect is observed, stop him at once. If not, he will be lost. Do not drive around the block expecting to get him later.

6. Do not give up too quickly; be certain that nothing has been overlooked. Be diligent and thorough. Remember, a closely hunted criminal will hide.

7. When convinced that the criminal is not in the assigned quadrant, report to the dispatcher for further instructions.

8. Do not go to scene of the crime unless instructed to do so. Even though a description has not yet been broadcast, continue to work your quadrant.

9. Do not visit or ride with any other officer assigned to the same or an adjoining quadrant.

10. When instructed to go directly to the scene, undertake search of quadrant immediately and without further instruction as soon as it is learned that the criminal has left the scene.

E. Miscellaneous

1. If the criminal has just left the scene at the time the call is received the same procedure will be followed except that the patrol sergeant or any other superior officer will immediately search the vicinity to make certain the criminal is not in hiding.

2. In the absence of either the beat officer or the special investigator, the one present will perform the duties of the other.

3. In the event of a crime where a curious public may interfere with the investigation or destroy evidence, the ranking officer will post officers to keep the crowd back, using a rope to establish a line when necessary.

4. In serious crimes, when the detective usually assigned to that type of case is available, the dispatcher will send him to the scene and the officer on the beat will assist him in the investigation. Otherwise the same procedure shall be followed.

5. A detective shall perform any duty in connection with a crime just committed to which he may be assigned by the dispatcher.

6. When a crime has been committed, officers will not spend their time at the station nor at the scene of the crime but will engage in the task of searching for the criminal. They will not give up the search until instructed to do so but will keep in close contact with headquarters by telephone or radio. They will contact everyone who may be of assistance in obtaining or providing information or evidence.

7. In trying doors and windows and in the act of surrounding a building containing criminals, remember that the object is to capture the criminals.

8. Every officer assigned will write a report on observations and action taken. This applies also to officers who do nothing but search a quadrant.

9. Since a yegg operating on a safe as a rule has a lookout behind a signboard, in a car, or hidden in some other likely spot, when an officer observes a man working on a safe he will not disturb him if the officer has not been observed, but will telephone immediately for assistance, and then return to the scene quickly and quietly on foot in an effort to prevent escape before the place is properly surrounded.

10. Never expose yourself to unnecessary danger. Take advantage of every natural cover and advantage. In case of a gun battle in the open where cover is not available, fall to the ground. Always take deliberate aim in shooting. Never shoot while running.

Field Interrogation

Police forces have been stopping individuals for many years and inquiring as to their identity and what they are doing, but accomplishing this in a systematic manner and recording the information is a relatively new development. There are many resulting values from this plan. First, evidence of a crime may be discovered. The person checked may attempt to escape at the time he is first stopped, may be carrying stolen goods, or may have them in his car. Second, a number of traffic violations are discovered. The person checked may be intoxicated, lack a driver's license, or not have the car properly registered or equipped. Third, this plan discourages criminals. Once they have been stopped and identified by the police, they are less likely to commit a crime, certainly not in that area because the police know who they are and when they were in the area. Fourth, this will assist in apprehension if a crime is committed in spite of the field interrogation and it may prevent establishing a false alibi. A review of the field interrogation records will show who was in the area and the modus operandi files for these individuals can be checked to see if they are logical suspects. Fifth, considerable material will be added to the files of known criminals showing who their associates are, the description and license number of the car they are currently driving, and their current address. Sixth, this has a good public relations value. An honest citizen will appreciate the worth of this system and an efficient and polite police officer will make a good impression on him.

Procedures for field interrogation must be carefully developed stating clearly who is to be checked, the procedures to be used and how the information is to be recorded.[14] Figure 23 is an example of a field interrogation form.

An effective supplement to this plan has been developed by one small town police chief. When a field interrogation has been made of juveniles in an automobile and from other towns, he writes a friendly letter to the father of the juvenile who has the car,

---

[14] See Allen P. Bristow, *Field Interrogation* (Springfield, Illinois: Charles C Thomas, 1958).

FIELD INTERROGATION CARD

LAST NAME	FIRST NAME		MIDDLE NAME		NUMBER	
ADDRESS					COL.	SEX AGE
HEIGHT	WEIGHT	EYES	HAIR	COMPL.	OCCUPATION	
DATE AND PLACE OF BIRTH				DR. LIC. NO.		STATE
MAKE AUTO		COLOR		LIC. NO.		YEAR
WHERE OBSERVED			TIME		DATE	
ASSOCIATES				ADDRESS		
1.						
2.						

Figure 23 -- Field Interrogation Card

thanking him for allowing his son John Jr., driving the blue 1959 Dodge sedan, license number 52-2750, to visit the chief's town in company with (and here he names the other occupants). He closes by saying the boys were well behaved and hopes they can visit again. Because many of the fathers do not realize their son and their car was that far afield, the effect has been to reduce the number of juveniles riding around this small town late at night with a resultant decrease in juvenile offenses.

Police Dogs

While police dogs have been used for many years in Europe and from time to time in a few cities in this country, there has been a very definite increase in the use of police dogs in this country in the past few years. Cities using police dogs in patrol work include Atlanta, Baltimore, Houston, Richmond, Springfield (Missouri), St. Louis, St. Paul, Salt Lake City, Washington, D.C., Amarillo, and Denver. However, Dearborn and Detroit, Michigan; Portland, Oregon; and Berkeley, California, have used police dogs in the past but no longer do so.

A number of points are in favor for police dogs: (1) Because of their excellent sense of smell and hearing they will detect a person that would not be discovered by an officer. (2) They are fast and agile and can overtake anyone much more rapidly and readily than an officer. (3) They are good protection to an officer not only in discovering persons but in preventing and repelling attacks. (4) They can hold an offender while the officer searches a second person or summons assistance. (5) They are useful in handling riots or disorderly crowds because most people fear a dog. (6) They can trail escaping offenders or lost persons under many circumstances.

On the other hand, there are a number of objections to the use of dogs. (1) The cost is always an objection to anything in police work. While the use of dogs is too recent a development to have a great deal of cost experience, the figures in Atlanta show that the cost for the first year is about $1,000 per dog dropping to $600 after this. (2) There is considerable inconvenience in training, housing, feeding, and maintaining the dogs. (3) They can work with only one officer and must live with him. As a result, they share his time off, vacation and sick leave. (4) While they are trained not to attack a man in uniform, they might attack a plain-clothes officer also answering a burglar or prowler call. (5) There is a danger of the dog attacking the wrong person or excessively injuring a minor offender. (6) They are limited as to types of duty and areas where they are most effective. While riding in a patrol car, for example, they are of little value.

The cities that are using police dogs are enthusiastic about this new development. Many of them have done a very careful job in planning the use and in training the dogs and officers. St. Louis, for example, sent several officers to England to receive training and bring back trained dogs. The London Metropolitan Police has 270 dogs and has had considerable experience in this field. This is a subject that should be studied carefully by the police chief to determine if police dogs can be used to advantage by his patrol force.

Relation of Police to Private Patrolmen

The patrol division must maintain a satisfactory working relationship with private police groups. While it is not feasible to dwell at length on the origin, duties, and types of private police, it is necessary that the police chief understand the various private police agencies in his community.

The organization of private police bodies may have come about as a result of a breakdown in regular law enforcement. In the frontier days when law enforcement was feeble or nonexistent, bodies of citizens or vigilante groups were organized to maintain law and order. Similarly, in many of our cities, private police agencies have flourished because of the inability of the regularly constituted police agency to provide the standard of service expected by certain citizens, particularly those who maintain commercial establishments or large estates.

A distinction should be made between private watchmen and private policemen. Both are classed as private police, but there is a real functional difference between them. Private watchmen act only to protect the property of a single employer, patrolling to detect and prevent fire, theft, or sabotage and exercising control over that property and such persons as come upon it. Railroad police, plant guards, store detectives, and warehouse guards are examples of private watchmen.

Private policemen work for many employers and are able to exist either because some citizens do not have confidence in the municipal police or because they desire the sense of additional security that is provided by a special officer who inspects their premises occasionally. The small monthly fee for the services of a private policeman may seem a reasonable cost for this additional security. An unregulated private patrol, however, is open to serious abuses. Unethical agencies or individuals may use pressure or threats to solicit customers or they may even work with criminals.

Whether private policing is well established, or just getting started and conditions in the community justify its continuance, each private officer and agency should be strictly regulated by means of the licensing powers of the city. An ordinance covering all essential points of control should include the following:

1. Every applicant should be required to apply for a license and should be thoroughly investigated as to the truth of statements in his application, his character, and any previous criminal record.

2. No license should be issued to anyone previously convicted of a felony or lacking in good moral character.

3. Every applicant should be fingerprinted, photographed, and required to post surety bond. When licensed, he should be required to carry an identification card issued by the city and containing his photo, prints, and signature.

4. Every licensee should be required to furnish an up-to-date list of customers to the chief of police at least semiannually.

5. Licenses should be renewed annually and be revocable at any time, for cause.

Other desirable provisions which appear in some city ordinances specify that the power to arrest of private patrolmen is only that provided for private persons under state law, and that patrolmen may carry weapons only in accordance with statutes and local ordinances. They also describe procedures for private police in reporting crimes and turning in lost or stolen property which they may recover, set license fees, and provide for uniforming. One representative ordinance requires all private patrolmen to wear the same style of uniform which must be different in design and color from that of the regular police.

Chapter 8

CRIME INVESTIGATION

Because of the chance occurrence of crime and the necessity for immediate investigation, once it is known, no single unit of the police department can be charged with the duty of crime investigation in its entirety. The time and place that crime will happen are seldom known to the police. No statistical service or psychological data enable the prediction of the exact hour and location of a specific crime.

For these reasons crime investigation must of necessity be carried on from time to time by all policemen. The patrolman on the beat may, through his knowledge of the fundamentals of this type of inquiry, be able to discover and preserve evidence leading to the arrest and conviction of the perpetrators. The patrol force is almost invariably the first unit of the department to be represented at the scene of a crime, and the duties which it performs at such times are of great importance to a successful investigation.[1]

The Investigation Process

Since all branches of police service and nearly all members of the force are engaged to a greater or lesser degree in some form of investigation, an analysis of the investigative process will assist in organizing the department in a manner to facilitate the effective performance of this important police task.

The ultimate objective in the investigation of a crime is the conviction of the perpetrator. Its achievement necessitates proof in court that a crime was committed and that the perpetrator did in fact commit it. All efforts should be directed toward this end. The police therefore must ascertain the facts of the crime (the answers to the questions who? what? where? when? why? and how?) and the identity of the criminal. They must identify and arrest the perpetrator and discover witnesses and physical evidence that may be used to prove the charge in court. Recovered stolen property provides additional evidence of guilt; the return of stolen property to its rightful owner is a further police responsibility quite separate from its use as evidence.

The duties of the police, when a crime has been reported to them, consist of the following:

1. Direct action (noninvestigative in character) consisting of (a) arresting the perpetrator at the scene or pursuing him if apprehension seems likely, (b) caring for critically injured persons, and (c) protecting (guarding for the purpose of preserving intact) the crime scene and all physical evidence.

---

[1] In the preparation of this chapter the editor has drawn heavily on the ideas expressed in a chapter of the same title in O. W. Wilson, *Police Administration* (New York: McGraw-Hill Book Company, 1950). With the special permission of the publisher.

2. Preliminary investigation consisting of (a) interviewing the victim and witnesses present at the scene, (b) transmitting information (facts of the crime and the identity of the criminal or a description of him and of stolen property) to headquarters to expedite the pursuit and capture of the criminal, the recovery of property, and the preparation of the necessary records, (c) searching for and interviewing witnesses not at the scene, (d) investigating leads uncovered up to the point that delay would not jeopardize the success of the investigation, and (e) discovering and interrogating suspects and arresting them when there is evidence of guilt.

3. Searching for, recording, preserving, and transporting physical evidence to the crime laboratory or other competent examiners. Evidence may be recorded by photograph, sketch, or notes; some evidence (such as latent fingerprints) may require clarification by development through the use of powders, liquids, or fumes. Evidence may be preserved in its natural state (in suitable vials, jars, cellophane envelopes, boxes, or other containers) or in solution, and some by the use of a special lifting tape. Evidence must be identified (as to where, when, and by whom it was found), marked to assure that its identity can be legally established in the future, and labeled to facilitate the control of its possession. It must be transported to the examiner in such a way that its original state is not altered by contamination or mutilation or as the result of not being kept at a suitable temperature.

4. Continuation of the investigation from the point where the preliminary investigation was discontinued. The investigation will include: (a) review, consolidation, and analysis of the reports of officers relating to their action and discoveries in the first three steps; (b) further interview of the victim and some of the witnesses (such reinterview is desirable in all but minor crimes; it often provides additional important facts discovered or recalled since the preliminary interview; it also usually favorably impresses the victim with the interest of the police and the thoroughness of their investigation); (c) identification of the crime (through the *modus operandi* of the perpetrator in a manner described in Chapter 12) as being similar to other crimes of the same type that may have been committed in the local community, the surrounding territory, or elsewhere in the state or nation; (d) search of pawnshops, secondhand stores, and other places where loot may be disposed of; (e) investigation of the activities of persons in the community or nearby who, by reason of their previous criminal acts, may be considered likely suspects; (f) obtaining information as to the perpetrator and the disposition of the loot from elements in the community who may be informed on such matters; (g) planning (and perhaps directing) organized police action directed at discovering additional physical evidence or witnesses, the loot, or information relating to persons who may be suspects; and (h) planning the dissemination of information (beyond that routinely provided by department procedure) relating to the crime, property stolen, the criminal, or suspects.

5. The apprehension of the offender. This may involve surveillance of places where the criminal is likely to go to obtain medical or financial aid, food, clothing, shelter, transportation, mail, personal belongings, and so on, and planned raids that may require a strong force; the raids may be made locally or in some outside jurisdiction. Apprehension may also involve the transportation of the prisoner from some outside jurisdiction (responsibility for which rests with the police in some states but not in others); it may involve the imposition of some restrictions on the liberty of the prisoner to obtain bail or to communicate with other prisoners and persons on the outside.

6. Preparing the case for presentation in court. This involves the interrogation of the perpetrator, the taking of statements from him and sometimes from the victim and

witnesses; the preparation and organization of physical evidence to be introduced in court; and of other relevant matter to be offered in testimony by criminalists and witnesses.

The Assignment of Investigative Duties

The investigative duties listed above must be assigned to specified divisions and other operating units of the department in order to fix precisely the responsibility for their performance. Neglect through oversight as well as friction through duplication of effort are thus minimized. The selection of the unit to which each duty will be assigned should be based on three considerations: (1) Economy of manpower. Police manpower is expensive and operations should be planned that will use it to best advantage. (2) Immediate availability of service. Time is of the essence in crime investigation; minutes, sometimes even seconds, make the difference between success and failure; the likelihood of success in apprehending and convicting the criminal usually decreases approximately in proportion to the time that has elapsed since the crime was committed. (3) Effectiveness of performance. The several investigative duties require skills that vary in nature and degree; all other factors being equal, the assignment should be made to the unit that is best qualified to perform the task.

In order to apply these three principles, consideration should be given to the performance of investigative tasks by men who are already on duty (in addition to their present duties) in order to make unnecessary the assignment of additional men who may spend much of their time idly waiting for an occurrence to call them into action. When such additional assignment of men seems indicated, however, other duties should be imposed upon them that will not interfere with their primary objective and that will keep them profitably employed during their entire tour of duty. Delays incident to locating, and bringing to the scene specialists who may be off duty, on other assignment, or at headquarters should be avoided as far as possible.

Other factors to consider in appraising the suitability of a unit to perform a task effectively include the following attributes of its members: skill gained by training and experience; freedom of movement; dress; information sources; and knowledge of the identity, location, activities, and associates of criminals and of persons who may assist criminals in some manner in committing the crime or in disposing of the loot.

Direct Action

Direct action is now and always has been primarily the responsibility of the patrol division in all police departments. No other division is as well suited as patrol to take direct action when a crime has been committed.

Preliminary Investigation

The patrol division is likewise the logical division to make the preliminary investigation of crime. Its 24-hour, jurisdiction-wide, radio-equipped patrol makes it especially well suited to this purpose. The investigation is made immediately; delays are thus avoided — delays incident to dispatching investigators from headquarters, to locating specialists who may be on another assignment, and to investigating by detectives who may not report for duty for some hours (as often occurs when crimes committed at night are investigated by detectives the following day).

Preliminary investigation by the patrol division relieves the detective division of a great deal of routine preliminary spade work; the time of these specialists is thus conserved, permitting their special talents and facilities to be focused on the investigative tasks that need them. This procedure also provides the patrolmen with valuable experience and training in interrogation and investigation; they are thus prepared for future assignment to the detective division, and executives may select the most competent for this assignment on the basis of demonstrated ability.

Physical Evidence

The search of crime scenes for physical evidence, and recording, preserving, and transporting it to the examiner, requires special equipment and the development by training of skills in its use and in other techniques — skills that can be maintained only through frequent performance. These duties should not be imposed on either the beat officer charged with the preliminary investigation or the detective responsible for its continuance. It is not practical to train all patrolmen, or even detectives, in the requisite techniques. There is not sufficient work of this character for either patrolmen or detectives to maintain the necessary skills by performance. To provide each patrolman or detective with the needed equipment would be costly and its possession would be bothersome; for them to go to headquarters to pick up the necessary equipment would be a time-consuming undertaking. Also, the search for physical evidence by either the patrolman or the detective would interfere with other equally important phases of the investigation.

Neither should the physical evidence task be imposed on either the identification officer or the criminalist (the laboratory examiner). Few departments have a sufficiently large staff of these officers to permit the assignment of one to each shift; usually they work during the day time. When these officers are not on duty, crime scene searches must either be postponed for some hours until they report for duty (a needless, unforgiveable delay that invariably lessens the likelihood of discovering the preserving evidence) or one of them must be located (at his home or place of recreation), a car sent to transport him to headquarters for his equipment and then to the scene, which also causes delay.

This latter procedure is also an inconvenience for the officers who are currently engrossed in the investigation and heavily loaded with tasks arising from the commission of the crime; it is likewise an inconvenience and an imposition on the officers who are called back to service during their normal rest period. For both of these reasons operating personnel do not call on these officers in every case; the scenes of only the most important crimes are searched, and consequently much physical evidence is not discovered, recorded, and preserved.

Special investigators should be assigned to each shift to perform duties related to the search of crime scenes for physical evidence.[2] Each special investigator should be supplied with an automobile furnished with essential equipment. Two weeks of full-time training is adequate to qualify an otherwise well trained patrolman to take satisfactory photographs, make simple preliminary tests, prepare casts, sketch and otherwise record physical evidence, and mark, label, preserve, and transport it to headquarters.

---

[2] D. J. Finney, "Police Duties at Crime Scenes," *Journal of Criminal Law and Criminology,* July-August, 1936, pp. 231-48; and September-October, 1936, pp. 412-41.

The Detective Division Investigative Duties

The remaining investigative duties, viz., the investigation from the point where the preliminary investigation was discontinued, the apprehension of the criminal and the recovery of stolen property (when these tasks have not been accomplished by the patrol division), and the preparation of the case for presentation in court (assistance to the prosecutor) are clearly the responsibilities of the detective division. These tasks are now and always have been basic detective duties. When the patrol division fails, the ultimate responsibility for the apprehension of the culprit and the recovery of stolen property should rest on the detectives. When the patrol division does arrest the perpetrator and recover property, the detectives still have the responsibility of continuing the investigation so that all evidence will be discovered, suitably organized, analyzed, and prepared for court presentation in the most effective manner. Furthermore, in any case, detectives are responsible for gathering information which may result in clearing other crimes and, in some instances, prevent the occurrence of additional ones.

Relationship of the Detective Division to Other Agencies

While the detective division is held ultimately responsible for the recovery of stolen property and the clearance by arrest and successful prosecution in court of crimes assigned to them, some investigative duties are properly the responsibility of other operating units. Also, there are certain offenses the investigation of which is made the ultimate responsibility of other divisions: i.e., vice, juvenile, and traffic.

In order to assure the effective investigation of all crimes, therefore, it is essential that the relationships between the detective division and the other operating units should be precisely defined by departmental regulations. When all members understand the relationships and the allocation of duties among the several units, the likelihood of oversight and friction is lessened.

Department regulations should also stipulate that all police officers, regardless of the unit to which they may be regularly assigned, have a responsibility for taking suitable action when violations come to their attention in the absence of members of the special unit ordinarily responsible. Exceptions, so far as officers in plain clothes are concerned, are sometimes specifically made for misdemeanor traffic violations.

Patrol Division

In addition to making the preliminary investigation of crimes, patrolmen should serve as eyes, ears, and legs for the detective division. The patrol division may be used for surveillance, to serve warrants and bring in suspects and witnesses, and to perform a number of tasks for the detectives that will increase the time available for tasks that require their special skills and facilities. Patrolmen should be urged also to seek additional information relating to crimes committed and the activities of criminals on their beats, even some time after their occurrence, and should perform all of the tasks related thereto that come under the previously given definition of preliminary investigation. Duplicates of investigation reports made by patrolmen, on cases assigned to the detective division, keep detectives informed of the investigative activities of patrolmen.

It is to the advantage of individual detectives, as well as of the division, to have patrolmen working in this manner; more cases are cleared by arrest and a greater proportion of stolen property is recovered when, in addition to the detective regularly assigned, numbers of patrolmen also work on the case. Detectives may stimulate the interest and participation of patrolmen by keeping them currently informed of the presence, identity or description, hangouts, associates, vehicle, and method of operation of each criminal known to be in the community. Patrol participation is also stimulated and friction avoided when the detectives scrupulously give credit to patrolmen for work done by them; best results are attained when the detectives give the principal credit to the patrolmen. When detectives, without protest, permit credit to be given to themselves for arrests and other work done by patrolmen, they cannot expect cooperation.

Supervising and command officers in the patrol division should urge patrolmen to participate in crime investigations; they should guide them in this work and further stimulate their interest by seeing that patrolmen are commended, by themselves and the chief, for outstanding investigations and arrests. Praise before their fellow officers, commendation on the daily bulletin, and news items giving them the credit, are helpful.

While patrolmen should be held responsible for crimes committed on their beats, they should not be held to account for the clearance of these crimes by arrest or the recovery of stolen property. To do so necessitates giving them commensurate authority which includes freedom to neglect their regular patrol duties by making investigations that take them off their beats for protracted periods of time. To do so is also tantamount to requiring them to work overtime; otherwise the investigation would lag until they return to duty 16 or more hours later. Instead, the preliminary investigation should be a patrol division responsibility; an investigation not completed by one platoon may be continued by the next when their efforts are suitably coordinated.

Special Investigators

Special, or uniformed, investigators, charged with the search of crime scenes for physical evidence, should be assigned to the patrol division for four reasons: (1) They may then be used to supplement the regular patrol in areas where needed when not engaged in their physical evidence tasks. (2) They are then under the direct supervision of the officer charged with supervising patrolmen on street duty, thus assuring more effective supervision (so necessary for the most effective work) than though they were assigned to any other division. (3) Their operations are intimately related to the preliminary investigation of crimes; the probability of the successful conclusion of the investigation during the preliminary stage is enhanced when the patrolman and the special investigator work as a team, both under the direct control of the same supervisor. (4) The special investigator should search all crime scenes (where there is any probability of finding physical evidence), and while the preliminary investigation of all of these crimes should be the duty of the beat officer, their ultimate clearance in some cases is the responsibility of some division other than the detective division. The search for physical evidence, like the preliminary investigation, is a field service performed for all divisions; it therefore more logically belongs in the patrol division than in a special division.

Many departments now have officers in accident investigation cars make investigations of traffic accidents including the search for physical evidence; the chief accident investigator in the traffic division follows up on these investigations in the same manner as the detectives follow upon the preliminary investigation of crimes by patrolmen. A first step toward the creation of special investigators in these departments is the assignment of the task of searching crime scenes for physical evidence to the accident investigation crews. When this is done, the analogy between the preliminary investigation of crimes and accidents will usually become so apparent as to result in the assignment of the special investigator to the patrol division to search both crime and accident scenes for physical evidence while the beat officer (with such assistance as may be needed) makes the preliminary investigation of both crimes and accidents. This transfer has the further advantage of assuring a more continuous supervision of the members of the crew, especially on the dog watch, than is possible when they are assigned to the traffic division.

If the accident investigation crews, when given the responsibility of searching crime scenes for physical evidence, are not transferred to the patrol division, they are likely to undertake the total preliminary investigation of crimes. The beat officer, because he is not made a party to the undertaking, then loses interest in the project, feels little or no responsibility for its successful conclusion, is not likely to be alert for information and suspects, is less impressed with the seriousness of his failure to prevent the occurrence, and no longer will serve effectively as the eyes, ears, and legs of the detective division. The department then will not operate as a well-integrated machine. Neither will the patrolman have so great an opportunity to develop interrogative and investigative skills through practice and experience, nor will the executives of the department have so great an opportunity to select patrolmen, on the basis of demonstrated ability, for assignment to the detective division and to other investigative jobs.

In cities of less than 100,000 population, one special investigator on the evening shift (which has the heaviest load) is adequate. In addition to their physical evidence tasks, the special investigator on the dog watch may be assigned to patrol the lightest beat if it is centrally located, and the one on the day watch may be given the duties of chief accident investigator. In larger cities the need is likely to be sufficiently great to justify the assignment of two or more special investigators on the evening shift and, at first, relieving the other two of their additional duties. In large cities there will of course be need for a greater number on all shifts.

Juvenile Division

Cases that should be assigned to the juvenile division are discussed in Chapter 6. When these assignments are clearly understood by both the detectives and the juvenile officers, relationship problems in their investigation are unlikely. Difficulty is sometimes found, however, in cases regularly assigned to the detective division, when the offense is committed by a juvenile or both a juvenile and adult are involved. The line of demarcation should be based on the act of apprehension. This act should be the responsibility of the detective division; the treatment and disposition of the juvenile offender should be left to the juvenile division. By so segregating the responsibility, the detective division interest in the clearance of their cases is safeguarded, as is the interest of the crime prevention division in the treatment and disposition of the offender.

These two divisions have a common ground of interest which is best covered by close cooperation; officers from both divisions should work as a team where the status of the offender is clearly established as a juvenile. Until this fact is established, the responsibility rests entirely in the detective division. This responsibility is not evaded nor shared by determining that the offender is a juvenile, but is joined in by the juvenile division at that moment.

Vice Division

The practice of placing the responsibility for the investigation of all offenses resulting from commercialized vice (including narcotics, gambling, prostitution, and liquor control) in a unit separate from the detective division is a wise one. It provides the necessary specialization, but more important still, this practice frees the officer charged with the investigation of criminal offenses from a responsibility, the very nature of which takes from him valuable information sources. A detective charged with the enforcement of regulations governing prostitutes and gamblers is not in the best position to obtain information valuable in the clearance of his criminal cases. If he is energetic in his enforcement of these regulations, all offenders in this field will be his natural enemies. If he attempts to maintain a friendly relationship with these persons, he must, by the nature of things, be failing in the performance of his duty. By placing this responsibility in an entirely separate division, detectives charged with the investigation of criminal offenses will have information sources that would not otherwise be available.

Jail Division

While the jail division will be entirely separate from the detective division, it is important that the detectives have assurance that their prisoners are held in custody under charges and conditions best suited to assist in the investigation. Department rules must establish authority for holding prisoners during the investigation or incommunicado.

Records Division

The records division is the coordinating unit that binds all other functional divisions of the department together. The records division should include criminal records, thus making identification officers a part of this unit rather than a separate unit or a part of the detective division.

There is a tie between the investigation division and the records division. Some departments feel that investigators are so closely dependent on records that the investigation division must have immediate control of its records in order to be effective. It is better practice, however, to centralize record-keeping activities in a single division, with the clear understanding that the records division will be fully cooperative in supplying the investigation division with the records it needs. Needless duplication of records should be avoided, but often duplicate copies of case records will be required, as the investigation division will require one copy as long as the case is open. The records division in turn is completely dependent on investigators for accurate and complete reports on which a satisfactory records system must be based.

The Crime Laboratory. The crime laboratory and the lie detector operator should not be a part of any line division but should be a part of a service division. They provide a service to all operating units of the department, and this arrangement gives greater assurance that their services will be made available in proportion to need and makes less likely influences that might impair the objectivity of their conclusions.

Federal, State, and County Agencies. The facilities of a large number of law enforcement, investigative, and other agencies should be utilized by the local police in their investigation of crimes. Federal police agencies are of immeasurable assistance in the investigation of crimes that are violations of both federal and state law; in addition, most of them stand ready to assist informally in local crime investigations even though the offense is not a federal violation. Postal inspectors (as well as the local post office officials) are especially cooperative in assisting the police in tracing and locating fugitives. Federal narcotic agents are likewise ready to assist in narcotic violations, and secret service agents render aid in the investigation of cases involving the counterfeiting or forgery of United States coin, currency, and other documents. The immigration service, alcohol tax unit, intelligence unit of the Internal Revenue Service, and U. S. Customs Service also prove helpful in the investigation of some crimes and the disposition of some criminals. The FBI provides the widest service to the local police of all the federal police agencies. In addition to a large number of offenses over which they have jurisdiction, this agency serves as a clearinghouse for criminal identifications and disseminates information regarding persons who are wanted by sending wanted notices and the *Fugitive Bulletin* to local forces.

Most states have one or more state investigative agencies with facilities usually at the service of the local police. The state police, identification bureau, crime laboratory, criminal investigation bureau, and narcotics bureau are examples of police agencies found in many states. In addition, there are other state investigative agencies, not so precisely concerned with the enforcement of criminal law, whose facilities the police may use. Examples include the motor vehicle department, highway patrol, alcohol control agency, fire marshal, game wardens, and other agencies having inspectional duties. Both state and county probation and parole offices likewise are in a position to render valuable assistance.

At the county level the sheriff plays an important role in law enforcement which must be coordinated with the efforts of the local force. The coroner or medical examiner likewise enters the scene in cases of suspicious or violent death. The county prosecutor also is available to assist in crime investigation with advice and with the assistance of investigators who are appearing in increasing numbers on the prosecutor's staff.

Contacts with other enforcement units or criminal matters or in missing person cases, wherever located, are normally made through the detective division. The interchange of requests for service of warrants of arrest, for investigations concerning the whereabouts of wanted persons, and similar services are matters of daily occurrence in a large police department. A reputation for service regarding such requests is beneficial to the long-time effectiveness of any police unit. It should also be added that although criminal correspondence may originate in the detective division, it should flow through the records division so that reports and records will be complete and the operation of the follow-up system will be facilitated.

Private Detectives. It is beyond the scope of this volume to treat exhaustively the organization, work, and methods of operation of private detectives; only brief mention is made of the relations between the investigative unit of the police department and the private detective agency.

The executive officer of the investigation unit should have a list of private detectives in his jurisdiction. It is wise to maintain friendly relations with these operatives as they may be able to assist by furnishing information in some criminal cases. Because the work of private detectives often parallels the investigative work of the police, relations with private detectives give rise to friction at many points. Many police administrators feel that the existence of private detective agencies is a challenge to modern law enforcement, but there will probably continue to be employment for private detectives because the regular police function is restricted to criminal activity.

Most states provide for the licensing of private detectives. Such statutes commonly provide for the posting of a bond by the private detective and certain restrictions concerning his operations. Any system of local control should be based on the state law. If there is no state control, it will usually be possible to enact local legislation providing for a licensing system.

The Crime Laboratory

It is not the purpose of this volume to discuss in detail the scientific analysis of criminal evidence, which is given intensive treatment in a number of highly technical books.[3] Nor is it the purpose of this section to suggest that every police detective become a Philo Vance or a Sherlock Holmes who solves all crimes in the laboratory with the aid of superhuman mental powers of deduction. It is true, however, that science has been injected profitably into the routine work of crime investigation. In fact it was one of the greatest modern scientists, Sir Francis Galton, who introduced the use of fingerprints as an unfailing method of identification. This is only one of the many contributions which science has made to police work in recent years. For example, scientific techniques are available for the analysis of such evidence as: blood and seminal stains, dusts, soils, fibers, gunpowder, firearms, dyes, stains, documents, and tire marks.

Every mark and every piece of physical substance, no matter how minute, left at the crime scene, may aid in the identification of the criminal. One of the greatest advances in crime detection in recent years has been made in this field of identification through laboratory analysis of evidence formerly ignored. By using the objective approach of science, the statements of witnesses and the hypothesis of the investigator can be tested and the truth of what took place in a criminal activity more closely approached. Scientific aids have developed both because of the strides made generally in scientific fields and because of the increasing use of science by criminals themselves. The police must keep ahead of the criminal if their work is to be effective.

Scientific Techniques

The relation of scientific resources to criminal investigation and the scientific techniques which are being utilized by modern police departments are indicated in the following paragraphs:

Chemistry. Chemical analysis may reveal the identity of an unknown substance, the contents of an explosive, or the presence of poisons in human organs. Chemical and physical analysis of soil, glass, safe insulation, and paint may establish the relationship between these substances found on the person or in the possession of a suspect and similar material from the crime. Chemical and serological analysis of blood stains may determine whether a stain is blood, the animal species, and the group or type to which the blood belongs. Identity with the victim's type is not conclusive, but in certain situations nonidentity with the suspect's type may serve to refute an alibi or exonerate a suspect.

Every firearm makes distinctive marks on the bullets fired from it, but it takes a comparison microscope to differentiate the markings of weapons having similar class characteristics. The microscope is useful in the analysis and identification of substances of biological, botanical, or chemical origin such as fibers, hair, seeds, leaves, or spermatozoa. As a general tool, microscopy is employed in the comparison of tool marks, the study of questioned documents, and on any other problem where the unaided eye is ineffective in detecting the necessary uniqueness of certain aspects of the evidence.

---

[3] An excellent treatise for the police officer will be found in Charles E. O'Hara and James W. Osterberg, *Criminalistics* (New York: The Macmillan Company, 1949).

Photographic records of a crime scene or other evidence preserve details and may detect evidence that escapes the human eye, particularly when filters, ultraviolet or infrared radiation, or special emulsions are used. Even the most careful observation by an investigator may fail to discover evidence later revealed by photography. Photographs, together with sketches and scaled drawings, show the relationship between objects in a way that is far superior to a verbal description.

Police photography need not be confined to the "snapshot," picture-for-the-record class. Growing use of color film, aerial photographs, silent and sound movies, as well as photogrammetry have extended the usefulness of this recording media. Photography as a crime prevention and crime detection agent has become an important tool. Hidden cameras to record criminal proceedings; telephoto pictures of a surveillance; movies of drunk drivers, confessions, and re-enactments; and the quieting effect of the camera at a riot, are a few of the extensions of this technique by progressive departments. Unfortunately it must be noted that too large a percentage of police photography fails to measure up to the quality necessary for even minimum utility. Photography is "practiced" by a large segment of the population in an off-hand manner, but this should not permit police photographers to relax their self-criticism.

The use of photographic equipment to develop pictures on the spot is increasing rapidly. Because a minimum expenditure is required, a darkroom is not needed, and because only a short training period will qualify an officer, this method of photography is well suited to small departments. Because of the convenience of having a finished print in one minute, this system also is of value to large forces for many sorts of record shots. With a supplementary lens system and a copying device, satisfactory pictures of latent fingerprints and other small bits of evidence are readily made. Identification photographs can be made and duplicated rapidly, and black and white slides can be made either from a photograph or from the original scene. If the officer makes a mistake, he sees it as soon as the print is developed and can take a second picture at once. While this system of photography can not do all of the things a photographic laboratory can, it has many advantages in police work and can be used as the basic method in a small force or to supplement the equipment of a large department.

Medicine. Medical assistance is, of course, one of the oldest scientific aids in criminal investigation. The pathologist helps in determining the cause of death; the nature of the blow, stab, cut, and weapon, and sometimes the circumstances that led to wounds and fractures; reason for illness; drug addiction; presence of poison; time of death; and additional facts of value.

Casts of Impressions. Plaster of Paris, moulage, and other substances are used for making casts to reproduce such evidence as footprints, tool impressions, and tire marks. Such casts are invaluable in laboratory comparisons and in preserving such evidence for judge and jury.

Instrumental Analysis. Through the use of infrared, ultraviolet, and visible absorbtion spectroscopy as well as emission spectroscopy, the identification and comparison of evidence can be extended to micro traces. Additional techniques, borrowed from the field of physics, such as x-ray diffraction and x-ray spectroscopy enable the crime laboratory technician to analyze minute specimens on a nondestructive basis. Although these instruments require a high initial investment, their usefulness in competent hands extends over many years.

Psychiatry and Psychology. Psychiatry and psychology are helpful to the police in analyzing emotionally and mentally defective criminals and juvenile delinquents and planning a program for their treatment, in discovering the mental and emotional condition of some felons, and in appraising the personality of candidates for appointment to the police force. These skills also may throw light on the method of operation of the perpetrator, reveal his motive, discover the effect of drugs, alcohol, and fatigue, and lead to an understanding of the cause of some crimes.

Lie Detector. Deception tests are of great aid to the police in investigation work, although they do not constitute evidence which is admissible in court. The most widely known deception test is the polygraph, or lie-detector, which was perfected after extensive experiments by Leonard Keeler. This instrument consists of units which record respiratory changes, pulse rate, blood pressure, heart action, and changes in the electric conductivity of the skin while the suspect is being questioned. Significant changes in these body reactions give the examiner highly reliable leads as to when the suspect is lying.[4]

It is of some interest that one police department has used the polygraph in the routine examination of transient vagrants and other suspicious characters not being questioned with reference to specific crime. By this procedure the police have discovered a number of escaped convicts and persons wanted for crimes committed in other jurisdictions. In some cases stolen property was recovered before the crime had been reported to the police authority in the jurisdiction where the crime was committed. It is important, however, to observe the warning that the technique is reliable only when used by trained persons.

Mention may also be made of the use of so-called "truth serums" which depress the inhibitory power and may result in the revelation of the truth. The application of these drugs to the subject produces a kind of coma in which he may be less able to deceive. The treatment has some value in learning the identity of amnesia victims. Developments in this use of drugs are being followed with interest by progressive police administrators.

Dangers of Pseudoscientific Methods. The rapidity with which science has been injected into crime investigation has its dangers as well as its assets. Cloaked by the disguise of scientific terminology, quacks may sell unscientific devices to police departments, and the police are often confronted by unscientific evidence introduced by unscrupulous lawyers using pseudoscientists as witnesses. The fact that the legal and scientific status of new types of evidence is so uncertain contributes to the confusion of courts and law enforcement agencies in this field. There are recognized and reputable journals which report faithfully reliable experiments and conclusions in police science, and it has been suggested that there should be a national committee of jurists and scientists who would be responsible for verifying the validity or nonvalidity of scientific techniques which may be used to support evidence in criminal cases. Failing the establishment of some such body the police must be cautious to avoid scientific methods whose validity has not been conclusively determined. This warning, however, should not deter the police from progressively utilizing those techniques which are valid beyond any reasonable doubt.

The Availability of Scientific Resources

From the preceding paragraphs it may be seen that some criminal investigations may be facilitated by the use of techniques and skills developed in any of the physical sciences. Since any substance might become physical evidence in some case, all of the

---

[4] Fred E. Inbau and John E. Reid, *Lie Detection and Criminal Interrogation* (Baltimore: Williams and Wilkins, 1953).

body of scientific knowledge might at some time prove useful. To provide a crime laboratory with a staff skilled in every scientific field and supplied with the equipment and standards needed to conduct their examinations is obviously impossible in even the largest law enforcement agencies. Instead, all crime laboratories should be equipped to make examinations frequently needed, and those beyond their scope should be handled by university, governmental, or industrial laboratories.

The facilities of the FBI crime laboratory (one of the most completely staffed and equipped in the country) are available to all law enforcement agencies. Many states maintain crime laboratories for the convenience of state and local enforcement officers. In addition, large police departments frequently have excellent crime laboratory facilities that are available to near-by smaller law enforcement agencies.

No matter how extensive or limited the laboratory service of a department may be, its head should inventory the services available in the community, surrounding area, and state that may be relied upon in crime investigations that necessitate an examination of physical evidence beyond the capacity of the local force.

Laboratory Service in the Small Department. Crime investigation involves ascertaining facts from the examination of physical things as well as persons, and investigation that is restricted to the interrogation of persons must be considered seriously inadequate when there is physical evidence available for examination. It follows logically, then, that even the smallest department, if it hopes to make thorough investigations of crimes, must provide facilities and develop procedures to assure the search of crime scenes and the recording and preserving of physical evidence. It must also arrange for the laboratory examination of physical evidence.

Small departments interested in establishing a crime laboratory must consider a number of things. Foremost is the choice of personnel. It is a common practice to select a young officer with rudimentary training in science and assign him to the task of developing a laboratory. This procedure is adequate provided he is restrained from engaging in laboratory examinations and is confined to problems related to collection and preservation of evidence. Most of the analyses conducted in a crime laboratory require thorough grounding in chemistry, physics, and biology without which the probability for errors in techniques or choice of method is great. Furthermore, after one laboratory has handled the examination of an item of evidence, a second laboratory is reluctant to accept this material and rightly so since, in a sense, their reputation may be endangered by erroneous diagnoses based upon contaminated evidence.

Many fine laboratories in the past have evolved from the identification office, adding photographic facilities and laboratory as needed. Today the array of techniques and instruments available are beyond the knowledge and training of the identification officer. Not only must the evidence be processed by the correct method, but the results of the examination must be interpreted as to its value to the investigation. In the light of these precautions, the small department may still have locally available facilities by employing graduates from any of several universities training technicians for the field of criminalistics. This may be the core around which a laboratory will grow.

Personnel represent only one of the major considerations. The administration should consider case load. Will there be enough examinations to justify a laboratory? Can adequate space be provided? Cramped quarters will seriously impair the efficiency of the unit. Do all considerations above named justify the capital investment and the continued budget for current needs and growth? A properly equipped local laboratory can represent a saving in investigation time and bring to bear the services of science on cases that might not warrant transportation of evidence to a distant agency. A laboratory established on a county, intercounty, metropolitan, or some other basis is the best solution to the dilemma facing the small department. Although tempting, the public relations value of technical facilities which represent no more than a "sign on the door" should be avoided. If this is the major desire of the administration, it should go no further with the project. A laboratory is *not* the panacea for local crime; it is rather a *service* to criminal investigation.

A crime laboratory is more than fingerprints, casts, and photography. To cope with the diversification of evidence collected in a moderate-sized city, an investment of $25,000 or more may be necessary. In order to recruit properly trained laboratory personnel and to keep these technicians after they become thoroughly experienced, a department must be prepared to pay salaries equal to top ranking police positions.

Faced with the problem of compromising need with limited budget, the small department should survey its needs for collection and preservation of evidence, solve this need with trained, properly equipped crime scene investigators, and then rely upon larger state or federal laboratories for analytical assistance.

The Investigation

The investigation of a crime may now be considered in greater detail. Crime usually involves several phases. At the outset, the first officer at the scene must attend to any problems of first aid, collect and segregate witnesses, apprehend the perpetrator, preserve the crime scene, and summon assistance. The nature and circumstances of the case will determine the order in which these things might be accomplished. In small departments the entire investigation will be handled by the patrol force. In larger departments, after the first phase is completed, the investigation will be conducted by specialists. The entire procedure should be a systematic, coordinated effort by all of the personnel involved. Whether direct action and the preliminary investigation, including the search for physical evidence, should be the responsibility of the patrol division will depend upon the size and structure of the department involved.

It is apparent that the level of performance of these tasks is dependent on the competence of the officers so engaged. Competence is increased by careful selection for appointment, thorough training, and suitable supervision. Emphasis must be given to the important role of patrol supervisors in the preliminary investigation; their judgement and activity in directing their force in the performance of these tasks will influence the result more decisively than the competence of individual patrolmen. Strong and competent leadership in patrol will assure a level of performance by average patrolmen that will clearly justify their preliminary investigation of crimes. When the platoon commander and his patrol sergeants are as able investigators as detectives (and they should be), and are also superior leaders, they are entirely competent to make the preliminary investigation of any crime, utilizing their patrol force to carry it out.

As previously stated, the purpose of the investigation is to convict the perpetrator. This involves establishing that a crime has been committed, identifying the criminal, apprehending him, and gathering evidence to prove the charge in court. These objectives are achieved by means of facts discovered by the examination of persons and things. The patrol force, therefore, should proceed to discover persons and things from whom pertinent facts may be obtained.

The Preliminary Investigation

At the scene of the crime the investigating officer will first determine that an actual offense has been committed. This in itself may require considerable investigation. The citizen reporting may be in error, the "stolen" article may be lost or mislaid, the "assaulted" drunk may have fallen off of the curb, or the circumstances may have been intentionally altered to simulate a crime for any of many reasons. A painstaking investigation will be made to reconstruct the crime as completely as possible. The exact manner in which the crime was carried out, as well as the preparatory steps made by the criminal, may be important to the investigator in order to establish the motive of the crime and to identify the perpetrator.

The investigator can leave no stone unturned in his search for persons who may have witnessed the crime or who have some direct knowledge of it. Since often these witnesses are unwilling to come forth, the investigator must search them out and, by adroit interview, get their testimony. Often the victim of the crime is the best witness, and if such is the case, he should be carefully questioned and his statements and impressions carefully recorded before time can distort his memory. In the questioning of possible suspects or witnesses the detective must avoid any use of force, threats, or mental or physical coercion. The suspect may be innocent; a statement extorted by such methods is illegal. It must be remembered that the aim of the questioner is to bring out the facts and not to establish the guilt of the suspect by playing up information which points to his apparent culpability and playing down items which indicate his innocence. The investigating officer should bear in mind that the duty of clearing an innocent person who may be suspected is as important as convicting the guilty, and it pays equal human dividends. Any questioning should be without bias — objective rather than subjective.

The Search for and Preservation of Physical Evidence

The term physical evidence includes any physical thing that may be found at the scene of a crime. No one, not even the skilled prosecutor, can tell exactly what evidence may be admissible in court. Therefore, it is incumbent on the investigator to search the crime scene carefully for all physical things that may be connected with the crime. The means of entrance to a building; tool marks; debris left by the perpetrator; impressions left by the body of the perpetrator, such as fingerprints, footprints, and so on; the object of the crime; and a host of other material facts may be found at the scene of a crime. After the crime scene has been minutely searched, the evidence found must be carefully marked and recorded. This duty is especially important since the evidence is likely to be presented in court. The exact spot where the piece of evidence was found, its relation to other objects near by, and the physical characteristics are some of the things that should be recorded.

The investigator must be able to identify positively the evidence later in court, and if there are no identifying marks on the evidence, he should mark it. Some physical evidence cannot be moved or preserved for presentation in court; in these cases photographs, diagrams, or casts should be made to reproduce or record the evidence. Transporting the evidence from the scene of the crime and storing it pending its examination by a criminalist present technical problems to the investigator. It is not the purpose of this text to train the investigator in his duties but merely to point out the importance of these operations. The reader, who may be particularly interested in the care and preservation of physical evidence, has a host of material at his disposal which deals with this phase of investigation.

The Chain of Possession. In order to establish the authenticity of physical evidence and thus gain its admission in evidence, it may be necessary to produce in court the person who discovered the evidence and every other person who at any time had the evidence in his possession. For this reason it is important that the investigator establish the identity of anyone who gives or points out to him any physical evidence found at a crime scene. It is equally important to record the identity of every person through whose hands the evidence passes. The number of persons who handle physical evidence should be held to a minimum; as it is increased, the number who may need to be produced in court is increased; the probability of the defense attorney raising doubt in the minds of the jury as to the credibility of any one is increased; and the chances of mutilation, contamination, and loss through careless handling and the opportunity for deliberate alteration or substitution are also increased.

Since the laboratory staff usually is not on duty at night, provision should be made for the safe storage of physical evidence brought in by the special investigators without the need of placing it in the hands of other officers. This may be done by providing each special investigator with a secure cabinet with a lock.

Continued Investigation

Many detective divisions are defective in their system of subsequent investigation after the initial inquiry. Reports of minor crimes are often dismissed with a perfunctory examination by the officer on the beat, and nothing more is done about the matter unless the complainant protests. Then, after the clues have been destroyed in whole or in part, a detective may be sent out to appease the irate citizen. Serious crimes are sometimes handled in the same slipshod fashion.

The detective division has the important responsibility of continuing the investigation beyond the preliminary stage. The efforts of the patrol division must be analyzed. Evidence which does not appear in the course of the initial investigation may be discovered later. Witnesses who have nothing of significant value to reveal when first questioned may have pondered the events and established important connecting links between hitherto minor items of information. Caution may have been allayed by the lapse of time, and some previously unsuspected person may have talked or acted in such manner as to reveal evidence of guilt. The proceeds of a crime, where money or valuables have been taken, may appear in the form of extravagant or unusual spending on the part of one who has no obvious legitimate source for such funds.

These opportunities should not be overlooked; in the interest of competent police administration they cannot be ignored. A crime unsolved after the first investigation should not be filed without further ceremony, to be revived only as the result of a newspaper scoop or at the insistence of some dissatisfied relative or victim.

The success of the detective division in identifying and apprehending the criminal, recovering stolen property, and preparing an airtight case for prosecution is dependent on the thoroughness of its continued investigation. The follow-up method presented in Chapter 12, "Records," will insure continuing and complete investigation.

Identification of Offenders

The criminal commonly flees the scene of the crime, if possible. A distinctive description of him should be obtained from the persons who are best able to relate his distinguishing characteristics. Sex, age, build, weight, height, shape of nose, complexion, kind of lips, color of hair and eyes, shape of ears, nationality, occupation, degree of baldness, birthmarks, skin blemishes, gait, speech, amputations, peculiar habits, description of clothing, jewelry worn, and direction and manner of escape are important. Unique or unusual characteristics have great value in identification. The above information should be broadcast without delay; photographs, criminal and police records, and fingerprint classifications should be given when available.

In addition to these more personal means of identification, mention should be made of identification through secondary items of evidence: latent fingerprints, footprints, toolmarks, and lint or buttons from clothing. Trade and secret marks, such as those employed by laundries, furriers, and rugmakers, may be important clues in criminal identification. Clothing labels, jewelry, and dental work may also provide leads. Letters, cards, and bankbooks may yield their story promptly or later. The method of operation of the criminal may also have important value in his identification, as explained in Chapter 12.

Recovery of Stolen Property

Where property has been taken in connection with a crime, the most accurate available description should be furnished for police broadcast. Case and movement serial numbers of watches, engraved initials, scratched marks or inscriptions, hat and clothing labels and sizes, laundry marks, and similar distinguishing means of identification are valuable. Make, model, year of manufacture, engine and factory serial numbers, license plate number, and special equipment, make possible the identification of an automobile used in connection with a crime. The recovery of stolen property will require effective contacts with, and control over, legitimate pawnshops as well as the unlawful pawnbroker who serves as a fence for goods that are "hot."

Apprehension of Offenders

All criminals must be supplied with the essentials of food, clothing, shelter, and perhaps medical care. The more that can be learned as to the suspect's source of these necessities, and the more intimate the picture which can be obtained of his habits, the easier it will be to identify and apprehend him.

Where a serious crime is discovered promptly and a distinctive description of the perpetrator is obtained, the means of escape from the municipality should be immediately and intensively placed under surveillance. Bridges, railroad and bus depots, airports, highways, and waterways should be watched. The cooperation of adjacent police departments should be asked toward the apprehension of the fugitive. In many cases it may also be profitable to enlist the cooperation of county, state, and federal law enforcement agencies, and in special cases aid may be received from specialized agencies in both public and private work. In many areas the police may use a highly organized system of blockade which will depend on the cooperation of other police departments.

In the apprehension of criminals the police must be informed on the law and trained in the technique of arrest. This will require instruction in the use of force and the limits of such force, when help should be secured from citizens or the rest of the force, how to minimize danger, the control of intoxicated or otherwise unruly prisoners, the times when a warrant is required for an arrest, the policeman's lack of power to release an arrested prisoner on his own authority, and the proper treatment of women and children prisoners.

PROSECUTION REPORT

Trial Court No.   Preliminary Court No.   CASE NO.

Person arrested: ....
Alias: ....
Copy of criminal history sheet attached: Yes......... No.........
Date and time of arrest: ....
Where arrested: ....
Arresting officers: ....
Circumstances of arrest: ....

What he said when first arrested: ....

Did he sign a written statement: ....
Did he admit the crime orally or in writing: ....
Crime committed: ....
Where committed: ....
When committed: ....
Name, address, and telephone of victim: ....
Details of crime...............

Property stolen: ....
Circumstances of recovery and disposition: ....

Description of evidence and how marked: ....

Disposition of evidence: ....
Names, addresses, and telephone numbers of witnesses: ....

Immediately on issuance of a warrant the detective assigned to the case shall fill out this prosecution report in quadruplicate and route as follows: white original to prosecuting attorney; yellow duplicate to records division; blue triplicate to chief of police; pink quadruplicate to division responsible for its preparation. There shall accompany each of these copies a witness report of similar color and heading containing on the left the name of each witness and on the right a statement of testimony to be offered by him. The statement of testimony shall have a two-inch margin at the left. As many witness reports as are necessary to contain all of the testimony to be offered by all of the witnesses shall be used. As additional witnesses or testimony are obtained, additional witness reports shall be prepared and routed as indicated above.

Source: O. W. Wilson, *Police Records: Their Installation and Use* (Chicago: Public Administration Service, 1942), p. 99.

Figure 24 — Prosecution Report (8-1/2 x 11 or 8 x 10, to be folded to 8 x 5 inches)

Prosecution of Offenders[5]

Although the prosecution of offenders is not directly a function of police investigators, their assistance is essential to the prosecuting official. We have already stressed the necessity for thoroughness in the collection of evidence and testimony as an essential to successful presentation of the case in court. To be of greatest use to the prosecutor, this evidence and testimony must not only be collected, it must also be prepared in orderly and intelligible form. In many minor cases the prosecutor knows nothing about the case until he steps into the courtroom on the day of the trial. In such cases he must rely upon the police investigators to have all the evidence marshaled for him in brief and readable form. A prosecution report (Figure 24) facilitates organization and presentation of this material in a readily usable form.

The prosecution report is prepared immediately after filing information or issuing a warrant by the detective handling the investigation and responsible for the preparation of the case for trial and its presentation in court. Attached to the prosecution report are additional sheets carrying brief resumes of the testimony to be offered by each of the witnesses.

The prosecution report ordinarily is prepared in quadruplicate. The original is forwarded to the prosecuting attorney; the duplicate is filed with the case immediately back of the case sheet; the triplicate goes to the chief of police (this copy may be omitted in departments of fewer than 75 men); and the quadruplicate is retained by the division responsible for its preparation. When cases are disposed of, the detective copy, with a notation of the disposition inserted in the margin, is sent to the chief. In minor cases, a simpler procedure may be used.

---

[5]O. W. Wilson, *Police Records: Their Installation and Use* (Chicago: Public Administration Service, 1942), pp. 98-101.

The prosecution report serves a number of purposes. It provides the prosecuting attorney with the facts of the crime, the criminal history of the defendant, and the evidence to be presented and by whom. Examined before the trial, these facts enable the prosecutor to discuss the case intelligently with the police, to advise them regarding additional investigations, and to determine which, if any, witnesses he wishes to interview before the trial.

The prosecution report consolidates in a single document all the information relating to the case which has been obtained by the members of the department without regard to the division to which they are assigned. The act of preparing the prosecution report forces the detective responsible for its preparation to review the case. This review clarifies his thinking on the case and prompts an evaluation of the evidence to be presented in court. This critical analysis frequently causes the officer to make additional investigation along lines that had not previously occurred to him.

The prosecution report permits the commanding officer to examine critically the work being done by his subordinates. The examination of individual cases may indicate points that should be strengthened. The examination of the cases prepared by the various detectives over a period will prove useful in determining weaknesses in the staff.

Finally, an inspection of a sample of prosecution reports as they cross his desk permits the chief to know the quality of work being performed by the investigating officers. The notation as to disposition of the case in court, inserted in the margin of the detective division copy, serves to inform him of the results being obtained through the work of the investigating officers.

The role of the police investigator extends even to the conduct of the trial. Criminal investigation is intimately related to court procedure. Everything that is done in the investigation of a criminal case is done with due regard to the prosecution of the criminal in court. Evidence must be not only that which is legally admissible and which is sufficient to secure a conviction but must be convincing to a jury. The police themselves must serve as witnesses; they not only must be familiar with fundamentals of the laws of evidence and court procedure but must be psychologically on guard to withstand the harassing tactics of defense attorneys who seek to confuse and trip them.

The investigator and perhaps the patrolman who had first contact with the case will be key witnesses for the state. Their general conduct in court, their demeanor on the witness stand, and their ability to supply information and to answer questions are therefore important both to the successful prosecution of the case and to the prestige of the police department with the judiciary and with the public.

The Detective Division

The requirements of investigation demand that a separate division of the police department be responsible for the final clearance of crimes by the arrest of the perpetrators and the recovery of stolen property; this division should likewise be charged with the staff supervision of investigations by patrolmen and should develop procedures that will increase the scope and effectiveness of patrol investigations.

The size of the division should be determined by the work load. The patrol force is the backbone of the department and its largest division; it should be utilized to the utmost in all crime investigations, and the size of the detective division should be held to minimum requirements in order not to deplete the patrol force.

Detective Qualifications

The desirable characteristics of a detective differ in degree rather than in kind from those previously stipulated for members of the patrol force. Like the patrolman, the detective must have energy, persistence, courage, resourcefulness, initiative, intelligence, imagination, alertness, discriminating observation, memory, and judgment — only to a greater degree.

A number of more or less particularized traits are desirable in a detective. Some of these can be learned by training or experience; others are innate and should be looked for in the selection process. The more important of these traits can be listed briefly. A knowledge of practical psychology — of how human beings react in normal and in criminal situations — is of great value to a detective. He should have a healthy skepticism to prevent his being "taken in" easily. He should be able to recognize crimes, that is, to distinguish between an actual and a simulated crime. He should have adaptability and wide interests to enable him to get along well and to mingle easily with the many sorts of people he must deal with in his investigation work. He must be practiced in the arts of misdirection — the ability to pass quickly from one role to another, which requires versatility and presence of mind. He must know the best way of questioning people to gain the information he needs. He should be able to spot criminal types and recognize criminal behavior, and from the lineup he should learn to recognize on sight suspects who have been arrested.

Most crimes are solved not by superhuman detective brain power but by intelligence, hard work, and information. In investigation, then, there must be an active, intensive, tireless, territorially limitless search for facts — facts that will prove the crime and identify its perpetrator in court. This work brings a man in contact with every field of human endeavor and makes demands upon his every resource of mind and body. He must be familiar with sources of information and know how to gain access to them. A good detective carefully and selectively cultivates his sources of information. In the area in which he normally operates, he makes it his business to get acquainted with tradesmen, service people, and others who might prove useful to him in an hour of need.

There should be a daily accounting of the detective's assignment records and of the follow-up investigations which have been ordered. Periodic reappraisals need to be made of the functioning of the unit as a whole as well as of the service value of the men of the division. Standard service ratings should be made as often as twice a year, quarterly if possible. A certain number of men will ordinarily render themselves undesirable as detectives either by misconduct or incompetence; they must be replaced.

Selection

If selection methods described elsewhere in this volume have been used in the initial recruitment of members of the police force, patrolmen already possess some of the qualifications of a good detective. Additional qualifications which have been sketched above cannot at the present stage of testing techniques be examined on an objective basis, and selection must largely be based on a common-sense appraisal of traits common in good detectives. Preliminary investigations by patrolmen prepare them for detective service and provide executives an opportunity to discover those who possess the requisite qualities and excel in performance. While written information tests should also be used in the selection, care must be observed not to assign too great a weight to the results. Political preferment should, of course, play no part in the assignment of patrolmen to detective work.

The investigation division is a proper goal for the ambitious member of the patrol force. The prestige and larger freedom and opportunities of this unit rightly attract the man who wants to get ahead, and assignments to it and within it should be based entirely on demonstrated qualifications.

Training

Detectives will require as much specialized training as other members of the force. The subjects with which they must be particularly familiar include criminal law, evidence, court procedure, techniques of investigation and interrogation, modus operandi, observation, portrait parle, property description, report writing, and the use of science in investigation. Training opportunities have been described in Chapter 5, but the facilities of the Federal Bureau of Investigation and the Southern Police Institute may be mentioned again in the training of municipal officers for detective work.

An attempt to treat law in any detail would be inconsistent with the major purposes of this text, but it should be noted that over the past 20 years state and federal courts have shown pronounced concern as to individual rights. The trend has had a very restrictive effect on some law enforcement practices. Numerous court decisions have left imprints on activities of all line units, but they have posed more problems to detectives than to officers of other operating units. For that reason, and because law is as basic a tool to a police officer as is a rifle to an infantryman, greater emphasis must be placed now and in the future on legal rules affecting investigative methods. Arrest, search and seizure, confessions, self-incrimination, and wire tapping can be regarded as particularly troublesome areas.

Good techniques in making an investigation are not enough. Evidence gathered during the course of an investigation must be of a kind that will be admissible in court. Investigators must be adequately trained in the law to perform duties intelligently and in a way that will tend toward striking a better balance between the rights of the individual on the one hand and the rights of the people on the other.

Rank and Pay of Detectives

As was pointed out earlier in this chapter, the differences in the duties of police patrolmen and detectives are more of degree than of kind. For this reason some police administrators feel strongly that there is no need for a position classification of detective as part of the city's over-all personnel system. These administrators hold that police officers should be assigned to the detective division from the patrol division and retained in this service on the basis of demonstrated performance. Such officers assigned to the detective division would retain the rank formerly held, be it patrolman, sergeant, or higher rank. The police chief then is free to transfer detectives back to the patrol division or reassign them to other divisions of the department to meet the needs of the service at any time. Such assignments and reassignments would not necessarily be a reflection of a police officer's inability to do detective work. On the other hand a police officer who is inadequate as a detective can be returned to the patrol force where his work is satisfactory.

A contrary opinion is held by some police administrators and by many police patrolmen and detectives. These police officers feel that detective work, because of its specialized nature, warrants a different and higher job classification than the work of the regular police patrolmen. They hold that the work of the detective warrants a promotion and that classification, rank, and pay should be commensurate.

No formula can be provided to solve this problem because so much depends on the organization of the police department and the needs of the community it serves. The best that can be done is to suggest three generalized approaches.

In large cities it is likely that there will be need for the class of positions of "Detective." There will be sufficient investigative work to warrant full-time assignments to a considerable number of men. The pay can vary from that of the range of police patrolman to the range for police sergeant. In most cities, however, the pay range should not be *substantially* higher than that for police patrolmen.

In large cities it may be desirable to give police patrolmen temporary assignments to plainclothes work of an investigative nature that may range from a few days to several months or more in duration. Patrolmen on plainclothes assignments would operate out of district stations and report to district commanders. They would work in cooperation with detectives from headquarters where there is a need for more investigative personnel at certain times or in certain areas.

In medium-sized cities the class of positions of "Detective" can be established with the number of positions assigned to this class held to an absolute minimum. Considerable reliance would be placed on temporary investigative assignments that would be handled by police patrolmen.

In smaller police departments, the class of "Detective" is not needed. The volume of work does not justify it. The investigative assignments can be handled as part of the day-to-day work of police patrolmen, sergeants, and other departmental personnel.

Regardless of organization, position classification, and rank, the work of police detectives should be scrutinized carefully and thoroughly. There is no branch of the police service where the accomplishments of policemen may be as accurately measured as is the case for detective work. Advantage should be taken of these reliable and objective measures of performance. Incompetent and indifferent officers should not be permitted to remain in positions where they block effective police operations. Officers should be assigned and retained in detective work only on the basis of demonstrated performance.

Assignment of Cases

The case for complete specialization in the detective division is clear. If the detective force is limited to only two men, the entire assignment should be equally divided between them on the basis of types of crimes. The assignment of cases in rotation, thus avoiding any possibility of specialization, is an undesirable practice.

The reason for this specialization is obvious. Criminals tend to follow well-defined lines of operation. Bad-check artists, bank holdup men, and safe burglars, like all other criminals, are proud of their profession. Bunco men nearly always continue to be bunco artists. Pickpockets likewise specialize in their line. Professional criminals usually do not change their line, because to do so they would have to learn a new "game." Equally important, detectives working with only one or a few types of crime become increasingly expert in looking for the clues found in that sort of offense. They become expert in the law in their particular specialty, learn the associated criminal jargon, and develop a wide acquaintance with the criminals operating on the other side of their field. They often can tell offhand, by reading a report, what class of criminal is operating and, by the process of elimination, narrow the possibilities to a few suspects.

The degree of specialization among the bureaus or sections of a detective division will depend upon the kinds and numbers of crimes which the division must investigate and the personnel that are available. There may be a homicide bureau and one to investigate auto thefts. It may be necessary to concentrate supervision of pawnshops and second-hand stores in one unit. Bomb outrages, arson cases, shoplifting, bunco artists and pick-pockets, bogus checks and forgeries, safe blowing, and loft burglaries may each require the attention of a separate section if their occurrence is sufficiently frequent. Such units should be created only in response to a real need and consolidated with another unit when the need has passed or has ceased to be acute and continuous.

Detectives should carry equal work loads. A serious case may require as much work as several minor cases; this should be recognized by the commanding officer responsible for the assignment of cases. Temporary inequalities of work load should be adjusted by reassignment of some cases to detectives currently enjoying a lighter load.

The detective force must be completely mobile. Therefore detectives should not be assigned permanently to geographical districts. Detectives should be available for work in any part of the city which requires their services. It may be necessary, however, to assign some members of the detective division to substations in the largest cities.

Hours of Detective Work

Detectives should work during business hours as far as possible. It is during these hours that they are most easily able to get in touch with victims, witnesses, and others. Detectives who work night hours, therefore, do not usually perform the previously described continuing or follow-up investigation. They are really only conducting the preliminary investigation that should normally be performed by patrolmen. The continuance of the investigation that they initiate (as a preliminary investigation) must be done by the day crew; otherwise specialization would not be possible nor would the investigation be as thorough and complete because the hours are not so well suited to inquiry.

Frequently the specialized detective, who ordinarily works during the day, finds it desirable to work at night. This he should be permitted to do when the requirements of his investigations make this necessary. Occasionally, crimes committed at night seem to justify the immediate attention of detectives. With a competent patrol force, this will occur infrequently. The detective division head should outline to the patrol division circumstances under which notice should be sent to him or to other designated members of his force. The head of the patrol division and his platoon commanders should determine, with the detective division, the point in the investigation of various types of crimes at which the detective division should be notified.

Supervision of Detectives

Detectives are given greater freedom of movement and discretion in action, and operate under less continuous personal supervision of their superiors, than officers in any other branch of police service. The nature of detective service makes this apparent laxness in supervision and control necessary; undue restrictions would impair effective detective operations. It is because of this freedom of action that detectives in some departments have earned unenviable reputations as loafers. Detectives must be trustworthy officers who can be relied upon to work with minimum supervision — who will not take advantage of their freedom to neglect their investigative duties.

The necessity of freedom of movement in detective service, and the fact that a control that does not impair operations is difficult to achieve, makes it important that consideration be given to the development of procedures that will assure suitable supervision without interfering with the job to be done.

Beyond the duplicates of complaint sheets and investigation reports submitted by patrolmen (described in Chapter 12), there are three records that should be maintained by the detective division in order to facilitate the control of their members and measure their accomplishments.

A daily attendance record or call sheet should be maintained by the division secretary to record the attendance and routine hourly telephone or call-box calls. In conjunction, a system should be set up so that the whereabouts of each detective can be established at any time. So far as possible, the telephone number over which he may be reached should be recorded.

A monthly summary sheet furnishes a day-by-day record of the activity of each detective. This summary, to be maintained by the division secretary, is available for inspection by the head of the division at any time during the month. When a case from a previous month is cleared or property is recovered on it, an entry is made on the summary of the current month, the date serving to distinguish current cases from those of previous months. The summary provides information for each case on its current status and disposition or clearance.[6]

A ledger should be maintained to record and account for the disposition of all cases filed in state and federal courts by the detective division. A page or section of the ledger should be devoted to each class of crime or to all crimes assigned for investigation to each detective. The sheets should be divided into columns headed as follows: (1) date of arrest; (2) case number; (3) name of defendant; (4) date disposed of; (5) court and docket number; (6) plead guilty: same or lesser charge; (7) trial result: guilty, not guilty, hung jury; (8) dismissed. Entries in columns 6 and 7 should indicate whether the plea was to the same or a lesser charge and the trial result.

The initial ledger entry is made when a complaint is filed with the court; receipt of the prosecution report (previously mentioned) serves to initiate this action. At the same time a disposition sheet is filled out and filed either in the front of the ledger or in a separate file. On the last day of the month, all disposition sheets may be given to a detective charged with determining the disposition of cases not yet reported. When the disposition sheets are returned, suitable entries are noted in the ledger on disposed-of cases and the disposition sheet is forwarded to the records division for filing with the case. Disposition sheets on undisposed cases are returned to file for subsequent check at the end of the following month.[7]

Measuring Effectiveness of Investigation Division

The chief of police wants to know if the investigation division is being properly supervised and if it is fulfilling its functions. The effectiveness of this unit can be measured; the chief has means of checking detective accomplishments. By means of follow-up control and by spot checks he can determine if complete reports are being submitted and if they are being submitted promptly; and the thoroughness of investigations is reflected in written reports and the recovery of stolen property, as well as in the clearance of cases by arrest. Résumés of individual investigation will reveal whether the detective has prepared a complete, strong case for the prosecution, whether he has secured satisfactory statements from witnesses, and whether he has prepared physical evidence for presentation in court.

---

[6]*Ibid.*, pp. 143-44.
[7]*Ibid.*, pp. 101-104.

The detective division has the function of apprehending criminals, recovering stolen property, and convicting criminals in court. There are three measures of its effectiveness and of the effectiveness of individual detectives:

1. Percentage cleared by arrest. The percentages of crimes investigated by detectives which are cleared by arrest of the perpetrator. Percentage clearances by arrest are obtainable from the detective monthly summary.

2. Percentage of stolen property recovered. The percentage of stolen property recovered is expressed in terms of money value, or in the case of stolen automobiles and bicycles in terms of number of items.

3. Percentage convicted. The percentage of persons who are convicted of offenses investigated by detectives is a measure of detective effectiveness in preparing cases for prosecution. In evaluating this percentage, it is desirable to consider types of offenses rather than totals in order to appraise the disposition of cases on the basis of their seriousness. Detective efficiency is not the only factor influencing this percentage. The other factors, especially the prosecution and the court, are not to be ignored, but usually their effectiveness may be considered to be fairly constant.

Progress in Criminalistics[8]

The most important trend in crime investigation today is unquestionably that toward more and better training for investigators. If this were the only progress being made, it would still portend a brighter future. In addition, like the other applied sciences, crime investigation is slowly but surely adopting many of the advantages of fundamental science and technology which can serve it. As with other applied sciences, overenthusiasm, inadequate understanding of the problems, and the normal failures of human judgment have led to extravagances in some instances and to over cautious conservatism in others. The advances have been many and significant, but at times they have outrun the growth of fundamental philosophy and balanced understanding. These must develop before a new technique, instrument, or approach can be fitted solidly into its proper niche and be viewed in its correct perspective.

Training

That crime investigation is more than normally susceptible to failure of perspective and judgment follows from the fact that its acceptance as a true profession is not yet universal, and its practitioners are by virtue of necessity largely self-trained, half-trained, or untrained. There is as yet no generally accepted type of standard training as is found in the other professions. Where efforts have been made to develop adequate standard training, it is given and administered by persons who themselves are not its product. Thus, educators in this field are still struggling to fashion curricula that are sound, logical, and inclusive, and at the same time adapted to the practical needs of law enforcement agencies. The struggle of the latter with inadequate financing, public indifference, political complications, obsolete regulations, unsuitable applicants, and related difficulties tends to handicap the effective cooperation that is desired by both educational and law enforcement administrators.

---

[8]This entire section appeared originally as an article by Paul L. Kirk, "Progress in Criminal Investigation," *The Annals of the American Academy of Political and Social Science,* January, 1954, pp. 54-62, and is reprinted with permission of the author and the publisher.

That the situation is nevertheless hopeful is proved by the enthusiastic efforts of both groups to achieve a solid basis of cooperation. Medicine, and more recently the law, had to struggle through similar difficulties in standardizing their training programs and developing acknowledged and respected professions. Their great measure of success and the smaller but significant degree of success in professionalizing crime investigation point to continued progress in this direction. Time is needed, accompanied by the continued efforts of the large group that is truly interested in developing in this area the professional standards of training, ethics, and effective practice that are needed.

Numerous colleges and universities offer police training at various levels, and the number of them is increasing. The graduates of such curricula, after obtaining sufficient practical experience in police work, may be expected to raise significantly the standards of police operation. The proportion of police officers who can take advantage of advanced training will remain small for many years to come, and the large remaining group should have the opportunity to receive high-quality in-service training. Local police schools are meeting this need in some places, and the state and federal agencies are partially effective in larger areas; but it is here that a tremendous unfilled need exists. The operation of such schools requires financing and local cooperation to a degree that is not obtainable in many regions. Increased public support of this effort is greatly to be desired.

The laboratory investigator requires extended training at the college level. In-service training can never be sufficient. And colleges cannot be effective in giving the necessary training if the time is restricted to less than a full four-year course. A longer curriculum is preferable. Intelligent and eager police officers have achieved significant results in very limited specialties by self-training, but to encourage this trend is to retard the more significant progress toward making criminalistics a truly scientific and professional subject. Criminalistic training and police training are quite different, even though they occupy common ground in some respects. The necessary knowledge of the basic sciences cannot be imparted rapidly by means of short courses or a little spare-time study.

Identification as a Science

The science of criminalistics is largely the science of identification. Every method of identification — chemical, physical, biological, microscopical — is a potential tool. Items of evidence must be identified as to nature and as to source. The fiber must be found to be in turn a hair, a human hair, a head hair, and a hair of John Smith, if the facts can be made to yield their maximum information. The material must be identified as glass, and as glass from a specific broken window. Progress in this field has been marked and sometimes almost spectacular because of the constant availability of new techniques, instruments, and compilations of data that flow from the laboratories of the physical scientists.

Applications of the methods and data of the physical sciences have been discouragingly slow at times because of the small amount of research in the field of criminalistics as such. Educational institutions in which research in this field is a recognized function are few and inadequately staffed. The crime laboratories are overburdened with case work and often are poorly staffed and equipped for research. It is probable that no other applied science today has so little research output, in toto and possibly per capita, as criminalistics.

The picture is made even more dismal by the residual tendency of practicing investigators to consider their profession as a trade rather than a science, and to hide their

specialized knowledge under the bushel basket of "trade secrets" rather than to disseminate it in the spirit of research science. One is always tantalized by the speculation as
to how much is actually known, and how impressive an array of criminalistic skill could
be compiled if all investigators were to pool their knowledge in a single repository such
as is typical of any good scientific library. An even more unfortunate situation is the encouragement by certain investigative organizations to pool information within the organization but keep it secret from all but the elect. The suspicion that such semisecret information may not be worth revealing can at times be confirmed.

Instruments Versus Skills

Instrumentation has been the most conspicuous focus of attention by laboratory investigators, and to a large degree general police investigators as well. Every convention
of law enforcement organizations is likely to see featured a tremendous variety of special
instruments which will include a ridiculously complex array of fingerprinting equipment
with perhaps ten kinds of powder, about two or three of which will be actually used, and a
bewildering list of tools, the function of which is largely concerned with the profit of the
manufacturer. Here also are pocket wire recorders, infrared scopes, easily concealed
cameras, and much other paraphernalia of the private detective who is far more interested in obtaining evidence for divorces than in solving crimes.

While all of these devices have legitimate and valuable uses, the overemphasis on
such investigative aids tends to obscure the more fundamental requirements placed on the
investigator — thoroughness, common sense, care and thought in approaching the problem,
and a definite and deliberate plan of action designed to achieve the desired result. In
short, the tendency to substitute gadgets for skilled personnel is the most serious mistake that can possibly be made.

In the Laboratory. Though the conditions are different, a similar tendency exists
in the crime laboratory. There, the instrument is essential to operation. Optical devices
extend the range of the eye to perceive minute details that allow identification. Physical
devices provide information for which no special senses exist in the human body. Chemical tests reveal the fundamental nature of materials. All of these require instruments
and equipment.

No other instrument or combination of instruments has made so intense and lasting
an impression on criminal investigation practices as has the microscope. Without the
lenses of a variety of common and special microscopes, most of the identification work
of the crime laboratory would never be accomplished. The spectrograph, the spectro-
photometer, and the X-ray diffraction camera have supplied additional vital information
regarding the identity of materials that could not be readily duplicated otherwise. Ultraviolet and infrared radiations with the necessary accompanying instruments are essential.
The camera makes visible to all the results obtained by most of the other instruments.

To a great extent the laboratory investigator must be an instrumental specialist.
On the other hand, undue stress on instruments in some laboratories has inevitably led
to a complete failure to appreciate that no instrument is ever any better than the man who
operates it. Unskilled and ineffective personnel equipped with every conceivable instrument cannot solve crimes. Skillful, effective personnel with a bare minimum of instruments will still solve a high proportion of crimes submitted to them.

The average crime laboratory has not an adequate budget to acquire the instruments
that it could employ profitably, but an even more serious deficiency is that it often does
not have investigators with sufficient ability to utilize even the most commonplace

instruments to the best advantage. This error is doubly compounded in the occasional laboratory that has more money than it can spend legitimately. In such a laboratory a discussion developed as to whether two electron microscopes or only one should be purchased, even though no person present knew how to operate such an instrument. Moreover, no one has yet suggested a single significant application for one in identification work. While this situation is understandably rare, it is not absent in the field, particularly in laboratories supported by federal funds.

An instrument need not be complicated, rare, or expensive, to be effective. Biochemists made enormous investments in ultracentrifuges, elaborate extraction apparatus, complex diffusion and molecular distillation equipment, and other expensive apparatus to fractionate complex biological mixtures. Today, a simple column of adsorbent or a sheet of filter paper and some common solvents are producing fractionations so much more spectacular that the biochemist has become largely a chromatographer. By adding a five-cent sheet of filter paper to a simple electrolytic apparatus, zone electrophoresis was accomplished with the saving of about five thousand dollars' worth of equipment previously held necessary to obtain the same information.

This is a valuable lesson on the importance of simplicity and ingenuity, as well as a strong indication of the necessity for being alert to new and valuable developments. With few exceptions, laboratory investigators have completely disregarded both chromatography and zone electrophoresis as crime investigation techniques, and have substituted expensive instruments for ingenuity and simplicity. Their most important instrument is still an ingenious and functional brain.

Personal Identification Still Invites Research

It is obvious that the final aim of all identification methods is to identify a person. While indirect identification is the most likely to be possible, it would be more satisfactory to utilize direct identification of the person if it could be done. Eyewitness testimony is so erratic and undependable, as is well known by all experienced investigators, that the fingerprint has long been the indispensable technique of direct personal identification. Criminals also know this, and are commonly able to prevent identification by avoiding contacts that would leave latent prints.

Criminalistic research has indeed been so sterile in finding better methods of identification by direct means that the initiative appears already to be slipping from those most interested. Fundamental scientists, not even concerned with personal identification, are already reporting that blood is individual. Others are reporting the individuality of semen and hair is far on the way toward being proved to be individual. How many times the expert testifies to the presence of O-type blood on a suspect's clothing and then has to admit that nearly half the population has O blood! The day is soon due when he can say that the suspect has on his clothes the blood of the victim and nobody else, or that the victim carried semen or a hair from the suspect and from nobody else.

The techniques are largely available, the fundamentals of the field are already well known in some quarters, but the laboratory investigators are still sitting on the side lines. The writer has a strong feeling that this is due at least in part to the gradual crowding of enthusiastic, scientifically trained amateurs from the field as the large, highly organized laboratories take over the practice of the profession and diminish the contacts with the wider scientific circles. Except when a large organization is directly organized for research, research will be stifled. There, the pay check and the time clock tend to replace the thrill of accomplishment and the constructive imagination of the worker.

Fingerprint technique, though highly standardized and universally practiced, made its most significant advance through the early work of amateurs — Sir Edward Henry and some others. Little by little, the technically trained amateur with a real understanding of the specialized fields of biology, chemistry, and physics is being crowded from the crime investigation field without having his research ability replaced by that of the practicing laboratory investigator. Though the movement toward professional standardization itself constitutes progress, it would be tragic if the very seeds of continuing progress in the larger field were lost in the process.

It is time that the large and well-equipped laboratories, and even the small ones, give serious attention to this situation. They must remember that the more intelligent criminals are ever on the alert for better methods of thwarting the law. In the war on crime, the agents of the law must maintain the lead in the development or be forced to ultimate failure. Financially, the criminal has the lead by a large margin. He also leads in numbers. The only advantage enjoyed by the agents of the law, aside from perfunctory support by the large majority of the public, is access to superior technical facilities. The most potent of these is research — a fact which must be realized and acted upon if progress is to be sustained at a sufficient rate to continue effective law enforcement.

Crime Laboratories

Because of misunderstanding of the proper and necessary functions of crime laboratories, their proper integration into the law enforcement program is often not accomplished. The inevitable result is that the laboratory does not deliver the service of which it is capable, and dissatisfaction arises with its existence, when it should apply only to its operation. Sometimes miracles are expected from the laboratory by the overenthusiastic but more often the laboratory is neglected or bypassed by the police or the administrators who do not understand it and may be suspicious of it.

Poor functioning of such a laboratory is sometimes explained as being due to poor facilities. Far more often the real cause of the situation is inadequate personnel, or poor coordination of effort with the police investigators. The latter may not be adequately informed as to what the laboratory can do to help them, and they usually have a very limited appreciation of the nature and value of physical objects as evidence. Uncollected evidence cannot be made to assist in solving crimes. In a very large majority of cases, most of the valuable physical evidence is never collected, and the little that is recovered may often be inadequate to establish proof. When this occurs it is often listed as a laboratory failure, when in fact the laboratory never had a chance.

More serious, though less common, than the failure to obtain all the physical evidence is the inclination to destroy it. This is encountered on the part of police officers who do not realize its value, and has been known to occur in the laboratory itself on the part of technicians who lacked the necessary ability and/or inclination to deal intelligently with it. A very bloody garment is not a pleasant object to examine, and it is far easier to destroy it than to preserve and test it; but any laboratory in which this could occur requires immediate overhauling.

The Local Laboratory. The cost of the laboratory and the physical and organizational difficulties of establishing local laboratories have been major deterrents to their installation in many places, especially in medium and small cities. It is tragic when misunderstanding of the true nature of the difficulty is not appreciated and leads to delay in an obviously valuable acquisition. A small but efficient laboratory can be equipped for less than ten thousand dollars, even at today's inflated costs. It can operate on a total annual budget, including salary for a skilled laboratory investigator, of five to ten thousand dollars and provide excellent service in 90 per cent or more of the cases requiring laboratory study. When it is realized that the police force, by increasing its efficiency, can actually save the salaries of additional officers otherwise necessary to carry a heavy investigative load, the total outlay may be written off entirely in the saving effected.

Even more significant is the saving in terms of court trials. A remarkably large proportion of guilty suspects, when confronted with a laboratory report that demonstrates their guilt, will plead guilty and save the cost of a contested trial. Even standing alone, this saving is probably more than enough to defray the cost of a small laboratory.

Aside from the less tangible but no less real fact that the proportion of convictions nearly always rises sharply when laboratory testimony is employed, there is ample argument for many laboratory installations in police departments today. The significant question now is whether the police department can afford to be without the laboratory, rather than whether it can afford a laboratory.

The Central Laboratory. There has been a marked tendency in recent years toward the establishment of central laboratories by states and various agencies of the federal government. Success in meeting many of the needs of law enforcement agencies is indicated by the considerable expansion of these laboratories when they have operated over a period of time. Along with this movement there has also developed a tendency to depend on them for all laboratory work, and at the same time a feeling on the part of administrators of such laboratories that they should monopolize the laboratory work of the area served. While their services have markedly improved law enforcement as compared with the conditions prevailing in their absence, it can be demonstrated readily that these laboratories do not furnish a complete or ideal answer to the laboratory problem.

Proper functioning of any laboratory requires close coordination and exchange of information between the police investigator and the laboratory investigator. This starts with the collection of the evidence itself, which usually cannot be evaluated without full and complete understanding of the problems by both parties. It continues throughout the investigation. As each new fact emerges from the laboratory, it must be evaluated cooperatively to determine whether it is a significant finding regarding the crime or merely an extraneous fact which is totally unrelated. The laboratory may waste much valuable time studying materials that have no value as evidence, and the investigators in the field may overlook the most important evidence because they do not realize its potential value when examined in the laboratory. Further, they immediately apply the information obtained by the laboratory if they can receive it promptly.

Such close integration of effort is usually impossible when the central laboratory is involved. Only the police scientist is on the spot at the right time and in constant touch with the field investigation.

The small police laboratory, on the other hand, can rarely be provided with all the facilities that are associated with the central laboratory. Therefore, some types of examination cannot be made locally. Also, it is likely that the police scientist is more restricted in experience and training than his counterpart in the larger laboratory. The central laboratory can serve best as a cooperating agency that carries out those examinations which the police scientist realizes are desirable but which he cannot make. He, in turn, is in an excellent position to serve as liaison man with the central laboratory on the one hand and the police investigator on the other. He can assure that evidence is not overlooked or disregarded, that the preliminary examinations perhaps involving much sterile exploratory work are carried out locally and in close coordination with the police, and that all necessary examinations he himself cannot make will be properly done with a minimum of wasted time by the central laboratory personnel.

An additional and extremely important function attaches to the central laboratory, namely, the training and orientation work that must be performed in making local law enforcement officials conversant with the significance and handling of physical evidence. Uniformity of practice and of instruction cannot be achieved by working on the local level alone, even though the efforts of local laboratory personnel in indoctrinating local officials is invaluable. Coordinated programs of training for sheriffs and others are in operation in various states and are yielding most significant and valuable results. These programs require direction in part by the state or federal laboratory officials, who need not infringe on the local efforts being made in the same direction. The two aspects of crime laboratory work are thus complementary when properly organized and directed. It is a mark of poor administration if they ever become truly competitive.

Interviewing and Physical Evidence

The most extensive use of technical advances in the fundamental sciences has been made in the field of physical evidence examination. Investigation of persons rather than things is still handicapped by the same basic difficulties that complicate the precise application of economic or political laws and generalizations. A new instrument may be readily understood because it is conceived, designed, and built by people, and will be operated by people. Interviewing witnesses, on the other hand, involves understanding of the human mind and of human behavior. No mysteries of science are so profound as these. The skillful examiner who can interview a person and usually uncover the truth of an event is certainly operating more in the realm of the artist than in that of the objective scientist.

Uncovering the facts of a crime by means other than direct interview and examination of physical evidence in the strict sense requires an active and practical imagination and the ability to substitute the mental processes of the culprit for one's own. This type of mind, so valuable in the investigator, may be inherent, but is more often acquired by experience when the person has an aptitude for investigative work. Recognition of such a person, and provision of ample opportunity for him to acquire experience under stimulating guidance, are a prime necessity if good investigators are to be developed. Along with this must go sound common sense and training in the two most important phases of investigation — interviews and physical evidence.

In the field of the interview, the great progress in psychology and psychiatry, supplemented by the development of objective tests to expose deception, has led to material advances in this old and difficult art. As with the more objective field of criminalistics, these advances have attracted both overenthusiasts and scoffers. Here also, the middle road of cautious enthusiasm, careful testing and conservative application is the real goal. It is unfortunate that the objective tests for deception have been so widely misunderstood and misinterpreted, for they are the only known substitutes for a very profound knowledge of and ability in probing the human mind.

Lie-detecting Devices. The so-called "lie detector," or polygraph, is an excellent illustration of the confusion in popular thinking, which spreads into many police departments as well. It is not generally recognized that the polygraph is merely a device to detect emotional reactions of any type, but not to detect falsehood except as it stimulates an emotional reaction. Thus, it is the examiner and the question he asks that are important, and not the machine, which is merely designed to give a signal when a question stirs up an emotion. As in the laboratory, the machine is completely secondary, the operator being the important element. When this simple idea is finally grasped by investigators, courts, and the public, it will be safe to allow lie-detector evidence in court. Until then, training of operators and general education — not a change in legal attitude — should be the main objective.

Even more widely misunderstood is the so-called "truth serum," which is not a serum and has no relation to truth. The device of inhibiting the higher mental centers with a drug so that the normal inhibitions of the subject are suppressed is not new. Alcohol frequently does the same thing, though less efficiently. What emerges is not necessarily truth and may be pure gibberish; but it may also impart to the skilled operator information not otherwise obtainable. Here again, the emphasis must be entirely on the operator, not the device. This points as before to training, practice, experience, and more training of investigators in this, as in the other specialties of investigation.

Nontechnical Police Personnel

By any criterion, the police investigator is the most important person in the complex chain of crime investigation. The psychiatrist, the police scientist, and the lawyer supplement his efforts, but the case normally is solved or not solved depending on the ability, persistence, and skill of the investigator. In order to increase the probability of his ultimate success, he should have access to the best laboratory possible, and the training necessary to utilize it fully. He should have the services of skilled operators of detection-of-deception methods, and the training necessary to profit from them. His selection should be by persons who have a thorough understanding of the job requirements and a profound appreciation of the inherent qualities necessary for good investigators. The examiner may be a good psychiatrist, or a thoroughly competent police executive, but it should not be just a personnel board or civil service commission with a list of confusing and ambiguous questions gleaned from an obsolete textbook.

Above all, the investigator should be given the opportunity and the incentive to receive all the training possible and the best grade of training available. Low standards of training that too often prevail should be improved, and new training instituted. In this direction only will lie progress, progress that is now being seen in certain quarters where training is relatively good, and which stands in sharp contrast to that in other regions where training facilities are inadequate and where police are not encouraged to obtain even that which is available.

Not only will this lead to better police performance, but it will so increase police prestige that many of the other problems such as public indifference and poor financing will be markedly reduced. Professional standards and good performance can always demand and get their own terms. This will be evident in the police field, as in other fields, when the quality of police work is good enough to command respect and consideration.

Chapter 9

VICE CONTROL

The enforcement of laws relating to gambling, prostitution, narcotics, obscenity, and liquor is a police responsibility known as vice control. Operations and individual acts in the field of vice are made crimes and severe penalties are prescribed by state penal statutes and municipal ordinaces. Elaborate provisions are usually made in state statutes for the abatement of nuisances caused by the existence of vice conditions, even to the extent of punishing the owner for allowing vice operations on his property. Theoretically, therefore, such activities should be easily eradicated.[1]

However, vice often flourishes openly in spite of the law and the legal procedures established for its elimination; under all circumstances the enforcement of vice laws presents many difficult problems to the police executive. This is so because public opinion frequently favors laxness in the enforcement of vice laws — a laxity favored in part because of some real or fancied profit or other benefit to be derived from vice operations, but principally because of a failure of the public to understand the true significance and consequences of laxness in vice control.

Problems of Vice Control

It is the purpose of this chapter to explain for both the public and the police the significance and the consequences of laxity in the enforcement of vice laws, to explode the fallacious arguments used by persons who either do not think straight or have a selfish motive in fostering vice conditions, and to describe the manner in which the police should be organized and how they should proceed to control vice most effectively.

It is not the purpose of this chapter to deal with the moral issues of vice; the problem will be treated frankly as one of police administration. Also, the discussion is focussed on commercialized vice, i.e., vice-operations conducted for profit in contrast to vice offenses by individuals committed privately and not for money profit.

At the outset it must be said that the discussion of this police problem will strictly adhere to the principle of absolute repression of vice conditions. No half-way measure or concession is compatible with good police administration. Legalizing vice operations only multiplies the evils, and official sanction and regulation do not solve the problem. The police administrator must treat vice offenses in the same manner as other criminal offenses. There can be no compromise with commercialized vice.

---

[1] Much of the material in this chapter has been drawn from O. W. Wilson, *Police Administration* (New York: McGraw-Hill Book Company, 1950). With special permission of the publisher.

Characteristics of Vice Offenses

Vice offenses differ from other crimes in a number of respects. Vice offenses are usually continuing offenses in both time and place. This is necessarily so because vice operators are providing a service and the clientele must know where it is being offered; also the operation involves a continuing series of acts, each of which is a separate violation.

Absence of Victim. Vice offenses usually lack a victim in the sense of someone who complains that he has been injured by the criminal act. In contrast to most crimes where the victim complains bitterly (confidence games are sometimes an exception), in vice offenses the customer is a willing participant who does not consider himself a victim except when he becomes diseased or is dealt with fraudulently.

In prosecuting criminals, the police experience their greatest difficulty in offenses against the public at large (in contrast to crimes against persons or property) where there is no individual private person injured by the criminal act who is prepared to charge the defendant in court with having committed the offense. Vice offenses come within this category. This is one reason for the difficulty of eliminating vice.

Vice Organization. Services offered to the public in the field of vice usually require the work of a number of persons. For prostitutes to flourish there must be quarters, madames, procurers, and pimps; for gamblers to prosper there must be games with dealers, bankers, and cappers, and men to place and service gambling equipment; for narcotic peddlers to operate there must be a source of supply. Vice operations, in contrast to most other types of crime, are not usually one-man operations; when they are, vice conditions in the community may be considered to be under reasonable control.

When more than one person is engaged in an undertaking there must be organization. Someone must plan the operation; furnish any needed funds, quarters, equipment, and supplies; hire employees; and direct the operation.

To arrest individual prostitutes and pimps and ignore the madame and those above her; to prosecute the individual gambler employed to operate the game and permit his employer to go scot free; to confiscate gambling equipment and pay no attention to the organization that places and services it and takes the lion's share of its profit; to jail the narcotic addict and peddler and not go after the source of their supply — all such procedures are superficial. They do not attack the root of the problem; they harass but they do not destroy the vice organization.

The police must continue to harass vice operators by arresting and prosecuting their employees and agents and confiscating their equipment. But they must do more than this if they are to eradicate commercialized vice. As in killing a snake, they must smash the head of the vice organization if its operation is to be stopped. The police must direct their efforts toward identifying persons at higher levels of operation and gathering evidence to prove their criminal operations.

The identities of the head and of those at high levels in the vice organization are frequently not known. Sometimes the identities are so cleverly concealed that they are difficult to discover and prove. This is another reason why the police experience difficulty in eliminating vice from their communities.

Third-Party Profit. If the money profit from vice offenses were restricted to the individual prostitute, gambler, bookie, narcotic peddler, or proprietor with gambling equipment on his premises, the situation would not be so difficult for the police. Their identities are not readily concealed; their operations are easily discovered; their convictions are not ordinarily difficult.

But the persons who deal directly with the customer do not keep all of the proceeds. A share must be paid to someone "higher up." It is this nebulous "higher up" whose identity is so difficult to prove who makes vice operations especially vicious. It is he who expands the operation to increase the profits, who dresses vice in its most attractive form to lure the indiscriminate, who recruits new devotees to add to his profits.

The third-party profit puts the commerce into vice; without it, vice operations would not reach such huge proportions. The third-party profit is made possible through organization; it also makes the organization possible. The third-party profit is an important factor in making vice control difficult for the police.

Tremendous Vice Profits. In vice, as in industry and commerce, the head of the organization is in a position to take the largest profit. He may have operating for him hundreds and sometimes thousands of bookies, gamblers, proprietors with his equipment, prostitutes, madames, or narcotic peddlers. Each of these is engaged in a continuing series of criminal acts, each one of which results in unfailing monetary gain. The total number of criminal acts mounts into the hundreds of thousands. The head of the organization receives a per cent of the profit on each act. Though in small percentage, the "take" swells to enormous proportions in the aggregate.

The general public is unconscious of the tremendous sums of money that are diverted from normal business channels in this manner. For one reason, the public is not inclined to look beyond the amount involved in one single act; when they lose 50 cents or a dollar in a slot machine they are inclined to consider it chicken feed; they fail to see that apparently trifling sums add up to astronomical proportions. For another reason, when the tremendous sums that are thus taken are quoted, their very size leaves the public cold. These figures, like the figures of the national debt, are beyond the comprehension of most people.

The tremendous profits in vice are used to circumvent the law. Funds are available to corrupt, to influence, to bribe, to compaign, to employ the best legal talent, to elect friendly officials, and to remove unfriendly ones. Vice profits add to police difficulty in the control of vice.

Relationship of Vice to Crime

Communities in which vice flourishes attract criminals. The emotionally unstable character of criminals and their usual lack of home ties causes them to seek recreation in vice establishments; their profits from crime are usually squandered in some form of vice. The channels of influence which enable vice to operate in the community are frequently useful to the criminal seeking immunity from punishment for his criminal acts. The vice operator is also criminal (although of a different type) and welcomes other criminals and sometimes assists them in disposing of their loot, obtaining weapons, and planning further depredations.

The presence of criminals in a community invariably increases the amount of crime. The community in which vice flourishes nearly always has a higher crime rate than others. Vice operations also create other police problems. Vice establishments and districts containing them are frequently the scenes of murders, assaults, and drunkenness. Private persons, when victimized by their vices, sometimes commit suicide, embezzle funds, and commit a variety of other serious offenses. The existence of vice in a community, therefore, greatly increases the task of policing. It is for these reasons, among others, that the police should interest themselves in the eradication of vice. To do so simplifies their other police tasks.

Vice and Organized Crime.[2] Organized crime is the combination of two or more persons for the purpose of establishing by terror or corruption, in a state or city or section of either, a monopoly or virtual monopoly of criminal activity in a field that provides a continuing financial profit. Crime is organized by gangsters. Continued criminal operations uninterrupted by police interference, or with police interference rendered comparatively innocuous by dismissals and indifferent prosecutions, necessitate the corruption of public officials. Monopolistic control necessitates killing intruders to eliminate those who attempt to muscle in on the profitable venture and to warn others who may be likewise tempted.

Tremendous illegal profits make organized crime possible; otherwise public officials could not be easily corrupted and the risk of killing and of being killed would not be justified. Hugh profits in gambling, prostitution, narcotics, and liquor control make these the fields of organized crime; in them racketeers attempt to establish monopolies by corruption and terrorism.

Vice and Political Corruption. The field of vice is the seed bed for organized crime. The community in which vice flourishes is either politically corrupt or will be tomorrow. This is another fact the public seems unable or unwilling to comprehend. The citizen who plays a slot machine or indulges in any other form of vice has difficulty seeing the inevitable relationship between his act and the corruption of his government.

Corruption in the administration of criminal justice further increases the difficulty of the police in eradicating vice; once organized crime becomes entrenched in a community, it is exceedingly difficult to root out. The failure of the public to see the relationship between vice and political corruption adds to the difficulty.

Character of Vice Operators. Vice attracts operators of undesirable character. Although bankers and other persons of sound character have at times owned and rented property for vice operations and hence have profited from the illegal activity, as a general rule men with high principles and good reputations do not engage in vice operations, even when legalized. Instead, the operators are usually persons of questionable reputation, often with criminal records. The proportion who have served time in penitentiaries is high.

The community in which vice flourishes has attracted to it, as vice operators, persons of undesirable character; vice operations provide these persons large profits which make them influential in the life of the community. The presence of such persons further increases the difficulty of the police in eradicating vice.

Division of Community Opinion. Community opinion as to the enforcement of laws relating to vice is invariably divided. The majority (and it is usually a very large majority) is indifferent to the problem. They may indulge in some apparently innocuous vice activities on special occasions but so infrequently that they do not feel justified in demanding the continuance of the operation in the event it is forced out of business by the police. On the other hand, they have no strong objection to its continuance, and they fail to understand the political significance of vice operations. Theirs is a passive role.

On either side of this group a small minority is found who are sometimes very vocal and otherwise influential. At one extreme are those who demand that all vice be eradicated. This crusading group is usually concerned principally with the moral aspects of the problem; their fervor sometimes leads them to be so intolerant of vice as to demand that the police, who are unable to rid the community of all thieves and other

---

[2] *Ibid.*

criminals and who cannot hope to prevent all crime, should completely rid the community of all vice. This, of course, is impossible. The demand, however, and the pressure of this group, sometimes works to the disadvantage of a police executive who is doing all that can reasonably be expected to eliminate vice. After all, if all members of the police force devoted all of their time to vice, there would still be some vice offenses. The police cannot prevent all crime, all accidents, nor all vice offenses.

At the other extreme is another minority group interested for selfish reasons in "opening up" the town. They do not want enforcement; they want the police to permit vice to operate; they exert their influence (and sometimes it is powerful) in this direction. This group usually does not attempt to have the laws changed; the law, when administered to their advantage, will serve to protect them from intruders.

This is the group that causes the police most of their difficulty in enforcing laws in the field of vice. They usually have money to employ the best legal counsel, to bribe and to corrupt. Pressure on the police to relax enforcement may come from the executive head of the city, the governing body, the budget-making body, the press, and influential citizens. It is a sad commentary on police control in this country that sometimes the influence is sufficiently great to result in the removal of police executives who insist on enforcement. When laxness cannot be accomplished through the police, the influence is directed at the prosecutor or the court; when successful, police action is thus made harmless.

This division of public opinion makes the police task even more difficult. The police are nearly powerless without the backing of the large majority who all too frequently are content in their passive role.

Fallacies Relating to Vice

A number of fallacies relating to vice have been foisted on the public. The small minority in the community who favor lax enforcement promote these fallacies in the hope of winning the support or avoiding the active opposition of the great majority who play the passive role. The general public will abandon their passive role and support the police in their enforcement efforts only as the true character of vice is made apparent to them. The police, therefore, should do all that they can to explode these common fallacies.

Legalization Fallacy. A surprisingly large number of ill-informed persons believe that the principal evils of vice could be eliminated by legalization. This supposed "cure" is proposed with special frequency in the case of gambling; it is sometimes suggested for the other fields as well.

The validity of this "cure" is based on the false premise that vice activities are good for people. If the vices were good for people, if children would become healthier and more useful citizens with improved characters and higher principles if they were taught to gamble, drink, use narcotics, and consort with prostitutes, then it would be desirable to make these facilities readily available. But this premise is false. Indulgence in the vices does not make either children or adults better citizens; the reverse is true. When this is agreed, and it must be agreed because it is true, then it becomes apparent that less gambling, drinking, drugging, and prostituting is for the common good, and such facilities should be discouraged rather than encouraged by legalizing the acts.

That the vices are not good for people can be asserted without moralizing. The record of the consequences in each field speaks for itself. No group in the community sees the sordid consequences of vice so clearly as the police because they are forced to contend with the results.

Another frequently offered argument for legalization is that it would eliminate corruption — that corruption springs from the unenforceability of a "bad" law. The record of legalized vice in this country explodes this reasoning. Gambling was once legalized in many parts of our country; corruption invariably followed in its train. Prostitution has been legalized in many of our cities in the past; invariably it played a part in the corruption of officials. This is true in part because of the type of persons who are attracted to the operation. The best citizens, the men of highest principles, have not been the ones who have operated vice establishments when their operation has been legal. On the contrary, persons who have run gambling games and houses of prostitution have invariably been unprincipled rogues who have grown rich preying on human weaknesses. Even today a check of the background of persons who are associated with the operation of legal bars and taverns discloses many with long criminal records in spite of the legal prohibition against their being licensed to operate.[3]

Vice and Business. Many businessmen have been led to believe that vice in a community enhances its prosperity; that persons thus attracted to the community spend their money in legitimate trade. Studies have disproved this contention. The presence of vice establishments diverts much of the money in the community that would otherwise go into legitimate trade. The businessman, like the general public, seems unable to comprehend the proportions of this diversion. The sums of money that flow into the coffers of vice operators, with a "take" frequently going out of the community to the head of the organization, reach tremendous proportions. If businessmen could be made aware of the loss they suffer to vice operators, they would strongly support the police in their enforcement of vice laws.

Prostitution and Venereal Disease. Uninformed persons sometimes argue that the most effective way to reduce the incidence of venereal disease is to place the prostitutes in houses where they may be subjected to regular medical inspection. Medical authorities consistently deny this contention. They insist that this procedure increases the incidence of the disease instead of diminishing it because the presence of the house makes more contacts possible. The prostitute may pass on infection from one client to others. She may become infected herself and infect hundreds of clients before her next inspection. The most effective way to reduce the incidence of venereal disease is to reduce the frequency of contact.

The more effective the police are in reducing the frequency of contact, the more effective they are in reducing exposure to venereal disease. Their efforts should be directed toward that end. Houses of prostitution, therefore, should be closed.

The United States Public Health Service, the Army, the Navy, and health authorities generally are now in agreement that the most effective way to combat the spread of venereal disease is to suppress prostitution.

Some persons also argue that when houses of prostitution are closed, the prostitutes are forced to scatter throughout the community and thereby are a greater menace than before. Checks made in communities that have restricted districts show that there are proportionately more prostitutes operating outside of the district than in communities where an honest effort is made to enforce the laws prohibiting the practice. Even though they were scattered they would not be able to make as many contacts as when they

---

[3] See Virgil W. Peterson, *Gambling: Should It Be Legalized?* (Chicago: Chicago Crime Commission, 1945).

operate in a house or in a restricted district, and the scattering would therefore reduce the incidence of disease.

Another argument offered is that when houses are closed and prostitution is suppressed the incidence of such sex crimes as rape, exhibitionism, sex crimes against children, and sex murders increases. This cannot be proved statistically. On the contrary there is some evidence that the incidence of these crimes decreases rather than increases when prostitution is repressed. Persons guilty of these crimes do not usually seek prostitutes for sex gratification.

Finally, it is contended that the sex act is essential for normal development and life. There does not seem to be medical authority for this contention. Even if it were true, however, it is not a valid argument for prostitution. The police, in enforcing laws prohibiting prostitution, are not eliminating the sex act; it may continue to be carried out without the evils of commercialized prostitution.

Vice Operators and the Police. Vice operators sometimes represent to the police their value as informers. They offer to keep the police notified of criminals who come to the community and of the identity of the perpetrators of crimes committed in their jurisdiction in return for the privilege of operating. In past decades some police officials operated in this manner, thinking that they could thus control serious crime and important criminals most effectively. The fallacy of their judgment was made apparent on many occasions. Today no informed police executive undertakes to combat crime in this manner.

Legalized Gambling.[4] The widespread incidence of illegal gambling disclosed by a Senate committee's investigations has resulted in the suggestion, made by many well-meaning and conscientious individuals, that the anti-gambling laws should be abandoned as unenforceable, and that the business of gambling should be legalized and licensed.

This suggestion appears to be premised on the dual assumptions that once gambling is legalized the crooks and the cheats will retire from the field and leave the operations of the handbooks, policy wheels, and the gaming rooms to honest and upstanding businessmen, and that public officials, who have previously been persuaded to ignore or affirmatively aid illegal gambling operations, will automatically prove incorruptible when entrusted with responsibility for controlling these same operations through a licensing system.

It seemed to the Senate committee that this statement of premises is sufficient to demonstrate how invalid they really are. It is the nature of the business of gambling, and not its legality or illegality, that makes it so attractive and lucrative for gangsters and hoodlums. The tremendous profits to be made from these completely nonproductive operations offer obvious attractions to the lawless and parasitic elements in our society. Legalization of gambling in no way diminished its attractions for underworld elements, nor did it prevent them from maintaining their domination of the field through intimidation and corruption.

Proponents of legalization often argue that the urge to gamble is inherent in human nature and that the enforcement of antigambling laws is an impossible and impracticable task. It is undoubtedly true that a great number of people enjoy gambling but the investigations of this committee have disclosed ample evidence of the evils which inevitably accompany the gratification of the desire to gamble. The fact that it is undoubtedly

[4] See *Third Interim Report of the Senate Committee to Investigate Organized Crime in Interstate Commerce* (Washington: Government Printing Office, 1951), pp. 192-195.

impossible to eradicate gambling completely would not justify the abandonment of attempts to limit the operations of the professional gamblers.

The history of previous experiments in legalization of gambling has shown that legalization results in an increase in gambling, particularly in increased participation by small-wage earners — the people who are least able to bear the inevitable losses. Wherever large-scale gambling has been carried on it has been the experience of law-enforcement officials that violence and crime increase in proportion to the size of the gambling operations. The promise of income to the gambling operator is sufficient to encourage large-scale intimidation and corruption in order to maintain a monopoly of the gambling operation. The losses incurred by victims of gambling have driven them to embezzlement, robbery, and other crimes committed by men desperately attempting to recoup gambling losses they could not afford to sustain.

If legalized gambling could be successfully divorced from the evils of crime and corruption, the state of Nevada would offer the most ideal climate for its operation. Nevada is a state with a small population, where gambling operations can be policed easily and the comings and goings of undesirables can be noted, and yet Nevada has found it necessary substantially to increase police surveillance as a result of the legalization of gambling and the accompanying influx of hoodlums, racketeers, and the other inevitable parasites who spring up like weeds wherever gambling operations are carried on.

While it is true that the revenue received by the state of Nevada in connection with the licensing of gambling in that state contributes somewhat to the rather meager finances of the state, it should also be noted that the revenue from such operations finds its way into the pockets of hoodlums. At the same time the taxpaying citizens of the state must foot the bill for large expenditures for relief and police protection, expenditures which are necessary accompaniments of the wide-scale gambling operations in the state.

It is often argued that it is impossible effectively to outlaw the operation of hand-books, lotteries, and other forms of gambling in states where pari-mutuel betting is permitted. The fact that a number of states have considered it desirable to permit on-track betting under conditions that are most easily subject to policing and control does not furnish any basis for the legalization of other forms of gambling which are far more likely to be dominated by underworld elements and most apt to lead to violent competition and criminal activity.

Those states which have legalized pari-mutuel betting have done so in an attempt to satisfy the gambling urge in the manner which can be most closely controlled and least likely to be accompanied by the familiar evils of gambling. While race-track wagering undoubtedly results in individual personal tragedies as a result of undisciplined betting, the damage can be more or less limited to persons who can better afford to incur financial losses. The operation of hand-books and other gambling establishments in places that are easily accessible to the workingman and the nonhabitual better results in the spread of the evils of gambling to increasingly larger segments of the population.

There is no sense or logic in legalizing the greater evils of off-track betting simply because it has been the considered judgment of a number of states that pari-mutuel betting can be controlled and operated without undue detriment to society. There has not been presented to the committee any plan for the extension of controlled gambling which carried with it a substantial chance of success. On the contrary, each plan for extending legal gambling appears to play into the hands of the gangster element.

In many communities the professional gambling element is synonymous with the gangster element. This is particularly true in the large cities which the committee investigated. In these cities much of the propaganda for legalized gambling can be traced to organized and professional gamblers. They have attempted through public relation channels open to them to persuade legitimate businessmen that an open town is good for business. They have succeeded in many cities in intimidating law-abiding citizens so that they are reluctant to enter into political campaigns against the candidates supported by the gangsters. Particularly in resort areas where wide-open gambling had the connivance of local police have these efforts been made to persuade the nongambling businessmen to support the gamblers.

Fallacy of Legalizing Drug Addiction.[5] Under Federal law the responsibility for the proper prescribing and dispensing of narcotic drugs rests upon the physician in charge of any given case. Without reference to the question of addiction, a physician acting in accordance with proper medical practice may prescribe or dispense narcotics for the relief of acute pain or for any acute condition. Mere addiction alone is not recognized as an incurable disease.

The clinic plan advocated by a small minority group in one section of the country, would radically change the present plan of enforcement and revert to dispensing narcotic drugs to drug addicts for the purpose of maintaining addiction. Under this plan anyone who is now or who later becomes a drug addict would apply to the clinic and receive the amount of narcotic drug sufficient to maintain his customary use. The proponents of the plan claim that the "dope peddler" would thus be put out of business.

This plan would elevate a most despicable trade to the avowed status of an honorable business, nay, to the status of practice of a time-honored profession; and drug addicts would multiply unrestrained, to the irrevocable impairment of the moral fiber and physical welfare of the American people.

Any plan which, like the one under discussion, tends to maintain and increase the spread of drug addiction is not only in direct contravention of the spirit and purpose of the international drug conventions, which the United States solemnly entered into along with 72 other nations of the world, but also constitutes a complete reversal of settled national policy of more than 20 years standing with respect to narcotic drug traffic control. This national policy is firmly rooted in the national legislation as interpreted by the highest federal court and supplemented by concomitant state narcotic legislation.

The supplying of narcotics to addicts merely for the purpose of maintaining addiction certainly constitutes distribution for abusive use even if taken over by practitioners, and to recognize such procedure as legal would be not only a gross repudiation of our international obligations but also a reversion to conditions prior to the enactment of national control legislation and a surrender of the benefits of many years of progress in controlling this evil, in which control the United States has been a pioneer among nations.

The answer to the problem is not, therefore, to accept narcotic drug addiction as a necessary evil and calmly proceed to ration with a daily supply each and every person who applies for the ration. It should rather be the provision by the states of facilities for scientific treatment of these unfortunates, looking toward a cure, coupled with vigorous and unremitting efforts toward elimination of improper sources of supply so as to facilitate complete rehabilitation of the reclaimed addict and prevent the addition of recruits to the ranks of these unfortunates. By scientific treatment is meant that professional treatment which includes confinement or restraint upon the addict to insure that

---

[5] See H. J. Anslinger and William F. Tompkins, *The Traffic in Narcotics* (New York: Funk and Wagnalls, 1953), pp. 185-191.

no surreptitious source of supply is available to him that would defeat the purpose of the attending physician.

The Federal Bureau of Narcotics has never approved ambulatory treatment of drug addiction, for the reason that experience has shown where the addict controls the dosage he will not be benefited or cured. Medical authorities agree that the treatment of addiction with the view toward effecting a cure, which makes no provision for confinement while the drug is being withdrawn is a failure, except in a relatively small number of cases where the addict is possessed of a much greater degree of will-power than that of the average addict.

The Vice Division

Suitable vice control is important to both the police and the public in every community. Consideration of the consequences of the failure to control vice makes the need apparent. Failure results in political corruption; criminals are attracted to the community and undesirable characters become influential; the crime rate is increased; and the policing task becomes otherwise more difficult. On the other hand, as vice is suppressed, the government is less likely to be corrupted; criminals are less likely to seek refuge; crimes become less frequent; and the task of the police administrator is considerably simplified. Also, as a part of the picture, in the community with suitable vice control, the public has a better understanding of the true significance of vice — of its relationship to organized crime and corruption. This is necessarily so because without this understanding the suppression of vice becomes almost impossible.

The Case for a Separate Vice Division

A vice division should be created in the police department if it is to suppress vice most effectively and thus enjoy the advantages of suitable control. Such a division permits the placing of responsibility for vice conditions; it assures a continuing and constant enforcement pressure undiminished by attention diverted to other duties; it permits the selection of members for the work who are qualified by interest, ability, and integrity, and their training in the special skills and techniques that differentiate vice control from other investigative work.

The specialization provided by a vice division enables the members of the vice division to study the legal procedure relating to vice control and to learn the identity, haunts, and methods of operation of persons engaged in vice activities. A vice division also concentrates information relating to vice and police action against it in fewer hands, thus lessening the possibility of information leaks and tip-offs.

The vice division should be completely independent of the detective division. When those charged with the investigation of serious crimes are also responsible for ferreting out and prosecuting vice violators, they are tempted to compromise their vice control efforts in exchange for information helpful in the solution of their criminal cases. Further, detectives who are conscientious in their vice enforcement have a lessened opportunity to obtain, from a useful source, information helpful in the clearance of their crime cases.

Specialization. Assignment to special units within the division is not usually desirable except in a very large city. Instead, the squad as a unit should direct its attention to all violations in the field. The first unit within the vice division to be specialized will ordinarily be narcotics investigation because the approach to this problem is somewhat different and the vast amount of knowledge needed is not easy to acquire except through specialization.

As mentioned earlier, the most effective way to deal with vice is to get the men at the top. In the case of gambling for example, this is not so easy to do, for the only connection between the operator of a crap game and the man at the top will be the money flowing up the chain of command. In narcotics, however, the man at the top is the supplier, and the narcotics go from him through a number of hands to the seller and the addict and then the money goes back up. The difficulty is that there are a number of steps between the top and the bottom, so it is a slow, difficult investigative process to establish this link. A narcotics investigator has an interest in the supplier who sells to the addict only in that he will lead him to his source, who in turn will lead to *his* source, and finally to the top. This is a full-time job, and a good narcotics officer will often work for months before he makes an arrest, but when he does, the effect is to put many suppliers out of business. This means that these officers must be free to continue their investigations, and they must often work under cover. To operate at their best they cannot be given other vice investigation assignments. This does not mean that they will not be of a great deal of value to the rest of the vice division for in making narcotics investigations for they will uncover considerable information on such people as prostitutes who also use narcotics, and on gamblers, bootleggers, and the like who are closely allied with narcotics users and distributors.

Relationship to Police Chief. Vice control requires the application of sound judgment; decisions must be made that often have far-reaching consequences. The vice division is in a position to break the head of the police department and sometimes the city administration itself. Changes in administration in city government frequently grow out of the mismanagement of vice control by the police.

The vice division head should report directly to the chief of police or to an assistant chief in a very large department. This close control of the vice division by the head of the department is justified because of the confidential nature of its work and its significant effect on the health and stability of city government and on the criminality of the community, and because vice operations involve such large profits that strong effort can be expected to corrupt officials and otherwise defeat its control. Even if only one officer is engaged in vice control, he should report directly to the chief of police.

Vice Control Responsibilities of Other Members of the Force

The creation of a special division charged with the suppression of vice in the community should not, however, relieve other members of the force of a continuing responsibility. While detectives may be relieved of the duty to ferret out vice violators and to investigate vice complaints, department regulations should require them and all other members of the force to take effective action in the absence of members of the vice division when violations come to their attention. Violation of law cannot be condoned by any member of the force. One caution must be expressed here. If there is not an open violation of a vice law, only evidence leading an officer to believe that there may be, no direct action should be taken; rather a full report of the circumstances should be made at once to the vice division. If this is not done, an officer by chance may discover a part of a narcotics operation, for example, that is already under investigation, and premature action may lead to blowing up the case before the investigation is complete.

The Patrol Division. Each patrolman should be held responsible for vice conditions on his beat. He should be required to take suitable action, under the direction of his supervising officer, against all vice violations coming to his attention; he should be required to investigate some vice complaints that do not justify assignment to the vice division; he should also be required to make frequent inspections of suspected establishments on his beat.

When the patrol division is thus actively engaged in the enforcement of vice laws, most of the outward evidences of vice are driven under cover. This is desirable because the critical public is then less conscious of the existence of vice, and, since fewer customers are then able to obtain the services, the amount of vice is effectively diminished.

The investigation of minor vice complaints, the elimination of the more readily discovered violations, and the driving of vice operations under cover by the patrol division conserves the time and energies of the vice division for their most important task — the investigation of the vice hierarchy for the purpose of identifying the operators and obtaining evidence that may lead to their conviction.

From the above it may be seen that the vice division should operate as a line unit in the investigation of important aspects of vice that are beyond the ability of the patrol division. It should also operate as a staff agency planning and directing the work of the patrol division in this field.

Hours of Work. Vice division members (except in a very large city) should work together as a team; their effective strength should not be dissipated by assignment to more than one shift. They should work flexible hours, selected by the head on the basis of need; on some days of the week certain hours will be more desirable than on others. Frequent change also confuses the vice operators.

Training. The members of the vice squad as well as other officers will need training in vice control. Federal and state laws and city ordinances need to be studied; methods of operation of prostitution, gambling, illegal liquor sales, and narcotics sales must be taught; the operation of the many gambling systems will need consideration for some of these are quite complicated; and the need for this operation and the responsibilities of each member of the force must be clearly understood.

Federal agencies are most helpful in furnishing instructors in their various fields. The Bureau of Narcotics of the U. S. Treasury Department, for example, has developed excellent training programs for local schools and holds an outstanding training course in Washington where city police officers will be admitted.

Enforcement Methods

Reliable methods of vice suppression and enforcement are well known to police departments and do not vary greatly from one city to another. The following methods are in general use and usually prove effective.

Gambling. Methods of control of gambling include:

1. Investigation of all complaints.

2. Constant inspection by plainclothes personnel, at irregular intervals, of taverns, bars, amusement centers and places where gambling is known to occur. Uniformed officers check such places as a regular part of their beat patrol.

3. Warnings are given at the time of inspection where it is believed that such a warning will prevent gambling.

4. Observing known gamblers to learn the location of gambling.

5. Using undercover agents to locate gambling and to gather evidence.

6. Conducting raids when the evidence warrants.

7. Holding the beat officer and his superiors responsible for gambling violations.

Prostitution. This form of vice can spring up in a community at any time in any of three different forms. First is the bawdy house with its madam and pimp which can start operations overnight, even in the better residential districts. Second is the streetwalker who operates in hotels and bars, or even on the street, sometimes as a free-lance or with a pimp. A variation of the streetwalker is the girl employed in a bar, dance hall, or commercial amusement center as a barmaid or hostess. The employment is only a convenient method to get customers for her actual profession. Call girls comprise the third group and work with bell-hops, taxi drivers, pimps, and madams.

Like other forms of vice, control of prostitution requires constant attention from the police. The places where prostitutes are known or suspected to reside must be frequently observed by all officers. Suspected or known patrons must be closely observed and followed when necessary to ascertain the location of places of prostitution. Unescorted women should be observed carefully in taverns and similar public places. The police can cultivate such sources of information as cab drivers, bartenders, bellhops, hotel room clerks, and other employees. To maintain the trust of hotel owners and proprietors of other establishments it helps not to publicize any particular place following an arrest.

Control of prostitution is much more effective when the case also includes the arrest and conviction of madams, pimps, and other third-party participants. Thorough surveillance and investigation may be needed to make a good case against a house of prostitution. This may require the use of undercover agents or informers.

Valuable leads can be obtained from health authorities through their records of venereal disease. Many such agencies are highly cooperative, and the former patron of a prostitute who got more for his money than he expected is often anxious to identify her, but rarely willing to appear as a witness. In some cities, a great many prostitutes are not prosecuted under the criminal law. Rather the women are checked for venereal disease under the authority of health laws; then if infected they are held under those same laws until cured, or if they have no previous record, released when past the infectious stage upon their promise to return at regular intervals for treatment. Upon failure to do so, the police pick them up, and they are held until cured. Holding for treatment is often a greater penalty than the fine or jail sentence that might be received, and of course the prostitute is free of the disease at least until her next customer.

Liquor. One important phase of liquor control depends entirely upon state law — that is, whether the state or city government has the authority for issuance and revocation of liquor licenses for package sale or sale for consumption on the premises. Where the state government has the authority and is using it properly, a major part of the police job is to report violations and furnish evidence to state inspectors to support suspension or revocation of the license.

A good program of liquor control in all cities should include the following police activities:

1. Applicants for liquor licenses should be investigated with recommendations made to the licensing authority prior to the granting of the license.

2. Licensees, bartenders, and waitresses and waiters should be photographed and fingerprinted.

3. Taverns, bars, and package stores should be frequently and irregularly checked by beat men and plainclothes officers.

4. Commercial amusement centers should be checked for sales to juveniles or for use of liquor by juveniles.

5. Sales outside regular hours should be checked.

6. The police should work closely with state and federal liquor law enforcement agencies.

It will be found that if there is a close and fair supervision of liquor sales that the greatest number of complaints of violations will come from tavern owners who call in to complain that they have to close promptly and why is it that their competition in the next block is still open?

Undercover Operators and Informers

The chief difficulty in prosecuting cases of commercialized vice is the difficulty of obtaining evidence and prosecuting witnesses. Frequently vice conditions exist in a given locality for a considerable time before the police are even aware of the violation. In most other crimes the victims are quick to report the commission of the offense, but this is not true of vice. Customers will not report against the existence of vice unless they feel that they personally have been unfairly treated or robbed. Even then, most such reports are anonymous; or when made in person invariably are accompanied by the statement, "I want you to clean up this situation, but don't use my name or expect me for a witness, because the publicity would ruin me." Under the rules of evidence hearsay is not admissible, and a search warrant cannot be obtained without a sworn statement as to the existing violation based upon personal observation. Under these conditions the police are at an impasse — they are aware of the violation but cannot proceed legally against it.

The police administrator must then bring his ingenuity into play. It is possible to move effectively against the vice problem and still not resort to illegal methods. Local laws and ordinances will govern somewhat the procedure to be taken, but some general methods are worthy of mention.

Undercover Operators. A method long used by the police in combating vice is the employment of undercover operators and informers to gather evidence of vice operations. In every community there are some persons who are willing to perform these services for compensation. This need should be realized openly by the police administrator and the legislative body. As a matter of fact, the withholding of such funds from the police is an effective control device used in some communities where the legislative body is not in favor of strict vice enforcement.

Undercover operators should be distinguished from informers. The undercover operator is a law-abiding citizen, selected on the basis of his reliability and competence, to seek information relating to vice operations in the community by association with, or observation of, persons engaged in these activities. The undercover operator does not ordinarily engage in these activities himself; rather, he poses as a customer or as an idler on the sidelines, and is thus able to learn the identity of persons engaged in vice and something about their methods of operation. While to use him as a witness in court will usually destroy his value as an undercover man, this may be done when the circumstances make such action desirable; the nature of his employment will not ordinarily impair the credibility of his testimony. The undercover operator should be paid a regular salary; it should not ordinarily be based on the evidence produced or the cases made.

Informers. In contrast to the undercover operator, the confidential informer or stool pigeon is not a law-abiding citizen. Instead, he is one engaged in vice or other unlawful activities who, by reason of his operations, is in possession of information valuable to the police in making a case, or he has associations with persons so engaged that enable him to obtain wanted information.

The informer is willing to furnish important information to the police for any one of a number of reasons. He may be in desperate need of funds and willing to sell his information for no other purpose; he may be motivated by jealousy or a desire for revenge; he may be caught by the police in a law violation and be willing to escape punishment by selling out his associates or other operators or by actively undertaking to get for the police information that they want. This latter procedure, sometimes called trading little ones for big ones, is a useful device for the police to use in working up in the vice hierarchy toward those at the top levels.

There is some risk involved in the use of confidential informers of the type described above. The informer may consider that his relationship with the police gives him some special privileges that amount to immunity from arrest for violations; some, in fact, enter into the relation for this specific purpose. The wise police officer, in dealing with an informer, will carefully distinguish between past and future violations; he is justified in overlooking not-too-serious past violations when by doing so he is able to obtain evidence which will enable the conviction of a more important operator.

But the police are never justified in granting immunity or special privileges to vice operators in exchange for information nor for any other reason. To do so places them in an untenable position; when the facts become known, questions of integrity are raised, not only by the public but by the police themselves. To do so is also an opening wedge for graft; when special privilege is used to obtain information, the next step is to use it for other rewards. There can be no compromise with vice nor with vice operators.

The successful use of confidential informers is dependent on the maintenance of a suitable relationship between them. The informer should be used only by the officer who develops him; the officer must conduct himself in such a manner that the informer will have confidence in him; he must avoid any action or word that may impair this confidence; he must not make a promise to the informer that he cannot fulfill. The officer must establish a friendly relationship with his informer, stimulated by common interests that should be developed and by flattering his ego; the officer should avoid demeaning the informer; he should not, for example, refer to the informer as a "stoolie" or "snitch." The officer must not reveal the identity of the informer to others and must arrange contacts which will avoid making the relationship apparent. He should avoid compromising his informer in any way; to do so may endanger his life and will certainly render him useless as an informer.

The character of the informer usually makes the information obtained from him less reliable than that obtained from an undercover operator. The informer is useless as a witness. Juries are quick to discredit the testimony of a person who is selling out his associates. Court appearance also jeopardizes the informer and should be avoided except in rare cases.

The police must recognize that the informer is double-crossing someone, and it may very well be the police themselves. For this reason the police must be wary in using the information so gained to avoid a frame-up against themselves or the object of their inquiry. They should also adopt the policy of not paying for information except on a C.O.D. basis after its reliability has been tested. The best manner of paying informers is by establishing a set fee for information that enables the police to make a specified type of case, the fee to be paid after the arrest has been made and evidence sufficient to convict obtained.

Pitfalls To Be Avoided. Officers assigned to the vice division should be aware of the hazards of the positions they occupy — not from danger of personal injury but of damage to their professional reputations. The head of the division should be alert to tighten operating procedures to lessen this danger. Care must be taken to avoid an appearance of a breach of integrity. The conduct of officers both on and off duty must be exemplary. They must be aware that there are influences at work, sometimes with large sums of money available to accomplish their purpose, that will not hesitate to go to any lengths to lessen the effectiveness of the police in the control of vice. They are constantly in danger of being framed and must avoid situations that make such action possible; they must do nothing that will discredit the integrity of the vice division.

Hazards in connection with the use of informers have been mentioned. Related thereto are hazards in connection with their pay. Procedures must be established for the disbursement of undercover funds that will assure secrecy and at the same time protect those who disburse the funds from charges of misappropriation. Care must likewise be used in handling contraband. Lost evidence in vice cases usually results in a dismissal of the case; such losses are frequently considered evidence of police connivance. Procedures should be established and facilities provided that will assure safe custody of all vice evidence.

Cooperation With Other Agencies. As pointed out earlier in this chapter, the most dangerous vice operations are wide-spread. The gambling in one city may be directed from another city hundreds of miles away. Illicit alcohol may be shipped in from another state, and narcotics will almost invariably be from out of town. As a result the vice division must have full and continuous cooperation with the proper federal and state agencies and with the vice divisions in surrounding communities. These other agencies will not only be able to furnish a great deal of information, but as in the case of the U. S. Bureau of Narcotics for example, will send in highly skilled agents and undercover men to assist local police. At the same time, locally developed information will be of great value to other cities and agencies. This is a problem controlled by a nation-wide criminal organization, and police operations must be equally well coordinated.

Recording Vice Activities

The nature of vice division activities requires secrecy in operations. The money profits involved in commercialized vice and the fact that such activities are sometimes supported by otherwise responsible citizens creates a difficult problem for the police. Since ready money is to be had for the sale of information about police vice control activities, investigations of commercialized vice are conducted with greater secrecy than are most other police activities, and safeguards are taken to keep information from persons who take no part in the investigation. Every member having access to information on cases under investigation by the vice division is subject to temptation, and when plans miscarry vice division personnel suspect that the information has been supplied by some member of the department.

Two plans may be used to keep vice information confidential. The first is to maintain a separate vice division records system for recording matters to be investigated by that unit. Cases with investigation reports submitted by vice officers and their undercover operators are retained permanently in the vice division quarters. Under this system regular complaint sheets, investigation reports, an exclusive vice division daily bulletin (only necessary in larger departments), and a separate number series are used.

When an arrest is made on a case already recorded in this system, it is handled like any other arrest, a new complaint sheet being made by the complaint clerk, with the usual resume on the regular police department daily bulletin. An investigation report, to be filed in the central records office, is then written by the vice division personnel. The vice division case number and such information as is deemed advisable are included.

The other plan, satisfactory in small departments, calls for the use of "silent" cases, which are retained in the vice division office until they are disposed of and are then forwarded to the records office for the usual indexing and filing. An index of cases for the current month is kept for tabulation of the monthly report. An arrest ledger similar to the prosecution ledger in the detective division is also maintained. An arrest on any vice charge by officers of any other division would be handled, so far as records are concerned, exactly like any other arrest except where circumstances justify further investigation by the vice division.

Under either plan, index files maintained in the division which are useful in present and future vice investigations are a location file of places which have given or may give trouble, an automobile license number file, a file of suspects, a file of contacts containing, alphabetically arranged, the names of persons who have supplied the police with useful information, and an undercover operators' file in which are placed daily reports submitted by undercover agents.

Obscenity and Pornography

This topic will be discussed here because obscene and pornographic material is apparently related to vice. In many departments, the enforcement of laws governing it is a duty of the vice division.

This is not a problem in which all aspects are well settled. The question of methods of control is less difficult than the one relating to determination of what should be controlled. In any case, police will receive many complaints about the sale or possession of certain magazines, books (particularly paperbacks), photographs, picture playing cards, motion picture films, comic book-type drawings, and various items with an objectionable theme. The police also will discover much of this kind of material in their regular duties. The question arises, what should and what can be done about it?

What is Obscene?

The commonly accepted meaning of obscenity, according to dictionary definition, is "something offensive to modesty or decency; lewd; disgusting; filthy; repulsive, as language, conduct, an expression, an act, etc." Pornography is defined as, "originally, a description of prostitutes and their trades; hence, writings, pictures, etc., intended to arouse sexual desire."

These definitions seem clear enough, but they are not easily applied to specific material. Where is the line to be drawn?

Certain of this material poses no problem. It is undoubtedly obscene or pornographic by anyone's definition, and the case is not difficult to handle.

There is, however, a wide area of controversy for certain materials, and there will generally be two major groups in conflict. One group, made up of highly respected church leaders and representatives of a number of other worthwhile organizations, will lead those who want to draw the dividing line near one extreme. Another group, equally vocal, will have a more diverse membership. It will include people sincerely interested in protecting the right of free speech and the accompanying right of a free press. There will be authors and artists with a sound interest in working with no limitations placed on their creativity. And there will be a group interested in the sale of the material in question. This group again will be divided with one part made of highly respectable publishers with a fear of excessive and unwarranted censorship and control of their publishing activity. The other group of publishers will not be so apparent but will use all of the arguments of everyone on their side. This will be the group that publishes the trash, that makes up magazines from press-agents' releases, never names its authors, and frequently changes the name and often the place of publication. Their only investment is in the pair of scissors and bottle of paste needed to make up the copy for the magazine.

The conflicting arguments furnished by these two groups will not make it easier for the police to decide what constitutes a violation of the law. Both groups are highly vocal, and many of their arguments will be more emotional than factual. If the police turn to the psychiatrist for an answer, they will find some division of opinion as to just how harmful pornographic material is, with many competent psychiatrists believing that its effects are often overrated, that it probably serves as a release from sexual tensions for many individuals. Evidence that this sort of material serves as a stimulant to sexual activity seems to be lacking. There do not seem to be cases where a rape is committed as a result of looking at pictures, although it is common police knowledge that many sex offenders have accumulated considerable amounts of this sort of material.

The law and the cases decided by higher courts are not much help either. The law is relatively new. While a few general principles appear, the exact interpretations are fuzzy, and each case seems to apply only to the specific circumstances presented to the court.

The Police Position. It is not easy to establish a sound police position. However, there are certain practices that are generally used by the police — and one that is generally discarded.

The discarded practice is police censorship. While there are police forces that are involved in censorship, their numbers are decreasing. In some cities this duty unfortunately is placed upon them specifically by law. In no case should the police act as censors. It is not a function of the police to advise by interpreting the law or by determining prior to an act that it would constitute a violation of the law when the many circumstances and conditions involved are properly a question for a court. In acting as censors, the police would in effect be answering a hypothetical question as to whether certain material constituted such a violation of the law that a court, reviewing all of the many aspects of the case, would make a finding of guilty.

In some cities, the police have acted as censors on an advisory basis. They have reviewed everything from books to painted neckties and recommended that they pass or do not pass. Then, the persons submitting the material have voluntarily not placed the objectionable material on sale. Again, this is not a police function. It may be a needed function, but up to now no one has worked up a system of censorship satisfactory to everyone, and it is not likely that this will ever be done. One major difficulty has been that it is too easy to go to an extreme — to censor anything that could be found objectionable, or to censor only upon a specific complaint. This is a complex question that cannot be fully discussed here, but one acceptable solution may be similar to the motion picture industry's solution that resulted in the formation of the Hays office many years ago. As a result of this voluntary censorship some states and cities have dropped their motion picture censorship boards.

The basic police function in relation to obscene or pornographic material is to receive complaints, as in the case of other offenses, and to discover the presence of such material as a part of their regular duties. The next step is to assemble evidence if there appears to be a violation of the law, and then, as with all police cases, to submit this evidence to the proper prosecuting authorities and cooperate with them until the case is disposed of.

The Difficult Decision. Hard core pornographic material poses no problem of definition or interpretation because by any standards it is on the face illegal. Usually no serious difficulties are encountered on the merits of the case in prosecutions brought for sale, circulation, and distribution of such material.

The difficulty arises when borderline suspected obscene material is brought into question. Here the prosecutor must look to court decisions as the necessary tools to adequately cope with this growing problem. In recent federal court decisions it has been held that the community itself sets the standard as to what is considered obscene, with the test being whether or not the dominant theme of the material taken as a whole appeals to the prurient interest.[6]

The federal decisions afford a large umbrella in the shade of which local, state, and city courts may function toward setting up a measuring standard to guide the police officer in his move against suspected obscene material.

Methods of Enforcement

At present, there are at least three proven methods by which the police officer, the prosecutor, and the courts may proceed against "dealers in depravity" for the sale, circulation and distribution of obscene and salacious material.

Action Against Material. The first method is, in legal parlance, an action "in rem." In other words, an action against the material itself.[7] This method is a statutory action which provides for the seizure of the obscene material upon court order; for notice and hearing; and, for disposition of the material involved by either ordering its destruction or ordering it returned to the owner. This type of proceeding is had before a court without a jury. Applying the community standard, the court sits as the conscience of the community and rules upon each piece of evidence suspected of being obscene. Once rulings are made the police officer then has the material, found objectionable, to use as a guide for comparison purposes in preparation of similar cases.

Besides the foregoing advantage, the "in rem" action normally allows more expeditious determinations than are obtained in a trial by jury through criminal proceedings against an individual. It should be noted too that once the determination of the obscene character of the suspected material is made by the court, through an "in rem" action, there is no bar to further criminal proceedings against the individuals involved in the sale, circulation, and distribution of the obscene material.

Injunction. A second form of proceeding that has been used with success, particularly in the state of New York, is an injunction against defendants, enjoining them from the sale, circulation, or distribution of obscene material. The injunction proceeding provides for the seizure of the material, for notice and hearing, and disposition of the

[6] U.S. v. Roth, 354 U.S. 476, 77 Supreme Court 1304.
[7] See Vernon's Annotated Missouri Statutes, Volume 38, Sections 542.380 to 542.420. In re Search Warrant of Property at 5 W. 12th St., Kansas City, Missouri v. Marcus, et al, 3344 S.W. 2d 119.

material by the court. The U. S. Supreme Court has upheld the legality of this proceeding.[8] A similar purpose may be served through injunction as by the "in rem" procedure. The injunction is an expeditious method of handling a given case where there are several defendants. Here again, criminal prosecution can be instituted after the court has adjudicated the character of the questioned material.

Prosecution. The third and most common method of handling suspected obscenity is by criminal prosecution against the purveyors for the sale, circulation, and distribution of the material. With the crowded criminal court dockets of today, this method is time-consuming and necessitates, somewhere in the proceeding, an adjudication of what is or is not obscene or salacious material. Prosecution does not necessarily achieve the ultimate purpose of removing such material from public availability, particularly while waiting for a case to be tried. The obscenity and pornography field of vice investigation demands serious attention and is of increasing concern to legislators and law enforcement officials on federal, state, and local levels.

---

[8] *Kingsley Books* v. *Brown*, 354 U.S. 436, 77 Supreme Court 1325.

Chapter 10

TRAFFIC SUPERVISION

The total traffic problem, measured by almost any yardstick, has continued to rise at a precipitous rate. Despite expert opinions of only a few years ago, vehicle registrations have not begun to "level off." The two-car family and the compact car have created tremendous demands. The move to suburbs continues. Many older highways have long since exceeded limits for safe and expeditious travel. New highways are generating increased traffic and demands for travel. The total number of accidents continues to rise, along with the costs of accidents, of insurance, and of services to car owners. Demand for parking space is at the crisis stage in some cities, and congestion has become a "normal" way of life. In almost all cities today, traffic constitutes a major problem if not *the* most important problem facing the community.

Progress and Problems

Police service as a whole has made many important gains in dealing with traffic problems over the past decade. These cannot be ignored. But at the same time it cannot be denied that some ground has been lost. New devices and techniques have not proved to be panaceas. Total police resources for dealing with the police part of the problem have not kept pace with the increase in the problem. It is becoming increasingly difficult to find qualified police applicants, and the costs of police service are rising faster than the overworked tax dollar can effectively meet. Short-cut or "make do" methods have taken the place of sound comprehensive programs because of sheer overloading of demands upon harrassed police departments.

There is a greater need than ever to take a close, critical look at the ingredients of an effective police traffic program and at traffic enforcement policies to avoid compromising obligations or diluting standards of effective police service. Solving the traffic problem will demand not only greater police effort than has ever been put forth, but more carefully aimed and more competently directed police effort.

The Highway Transportation System. The total responsibility for developing and maintaining an efficient highway transportation system has been divided into eight major areas of group — or agency — responsibility:

1. Legislation — Setting up the laws, ordinances, and regulations to define and govern traffic movement, behavior of users, and conditions of road use.

2. Accident Records — Obtaining, processing, and analyzing facts of accidents so that all agencies interested in and responsible for traffic safety and convenience will be better informed.

3. Education — Teaching drivers and pedestrians how to behave in traffic.

315

4. <u>Enforcement</u> — Supervising road users. The police part includes accident investigation, traffic direction, and traffic law enforcement. The court part is the adjudication of charges.

5. <u>Engineering</u> — Includes automotive design and manufacturing, design and construction of highways, and development and installation of traffic controls or "traffic engineering."

6. <u>Motor Vehicle Administration</u> — Controlling and improving drivers through examinations and licenses, controlling vehicles through registration and inspection, and maintaining useful driver records.

7. <u>Organized Public Support</u> — Getting people working together to support safety and the official agencies and their programs.

8. <u>Public Information</u> — Keeping the public (especially road users) aware of traffic problems and dangers, and of progress being made against them, through all available support groups and public information media.

<u>Role of the Police</u>. The police came into the picture early in the development of highway traffic, when it was first necessary to enforce rules of the road. Later, the concept of the "three E's" developed for engineering, education, and enforcement. Much of the direct work of traffic engineering and safety education was taken on by the police, since there were no officially constituted agencies to do the job in most communities. The public generally does not understand the limitations of police authority and responsibility, much less the complexity of highway traffic management. It is no wonder that to the average motorist the traffic policeman symbolizes the practical aspects of the traffic problem.

The police department is only one of many official and nonofficial groups responsible for highway traffic management. However, the police must not be held responsible alone for its failures or its successes. Unless all concerned fully understand their parts in the traffic program, the police can easily be saddled with responsibilities or activities which belong elsewhere or forced to compensate for the failures or shortcomings of some other agency. This results in lack of over-all integration of a community traffic program, undue emphasis on the policing role, and a severe strain on police facilities.

It is both natural and proper that the police exert leadership in solving traffic problems; but they must take steps to clarify their position in relation to the work of other traffic safety agencies and seek to do the best possible job in their own areas of responsibility.

The Nature of Police Traffic Supervision

A well-rounded police traffic program cannot be described by the word "enforcement" alone, as enforcement is only one of the jobs to be done by the police. Traffic supervision is defined as: "Keeping order on streets and highways within existing regulations, to make their use safe and expeditious." Highway traffic supervision is essentially the traffic work of the police agencies. It has three main direct functions which require police powers: (1) police traffic accident investigation, (2) police traffic direction, and (3) police traffic law enforcement. These, then, are the three primary traffic functions of the police.

Traffic Accident Investigation[1]

Webster defines investigation as "the act of investigating; thorough inquiry; research. . . ." Police traffic investigation is defined as "determining what happened and who and what was involved in a traffic accident, usually at the scene of the accident." (In its broader meaning this includes some activities in connection with the emergency.)

Officers employed in traffic accident investigation must take any necessary steps to prevent accidents from becoming more serious. This may involve placing lights to warn approaching vehicles; giving first aid, summoning medical help, and providing for transportation of injured persons; putting out fires and taking precautions against their starting or spreading; preventing pilferage or loss of goods from vehicles or persons involved in the accident; directing traffic and controlling bystanders; and seeing that the roadway is left in good condition. The investigator himself may not do all of these things, but he frequently must see that they are done.

Responsibility of the Officer. The officer investigating an accident must find out what happened. This is usually done through interviewing participants and witnesses, either at the scene or at some other place where they may later be available; noting (and preserving) physical evidence, such as the position of and damage to vehicles, injuries to pedestrians and occupants, marks or materials on the roadway, and marks on or damage to fixed objects; and examining or testing drivers, pedestrians, and vehicles. The latter may include testing drivers and pedestrians for intoxication and testing vehicles for mechanical condition.

The officer investigating an accident must form an opinion as to why the accident happened, evaluating the effect of remote as well as immediate circumstances, and he must make records of the facts and conclusions developed from his inquiry and examination. The latter usually includes summarizing the facts of the accident on a standard form; making sketches and diagrams, and taking photographs to show the position and condition of places and things involved; noting tests and measurements; and reporting any special circumstances or opinions for official records.

Police officers, in connection with accidents, often must do something about the two other primary traffic functions of the police, namely: direct traffic and control bystanders the same as in connection with any other emergency, and enforce traffic laws by making traffic arrests in connection with the accident where evidence warrants it.

Prevention. To be considered as police traffic accident investigation, the activity must include the formation for accident-prevention purposes of an independent, official, recorded opinion of the circumstances and manner of occurrence of a traffic accident. Thus an accident investigation must seek out readily available and pertinent information from participants, witnesses, and physical evidence. Accidents rarely can be considered as having been investigated unless the vehicles are inspected, the location studied, and the drivers examined. The investigation must reconcile conflicting information and substantiate or discredit all doubtful information to reach a well-supported idea of events and circumstances, and it must summarize systematically, in writing, conclusions as to how the accident happened.

Elements of Good Investigation. The handling of an accident or its reporting by

---

[1] See *Traffic Accident Investigator's Manual for Police* (Evanston, Illinois: The Traffic Institute of Northwestern University, 1957).

"investigators" does not necessarily constitute an investigation. This is particularly true if it involves merely receiving reports (even required reports) from one or more drivers; taking information from drivers and recording it on official forms; securing additional information on names, addresses, or connections of drivers, owners, injured persons, or witnesses; or visiting the scene only to give first aid, direct traffic, clear the roadway, and obtain general information. Police administrators under the delusion that the mere handling or reporting of accidents is, in fact, accident investigation are likely to commit serious errors in the management of this activity.

Good accident investigation will serve three general purposes. The first is to get facts to form the basis of all accident prevention programs, not only of police programs but also those of the many other agencies working for the prevention of accidents — the engineers, educators, motor vehicle administrators, public information people, and legislators. Its second general purpose is to determine whether violations of law occurred in the accident and to gather the evidence to support prosecution of the violators. Its third general purpose is to get the facts so that those involved in accidents can properly exercise their rights under civil law.

Good accident investigation will require enough personnel, however organized, to do the activity properly and attention by management to its needs in equipment, supervision, and training. Such training must include the purposes of the activity as well as its procedures and techniques. Management must review and evaluate investigation activity at least as carefully as it will review and evaluate other critical police operations. But most of all, management must use the data derived from accident investigation and assure the receipt of such data by other agencies needing it. Otherwise this important stimulus to good accident investigation will be lost, and the data-gathering function will degenerate into futile activity.

Traffic Direction

Police traffic direction is defined as: "Telling drivers and pedestrians how and where they may or may not move or stand at a particular place, especially during periods of congestion or in emergencies. In its broader meaning, this includes all police activities in taking charge of street or highway traffic." Officers employed in traffic direction will ordinarily do three main things:

1. They will answer inquiries, especially concerning local regulations and how to reach places or routes. Because of their availability to the public, traffic officers are called on for this service far more frequently than are other uniformed officers.

2. They will expedite traffic flow by telling drivers and pedestrians what to do and what not to do, especially when and how to move at an intersection of streets whenever or wherever hazards or congestion make using the streets dangerous or difficult, and assume responsibility for all manual direction of vehicular traffic.

3. They will at times make emergency rules for the flow of traffic, when usual rules are inadequate or special regulations have not been set up to meet unusual or unexpected traffic conditions.

Responsibility of Administrator. The traffic direction function is one that is all too frequently overlooked by the police administrator. He can see the need for special planning and attention to unusual or special traffic movements, such as those involved in parades, athletic events, or disasters, but he frequently fails to see the need for this degree of attention to the everyday expedition of traffic flow, as, for example, the demands of daily peak-hour traffic. This shows up in poor selection of men for this work, in inadequate training, in lack of instruction in the over-all traffic flow needs of the area, in failure to establish sufficient guides for these officers in making decisions to cover emergency situations, in inadequate supervision or provisions for relief, and in failure to utilize direction officers to their fullest capacities in meeting the broad demands of traffic and police service of the community.

Where traffic is heavy enough to create some measure of congestion throughout the day, it is usually best to assign intersection officers on a more or less permanent basis. Directing traffic requires special techniques and standardized signals and gestures must be learned. The art of maintaining smooth flow through an intersection and preventing the formation of traffic jams is one which is mastered only through training and experience.[2]

Even where traffic lights are installed, it may be necessary to provide officer supervision of the intersection to supplement their operation, to maintain obedience to the signal, to prevent jaywalking, and to take over when the load exceeds the ability of the mechanical signal to handle the situation. While a specialized function, traffic direction may conveniently be combined with that of parking supervision. The latter will supplement traffic flow needs during the peak periods, and the intersection officers can devote their attention to vehicle parking during the off-peak periods when special intersection control may not be needed.

Traffic Law Enforcement[3]

In its broad meaning police traffic law enforcement includes all activities in connection with patrolling streets and highways for traffic supervisory purposes.

Police officers on patrol look for pertinent defects in the behavior of people, especially of drivers and pedestrians, defects in vehicles and their equipment, and defects in roadway conditions. Enforcement work then does not begin with a condition or behavior requiring police attention but with looking for such conditions or behavior. What to look for and how to look for it becomes as important for enforcement work as the specifications in laws and ordinances.

Police officers usually start appropriate action at once to prevent such defects from endangering or inconveniencing users of the streets and highways, to remedy such defects, and to discourage their repetition. Appropriate action under various circumstances can mean anything from an oral admonition to physical arrest and incarceration.

Enforcement action is not produced by patrol activity alone. An important and necessary part of enforcement results from the investigation of accidents. If enforcement of any type is justified as a deterrent, on the basis that it can and does prevent accidents, then the taking of enforcement action after an accident has occurred is the most reasonable and fair type of enforcement. Such action makes direct application of enforcement to a specific act or condition which was a cause of an actual accident. Still other enforcement actions result from the follow-up of complaints requesting police attention.

Traffic law enforcement has as its primary objective the creation of a deterrent to

---

[2] See pamphlet series on *Directing Traffic* by the Traffic Institute, Northwestern University, Evanston, Illinois.
[3] See "Traffic Law Enforcement Series" of unit publications (to be compiled into an enforcement manual) by the **Traffic** Institute, Northwestern University, Evanston, Illinois.

violators and potential violators of traffic laws and regulations. One of the important kinds of deterrent thus supplied is the fear of fines, imprisonment, or loss of driving privilege. Another deterrent force is the loss of prestige, or embarrassment, due to social factors. Still another is in the positive area of good citizenship or good parenthood — doing what is right and setting an example. The possibility of involvement in an accident is yet another kind of deterrent. Traffic law enforcement should contribute to all of these deterrent forces and seek to build the positive deterrents as well as to restrain those who may need restraint.

Of all the controlling forces and factors supplied by the many agencies in their various areas of responsibility in the big picture of highway traffic management, the function of enforcement is unique. It is the one force that seeks to change human behavior directly, individually, and constantly. Enforcement is far more than an application of a given traffic law or regulation to a given situation. It requires understanding of the purposes of traffic laws, of the intent of such laws, and of the interpretations which can and may be placed on them by the courts, the police, and the public. To change human behavior requires an understanding of some of the complexities of that behavior, what it is that makes people behave as they do, and how enforcement can operate to influence the change.

If enforcement is to produce the desired deterrent effect, the public must hold the belief that traffic laws are sound, just, and reasonable; the belief that the police are everywhere and constantly on the job, observing the behavior of all drivers; the belief in the certainty of police action — that if a violation is observed by or known to the police, enforcement action will be taken; and the belief that court action will be prompt and result in adequate penalties for the guilty.

The establishment of an enforcement program, methods of attaining high quality and proper quantity of enforcement, and how enforcement activity can be evaluated will be treated in a separate section.

Staff Functions To Aid Traffic Supervision

The three principal ways in which the police directly attack their objective of reducing accidents and congestion have been examined. In order to perform these activities properly, the police must do many other things in addition to the general and special staff services needed to operate the department as a whole.

Traffic Records. First, they must give special attention to traffic records. The kinds of facts needed for the traffic program are quite different from those needed for general police operations. The practice in many departments of burying traffic data in the general mass of departmental records should be reviewed and revised to make possible the best use of this information. The various clerical processes, such as indexing, tabulating, and filing, are much the same for traffic reports as for reports of other police activity, but the special purposes and uses of traffic data demand that they be given special attention by trained people. Otherwise such data will end up as mere compilations of facts and activities.

This should not be taken to mean that the traffic division should set up its own record system, but rather that the handling of traffic records by the records division should follow approved practices so that the data accumulated can be applied. The duties of the records division are largely mechanical. They will include the proper filing of the material and the clerical work needed to reduce data to tabular form, but the determination of the data needed, interpretation of the data, and the application to the traffic problem will be a function of the traffic division. Copies of some traffic records will need to be retained in the traffic division. For example, copies of the accident investigation forms will be needed for analysis of individual intersections, and copies of hit-and-run reports will be needed while the investigation is in progress.

In order to get sufficient information, or information of the right type, it may often be necessary to develop special reporting procedures or forms so that the accident investigators and enforcement officers will report the special facts needed. Some problems may require special studies of certain locations or situations, such as a compliance checks and collision diagrams ordinarily thought of as being in the realm of engineering.

At all stages in their processing and routing, traffic reports and data must be made to serve useful and productive purposes. For example, in the indexing process, usually done in order to facilitate locating a given report or case, the indexing of traffic reports may be incorporated with the "personal identification" process, to accumulate for each person involved in a traffic case a continuous and complete record of his traffic history in the community. In taking off or tabulating the many classes of information contained in traffic reports, the numerous uses such data can serve in the over-all traffic program must be kept in mind. Data are used by the engineers, educators, courts, driver license administrators, and public information specialists.

Mechanical data processing has been used in many police departments for the past quarter-century or more. Mechanical and electronic data processing has now become standard in large departments, because of the increased volume of incidents (accidents, citations, etc.) and because of demands for increased refinement of facts relating to such incidents. The old manual processing methods would no longer meet demands, particularly in getting essential information to the administration while it is still current and useful. Many smaller departments can now avail themselves of modern data processing systems either through rental or purchase of modest systems or through a cooperative use of systems now used by many cities for other areas of municipal administration. Their principal advantage lies in the increase in the number of compilations and relationships of available facts which may be made in a short time. It must be remembered, however, that data processing is no substitute for analytical competence; in fact, it is a challenge to increasing imagination and competence.

The compilation of traffic data is useful only if it serves to provide answers to problems and guides to programs of action to reduce accidents and congestion. The key activity in making traffic data useful is the analysis of traffic records. The work of the analyst begins largely where the clerical work of compiling and summarizing ends. The analyst must examine and study all the pertinent facts in all their relationships to traffic problems and traffic activities of the police. He must look not only for the nature of problems, but must seek the explanation of why and how the problems came to be. This must be followed by developing possible solutions to the problems in terms of police activity. He has the critical job of evaluation and of suggesting or recommending courses of action to keep the traffic program directed toward its objectives. The analyst, therefore, must be skilled not only in statistical methods and interpretations but also must have a sound and comprehensive knowledge of traffic programs and police traffic operations in the field.

Training. The men who are to have any part in the traffic program must be selected properly and given adequate traffic training. An officer selected for traffic work first must be a good police officer. He will be called upon frequently to do general police duty in all sorts of emergencies. He must have a conviction that traffic duty is in no sense less important or essential to the community than is general policing; he must have stamina to withstand trying duty in all kinds of weather; and he must have patience to maintain control in vexing situations.

The traffic administrator must prepare these men for traffic duty by seeing that they have a specific traffic training program. It is not enough that patrolmen be trained in techniques of accident investigation, traffic direction, and enforcement in a general departmental training program, although the rudiments of these must be included for all recruits. Even at the recruit level men must be trained in the purposes of these activities — their general as well as specific objectives — and how such activities can be made to produce the maximum return for the time and effort expended.

Real traffic training requires enough time devoted to the study of specific traffic subjects to give the officer an adequate basis of understanding, both of requirements and of techniques. At the operational level there should be a minimum of 70 hours for specialized accident investigators, 70 hours for enforcement officers, and 35 hours for intersection officers. An additional 70 hours of supervisory training should be provided for officers who oversee traffic operations. Of far more significance than the number of hours devoted to training are such considerations as: the determination of training objectives for each unit and each course of training, the development of a desirable training "atmosphere," and the maintenance of instructional and performance standards.

There should be planned retraining of traffic personnel, to re-emphasize essentials and provide for the dissemination of new thinking or methods and the elimination of problems or weaknesses which are revealed. All training should be supplemented by day-to-day supervision and guidance by officers thoroughly qualified and properly motivated for traffic work.

Proper attention must be given to all areas of information the officer will need to do his best job in traffic. These are: (1) laws and ordinances dealing with traffic, their practical application and interpretations; (2) principles of why the job is important and why it must be done in an effective way; (3) policies to guide all men alike in given situations not covered by a law or order; (4) procedures to be followed in given situations; (5) techniques of traffic direction, accident investigation, and patrol; (6) general personal upgrading in conduct, ethics, understanding human behavior, tactics, attitudes, court testimony, and similar matters; and (7) expression through various accident and activity reports, testifying in court, and dealing with the public.

Not all of this can be given the recruit. At this stage the new officer is so occupied in acquiring new knowledge that the importance of traffic operations may be missed. Once he begins to settle into his job, his real traffic training must be commenced. It is far more important to make him a good all-round policeman during his first year or so than to shape his service in any one direction.

Because of the growing importance of the traffic function it is increasingly important that specialized and advanced training be given those who are to play important parts in the program. This applies particularly to the analyst and to specialized units and to the supervisory and command personnel who will put the program in operation.

There are many ways to get this training even if a department does not have enough men to be trained, or the necessary facilities, to warrant setting up its own detailed and extended training operations. Neighboring communities are banding together and cooperating their traffic training needs. Many states now open their police training facilities to city officers, and some large cities are doing likewise for their smaller neighbors. The Traffic Institute of Northwestern University and the Field Services Division of the International Association of Chiefs of Police will provide on request specific training to departments or groups of departments at cost. Universities in many parts of the country are offering traffic training, either as part of their regular programs or in cooperation with such agencies as the Traffic Institute and the IACP. Such regional training opportunities are increasing each year.

In recent years specialized traffic training opportunities have been vastly increased, not only through local and regional programs but through formal training courses at various traffic training centers. The Traffic Institute, for example, offers a nine-month program in traffic police administration. Grants-in-aid are made to police agencies to enable them to send qualified officers for this comprehensive program of traffic training. This is supplemented by one to five-week unit courses in records, chemical tests, personnel management, accident investigation, enforcement, traffic flow regulation, and other subjects. In some areas automobile clubs and local traffic safety associations are providing funds to aid police departments to obtain this kind of training.

Technical Aids and Services. In addition, the police must avail themselves of technical aids or services developed by modern science if they are to realize their full potential. This means specifically such important tools as chemical tests for intoxication, not as a substitute for sound investigative techniques and objective reaction and behavior tests, but to supplement such investigation and testing, or to put the "clincher" on many cases which might otherwise be impossible to prove.

Care in selecting the right kind of testing techniques or device is extremely important, but of even greater importance is the proper training of personnel to use the tests or supervise their use and the indoctrination of public and courts in their acceptance. Nothing but failure awaits the department or the administrator buying chemical testing devices in the expectation that the devices themselves will get convictions in drunken driving cases. The improper or inconsidered use of such devices or techniques will not only backfire against the individual or department so using them but it may even cause public reaction against chemical testing in general. Such instances have happened in large and otherwise progressive cities and must be guarded against.

Other special scientific aids include tests for the detection of deception. The lie detector can have important application in hit-and-run investigations. The many tests and techniques developed by the physical sciences for the examination and identification of physical materials are of great value.

It is not necessary or recommended that all police departments establish or develop full-scale scientific laboratories or hire expensive technicians to have such services available. Almost every community has qualified technicians serving in education, industry, medicine, or general research who are ready and able to assist the police in their respective fields. There are in most large cities extensive laboratories available to neighboring communities, in addition to central facilities provided by state and federal governments. But it is recommended that the police administrator investigate ways in which scientific or technical aids can improve traffic service and provide the leadership, training, and supervision needed to enable his department to take advantage of the many scientific devices and techniques available.

Supporting or "Cooperative" Traffic Activities

In order to be fully effective, traffic supervision needs the support of certain other activities. Some of these, which are ordinarily the duties of agencies other than the police, may have to be assumed as part of the police function if the other "responsible" agencies fail to perform them.

1. Certain Kinds of Traffic Engineering. The reference here is not to the broad

problems of research, technical design or construction, or physical maintenance of highways and control facilities, which are in the province of traffic engineering, but rather to those activities of an engineering character which the police may be qualified to perform. Examples are such services as determining parking requirements and restrictions, planning special traffic movements in connection with emergency or temporary conditions, and the placement and maintenance of traffic signs and other control devices.

All traffic engineering services should be provided by the engineering agency. If the community cannot afford a full-time qualified traffic engineer, then some junior member of the city engineer's staff should be trained and assigned to provide them, or a part-time or cooperative arrangement can be worked out between neighboring cities or among a group of cities. But enforcement and traffic flow cannot function without some minimum engineering controls, and if no one else is going to provide them, the police must. In general, police participation in the engineering function should be limited to furnishing the basic data on accidents and enforcement to assist the engineer in his work, and perhaps the assignment of someone to maintain a continuing working liaison with the engineer's office. If city administrators cannot recognize the need for separation of the police and engineering functions, then police management must take the initiative in working toward that end.

2. Educational Activities. Certainly there is an important kind and amount of safety education in all traffic supervisory activities performed by the police. But this is an expensive as well as a haphazard form of education and cannot take the place of a sound, planned traffic educational program in a community.

It is not the responsibility of the police to provide elementary training to the public in safe walking habits; nor are the police responsible for providing predriver training in any of its parts to would-be drivers. The jobs of providing the community with general information on safe driving and safe walking practices, and of retraining drivers with known defects, are again not part of the official duties of the police. All these are the responsibility of other agencies and the community as a whole, in line with the responsibility to develop good citizenship, ethics, morals, and practical preparation for living. But, as in the case of minimum engineering controls, someone must provide a minimum of general education and information if the police job of traffic supervision is not to be overwhelmed before it can be started.

The police will be expected to cooperate in safety education, lending their name, facilities, and personnel to assist in developing the program and bringing it to the community. Such cooperation cannot be allowed to develop into anything approaching full responsibility, both because the police basically are not qualified as educators, and because the police have other urgent duties requiring their attention.

Much of the reluctance of police officials to surrender control or influence in the areas of safety education and traffic engineering undoubtedly stems from a faulty concept of the "Three E's." At a time when there was little traffic engineering, as it is known today, and when safety education was beginning to be recognized as essential to a traffic program, the police took a major part in promoting this philosophy of traffic control. Instead of recognizing the concept for what it was, the division of responsibility, many police and traffic administrators sought to adopt the three E's as the basis of the police traffic program. When the educational factor of police traffic work is allowed to be the dominating objective, the true function of enforcement loses its meaning, and enforcement programs lose their vigor and effectiveness.

3. Activities Relating to Prosecution of Violators. It would serve little purpose to

detect and apprehend traffic law violators if the prosecution of such violators were neglected. Prosecution is more than calling cases in court and naming charges which have been filed. It involves careful examination of the facts for and against the accused, examination and interpretation of the evidence to support those facts, and placing proper charges and marshalling witnesses before the case is heard in court.

The police part of traffic law enforcement carries over into assisting the prosecution of offenders by securing statements from witnesses, filing complaints, summarizing information available for prosecution, serving warrants for those who fail to appear, and testifying in court and other hearings.

Clearly the prosecution of cases is a job belonging to a designated and qualified prosecuting officer, with the police serving only to support and assist him. Frequently the prosecutor will have special assistants or investigators who will assist him, but this in no way relieves the police of responsibility to carry an investigation through to its completion, to place appropriate and supportable charges, and to have all information and evidence ready for use.

Steps in Developing a Basic Program

The essential traffic duties of the police do not necessarily constitute a program. In order to convert activities into a program it is necessary to know the what, when, and where of the problem, and to set some kind of reasonable and attainable goals. Activities need to be properly integrated, controlled, and coordinated to steer them in the desired direction with the desired speed and force.

Elements of a Program

A program is good or bad, effective or ineffective, principally in relation to how well it meets its objectives. Activity for activity's sake, as "window dressing" or public relations, or activity which is unplanned and unguided, can be effective only by accident. Police service has too large and important a job to do to afford the luxury of mistakes or of catch-as-catch-can operations. As a constant standard of evaluation, the ultimate sum total of service rendered, through results achieved, must be the yardstick.

Get the Facts. The responsibility for developing a program lies, of course, at the top level of police traffic management. The man at the top must first know what is occurring to create the problem. Facts about traffic accidents are obtained from the investigation of accidents. To prevent accidents the police must be able to predict when, where, and how they are likely to occur. Predictions based on a sampling or small amount of data can be misleading. The first requirement, then, is complete and accurate reporting.

Study the Facts. Thorough investigation of accidents, with good reporting, will produce a mass of factual data. To be useful, the data must be processed and put into significant form — tables, graphs, summaries, percentages, and rates. Study of such data will reveal not only the details of the problem but also something about what has created the problem — what circumstances, what conditions, and what behavior are producing accidents.

Base Program on Analyzed Data. Sound planning of police traffic activity depends on the highest possible degree of accuracy in forecasting or anticipating what the problem will be and what effect the activity will have on the problem. From the study of data, it is possible to at least estimate the situation at some given time in the future. If local data cannot supply the answer, officials can borrow from the experience of other comparable cities. Much of these data have been consolidated by such agencies as the National Safety Council and the International Association of Chiefs of Police and form reasonably sound bases for planning.

Planning the program must include planning for objectives. For example, since the traffic problem cannot be solved overnight, what does the city ultimately hope to produce through traffic activities? By how much should a city reduce accidents in a given time? By how much will enforcement pressure need to be raised to do this?

Planning the program poses many other management problems. For example: What policies are sound? What organizational pattern shall be adopted? What are the advantages and disadvantages of specializing the traffic function, or of specializing any or all of the activities which comprise the traffic function? How many men are needed in order to provide the traffic services the city plans to provide? How should they be distributed among the various activities, if they are specialized? How many additional men, if any, will be needed if the city does not specialize but adds a traffic program to the general patrol force? How shall men be distributed areawise and timewise to meet the anticipated problem of when and where accidents are expected or occur? What violations should be given priority attention? And what needs to be done to inform and prepare the public for the program which is planned?

Apply Corrective Measures. This is the "attack" phase of the program. In police traffic supervision this attack is essentially through enforcement, so that the selective enforcement program forms the spearhead of the attack — the strategy by which police seek to make enforcement work most effective. Because of the importance of the principle of selectivity in enforcement, and the need to achieve the right quality and quantity of enforcement, the enforcement program and its evaluation will be treated in a separate section.

Control and Coordinate the Program. The complexity of the problem, involving numerous police activities and many nonpolice agencies, demands that efforts be coordinated. Within the police department this means giving sufficient management attention to keeping the important activities in balance and not allowing each activity to run itself according to the individual thinking of the officers engaged in that activity. Coordination with outside agencies should be based on the pattern set out by the President's Highway Safety Conference[4] reports and recommendations and through the coordinating agencies established in the community.

Evaluate Results. At all levels of management — supervisory, intermediate command, and top management — evaluation must be a constant factor, feeding back into the planning or execution of the program an assurance that things are going right or indicating what needs to be corrected. If no real evaluation is done except on an annual or other long-term basis, many things might have been going wrong for a long time before being discovered.

Ingredients of the Enforcement Program

Traffic law enforcement by the police means all police acts or operations which relate to observing, detecting, and preventing traffic law violations and taking appropriate action. It does not stem from arrests or citations alone. It is also provided by keeping drivers and pedestrians from committing minor and often unthinking violations, such as prohibited turns or jaywalking. It is not possible in this brief discussion to go into the

---

[4] Available from Superintendent of Documents, U. S. Government Printing Office, Washington 25, D. C.

details of how, when, and where each different kind of enforcing action is most effective and appropriate. Emphasis is placed here on how the enforcement efforts of the police can be made most productive.

Enforcement Policies. Enforcement objectives must be implemented through sound and adequate enforcement policies. In the many controversial areas of decision-making, and to guide police officers in putting into effect the kind of enforcement program envisioned by the administration, clear statements of policy will help to resolve doubts in determining administrative intent. Critical areas in enforcement which need policy guidance include:

1. Tolerances. Enforcement tolerance may be defined as that margin or degree of deviation which is needed to assure that a violation has in fact occurred, allowing for reasonable human and mechanical errors in the measurements which must be made. Such deviation does not weaken enforcement but strengthens it by eliminating reasonable doubts or "borderline" cases.

In speed enforcement, for example, it may be possible to measure speeds within close limits, but from a practical standpoint precise measurement is difficult and courts are hesitant to convict on a pure technicality. Usually, a leeway of five miles per hour is reasonable to assure that the legal limit (in the case of absolute limits) has been exceeded; allowing much more than this amount would actually be an extension to or a deviation from the law, which is not within the authority of the police.

In stop-sign enforcement, while the laws in most jurisdictions require a "full stop" at certain designated places, the exact point of stopping cannot readily be measured, nor is it always readily determinable by the police officer or the driver that the vehicle actually did not stop.

In measuring clearance distances -- required distance for displaying turn signal, in overtaking and passing, in keeping within a driving lane, or in parking regulations — it is not always clear as to precisely what reference points are used in measurement, or how an officer is to measure the distance. For instance, how can he measure accurately the distance in which a turn-signal is displayed before turning?

In time-limit parking, the offense technically occurs after the termination of the time limit specified — theoretically on the first tick of the watch. But practical considerations demand that some leeway be established; metering clocks are not chronometers, and the precise recording of times is difficult. It is general practice to make checks at such frequencies as will (1) reasonably ensure desired turnover in parking space, and (2) leave no doubt as to a violation when it does occur.

Recognizing such problems, the administrator must examine traffic regulations and decide what guides can be provided to men in the field to assure reasonableness and uniformity in their application. Tolerances should never be made public, or be so "reasonable" as to defeat the intent of the law. Where excessive tolerances appear to be warranted, in view of the undue restrictiveness of a regulation, the regulation itself should be reviewed. The police agency must exert positive leadership in working for needed revisions.

2. Warnings vs. Citations. The issuance of warnings for traffic violations is an unresolved issue among police administrators. Agreement appears to be clear, however, on at least these two major points: (1) Warnings serve a definite purpose during a "break-in" period, when new regulations take effect or when enforcement is being accelerated, for both educational and deterrent purposes. (2) Warnings lose their effect if issued promiscuously where citations are indicated, or if enforcement officers are given complete

freedom to "excuse" violations on the basis of the driver's good intentions or frivolous excuse, or the officer's desire to be a "right guy." The police administrator should establish clear-cut policies and detailed guides as to the circumstances under which warnings (oral or written) may be issued, and those when stronger enforcement action is required.

3. The "Unintentional" Violator. Police administrators must be aware of the need to deal as strongly with "unintentional" violators of law as with intentional violators. The intentional violator usually takes a calculated risk regarding his unlawful action, so he is observant as to the hazards and circumstances present (including the presence of a police unit). The unintentional violator, on the other hand, is unaware of the hazards he is creating or risking by his unlawful behavior, and he is therefore not alerted to taking quick and appropriate evasive action in a critical situation. He needs strong discipline to develop practices and habits of alertness to driving conditions and his driving obligations. The practice of in any way excusing unintentional violations tends to weaken or undermine the effectiveness of enforcement as an accident-prevention tool.

4. Multiple vs. Single Charges. Writing citations for each and every offense possible, sometimes called "throwing the book" at an offender, is ordinarily discouraged. It is usually best to single out the most serious and most readily provable offense committed, and develop a case around this offense. A record of the other offenses should be noted on the record copies of the citation or in the officer's notebook.

If the offenses are serious and all part of a continuing action — such as fleeing from a patrol car, or a combination of speeding, disregarding signals, and violating right-of-way — it is often advisable to employ the charge of reckless driving. This charge should never be used as a catch-all, however, for every time a series of violations occurs. Separate charges are advised for all serious offenses where mandatory penalties may be provided, or where separate serious violations have occurred not in direct sequence or in relation to each other.

5. Enforcement Needs vs. Public Necessity. Policy must be established as to what conditions or circumstances should require the stopping and citing (or arresting) of drivers of public safety and convenience vehicles — emergency cars, public conveyances, public utility vehicles, etc. The laws are clear regarding their application to such vehicles, but many abuses are committed in the name of "emergency" or "necessity." Improper parking, improper turning, speeding, and many violations of rules of the road are often condoned or overlooked. Guides must be provided to reduce these abuses to a minimum yet not create undue interference with real emergency missions. All agencies affected should be in agreement as to these policies and practices.

6. Physical Arrests in Traffic Enforcement. Ordinarily physical arrest is not required in traffic enforcement. Administrative guides should indicate the circumstances under which physical arrests are to be made — as, for example, in cases where some other crime is involved or revealed, the driver cannot identify himself or has no license, where there is interference with authority of the police, or in serious offenses where the penalty is revocation of license.

7. Fixed-Position Speed Measuring Devices. It must be clear to every police administrator that such devices as radar, and a host of timing mechanisms, serve one basic purpose only — to measure more precisely the speed of a vehicle or vehicles on the highway. They cannot be considered as self-enforcing devices or as a substitute for a patrol officer; they are only aids for obtaining more precise evidence of speed. The manner in which such evidence is used is an important consideration, therefore a policy must be established. It is detrimental to enforcement to use them to "shoot fish in a barrel," in

order to increase enforcement revenues, or to establish a record for the administration. The equipping of some patrol vehicles with these devices must not serve to lessen the speed enforcement efforts of patrols which are not so equipped, or to give undue emphasis to speed enforcement in the total enforcement program. Properly employed, these devices can help to reduce conflicts based on actual speed of the suspect vehicle and many of the hazards of the "pace and pursue" methods of enforcement.

Selective Enforcement. As defined in the Enforcement Report of the President's Highway Safety Conference: "Selective enforcement is enforcement which is proportional to traffic accidents with respect to time, place, and type of violation." It is not only logical and efficient; it is necessary. Police manpower is so limited that it is impossible to give adequate attention to all times and places. Efforts must be concentrated on certain phases of the problem; the best basis for determining such concentration is accident experience.

No police department has sufficient personnel to enforce all traffic regulations at all times and in all parts of the city at the same time. Even if it were possible, it would not be wise to do so. Not only would the cost be prohibitive, but such complete enforcement is unnecessary and would be repudiated by the public. The basis of selective enforcement is complete and accurate information relating to the times and places of accidents and the violations predominantly involved.

Adequate spot maps of accidents must be provided. Many police administrators like to keep several different spot maps for the same period, and break them down by time of day, kind of accident, and other factors, or to keep such maps for a month or quarter-year, and then begin anew. Most recent research indicates, however, that these refinements are not justified or necessary. Studies indicate that the greater the mass of information compiled, the more nearly accurate the forecasts will be.[5]

Since the forecast of where accidents are likely to happen is rarely better than 80 to 85 per cent accurate, and since police departments cannot match enforcement with accident expectancy even this well, it is unnecessary to attempt to match frequent and changing accident experience bases. This means in brief that a single spot map, kept for as long a period as will show significant accident experience and distribution, is better than several different maps, or maps for short periods of time, which will give inadequate and perhaps completely false pictures of what may be expected in the future.

Supplementing accident spot maps, the administrator must provide for careful and intelligent interpretation of all accident statistics. From these he can determine with some assurance where the high accident locations are, what the peak periods are of the day and the week, with subpeaks and valleys also clearly identifiable. He will know the leading violations associated with accidents and how they compare in frequency. In other words, he will be able to obtain all the necessary and pertinent facts to attack the accident problem through enforcement if: he obtains (1) maximum accident reporting by the public, (2) the best possible investigation of accidents by his officers, and (3) makes intelligent and orderly inspection of the data compiled from the reports.

Thus armed, the administrator marshals his forces. First, what manpower is available for traffic enforcement? Not only the men normally assignable to traffic patrols, but what percentage of the time of all other officers, traffic personnel, and general police officers alike, can and should be devoted to traffic enforcement? The administrator must

[5]Studies made by James Stannard Baker, director of research and development, the Traffic Institute, Northwestern University, based on accident experience in Cincinnati and other cities.

recognize that responsibility for traffic enforcement belongs to the entire department even though certain special and detailed assignments may be made to traffic personnel. This fact must be driven home to the entire department, through all commanding and supervisory officers, and through department policy which is clearly established, carefully expressed, and attentively executed.

A cardinal rule for all administrators, regardless of the size of the force, is to guard against weakening the effective beat strength of the traffic assignments for escorts, errands, chauffeuring of official visitors, and other miscellaneous jobs.

Time Distribution. Assignment of available personnel (including the portion of non-traffic officers' time which is to be devoted to traffic enforcement) is made as nearly as practicable in proportion to the time frequency of accidents. Since it is not feasible to stagger working hours to an infinite degree, the matching of manpower to accident distribution can never be done exactly. By using four-hour blocks of time the accident curve and the assignment curve can be approximated closely enough, however, and for departments of limited personnel this will be necessary if any sort of matching is to be obtained.

The administrator must keep in mind the weekly peaks and valleys as well as the daily shifts in volume. For practical purposes, and in most cities, he can average the distribution for the five days from Monday through Friday, and use one plan of personnel assignment for those days. Saturday and Sunday present entirely individual problems, and the weekday distribution of personnel will be found unsatisfactory for week ends. In taking the personnel inventory, the administrator must take into account the net available working strength rather than the total number of men on the roster, with allowances for days off and for at least eight hours off duty for individual officers between any two consecutive shifts. Split shifts should be avoided.

Little attention needs to be paid to seasonal changes in volume, as the percentage distribution of accidents throughout the week tends to follow the same general curve even though over-all volumes may show considerable change in some cities, as influenced by winter hazards, tourist traffic, school traffic, and other conditions or factors. Personnel assignments should be on a percentage basis rather than a strict numerical basis. The numbers of men available during peak seasons can be in part controlled through the assignment of vacation periods of the force.

Area Distribution. Area distribution of traffic enforcement units during any given period is based on the area distribution of the accident problem during that time. There will be many practical limitations on how areas may be divided effectively. If the units to be assigned are full-time specialized traffic units, then the principal factor is the number of accidents in the area, but if the units working are not specialized then the traffic work load must be combined with the service requirements of general policing.

The total number of beat areas should be at least equal to the number of traffic enforcement units available for assignment at the maximum period, with two or more beats assigned to a unit when fewer units are available. Often it is desirable to assign units to line patrol rather than to area patrol, if the problem on a given street or route is important enough. Another device is to overlap patrol areas at points of heaviest load or along main arterials so that added attention is given to this need. In these cases it is most important to have the units clearly understand their joint responsibility.

Predominant Violations. After making a tentative distribution and assignment of men as to time and area, the next step is to give them instructions on the kind of work they will do. Accident data will provide a long list of violations involved in accidents during a given period. From this list it is possible to determine the frequency with which specific violations occur, expressed in terms of per cent of all violations noted. At the top of this list normally are some four to 10 violations that constitute the major percentage of the total; perhaps a few others occur with sufficient frequency to be important. These violations are called the predominant violations in accidents. The principle of selectivity says that enforcement must be directed against the predominant violations somewhat in proportion to their frequency of occurrence.

In applying this principle enforcement officers issue traffic citations in approximate proportion to these predominant violations. It is hardly necessary or advisable to try to match enforcement on a daily, weekly, or even monthly basis, to these predominant violations. It is important only that over-all enforcement, on a long-term basis, approximately match these violations. One important objective of selective enforcement is to assure that enforcement against certain violations needing attention will not be overlooked entirely. For example, pedestrian violations cause most pedestrian accidents, yet in many departments little if any enforcement is made against pedestrians.

The enforcement bulletin is one practical device to carry selectivity objectives to the men in the field. On this bulletin, issued at least monthly are noted the pertinent facts about accidents — when, where, how many, how severe, and so on — with a listing of the predominant violations involved. The bulletin serves only as a guide, and to make it work all supervisory and command personnel must constantly evaluate the activity of officers, individually and collectively, and shape their enforcement efforts accordingly. Selectivity does not mean that lesser or "nonpredominant" violations go unchecked. The "all other" category is often large, and officers must be impressed with the need for taking appropriate enforcement action for all violations coming to their attention whenever possible. Talks at roll-call, in meetings, general orders, detailed notices, conferences, and training classes form some of the other ways in which the principles and practices of selectivity must be carried to the men.

Quality of Enforcement

Enforcement work of a department may be fully selective as to time, place, and type of violation, yet not be effective in reducing accidents. In addition to selectivity, then, something else is needed. Selectivity does not indicate the quality of enforcement in terms of the individual worth or effect of a given traffic arrest or contact; nor does it tell how much or what quantity of enforcement is needed to provide sufficient deterrent effect to highway users.

Quality a Goal. Good quality of enforcement means providing maximum deterrent to violations of law for each enforcement action taken. It means accomplishing the objectives which justify enforcement — namely, preventing accidents and delays — in the most efficient manner possible. It means increasing the efficiency of personnel and obtaining maximum return for time and effort expended. Selectivity is one of the means of obtaining quality. But full quality in enforcement depends upon many other factors, and it is influenced by caliber of personnel, the kind and extent of training, good equipment, good procedures, good courtroom facilities and personnel, and many other factors. The total quality of enforcement is not easily measured. Because it cannot be measured, utmost attention must be given to all the details which tend to promote the quality of enforcement.

Many administrators have found that increasing the number of enforcement actions, without regard to quality or selectivity, may actually tend to detract from, rather than add to, the desired objectives. Promiscuous arrests are usually interpreted by the public as "drives" and evidence of an officer "quota" system. The public rightfully resents these efforts. Where sheer quantity is the goal, officers tend to issue more and more citations under circumstances where they are less and less warranted. The pettiness of some arrests aggravates the situation. The bad effect of wholesale arrests is that they do not bring about the compliance intended; the processing of traffic violations may become jammed under the overload; the courts and prosecution can give less time to serious cases; the quality of justice may slip; and the number of convictions goes down. Thus not only does the public resent the police, but it becomes contemptuous of the courts as well.

On the other hand, high-quality enforcement, even in relatively small amounts, has an important deterrent effect upon would-be violators. Through high-quality enforcement contacts the officer singles out for attention the kinds of violations which might result in accidents. Even the average motorist, with his inherent dislike of the "traffic cop," can see the appropriateness of the officer's actions where the violation is clear-cut and significant. He understands why the officer has stopped him (or the other fellow), and his resentment is held to a minimum. As the department's enforcement program is understood by the public, and as its reasonableness and basic fairness are demonstrated, it becomes more acceptable. This is the root and essence of securing public acceptance and compliance. It minimizes opportunities for resentment of the department's program and action.

Good quality in enforcement does more than build public acceptance. It is the essence of efficient operation, since the officer is doing his best work in the most effective way. He thus has more time to devote to over-all supervision and patrol. He is better able to cover a larger area, or make more frequent patrols of a small area. He is in a better position to evaluate over-all conditions and to focus attention on situations needing action most. With his nose constantly buried in a citation book, in an effort to write a maximum number of tickets in a given time, he is quite likely to permit the "big ones" to get away more frequently than if he devoted more time to patrolling, observing, and evaluating the situation.

Use of the enforcement index (as discussed later) in gauging the amount of enforcement needed to keep accidents on the decline, presupposes the attainment of desired quality in enforcement — that the actions taken by the officers are not only appropriate under the circumstances, but that they also are carefully aimed to have the greatest effect in preventing accidents.

Phases of Enforcement Actions. Of all traffic violations occurring, it is possible to take police enforcement action against only a relatively small percentage of the total. Thus it is important that this small percentage be made as effective as possible. Examination of an enforcement action, phase by phase, indicates where quality might be improved.

1. Detection. Improvement in detecting traffic violations can be developed in much the same manner as detection and observation of all matters which come under the jurisdiction of the police. Those factors which have special importance in traffic patrol include: (1) the basic preparedness of the officer for patrol — knowledge of general policing methods, appreciation of the function of patrol, knowledge and interpretation of traffic laws, understanding of departmental traffic policies, knowledge of the department's over-all traffic program and objectives, and understanding of specific purpose and assignment; (2) use of tactics enabling him to make patrol more effective; mixing the form of patrol; varying the timing and route of patrol; using "at rest" patrol tactics at carefully selected times and places; using "open" vs. "inconspicuous" patrol methods; concentrating on locations of high potential in violations or accidents; utilizing all potential sources of

information available on a beat; utilizing the best means of observation; recognizing the
tell-tale signs of potential violations; choice of best patrol speed under varying circumstances; choice of best position in the roadway for patrol effectiveness; and keeping the
safety of the patrol officer and the public always in mind.

Limited access expressways or "freeways" are being built at an increasing rate
within municipal boundaries. The special problems of policing limited access highways
must be recognized and taken into consideration. Not the least important of these problems are the techniques of detection and apprehension of violators. Police administrators
should make a special effort to keep abreast of developments in this area.

2. Apprehension. Once the violation is detected, and the officer has decided to take
action, he must overtake and stop the violator and complete the action decided on. This
often involves: (1) Pursuing the violator: selecting the best spot from which to take off
in pursuit; identification of the violator's vehicle in case he should be temporarily lost in
traffic; getting into the stream of traffic safely yet swiftly; pacing the violator's vehicle
properly and overtaking the violator's vehicle as soon as it can be done safely. (2) Stopping the violator: selecting the place to stop; and approaching the stopped vehicle with
regard to the officer's safety and ability to control the situation. (3) Dealing with the violator: recognizing that human relationships involve many complexities; minimizing the
sources of human irritation which occur between officer and violator; and keeping officer
conduct above criticism. (4) Taking appropriate enforcement action: knowing the basis
for the kind of enforcement action which is appropriate; identifying the violator and vehicle; checking the violator's driver license; and informing the driver of intended action.
(5) Completing the contact: assuring that the violator knows what is expected in future
similar situations; informing him, if asked, where to dispose of present charges; and
assisting him to get back into traffic. These two phases of enforcement actions, detection
and apprehension, are clearly the responsibility of the police.

3. Prosecution. Here is the juncture between the police part and the court part of
enforcement. What the police are expected to do in this area already has been discussed.
How the police can further improve quality through coordination and cooperation with the
prosecutor will be discussed in the last section of this chapter.

4. Adjudication. Officially, the police participate in determining the guilt or innocence of an accused person only through the placing of appropriate charges based on sound
evidence and in proper testimony in court. But there are many things that can be done by
the police outside the courtroom to help improve the quality of decisions. These also will
be discussed later.

5. Penalization. This is the final phase in enforcement action. The police exert
but little official influence, and none of it directly, in determining the nature or severity
of penalties which are appropriate in various cases. The best way to assure that violators
found guilty are appropriately penalized is to bring in sound cases and to present them
properly. Another means is through keeping adequate records and providing the court
with the complete traffic history of the person charged in court, showing how many times
he was involved in a traffic accident, and what action resulted, and in presenting a record
of the accumulation of violations committed by this driver and his accident record over a
period of time. Still another means is to provide the judge periodically with summaries
and interpretations of the accident situation, so that he will be better aware of the specific
needs for and results of traffic law enforcement.

Quantity of Enforcement

In discussing quality of enforcement in the preceding section, it was shown that when a city fails to assure the right quality of traffic enforcement, or fails to control its quantity, there is no assurance that enforcement work is serving its intended purpose. What then about quantity of enforcement? How many traffic arrests and citations will constitute the right amount to meet enforcement requirements and yet not go too far?

A Local Choice. Within certain limits the question of the right amount will have to be determined for each individual city by each individual police department. It is that amount of enforcement that will in fact create a measurable increase in general compliance with traffic laws and bring the number of accidents down. Enforcement of traffic laws by arresting and citing violators will up to a certain point tend to deter drivers and pedestrians from committing violations and thus prevent accidents. There is a point below which the amount of enforcement is too small to have any effect, but it is also possible for the amount of enforcement to reach a point where additional enforcement will not result in additional deterrence. When the volume of traffic arrests and citations goes beyond this point, additional enforcement will not materially reduce the number of accidents.

This point is known as the "saturation point" or as the "point of diminishing returns." It will vary from city to city and sometimes from year to year. It is influenced by the kind of enforcement and by all the factors of quality previously discussed, but it is also influenced by external factors over which the police have no control. For example, in small residential cities having little out-of-town or out-of-state through traffic, a relatively small amount of traffic enforcement has an important effect. In larger cities, and in cities having a high per cent of itinerant traffic, it may take a tremendous volume of arrests to bring accidents down. When a city begins to increase enforcement pressure the volume of traffic arrests may have to be increased to a high level before any effect is noted. Then, as people begin to comply and accidents go down, a lesser volume may be adequate.

Enforcement Index. Examining this more closely, it is found that what is being done is raising or lowering the volume of enforcement in relation to the number of accidents. This relationship is expressed in a practical mathematical form called the "enforcement index." This index is determined by dividing the number of convictions with penalty for hazardous traffic violations during a given period by the number of fatal and personal-injury accidents occurring during the same period. This is expressed mathematically as follows:

$$EI = \frac{\text{Convictions with Penalty for Hazardous Violations}}{\text{Number of Fatal plus Personal-Injury Accidents}}$$

In the "index," convictions with a penalty are used because without the conviction and penalty, there will be little real deterrence. Hazardous violations are used principally because they are the violations most likely to result in accidents and because some uniform and reasonable base is needed. Fatal and personal-injury accidents are used primarily because the completeness of reporting these accidents is much higher and more consistent than is the reporting of property-damage-only accidents.

Practical experience has shown that an enforcement index of about 20 is a minimum effective level for most cities. But the best rate for any given city must be determined individually. Some cities have found that an index of somewhat less than 20 is adequate; other cities have needed to increase the index to 40 or 50 before real results have been obtained. Only by experience and by careful study of the long-range effects of planned enforcement can the traffic administrator determine an index appropriate for his community. He may have to experiment by gradually increasing the index to a figure considerably higher than he expects to finally accept and then gradually decreasing it, observing the effects of this control. This is analogous to the action of a gunner who "brackets" a target with test shots in order to correct for range and windage, before aiming for a direct hit. As accidents decrease, the volume of arrests may be proportionately decreased in order to maintain the desired index.

The enforcement index is a management tool and nothing more. It is not an end or a goal to be sought in itself. It is not a proper means of comparing one city with another. In no case should the index, either in principle or in designated figures, be publicized or made general information.

An administrator should never seek to increase volume without considering other major factors. Police officers must be capable of increasing volume without decreasing quality. The public must be prepared for the increased pressure, and the pressure should be applied gradually, increasing it a little at a time, so that the program does not take on the aspects of a "drive." The prosecutor and the court must be ready, willing, and able to handle the increased load without resisting the program or becoming swamped by it. To do otherwise would be to doom the program to failure before it has a chance to succeed.

Evaluation of Enforcement

Management needs ways to measure the quantity and quality of traffic supervision. Ultimate evaluation, as already indicated, must be made for each city for itself, based on its own problems, its own needs, and its own collective desire to apply the corrective forces needed. The police administrator must know how closely police efforts are being directed toward objectives, how thoroughly and how well the officers are doing their individual and collective jobs, and what effect the program is having in reducing accidents.

Administrative Tools. To obtain the information necessary for accurate measurement and intelligent appraisal of the program's effectiveness, the administrator should establish a series of information reports. Some of the more important of these are:

1. Officers' Daily Activity Report, submitted by each officer to his superior at the close of each tour of duty, showing by breakdown what he did during the working day, and the totals of actions taken.

2. Daily Traffic Summary, showing daily the totals of accidents and enforcement for the past 24 hours and for the month or year to date. Breakdown will be by type and severity of accident, and by kind of enforcement action and type of violation.

3. Personnel Report, to show the effective daily personnel strength of the traffic division, and the reasons for men being off-duty or not working on traffic assignments.

4. Monthly Summary of the individual officer's performance, summarizing his activities by kind and number of cases assigned, by the quantity and nature of traffic citations and warnings issued, and by the conviction rate attained.

5. District (and/or Watch) Summaries, summarizing for all officers of the unit or shift the information contained in individual summaries.

6. Traffic Safety Report of the Department, totalling all accident and enforcement data for each month, for the year to date, and for the preceding (or other) year.

7. Periodic law observance checks, by officers in civilian clothes in different key or problem locations throughout the city to correlate the recorded enforcement information with the actual compliance by drivers.

This information should be supplemented by spot maps, tables, charts, and graphs to record enforcement for hazardous violations in the same manner used in keeping the data for accidents. This gives visual and tabular indication of how well the enforcement is matching the accidents it is supposed to prevent. The closest proportional matching throughout the measurements indicates the greatest selectivity in enforcement.

Many police administrators do not know how to determine an estimate of their needs or how to measure or evaluate the progress being made. This is especially true at the outset of a program, when they may suffer not only from lack of administrative experience but also from a lack of enough information or the right kind of information about the problem.

Rates and Measures. To meet this need, professional police administrators have agreed on a limited number of rates and measures that are sufficiently well established to be of use to cities. While these guides will be helpful in many cases, they cannot be taken as absolute or conclusive measures of satisfactory work. They cannot yet be considered as "standards" because terminology and record keeping have not been standardized to permit fixing reliable recommended values. With more experience and more uniform records, standards may someday be established. In the meantime, the figures offered represent generally the best informed opinions (see Table 5).

Satisfactory performance, or a reasonably healthy condition, is indicated by the rates shown in Table 5. If the actual figures in a community are consistently better than these rates, then any significant improvement probably would be difficult and costly. It is likely that other things could be done to better advantage than trying to raise this value. If the actual figures in a community are substantially less than these rates, then improvement should be fairly easy and profitable. In every case local experience and evaluation is essential. The final proof, of course, lies in whether accidents are actually being reduced by the program.

No numerical values were inserted in Table 5 for "Pedestrian Enforcement Rate" because of general inability to agree on classification of what properly constitutes such enforcement. For example, to what extent should the arrest of pedestrians under the influence of liquor (a large volume of arrests in most cities) count as being in the interests of traffic safety? Need the arrest be made on the highway, or just anywhere to have effect? Listing of the rate is included, however, because of the importance of keeping pedestrian enforcement in the forefront of attention, regardless of ability to measure its effect adequately. It is suggested that each city experimentally determine this rate and seek to find an effective figure for its own situation.

Evaluation of activity must go far beyond the study of rates and measures. In order to make intelligent use of such rates the police administrator must know as much as possible about the factors which influence performance. This goes back to the matter of quality, and because it is impossible to measure all the factors, or give them a weighting in over-all evaluation, it is important to maintain maximum quality in every activity and every phase of operations.

To improve effectiveness, any evaluation must be used by management to more closely direct and guide the activity. This may involve but minor steering or correction at times; at other times it may involve major changes or realignment of activities and objectives. The more frequently evaluation is made of things that are likely to go wrong, the less likely it is that any drastic revisions of the program will be needed.

Table 5

Traffic Enforcement Rates for Cities

Item[1]	Minimum Effective Rates[2]
1. ACCIDENT SEVERITY OR REPORTING RATES	
a. Personal-injury accidents per fatal accident	55
b. Damage accidents per fatal accident	200
2. ACCIDENT INVESTIGATION RATE	
Accidents investigated per 100 accidents reported	95
3. ACCIDENT ARREST RATE	
Investigations resulting in arrests per 100 accidents investigated	55
4. ACCIDENT VIOLATOR ARREST RATE	
Persons in accidents arrested per 100 accidents investigated	60
5. HIT-AND-RUN CLEARANCE RATE	
Hit-and-run cases cleared per 100 cases known	85
6. HIT-AND-RUN ARREST RATE	
Hit-and-run drivers arrested per 100 cases known	80
7. THE ENFORCEMENT INDEX (OR RATE)	
Convictions with penalty paid for hazardous traffic law violations per motor-vehicle traffic accident resulting in injury or death	20
8. CONVICTION RATE FOR ACCIDENT ARRESTS	
Convictions per 100 arrests made in accidents	95
9. TRAFFIC CONVICTION RATE	
Convictions per 100 arrests for hazardous violations	95
10. PEDESTRIAN ENFORCEMENT RATE	
Pedestrians convicted for pedestrian traffic offenses per 100 pedestrian accidents	--[3]

[1]All quantities used in computing these rates must be based on the uniform definitions of terms.

[2]These are general only, and do not necessarily apply in every city. Local experience and evaluation should be developed whenever possible.

[3]There is no consensus on a desirable rate, but each city should attempt to develop its own standards.

Organizing the Traffic Function

Thus far this chapter has discussed the traffic function, traffic activities, and traffic personnel without regard to their specific place in the department. Everything that has been said applies with equal force to all police departments, regardless of size or organizational form, where police officers have traffic duties. The question arises as to where in the department the traffic function belongs, whether there should or should not be a specialized traffic division, or specialization of any of the work of the police which is in the nature of traffic service.

Development of Specialized Traffic Divisions

City police departments gave attention to traffic late in the 19th century with the assignment of bicycle-mounted police to apprehend speeding cyclists. Even prior to this, police had been engaged in traffic supervision, principally at intersections. In the main such duty was delegated, along with other duties, to patrolmen from the uniformed force.

With the advent of the motor car came new problems in street and highway traffic. The police motorcycle replaced the bicycle, and traffic forces were expanded to include foot patrolmen regularly assigned to direct traffic at intersections and effect some control of parking. Horse-mounted police frequently were used for parking control. Early motorcycle squads concentrated principally on enforcement of speed laws.

But accidents and congestion continued to grow, as did public demand for improvement of conditions (always directed at the police). Some administrators saw the need for sounder procedures in investigation, recording, analysis, and assignment of force to permit concentration of specialized enforcement effort.

By the late twenties, and in increasing numbers in the early thirties, in cities where specialized police traffic divisions or bureaus had been established, accidents were investigated by trained, selected police, traveling in specially equipped vehicles. Enforcement, reporting, and analysis were also being developed into effective specialized functions. Some traffic divisions consisted only of administrative staffs responsible for traffic planning, and in their staff capacity they supplied traffic data to the uniformed force; but most of the newly created specialized bureaus were centralized line operations.

Favorable Results from Specialization. Cities administering traffic enforcement through a specialized police traffic division have generally enjoyed favorable experiences in terms of safety. This has been brought about without any demonstrable loss in the control of vice and crime. In fact, the officers specially assigned to traffic frequently were, and still are, outstanding in nontraffic criminal apprehension. On the other hand, many cities without specialized traffic divisions have also obtained good results due to outstanding police administrators and well-trained forces.

The rise to a rate of 15.9 deaths per one hundred million vehicle miles of travel in 1935, and the killing of almost 40,000 people in traffic accidents in the United States in 1941, emphasized the need for positive, concentrated action. Through the forties and fifties the specialized traffic division increasingly was adopted as a weapon against this rising problem. Most cities with specialized traffic divisions have continued to reduce their rates and gross losses and have contributed importantly to the reduction of the national traffic death rate to 5.6 deaths per one hundred million vehicle miles in 1959, the lowest rate in history.

Specialization Needed. Few American cities today, other than the very smallest, can successfully deal with traffic supervision without the establishment of a specialized traffic division, including accident investigation, the recording and analysis of data (in coordination with a central records system), traffic enforcement patrols, motorized parking and movement supervision, and intersection control. Some of the arguments for specialization are:

1. A traffic division assures attention to the problem in proportion to its importance.

2. The chief of police can place definite responsibility for the satisfactory performance of traffic functions.

3. A traffic division stimulates police interest and activity in the traffic field, developing an esprit de corps within a selected group of officers that produces pride of "workmanship."

4. Specialization promotes skill and ability in dealing with technical and complex operations. Traffic is a specialized problem requiring special aptitudes and training. When a department has officers devoting full time to traffic duties, specialized effort tends to increase effectiveness and chances of success.

Degrees of Specialization. There is no formula to determine how large a police department should be before it specializes in traffic activities, or what degree of specialization is appropriate. Cities of 50,000 population and up generally can improve effectiveness by line specialization, but many cities of 25,000 or smaller have full-fledged traffic divisions working successfully. On the other hand, many cities do not have a line traffic division and are also doing outstanding work.

There are many levels and degrees of specialization. In a strict sense, specialization within a police force actually commences when a one-man police department adds a second officer. This is the beginning of some division of duties and responsibilities, mainly between management and operations. Keeping this point in mind, one can examine the transition in specialization of traffic activities that might take place.

Specialized attention to traffic work usually begins with establishment of a special staff unit or agency, often just the part-time attention of a single employee to the functions of analysis, planning, and coordination of police traffic activities. All line traffic activities are performed by the general uniformed force, and traffic records keeping is consolidated with central records.

In the second degree of specialization the same type of special staff agency exists, but in the field are traffic units that divide their attention between accident investigation and traffic patrol, and which perform some of the other traffic field services on demand. A major part of general traffic services in the field is still performed by the general patrol force, with the specialized units spearheading the work. Traffic records are still consolidated with central records in most organizations of this type.

The third degree of specialization includes generally the extension of specialization to other field services as, for example, the establishment of a unit or units to control congestion in the central business area and for parking enforcement and intersection control. There may also be a separation of accident investigation units from enforcement units. The analytical and planning agency has attained full-time status, with perhaps the addition of a clerk to process accident and enforcement reports and to set up the consolidation of traffic facts. In this stage there is need not only for supervision over traffic line activities but also for intermediate command levels having management over the traffic function. Here is the first real division status of traffic, with line command having rank and status equal to that of the commanders of other divisions.

The fourth stage brings not only the inclusion of all traffic functions within the traffic division but also varying degrees of specialization within the division itself. The degree or extent of specialization here usually depends upon the size of the over-all operation and the amount of work demanding specialized attention. Many departments commit the error of overspecialization at this stage, with the unhappy result that coordination is lost, manpower is wasted, and the focus of attention is on activity rather than program.

Inherent Dangers in Specializing. Some reasons why police administrators must be wary in specializing the traffic function are:

1. Specialization of the traffic function may lead to exclusion. The traffic officer may consider that his work begins and ends with traffic and does not include general and equally important police duties. Carried further, accident investigators may believe they are above and apart from other traffic officers, and intersection officers may tend to ignore significant violations under their very noses, because they are assigned to direct traffic.

2. Specialization may be carried too far, once it has been started. Success with limited specialization may tempt the unwary administrator to specialize to an unwarranted degree, thus aggravating manpower wastage and other abuses.

3. Specialization may create undesirable cliques or factions within the department. Petty interdivisional jealousies may be generated over working conditions, recognition, and other factors. Misunderstanding may develop into misguided loyalties that can pull the department apart and destroy its effectiveness.

4. Specialization may overemphasize certain tasks at the expense of others; by calling attention to the importance of a specific job it may imply that other jobs are less important and therefore need not be done.

5. Specialization imposes additional or more complex problems of supervision and coordination, especially where the specialized units are numerous and small.

Close examination of these arguments shows that they often constitute a case against weak leadership and poor management, which may not be so clearly identified in a nonspecialized force. Because specialization allows for closer scrutiny and more critical evaluation of work through clear definition of activity and responsibility, defects in management can more readily be detected.

Establishment of a specialized traffic division (or of a detective division, for that matter) must not result in the development of separate operational forces within the department. This can be avoided through clearly enunciated policy and directives, implemented by supervision and training. There is too often a tendency toward separation of functions — even a disinclination to cooperate. This can and must be overcome.

The tendency toward separation has been abetted in some departments having specialized traffic divisions by the creation of traffic ranks, sometimes under civil service. This deprives the administrator of flexibility of assignment and gives impetus to the tendency toward separation of the responsibility and function and thus increases the problems of coordination. The civil service "Traffic Sergeant," for example, is not strongly inclined to require his men to be alert to nontraffic violations, incidents, or crimes.

Important progress toward better traffic action by the general patrol force has often resulted from rotating supervisory and command officers from traffic to corresponding positions in patrol. Detroit, for example, substantially improved the quantity and quality of traffic law enforcement in its precincts when a number of sergeants, lieutenants, and inspectors (precinct commanders) were assigned to general patrol duty from the traffic bureau.

Specialization Alone Not Enough. Experience with established and well-directed specialized traffic activities indicates that they are potentially productive and economical means of combating the growing traffic problem. But many specialized traffic divisions are producing only a part of the result one might expect in light of their manpower, equipment, and budget.

In these instances better management is needed, and this requires better-trained administrators. The chief of police in many such cases dares not despecialize and decentralize this responsibility to his precinct commanders, because even a higher administrative skill is demanded to administer a dispersed multipurpose operation. Generally, at the district level of command, managerial resources are lower. The police have learned the hard way that organizational form is no answer to the need for effective management — that it usually does not solve administrative problems.

Some cities, possessed of outstanding police leadership and a high state of police training, morale, and competence, are successfully meeting the problem without specialization. They are, for the most part, smaller cities. The future should bring more and better personnel, both administrative and operational. Some of the larger cities may then begin to despecialize without loss of efficiency in this important area of police service.

While bringing the traffic problem under control through a specialized division, intensive training and indoctrination of the general patrol force should be undertaken, so that it may effectively provide an increasing proportion of traffic enforcement, with corresponding reduction in the motorized traffic enforcement patrol. How rapidly this can be done, and to what ultimate degree, depends upon the quality of the force and its command, the sufficiency of its training, and the coincidence of the demands for other police service and traffic service as to time and place.

Ultimately, particularly in the small and medium-sized cities, even the highly technical function of accident investigation may be performed well by general investigators of the patrol force. In many jurisdictions, however, this is too much to expect in the foreseeable future.

Coordination with Official and Nonofficial Agencies

The first part of this chapter examined highway traffic management and reviewed the many agencies and controlling forces, in addition to the police, that are responsible for its functioning. The segment of responsibility belonging to the police was then separated and examined as to the nature and function of each of its parts. Finally, the police traffic program was outlined and it was shown how it is developed, activated, and controlled. Now, in a sense, this process must be reversed. The question here is the position of police traffic supervision in the community program so that the whole will operate in full harmony and integration. As far as this affects the chief of police, what does this mean?   A look at the interlacing responsibilities and functions of the police and other agencies in the community is the first step.

Police and the Traffic Engineer

The police have a liaison relationship to the traffic engineer. From a practical standpoint, traffic engineering may be divided into three general kinds of activity:

(1) research concerned with flow studies, congestion problems, parking problems, location hazards, and similar technical studies; (2) technical engineering problems of design, construction, serviceability, technical installations (such as signals and channelization) and their maintenance; and (3) mechanical operations of routine maintenance and inspection of facilities, such as erecting signs, painting street lines and curbings, setting out barricades for special controls, and similar activities.

The police contribute importantly to traffic engineering research by collecting information from accidents and congestion. In addition, all reports referred to the police by citizens or submitted by patrol officers on hazards or other conditions needing attention must be brought to the attention of the traffic engineer.

Liaison Necessary. Interchange of information cannot be effectively and continuously maintained without specific and clearly defined working relationships. If the police do not have an officer with an assignment to maintain such liaison, it is a management responsibility to see that the system of routing and receiving information between these two agencies is developed and maintained. Such a system should include a follow-up to show what action was taken on data submitted.

While the police can offer little assistance in technical matters relating to design or installation of facilities, the police should develop an understanding of such matters and have an opportunity to review plans before an actual installation is made. The engineer with all his technical qualifications may still overlook some factor having an important bearing on police work. The police will be required to patrol and to enforce the laws, and if the proposed facility will create unusual or difficult problems for the police it is better to recognize and discuss them before the facility is installed than to wait until the problem becomes acute.

Particularly in the planning stage, when new controls or installations are being considered, the police and the traffic engineer must work closely together. They are striving for the same objectives — safe and efficient movement of traffic. By joint planning they can agree on the means of achieving these objectives and present a united front in the procurement of funds, legislation, and public support needed to implement a program.

Interdependency of the police and traffic engineer also shows up conspicuously in the realm of mechanical installations and maintenance. Parking meters which are out of order, signs which are down or illegible, curb markings which are faded, or channel stripes which have been worn away, pose unnecessary burdens on the police. Not only is supervision over such rundown facilities hampered, but the public interprets the limited action of the police as a general letdown in supervision and enforcement.

While many engineering facilities serve to reduce the work of the police by reducing accidents, by expediting traffic flow, and by minimizing enforcement requirements, the police must still be responsible for traffic supervision over such facilities. This is particularly true at the initial stage, when new signal systems are installed, when new through arterials are opened up, or when new traffic flow patterns (such as one-way streets) are adopted. Even the best and most expensively engineered systems will continue to need supervision if they are to function as intended, because the human element, which cannot be "engineered," will always remain.

Police and Safety Educators

Relationships between the police and educators are much the same as between the police and the traffic engineer. It has already been pointed out that the job of educating the community and its drivers in matters of traffic safety and behavior cannot be fastened on the backs of the police, although police cooperation will be expected and welcomed, and the police will incidentally provide important educational influences through the three basic traffic functions. Nevertheless, because of its high public relations value and because of the need to maintain operational liaison with the education agencies, the police frequently set up a permanent "traffic education bureau" or unit and give it heavy publicity.

Educational Phases. The education of both drivers and pedestrians may be separated into three main phases: (1) the initial phase, education of the beginner; (2) the continuing or "in-service" phase, directed toward improvement of driving and walking practices; and (3) the remedial phase which attempts to correct specific individual defects, usually of drivers rather than of pedestrians.

Initial traffic training must be done in the home and kindergarten, when the child is first being taught how to walk and play safely out of doors. It continues up through the grade school, along with predriver conditioning and indoctrination. By the time the youngster reachers senior high school age he is ready for formal driver education. Classroom training is roughly equivalent to ground-school for aviation cadets. Safe driving practices and habits are taught, along with traffic laws and rules of the road. Then the student must study both the driver and the car, learning about attitudes, mental and physical limitations, and the forces involved with a car in motion. Finally he is trained in actual driving techniques, supplemented by supervised driving experience. When he at last "solos" and gets his license, the initial training phase is over.

Once he becomes a driver he must continually be reminded of the need for compliance with traffic laws and safe driving (or walking) practices. This is developed through supervision and enforcement by the police and courts; continual publicity through newspapers, magazines, radio, television, motion pictures, and public talks; and through specific publicity in the form of posters and safety campaigns. In this phase fleet operators may provide in-service training schools for their drivers, high schools and colleges may conduct special educational programs, and community service organizations may lend their aid.

Phase three takes the driver, after he has demonstrated seriously faulty driving practices or attitudes, and attempts to rehabilitate him as a safe driver. This may be done through a "traffic school," often in lieu of other corrective or penalizing action, or through the operation of psychological and physiological clinics for faulty drivers. Driver license administrators work importantly in this area, seeking to learn which drivers need attention and to apply corrective measures. Pedestrians need this retraining also, but unfortunately the means to assure this have not yet been developed. The only way to deprive a pedestrian of his "walking license" is to jail him, and that is hardly a practical solution.

Police Participation. How do the police participate in the initial training phase? Certainly not by undertaking to replace the home or the school in this work. Certainly not by setting up the program for the home and the school or by dictating to the educational authorities what they shall teach and how they shall teach it. Through the "traffic education bureau" or other working liaison, the police must learn of programs and objectives of the educators, and in turn keep the educators advised of police programs and objectives. Specific training needs which the police may recognize can thus be referred, desirability of police assistance in specific areas of training can be made known, and mutual problems can be solved. For example, the police may be asked to discuss their function in supervising traffic and perhaps some of the details of the enforcement program. Or general safety instruction may be given realism by police review of accidents involving the safety principles being discussed and identification of the behavior or violations which led to the accidents.

If there is no educational program operating in the community, the police must show why it is important and perhaps how such a program can be set up. But once the program is established, the police must withdraw from any semblance of control, or conflicts and frictions disastrous to both agencies may result.

In the second or continuing phase, the police make their greatest direct contribution. This is particularly true for drivers or pedestrians who may never have had formal training in traffic safety. All traffic supervision — such as indicating and requiring correct behavior at intersections, pointing out what was done wrong when an accident resulted, issuing citations or warnings when violations are detected — must seek to correct and prevent faulty behavior or conditions.

Police frequently make the mistake of undertaking or assuming full authority and responsibility for traffic safety education in the continuing phase, rather than working through or with a central community agency such as the local safety council or traffic committee. Thus the police sometimes run their own poster program, seasonal safety campaigns, and general safety promotion without consulting or advising the community agency. If safety education ever is to be recognized as a community responsibility in contrast to a police responsibility, this kind of independent and unilateral operation must cease. However highly motivated, or whatever small measure of success these police efforts achieve, the community as a whole must participate. All official and nonofficial agencies in the community must accept their share in this work, with all efforts combined into a unified and coordinated program.

Police participation in the third phase of safety education is much the same as in the first phase, one of interested cooperation. One important difference is the responsibility of the police to assist in keeping the records which will reveal those who need driver improvement, and to report such information to the appropriate authority.

Police and the Prosecutor

Because of the close coordination needed, it is important that official and personal relationships between the police and prosecuting officer be the very best. Personality clashes between these two can wreck an enforcement program almost as effectively as if no prosecution were attempted in the first place.

It is important that these officials understand each other's viewpoints and problems and attempt to reach agreement on over-all policies and methods. Frequent conferences and informal meetings may help to cement these relationships. They should be followed by wholehearted and sincere fulfillment of mutual obligations.

Liaison with Prosecutor. The prosecutor should plan his activities in court to reduce unnecessary waiting by the officer. He should anticipate delays and lengthy trials and inform the officer when his appearance will not be necessary. This loss of time, frequently at the expense of the officer's off-duty or leisure time, is one of the principal reasons why police are not more aggressive in traffic enforcement.

The prosecutor should understand the department's program of selective enforcement and its accident prevention objectives. He should seek to match these objectives by giving proportionally more attention and time to the serious classes of violations and to charges arising from accident investigations. Policies to eliminate any semblance of "fixing," to reduce the nolle prosequi of cases, to assure vigorous follow-up of defendants who fail to appear, and to reduce the number of cases needlessly lost in court, should be closely coordinated between the police and the prosecutor.

Police and the Court

As in his dealings with the prosecutor, the traffic administrator can develop relationships between the police and the court to produce improved understanding of the needs and functions of each. For example, the importance of maintaining a united and serious attitude toward drinking drivers and traffic violators who repeatedly commit hazardous violations should be understood. The "nonfix" system, improved court attitude toward officers in court, improved courtroom facilities, improved courtroom atmosphere, and speedy but unhurried trials are necessary if the benefits of enforcement are not to be lost at this stage.

Judges rarely will refuse to assist the police when asked to suggest methods of improving police appearances in court and in their presentation of testimony. Judges will also be quick to respond to calls for help in training officers in legal subjects, especially in areas where they have been evidencing trouble in court.

Liaison with Courts. It is important that police understand their own limitations and the proper function of the court. Police are frequently sensitive and critical of court action which doesn't match their own beliefs of what the action should have been. Even where the situation seems hopeless, because of political motivation by the court, the police cannot afford to throw in the sponge. Rather, they must work even harder to develop and maintain a standard of quality in every action and phase of enforcement. Public pressure will eventually tend to correct this situation. But in the typical or average situation the police can do much to stimulate appropriate penalties in traffic cases.

Monetary fines should never be developed as a money-making device for the city. This could effectively destroy whatever merit there has been in seeking to increase the level of penalties as a deterrent force. In order to prevent any public impression that traffic enforcement is for the purpose of raising money, all agencies involved should minimize the revenue factor in reporting or summarizing enforcement activity. This in no way means that individual fines should not be given full publicity for public information and general deterrent purposes.

Traffic Bureaus. Another aspect of coordination with the court comes through the relationships of the police to the violations bureau. Whenever possible, this activity should be run by the court. The principal reason for removing it from police control is to separate the executive and judicial phase of traffic law enforcement. It is just another example of the nonpolice functions the police have been saddled with.

A good "nonfix" citation system is more readily attainable when the violations bureau is not under the control of the agency that issues the citations. Also there is less tendency for the public to attach any revenue-raising motive to the enforcement work of the police. It is important, then, for the police to refrain from meddling or applying "pressure" in the processing of citations. The police and the traffic court can pool their efforts and information in keeping violators' files, checking on repeaters, posting "stop" or "wanted" notices in their files, and keeping alert for persons who have failed to account for past citations and whose addresses are unknown.

Police and the Traffic Commission

The traffic commission, as described in the Model Traffic Ordinance, is an official body consisting of representatives of the official agencies having an interest and responsibility in the traffic problem. Such a commission may be needed to get satisfactory results through coordination where individual liaison and coordination alone do not prove effective.

Representation. The traffic commission should include representatives of the police department, traffic engineering agency, school authorities, traffic court (and prosecution), planning authority, and others with official responsibilities. Such a body could become the principal coordinating force in a community traffic program. Here in one group and around a single table are all the agencies having official problems needing common consideration. The Model Traffic Ordinance states:

It shall be the duty of the Traffic Commission, and to this end it shall have the authority within the limits of the funds at its disposal, to coordinate traffic matters, to carry on educational activities in traffic matters, to supervise the preparation and publication of traffic reports, to receive complaints having to do with traffic matters, and to recommend to the legislative body of the city and to the city traffic engineer, the chief of the traffic division, and other city officials ways and means for improving traffic conditions and the administration and enforcement of traffic regulations.

Nonofficial Agencies and the Police

Police relationships and coordination with some of the nonofficial agencies concerned with traffic management are discussed here.

Police and the Press. Police public relations is carried on largely through the press, which includes the newspapers, radio, and television. Since only a few people become directly involved with the police, and not very many will know by first-hand experience or observation what the police are doing or seeking to achieve in traffic supervision, most citizens must form opinions and develop attitudes about the police from what they read or hear.

Through the press the community learns about traffic problems, accident facts, police enforcement policies and programs, and other "public information" in traffic. Public information is as vital a force as any of the official control forces in reducing accidents and congestion. All police information given the press relating to traffic matters, especially that in the form of statements, must be carefully considered. For example, in informing the public of the aims of the police department, a clear statement of its enforcement policy should be made.

This will probably take the form of an announcement that motorists who violate traffic laws cause accidents; the department must prevent accidents; and its method will be by the arrest of violators, who will themselves determine by the number of accidents whether arrests must increase or be allowed to decrease. Ample notice should be given the public when a new highway is to be opened, a two-way street made one-way, U-turns eliminated, other turns prohibited, stop signs installed, or parking regulations changed. The driver prepared for a change is much less likely to be disgruntled about it and much more likely to cooperate.

It is not enough to give the press statistical information in the form of graphs or tables to report what is taking place in traffic. Few newspaper or radio writers have the experience or the time to analyze the information to see its full or true significance. This results in faulty interpretation of the information and false understanding by the public. In presenting periodic or special reports on traffic conditions, the wise police chief will summarize, preferably in writing, the significance of the facts presented. But woe unto him who uses this device to deceive the public!

Police and the Safety Association. In all municipalities a traffic safety association (or citizens' advisory committee) is needed in addition to the more formal and official traffic commission. Its purpose is to gain public support for programs of official agencies. The official agencies, as authors of a plan, cannot gracefully promote them by the same means available to a safety association. Association publicity can bring to the community's attention national, state, and local traffic accident facts. The association can stimulate the emotional reaction often needed to stir the public to an appreciation of the problem.

While its membership should include representation of the official agencies, the association should consist principally of representatives of civic and service groups, women's clubs, veterans' organizations, church and neighborhood groups, automobile agencies, parent-teacher associations, and others.

Since it is an unofficial and public-contact group only, the safety association or committee cannot take on any of the regular functions of the official agencies or of the traffic commission. To attempt to do so would weaken its status and effectiveness in the areas where its operations are justified and needed. It properly should act as a cushion between the community and its official agencies, interpreting to each the views and desires of the other. In this sense, it should have much the same status as that held by the chamber of commerce in relation to the business community.

One important product of the safety association is the coordination and clearing of plans or programs before they reach the "official action" stage. Here in a less restricting atmosphere all participating agencies and forces can reach full understanding and agreement, all conflicting or irritating matters can be ironed out, and much of the real program of the community can be developed.

Summary

To realize its full potential of providing service to the community through its traffic supervisory function, the police department must:

1. Recognize the extent of the traffic problem and its importance to the community.

2. Know and appreciate the part that should be played by the police in reducing the traffic problem, in concert with all the official and nonofficial agencies involved.

3. Be able to perform each of the traffic activities which constitute police traffic supervision to a highly effective degree, recognizing the true nature and objectives of each activity.

4. Be able to integrate such activities into an effective police traffic supervision program, with full management attention to planning of such a program.

5. Deliver the program in the most efficient manner, through effective organization, supervision, and control, recognizing the worth of specialized attention where such specialization will improve service.

6. Coordinate the police program and its activities with the efforts of other community forces working on the traffic problem, not seeking to dominate any of the fields in which the police should play a supporting or cooperative role only.

7. Lean on the official and nonofficial community action and public-opinion groups for guidance and assistance and for community stimulus and response.

Chapter 11

COMMUNICATIONS

Policemen in 17th-century England carried bells or lanterns which served to identify them and to give warning or summon assistance. The 18th century saw little improvement in police signal contrivances. Police instructions of the late 19th century directed the officer to give three blasts on his whistle or three raps on the pavement with his baton (night stick) when help was needed. His alarm was taken up by the officer on the adjoining post and passed in similar manner to the next policeman, thus forging a chain of communication. In time of great need the officer was authorized to discharge his revolver three times in the air.

The whistle, night stick, and revolver still have a place as signal and alarm devices in connection with police duties, but various electrical instruments now provide long-distance communications. The telegraph, recall light, telephone, teletype, wireless telegraphy, and radio — all electrical appliances — accomplish the purpose with infinitely increased efficiency. It is the purpose of this chapter to examine the function of communications systems in the police department.

History and Significance

A review of police-radio history reveals rapid progress in a relatively short period of time. The Pennsylvania state police was the first police organization to make practical use of radio when it established radio-telegraph communication between Harrisburg headquarters and its field stations. After experimenting with broadcasts to police cars by a commercial radio station, the Detroit police department in 1929 was issued the first police radio-telephone license which enabled dispatchers to talk to patrol-car drivers by short-wave, one-way radio.

During the 1930's a substantial number of police departments installed radio transmitters at their headquarters with receivers in their patrol cars. The last half of this decade witnessed the development of two-way police radio communication which proved to be almost as revolutionary as the adoption of the one-way system. Two-way radio enables the car to talk to the station as well as the station to talk to the car. In this system the station transmitter is on one frequency or wave length and the mobile units operate on a different frequency. Two channels are thus required.

Shortly thereafter three-way radio systems were developed. These permit transmission from station to car, car to station, and car to car. Some three-way systems are adaptations of the two-way system; car-to-car transmissions are made possible by a switch on the automobile transmitter which places in operation a second crystal on the same wave length as that of the headquarters transmitter. The most common three-way system has the station and mobile units on the same frequency. Only one channel is thus required. This arrangement permits complete three-way communications in which each

radio car within range can hear all calls transmitted by the other cars. This characteristic is advantageous in small communities.

While voice communication received principal attention during this time, radio-
telegraph was also developing in the form of an intercity network, a necessity since the
police were prohibited from using for intercity communication frequency channels that
were assigned for the primary purpose of communicating with mobile units. The police
radio-telegraph network provides nationwide communication facilities that are independent of private-corporation services.

Radio transmission of fingerprint records and photographs and facsimile machines
which copy a message from headquarters to the patrol car in the absence of the driver,
as well as many adaptations of television will no doubt be common in police departments
in the not-distant future.

Probably the greatest advancement in police effectiveness and efficiency during the
past century has been effected through improved communications. Police radio equipment
has become so inexpensive that it is within the range of the smallest department. Future
developments in police communications are almost beyond imagination. The basic philosophy in communications is that the police must have at least as good means of communication as are available to the criminal.

Significance of Communications

There is hardly a single police action taken that does not involve some sort of communication. Practically all requests by citizens for police service are made by telephone;
police officers on street duty report to headquarters by telephone; radio communication
is maintained between the dispatcher and the officers in the field; communications between
various police departments may be made by long-distance telephone, radio-telephone,
radio-telegraph, teletype, or commercial telegraph. Communications with the police
headquarters building may involve a building telephone exchange, interoffice communication system, or some mechanical means such as pneumatic tubes.

The broad purpose of a police communications system is to enable supervising officers at headquarters to maintain contact with personnel at their command and translate
into action those measures necessary to protect the lives and property of the community.
The system is often called the nerve center of the department. Orders originating at
headquarters are received at various points in the community by the field force and carried into execution. Complete unity of command is thus theoretically possible.

Mobilization in Emergency. With the commanding officer of the department at the
helm and in control of all communication facilities, the manpower of the entire department
can be mobilized and concentrated in a major emergency. Such mass activities of semimilitary nature are seldom brought into play. A great fire, flood, tornado, earthquake,
epidemic, war, strike, or disorder may, with little or no warning, call them into being.
Preparedness should be the watchword. Emergencies which are more frequent include
bank or payroll robberies, hit-and-run driving, street or store stickups, murders, and
other crimes requiring immediate action.

Mobilization for Routine Duties. Quite aside from the major catastrophes, for which
the police communications system should be ready, are the hourly demands made by the
force upon its facilities. There are countless duty calls from the patrolman on the beat
to his station. These are made to give the commander an opportunity to communicate
orders to his men on patrol, if there is such need, and to provide a system of supervision

to make sure the patrolmen are safe and on their jobs. Or, the patrolman on post may call for information, further instructions, or reinforcements. The number of these routine and minor emergency calls is legion. They are a necessary and integral part of the administration of a police department. The communications system must provide facilities for the uninterrupted service of these calls.

Communication Needs. Specifically, the services that a communication system must provide are these:

1. The communication of citizens with the police in order that complaints may be promptly received.

2. The communication of police headquarters with the individual policeman: to transmit to him routine and emergency orders and information useful in the apprehension of criminals, and to supervise and control his operations.

3. The communication of policemen with other policemen and with police headquarters: to give information, to request assistance, and to acknowledge receipt of orders.

4. Communication between police departments and other law-enforcing agencies for the exchange of information.

5. The internal communication needs at police headquarters and between headquarters and district stations.

Essentials of Communications System

It is essential that the exact requirements for all types of communications be ascertained and that means be chosen to meet the requirements efficiently and economically. Several factors must be considered in establishing a police communications system in order to assure that it will accomplish its purposes effectively. These are discussed in the following paragraphs. Decisions as to the location of its mechanical and human controls and the place of the system in the organization structure should be made only in the light of a full knowledge of these important elements; they will be considered in a later section of this chapter.

Dependability. Maximum dependability must be assured in a communications system. Upon its continued operation may depend the safety of the lives and property of the community. Communications failures deprive the police command of prompt service from all or part of the force and thus jeopardize its effective strength. Any interruption, however brief, is fraught with the danger that an emergency might arise at that time.

Provision should be made for the disaster-proof operation of each component unit of the communications system. The system should be free of every conceivable physical hazard which might in an emergency put it out of operation. The possibility of damage to equipment or interruption of power supply by flood, fire, cyclone, or by rioters, criminal gangs, or saboteurs who may overpower the operator or disable the equipment all need to be foreseen and planned for. In its location and construction, proper consideration should be given to safeguarding the system at all vital points and to effecting quick repairs when damage renders the service inoperative in part or in whole. Carefully laid plans toward these ends, if wisely formulated and recorded in advance, may themselves result in the saving of lives and the conserving of property.

The dependability of radio transmission has improved steadily. Today, fixed transmitters seldom give trouble. Radio propagation disturbances are almost never severe enough to disrupt communications, but there are times when communications may be interrupted due either to actual equipment malfunction or to some unforeseen mishap, such as a general power failure. It seems desirable, therefore, that even with a completely motorized force, radio should be supplemented by some simple and inexpensive means of communication.

Every effort should be made to safeguard the headquarters transmitter from failure at a time of emergency. An auxiliary transmitter should be available for immediate operation in the event of failure of the main transmitter. In some cases it may be desirable to have the auxiliary transmitter removed geographically from headquarters in order that in the event of disaster in the police building, communications could be continued from some other location. An emergency power supply consisting of small generator operated by a gasoline or diesel motor should be available in the event of failure of the electric supply.

Speed. The rapidity with which communication can be established between various units is of tremendous importance. Immediate arrival of police officers at the scene of a crime not only gives better protection to citizens but also may diminish the seriousness of the offense. The officer can often capture offenders in the act of committing a crime or near the scene, thus saving the investigative division endless labor and expense in identifying and apprehending offenders and preparing a case against them. Witnesses may be available for questioning at the scene while their impressions are still fresh in their minds. Information thus obtained results in more certain convictions with less cost to the taxpayers.

In most instances, once communications have been established, only a short time is required to transmit or to receive the required information. It is the initial establishment of this link, however, which is sometimes frustratingly time-consuming. Various existing or proposed methods to significantly shorten this time lag are herein described.

Some method, preferably an instantaneous one, should be available to keep the patrolman in constant touch with headquarters. While he is in a radio-equipped vehicle this condition is met. If he is out of his vehicle, the following methods are available and are used by various jurisdictions:

1. Selective Calling System. This activates either the vehicle horn or a red light dome mounted on top of the vehicle. This method limits the distance that a patrolman can be from his vehicle, and the radio equipment must be left turned on. However, this system is practical. A number of municipalities in California have portions of their fleets equipped with such devices. Oakland, for example, has had the equipment mounted in 50 vehicles since 1958. Cleveland, Ohio, also has found this system very effective.

2. Red-Light Recall System. This consists of electric red lights mounted in fixed positions throughout or in certain portions of the city, usually at locations visible from many directions. Coded numbers of flashes produced by manual or automatic equipment at headquarters signify the need for the patrolman whose code is flashed to get in touch with his station. This method in conjunction with the telephone was once quite widespread. The advent of radio, however, enabled quicker initial contact, thus precluding further installations in new and growing municipalities. Existing red-light systems, however, furnish a method for signaling patrolmen on foot or provide a means of communication in those municipalities which are too small to accommodate a licensed radio system. The main drawback of this system is its high initial cost.

3. Loudspeaker Attachment. A common and inexpensive method of signaling a patrolman outside of his vehicle is to mount a loudspeaker externally and connect it to the radio receiver. This permits patrolmen who are writing citations or investigating collisions to hear all radio messages.

4. <u>Pocket Receivers</u>. A proposed system which consists of the modification of or the addition to existing vehicular radio equipment enables the automatic retransmission of all messages on another frequency by low power equipment in the vehicle to a small pocket receiver carried by the patrolman. This radiation would be either on a special frequency or of such a low power as to fall within the category of "limited radiation devices" as defined by the Federal Communications Commission. No such system as this is known to be in operation at this writing.

The most satisfactory method from the standpoint of flexibility and speed consists of the use of transistorized pocket receivers on the police frequency. If both the cars and the station are on one frequency (three-way), the patrolmen never need be out of touch with what is happening.

Receivers of this type also may be utilized by foot patrolmen for functions such as stakeouts, parade direction, or in a variety of situations wherever communication previously was either cumbersome or impossible. In 1958, the New York Police Department initiated the use of pocket receivers for city park patrolmen.

These receivers are available in the frequency ranges of 30-50 megacycles and in the 150 megacycle band. The weight of the latter units is about 10 ounces. Battery life varies with the manufacturer and model with a representative value of 150 hours minimum and 250 hours expected life in a certain model which has selective calling included. The price of these units (about $300) is perhaps the only deterrent to their widespread use. A miniature transmitter is also available but its range is limited due to its low power. Its present price (about $160) is generally justifiable under certain circumstances in large police departments.

<u>Reporting</u>. The preceding material has dealt primarily with methods which can be used to shorten the span of time necessary to pass information to the patrolmen on the street. The following methods can be used to shorten the delay between the time of offense and the report to police headquarters:

1. <u>Education</u>. The public can be educated by means of publicity media to report serious felony crimes immediately and to readily furnish other required information such as the description of the responsible persons, the direction of flight, and other pertinent information.

2. <u>Separation</u>. The police department can arrange with the telephone company for the installation of two distinct telephone numbers: one for carrying routine business calls, and one for emergency calls. A department which has answering facilities for emergency lines at the complaint desk takes immediate action on emergency calls rather than having them routed from a switchboard located elsewhere. Departments with only one number may have special emergency lines connected directly from the telephone company. Persons dialing "operator" and asking for emergency police assistance are connected on these special lines; incoming calls on these lines are processed immediately.

3. <u>Direct Calls</u>. Some departments have facilities for transmitting the incoming complaints directly to the patrol units, especially in emergency situations. This saves time as the dispatcher need not repeat all of the information, and by his judicious choice of questions he alerts all of the patrol cars and has officers on their way before the complainant finishes his conversation.

4. <u>Silent Alarms</u>. A silent alarm is one which gives no indication of its function or presence to the person who trips it. At a centrally located alarm board a buzzer sounds and a light gives the location of the alarm origin. If the alarm board is located in a

commercial installation, the operator on duty calls the police department to report an alarm from a certain location. If the alarm board is located at police headquarters, usually next to the dispatcher, the location of the alarm is broadcast immediately. However, most alarm boards located in police communication centers are limited to financial institutions or places of business that are subjected to frequent robberies. This is due primarily to space limitations and, secondarily, to avoid competition with private alarm companies.

Another type of silent alarm, recently proposed, utilizes a low-powered radio transmitter on the police frequency. A code wheel, tone generator, and possibly a timer, are built into the transmitter. The equipment is constructed in such a manner that it is silent in its operation. Its primary function is as a temporary robbery or burglary alarm, to be installed in commercial establishments that are determined by the police to be immediate robbery or burglary hazards. Upon being tripped, such an alarm transmits a prearranged sequence of tones directly to the patrol cars in the vicinity. The advantage of such alarm systems is their rapid installation: they are not connected to a central board by wire. Too there is a negligible lag of time between the alarm and the response by the patrolmen. A timer, if installed, turns the transmitter off after about a minute of operation to permit normal police broadcasting.

In summary, it is well to emphasize that the rapidity with which communications are established bears a direct relationship to the efficiency with which a law enforcing agency operates. Although the foregoing information has been concerned primarily with reducing the lag between the time of the offense and the arrival of officers at the scene, other phases of police communication, notably intercity, intercounty, and interstate, may well be re-examined in order to route radio messages with a minimum of delay. The latter systems are described in other portions of this chapter.

Accuracy. Accuracy in communications is also essential. A garbled order is misleading and may result in waste of time and effort or, still worse, cause a serious error which may lose prestige for the police and involve unnecessary hazards to persons and property. The correct sending and receiving of police messages should be assured by suitable mechanical installations, well-planned operating procedures, trained operators, and continuous supervision.

Secrecy. To reveal the substance of police communications sometimes destroys their value. Violators and their interested aides are usually aware of the tactical advantages to be gained through a knowledge of what the police are going to do. When criminals discover police plans, the police lose their tactical advantage. Secrecy should be sought for messages most likely to involve the department's effectiveness. Leaks of confidential information should be vigilantly prevented and detected.

Police information often has a substantial cash value to certain classes of people, such as lawyers and garage and ambulance owners who may indulge in "ambulance chasing." Their identity and methods of operation are usually well known to the police. The federal regulations governing radio provide a basis for regulating persons who might have motives in receiving police messages. Section 605 of the Communication Act provides that it shall be unlawful for any person not entitled to receive information by radio, to use it for his own benefit, or to publish it or in any other way to divulge such information. The police department should distribute this regulation to possible offenders and point out that any infractions will be prosecuted.

Effective Cooperation. Police departments in this age of fast transportation and faster communications have learned that they cannot live for themselves alone — unless they wish to be left hopelessly behind. Criminals speed in high-powered motor cars and avail themselves of every rapid communication facility with complete disregard of political boundary lines.

This suggests the need for effective cooperation between political units in their efforts to capture and suppress lawbreakers. To accomplish this in greatest measure a survey should precede the installation or revision of a police communications system in order that it may be tied in with the established neighboring facilities wherever possible. Plans should be formed to avoid unnecessary delay if the department, suddenly faced with a major emergency, should need to call upon a neighboring department for the temporary use of its communications facilities.

Radio Communication with Police Cars

Radio has the above-described essentials of the ideal communication system more completely and in higher degree than any other system of communication available to the police. Analysis of one- two- and three-way systems reveals that some of these systems have the essentials in greater degree than others. For example, one-way radio does not permit headquarters to check on the location of cars or to make certain that orders have been received or carried out. For these purposes it must be supplemented by a two-way radio or telephone system.

The two-way radio system can therefore add immeasurably to the usefulness of radio communications. It provides a way to keep in virtually constant potential contact with auto patrolmen, who have largely replaced the foot patrolmen in many cities. It provides a means of controlling and diverting traffic on a city-wide or state-wide scale by coordinating the services of airplane observation with surface-control forces at times of holiday traffic congestion or during parades and other group activities.

The auto patrolman may contact the headquarters staff for further information concerning an alarm received, request a check-up on an auto registration, or call for help to surround a building or head off a fleeing auto. With two-way radio the auto patrolman can report back in service from an assignment without stopping to "pull a box" and telephone in. Today, most of the one-way communication installations have been replaced by the modern and useful two- and three-way radio systems.

Three-way communication provides some advantages over two-way systems. It enables a supervisor in the field to direct other mobile units from his car. In addition, should the station transmitter fail to function, a mobile transmitter can be used for dispatching. Cities using the three-way system have been able to render better police service because of the flexibility of this type of system. More criminals have been caught than otherwise would have been apprehended because mobile units in three-way systems were able to monitor all radio calls and could thereby assist each other in blocking escape routes and capturing criminals without waiting for the slower two-way system which requires messages between mobile units to be relayed through the station transmitter.

Three-way systems not controlled from headquarters create problems that make rigid supervision essential. One is the danger that officers in patrol cars will use their radios to communicate with one another on matters that do not relate strictly to police business or that do not justify the use of radio time. Transmissions from cars may also, in some circumstances, interfere with the reception of messages from the central transmitter. A second problem created by the use of three-way communications is related to jeopardizing the principle of unity of command. When the central dispatcher, field supervisors in the field, and patrolmen in cars engaged in an operation all undertake to direct the efforts of the field force, confusion may result. The seriousness of these problems may be lessened somewhat by suitable regulation and strict supervision.

Characteristics of Two and Three-Way Radio Systems

Two and three-way police radio communication setups are not all of the same type. From a technical standpoint, they may be divided into simplex, duplex, and triplex systems. In a simplex system, the headquarters and mobile unit transmitters operate on the same high frequency channel; in the duplex systems, the headquarters and mobile unit transmitters operate on different channels. Duplex systems may be further divided into two distinct types: (1) those in which the headquarters and mobile unit transmitters operate on frequencies within the high frequency spectrum, but on different channels; and (2) those in which the headquarters transmitter operates on a medium frequency and the mobile unit transmitter on a high frequency.

In simplex (three-way) systems, mobile units may intercommunicate directly with other mobile units without the assistance of the headquarters transmitter. In a duplex (two-way) system, mobile units may not intercommunicate as their receivers are usually fixed on the frequency of the headquarters transmitter. Intercommunication between mobile units is possible in a duplex system, as previously mentioned, by the use of a second crystal which will enable the car transmitter to emit messages on the same frequency as the headquarters transmitter, and also by an arrangement at the headquarters station to provide for picking up and rebroadcasting the signals of the mobile units. Such an arrangement is called a triplex system.

Basis of Choice. The relative merits of these different systems depend to a very large extent upon particular circumstances and the regulations laid down by the Federal Communications Commission for the use of radio transmission. The following factors should be kept in mind in choosing a system:

1. If a medium frequency, one-way transmitter is already in use, a duplex (two-way) system can be provided at a fraction of the cost of a simplex (three-way) system.

2. A duplex system requires two channels, and with increased crowding the Federal Communication Commission may at some time discourage its use.

3. In a large city the number of police cars will be so great as to require several channels in any case.

4. The radio system should be coordinated with police radios in surrounding communities.

Legal Use of Police Radio in Making Arrests

Police officers in making use of information received by radio must usually act quickly to prevent the escape of accused persons. Such arrests have been upheld in cases where a felony has been committed and the information transmitted by radio constituted a reasonable ground to suspect that the persons arrested committed it. No court cases have been reported involving the use of radio information in arresting misdemeanants.

The usual rule that arrests for a misdemeanor can only be made when the offense is committed in the officer's presence seems too strict to meet present-day situations. Police officers frequently arrest on misdemeanor charges when they do not witness the wrongful act but instead receive information of it by police radio. The courts will undoubtedly give reasonable interpretation to the usual rules relating to arrests for misdemeanors when the arrests are made on information received by radio; otherwise new rules to cover this situation must be provided.

Radio Frequencies

The adoption of high frequencies and frequency modulation has improved the effectiveness of police radio.

Very High and Ultra-High Frequencies. The division between high, very high, and ultra-high frequencies is somewhat arbitrary, especially the boundary between the very high and the ultra-high. However, at present, it is generally agreed that 30 megacycles to 300 megacycles is the region of the very high frequencies and that 300 to 3,000 megacycles are the ultra-high frequencies. Transmission in the region above 30 megacycles is limited by the curvature of the earth and approximates, but is not necessarily equal to, the "line of sight," or the optical horizon. This propagation characteristic enables many communities throughout the country to operate on the same frequency without mutual interference. Separations on the order of two hundred miles are feasible in flat countryside.

Three frequency bands are commonly used for police base and mobile equipment in the region above 30 megacycles: 30 to 50 mc., 150-164 mc., and 450 mc. Other bands exist, but their use is limited. Most equipment commercially available is constructed for these bands, each of which has certain propagation characteristics to be considered when choosing a system.

The greatest mobile-to-base coverage may be expected in the 30-50 mc. band because transmitter power output in mobile units is higher in this range than for the higher bands; certain types of obstructions have negligible effect upon propagation; and receiving equipment is more sensitive in this region. Because of the greater range, the separation between station locations must be increased and the number of channels available for assignment is limited. This band is widely used by state and county law enforcement agencies since the area they normally cover is larger than that of a municipality. The most serious disadvantage of this band is the occasional interference from distant stations on the same frequency which usually occurs during the daylight hours. This interference is caused by ionospheric conditions which return the signal to earth from a location thousands of miles away. In some instances the strength of these signals may be greater than that from the local mobile units. Instances of interference between such widely separated points as Illinois and Venezuela have been reported. Use of this band should be limited to those instances where sufficient coverage cannot be affected by other frequencies.

The 150 mc. band is the most widely used for police communication within a municipality. This frequency region is not affected by ionospheric conditions. By properly choosing the transmitting and receiving site or sites, complete coverage may be given to almost any city. Since the height of the station antenna determines the distance to the horizon, locating the station equipment on a mountain top or in a tall building affords the best coverage. In most cases it may be said that the distance to the optical horizon limits the maximum reliable range of the station. Also, more channels are available in this region as is explained in this chapter. Large intervening objects or hills cut down the range, but this problem is normally solved by locating the equipment on the highest object or hill, using a number of receivers scattered throughout the area to be covered, and feeding the audio signals over leased telephone lines to headquarters. Often the amount of power necessary at the base transmitter can be reduced by locating the transmitter at a high point. A California municipality of 100,000 population was able to afford considerably greater coverage from a transmitter of 20 watts output located at 1,800 feet elevation than from a 250 watt base station with a quadruple power gain antenna located 200 feet above street level.

The 450 megacycle band has approximately the same characteristics as the 150 megacycle region except that in certain cases the range is less because generating a given amount of power output requires more battery drain in the mobile equipment and receivers are not as sensitive in this band as in the ones previously described. In certain cases, especially among concrete buildings, the coverage is better because, under such conditions, the shorter waves are reflected and scattered beneficially. In general, this equipment is more expensive and requires careful maintenance. Frequency allocations within this band are detailed in another section of this chapter.

Frequency Modulated Police Radio Equipment. Due to demonstrable advantages of frequency modulation over amplitude modulation, most police radio installations consist of frequency modulated (FM) radio equipment. The chief advantage of FM equipment for police work is reduction of noise from man-made and natural sources such as electrical devices and thunder storms. Two major benefits are derived. The system is more reliable because of the utilization of low signal levels within the service area, and the effective radius of communication is increased, making it possible for mobile units to cover wider territories.

The danger of "dead spots," which has long been the bane of radio servicemen using medium- and high-frequency amplitude-modulated (AM) systems, has been largely eliminated in the use of FM by reducing the noise level below the signal level so that greater receiver sensitivity can be used, thereby increasing the service and reliability of the communication system. Another advantage of FM is that it operates in mobile units with less input power than does the amplitude-modulated equipment. The advantages can be summarized as: greater coverage with less noise, increased reliability, virtual elimination of "dead spots," greater intelligibility, and lower operating and maintenance costs.

Federal Regulation

The Federal Communications Commission is vested with regulatory power over the use of air channels for radio purposes. No radio transmitter can be operated in police service except under license granted by this body and by similarly licensed operators.

Radio Station License. Agencies desiring to install and operate any transmitting equipment must first submit an application for station authorization. Under the rules governing public safety radio services, which were issued December 18, 1953, the Federal Communications Commission may subsequently issue either a construction permit only or construction permit and station license simultaneously.

When a construction permit only has been issued for a transmitter and installation has been completed, the permittee may test his equipment after he has notified the engineer-in-charge of the local radio district at least two days in advance of the test date. After testing, but prior to the date when the transmitter is used for operational purposes, an application for station license must be forwarded to the Commission. The transmitter may then be used as though licensed, pending Commission action on the application.

When a construction permit and license for a new transmitter are issued simultaneously the licensee must notify the engineer-in-charge of the local radio district of the date on which the transmitter will be placed in operation. When a construction permit and modification of license are issued simultaneously, operation may be commenced without notification to the engineer-in-charge, except where license has been granted to operate on a new or different frequency.

In considering an application for license to broadcast, the Commission is required by statute to apply the test of "public interest, convenience, and necessity." The burden of proof rests upon the applicant to establish the need on this basis. The commission has designated certain frequencies sufficiently far apart to avoid congestion and assure minimum interference.

Operator's License. At least one licensed operator must be on duty when the transmitter is being operated. The commission may give permission to locate the operator at the control point where the transmitter is remotely controlled. Mobile (car) transmitters are operated under the supervision of the headquarters operator and are not required to have licensed operators.

Municipal, county, and state police radio stations using voice transmissions, regardless of power, may be operated by personnel holding a restricted radio-telephone permit, providing they are restricted to the handling of only the instrument controls that are absolutely necessary to operate the station and which do not otherwise affect the emissions of the station. All transmitter adjustments which may effect the proper operation of the station must be made under the supervision of a person holding a first- or second-class commercial radio-operator license, either radio-telephone or radio-telegraph.

Furthermore, if the police agency operates a two-way system, licensed operators are not required in each patrol car provided that an operator holding a restricted radio-telephone permit is on duty at headquarters to supervise the emissions of all such stations so as to insure proper operation in accordance with the station license.

Where the radio system is furnished by the telephone company, the licensee is still the police department using the service, and the day-to-day operation remains vested in that department. However, the telephone company will assist in the preparation of applications, construction permits, and any other data required by the Federal Communications Commission.

Frequency Allocation. There has been and continues to be an increasing demand for radio frequencies. During the past several years there has been a tremendous increase in the number of television broadcasting stations and in the use of radio transmitting and receiving equipment by public utilities, taxicabs, railroads, and others. The rapid growth of police radio stations is illustrated by the fact that on June 30, 1945, there were 2,643 licenses outstanding in the police service. By June 30, 1953, the number had increased to 8,005 licenses — more than a threefold increase. This growth is typical of all of the radio services.

Competition for the use of frequency channels is very keen, and it is necessary periodically for the Committee on Radio and Communication of the International Association of Chiefs of Police and the Associated Police Communications Officers to represent the police interests before the Federal Communications Commission in order to insure adequate frequency allocations for use by law enforcement agencies.

Federal, International, and Legal Restrictions. In allocating frequencies the Federal Communications Commission is constantly faced with important problems. Many police officials fail to understand and appreciate the limitations imposed upon the Commission.. The Commission derives its authority and jurisdiction from the Communications Act of 1934. Broadly, the Commission has the authority not only to assign stations but more generally to determine the broad frequencies under which the various services, including commercial broadcasting, television, police, marine or aviation, may operate. However, the Commission has no absolute power in that field, because the Communications Act provides that the Commission shall only have jurisdiction over those frequencies which are not reserved by the federal government. The President of the United States, exercising his prerogative through the Inter-Departmental Radio Advisory Committee, has the authority to assign frequencies for use by the federal government.

International implications further complicate the situation. This country cannot use all available frequencies because the frequency-allocation needs of other nations must be considered. Since radio transmissions in one country can interfere with communications in other countries and at sea, the need for regulating certain frequency allocations on a world-wide basis is obvious. International conferences have made frequency-allocation agreements on a world-wide basis which have been legalized by international treaties. The Federal Communications Commission has no authority over the use of frequencies reserved for other use by such treaties.

The Federal Communications Commission has frequently been criticized for not making more radio channels available to the police. As was previously indicated, the Commission's authority to assign frequencies throughout the radio spectrum is not absolute. Even after the Commission does assign frequencies and issues licenses, certain legal problems sometimes arise. Any person interested in the assigned frequency, or any licensee who feels his property rights are jeopardized, may appeal to the Commission for a hearing and can then, if desired, go to the courts to have the ruling of the Commission set aside.

Engineering Problems. Engineering problems also enter the picture. Certain radio frequencies characteristically have skip effects. At certain times, particularly during the night hours, patrol units in some cities receive transmissions from stations located in distant parts of the United States. An example may be illustrative. The dispatchers in Wichita, Kansas, were sometimes unable to receive transmission from the patrol units during the time that the dispatcher in Piedmont, California, was transmitting because of the interference created. It is a difficult and trying procedure to designate frequencies on a nation-wide basis for the purpose of eliminating interference caused by radio-skip characteristics.

Harmonic relationships present another engineering problem. A radio station operating on one frequency may create interference with another station operating, for example, on a frequency twice as high. If the two stations are located in the same area, there is a probability that sufficient interference will prevail which would prohibit satisfactory communications.

Power limitations must also be considered. If a police station in a particular locality has more than sufficient radio power to cover its own area, it may interfere with police broadcasts in a nearby community that uses the same frequency.

A radio-station transmitter has an area of interference which extends far beyond the area within which its messages are clear enough to be of practical service. A transmitter, for instance, may have a service radius of a short distance but an interference radius of many miles. Police-car transmitters, operating on a lower power output, have a correspondingly smaller range of interference.

The larger the area and population to be served, the more messages must be broadcast. A large area cannot be served on one frequency without overloading the channel, thereby causing undue delay in transmitting emergency messages. Therefore, in order to provide adequate air time for two-way communications, large cities have been forced to operate headquarters transmitters on more than one frequency. In cities using several frequencies, mobile units are sometimes separated by frequency on a geographical basis; in other cases the frequency separation may be dictated by function. Thus traffic cars and motorcycles may be on one channel; detectives and administrative personnel may be assigned to another frequency.

A recent survey in California indicated that a channel becomes loaded to capacity when occupied by an average of 37 mobile units. This does not preclude heavier channel loading but it indicates that difficulty may be encountered if loading of the channel is increased above this level.

Police Frequency Allocations. The radio spectrum extends in frequency from 10 kilocycles to 30,000 megacycles and above. These frequencies have widely different characteristics, and only a few are suitable or available for police work. The current frequency allocations for the police service are listed in Part 10 of "Rules Governing Public Safety Radio Services" which constitute part of Volume V of the Rules and Regulations of the Federal Communications Commission. These allocations are constantly undergoing revision, not so much in assigned frequency as in technical standards and allowed usage. Whenever a new frequency is desired, the latest revisions should be checked to determine the current status of police allocations. As of August, 1959, a total of 96 frequencies were available for municipal police use in the 40 mc. and 155 mc. ranges, and 38 additional frequencies existed for such use in the region between 453.05 to 458.95 megacycles.

Paragraph 10.255 of the rules, listing the frequencies available to police, states that all frequencies from 1610 kilocycles to 2490 kilocycles now in use by the police may be subject to change when the Atlantic City table of frequency allocations below 27.50 mc. comes into force. Having been forewarned in 1949, the majority of departments that formerly used these medium frequencies have converted their equipment to the very-high frequencies allocated to police services by the Commission. As of 1960, there were still a few medium-frequency AM police radio stations in use, primarily operated by county and state agencies.

Recent FCC rulings have established a large number of "Radio Services" with a corresponding increase in the number of channels required. This brought about the creation of new channels by sandwiching them between existing ones. As a consequence technical standards governing the stability of transmitters and the bandwidth of their emission were tightened. In addition, specific deadline dates were established to enable the various agencies to amortize their equipment over a period of years. The common name for these rulings is "Split Channel Regulations." Specifically these rules state that the transmitter should be 10 times better in regards to frequency stability than it was before, the bandwidth should be one-third the previous width, and certain other technical standards should be met. The deadline for the reduced bandwidth was August, 1960. The final deadline for stability, pertaining only to old equipment, is October 31, 1963. Needless to say, newly purchased equipment must meet these standards.

In the past it has been the practice of small municipalities to use one frequency for both police and fire, and sometimes for other city functions. With the establishment of the "Local Government Radio Service" frequencies it is now possible to have all non-public-safety functions licensed for a separate radio system. The use of police frequencies to transmit fire department radio messages will become illegal as of October, 1963; however, regulations permit monitor receivers in order to coordinate fire and police activities.

Upon first glance at the FCC frequency allocation table it may seem that there are many more frequencies for police use than are mentioned above. But upon closer examination, various conditions governing their use become evident. Certain bands are available only to state police; other wavelengths are not licensed for base stations; power limitations exist which permit only portable equipment on some frequencies; and certain allocations are authorized only if their use does not cause harmful interference.

As mentioned previously, competition for the use of radio channels is very keen. Only through some form of voluntary frequency allocation coordination among the organizations representing police interests before the FCC has there been success in assigning frequencies on a minimum interference basis.

Telephone Communications

A police department must have a means of communication in addition to its radio system. Even with a complete two-way radio there is need for: (1) a means for citizens to contact the police promptly; (2) a means of communication between policemen and headquarters in case of failure of the radio system and unavailability of a public telephone or for purposes of secrecy, for less urgent and more lengthy conversations, and for conversation with those at headquarters who do not have radio broadcasting and receiving facilities; (3) a means of communication to supervise the operations of officers by providing a check on their location. Most citizen communications needs are met by the public telephone system. A suitable network of call boxes meets many of the above-listed police needs.

Major Systems

The two principal elements in a purely local communication system are the call box and the headquarters telephone systems.

Call-Box System. The most economical method of providing a call-box system is to lease the service from the public telephone system. The call boxes provide telephone service for patrolmen when public telephones are not available. In several cities, including Philadelphia, police call boxes are left unlocked so that they may be used by citizens to report emergency conditions to the police. This plan has been highly successful in communities where it has been employed.

The supervisory function of the call-box system has been strongly urged. If the patrolman is required to call in at stated intervals from specific points there is assurance that he has at least covered his beat and is safe. Routine calls provide a minimum of supervision, however, and must be supplemented by the work of patrol sergeants and by study of the performance records of patrolmen. The weight of opinion is that if a call-box system can be provided at a reasonable cost it is probably desirable. The desirability increases with the amount of foot patrol, the size of the department, and the need for strict centralized supervision over policemen and patrol sergeants as well.

In at least one modern police department (Berkeley, California), a recall light system is used in conjunction with the police boxes and radio. In this city the officer on each beat is required to spend part of his time on foot patrol away from his car. Therefore, each time a radio broadcast is made the recall light and police box systems are used to contact the beat officer in case he is out of hearing of his radio receiver.

The city-owned call-box system for police use was a preferred method of signaling before the widespread use of police radio. The cost of the installation and maintenance of such a system nowadays, however, is considered prohibitive in most cities. In fact, in recent years some cities have abandoned their private call-box systems because of the prohibitive operating costs and have substituted regular telephone service. The use of telephone company-owned call-box systems is becoming increasingly popular.

Before installing call-box facilities the department should investigate the relative costs and adequacy of service that could be provided under these different arrangements. There should not be overlooked, also, the possibility of including in the telephone company franchise a provision for free transmission of police alarms and reports.

Headquarters Telephone System. A fact not commonly known is that the telephone company will undertake a survey free of charge to determine the adequacy of trunk lines coming into the police department. It can be safely said that most police departments do not have adequate telephone facilities. Ordinarily, when a citizen calls police headquarters he is reporting an emergency situation, or at least a situation which seems to him to be an emergency. If he is baffled time and time again by receiving the busy signal on the telephone, he cannot help but feel that police service is inadequate.

In addition to the provision of ample physical facilities for handling peak telephone loads coming into the police department, there must be promptness in answering police calls. As mentioned above, a citizen calling headquarters wants immediate service. If the phone is allowed to ring a number of times before the call is answered at the police station, the citizen receives the impression of a lack of interest in his individual problem. Promptness in answering telephone calls may be stimulated by effective supervision of communications personnel. It is a problem deserving the serious attention of the police administrator.

Extensions are provided from the PBX (private branch exchange) switchboard to the various police officers at headquarters and to district stations. There should be tie-lines to the fire department headquarters, city hall, and to some other city-leased private branch exchanges in the community. For example, a tie-line may connect the city hospital or any institution, public or private, with which the municipality may have an arrangement for ambulance service.

In the large city with district police stations it is important that all calls be routed to the central complaint room to strengthen control and thus assure effective disposition in the shortest possible time. In order to make every possible provision against unnecessary delay in the receipt of a call for police service, arrangements should be made for the designation of a telephone number of characteristic and easily remembered numerals for the central complaint room. Chicago, for instance, employs "POLICE 1313," and New York City uses "SPRING 3100." The cooperation of the local press and radio should be secured to publicize the number at every opportunity. District stations should not be listed in the telephone book.

The use of other intradepartmental communication should not be overlooked. The police headquarters building in Berkeley, California, is an outstanding example of modern interoffice communications: an interoffice sound system and a light system for calling officers have been installed. Where there are district stations, teletype may be used to transmit orders from central headquarters. Within the headquarters building physical transfer systems may even be installed such as pneumatic tubes and dumb-waiters for the transfer of messages and records between offices and floors.

Communications in the Small Department. The small police department has neither the need for, nor the ability to finance, an elaborate communications system. The advantages of one-way radio can often be obtained by arrangement with a neighboring municipality, the county sheriff, or the state police to transmit police messages which are telephoned to them. The only cost which the city need then incur is the installation of receivers in police cars and the cost of telephone calls to the dispatcher.

When police are not radio-equipped or have a number of foot patrolmen, a recall system is desirable. This can usually be arranged by installing red signal lights on conspicuous buildings in the city.

When someone is not on duty at headquarters at all hours, arrangements should be made with the local telephone operator to act as "communications officer." When it is impossible to reach headquarters, she should be instructed to operate the recall system and transmit any complaint or information to the patrolman when he is reached. This plan is not feasible, however, with the dial system. Another possibility is to have calls received by some other city department where someone is on duty 24 hours a day, as for example, a municipal light plant, sewage disposal plant, or water works.

Small cities, unable to justify sufficient personnel to keep the police station open 24 hours per day, can switch police telephones to a nearby police radio station. The dispatcher can then transmit the messages to the police cars on duty.

In order to signal to officers in police cars while they are on foot patrol or other assignment, a red light can be installed on top or inside the police car which can be turned on by the dispatcher by means of a selective calling device. By remaining within view of the police cars, the officers may determine at once when they are needed.

Interregional Communication

Thus far the discussion has been limited to communication within the city — or at most within the metropolitan area if a regional radio system is operated. But criminals respect no such boundaries. Their activities may range over a whole state or several states. If the police are to be effective, they must provide for the free interchange of information between departments. Interregional communication has been developed by means of three instruments: teletype, radiotelegraph, and the Speedphoto transceiver.

Teletype

The telephone-typewriter system is an electrically operated typewritten communication service which transmits printed messages over telephone wires from a sending teletypewriter machine to a similar receiving instrument. The sending device may be so arranged as to cause the message to be received simultaneously by all machines directly connected with the circuit, by a group, or by any individual machine.

The teletype system which is quite reliable in its constancy of operation, has particular value in that it produces a written record which is reserved for the eyes of the police alone. By the installation of a return-light apparatus and telephone panel, a check upon the receipt of the message may be effected and the presence of mechanical trouble indicated. A high degree of certainty in the transmission of messages is attained by this method.

Separate teletype machines are used to send and receive messages. While larger departments will want both sending and receiving facilities, smaller police forces will require only the receiving set, inasmuch as occasional outgoing messages can be telephoned to a department with sending equipment. Sending equipment should be installed only in the central complaint room of a department.

The first state-wide police teletypewriter system was installed by the Pennsylvania state police on December 23, 1929. There are today 128 police departments connected together in the New York state teletype network. The California Department of Justice is the nucleus for a comprehensive police teletype network which now comprises 251 stations.

The interstate aspects of police teletype systems are also important. For example, the Pennsylvania state teletypewriter system is now an integral part of a 14-state teletype network comprising 1,000 points of communication, thus establishing an extensive regional police communication system. The California teletype system provides direct teletype connections to the state police in Medford, Oregon, the police and sheriff's department in Reno and Las Vegas, Nevada, and the sheriff's department in Yuma, Arizona.

The realization of maximum results in the operation of a teletype system requires careful planning and supervision. Only certain classes of police information should go on the teletype. Alarms, such as murders, manslaughters, robberies, escapes, and burglaries, are usually broadcast by teletype. Under appropriate circumstances, other information may also be sent such as alarms concerning stolen automobiles or other property, missing persons, reports of unidentified dead, arrests of criminals, and unidentified recovered property.

The number of stations brought into the broadcast area in connection with any single alarm depends upon the importance of the information and its possible value to the stations informed. Rules must be formulated to regulate the composition of alarms, provide for uniform abbreviations, and designate the exact procedure to be followed in every predicable emergency or routine operation. Clear instructions should be given and carried out to prevent cluttering the teletype with unsuitable messages. Administrative check-ups should be made at periodic intervals to make certain that only those items which are properly the subject for teletype transmission are regularly placed on the system.

Adequate evidence is available in the statistical reports of the New Jersey and Massachusetts state police to demonstrate the service value of teletype. Open to the municipal police for the asking, the system has encouraged the cooperation of law-enforcement agencies on a regional basis in those states where the pioneering has been accomplished by the state police. Notable examples of teletype's emergency utility could be recited from the records of units employing it.

In a "Manual of Practices and Procedures — State Teletypewriter System" the California Department of Justice, under date of January, 1954, has set forth the definition of terms, authorized abbreviations, sample message forms, file classifications, and code signals which have been found necessary for the regulation and operation of the California system. This manual would be a useful aid to any agency contemplating a teletype installation or in need of regulatory refinements in the operation of its present system.

As with the police signal system, regular inspections and swift and competent repair facilities should be provided so that the maximum continuous service may be obtained from the teletype system. The advantages of the teletype over the radio are found in the greater accuracy, certainty, and permanency of its written record and in its secrecy — its messages are received only by those for whom they are intended.

Radiotelegraph

In 1937 a plan was formulated for a nationwide intercity police radiotelegraph system. Nine channels between 2804 and 7935 kilocycles were set aside by the Federal

Communications commission for this radio-telegraph network. Six of the frequencies are working channels and three frequencies are for calling purposes. In 1957 the network comprised 104 stations. This is an invaluable law enforcement communication system connecting 46 states, and far greater use should be made of this facility by all police agencies.

Description. The country is divided into zones which in most cases are the individual states. One station in the zone is designated as the key station, and all interzone or interstate police communications are transmitted through it. The other departments that desire intercity communication may route their messages through the key stations.

Telegraphy offers the advantages of greater speed and much lower cost than teletype. Successful experiments have been conducted with radioteletype, that is teletype using wireless rather than telephone for the transmission of the electric signals.

Each city should participate in any regional communication system available to it. If the area is served by teletype, equipment should be rented from the telephone company. In the event that teletype is supplanted by radiotelegraph, no loss will be sustained.

Among informal agencies of regional communication, amateur and naval reserve facilities should be mentioned. Though not a part of the ordinary system of police communications, their value in time of disaster can be great. The police department should plan to utilize such agencies in time of emergency.

The Speedphoto Transceiver

One of the most significant and certainly one of the most interesting advancements in scientific crime detection is the Speedphoto machine. Essentially this is a facsimile device which will send or receive pictorial matter. The most common use of Speedphoto is to get quick access to the FBI's massive file of fingerprints.

The transceivers produce either a negative or a positive of a size 7.5 by 9 inches. A law enforcement agency possessing a Speedphoto transceiver can telephone to another agency with a transceiver and converse about the request for assistance. Next, both transceivers are connected to the telephone line and the long distance operator is advised not to monitor the call. If the operator opens the key, as is ordinarily done to see if the parties have finished, the picture is fogged. What goes over the wire, instead of conversation, is a whining noise. The machine converts the lights and shadows of the photo into sound. The machine at the other end turns this noise back into a picture. These machines are extremely useful as a means of telephoning pictures of individuals, fingerprints, handwriting samples, and tire tracks.

Utilization. The police Speedphoto network came into being following the experimental use of news wire service facilities for the transmission of police photographs. The Speedphoto equipment is essentially the same as that used by the press wire services. The experiments were successful and engineers designed apparatus which could be standard police equipment.

The equipment is presently in use in New York, Chicago, Boston, Philadelphia, Detroit, Newark, Seattle, Columbus, Toledo, St. Paul, St. Louis, Baltimore, Los Angeles, Miami, New Orleans, and other medium-sized and large cities. Also in this network are the state police of New York, Connecticut, Michigan, Texas, the California State Bureau of Criminal Investigation, and the FBI. Some of the units serve a large territory. For example, St. Paul police make their equipment available to police anywhere in that region.

Cost. Speedphoto machines are expensive. If purchased outright they cost around $3,000. Usually they are leased for $100 per month. Law enforcement agencies unable to afford the purchase or lease price of a machine may be able to take advantage of the wire service equipment possessed by a local newspaper office. In considering the cost of such facilities, it must also be admitted that solving crimes has always been an expensive business. If police departments can step up the process of catching criminals they can save on the heavy cost of investigation.

Before Speedphoto, the fastest way of making a fingerprint check with the FBI was to send the fingerprints by air mail. By mail a considerable delay is inevitable and this time element is highly useful to criminals. By Speedphoto, fingerprints of criminals can be transmitted from any point in the country and can be received by the FBI in about 9 minutes. When the FBI receives fingerprints by telephone, the local police get a response, as a general rule, in less than one hour. This means that in less than one hour the police can many times accomplish what by older methods often took about one week. This represents a very sharp change of odds. The police can thus get off to a faster start and may be spared long hours of investigative work.

Some police officials look on the picture machine as a fancy toy, the most expensive substitute ever invented for the four-cent stamp. However, others regard Speedphoto as the most important improvement since the adoption of the police radio and the only major advance in many years. It will suffice to say that the picture network across the country has been operating and growing and its future use in important cases will become standard operating procedure for most law enforcement agencies.

Telephone Company Communications Services

Telephone companies are engaged in the provision of all types of communications services — telephones, of course, but also teletype, call boxes, and radio. Upon request, telephone engineers will study police radio and other communications problems at no cost to the prospective customer and, based on analysis of requirements, submit recommendations for an integrated system. In cases of existing systems, telephone companies have in a number of cases purchased the facilities, modernized them, and then rented the system to the police department. Under such arrangements the capital outlay and expense of maintenance, depreciation, and engineering are eliminated, and the monthly rates cover the provision of the entire service.

As a part of their customer service, telephone companies make available on a continuing basis complete maintenance as well as engineering reviews to insure that the system is kept abreast of developments in the communications field. One organization whose sole business is communications thus assumes the responsibility of providing complete and effective communications under the direction of the police department.

Police radio systems provided by telephone companies are of all types and sizes. One of the largest, operated by the New York state police, has 48 base stations and 422 mobile units. The Pennsylvania state police have a system of 76 base stations with 360 mobile units. The Newark, New Jersey, police department has three base stations with 99 mobile units. The Montgomery County sheriff at Clarksville, Tennessee, has but one base station with one mobile unit.

Place of Communications in Organization

The communication system has been considered thus far from the point of view of the line officer — the man working in the field and his supervisor — whom it serves. What about the administration of the system itself? How should it be set up? What is its place in the departmental organization?

Three aspects of communications must be distinguished: (1) maintenance of the physical equipment, (2) coordination of police work and dispatching of officers, and (3) preparation of original complaint records.

Maintenance activities will be carried on in the same way as maintenance of any other departmental equipment. In a large department, the maintenance division will take care of this function. In a smaller department, the particular arrangement will depend upon the personnel available. Maintenance of the radio transmitter, for instance, might be the task of a particularly qualified officer acting also as desk sergeant during the "dog watch," when there is little action. Or it might be arranged by contract with a local radio technician.

Location of Communications Unit

The location of the dispatching activities of the communications unit presents an interesting problem of interrelationships. Since one of the important tasks of the communications unit when complaints are received is to take appropriate action by dispatching officers or transmitting information to the proper division, the communications officer is in constant contact with patrol officers. But he is also the means of communication for other line divisions such as investigation, prevention, and traffic. Communications may, therefore, be considered an auxiliary service which should be organized on that basis.

Logical Assignment. Because the communications center prepares the original record of complaints received, it is recommended that it be located in the records division under the control of the records officer. This insures complete and accurate reporting and prevents possible suppression of complaints when such action might be considered advantageous by any line division which controlled the dispatchers. It is also convenient for the communications unit to be located physically in the records division where the communications officer has easy access to the records.

It may be thought that placing the records officer in charge of communications hampers the control of the heads of the line divisions who are concerned with effective and prompt dispatch and mobilization of men whenever an emergency occurs. The interests of the patrol, investigation, and traffic divisions can be protected to a very large degree by the careful formulation under the guidance of the chief and the commanding officers of the department of specific rules and regulations which will govern the communications officer in the mass of routine cases. Whenever a case arises which is not covered by the methods and procedures laid down in these regulations, it should be referred at once to the ranking officer at headquarters for a decision. In no case should the communications unit be decentralized by districts, with the possible exception of the call-box system.

To sum up, the arguments for attachment to the records unit have been stated as follows:

Desk sergeants or dispatchers (like records clerks who perform a service for all operating divisions) should be attached to the records division because they form a link in the records and reporting system. The control of communications by a central service agency instead of an operating division is essential to accurate crime accounting. Since the central complaint desk at which the desk officers are located should be an integral part of the records division layout, the supervision of these officers by the head of the records unit is both natural and easy....

Making dispatchers or desk sergeants responsible to the records division is protested by some police executives on the ground that such assignment violates the principle of unity of command by placing operating division subordinates under the control of two masters: the dispatcher and the commanding officer of a line division. This criticism would not be eliminated by assigning dispatchers to an operating unit, since dispatchers must serve the personnel of all operating divisions whether patrol, traffic, or detective. Actually, the dispatcher has no power of command in his own right; he merely acts for the commanding officer whose personnel is being directed. He may not depart from established policy and practice without consulting that commanding officer. Departmental regulations governing these matters, drafted with the participation of the heads of the operating divisions, will safeguard their interests. Unusual situations are referred by the dispatcher to the commanding officer in charge of headquarters.

Some departments assign dispatchers or desk sergeants to an operating unit, usually the patrol division. This arrangement does not alter the pattern of records that must be kept, but merely transfers certain records tasks to another unit; the same duties will be performed by these officers regardless of the division to which they are assigned.[1]

Small Departments. In the smaller departments, communication will usually be the responsibility of the desk sergeant of each platoon. In this case there will be no single communications unit, but the desk sergeant will be responsible to the officer in charge of the patrol division during his tour of duty. In the very small department communications will be the task of whichever officer is regularly assigned to headquarters duty. If headquarters is not continuously manned, an arrangement should be made with the local telephone company to have the operator contact officers when they are needed.

Communications Center

A central communications room in the headquarters building is required to house the terminal and broadcast control facilities of the entire department. Only in this way can effective patrol control be realized. Careful planning should be given this branch of the service which must serve or stand by ready for instant service every minute of every day. No reasonable provision which may anticipate an emergency is too costly, and no routine convenience designed to relieve the burden of eternal vigilance is too pampering, as an administrative act of foresight.

Facilities and Services. The communications center should provide adequate space for all of the necessary equipment. There will be the signal desk, as the terminus of the patrol box system, and its associated testing panel; the telephone company-owned private branch telephone exchange; the teletype sending and receiving machine; and the microphone and radio transmitter control devices, or remote control circuit instruments. There may be an automatic private (PAX) telephone system more or less closely associated with the communications center. A radio receiver to monitor the messages of an accommodating station will be necessary if the broadcasting is accomplished by another police department as the result of a telephoned alarm. If two-way radio is employed, a receiver will be required to pick up the messages from the cars. When it is desired to monitor state police alarms, still another receiver will be required to tune into them.

Arrangements must be made to receive the private bank and business-house alarms coming directly into headquarters from these sources. There must be a place for the fire alarm tapper. Telephone tie-lines to the city hall, fire department, ambulance headquarters, and any other departmental telephone company-owned private branch exchange should be provided.

---

[1]O. W. Wilson, *Police Records: Their Installation and Use* (Chicago: Public Administration Service, 1942), pp. 13-15.

Special Provisions. The operating continuity and safety of the communications center should be considered in determining its physical location. Bars may be wisely provided for the windows, and steel roll-down shutters for exterior and interior openings may guarantee continued service during a period of mob violence. Noise as well as dust may be eliminated, in large part, by double windows equipped with room silencers and air filters.

Walls and ceiling of the room should be acoustically treated because noise causes strain and mental fatigue, which may contribute to human errors. The teletype machine should be encased in a soundproof box and the patrol box registers similarly silenced.

The operating personnel should be trained in civility, clear enunciation, and alert service. Tact and resourcefulness will be required in handling the complaints of the citizens and in providing satisfactory police service. A control board to show instantly the location of radio cars is a necessity in most municipalities.

Central Complaint Room in Oakland. A larger police department naturally will require more complicated arrangements, although the principle of central handling of complaints is equally valid. The central complaint room established in the Oakland, California, police headquarters is the result of intensive analysis of the requirements of the communications system in a large city.

The station radio messages are transmitted to mobile units on one radio frequency. Mobile transmitters in patrol units operate on a second frequency, and other units, including detective cars and motorcycles, operate on a third frequency. This is a two-way radio system in that mobile units can only receive messages which are transmitted by the dispatchers. When the equipment was originally installed, a three-way system was considered but the plan was rejected because it was apparent that insufficient air time would be available for the station transmitter if officers in mobile units were permitted to broadcast messages to each other. All radio messages are recorded on a dictating machine which is actuated by broadcasts from the station and mobile transmitters. This method of keeping a log of messages has been approved by the Federal Communications Commission.

The radio room is located in an air-conditioned and sound-proofed room at police headquarters. Protection of the facilities was enhanced by locating it in a place which is almost inaccessible to the public and, further, by securing the door to the room with an electrically operated locking device which can be controlled only by communications personnel.

Four telephone operators and two radio dispatcher positions are arranged on one side of a long table. Mounted on the wall near the dispatcher positions are two large maps of the city. Both map installations contain numerous small electric light bulbs which are controlled from a three-position switch panel located between the two dispatcher positions. Each bulb represents one mobile unit. If the unit is in the field and is available for assignment, the bulb is switched to a green color. If the unit is on an assignment, the bulb is switched to a red color. The bulbs are located on the maps in relation to the patrol beats and assignment areas of specialized field units.

Street names are arranged alphabetically on a rotary drum file to indicate the beat number for any given street address in the city. A rotary file has been installed at each telephone operator position. Incoming calls for reception of citizens' complaints are received on telephone trunk lines which terminate in key cabinets. A telephone operator receiving a complaint writes the details on an assignment record sheet and specifies the number of the beat where the complaint originated. The date and time received are placed on the reverse side of the record by stamping the sheet in an electrically operated clock. The record sheet is then placed on a conveyor belt which carries it to the radio dispatcher positions.

The dispatcher selects the mobile unit to be assigned to the complaint and indicates the number of the unit detailed on the record sheet. After broadcasting the information, the dispatcher stamps the time of broadcast on the sheet. When the officer detailed to the complaint has finished with the investigation, he reports the information to the dispatcher who then writes a brief description of the disposition on the sheet and stamps thereon the time that the assignment was completed. The assignment record sheets are forwarded to the records section from which point the subsequent offense reports and records on supplementary offense reports are controlled.

The telephone operator position adjacent to the dispatcher positions maintains liaison with the other operators and with the dispatchers. In addition to serving as a relief dispatcher and telephone operator, he monitors the broadcasts from the fire alarm board and from nearby law enforcement agencies. He also handles the telephone and interoffice communication system messages between the radio room and other functional units of the department.

The sergeant in charge of the communications section has a desk in the radio room which is located in such a position that he has a complete view of the entire facility and can render any assistance or supervision that is warranted. A master control panel on his desk enables him to assist with or to control the telephone and broadcasting equipment.

A bank robbery alarm board is located in the radio room. When an alarm sounds, a member of the communications staff determines from which bank the alarm came by means of a small lighted bulb on the panel board. The name and address of each bank is listed on a name strip beneath each light bulb.

The Oakland teletype system consists of two transmitters. One is connected with the statewide teletypewriter circuit and the other one is connected to the two precinct stations and certain other divisions within the department.

Centralization of Communications

A trend to departmentalize the communications function is beginning to develop, especially in counties. Most such organizations are headed up by an administrative officer who is usually responsible to the managing authority of the governmental unit.

The communications administrator is responsible for the planning, operating, purchasing, budgeting and related functions of his department. He must have a clear-visioned appreciation of all the communications needs of the governmental organization he serves and must be able to instill in the employees under his jurisdiction the concept that communications is a service to the political entity as a whole.

An intelligently developed communications department will give maximum service at a minimum cost and will overcome some of the operational difficulties that crop up when a dispatcher may be faced with the dilemma of divided allegiance.

Communications Center in Monterey, California. In this city of 23,000 inhabitants the city communications center has been placed under the jurisdiction of the chief of police. This system carries out all city communication functions. The center is equipped with two switchboards that are side by side and so connected that either operating position may operate both boards. One board has four incoming police and three fire trunks and the extensions to the police offices, street boxes, fire offices, and three fire houses. The other board has seven incoming city hall trunk lines and the extensions to all other city offices. The switchboards are operated by two operators during business hours and by one operator after the city offices close. The operators dial all outgoing telephone calls. A bell signal in the police records office summons additional help in an emergency.

All of the municipal radio communication load is handled by the center. A microphone on a swivel is mounted between the boards and either operator may broadcast to the 39 mobile units. The transmitter can be operated with a hand or foot switch. All police and fire units and many other city units that coordinate with the protective services are two-way equipped.

An important center function is the dispatch of fire apparatus. A Gamewell transmitter and register is installed to the rear of the operating position to assist the operator. Kardex locators and a public-address microphone are associated with the register. Loudspeakers are installed strategically in the fire houses in addition to the customary gong and register.

The center handles about 22,000 radio broadcasts, 28,000 telephone transactions, and 35 fire calls each month. The coordination has proved effective and real savings have been made through:

1. Careful recording of long distance telephone calls.

2. Response of all firemen to fire calls due to the elimination of the necessity of a fireman remaining in the fire houses to answer the telephone.

3. Central coordination of all emergency functions when vitally needed.

Central Radio Terminal in Salt Lake City. A centralized communications system, even for a large city, permits considerable economy due to elimination of a technical staff with instruments and equipment for each city department having radio facilities. It also allows greater flexibility in using the facilities between departments and in protecting the service against equipment failures.

The radio terminal in Salt Lake City is an example of a centralized communications system for all departments in a city of about 200,000 population. The terminal building is located near the center of the area served. It has no contiguous buildings, and provision has been made to insure that contiguous buildings will not occupy adjacent space in the future. The building houses radio facilities that provide three-way radio service on different channels and to several city departments. It also contains testing equipment, a work shop, auxiliary-power unit, and a modern garage for installation and maintenance work on mobile units. Various departments perform their own dispatching from their respective headquarters and control the facilities at the terminal building by means of land lines.

Salt Lake City is using three-way radio, which means that each car can hear and talk with other cars as well as with central dispatchers. This method requires the cars and base transmitter to all be on the same frequency; it requires more training and discipline for car personnel than the two-way method whereby cars can only hear and talk with central dispatchers.

Because of the number of units, which are too many for one channel, two channels are used. All units on a channel may have three-way communication with units on that same channel but do not hear units on the other channel. Cars are put on a channel in accordance with the type of work they do. For example, one channel serves the fire department, police traffic division, police ambulances, municipal airport, signal system maintenance, and the traffic engineer. Another channel serves police plainclothesmen, police radio patrol, auto theft division, fingerprint and photography, juvenile division, and the antivice division. Each of these groups is doing a common type of work and they must work closely in conjunction with each other. Central dispatchers can work with either group separately or can talk to both at the same time. This permits the channels to operate independently and simultaneously, or to be tied into one single operation whenever that is required.

Police dispatchers normally handle one channel, each independently of each other, but can instantly talk on both at once for disseminating general information or to allow a single man to take over both channels for short periods when required. Some dispatching points, such as the municipal airport or fire department, are equipped only for the single channel with which they are concerned; other dispatching points are equipped to handle both. The automotive units of command personnel are equipped for both channels, so that these men may direct or participate in incidents on either channel. At the police dispatching room, both channels are continuously monitored by recording equipment, so that the actual voice-record of the system's operations is always available for review and preservation.

The heart of such a system is the control equipment and control lines from the various dispatching centers. At the terminal these controls may be switched at will to handle various transmitters and circuits. In this way, protection of service and expansion of facilities are always easily handled. The control system provides an "intercom" circuit joining all dispatching points so that they can easily talk with each other without going on the air, and it provides suitable indicators so that each dispatching point can know when it is in control of the air. Users on the same channel are interlocked, so that only one at a time can get control, and while normally the two channels are independent they are interlocked so that if any dispatching point is using both at once no other user can cut in until he is through.

At the terminal are also facilities for a low-frequency system for civil defense and auxiliary police service; this transmitter is licensed in the FCC disaster communications service. Facilities are provided so that this transmitter may be used to communicate with amateur stations and special mobile units in the area.

A few other noteworthy features at the terminal are the underground feed for power and for telephone cable, to eliminate radio interference and for increased mechanical protection; the provision of auxiliary power such that the station may operate indefinitely by generating its own power from gasoline; and the provision of receivers located at strategic points within the area but controlled from the terminal. The terminal provides communications from police dispatchers to police car units; from fire dispatchers to fire units; from municipal airport control tower to ambulances and fire apparatus operating in the field; from substations, alarm systems, and maintenance shops to all types of mobile units; and from civil defense centers to amateur mobile units and home stations. Altogether, 195 mobile units are handled, along with 14 fixed units, and numerous handi-talkie, walkie-talkie, and motorcycle sets.[2]

The Future of Police Communications

At this point it may be well to review the communication needs which were listed

---

[2]This section, except for the first two paragraphs, is from F. Clark Sanford (former chief of police at Salt Lake City), "Improving Radio Service Through a Central Terminal," *FBI Law Enforcement Bulletin*, May, 1954.

at the beginning of the chapter and to see to what extent the systems which have been described fulfill those needs.

1. Communication of citizens with police is adequately taken care of by public telephone. Some cities leave their call boxes unlocked and available for public use.

2. The most satisfactory means of communication from headquarters to policemen is radio. It makes possible the swiftest transmission of information and orders. In the absence of radio, a telephone recall system is almost indispensable, and unless the radio is two-way, regular reporting at call boxes is an essential means of supervision. The same is true wherever foot patrol is used.

3. The need for rapid communication of policemen with headquarters is again best satisfied by two-way radio. In the absence of such facilities, telephone is necessary.

4. Communication among law-enforcement agencies involves (1) regional police radio systems, (2) teletype, and (3) radiotelegraph.

5. Communication among headquarters officials is supplied by the telephone, other forms of interoffice communication, including such devices as pneumatic tubes, and teletype if there are districts.

Simplified systems for small communities have been suggested which involve use of radio transmission facilities of neighboring cities or state police, use of the telephone, and installation of simple recall systems.

Dependability in police communications is obtained by guarding against all possible emergencies. Duplicate equipment, independent sources of power supply, and composite systems of communication employing radio, private telephone, and public telephone decrease the reliance on specific pieces of delicate equipment and destructible wires and minimize the danger of breakdown.

Radio communication is sufficiently secret for most purposes, but where additional precautions are needed, telephone and teletype can be used. Radio, too, provides the speed that is indispensable to police work in a world of rapid transportation.

Means of communication are undergoing constant change and development, and only continuous and intensive study can keep one abreast of the technical and legal phases which affect the use of communication devices. No effort should be spared to maintain a modern and effective system, for communications can be a strong offensive weapon in the war of the police against crime.

New Developments

Police administrators and radio technicians should keep abreast with developments in the rapidly changing methods of communication in order to take advantage of the progress made in this important field of police endeavor. The police can be truly effective in their war against crime only so long as they remain alert to the latest technological advances and utilize all of the facilities which are practical.

Radio Teletypewriter Broadcasting. Although teletyping messages by radio has been used for several years by both military and commercial communication agencies, there is very little development of this means of communication in the law enforcement field.

A number of law enforcement agencies operate limited radioteletype systems over their own microwave facilities, among these being the New Jersey State Police, the

Washington State Police, the Virginia State Police, and possibly a few others. However, long distance radio teletype, although technically quite feasible, has not been initiated on a regular basis. A system such as this would have a greater message handling capacity than the present radiotelegraph network and would not require the trained radiotelegraph operators now needed.

Miniature Transmitters and Receivers. For several years technicians have been working toward the development of receivers and transmitters which routinely can be carried by foot patrolmen. Recently much progress has been made, and several companies are devoting their attention to this field. With the development of printed circuits and the use of transistors to replace radio tubes, undoubtedly the wrist watch radio will become a reality within the next few years. Present miniaturized equipment, although not exactly "wrist watch" in size, is sufficiently small to be carried on a person, the transmitter being clipped to the belt. It is expensive; the entire two-way unit presently (1960) sells for approximately $480. The receiving set which can be carried inside a shirt pocket is described more fully in the forepart of this chapter.

"Handi-Talkie" or Pack Transceivers. "Handie-Talkie" equipment has been on the market for several years. Most police departments, however, have been slow in adopting it. Essentially they are portable FM two-way radiotelephone packs that consist of a completely self-contained crystal controlled transmitter and receiver including battery power supply, antenna, and handset. Loudspeaker operation is provided for noisy areas. These pack transceivers will normally operate for 40 hours with one supply of batteries employed in a duty cycle of 8 hours operating and 16 hours off. They come equipped with carrying straps. Weather resistant carrying cases can be obtained as well as headsets, microphones, and auxiliary power supply for operation from either six volts direct current or 110 volts alternating current.

This equipment is especially useful in conducting police operations involving large-scale traffic congestion and civil disturbances. Pack transmitters have been found helpful also on "stake-out" work. The Cleveland police department has reported unusual success with this type equipment in dealing with merchandise thefts from automobile by narcotic addicts. Patrol officers made numerous on-view arrests, but the majority of all cases were lost in court because the patrol officers usually did not see the person arrested break into the car but did see him running away from a car and carrying merchandise.

Automobiles containing merchandise were observed by Cleveland police from concealed observation points by officers equipped with pack transceivers. Police pursuit cars were stationed five or six blocks away from the observation officers. The officer at the observation post transmitted information to the pursuit car when anyone approached the automobile which had been "staked-out." The pursuit car would approach nearer to the scene but would not make the arrest until directed to do so by the observation officer. The use of portable radio equipment was credited with reducing this type of crime from over 300 cases per month to an average of about 80 cases per month.

Selective Calling System. Interference created by increased use of the necessarily limited radio frequency spectrum threatens the usefulness of some channels. The basic solution to the problems of interference in the shared use of radio channels depends upon the development of more efficient means of transmitting information over a limited band of frequencies. However, most of the evils of interference can be minimized or eliminated by some form of selective calling system.

A selective calling system consists of a station coding unit which is attached to the transmitter and a receiver decoding unit attached to each receiver. Such a system permits calling each receiver individually or activating a whole group of receivers at one time. In police service, radio is used primarily for dispatching, and communication is desired primarily between a central station and several patrol cars. While the patrol car receiver must be on at all times, no mobile unit is actually in use more than a small portion of the time.

The receiver output then is largely composed of: (1) transmission to the patrol cars to which the radio belongs, (2) interference from other patrol cars sharing the same band, and (3) radio frequency noise, man-made and natural. Transmission to patrol cars which is of no concern to a particular car can be classed with the other undesirable reception as "chatter." "Chatter" causes driver fatigue.

In areas where the nuisance interference of "chatter" needs to be reduced, a selective-calling system can be used to silence receivers except when communication is desired. Reliability of communication is thus increased. When an officer in a patrol car is required to pay attention to all radio broadcasts in an area serviced by numerous police cars, it is inevitable that some messages will be missed. With a selective-calling system, he need hear only pertinent messages.

Further, when a message is directed to an officer when he is out of his car, he is likely to miss that call. If a calling system were used, he would find his radio on when he returned to his car and would know that there had been a message for him during his absence. He can then call in by radio for a repetition of the message. As has been pointed out previously, selective-calling systems can be used to turn on red lights on top of or within police vehicles or to operate other signal devices to attract the attention of patrol car officers.

In addition, selective-calling installations which operate on a two-way basis will undoubtedly become standard equipment in all police radio stations in order to silence station receivers used in monitoring point-to-point broadcasts except when a message is being directed to the particular station. Present-day radio interference and radio chatter has a deleterious effect on the efficiency with which radio dispatchers can perform their transmitting and other duties.

Television. Industrial closed-circuit television has become a reality and can be used to increase the efficiency of law enforcement and save large-city police departments thousands of man-hours every year. This was demonstrated for the first time by the New York police department. Using a small industrial television camera and a microwave radio link, the police transmitted images of the daily "line-up" of suspects from the police headquarters in lower Manhattan, where the "line-up" is conducted, to the department's Brooklyn headquarters, about seven miles away. At the Brooklyn end a large group of detectives and police officials witnessed the "line-up" on the screens of modified table model TV receivers.

In the Houston, Texas, city jail, eight industrial camera chains (camera and combination power supply, control, and monitor unit) have been used. Applications there include monitoring of cell corridors and work and recreation areas. In another instance, the same type of equipment was used by Los Angeles police to trap thieves suspected of stealing merchandise from a shipping platform.

Television can also be used for communicating photographs of wanted or missing persons and other pictorial information to district stations. It would also enable police commanders and other officials to address almost the entire police force simultaneously with any message of sufficient importance.

Public vs. Private Ownership of Police Radio Systems

One of the problems in radio communications facing police administrators today is whether the political entity should own and maintain the radio communications system or whether it should be sold to commercial interests and leased back to the police with a maintenance contract. A similar problem relates to the service and maintenance of police-owned radio equipment by private contract or by city employees.

The police should consider these problems carefully before engaging a private-ownership installation or private-maintenance contract. The primary question which must be answered is whether private ownership will provide the police service with workable communication facilities on an uninterrupted basis. Other questions which must be resolved are:

1. Can the commercial interest provide all the necessary facilities and maintenance service?

2. When will needed facilities and maintenance be provided?

3. What will be the plan for providing service during an emergency involving perhaps a disaster or war emergency?

4. What will happen to the maintenance program if the commercial interest becomes strikebound?

Continued study of the problems inherent in private service of police communications is needed to decide whether such ownership and maintenance is advantageous to the police service.

Communications and Civil Defense

Police communication is an important factor in civil-defense planning. Several communities and some states have already formulated plans to use the police communication system as an integral part of the civil defense communications network. Others are planning to use it as an adjunct to their civil-defense system. Such use of police communications facilities is of serious concern to the police administrator whose communication facilities are already frequently over-taxed by routine police business. He must consider how he may increase its efficiency so as to be able to render assistance to other governmental agencies in the event of an enemy attack or the occurrence of a natural disaster.

Of prime consideration should be the expansion of present radio facilities so that they may be utilized more fully in the event of emergency. The majority of communication systems are adequate for normal police business but experience has indicated that they do not have the capacity to deal with major disasters. Also, while most systems have some degree of protection against damage and breakdowns, few are protected against the type of destruction that could occur under war conditions.

Communications are so vital to every phase of civil defense that the police should take steps to protect and improve the services they have and expand these services as much as possible. Objectives have been offered by the Committee on Radio and Communication of the International Association of Chiefs of Police as a guide for the coordination of the police radio services in civil defense planning. The following paragraphs are a presentation of the committee's findings and conclusions.

Our first basic objective, that of expanding our present police radio system to the fullest extent and providing protection against damage by bombing or sabotage may be summarized as follows:

1. Proper supervision.
2. Efficient operating personnel and techniques.
3. Auxiliary power plants.
4. Providing operating facilities at remote controlled transmitters with alternate facilities for communication with these new operating points.
5. Expert maintenance and additional facilities for maintenance both as to personnel and material.
6. Auxiliary or duplicate base stations.
7. Decentralization and dispersal.
8. Mobile base stations.
9. Coordination with various other radio services.
10. Amateur radio and disaster radio services.

Supervision. To maintain the highest degree of day-to-day efficiency, a communication system must be constantly supervised by experienced personnel, possessing an over-all knowledge of all types of communications. Where several stations are operated as a part of a coordinated system covering several municipalities or state or county agencies, it would seem desirable in the interest of efficiency to appoint one supervisor, authorized to exercise complete supervision of the operational personnel of the entire coordinated system.

Operating Personnel. Radio stations, especially in the police service, should be operated by persons possessing extreme calmness when confronted with an emergency, thoroughly familiar with the geography and roads of his area, and who may give orders and directions with authority. He cannot be hampered during disaster operation by any other duties, such as answering or making telephone calls. He should have an assistant to make the necessary written notes and messages. Messages must be short, concise, and without unnecessary wordage. A simple code system might be desirable so as to cut transmission time to the minimum as well as for security reasons. As far as possible, only experienced operators should be used.

Auxiliary Power Plants. During peace time we are apt to depend entirely upon commercial electric power and many of our radio systems are without any emergency power source. Commercial power lines and generating plants are most vulnerable to damage; therefore, an emergency radio system loses its value unless a means of emergency power is available. The emergency power system should be sized so as to be able to carry the radio loads plus any required lights, continuously.

Operating Remote Controlled Transmitters. Some police radio stations are remotely controlled by means of leased telephone lines. Such circuits, often passing through telephone central offices and strung on overhead pole lines are extremely vulnerable to all sorts of damage. Some means of operating such remotely controlled transmitters directly from the transmitter point should be established. Experienced personnel at the operating point and a means of linking the transmitter location with headquarters, or alternate headquarters and civil defense control centers, other than by wire, should be provided.

Maintenance. Most public safety radio systems are maintained by full-time technicians, well equipped with suitable testing equipment and tools. However, there are a great many smaller systems where maintenance is provided under contract with a radio shop, sometimes located in a distant city. Failure of a radio system so maintained, during a serious disaster, may pose a very serious problem. Those in charge of such radio systems should determine how quickly repairs could be made to their system. Some improvement might be indicated in the interest of civil defense. Perhaps an auxiliary base station transmitter or several spare mobile units, as well as spare tubes, vibrators, etc., for quick replacement in radio cars would provide the added safety factor in maintaining uninterrupted radio service.

Auxiliary Radio Equipment. Duplicate or auxiliary base station transmitters and receivers are most important, especially in the larger departments. Serious consideration should be given to establishing such a duplicate base station at a decentralized point. Auxiliary equipment should include everything necessary to establish an auxiliary base station. Transmitters and receivers are only a part of the equipment necessary. Portable antennas, power generators, spare parts, etc., are all necessary. Such auxiliary and spare equipment should, of course, be decentralized.

Decentralization. The importance of dispersal and decentralization of emergency communications equipment should be given careful consideration. In view of the present world crises, it is absolutely essential that careful thought be given that such emergency equipment be dispersed to points outside of any possible bombing target area. In the event of such decentralization, the following factors should be considered:

1. A good radio location.

2. Well outside the possible target area.

3. Sufficient room to handle the estimated number of persons who may report there.

4. Emergency power units including spare units.

5. Proper heating, sleeping, and kitchen facilities with a good stock of food, blankets and fuel for both heating and emergency power units.

6. Sufficient radio equipment to handle police, fire, and auxiliary radio systems in the area. Liaison radio channels with the military, Red Cross, civil defense control centers, civil air patrol, and commercial radio stations should be considered by police if such liaison is not available through the local civil defense control center. The disaster radio service using the 1750-1800 kc. band should be considered for this purpose. Amateur radio operators are an excellent source of manpower for operating the many radio channels required for such a program.

7. Spare parts for all equipment should be stocked and one or more radio technicians on duty. A sufficient number of telephone and teletype circuits should be provided, served from two telephone exchange areas if possible. Such a place should be capable of complete radio operation, should commercial power or telephone facilities be destroyed. Consideration should also be given to the fact that it might be necessary to maintain such a place for a number of years; therefore, some degree of permanency should be considered.

8. Frequent drills should be provided. Everyone participating should know his job to perfection. Complete secrecy should be maintained. Only those actually assigned to the decentralized communications center should have knowledge of its location. It would be well, where such places are available, to choose a place removed from main roads and nearby residences. Protection against sabotage and fire must be maintained. Some sort of fire and unlawful entry alarms should be installed and an adequate guard system maintained.

Mobile Radio Communications Units. Mobile radio trucks operating as base stations should be equipped with some telephone facilities so that temporary lines can be connected when possible. In some cases, facilities for a small switchboard may be desirable. Desk space for a commanding officer should be considered.

Coordination With Other Radio Services in Civil Defense. Complete coordination of, and liaison with, all the radio services not only within a community but also at the area, state, and interstate levels is a most important factor in establishing an efficient civil defense communications system. To acquire unity of purpose, fullest utilization of available radio channel space and to provide speedy, accurate, communications, all of the facilities must be completely coordinated. This may be accomplished at the community level by the public safety services monitoring each other. This is already a well established practice in many radio systems. This plan should be carried out right up through the area level as well as the state and interstate levels.

Amateur Radio for Auxiliary Police Communication. The radio amateur can be of great assistance by using the amateur frequencies designated for civil defense participation. Many of the radio amateurs are willing and able to provide experience and equipment to establish auxiliary police and civil defense communications channels to tie in the community with the area, state and interstate levels. They should be encouraged.

The Federal Communications Commission has issued rules and regulations for a disaster radio service. One of the requirements to license a station in this service is, among other things, that it be a part of an organized network, capable of coordinated, unified operation in time of disaster. Police Radio Control points could use this service for liaison with Civil Defense Control Centers.[3]

---

[3] John A. Lyddy, "Report of Committee on Radio and Communication," *The Police Yearbook, 1953* (Washington, D.C.: International Association of Chiefs of Police, 1953).

Protecting the Communications Center Against Disaster

The radio facilities of the Los Angeles County sheriff's department are an excellent example of a communications system designed to be fortified against unpredictable catastrophes. Every practical precaution against loss of radio communications in time of emergency has been taken.

The sheriff's department operates 250 vehicles and two airplanes, and these units are dispatched through a partially underground, reinforced-concrete communications center. The center facilities are complete and comfortable and stocked with provisions so that the staff can continue operating without leaving the center during an emergency.

Administrative officials responsible for coordinating relief work can receive and review reports in a disaster communications center in one part of the building. Telephone lines have been installed to reduce the radio traffic load under emergency conditions.

Other parts of the building accommodate a radio operating room, a complete drive-in service and repair shop, an emergency engine-driven generator, and offices for the staff. An auxiliary antenna, ready for operation, has been installed underground. Hydraulic pressure can be applied to raise it to a height of 50 feet above the ground. In order to cover the large area served by the sheriff's department, three remotely controlled base stations are operated from the central communications center. Because of the vulnerability of overhead wires, the three remote stations are controlled over separate microwave spans. A radio alarm signal announces the approach of a trespasser at the communications center.

In the event it is necessary to abandon or increase the facilities of the center, an emergency mobile communication center can become operative immediately. The mobile center has a 250-watt station, monitoring receivers, space for conferences, sleeping accommodations, cooking facilities, and a one-month supply of provisions. Electric power is provided by two three-kilowatt generators. When the unit is in motion, the 30-foot sectional antenna is carried inside the trailer.

Chapter 12

RECORDS

Accurate and complete police records reveal in words and statistics a picture of most police problems and activities, at least such parts of police work as contribute to the protection of life and property and to harmonious human relationships. Such records should reflect the need for police service and the effort of the police to provide the needed service. It is imperative, therefore, that all incidents reported to the police be promptly and correctly recorded for current reference and review and for subsequent analysis.

The nature of police work justifies emphasis on criminal records, but records of other essential activities of the department must also be maintained. Together these records assist in the intelligent supervision and review of the work of the department and provide the necessary requisites of judicial proof.

To be fully effective a police records system must: (1) be comprehensive and include every police incident; (2) be adequately indexed to permit ready reference; (3) be centralized to provide adequate control and maximum utilization of clerical personnel; (4) be as simple as is possible, consistent with adequacy; and (5) lend itself to summarization and analysis to permit periodic appraisal of police services. Such a system will permit police records, reports, and analyses to be used as significant tools of management, supervision, control, policy-making, and operation.

Records in Police Administration

When it tries to recall events, the human mind loses a considerable number of the details. For this reason, among others, it is important that an accurate written record be made immediately. The report should be sent forthwith to a central records division where it should receive a serial number, be indexed, and be placed in the appropriate file. Such procedure places all records under unified control.

Prompt submission to the records division of a copy of each report also reduces the possibility of collusion and alteration of the records by operating personnel. Further, a record of events, when freshly made, is more likely to reveal the spontaneous responses of the witness than a report which is days or hours old — into which may creep the unseen hand of an interested lawyer, conniving politician, pleading friend, or the fear of hurting an interested party whose potential influence was at first unknown. Prompt reporting will prevent many of these potential irregularities.

Unless data are recorded in a logical and systematic way, it is impossible to fully coordinate large masses of facts, especially if those facts are gathered by a number of persons. Most of the information which enables a police department to find the perpetrator of a crime would be utterly useless if not recorded uniformly and integrated by a system of records. Information gathered in investigations, therefore, must be promptly recorded, indexed, and filed as part of a total system which facilitates further investigation. Indexes make possible the rapid access to such information and the accurate identification of property and persons.

Records and Administration

Records are a means of supervision and control over police officers. Suitable follow-up assures proper action in each case. The performance of officers in preventing crime, making arrests, and observing conditions on their beats also is reflected in the records system.

Basis for Analysis. Without records and a regular system of reports, those in charge of administering a police department cannot have a complete picture of the activities and needs of each unit. Since records provide a ready means for the analysis of the internal and external problems of the department, an administrative officer must be supplied with means to see a problem at close range and to understand its requirements thoroughly, or his supervisory control is diminished severely. Generalities in orders do not serve to accomplish results in police work any more than in other service units. Instructions must be clear, concise, and authoritative.

Performance and Trends. An adequate records system will yield the reports which reflect the status of the department. Records will tell the administrative head what his department is accomplishing and what kind of job it is doing — the quality of the work as well as the quantity. Until such facts are known to the proper supervisors an effort cannot be made to correct errors and prevent failures. Records will show what has happened in the past and will reveal the trends which are so important in the diagnosis of forthcoming needs and the formulation of plans for future growth.

A major value of a police records system, then, is that it permits responsible officials to face facts and study reality. After that, effective action is in their hands.[1]

Records Division

A central records division to which original or authentic copies of all reports are transmitted without delay establishes the basis for an indispensable form of administrative control. A master file, once begun, can be employed to follow through on investigation reports and the disposition of any police matters. In addition to preventing an inquiry from being pigeonholed and forgotten, this system provides a control feature which is a constant stimulus to prompt and effective police service. The head of the central records division should hold rank equal to that of other division heads since he will have occasion to be in touch with them regularly, and his effectiveness would suffer if he were of inferior rank.

The records will be used by all divisions of the police service — investigation, patrol, traffic, vice, and juvenile — but they should be centrally maintained and administered. Only in this manner can complete control be secured and full access to records be guaranteed to all branches of the service. If separate copies of records are wanted by a special division (or outside agency) arrangements can be made to supply them, but in no case should the administration of the records be decentralized. Since identification records

---

[1] The procedures set forth in this chapter are based primarily upon the records systems installed in numerous cities by Public Administration Service, 1313 East 60th Street, Chicago, and upon those outlined in O. W. Wilson, *Police Records: Their Installation and Use* (Chicago: Public Administration Service, 1942), 336pp.

will be included among the central files, identification activities also should be performed by the records division.

Police records are essential to the success of operating divisions. At any hour of the day or night the records division should be accessible to a responsible officer who is well acquainted with the filing system. For this reason, a central location is preferable.

Every member of the force will contribute in some degree to the records of the department. To assure maximum uniformity the system should be as simple and understandable as it can be made, consistent with adequacy. Unnecessary complexity in records and reports is wasteful of time and may defeat the primary purpose of the record.

What information is to go into records and the precise procedures for preparing, indexing, routing, and filing them should be stated in regulations governing reporting and records operations.[2] These should be prepared by the records division and issued as general orders by the chief of police. This is essential since the records division is dependent for adequate reporting upon officers who are not subject to its direct control. Training programs should acquaint officers with the operation of the records system and should provide instructions for improving note-taking and report-writing.

Classes of Police Records

Police records, other than administrative records, may be divided into three general classifications: (1) case or complaint records; (2) arrest records; and (3) personal identification records. The case or complaint record is the master record, and the arrest and identification records are geared to it. Each is numbered serially; therefore, there are case numbers, arrest numbers, and identification numbers.

Case Records. This record contains information regarding complaints and reports received by the police from citizens and other agencies, and actions initiated by the police. In addition, any property records and correspondence relating to a particular case are filed with it.

Arrest Records. These originate at the time of booking. In this classification are all records relating to the control of prisoners, court procedures, and release of prisoners.

Identification Records. These consist largely of the fingerprints, photographs, criminal history records ("rap sheets"), and personal and descriptive data of arrested persons.

In addition to the three basic types of police records there are also miscellaneous records which include departmental memorandums, sick leave reports, reports of special services, maintenance reports, and possibly some others. The most common police records in descending order of their importance are indicated in Figure 25.

Case Records

The case record is the heart of any police records system. It is concerned with recording crimes and other incidents reported to the police and is used for controlling investigations through the filing of additional reports. It is the basis for an analysis of offenses and the methods by which they are committed.

A case records system is necessary to assure satisfactory disposition of each case.

---

[2] *Ibid.*, pp. 272-87, contains the records operations of one department as an example.

	CASE RECORDS	ARREST RECORDS	IDENTIFICATION RECORDS	MISCELLANEOUS RECORDS
Essential in every department.	Case sheet Investigation report Daily bulletin	Record of arrest Prisoner's property receipt Citation	Fingerprint card F.B.I. criminal history sheet	Department memo Note on bulletin Sick report Daily summary
Important but not essential in departments of fewer than 20 men.	Radio log Motor vehicle accident report Preliminary report Auto larceny report Bicycle larceny report	Police court disposition Federal and state court disposition Cash receipt Daily jail sheet Motor vehicle intoxication report	Description card	Follow-up indicator Call sheet Personnel status record Special service report Daily attendance record
Less important; essential only in departments of more than 50 men.	Persons wanted form Receipt for property Property record	Prosecution report Defect notice Held for investigation	Photo description stamp	Daily vehicle report Beat assignment sheet Traffic beat card
Useful but not essential to records system; desirable in departments of more than 50 men.	Case memo Auto receipt	Cash book Notice to court clerk Commitment and order for release Moving violation warning Parking violation warning		Detective summary Patrol sergeant's daily report Monthly patrol report Juvenile case history sheet Monthly vehicle maintenance report Store report Vacation home report
Optional; still less needed.	Daily polygraph report Polygram envelope Laboratory report Reassignment sheet	Request for internment Injured prisoner report Prisoner's personal property report	Photo order	Bicycle registration card Property registration Traffic engineering report Work order Tire report Charge-out slip

Figure 25 -- Common Police Records

An incident calling for police action is reported, usually by telephone; essential facts are briefly recorded on scratch paper or a memo blank; officers are dispatched; the facts known at this time are typed on a case sheet; and a résumé of the incident is recorded on a daily bulletin.

The dispatched officers record all information regarding the incident and the results of their investigations in notebooks. Before the end of their tour of duty, they prepare investigation reports summarizing in a concise manner all of the facts concerning the case, recording on the report the case number which they ascertain from the daily bulletin. Then the investigation reports are sent to the records office where they are attached to the case sheet. The case is indexed, inspected by the follow-up officer, and filed.

Case Sheet

The case sheet (Figure 26) is the basic record of offenses and has three major purposes: (1) it serves as a foundation or base on which to build the record of the case, since all other items are attached to it; (2) it aids as a control device by recording assignment and follow-up information; and (3) it records statistical information in a uniform, readily obtainable manner.

A single copy of the case sheet is all that is necessary in those departments having no specialized divisions, although some small departments make duplicates and use them for the daily bulletins. In larger departments, it is desirable to have duplicate sheets for those cases assigned to a specialized division such as the detective or juvenile division. At the time of its preparation, the original copy of the case sheet is routed to the records division where it serves as the beginning of the file on the case. In those cases where a

CASE SHEET

INCIDENT	CLASSIFICATION	CASE NO.

Victim ....Prelim. rept. by..
Address ....Ph...............Spec. invest. ....
Business or institution...Other officers..
Address ....Ph...............Detective ....
Where committed ....
When ....Persons arrested..
How ....
....
....Arrested by.....................................Date...............................
....Connect with Case No..
Person suspected...
Reported by ....
Address ....Ph...............
Reported to...Platoon and beat..
Time reported...Patrol officer received complaint by: Radio ☐   Box ☐
How reported: Ph. ☐   Person ☐   Letter ☐   Telegram ☐   On view ☐   At station ☐   Citizen ☐

Property stolen: Duplicate to...
                                 Classification index card corrected:
                                 Cleared by arrest....................Date....................Clerk.............
                                 Property recovered—Val. ....Date....................Clerk.............
                                 Unfounded ....Date....................Clerk.............
                                 Classification changed.............Date....................Clerk.............
                                 F. U. officer notified................Date....................Clerk.............

Indexed	*Inspected*	*Closed*
Clerk	F. U. Off.................	F. U. Off.................
Date	Date	Date ....

Figure 26 — Complaint Sheet (8″ x 5″; may also be 8-1/2″ x 11″)

duplicate is prepared, the duplicate is routed to the specialized division that will perform additional work on the case. Larger departments may require still additional copies.

Need for Uniform Reporting. Uniformity in classification is essential for reporting and other statistical purposes. The following five-part classification is recommended:[3]

Part I cases: Reports of offenses listed as Part I crimes in *Uniform Crime Reporting Handbook*.[4]

Part II cases: Reports of offenses listed as Part II offenses in *Uniform Crime Reporting Handbook*.

Part III cases: Reports of lost and found persons, animals, and property.

Part IV cases: Casualties, including traffic accidents,[5] other accidents, suicides, bodies found, sick cared for, and mental cases.

Part V cases: Includes all cases that do not come within the first four categories. Included are requests from citizens and public and private agencies that require some police action; general orders; special orders; and violations of rules and regulations.

When To Use? All occurrences in the following categories should be recorded by the preparation of case sheets.

---

[3] *Ibid.*, pp. 255-66.
[4] United States Department of Justice, Federal Bureau of Investigation, *Uniform Crime Reporting Handbook* (Washington, D. C.: FBI, 1960), 55pp.
[5] The classification developed by the National Safety Council should be used.

1. Warrants, subpoenas, and arrests[6] in which a record of arrest is prepared, with the exception of multiple arrests for which a single case sheet suffices.

2. Calls on which officers are dispatched, except those which are merely requests for information which result from traffic violations not endangering life or property, or which are handled by a special service report.

3. Violations of federal and state laws and city ordinances (except traffic violations recorded by citations) reported by citizens or other agencies or known in any other way by a police officer. Exceptions are made for city ordinance violations which are observed by the police (not those reported to them) in which action consists only of a warning which is accepted without protest.

4. Cases of lost and found persons, animals, and property.

5. Automobile accidents, personal injuries, bodies found, suicide and suicide attempts, and damage to public property.

6. Cases in which a police officer is involved in any way in the damage of public or private property or the injury of any person.

7. Miscellaneous cases, general orders, special orders, violations of rules and regulations, and any case on which a commanding officer desires a case sheet.

A separate case sheet is required for each crime or incident. It makes no difference whether the complaints are reported by telephone, by letter, in person at the public desk, to an officer on duty, or otherwise. The case sheets are registered by stamping a serial number on each; when so registered the case sheet becomes a part of the records system. There should be a consecutive series of numbers to be assigned by the desk officer. The serial number identifies each case and all other papers and reports relating to it and serves as a basis for filing.

The desk officer receiving the call need not obtain detailed information from the complainant but should merely secure the information needed to prepare the case sheet.

Daily Bulletin

A daily bulletin is needed to keep all members of the force informed concerning police operations, assignments, and administrative instructions.

The bulletin should carry a brief résumé of each numbered case, the name of the assigned officer, a description of missing persons and persons wanted, and information of general interest to members of the department. It should be an up-to-the-minute,

---

[6] Some departments, in order to minimize records work, use the record of arrest as a combination case sheet, record of arrest, and investigation report on minor Part II arrests. This practice is not desirable for the following reasons: (1) Frequently, the arrest marks the start of the investigation, rather than the completion. If no provision is made for follow-up and additional investigation reports, arresting officers will be prone to discontinue their investigation prematurely. (2) No provision is made for filing additional investigation reports as may be written. If they are filed with the arrest record, the arrest record file becomes a combination arrest record and case file, which is undesirable. If a copy of the record of arrest is used as a case sheet, with a case number assigned, an irregular and clumsy procedure is being substituted for a uniform practice of preparing a case sheet. (3) Classification index cards prepared from the case sheets are used in tabulating data for summaries and monthly reports. These tabulations will not be complete unless index cards are made on each case. To locate arrest records in those instances where case sheets are not made in order to prepare classification index cards involves more time than preparing the case sheets in the first instance. (4) Since such Part II crimes as kidnapping, arson, forgery and counterfeiting, and embezzlement and fraud are sufficiently serious to justify an intensive investigation, a case sheet must be prepared in these instances. It is difficult to designate those offenses which should be recorded on a case sheet and those for which case sheets are not prepared.

running account of all matters of police interest and should be made up continuously as cases are reported so that it will be as nearly current as possible.

The officer who prepares the case sheets may produce the daily bulletin on a typewriter as cases are reported and case sheets executed. In this manner, the daily bulletin becomes a chronological cross-reference to the case file. An appropriate number of copies may be made, using thin paper, so that each division in the department may receive a copy.

In large departments the daily bulletin may be duplicated by mimeograph or some such process, each officer then being presented with a copy when he reports for duty. The volume of cases in these departments makes impractical the recording of events on the daily bulletin. Consequently some other device is then needed to assure that officers are notified of their assignment to cases. In departments with district stations there is need for a supplementary bulletin to inform district personnel of police operations in their jurisdiction. As mentioned above, in small departments an additional copy of the case sheets may be used as the bulletin.

Investigation Reports

When the investigating officer has made inquiries concerning a case, taken necessary action, and obtained the available facts, he must report his findings and action. He normally does so by preparing a written report. Investigation reports may be prepared on blank paper of the same size as the case sheet, although some departments have a specially designed investigation report form (as shown in Figure 27) upon which to record

PRELIMINARY REPORT

Date........................CASE NO..................

Victim ....
Residence address.................................Phone...............
Business or institution...
Business address..................................Phone...............
Where committed...
Person attacked...
Property attacked...
How attacked...
Means of attack...
Time of attack..
Object of attack..
Trade-mark ....
Vehicle used...
Details of offense:

Persons suspected

Has persons-wanted form been made?

Persons arrested

Description of property stolen

Value $
Disposition of property: (Including tag no.)
Carbon copy to detective div. ( )

....Officer

....Date and hour

Figure 27 — Preliminary Report Form
(8″ x 10″)

If a preliminary report to fit into an 8″x5″ file is desired, the form used is 8″x10″ and folds to 8″x5″; another commonly used size is 8-1/2″x11″.

Figure 27 — Preliminary Report Form
(Reverse)

This is the reverse of the Preliminary Report, which is printed to be turned up from the bottom.

the details of certain types of offenses. Printed investigation report forms insure a more complete report, for the captions serve as a guide to the officer and may even assist him in the direction of his investigation. An investigation or progress report on blank paper with appropriate notations in the heading showing the case number, date, and heading of the case, may then be used to report all subsequent facts relating to the investigation. Each officer should submit an investigation report if he does any work or has any information on any complaint regardless of whether he is assigned to it or not; or, if he is assigned to any case, regardless of whether he has done any work or has any information on it. An officer by assignment to a case should make an additional report on the case either at the end of each tour of duty or at a specified date, even though the results were negative.

Dictation Equipment. The use of dictating equipment to facilitate reporting by investigating officers is becoming increasingly popular. Some departments have arrangements that permit patrolmen to report the results of their investigations by telephone, the information either being recorded or taken down immediately by a typist equipped with a telephone headset. Substantial time can be saved by detectives through the use of dictating equipment. With increased salary costs and payments for overtime work, the use of such equipment is an economy. A records division typist may be assigned to transcribe the reports in readiness for signature by the reporting officer at the end of his tour of duty.

Outline of Content of the Investigation Report. Because of the necessity of securing complete information on the investigation report, an outline similar to the following should be utilized as a guide to assure uniformity.

I. Synopsis

A brief resume which will permit a supervising officer to determine in a general way the subject matter of the report by reading the first sentence.

II. Detailed Facts
    A. Facts as observed by the officer
    B. Facts as reported to him by witnesses
    C. Opinions of citizens
    D. Descriptions
       1. Description of property
          a. Article
          b. Trade name
          c. Material
          d. Form
          e. Physical measurements
          f. Sensory description
          g. Design
          h. Identifying marks (letters, numbers, etc.)
          i. Condition (including age)
          j. Value
             1. Cost
             2. Present value
       2. Description of persons
          a. Name
          b. Sex
          c. Color
          d. Age
          e. Height

        f. Weight
        g. Build
        h. Hair
        i. Eyes
        j. Complexion
        k. Occupation
        l. Nativity
        m. Beard
        n. Dress
        o. Marks
     3. Modus operandi

III. Results

    A. Analysis
    B. Conclusions
    C. Recommendations

IV. Disposition: Temporary or Final

    A. Property
    B. Persons: suspects, prisoners, injured
    C. Case

V. Final Interview with Complainant[7]

The original copy of all investigation reports should be routed to the records division to be attached to the case sheets; the duplicate copy should be routed to and retained by the specialized division which has charge of further investigation on the case.

Special Forms. Some police departments use special forms for auto thefts, bicycle thefts, burglaries, and other classes of offenses. These forms are of value as guides for collection of information of pertinence in the investigation of a certain type of offense.

Such forms also expedite the classification and processing of cases susceptible to being fully reported on by the preparation of one form. For example, the Berkeley, California, police department has devised a miscellaneous service complaint form (Figure 28) that is designed to accommodate a report on a variety of called-for services. The reverse side of this form has space for a brief report by the officer assigned and for review by the sergeant. Officials of this department estimate that this form is executed in 18 to 20 per cent of all reports made to the police which require field investigation time.

Case File

As soon as case sheets are prepared, all of the investigation reports and other documents dealing with a case are clipped together or assembled in a folder. This accumulation of records is called the case file and is one of the principal features of a satisfactory records system.

Once assembled the method of filing case records may vary with the size of the form which, in turn, is influenced by filing cabinet size. Some departments use letter-size complaint forms and employ letter-size manila folders in their case files. Others, using 5 x 8-inch forms, staple or clip the various reports together in the file without

---

[7] This outline has been adapted from lecture notes supplied by William A. Wiltberger, director, Police School, San Jose State College, San Jose, California, as quoted in Wilson, *op. cit.*, pp. 67-68.

MISCELLANEOUS SERVICE COMPLAINT   No.

NAME_____Address_____Phone_____
       (First)   (Middle)   (Last)
                                                                  Date & Time
Location_____Plat._____Beat_____Report Rec'd_____

IF CONDITION IS NOT TRULY REPRESENTED EXPLAIN UNDER 'DETAILS'

Conditions Reported
INSTRUCTIONS: This form shall not be used for: Missing Persons; Where an arrest is made; Where property is lost, found or taken into custody, other than routine auto tows; Where supplemental reports are necessary; Casualties resulting from motor vehicle or traffic accidents, falls of persons on city streets, suicides or attempted suicides, dead bodies or where criminal acts are involved.

1. ☐—Noise abated. Caused by ( ) auto; ( ) dog; ( ) party; ( ) poultry............
2. ☐—Domestic complaint, non-criminal, settled to satisfaction of complainant............
3. ☐—Suspicious circumstance (indicate nature under 'details')............
4. ☐—Civil Matter (indicate type under 'details')............
5.*☐—Taken to Hospital by police ambulance (name of ambulance crew)............
6.*☐—Taken to hospital by Officer............
7. ☐—Suspicious auto; investigation indicated report unfounded............
8. ☐—Frightened person............
9. ☐—Suspicious person. Responsible interviewed; report unfounded............
10. ☐—Miscellaneous Traffic (explain under 'details'): NS............VC............Car towed............Tag No............
11. ☐—Locked out; aided in gaining ontrance............
12. ☐—Bonfire. ( ) extinguished; ( ) has necessary permit; ( ) unfounded............
13. ☐—Police protection requested while complainant removes clothing/property............
14. ☐—Suspicious noise............
15. ☐—Service to householder (indicate type under 'details')............
16. ☐—Miscellaneous surveillance (indicate type under 'details')............
17. ☐—Hazards (dangerous condition), non-traffic............
18. ☐—Outside Departments' requests for assistance (indicate type under 'details')............
19. ☐—............

*On reverse side show complete names, addresses and ages of injured and cause of injury.

Signed_____No._____

OFFICER ASSIGNED_____By_____   Date & Time_____
314-710 10M 10-59 (Berkeley Police Department)

Figure 28 — Miscellaneous Service Complaint, Berkeley, California

folders. A few departments file the more lengthy records in folders or envelopes and staple or clip the records of less bulk. The results are the same; the most convenient method should be used. Case records are filed according to the serial number assigned to the original complaint. This serial number is used on all investigation reports, arrest records, index cards, and other materials referring to the case.

Accident Records

The casualty sheet (Figure 29) is prepared by the desk officer on reports of suicides, dead bodies found, sick people attended, mental cases, accidental injuries, and, in some departments, traffic accidents. The casualty sheet serves the same purpose and is filed in the same manner as the case sheet previously mentioned. The desk officer assigns a serial number to the report and posts the case on the daily bulletin.

The Accident Report. In order to provide more specific and uniform information on automobile accidents and to provide a basis for further study and analysis, a special report form is used for recording information on traffic accidents (Figure 30). This may be size 8-1/2 x 11 inches or 8 x 10 inches to be folded to 8 x 5 inches. Ordinarily the accident report will serve as the investigation report of the officer who investigates the accident. This report should be prepared for each traffic accident — fatal, nonfatal injury, or property damage — in addition to the casualty sheet which is prepared by the desk officer.

Some departments do not prepare a casualty case sheet on traffic accidents but use a duplicate of the accident report made by the officer for control purposes and assign a serial number.

CASUALTY REPORT		Case No.	
Kind			
Victim	Age	Investigators	
Address	Phone	Number Injured	
		Number Killed	
Date & Time Occurred			Day
Where Occurred		Platoon	Beat
What & How Occurred			
Reported by		Removed to	
Address	Phone	Removed by	
Reported to		Attended by	
Date & Time Reported		Ambulance Crew	
REMARKS			
Dispn.	By	Date	

Figure 29 — Casualty Report (8″ x 5″)

In the case of an accident occurring between intersections, if a nearby intersection was in any way a causal factor, the accident record is filed as of that intersection. If, however, the accident had no relationship to any intersection, the record is filed immediately behind the primary divider bearing the name of the street on which it occurred according to block number. In other words, all between-intersection accidents on Fairview Street will be filed according to block number immediately behind the primary divider for Fairview and in front of the accidents which have occurred at intersections on Fairview Street.[8]

Fees for File Search. Many cities are charging fees for producing information from police records for attorneys, employers, insurance companies, and other organizations, agencies, or persons having good reason to seek such information. Most cities began charging for such service when they recognized that the cost of finding and producing such information was mounting. Requests for accident report investigations are the most frequently furnished reports for which a charge is made.

Accident Location File. An accident location file makes available for analysis the reports of accidents that have occurred at a certain location. Since most automobile accidents occur at intersections, cards are placed in the location file by names of streets intersecting instead of by street names and numbers. The names of the streets are arranged alphabetically on the primary dividers. A copy of the investigation report of an accident that has occurred at an intersection is filed behind the primary divider bearing

---

[8] For a complete treatment of this topic see National Safety Council, *Filing City Traffic Accident Reports by Location*. Single copies free.

POLICE REPORT OF MOTOR VEHICLE TRAFFIC ACCIDENT

National Safety Council Chicago

TIME / LOCATION

DATE OF ACCIDENT ...., 19 .... Day of Week .... Hour .... A.M. .... P.M. ....

DO NOT WRITE IN THIS SPACE

No. ....

PLACE WHERE ACCIDENT OCCURRED: County .... City, town or township .... State ....

If accident was outside city limits, indicate distance from nearest town .... miles ☐ ☐ ☐ ☐ of .... North S E W City or Town

ROAD ON WHICH ACCIDENT OCCURRED .... Give name of street or highway number (U.S. or State). If no highway number, identify by name.

AT ITS INTERSECTION WITH .... Name of intersecting street or highway number

IF NOT AT INTERSECTION .... feet ☐ ☐ ☐ ☐ of .... North S E W Show nearest intersecting street or highway, house no., bridge, RR crossing, alley, driveway, culvert, milepost, underpass, or other landmark.

VEHICLE NO. 1

VEHICLE .... Year Make Type (sedan, truck, taxi, bus, etc.) License Plate .... Year State Number

Parts of vehicle damaged .... Vehicle removed to: .... By:

OWNER .... Print or type FULL name Address .... Street or R.F.D. City and State

DRIVER .... Print or type FULL name Address .... Street or R.F.D. City and State | AGE | SEX | INJURY

Driver's License .... State Number / Regular Operator's License ☐ / Other Type License ☐ / Specify Type and/or Restrictions / Date of Birth / Month, Day, Year

Total number vehicles involved ....

OCCUPANTS
Front Center .... Name Address .... Street or R.F.D. City and State
Front Right .... Address
Rear Left .... Address
Rear Center .... Address
Rear Right .... Address

VEHICLE NO. 2 or PEDESTRIAN

VEHICLE .... Year Make Type (sedan, truck, taxi, bus, etc.) License Plate .... Year State Number

Parts of vehicle damaged .... Vehicle removed to: .... By:

OWNER .... Print or type FULL name Address .... Street or R.F.D. City and State

DRIVER (or Pedestrian) .... Print or type FULL name Address .... Street or R.F.D. City and State | AGE | SEX | INJURY

Driver's License .... State Number / Regular Operator's License ☐ / Other Type License ☐ / Specify Type and/or Restrictions / Date of Birth / Month, Day, Year

OCCUPANTS
Front Center .... Name Address .... Street or R.F.D. City and State
Front Right .... Address
Rear Left .... Address
Rear Center .... Address
Rear Right .... Address

FIRST AID GIVEN BY: .... Injured Taken to: ....

DAMAGE TO PROPERTY OTHER THAN VEHICLES .... Name object and state nature of damage
Name and address of owner of object struck ....

CODE FOR INJURY (Use only the most serious one in each space for injury.)
K—Dead before report made.
A—Visible signs of injury, as bleeding wound or distorted member; or had to be carried from scene.
B—Other visible injury, as bruises, abrasions, swelling, limping, etc.
C—No visible injury but complaint of pain or momentary unconsciousness.
O—No indication of injury.

WITNESSES | AGE | SEX
Name .... Address
Name .... Address

Form Traffic 1 (Police) 1958 REP. 100M105909 TURN THE PAGE – COMPLETE BOTH SIDES Stock No. 321.16

Figure 30 – Motor Vehicle Accident Report Form (8-1/2" x 11")

KIND OF LOCALITY
(Check one)
- [ ] Apartments, Stores, Factories
- [ ] One-family homes
- [ ] Farms, Fields
- [ ] No marginal development

ROAD SURFACE
(Check one)
- [ ] Dry
- [ ] Wet
- [ ] Snowy or Icy
- [ ] .... Specify other

LIGHT CONDITIONS
(Check one)
- [ ] Daylight
- [ ] Dawn or dusk
- [ ] Darkness

ROAD TYPE
(Check one or more)
Driver		
1	2	
[ ]	[ ]	1 driving lane
[ ]	[ ]	2 driving lanes
[ ]	[ ]	3 driving lanes
[ ]	[ ]	4 or more lanes
[ ]	[ ]	Divided roadway
[ ]	[ ]	Expressway, parkway, toll road

WEATHER
(Check one)
- [ ] Clear
- [ ] Raining
- [ ] Snowing
- [ ] Fog
- [ ] .... Specify other

TRAFFIC CONTROL
(Check one or more)
- [ ] Stop sign
- [ ] Stop-and-go signal
- [ ] Officer or watchman
- [ ] R.R. gates or signals
- [ ] .... Specify other
- [ ] No traffic control

ROAD CHARACTER
(Check two)
- [ ] Straight road
- [ ] Curve
- [ ] Level
- [ ] On grade
- [ ] Hillcrest

WHAT DRIVERS WERE GOING TO DO BEFORE ACCIDENT

Driver No. 1 was headed [ ] [ ] [ ] [ ] on ....
           North S E W   (Street or highway)

Driver No. 2 was headed [ ] [ ] [ ] [ ] on ....
                                          (Street or highway)

Driver 1 2 (Check one for each driver)	Driver 1 2	Driver 1 2	Driver 1 2
[ ] [ ] Go straight ahead	[ ] [ ] Make left turn	[ ] [ ] Start in traffic lane	[ ] [ ] Remain stopped in traffic lane
[ ] [ ] Overtake	[ ] [ ] Make U turn	[ ] [ ] Start from parked position	[ ] [ ] Remain parked
[ ] [ ] Make right turn	[ ] [ ] Slow or stop	[ ] [ ] Back	

WHAT PEDESTRIAN WAS DOING   [ ] Along

Pedestrian was going [ ] [ ] [ ] [ ]   Across or into .... From .... To ....
                               (Check one) N S E W   (Street name, highway No.)   (N.E. corner to S.E. corner, or west to east side, etc.)

- [ ] Crossing or entering at intersection
- [ ] Crossing or entering not at intersection
- [ ] Getting on or off vehicle
- [ ] Walking in roadway—with traffic
- [ ] Walking in roadway—against traffic
- [ ] Standing in roadway
- [ ] Pushing or working on vehicle
- [ ] Other working in roadway
- [ ] Playing in roadway
- [ ] Other in roadway
- [ ] Not in roadway

CONTRIBUTING CIRCUMSTANCES

Driver 1 2 (Check one or more for each driver)	Driver 1 2	Driver 1 2
[ ] [ ] Speed too fast	[ ] [ ] Passed stop sign	[ ] [ ] Other improper driving
[ ] [ ] Failed to yield right of way	[ ] [ ] Disregarded traffic signal	[ ] [ ] Inadequate brakes
[ ] [ ] Drove left of center	[ ] [ ] Followed too closely	[ ] [ ] Improper lights
[ ] [ ] Improper overtaking	[ ] [ ] Made improper turn	[ ] [ ] Had been drinking

SHOW NORTH BY ARROW

INDICATE ON THIS DIAGRAM WHAT HAPPENED

Street or highway

Street or highway

Street or highway

DESCRIBE WHAT HAPPENED:
(Refer to vehicles by number) ....

....

....

....

....

....

POLICE ACTIVITY   [ ] A.M.

What was the source of accident information?

Time notified of accident .... [ ] P.M.
           Date   Hour   (Officer at scene, No. 1 driver contacted station, both drivers contacted station, etc.)

Arrests

Name .... Charge ....

Name .... Charge ....

Other action taken: ....

SIGN HERE ....

         Officers rank and name   Badge No.   Department   Date of report

Printed in U.S.A.

Figure 30 — Reverse Side

SPECIAL SERVICE REPORT

Beat No.............Date ....Hour .... A.M. P.M. Officer ....

Location ....Date ....Hour .... A.M. P.M.

TO RECORDS DIVISION:
Please notify the proper agency of the condition checked ☐   The proper agency was notified by beat officer ☐

BUILDING DEPARTMENT:
No Permit: Signs ☐   Construction ☐   Moving structure ☐   Tents ☐   Wrecking building ☐; Dust-producing material not wet down ☐   Awning interferes with pedestrians ☐.   Signs: Illegal ☐   Dangerous ☐   No permit ☐   In parking ☐   In "AB" residence districts ☐   Rag sign over public property ☐   Swinging sign ☐.   Moving Building: No permit ☐   Permit not signed by: Bldg. Insp. ☐   Park Director ☐   City Eng. ☐   Supt. of Streets ☐; In congested area ☐   Pavement damaged ☐   Stakes in pavement ☐   Improper barricade ☐   Improper warning signs ☐   Improper lighting ☐.   Fire Escape: Defective ☐   Dangerous ☐   Blocked ☐   No exit light ☐.   Public Assembly Exits: Locked ☐   Swing in ☐.   Rooming House: Rope: Defective ☐   Absent ☐   Improperly secured ☐; No direction placard ☐   No fire extinguisher ☐   Inside room ☐   No vent gas stove ☐   Only one exit ☐.   Construction: Street ☐   Sidewalk ☐   Curb ☐   Is damaged ☐   Blocked ☐; Improper: Barricade ☐   Warning ☐   Lighting ☐.

FIRE DEPARTMENT:
Gasoline stored ☐   Defective tank trucks* ☐   Fire hazard (list details) ☐.

HEALTH DEPARTMENT:
Duct emits fumes, dust, waste, grease ☐.   Food: Not protected ☐   Displayed outside ☐   Trash spilled in hauling* ☐.   Garbage Wagon*: Leaking ☐   Spilling ☐   Not covered ☐.   Dead Animals Transported*: Uncovered ☐   Daytime ☐.   Huckster* with wares uncovered ☐.   Dumping: Trash ☐   Vegetable matter ☐; Sewer stopped up on private property ☐   Unsanitary conditions ☐   Scrub water on sidewalk or street ☐.   Stock: Hogs ☐   Billy goats ☐   Other stock in viol. ☐.   Milk trucks not marked ☐.   Weeds a hazard ☐.

PARK DEPARTMENT:
Trees: Down ☐   Dangerous ☐   Need attention ☐   Low branches ☐   Branches fallen ☐; Damage to parking ☐   Cars on parking ☐.   Children playing games on school lawns ☐.

STREET DEPARTMENT: Defective street ☐   Dangerous ☐   Paving ☐   Curb ☐   Sidewalk ☐   Sewer ☐   Hazard ☐.

(Front)

FINANCE DEPARTMENT:
New business ☐.   Hand bills or samples: in cars ☐   to pedestrians ☐.   No License: Hucksters* ☐   Canvassers ☐   Distributors (samples, handbills, etc.) ☐   Vending machines ☐.   Produce truck checked* (list action taken) ☐.

DESICCATING COMPANY: Dead animal (list type)..

HUMANE SOCIETY: Animal mistreated ☐   Pick up animal ☐.

ELECTRIC COMPANY: Street lights out ☐.   Dangerous: Wires ☐   Poles ☐.

GAS COMPANY: Leaks ☐   Miscellaneous ☐.

WATER COMPANY: Leaking: Main ☐   Fire Hydrant ☐.   Valve box, meter box protrudes ☐.

MISCELLANEOUS:
Sweeping walk after hours ☐.   Washing windows after hours ☐.   Assistance to citizen (list nature) ☐.

TRAFFIC: Hazards ☐   J.T.P. needs instruction ☐   R.R. wigwag defective ☐.

CRIME PREVENTION DIVISION: Juveniles need attention ☐   Home conditions should be investigated ☐.

MAINTENANCE: Signs, signals, markings need attention (list under details) ☐.

DETAILS: ....

PERSON RESPONSIBLE: ....

ACTION TAKEN BY BEAT OFFICER: ....

***LIST INFORMATION ON VEHICLE:**
License ....Owner .... Address ....
Driver ....Chauffeur's license ....Address ....
Telephone notice to...of above agency.   Records Clerk................Date ....Hour ....

(Reverse)

Figure 31 — Special Service Report (8″ x 5″)

the name of the street the initial letter of which occurs first in the alphabet. If an accident, for example, occurs at the intersection of Fairview and Wooley Streets, the record will be filed behind the primary divider, Fairview, and then filed alphabetically according to the initial of the intersecting street. Secondary dividers bearing initials are added only when the number of cards is large enough to warrant them. It may be desirable to use secondary dividers bearing the names of cross streets at intersections where a number of accidents occur.

Miscellaneous Records and Reports

Other records are commonly used by many departments. The use of these miscellaneous forms will depend on (1) size of the department; (2) attention given to specialized activities; and (3) relative costs of forms and procedures. A brief description and summary will be given of some of the more important miscellaneous reports.

Special Service Report. A special service report (Figure 31) is used as a ready means of reporting conditions to be directed to the attention of other city departments. This is in keeping with the popular image that the police are the eyes and ears of the city and as such should render many special services. If officers report such conditions, other departments will be able to render better service and will be saved costly outlays by speedy action. The form is prepared by the officer in single copy, which goes to the records division. On receipt of the form, the records division calls the department concerned, describes the officer's observations, notes the time and person talked with, and files the copy.

Vacant Home Reports. Many departments inspect homes left vacant while the occupants are out of town. This service does not include inspection of unoccupied houses for sale or for rent. Citizens appreciate this service, which results in building a good sound relationship with the public in addition to serving as a crime deterrent. Departments usually inform their citizens of this service by newspaper notices, radio broadcasts, and departmental publications.

The preparation of a vacant home report, such as illustrated in Figure 32, is the responsibility of the complaint clerk. In the event the citizen notifies some other member of the department regarding his desire to have his home inspected by the police during his absence, information in sufficient detail to permit the preparation of the vacant home report is forwarded to the complaint clerk on a department memo.

The report is prepared in triplicate. One copy is filed by the follow-up officer under the date of expected return, and the other two are placed in a file subdivided according to the beats on the two night shifts. The latter file is kept by the complaint clerk for his own convenience and that of the patrol sergeants. The information as to vacant homes is noted on the daily bulletin, and patrol officers record in their notebooks those homes within their districts.

```
┌─────────────────────────────────────────────────┐
│              VACATION HOME REPORT                 │
│  Date of Departure..............Return..........  │
│  Name ..........................................  │
│  Address .......................................  │
│  Reported by....................................  │
│  Address .......................................  │
│  Reported to.................Date...............  │
│  In emergency, notify...........................  │
│  Address .......................................  │
│  Forwarding address.............................  │
│  Checked with officer by sergeant...............  │
│  Interviewed by sergeant, second platoon........  │
│  ...............................................  │
│  ...............................................  │
│  ...............................................  │
└─────────────────────────────────────────────────┘
```

Figure 32 — Vacation Home Report (5″ x 3″)

Store Reports. Store reports, such as that illustrated in Figure 33,

STORE REPORT

Store name...Address ....Beat ....

Manager ....Res. add. ....Phone....................

Asst. mgr..Res. add. ....Phone....................

Doors: adequate modern locks: front (Yes......) (No......); rear (Yes......) (No......); side (Yes......) (No......); adequate bars,
    grates, fastenings (Yes......) (No......). Windows: inadequate bars or grates: location....................................

Roof entry: none; adequately secured; inadequately secured; accessible; inaccessible..

Can officer easily reach all entrances without climbing fences, etc.?...

Is back yard lighted at night? (Yes......) (No......). Are blinds or shades raised so officer can see inside? (Yes......) (No......)

Safe: none; easily visible; poorly visible; concealed. Night light: none; over safe; not over safe...............................

Night watchman: none; private patrol; full time (name)..

Precautions taken against hold-up...

Alarm system employed..

Other protective devices...

Did you make personal investigation of points covered? (Yes......) (No......). Kind of store......................................

Suggestions made: Doors..

Windows ....Roof ....

Safe ....Night light..

List any miscellaneous suggestions on reverse...Officer..

Will your suggestions be followed? (Yes......) (No......) (Doubtful......). Date.....................................Hour..................

Figure 33 — Store Report (8″ x 5″)

serve a number of purposes. (1) They cause the patrol officer to make periodic contacts with businessmen on their beat in order to obtain the information. Policemen are sometimes reluctant to make such contacts, yet good public relations demand that the businessmen of the community be acquainted with the police. (2) They assure a periodic inspection of every commercial establishment in the city for the purpose of detecting and causing to be corrected such police hazards as improperly secured or barred doors, windows, and skylights; improper or inadequate interior and exterior lighting; safes and other valuables in a position where the patrolman is unable to see them easily from a window; and improper handling of cash, either when left on the premises at night or when being transported to a bank for deposit. (3) They provide the residence addresses and telephone numbers of the proprietor and his assistant should there be need for locating them in an emergency. To be fully effective, store report data must be kept up to date. This should be the responsibility of the day shift patrol personnel. In the event the proprietor is unwilling to comply with the protection recommendations, the store report is referred to the patrol sergeant who discusses the matter with the merchant. If the proprietor fails to comply with the sergeant's request, notation is made on the reverse of the store report, and it is forwarded to the records division.

Store reports are filed according to street number under the names of streets arranged alphabetically. The store report file is kept in a location convenient to the dispatcher in order that he may use information regarding the proprietor or his assistants in case of emergency at any hour of the day or night.

Arrest Records

The second major division of police records is that dealing with the arrest of

RECORD OF ARREST   Alien Nativity Race Sex Age   CASE NO.

Name ....
Address .... Platoon .... Beat.............
Date and hour of arrest.. Where arrested ....
Length of time in County.............State..........U. S...... Single ☐ Married ☐ Widowed ☐ Divorced ☐
Occupation .... Has prisoner been drinking? Yes ☐ No ☐
Charge ....

Arrested by .... Sight ☐ Warrant ☐ Other authority ☐
Booked by .... Trial date ....
Entered on daily bulletin by................................ Date and hour.....................
General index searched by.................................... Reported to ....
Previous record ☐ Traffic ☐ Wanted ☐ Not wanted ☐ Questionable ☐
Fingerprinted by .... F. P. file searched by............Rptd. to........
Previous fingerprint record ☐ Wanted ☐ Not wanted ☐ Questionable ☐
Circumstances of release ....
Release authorized by .... Date and hour ....
Court clerk notified of change of charge by Ph. ☐ Notice ☐ By............ Date and hour........
Court clerk notified of trial date by Ph. ☐ Notice ☐ By............ Date and hour........
Disposition .... Date disposed of ....

In case of change of charge or trial date, booking officer shall notify court clerk by phone and notice (or by notice only if time permits) unless disposition sheet is still at desk, in which case change may be noted thereon, further notification then being unnecessary. At one hour before court session, booking officer shall determine that clerk has all necessary disposition sheets.
   Release may be authorized by booking officer except where fingerprints have not been taken when necessary or where search indicates prisoner is wanted or there is question of his being wanted, in which cases release must be authorized by commanding officer. Except in questionable cases F.P. file need not be searched. General index file must be searched before release.

ARREST No.

Figure 34 — Arrest Record (8″ x 5″)

offenders, their control, and disposition. The scope of arrest records covers every step from the initial booking of a prisoner to his release from custody of the police.

The Arrest Record

An arrest record (Figure 34) should be prepared at the time a prisoner is booked at headquarters. The arrest record should include the following information: name and alias of the offender; physical description; nature of the offense charged; the name of the arresting officer; indication of whether the offender was released, and whether such release was on paying of bail; and an arrest number. Some departments require that a single fingerprint of the offender be placed on the arrest record, to assure proper identification.

The arrest records are filed by arrest number and cross-indexed by name and all known aliases. The name and alias index cards should bear the fingerprint classification and be filed in the general index file described below. The arrest record also should carry the serial number of the case sheet.

In arrests where there has been no previous complaint, the desk officer will need to make out a case sheet and assign it a serial number at the time of booking.[9]

[9] For a complete procedure on handling arrest records, see Wilson, *op. cit.*, Chapter 4, "Records Relating to Persons Arrested."

UNIFORM TRAFFIC TICKET AND COMPLAINT

CASE No.................... DOCKET No........................ PAGE No.....................

YOUR STATE, COUNTY, AND CITY PRINTED HERE } SS.

| No. 00000 |

COMPLAINT

IN THE MUNICIPAL COURT OF...

THE UNDERSIGNED, BEING DULY SWORN, UPON HIS OATH DEPOSES AND SAYS:

ON THE..............DAY OF.., 19........., AT ....M.,

NAME ....
(Please Print)

STREET ....

CITY - STATE ....

BIRTH DATE...RACE.........SEX.........WT.......HT..........

DRIVER'S LIC. NO.., DID UNLAWFULLY (PARK) (OPERATE)

MOTOR VEHICLE (REG. NO.)............................ STATE................. YEAR.............

MAKE...................... BODY TYPE........................... COLOR...............

UPON A PUBLIC HIGHWAY, NAMELY AT (LOCATION)..

LOCATED IN THE CITY, COUNTY AND STATE AFORESAID AND DID THEN AND THERE COMMIT THE FOLLOWING OFFENSE:

Six Principal Causes of Accidents

SPEEDING (over limit) (........m.p.h. in ....m.p.h. zone)	☐ 5-10 m.p.h.	☐ 11-15 m.p.h.	☐ over 15 m.p.h.
Improper **LEFT TURN**	☐ No signal	☐ Cut corner	☐ From wrong lane
Improper **RIGHT TURN**	☐ No signal	☐ Into wrong lane	☐ From wrong lane
Disobeyed **TRAFFIC SIGNAL** (When light turned red)	☐ Past middle intersection	☐ Middle of intersection	☐ Not reached intersection
Disobeyed **STOP SIGN**	☐ Wrong place	☐ Walk speed	☐ Faster
Improper **PASSING AND LANE USAGE**	☐ At intersection ☐ Between Traffic ☐ Lane Straddling	☐ Cut in ☐ On right ☐ Wrong Lane	☐ Wrong side of pavement ☐ On hill ☐ On curve

OTHER VIOLATIONS (describe)..

IN VIOLATION OF the (statute)(ordinance) in such case made and provided.

PARKING: Meter No......................... ☐ Overtime ☐ Prohibited area ☐ Double parking

☐ Other parking violation (describe)..

Conditions that Increased Seriousness of Violation

SLIPPERY PAVEMENT	{☐ Rain ☐ Snow ☐ Ice}	**CAUSED PERSON TO DODGE** ☐ Pedestrian ☐ Driver	**IN ACCIDENT** ☐ Ped. ☐ Vehicle ☐ Intersection ☐ Right Angle
DARKNESS	{☐ Night ☐ Fog ☐ Snow}	**JUST MISSED ACCIDENT**	☐ Head on ☐ Sideswipe ☐ Rear end
OTHER TRAFFIC PRESENT	{☐ Cross ☐ Oncoming ☐ Pedestrian}	☐ one foot	☐ Ran off Roadway ☐ Hit Fixed Object

AREA: ☐ Business ☐ Industrial ☐ School ☐ Residential ☐ Rural
HIGHWAY TYPE: ☐ 2 lane ☐ 3 lane ☐ 4 lane ☐ 4 lane divided

THE UNDERSIGNED FURTHER STATES THAT HE HAS JUST AND REASONABLE GROUNDS TO BELIEVE, AND DOES BELIEVE, THAT THE PERSON NAMED ABOVE COMMITTED THE OFFENSE HEREIN SET FORTH, CONTRARY TO LAW.

SWORN TO AND SUBSCRIBED BEFORE ME

THIS........DAY OF...................., 19.........

....
(Name; and title)

....
(Signature and identification of officer or other complainant)

COURT APPEARANCE:...........DAY OF.................., 19........, AT..............M.,

ADDRESS OF COURT...

Figure 35 — Uniform Traffic Ticket

Citations

Citations (Figures 35 and 36) should be issued to all minor traffic violators (except those who are given written warnings) who are residents of the state and who are not guilty of driving with flagrant recklessness, under the influence of liquor or drugs, or of using a motor vehicle without the permission of the owner. These latter violators should be arrested and booked. The same rule can be followed for violators from other states which have reciprocal agreements by which operators' licenses will be suspended or revoked on failure to appear in court to answer to any traffic charge.

The citation form shown in Figure 35 is the Uniform Traffic Ticket prepared by the American Bar Association and used in many states. It should be noted that the citation form also provides information for the court. This is an increasingly common practice and has the advantage of saving the time and forms needed to provide separate information. Some citation forms are now being printed on a paper so sensitized that carbon paper is not required. As a result, it is easier for the officer to write the ticket, and he has no problem of disposing of the used carbon.

Form. Citations bound in books of 25 sets provide convenience in filing and for carrying in the pocket of the officer's shirt or blouse. They should be in triplicate or quadruplicate and should be used in conjunction with a control ledger with each line bearing a number to correspond to each citation serial number. When a book of citations is issued to an officer, his name is entered in the ledger to indicate responsibility for the corresponding block of serial numbers. He must then account for all of them. Suitable columns in the ledger facilitate the preparation of monthly summaries of citations served, nature of charges, and court dispositions. Citations in the form of punched cards (Figure 36) are now commonly used, making it possible to use tabulating equipment to provide monthly summaries more expeditiously and in greater detail and to follow up failure to appear in court. The same serial number system of control is used.

Processing. The procedures used in processing and accounting for citations vary greatly throughout the country, but several minimum criteria should be met. The system

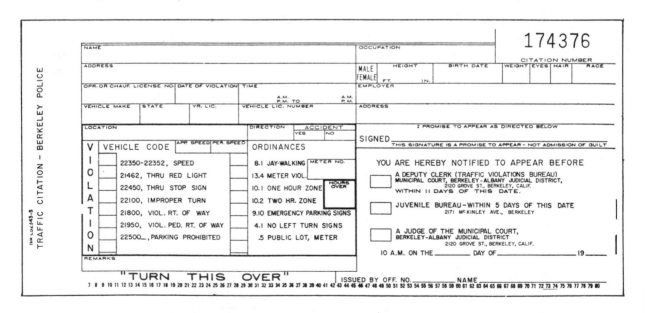

Figure 36 — Citation Form, Berkeley, California

should provide a permanent driving history of the offender, including a description of the offense and the disposition. It should assure that the case is disposed of in court. It should be fix-proof and should assure that points at which citations are being irregularly disposed of will be detected. Finally, the system should provide the court with the previous driving record of the motorist as a guide in disposing of the present case.

Citations Used for Other Violations. Citations may also be used in all minor cases of violations of ordinances if the identity of the violator is readily established, if he may reasonably be expected to appear in court, and if apprehension seems likely if the violator fails to appear. This procedure results in avoiding the unnecessary stigma of arrest and the necessity of transporting citizens who commit minor offenses. In addition to economy, the good will and public relations value of this device is a significant consideration.[10]

Other Reports Dealing with Arrested Persons

In addition to the arrest record, a number of other records are needed to assure suitable accounting and control of bail and fines, evidence, and of prisoners in custody.

For the control of prisoners, records should be used to assure: (1) the imposition of authorized restrictions on the privileges of prisoners (such as release on bail and communication with other prisoners and outsiders); (2) the placing of responsibility for such restrictions and for their removal when their purpose has been served, in order to lessen the danger of their abuse; (3) the accounting of prisoners in custody and their cell location, in order to discover and fix responsibility for the escapes and to aid in the investigation of reported mistreatment of prisoners which are sometimes initiated some days after the occurrence; (4) medical treatment for sick and injured prisoners and the protection of department interests in such cases; (5) the recording of court dispositions; and (6) the control of prisoners in transit from one lock-up to another. The use of these various reports is governed by conditions in the individual department. The physical location of the jail, size of the department, average jail population, jail regulations, and many other variable factors must be considered. For these reasons, no other arrest records are discussed here.[11]

Personal Identification Records

The third major division of police records embraces those records dealing with personal identification. Various devices have been employed to facilitate the recognition and positive identification of criminals.

Kinds of Records

Names and general descriptions do not suffice because false names can be substituted and many characteristics change with time or may be deliberately altered. When people remained in the community of their birth throughout their lives the problem of identity was not serious. Improvement of transportation makes it easy for people to move about; criminals may leave the community of their birth and lose themselves among strangers who know nothing of their character or reputation.

---

[10] Provision is made for some liberalization in the employment of a citation under such model codes as the Uniform Arrest Act (Section 9), the American Law Institute Code (Section 12), and the Federal Rules of Criminal Procedure (Rule 4a).

[11] They are discussed in detail by Wilson, *op. cit.*, pp. 94-116.

Bertillon System. The first substantial contribution to personal identification was made in the last half of the 19th century by an anthropometric system of classification devised by Alphonse Bertillon, whose name is commonly used to designate it. The theory of this system is that no two human beings are exactly the same size and that the human skeleton does not change appreciably after the 20th year. Measurements were made of the length and breadth of the head and of the length of the right ear, of the left foot, left middle and left little fingers, and the left arm and hand from the elbow to the top of the stretched middle finger. The height of body, width of outstretched arms, and sitting height were also taken, as well as the body weight. The Bertillon system is clumsy, time-consuming, and inexact, and it is no longer used. It has been replaced by the fingerprint system which is simpler and more exact.

Portrait Parle. Another contribution to personal identification made by Bertillon is called *portrait parle,* or spoken picture -- a clear word description. This system relies upon color, as of hair, beard, skin, and eye; shape, as of the head in its various parts and details; conditions and attributes, as of stoutness or thinness, voice qualities, body carriage, manner of dress, language facility and social position; and marks, such as tattooings, scars, moles, amputations, and deformities. The information generally recorded in this connection is the name, address, nationality, color, age, sex, height, weight, and occupation.

Portrait parle records numerous other details of appearance, mannerisms and habits, as well as place where the individual is likely to be found and a list of his personal associates. The portrait parle seeks to give an objective description of the criminal which will supplement the detective's memory for faces in identifying the criminal who is at large. It is still in use, with improvements, for this purpose.

Anatomical Descriptions. The department should develop index files of criminals according to physical description, scars, marks, missing or deformed parts of the body, and other unusual personal identifying characteristics. Tattoos are of particular value. Copies of index cards for persons missing and wanted should be included in this file.

Photography. Criminal photographs in profile and full-face, full length, and of groups of criminals, are valuable aids to officers who have good memories for faces. When supplemented by the portrait parle, the detective has information which can help him to pick up a wanted character on sight. Photographs also enable the victims and witnesses of some crimes to identify the perpetrator.

Photographs of criminals should be filed according to their criminal specialty in a visible-card file. It is desirable to place the photographs in order of date of birth because persons searching the file have at least a rough idea of the age of the offender. The reverse of the photographs can be used for recording a description of the subject, names and aliases, and the modus operandi most common to him. The same identification number employed on the fingerprint card is used for the photograph and appears on the index card. All prisoners who are fingerprinted need not be photographed; judicious selection reduces operating costs. [12]

Fingerprints

The fingerprint system is the most easily used and positive means of personal identification. Friction ridges on the finger and thumb tips (also found on the palms of

---

[12] For a complete discussion of photographing prisoners and other aspects of personal identification, see O. W. Wilson, *Police Planning* (Springfield, Illinois: Charles C Thomas, Publisher, 1958).

the hands and soles of the feet) furnish the means for this distinctive method of identification. It is believed that there are no two identical fingerprints; noted scientists have supported this view, and with hundreds of millions of prints on file (including those of identical twins) no one has ever reported the finding of identical patterns. Fingerprints are found on the four-month old fetus and are unchanged as recognizable patterns throughout life. The distinctiveness of fingerprints and the fact that they cannot be changed render the means of identification especially reliable.

Henry Classification. Although there are several systems of classification employed in reducing fingerprints to a simply expressed formula, the one devised by Sir Edward Richard Henry of the Metropolitan Police Force in London, published in 1900, is the basis for the system most commonly used in this country. The details concerning the classification system and its method of operation are available in the standard texts; time and space do not permit their exposition here.

The Henry system of classifying fingerprints, which is used with modifications and extensions in Great Britain, the United States, and other English-speaking countries, is based on the prints of all 10 fingers. The principal use of fingerprint identification is to identify persons who have previously been fingerprinted. By using the Henry classification it is possible also to compare latent prints left at the scene of the crime with those of known suspects whose prints are available.

Single Print System. Until recently it has not been possible by using a latent print left at the scene of the crime to make a search through large fingerprint collections in order to uncover the identity of an unknown suspect. This procedure, which obviously would be of great aid in criminal investigation, has awaited the development of a single fingerprint classification which would reduce the time and labor involved in comparing single prints. The Battley system of single fingerprint classification devised about 1930 by Harry Battley, a chief inspector of New Scotland Yard, London, gives promise of answering this need and providing the basis for single print collections. The increasing use of single prints only widens the scope of usefulness of this method of criminal identification. However, because of the time required to classify each of the 10 prints from a subject, single fingerprint files are usually limited to criminals who are likely to commit crimes where they will leave prints, for example, burglaries.

Latent Fingerprints. The police should give more attention to the search for latent fingerprints at crime scenes; they are frequently the principal evidence and are sometimes useful in identifying and convicting the criminal. Latent prints may be clarified by the use of special powders, liquids, and fumes; they may be preserved by photography, by lifting tape, or in their original state. Even though a single fingerprint file is used, latent fingerprints should also be filed according to the crime classification in a manner to permit easy reference by fingerprint technicians classifying current fingerprints. Copies of latent fingerprints should also be filed with the case.

Other Uses of Fingerprint Files. Fingerprints are employed chiefly for the identification of criminals but can be useful as well in the identification of dead bodies or persons suffering from amnesia and in cases of injury which produce prolonged unconsciousness. In such cases it is necessary, of course, that the fingerprints have been previously filed.

Clearance of Prints. All persons booked, with the exception of minor offenders not jailed and juveniles, should be fingerprinted promptly and their prints cleared through the Federal Bureau of Investigation at Washington and the state bureau of identification, if one exists. In this manner a valuable file may be built in the local department's bureau of identification to which immediate reference can be made for a suspect's criminal background. Immediate identification may be the means of connecting the suspect with a major crime committed elsewhere, though the subject may have been picked up only because of a minor violation. It is not ordinarily necessary to clear fingerprints through neighboring large-city departments.

Other Necessary Records

The criminal history and modus operandi files are valuable records. They help to solve many cases.

Criminal History File. The simplest, least expensive, and most readily searched criminal history file available in a police department consists of nothing more than the most recently received identification sheets from the FBI and the state identification bureau filed according to the local identification number. To maintain a letter-size folder in a filing cabinet for each fingerprint in the collection is expensive in terms of folder and filing cabinet costs and wasteful in terms of space. Material usually found in such folders belongs elsewhere. Extra photographs should be filed in the previously mentioned photograph file according to their identification number, and negatives belong in the laboratory or in or near the dark room, protected from deterioration and fire. Fingerprint cards should be filed by classification. Other material relating to the subject properly belongs in the previously described case file.

Modus Operandi. Because many criminals are known to have particular methods of operation (M.O.), it is often possible to classify criminals by their M.O. and sometimes to identify the perpetrator of a particular crime by the similarity between his M.O. and that used in other crimes with which he has been identified. For this reason, a growing number of police departments are maintaining *modus operandi* (Latin phrase for "method of operation") files in which the records of criminals who use similar methods are grouped and which can be searched to discover the perpetrator of a particular crime by its characteristics. The modus operandi system was first developed in the United States by the late August Vollmer, formerly a chief of police of Berkeley, California. The system has been used extensively in Europe, particularly in Great Britain.

The scope of the M.O. system as a method of identification is indicated by the type of information carried on the preliminary reports made by the investigating officers. The information that should be listed in the preliminary report and of value in a M.O. may be briefly summarized.

1. Date and time committed and the day of the week as exactly as possible. If the date or time is not known precisely, the interval during which the crime occurred should be shown.

2. Person attacked: the number of victims, their sex, age, and, so far as possible, their race and occupations. These entries are important because some criminals operate against a certain sex, age group, race, or certain types of professions.

3. Property attacked: the type of premises. If a bank was held up, the entry is "bank." Stores are described by type of business and whether independent or chain. Where a building is used for a number of purposes, the use of the particular room entered is specified first, and after that the general use of the building. Examples: grocery store under apartment; dentist's office at front of residence. Buildings used for residence purposes are described as to the number of families living therein and the type of building, as bungalow, apartment, club.

4. How attacked: the way in which the person or property was attacked. If burglary, property is attacked by breaking in. The point of entry, as rear door or first-floor side window, should be given. In robbery, state the method of attack as strong-armed, threatened, beaten. In worthless checks, drafts, notes, forgeries, and the like, state if by passing, forging, or raising, or if fictitious or fraudulent checks, drafts, or notes. In larceny, specify the place from which the property was stolen, as, for instance, cash register, clothesline, desk, kitchen.

5. Means of attack: the instrument, tool, device, trick, or method. In burglary, all tools should be described briefly but specifically. In robbery give the best possible description of the weapon. In larceny, the means may be carrying away, climbing adjoining premises, fence, ladder, rope, driving away, shoplifting, or with an instrument.

6. Object of attack: do not describe the articles taken in detail but rather state the general class to which they belong. (The articles taken should be described in detail, including serial numbers, in a subsequent portion of the report.) The object of attack by one criminal may be money only, another will take money and jewelry, or certain types of clothing, or silverware, and so on. In crimes against the person, not involving property, the object will be the motive rather than a material thing; for example, hijacking or illicit love affair.

7. Trade-mark or peculiarity: list the personal idiosyncrasies or methods of operation which may serve to distinguish the crime from other crimes committed in much the same fashion. Some men commit a robbery with no fuss and very little conversation; others make a great deal of noise and conversation. Some men turn on house lights in a burglary; others burn matches or use flashlights; some use no lights at all. Such items as committed during funeral, parade, party; assaulted occupant bathing; malicious damage to premises; poisoned dog; cut telephone wires; pretended to be blind or looking for employment, are all examples of the trade-mark. The more unusual or peculiar the trade-mark, the greater is its value in identifying the perpetrator of future crimes or in connecting a suspect with past crimes.

8. What the suspect said: exactly what, if anything, the criminal said in the course of committing the crime because words, phrases, or pronunciation may be peculiarly characteristic of a criminal's operation. This is particularly true in crimes committed against persons.

9. Transportation used: such descriptive details as are available, including the make, body, style, color, the year model, damaged or missing parts, accessories, as well as the license number. Some criminals use public transportation or leave on foot or bicycle. It is desirable to have as much information as possible concerning the method of travel or transportation used by the criminal in arriving at and departing the crime scene and the method used in transporting stolen property.

Modus Operandi File. Each card in the crime index (described below) should contain a summary of the modus operandi of the perpetrator. In its simplest form it consists of index cards showing the type of crime and two or three of its main features. The file has broader possibilities, particularly with the aid of mechanical tabulating equipment. A series of index cards on more than one modus operandi factor is prepared and filed according to guide cards for each such factor. A number of crimes may be identified as being committed by the same persons. Similarly when a person is arrested who is known to have committed one or more crimes in a particular way, it is a simple matter to assemble reports of all unsolved crimes committed in that same way and under similar circumstances. Many crimes can be solved in these ways.

Property Records

The purchase, care, and inventory of departmental equipment necessitates additional record forms and files. These were discussed in Chapter 3. The following discussion deals with prisoners' property and with lost, found, stolen, and recovered property.

The Importance of Property Control

Prisoners' property and other property coming under the control of the police department is frequently handled to the discredit of the police. An ironclad system for property control will do much to eliminate the opportunities for mishandling property and to assure citizens that their property is safely and properly controlled.

Assigning Responsibility. In order to place responsibility and eliminate mishandling, one officer of the records division should be named property clerk to have charge of found and recovered property coming into the custody of the department. Prisoners' property will be kept by the jail staff; small articles of evidence should be kept in cabinets under lock and key; and a safe or vault should be used for valuable property. Keys or combinations giving access to these storage places should be available only to two or three responsible officers. The booking officers will need to have a key for the prisoners' property locker.

Whenever property is received, it should be tagged. The tag should identify the property, its owner, the officer who received it, the date received, and the case number. A record of its receipt should be filed in the case file. A ledger, in which property is recorded as received, further tightens the control.

Property Identification

The records division should maintain a system for identifying lost, stolen, pawned, and found property, consisting of 3 x 5-inch index cards describing the articles which are reported lost or stolen locally or by circulars from other departments. Index cards of a different color on pawned articles and on found articles, the ownership of which is not established, are also filed. Prior to filing a card, a search should be made to determine whether the same piece of property has been previously recorded. In this way stolen and lost property will be immediately identified if found, pawned, discovered in possession of a prisoner, or if it comes to the attention of the department in any other way.

Index cards bearing the name of owners and serial numbers of bicycles and other property which has been registered with the police may be filed in the general alphabetical index for reference in the event of loss or theft.

Stolen Property Index. Descriptions of lost and stolen property where the serial number is not known should be indexed and the cards filed under the type of the article in alphabetical order. Care must be exercised in defining the types of articles because some articles may be called by a number of different names: for example, "looking glass" may also be indexed as "mirror." Some uniformity of selecting titles should be observed. A modifying or descriptive word preceding the class name should not be used except when it is so listed in any dictionary which may be selected as the standard. For example, a cigarette lighter would be filed under "lighter" and not under "cigarette lighter," whereas "drawing knife" should be filed under "drawing knife" and not under "knife." It is desirable to insert a definition of various articles on index cards which bear somewhat ambiguous names.

The number of dividers in the stolen property index file depends on the number of index cards and consequently should be added to as needed. In a small department a set of alphabetical dividers will suffice. Additional ones should be inserted when more than about 20 cards appear behind an alphabetical divider. Usually some articles will be recorded more frequently than others and dividers bearing the names of these articles may be inserted, as example, "watch."

Index cards should be removed from the files when the property is recovered and files should be overhauled periodically and certain cards removed. For example, cards over six months old describing perishable goods; those over two years old describing nonperishable food-stuffs, tobacco, and liquor; and those over five years old describing wearing apparel, linens, and bedclothes, serve no useful purpose after such a period of time. Cards describing articles of greater value, or articles not likely to be worn, consumed, or destroyed should be kept indefinitely.

Number File and Inscription Indexes. Number and inscription indexes aid in identifying property which bears identifying numbers, initials, monograms, or names. In the divisions of the index by number, the last three digits in the number are usually sufficient for filing purposes. Initials and monograms are filed according to the last initial in the description. The first initial is used as a secondary classification, and the second initial as the third classification.

The Auto Theft Index. An auto theft index is maintained separately for identifying stolen cars. The cards are filed by the engine number and by the license number. The auto theft indexes should be cleared of obsolete cards once each year. It is not necessary to maintain separate indexes for various makes of automobiles.

Filing and Indexing

The operation and maintenance of the above indexes, as well as any other files in the records division, is a technical task which, if allowed to become slipshod, is likely to destroy the effectiveness of the records themselves. If index cards are misfiled, they are difficult, if not impossible, to locate. Considerable supervision is needed to maintain the indexes in proper order. Rules should be promulgated which require that index cards should not be removed from the drawer, and the removal of other records should be strictly controlled. The best way to fix responsibility for filing is to designate one clerk to a single index and allow no one else to file in that index. The indexes should be gone through card by card every year or two to correct filing errors. This is especially important for the alphabetical index. Finally, spot checks should be made frequently of the work of the various clerks to determine that they are properly indexing names and other data appearing on the records which go through the records bureau.

The General Alphabetical Name Index. This is the department's first cross-reference to all cases and to other reports. It is maintained for the purpose of determining the case number, the arrest number, the identification number, the fingerprint classification, or the previous record of any person who has been the subject of police inquiry or action. A single alphabetical name index, rather than a separate one for each class of records (i.e., a complaint or case index, an arrest index, an identification index, and a correspondence index) is suggested for the following reasons: (1) there is only one index to be searched in determining whether the police have any record of the subject; (2) there is only one place to file alphabetically name index cards and the chance for errors in filing is reduced; and (3) a single index makes it unnecessary to duplicate index cards. (For instance, if a subject has his name appearing in one case, was arrested in another case, and fingerprinted for a license, it is not necessary to index his name on three separate cards as it would be if separate indexes were maintained.)

The following suggestions are offered as to which names should be indexed and included in the general alphabetical name index. Index cards should be made on all names appearing in a case. Index cards should be prepared when outside fingerprint cards are received and placed in the local fingerprint collection whether the subject is wanted or not. The preparation and filing of index cards on the names of persons wanted by other police agencies, as listed in circulars, depends upon departmental policy. Index cards should be made of persons placed on probation or parole and persons given licenses subject to revocation.

Index cards are arranged in the general alphabetical name index file in strictly alphabetical order. The index clerk should have at hand a telephone directory of a large city to be referred to in deciding the filing of doubtful cases. Since this index in medium-sized and in larger departments will contain hundreds of thousands of cards, it is important that the cards be filed accurately.

In addition to the alphabetical name index, the accident location index, and the stolen property index which have been mentioned above, other indexes may be used by the police department, depending on the volume of records and the personnel available. Among these are the driver index, which contains the names of persons who have been involved in accidents, who have been arrested or served with citations for traffic violations, or who have been given warnings for moving traffic violations. This file is useful in establishing the prior driving history of a traffic offender, particularly when a county or state agency does not provide such a service.

The Crime Index. The crime or complaint index contains an index card for each case reported to the police. Each index card is filed by classification of the complaint. As the status of the case changes (for example, if the case is cleared by arrest, property recovered, or other change takes place), these changes should be recorded on the index card. The index serves at least two purposes: (1) it aids in selecting cases which may have been committed by the same criminal, thus serving as a simple form of modus operandi file; and (2) it enables the records staff to locate a case on which the name and date have been forgotten when the nature of the complaint is known. It may also be used in the preparation of monthly police reports. At the end of the month the information in the crime index is readily tabulated. If the crime index is so used, guide cards should be inserted to divide the index so as to identify cases of the current month and previous cases.

Administrative Records

Since the police chief and his commanding officers cannot personally supervise all the acts of every member of the force they must utilize the aid of systematic controls and administrative reports. The records procedures described thus far will go a long way to control the work of the department. In addition, a good follow-up system is needed.

The Follow-Up System of Control

A regular, orderly system of checking on the disposition of all police business is an essential part of the records system. It increases the effectiveness of police operations by controlling all police matters that require investigation or other action, and by determining that the service rendered is effective and of high quality. It controls the work of individual officers and assures that all available information at the command of the department is brought to bear on each case. Effective police management is dependent on a suitable follow-up. A police department which relies solely upon individual officers to follow through on cases to which they are assigned cannot give satisfactory service. A system of follow-up expedites day-to-day business, catches the stray threads at proper intervals, causes action to be instituted at a stated time in the future, and generally aids in keeping the staff on its toes.

Simply stated, follow-up is a plan whereby every case report or other matter requiring attention is inspected to determine whether proper and timely action is being taken. The reading and inspection of cases and reports, while a tedious and time-consuming task, is a key job and must be performed by a dedicated, proficient person. In all but the largest departments the inspection of cases is not a full-time occupation for a number of individuals and consequently can be performed most economically and satisfactorily by assigning all follow-up activities to a single officer. He serves as the central analyst of all reports submitted by the force and calls the attention of the appropriate officers to errors, omissions, investigative incompleteness, and needed actions. He stands as a guardian over department policy and procedure.

Not all cases which the police investigate are closed as the result of initial action. Consequently, many cases stand in a pending status and are aggressively investigated in the attempt to successfully close them. Until such cases are properly closed their progress should be periodically checked by the follow-up officer and failures reported to a superior officer. Upon the follow-up officer, who is attached to the records division, rests the responsibility for checking, rejecting, and questioning all of the reports submitted to the division. His job is not to interfere with the actual work on the case, but only to take up with supervisory officers instances of incomplete reports and failures to follow prescribed rules and regulations and to suggest further steps, if needed, prior to final disposition.

The mechanics of the follow-up system consist of making out a 3 x 5-inch card on every complaint, arrest, or other matter which is not completely disposed of at the time of the original report. These cards are placed in a "tickler" or follow-up file according to the date (determined by department regulations) on which the investigating officer is to submit a supplementary report describing the results of his continuing investigation. This file has dividers for each day of the year separated into months. If the promised supplemental report has not been submitted on the designated date, the follow-up officer should send an indicator to the supervisor of the investigating officer (Figure 37). The follow-up card, bearing notation of the action, should then be filed for another follow-up at some later date, and so on until final disposition is made. This procedure applies to minor complaints, arrests, and departmental correspondence, as well as to serious crimes.

Relationship of Follow-up Officer to Other Officers. The follow-up duty involves referring cases through the line of direct control to ever higher authority. Such action frequently creates ill will since some superior officers resent having their judgment questioned and are offended when a matter is referred over their heads to a superior.

A clear understanding by superior officers of the secretarial and service nature of follow-up duties will do much to eliminate ill will. These officers should understand that the follow-up officer is not attempting to dictate their policies, or direct their men. For example, a secretary is obviously subordinate to his employer but is expected to call the employer's attention to correspondence which must be answered, appointments which must be met, and conferences which must be attended. It is not considered insubordination

FOLLOW-UP INDICATOR

.... CASE NO. ....

Attention ....Noted..........................Regarding ....

1. ☐ Not attached to case...

2. ☐ Report insufficient ....

.... Item.................

3. ☐ Should letter be written...? Yes ☐   No ☐

4. ☐ Should officer be assigned to follow up..

....? Yes ☐   No ☐

5. ☐ Discrepancy ....

6. ☐ What was disposition of property ☐ car ☐ ....Car in our possession...................days.

7. ☐ Should property item...................be released? Yes ☐ No ☐ Has owner been notified? Yes ☐ No ☐

8. ☐ Report indicates that it was not submitted at end of tour of duty. Item........................

9. ☐ Have suspect and all available information sources been checked? Yes ☐ No ☐

10. ☐ Report on indicator dated...not attached to case.

11. ☐ Has complainant been informed of action taken? Yes ☐ No ☐

12. ☐ Are details sufficient in item...................line...............? Yes ☐ No ☐

13. ☐ Is prompt action being taken? Has nuisance been abated? Yes ☐ No ☐

14. ☐ Should.. be run on polygraph? Yes ☐ No ☐

15. ☐ Should further investigation be made? Yes ☐ No ☐

Remarks ....

....

NOTE—Indicator shall be held by officer to whom directed until any necessary report has been received from officer involved. Indicator and any necessary report shall always be returned to records division at end of tour of duty. Indicator shall not be shown to officer involved. Officer to whom directed shall answer Yes ☐ No ☐ in every case where such answer is provided for.

Figure 37 — Follow-up Indicator (8″ x 5″)

to call these matters to the attention of the employer, nor does the action carry with it a command. The follow-up officer is in the same situation. Although he may suggest the advisability of certain procedures by questions, the decision regarding what is to be done is left to the superior officer. The follow-up officer has no direct authority over the personnel of the department. To give him such control would be a violation of the principle of unity of command.

The Duties of the Follow-up Officer. On the shoulders of the follow-up officer rests the responsibility of checking and inspecting reports and actions to reject, correct, criticize, and question. He must understand in detail the operations of each division of the department, the interrelationships of these operations, and the relationship of police functions to those of other municipal departments. He is the department diagnostician sitting with his finger on the pulse of activity, anxiously watching to be sure that no beat is missed. He needs to know every detail of the department's business; what should be done and what should not be done; how an investigation should be conducted and when it is completed; and what is expected from every officer regardless of rank. Obviously an ordinary clerk is not qualified to perform these tasks.

Specifically the follow-up officer has the responsibility of inspecting each case to ascertain that reporting regulations have been followed, and in particular that investigation reports: (1) are submitted promptly; (2) are completely executed, containing answers to the questions who? where? when? what? and how?; and (3) contain names and descriptions properly and completely recorded. He must also assure himself that proper and complete investigations have been made or actions taken, with particular attention to the following matters: (1) questioning neighbors and interviewing witnesses; (2) use in criminal investigations of all facilities in the department and available in the community, state, or nation; (3) complete investigation of each clue; (4) notification to other agencies, when this procedure is advisable; (5) sending letters reporting parole violations and reporting convictions which may result in the revocation of drivers' and other licenses; and (6) explanation to the complainant of the action taken by the department.

Making the Follow-up Effective. Much of the value of follow-up work depends upon the promptness with which action is taken. The bulk of reports reach the records office at the close of the day tour of duty. The next largest number of reports are received during the evening tour of duty. If the follow-up officer works during the day he will inspect these cases during the second day and the action taken by him may not become effective until the third day. The smallest number of reports is received during the tour of duty commencing at about midnight. Therefore if the follow-up officer begins working at midnight, follow-up action is taken that one day, and irregularities are detected and "kicked back" the day after they occur while the facts are fresh in the mind of the officer.

An officer superior in rank to the follow-up officer regularly should make an examination of enough samples of the cases in the file to enable him to supervise and check the follow-up work being done.

Pitfalls To Be Avoided. There is always the danger that officers may rely upon the follow-up system to such an extent that they lose some of their normal drive and efficiency in conducting investigations. They also have had a tendency to place too much reliance upon the follow-up officer in an investigation. They progress to a certain point in an investigation and then may adopt the attitude that if enough has not been done a kickback will come from the follow-up officer. If the matter gets by the follow-up officer, the investigating officer will have saved himself some work. Superior officers may have the same feeling — that since the follow-up system will catch all loose ends, why bother about careful supervision of either investigations or reports?

These attitudes are contrary to proper police duty and must not be permitted to develop. All officers must clearly understand that they are immediately responsible for matters assigned and that such responsibility cannot be passed to the follow-up officer. They must realize that the fundamental purpose of the follow-up officer is constructive assistance rather than arbitrary supervision. Officers must realize that if all police matters were promptly and properly handled there would be no need for a follow-up and that indicators are evidence of failure or carelessness.

Follow-up as an Aid in Evaluating Personnel. Follow-up index cards placed in a dead file as cases are closed are valuable in the compilation of personnel data. Monthly reports by the follow-up officer show for each officer the number of cases investigated and the number of indicators sent. This procedure gives some clue to the relative ambitiousness and efficiency of the officers; carelessness and indifference are quickly spotted; the relative efficiency of patrol sergeants may be judged by the efficiency of their men; and the degree of equality in the distribution of work may be estimated.

Principles of Follow-up. The principles to be followed in establishing the administrative relationships of the follow-up system may be restated as follows:

1. The head of each division (usually with rank of captain) and his subordinates are wholly responsible for supervising the work of the division. This supervision is carried out through individual case assignments and by personal supervision and guidance. The participation of the records division in the follow-up system in no way diminishes this responsibility.

2. The records division must be considered as a staff agency within the police

department. It has no power of control but seeks merely to aid each line division in making its work effective by follow-up on all police activities. The records division, therefore, never issues orders to a delinquent officer but communicates only with his superior by supplying him with information which will make his supervision effective and assure that no case is closed until all avenues of investigation have been explored on the basis of all available information. This procedure must be followed in order not to violate the principle of unity of command which decrees that no man can have two supervisors without confusion and disorder.

3. The individual officer is still responsible for investigating and reporting upon each case assigned to him and cannot relax his efforts because of the aid given him by his superior officer, or by the records division through his superior officer.

The personal relationships of a follow-up system are delicate. If not handled with tact and a sense of propriety, the records division may find itself unpopular because it is looked upon as always discovering deficiencies and reporting them to superior officers. If, in contrast to this, the records division can establish itself as an essential aid to effective investigation, any unfortunate impressions will fade away.

Personnel Records

Only a few suggestions are made with respect to personnel records since this subject has already been considered in Chapters 3 and 4.

Officer's Personnel Record. An individual personnel record should be kept for each member of the department. This record may be kept on a personnel status record (Figure 38), or it may be recorded on the front of a folder containing papers relating to the individual officer.

All complaints and charges preferred against the officer, reprimands, suspensions, and service ratings, as well as commendations for good work, should be placed in this folder. Likewise, all papers relating to the work and training should be included. Copies of the officer's fingerprints, picture, and other means of identification are also proper contents. In this manner all of the information relating to the conduct and work of the officer will be in a single available place. The history of his service on the force is thereby accumulated during his official career. The folders should be maintained in the records division or in the chief's office in small departments and in the office of the police personnel director in the larger departments. Because of the confidential nature of their contents, they should be kept under lock and key.

Other Records

There are a few general recommended procedures related to keeping other departmental records.

Department Memorandum. The department memorandum is intended as a means of communication between the officers of the department. It is not to be used where the subject bears a complaint number. It is employed like an interoffice memorandum and is used only for matters not provided for on some other form.

General Correspondence. All general correspondence not pertaining to a particular case is filed in a correspondence file. This file may be operated by the records division or as in some departments, it may be operated by a secretary in the chief's office.

Equipment Records. A complete inventory should be kept of police equipment, and

NAME		DATE APPOINTED			BIRTHPLACE		DATE		MARITAL STATUS		
Property Issued	Date Issued	Date Returned	Changes in Rank		Assignments	Date	Date	Address			Phone
			Date	Rank							
								CHANGES IN FAMILY STATUS			
								Date		Nature	

FORMER TRADE OR OCCUPATIONS	VIOLATIONS OF RULES AND REGULATIONS			LEAVES OF ABSENCE			
	Violation	Case No.	Action Taken	Date	Reason	Address	Return Date

Termination of Service	Date	Reason

(Front)

TESTS	SPECIAL DEPARTMENT TRAINING				EDUCATION		
	Subject	No. Classes	Date	Grade	Grade school completed	Yes	No
					High school diploma	Yes	No
					Year of high school completed		
					University degree		
					Attending university	Yes	No
					Total university credits toward degree		
					College major		
					College minors		
					Recruit training: Grade		
Special Qualifications					Additional training		

PERSONAL DESCRIPTION	COMMENDATIONS		DAYS LOST			
Hair Color Eye Color	NATURE	Date	Year	Illness	On-Duty Injury	Off-Duty Injury
Height Build Complexion						
Year Weight						

(Reverse)

Figure 38 — Personnel Status Record (11″ x 8-1/2″)

records of cost of maintenance and operation should also be kept. These records were described in Chapter 3.

Uniform Crime Reports

Under a congressional order issued in 1930, the Federal Bureau of Investigation has served as a central clearinghouse for national police crime statistics. The objectives in uniform crime reporting in summary are: (1) to present an "Index of Crime" composed of a relatively small group of offense classifications to serve as an indicator of the extent of and trend in criminality in the United States; and (2) the compilation of the total volume of all types of criminal offenses. For purposes of uniformity, crimes are grouped into two categories: Part I Offenses — major offenses that are most regularly reported to the police, including criminal homicide, forcible rape, robbery, aggravated assault, burglary, breaking or entering, larceny-theft, and auto theft; and Part II Offenses. Part II Offenses, such as traffic violations, prostitution, drunkenness, gambling, and weapons law violations, often do not come to police attention unless actually witnessed by an officer. Consequently the number of Part II Offenses known to the police in many cases will tend to approximate the number of arrests for such violations, not necessarily the actual number of such violations which have taken place.

The number of police agencies which voluntarily submits annual returns has increased regularly through the years. For example, in 1930, 400 agencies submitted returns while in 1958, 6,853 law enforcement agencies reported. The agencies cooperating in 1958 included 4,047 city police departments, 2,780 other law enforcement agencies, 15 state police agencies whose authority extends to criminal matters and which assume responsibility for specific reporting areas, and 11 departments in territories and other regions administered by the United States. These reporting departments represented 97.2 per cent of the urban population and 97.1 per cent of the rural population of the United States. Discounting incomplete returns and other reasons which invalidate annual crime reports, agencies forwarding reports for the full year represented 87.7 per cent of the population.

In accordance with the recommendations of a Consultant Committee on Uniform Crime Reporting in 1958, the Federal Bureau of Investigation has changed the crime reporting structure in several significant respects. Beginning in 1959, *Uniform Crime Reports* are published only once (instead of semiannually) each year, the report being released around September 1. Quarterly reports, based on preliminary tabulations subject to change, are issued for current information purposes showing trends and numbers of major crimes reported in cities of over 100,000 population. In addition, the Bureau now excludes from its reporting of major crimes negligent manslaughters (which are mainly the result of traffic accidents), larcenies under $50, and statutory (nonforcible) rape. Consequently, certain data relating to 1958 and subsequent years are not directly comparable to data published in earlier *Uniform Crime Reports*.

All offenses should be included in the *Uniform Crime Reports* compilation. This will comprise complaints made by citizens; police officers' reports; crimes known because of "on-view" arrests; crimes learned of by the prosecutor, coroner or medical examiner, sheriff, judge, or other enforcement, prosecuting, and judicial officials; or by any other means. This means that special effort should be made to obtain the submission of reports of crime to designated persons and agencies.

The Federal Bureau of Investigation encourages police departments to prepare and submit a monthly report disclosing the number of Part I offenses known to the police, the number of each offense known to be unfounded, and the net or number of actual offenses. In addition, the Bureau encourages police agencies to prepare and submit an annual return of Part I offenses by name of offense, number known to police, number unfounded, number cleared by arrest, number not cleared by arrest, and offenses reported "not cleared" in other years but now cleared by arrest. Annual returns constitute the basic documents for which *Uniform Crime Reports* are prepared.

Provision is also made for an annual report to the FBI concerning persons charged. This shows the number of individuals charged with offenses by the police and prosecuted. It includes both Part I and Part II offenses and lists the number of persons released by the police (who were not formally charged), total persons charged, number arrested (taken into custody), number summoned (or notified or cited), number of persons found guilty of the offense charged, and number found guilty of a lesser offense.

The data for these reports can be taken directly from the consolidated daily and monthly reports and involve practically no additional time or expense. Blank forms and franked envelopes are furnished without charge by the FBI, Washington 25, D.C. *The Uniform Crime Reporting Handbook*, mentioned earlier in this chapter, contains instructions, sample forms, and explanations for the preparation and submission of reports and should be on the desk of every administrative police officer. This manual is made available without charge.

The records system described in this chapter will not supply the information indispensable to the measurement of results unless certain consolidated reports and analyses are compiled from such a system. This information includes complete knowledge of crime conditions, results obtained from investigation, persons arrested and the disposition of their cases, distribution of personnel, and police problems in general. The chief of police and the chief administrator of the city should have placed at their disposal each day, month, and year a complete picture of the significant activities of the police department. Without knowledge of both the problems of crime and the effectiveness of the department in solving them, police administration can be little more than a haphazard operation which lacks definition and direction.

In preparing statistical reports, the standards set forth by the Committee on Uniform Crime Reports of the International Association of Chiefs of Police and presented in the *The Uniform Crime Reporting Handbook* and in the *Manual of Police Records*[13] should serve as a guide. Uniformity in these reports offers the police executive an opportunity to discover what other cities are doing and identify the methods which produce good results. The daily and monthly reports described below are based on the uniform classification of offenses and the tabular methods promulgated by the Committee on Uniform Crime Records, and in the accident field on the standard system adopted by the National Safety Council.

The Consolidated Daily Report

Because a copy of this report should be on the desks of the chief, the division heads, and the mayor or city manager each morning, the Consolidated Daily Report is sometimes referred to as the morning report. It shows briefly the crime and personnel conditions for the past 24 hours, with space for bringing the month's statement up to date, as well as for comparing the figures with those of the same day of the previous month and of the same month of the previous year. The daily report should be compiled by a records

---

[13] Federal Bureau of Investigation, *Manual of Police Records* (Washington: FBI, 1953). 56pp.

officer during the early morning watch from the complaint records, accident reports, and arrest records.

Since the volume of criminal happenings in moderate-sized cities is small, the most useful feature of this daily report, in addition to its comparative information, is the factual summary on the reverse side. Such a summary enables the chief and division heads to become familiar with the characteristics of crimes and other events during the past 24 hours. The information which it furnishes the chief has often paved the way for precautionary measures and saved the department embarrassment.

The Consolidated Monthly Report

From the standpoint of general police administration, the Consolidated Monthly Report is very important. It discloses crime tendencies and conditions as well as the effectiveness of the department in coping with them. As an up-to-the-minute appraisal of police work and problems, it covers personnel, results of investigations, accidents, and miscellaneous services. It affords sufficient comparisons with other periods to point out significant trends. The monthly report may be compared to the monthly operating or financial statement of a large corporation. It serves as a valuable aid to the chief and the division heads in evaluating the work of the force, planning new assignments, and directing attention towards areas deserving of greater patrol or enforcement pressure.

The monthly report may be distributed in the same manner as the daily report. In addition, some cities publish portions of the monthly report in the newspapers in order to stimulate police activity and to keep the public informed on trends and conditions. Since the part on personnel matters is for departmental use only, it may be omitted from publicity releases.

The monthly report is also a standard report form and is designed to serve as a source document for the compilation of the FBI annual crime returns.

The Annual Report

Just as the morning and monthly reports are indispensable for studying police work over a relatively short period of time, so the annual report is essential for analyzing police operations for the year. Further, this report has the important function of informing the citizens about their police department, both in their capacity as taxpayers and as persons whose cooperation must be secured for the effective execution of police work.

In addition to the information already described as a necessary part of the monthly report on strength and distribution of the force, number and disposition of persons charged by the police, and stolen and recovered property, the annual report will contain discussion and analysis of the long-range police problems.

Public Reporting. Enterprising police are making news rather than history in the preparation of their annual reports. Dry tabulations are giving way to charts, pictures, and other illustrations that catch the eye and tell the story of the problems and accomplishments of the department. Tables of figures are still as important as before in the administration of the department, but they may be relegated to a technical section of the printed annual report or given only limited distribution to interested officials.

Wherever practicable, the tables forming the basis for text and charts should provide a comparison, of at least two years' figures, showing the numerical change and the per cent of change. The placing of totals as the first items in a tabulation, rather than the last, adds to the interest of the table and aids the user.[14]

Special Analyses and Studies

The value of a records system does not depend so much upon the type of forms or upon the regular routine employed as upon the resourcefulness of the department in operating it. A sound police records system will permit police records, reports, and analyses to be used as significant tools of management, supervision, and policy-making. The forms presented here contain a storehouse of information which can easily be turned into effective weapons for solving police problems.[15]

Continuous study of the records and the information that they produce is necessary if the system is to be fully effective. It is for this reason that a full-time statistician is invaluable to a large department; such an employee can devote his energies to the problems of the department and keep the chief and other officials currently informed of results and conditions which otherwise would not be identified. His work also enables the department to put emphasis on preventing crimes rather than on concentrating upon them after they have been committed. If tabulating machinery is installed for analyzing offenses committed, persons charged, traffic accidents, and similar data, the records system can be particularly effective.

Purposes of Analysis

The numerous ends toward which these special analyses or tabulations may be directed are discussed below.

Revealing Unusual Problems. If the police are to be effective in solving crimes, all unusual factors must be identified at the time the crime occurs. Studies of the time of day at which offenses are occurring, the relative proportion of the various types of offenses, particular objects against which committed, locations in which a crime epidemic occurs, and so forth, should be constantly made by police officials through their records division. With such information, preventive measures can be taken.

Determination of the Number of Men Required. An analysis of the amount of crime committed, the number of investigations made, persons arrested, police hazards, and police duties permits an administrator to evaluate the adequacy of the strength of his force.

Proper Distribution of the Force. By analyzing such factors as those just enumerated with respect to various police units, precincts, and beats, it is possible to determine whether the patrol force is assigned and distributed effectively.

Apprehending Criminals. By maintaining proper records of offenses and criminals, a modus operandi file for identifying criminals can be maintained.

Ascertaining the Proper Disposition of Offenders and Causes of Crimes. Criminal histories are essential for police departments and social scientists. Statistics of the

---

[14] *Ibid.*, p. 53.
[15] The daily, monthly, and annual reports discussed above are to be considered the bare minimum. Much additional data must be compiled to provide suitable administrative guidance. Suggested forms for this purpose are found in Wilson, *op. cit.*, pp. 288-326.

social facts of offenders furnish information valuable in identifying the conditions and environment under which crime is most prevalent and in aiding to identify the causes of criminality. [16]

Analyses of Traffic Accidents and Violations. There is an obvious need for records of traffic accidents which show their location and cause. Until adequate records are available, intelligent steps cannot be taken to reduce accidents.

Crime Spot Map

A descriptive picture of the amount and distribution of crime can be obtained at once by means of the crime spot map. The materials used for its creation are simple, and the technique of maintenance is purely routine. As a graphic method of presentation of the current trends of crime, it is a highly useful tool of administration.

The materials consist of a large-scale map of the patrol area, showing clearly all streets and their names, and the block-numbering system. This is pasted to any material which will form a firm background and readily receive map pins. At the appropriate places, tacks or pins with distinguishable shapes are inserted as offenses become known to the police.

Colored tacks may be used to report crimes of particular significance. For example, it may be found convenient to represent murder, aggravated assault, robbery, burglary, larceny, theft, and stolen autos each by a separate color. If too many factors are shown on the map, however, its effectiveness is decreased.

Using the Map. At monthly or quarterly intervals the map may be photographed, the tacks or pins removed, and the process begun anew. The photographic record is most useful if specially shaped pin heads are relied upon to designate the classes of crime, since colors will not be recorded by the ordinary photographic process in such a way as to clearly differentiate the kind of crime meant to be represented.

Spot maps are useful not only in showing instantly where crime is being committed but also in revealing its character and proportions. Increase in crime in a police district is clearly shown, and a friendly spirit of competition may be developed between districts to brace the morale of the personnel in these areas and cause them to exercise more vigilance. Administrative action can be initiated promptly when the map reveals that a disproportionate incidence of some class of crime exists, and emergency measures may be adopted to curb the attacks.

Means of Data Processing, Tabulation, and Analyses

In addition to manually processing, various police data may be processed by semi-mechanical, mechanical, and, perhaps in the future, electronic methods. The use of these various methods depends in large measure on the size of the department.

Manual Means

The crime spot map gives a visual presentation of the distribution of crime, but if an accurate quantitative measure of the amount of crime in each area or similar data are

[16] For a comprehensive discussion of the problems and progress kindred to predicting delinquency, see Paul W. Tappan, *Crime, Justice and Correction* (New York: McGraw-Hill Book Company, 1960), pp. 479-91.

desired, a special analysis must be made of the case files. The simplest device is to use the classification index card, previously mentioned, although a master sheet may be used upon which any desired pieces of information may be tabulated, just as certain data are tabulated on the Daily and Monthly Consolidated Reports.[17]

Semimechanical Means

There are several semimechanical sorting systems which incorporate the use of specially designed punched cards and a sorting needle to facilitate manual tabulations of police data. The cards vary in size from 2 x 3 inches to 8 x 10 inches, depending upon the specific requirements of each activity which the cards are designed to record. Prepunched holes around the edges of the cards are coded by cutting away the remaining portion of the card between the prepunched hole and the edge. To sort cards, a long needle is inserted into one of the holes in a group of cards standing upright in a filing cabinet or on a desk. The needle, once inserted through the stack of cards, is then raised and those cards which have been notched and no longer have a hole in the position where the needle was inserted remain in upright position and are not lifted out on the needle. Unnotched cards, of course, remain on the needle, are lifted out, and thus the sorting operation is completed. Such semimechanical means may be used in sorting material for the preparation of statistical reports and similar tabulations as well as for identification and modus operandi.

Mechanical Means

Mechanical tabulating equipment (punched card) can be utilized for almost any type of tally, count, or analysis. Full benefit of such machine records depends upon the skill, ability, and dedication that a trained analyst devotes to a study of raw machine-produced statistics and the resultant course of action selected by police management.

Varied use is presently being made of mechanized record systems. For example, the Los Angeles Police Department uses mechanical devices in preparing in whole or in part such periodic statistical reports as the daily arrest bookings, weekly administrative report, traffic accident and enforcement summary, crime summary, deployment report, monthly crime activities report, monthly FBI report, quarterly report, semiannual report of arrests and dispositions, monthly crime and clearance report to the State of California Bureau of Criminal Identification and Investigation, and the annual review. Obviously not all departments could justify nor need consider tabulating such a variety of reports by mechanical means. Some departments may prepare only a few significant reports by using mechanical equipment and share the use of a machine with other departments such as health, fire, welfare, and accounting. Most American police departments, because they are small and do not process a significant volume of reports, need not consider mechanical means of data processing.

Mechanical punched card systems are designed to perform a variety of clerical work accurately and quickly by recording facts in the form of holes punched in significant positions in paper cards. In this fashion a punched card contains within itself the means for directing high-speed machinery to perform selected statistical, reporting, and accounting tasks. As the cards are fed through the various machines of the systems, the machine responses are controlled by what is read from the individual cards. Figure 39 is a copy of an 80-column arrest tabulating card as used by the Berkeley, California, Police

---

[17] Such master sheets are described in *Police Records: Their Installation and Use*, pages 207-11.

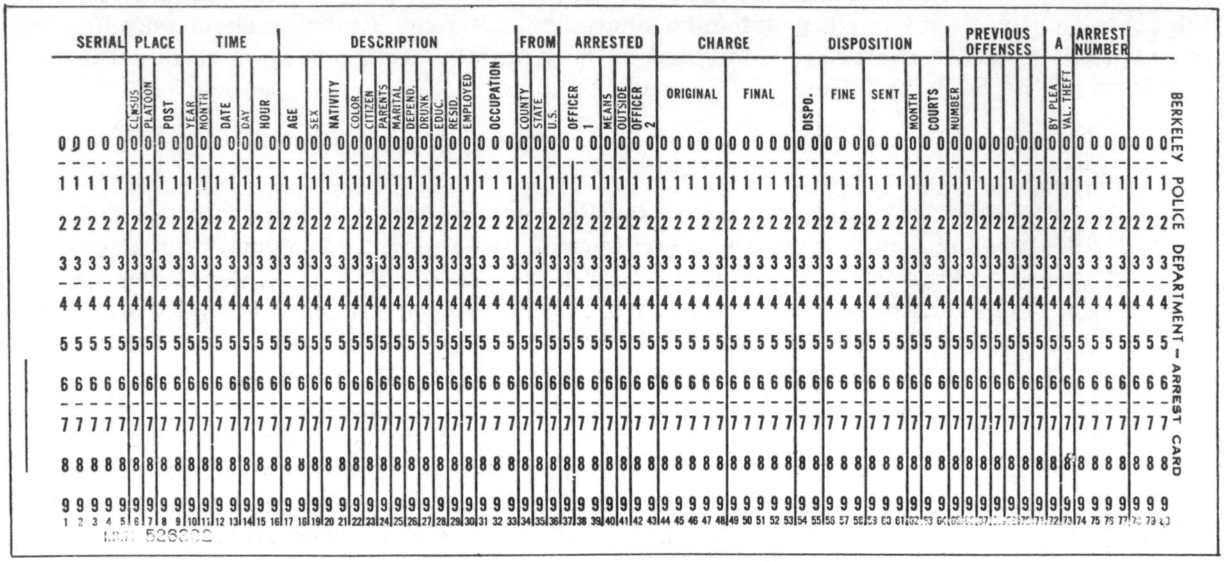

Figure 39 — Arrest Tabulating Card

Department. It is significant to note that almost every factor concerning the arrest is included on the card.

Machine methods, especially in larger police departments, permit a more accurate and prompt processing of data by facilitating the three steps kindred to every accounting or statistical job, whether machine or manual methods are used: (1) recording unit facts, (2) classifying such facts, and (3) summarizing them. In a mechanical system, the punched card represents a unit record. Several punched cards (or unit records) may be classified by directing a machine to group the cards systematically. A summary may then be prepared by refining and presenting the resultant arithmetical totals. [18]

Machines to punch, verify, classify, and summarize punched cards are basic, but other machines and machines which have optional features and variable capacities are available for more complex operations.

There is no ready formula available for making the decision to use a machine installation. Therefore, the police department must design procedures, estimate the anticipated volume of work, estimate machinery, personnel, and related needs, and consider the requirements of its potential applications. Then the department must translate such estimates into money. Finally, the cost factor must be viewed in consequence of, among other things: (1) the present cost of achieving the same ends; (2) gaining access to new facts; (3) the value of such new facts; and (4) the speed and accuracy with which reports may be prepared. It is fundamental that machine installations be geared to the needs of the user because a sound punched card application usually involves a large volume of work, multiple uses of unit facts, and standardized unit facts.

Electronic Data Processing

Electronic data processing equipment is being developed which some day may prove

---

[18] An informative introduction to the punched card world is contained in Burton Dean Friedman, *Punched Card Primer* (Chicago: Public Administration Service, 1955), 77pp. Several other texts describe the concept and use of punched cards in more detail.

practical to police purposes. As yet, the cost factor and questions of programming have not been resolved to the point where such systems lend themselves to general police use.

Pooling Information

If a thorough job of crime prevention is to be done, it will be necessary to pool the information gathered on police records with social data obtained from other agencies in the city such as population and economic statistics, welfare statistics, and many others. The same family, for instance, which is receiving welfare support may have a member who is criminally delinquent. Or the statistics on playground attendance may have an important bearing on the juvenile delinquency problem of a particular district.

The information possessed by the various social agencies can effectively be pooled through the coordinating councils which were discussed in Chapter 6. Data should always be gathered for districts whose boundaries correspond with the United States census tracts so that the fullest benefit can be obtained from the sociological statistics gathered by the Bureau of the Census.

Measuring Results

The remainder of this chapter will be devoted to the problem of measuring the effectiveness of the police department and of the procedures and techniques it uses. Measurements of effectiveness in traffic control were discussed in Chapter 10.

Measurement for results serves a number of important purposes. First, it is an indispensable basis for budget estimates. Second, it provides the information upon which the administrator can analyze the effectiveness of his procedure and methods and the efficiency with which work is executed. Third, accurate data on efficiency are the administrator's best defense against malicious or misdirected attacks upon his work. If the police administrator knows the facts about the amount of crime in the community, the hostile newspaper will have a hard time starting an imaginary crime wave.

The police are a service unit created to protect the lives and property of the entire community. This obligation is subject to the broadest interpretation, depending upon the needs and will of the area protected. It cannot, then, be considered a mere simple matter of hours worked, miles patrolled, or arrests effected, although these factors enter intimately and influentially into the problem.

The police service is complex. It has psychological, social, and economic elements. The normal and abnormal come within its purview. Like the present-day life with which it deals, it is complicated and sometimes inexplicable. A scale of quantitative measurements will never alone suffice. It must be qualitative as well because it deals with temperament and ideals and the public level of acceptance.

For example, there is no known method of determining how many crimes or traffic accidents are prevented by good police work, yet prevention is the keynote of all police activity. A commonly used measuring device is comparing crime rates or the incidence of traffic accidents among similar cities for a given period and in the same city for different periods of time. This is, in effect, a negative approach for it measures failures to prevent crimes and traffic accidents. Such comparisons can be used only in a very general way, for no two cities have identical police problems or needs. Furthermore, variations in reporting practices among police departments also affect the reliability of reported data.

Measurement of results presupposes that the objectives of police work have been established. The elements of the police function may be considered the police objectives: (1) prevention of criminality, (2) repression of crime, (3) apprehension of offenders, (4) recovery of property, and (5) regulation. A comprehensive measurement program must evaluate police activities in all of these directions.

Crime Rates

The discussion of objectives should have made clear that the first important information to be obtained by the police is the amount of crime in the community. Offenses can come to the attention of the police through a number of channels, including citizens' complaints, reports of police officers, "on-view" arrests, and offenses initially reported to the prosecutor, judge, or other officials. The rates of occurrence of Part I offenses are known with a fair degree of accuracy while most Part II offenses do not come to the attention of the police unless actually witnessed by an officer or reported to him.

How are Part I crime rates to be interpreted? Is a high rate of certain Part I offenses (such as robbery and auto thefts) to be charged against the police or against the community? The factors which influence the rate include population, area, identifiable police hazards, policies governing the assignment of personnel, police techniques in use, social, ethical, and economic conditions, location of the city in relation to other population centers, local laws and customs, quality and training of personnel in the police service, and the level of police service desired by the inhabitants. Not all of these factors are easily measured, and the way in which they react upon and sometimes tend to nullify each other is at best difficult to appraise.

On the other hand the police cannot entirely avoid responsibility for an unsatisfactorily high rate of crime. In the first place, efficiency in the detection and apprehension of criminals is an effective deterrent. Second, modern police administration does not narrowly limit itself to traditional techniques for dealing with crime but attempts to attack the problem at its origins. The police should be an active force in pointing out and remedying situations in the city which are responsible for crime. The amount of crime in the community is the only index which measures the extent to which this has been done. The rate of juvenile delinquency is probably the most sensitive measure of the effect of preventive measures, and there can be no doubt of the very close relationship between such delinquency and more serious offenses. At present, crime rates are best compared from time to time within the same city. Comparisons between cities should be undertaken with the greatest caution.

Somewhat more difficult is the interpretation of crime rates for Part II offenses — those not regularly reported. An increase in the number of arrests for speeding may indicate either that more people are violating the traffic ordinance or, what is more likely, that police policy with regard to speeding is becoming more severe. Of course the police administrator will be in a somewhat better position to know to what extent each of these factors is responsible, but even the police chief will have difficulty in interpreting figures submitted to him by his subordinates. To supplement the record of persons charged, a sampling procedure may be used to discover the frequency of offenses — for instance, by periodic "law observances checks" of traffic offenses or by using undercover men from outside the department to discover the extent of morals offenses.

Cases Cleared by Arrest

It has been noted that one of the most important means employed by the police in dealing with crime is the apprehension of offenders. The number of offenders arrested has an important relation, then, to police effectiveness. To have real significance this index must be related to the total number of crimes occurring and expressed as "percentages of cases cleared by arrest." But since, as we have seen, the total number of crimes is known only for certain major offenses — the first part of the Uniform Crime Reporting Classification — the index can be computed only for those crimes. Little is to be gained, furthermore, by attempting to use a single index for the total clearances of all these major crimes. Much more information as to the weak and strong aspects of police administration can be gained by use of the separate indexes. The "percentage of crimes cleared" can be used to compare police units with each other, as well as individual officers on similar assignments, to compute trends, and for month-to-month and year-to-year comparisons.

Recovery of Stolen Property

In cases of crimes against property, one of the duties of the police is to recover the stolen property. To measure the effectiveness with which this is accomplished, "the percentage of value of stolen property recovered" should be computed. Here again a breakdown according to type or property may be useful. It is especially desirable to keep a separate record of automobile and bicycle thefts and recoveries — recording them by number of cars and bicycles rather than value.

Convictions of Persons Arrested

The responsibility of the police is not discharged when offenders have been arrested. The police must assist also in obtaining evidence for the prosecution. Records should therefore be kept of the disposition of all persons charged. A low percentage of convictions may be interpreted in a number of ways: (1) poor gathering of evidence by police, (2) defective preparation and presentation of cases by the prosecution, (3) corruptness of prosecution, (4) arrest of innocent persons, (5) leniency or corruptness of courts, or (6) technical or involved legal procedure. The first and fourth factors are directly related to police administration. Although police responsibility is even further removed, some record should be kept of the percentage of convictions that result in fine or imprisonment.

Chapter 13

OTHER POLICE PROBLEMS

Foregoing chapters have dealt with the police functions of patrol, investigation, traffic, vice, and juvenile control. This chapter will deal with other aspects of the police job which are of major importance. First are the duties of the police in peacetime disasters; second, their responsibilities in war duties — civil defense; and third, the police in respect to labor-management disputes, minority groups, subversive elements, jail management, equipment, and junior traffic police.

The Police and Disasters

The police have a day-to-day responsibility to provide for security of the lives and property of the people of their communities and for the preservation of the public peace and order. They also have a responsibility for police preparedness against disasters which may result from conflagrations, earthquakes, tornadoes, storms, floods, explosions, or wrecks of common carriers. Organized preparedness is essential if order is to be maintained and normal functions and services quickly and efficiently restored. Only if the police successfully perform their emergency duties can the other agencies of government operate effectively in a disaster.

Before World War II, relatively few cities were well organized to meet the demands of a disaster. Frequently the police themselves did not have adequate plans for disaster operations. During the war, however, nearly every community of any size in the country developed some organization for civil defense. Some of these organizations performed with varying degrees of success under conditions of natural disasters. In the postwar years many of these civil defense organizations ceased to exist. In many cities, almost immediately, new or improved disaster organizations were formed. The federal government and many state governments have encouraged the perfecting of these disaster organizations. Civil defense, which is identified with defense against enemy attack as distinguished from peacetime disasters, is dealt with in a later section of this chapter.

Disaster Organization

A consolidation of certain activities, a temporary ceasing of some normal police duty, and a change in emphasis on certain normal services accompany police operations in disasters. Any police organization must, temporarily, be modified during a disaster. This modification should be planned so that it will not disrupt the normal chain of command and the placing of responsibility. In organizing for disasters it must be remembered that all of the resources of the community need to be mobilized if the best results are to be obtained and that the police department is only one of a number of participating agencies. Regardless of the organization, public agencies including the police operate under state and local laws, with definitely fixed statutory duties, many of which can be neither abrogated nor assigned to other agencies.

Example of State Law. An example of a state act adaptable to disaster operation is the Michigan State Civil Defense Act which, while designed for civil defense, also provides for natural disaster operation. In Michigan, the commissioner of the state police is the commander of the Michigan Civil Defense Emergency Task Force. This is a plan involving 10 state departments designed for relief and rehabilitation in a natural disaster where such disaster is beyond the control of local authorities. The Michigan Operational Survival Plan under the command of the governor and the state civil defense director is much wider in scope and is used for the enemy attack situation. In the Michigan Operational Survival Plan the state police are responsible for attack warning service, intelligence service, police service, and fire service.

The Role of Police. It is now generally accepted that a disaster program must be an extension of normal functions. Thus there is an increasing tendency to establish the disaster organization within the framework of the normal government structure. In more jurisdictions than not, the police play a predominant role in the organization. States or cities which have adopted effective organizational patterns doubtless were influenced by the fact that historically in the United States the police accept responsibilities of other agencies of government within their geographical jurisdictions in emergency situations.

Regular Personnel. In any disaster the effective strength of the police department will have to be increased in proportion to the size and duration of the emergency. The initial step to expand the local force is to reduce to the minimum all police operations not essential to the immediate disaster problem, and to assign, immediately, to the disaster situation all officers who thus can be spared from normal duty. The second step is the temporary cancellation of leaves and regular days off, and the recalling of off-duty officers. A third step is the immediate extension of the work day with tours of duty up to 12 or more hours. However, if it is estimated that the emergency will not be sharply reduced within a day, consideration must be given to relieving officers for sufficient rest periods so they will be effective when they are on duty. It is an operational error to summarily order all officers to duty without giving thought to the scope of the problem which will exist within 24 hours, three days, a week, or several weeks.

Auxiliary Personnel. The organization and use of civilian police have become so widespread since World War II that some semblance of their functions exists in a majority of cities over 10,000 population. Such a unit can help to improve police service. Properly trained, correctly organized, and judiciously controlled, it can supply a trained manpower reserve in times of extraordinary situations. Besides the obvious uses during disasters, such a unit can be used for traffic control during parades and sports events; handling crowds at rallies, fairs, and other events; and perhaps even assisting regular patrolmen in routine police patrol.

Perhaps the best way to define auxiliary police is to describe what they are not. Auxiliary policemen are not privately employed police, watchmen, or guards; private detectives; or civilian employees of the police department such as school crossing guards, radio dispatchers, or parking meter checkers. In addition, auxiliary police are circumscribed in duties and authority so as to protect the legal powers of the city police department and to protect the citizens from a group operating outside the law. Invariably, an auxiliary policeman has authority only while in uniform. When off duty he reverts to his status as a civilian. Thus, he is prohibited from making off-duty arrests, investigations, or inquiries. When a situation arises that requires police attention while an auxiliary policeman is off duty and out of uniform, a regular patrolman must be summoned before the auxiliary policeman can perform any police function.

Auxiliary policemen are usually assigned routine and nonhazardous duties. If he is allowed to carry a weapon on his person, it is usually by special authorization of the police chief. He normally cannot carry a weapon until he has familiarized himself with its use and has been able to fire a minimum qualification score. In some cases he cannot carry a weapon until he has completed a minimum amount of service.

As has been noted, the assignments of auxiliary policemen vary somewhat. Some cities use them only for civil defense. Others in varying degree of assistance to regular policemen at various functions. The frequency of assignment of auxiliary policemen to particular duties also varies, some cities using them only as the need arises, others assigning them to specific duty tours. As a rule, auxiliary policemen do not receive pay.

Most cities require some sort of minimum qualification for entrance into the auxiliary police unit, even if only a background investigation. The auxiliary police unit should be trained. Since the auxiliary police normally would not be continuously called upon, training should be held continuously and should not be a one-stage operation to be disposed of as quickly as possible. A part of continuous training is on-the-job assignments. These can be combined with classroom work. Such on-the-job training consists of accompanying an experienced officer on foot or motor patrol, engaging in minor police duties under supervision, and observing how various police assignments are handled. Correctly done, such a program will install a feeling in the auxiliary policeman that he is accepted as an integral part of police operations and is or will be relied upon to fulfill his duties.

The auxiliary police organization is separate and distinct from the regular police department and should function only upon the request of the police department or some higher authority and then under police department control. The rank and authority of individual members pertain only to the auxiliary. An auxiliary policeman has no jurisdiction over any regular police patrolman regardless of rank. The degree of organization of the auxiliary unit depends on the size of the unit.

Police Disaster Functions

The functions of the police in a time of disaster should be as clearly delineated as possible. The chief of police should develop plans and procedures to provide effective policing of a disaster and should be ready to implement these plans quickly when necessary. All local police matters should be handled by regular and auxiliary police forces operating directly under his supervision. He should establish and maintain coordination with other disaster agencies within his area of jurisdiction. He also should develop mutual aid agreements with the police of neighboring jurisdictions, with the sheriff's office or county police, and with the state police. He is responsible for the selection, training, deployment, and leadership of auxiliary police personnel.

The police disaster function should be integrated with some 14 functions more or less common to most police departments. It is the responsibility of the chief of police to integrate the special disaster functions into those functions with which he is already charged. These functions, for which the chief of police is directly responsible, are discussed below:

1. Administration. Through his normal chain of command, or through the chain of command established to cope with the special problems of disasters, the chief of police supervises all police department business and makes adequate provision for guidance in all matters not specifically assigned elsewhere in the department.

2. <u>Public Information.</u> He establishes regulations for the proper handling of newspaper, radio, television, and public relations for the department and gives guidance to his personnel in their relationships with the public. The police must keep open a channel of authoritative information to the local disaster organization, and, through that organization or directly, to the press and to the public. In a time of disaster, especially, dissemination of complete and accurate information to the public and the resultant public confidence in the disaster authorities are essential to successful operation.

3. <u>Personnel and Training.</u> Through the already established police recruit and auxiliary police procurement program, the chief of police augments his already established auxiliary police, provides recruit training for the new auxiliaries, and gives special and necessary training related to the disaster to his regular and auxiliary police. The individual responsibility of a police officer is tremendously increased in time of disaster. Both in normal times and in time of disaster, he often functions without direct supervision, and he must be prepared through adequate training to discharge his duties in many situations unaided by supervisory assistance.

4. <u>Procurement and Supply.</u> He is responsible for safekeeping of recovered property pending its return to owners; custody and control of property held as evidence; and procurement and storage of equipment used in police operations. Provision should be made for the regular stockpiling and, in emergencies, the procurement of essential items of communication equipment, police transportation vehicles and fuel, and special equipment.

5. <u>Records and Identification.</u> Although the general records keeping functions may be curtailed during the time of a disaster on a temporary basis, there may be an urgent need for the creation of special files on property in the custody of the police and on missing persons. Special files, planned for in advance, if necessary on a decentralized basis to facilitate the identification of disaster casualties, including persons and property may be required. Identification procedures should be closely related to the decentralized and master files. It may be necessary to issue passes and permits to key employees of government, business, industry, and the press. Experience has shown that the issuance and control of passes and permits in a disaster is a difficult process which merits advance planning of policies and procedures, and for the design of both short term and long term passes and permits. The maintenance of casualty and missing persons lists necessitates coordination with the American Red Cross and other agencies which use such lists during disasters.

6. <u>Communications.</u> The chief should provide for effective coordination of all commercial and some privately maintained wire communications systems, commercial radio and television systems, and two- and three-way mobile radio equipment. Provision should be made for possible use of an alternate headquarters, as well as for alternate communications systems, including police messengers. Police communication systems such as teletype, closed line telephone, and radio may have to be used in the early hours of an emergency as the sole communication facility available, until other communications have been restored. However, in the predisaster planning period coordination for the effective use of the several radio systems of the municipal departments should be established. It is essential in a disaster that police communication facilities be reserved primarily, for police use. To insure continuous service regular and alternate police headquarters should have adequate and alternative lighting facilities and independent power supplies.

7. <u>Transportation.</u> Provision and maintenance of police vehicular transportation is a function of the chief. He should not consider this equipment available for the movement of people or for other nonpolice functions. The mobility required to meet emergency

situations may tax police facilities severely, and plans should be made to provide for any necessary procurement in an emergency.

8. <u>Detention</u>. During a disaster the chief has a critical responsibility for providing suitable and secure places for the lawful detention of persons for the public protection, and for provision for alternate detention facilities. It is most important that adequate consideration be given to the proper protection of those detained, however, because their very condition of confinement under full physical security makes them unable to provide for their own personal protection. This is of special concern from the standpoint of conflagrations and the collapse of buildings. Both for the protection of the public and for that of the inmates, no jail facility should ever be left inadequately attended.

9. <u>Patrol</u>. The patrol force has the primary responsibility for the protection of life and property and for the preservation of order. While these functions are duties of all police, the number and deployment of patrol personnel make the patrol unit the basic element for these general services. Patrol units apprehend violators of every type; stand guard at critical points; set up antilooting units; conduct preliminary criminal investigations; transmit and enforce evacuation orders; perform traffic and regulatory duties as required; and provide many special services to the public.

10. <u>Traffic</u>. Largely through the traffic unit the chief has responsibility for the control and regulation of vehicular and pedestrian traffic. The traffic unit's principal function is to minimize delays through the relief of congestion and conflicts, and thereby to achieve orderly and efficient traffic movements.

11. <u>Criminal Investigation</u>. The criminal investigation unit continues to carry out its two basic responsibilities of conducting major crime investigations and of making indicated and necessary apprehensions. The unit may, however, greatly curtail its normal activities because of the requirements of a disaster situation. Special attention may have to be given to the activities of known criminals.

12. <u>Juvenile Aid</u>. There may be a virtual cessation of the normal activities of the juvenile aid unit so that it may concentrate on disaster-created problems involving missing persons, especially women and children. Its services will be utilized in coordination with all welfare services looking after women and children whose personal situations have been affected by the disaster.

13. <u>Vice Control</u>. Under disaster conditions, the police, especially the vice control unit, will act primarily in the area of vice control in assuring that stocks of drugs and alcoholic liquors are kept secure. Prices of both commodities may rise sharply and thus warrant unusual attention from thieves and burglars. The protection of the narcotics supplies particularly may be critical to the general well being of the community.

14. <u>Auxiliary Police</u>. In the time of a disaster the chief of police will have a special responsibility for the auxiliary police program. In addition to recruiting and training, he has the responsibility for morale and good discipline; arranging for uniforms and equipment; and maintaining a pool from which the auxiliary police can be assigned, as their services are required, to any division of the department.

All of these functions and responsibilities are performed and exercised in normal times, as well as in time of disaster. In a disaster there is simply an expansion of certain of the functions and a contraction of others. The degree of expansion or contraction largely depends upon the conditions in existence at the time of the disaster and in the area affected. A police department in normal or abnormal times, daily or even hourly, shifts functional emphasis, depending upon the type of community, and the changing characteristics of the problem. The key to successful police operation during a time of disaster is adequate advance planning, full dissemination of the details of planning to all personnel affected, and the ability to swing immediately from normal to abnormal operations.

Evacuation

The disaster organization "is responsible for activities concerning the evacuation of population including the designation of gathering points and assembly areas and planning the relocation. Related to this is the police responsibility to transmit orders for evacuation or for the restriction of movement of persons, and to enforce such orders. Except under the most urgent conditions no agency other than the police (or their auxiliaries under police direction) should be permitted to transmit local evacuation orders .... the police service provides an effective means of sustaining public confidence and morale by placing in the presence of the people a source of assistance, information and direction. When such an authoritative service exists, the public is less subject to rumor and false reports."[1]

Evacuation of civilian personnel is extremely difficult to accomplish. Long-time residents or workers in any given community are not inclined to move even under the urging of a police agency. This makes it imperative for the police to understand the legal implications of evacuation including those circumstances under which they may require evacuation, responsibility for property evacuated, and the safe conduct of persons moved. The police must be prepared to convince the people of the need for the move. The necessity for certain evacuations can be established well in advance of certain disasters. For instance, the time at which a river will overflow its banks or levees at a given location often may be determined precisely. In such case the residents must be psychologically prepared for the move so that the evacuation can be carried out efficiently and quickly.

Mutual Aid

There are many informal and formal mutual aid agreements[2] among municipal departments in the country. It is most desirable that such agreements be developed, preferably based upon the proper enabling legislation, so that in the event of a disaster the police in the area affected may be reinforced if necessary, but without reducing effective police strength in adjacent cities below foreseeable minimum requirements.

Mutual aid should be on condition that police personnel brought into an area would operate as an integral part of the police force in the area but under their own supervisory officers. Command responsibility in an affected area should rest with the chief law enforcement officer of the jurisdiction being aided, except that if martial law is invoked, civil police authority would be superseded by military command.

Police personnel assigned to mutual aid units should be subject to the disciplinary rules that prevail in the jurisdiction being aided; they should have the same authority and immunities as do the police whom they are aiding. It is not contemplated that auxiliary police would be employed in mutual aid activities. Such assignments would take auxiliaries away from their home communities and their normal vocations, perhaps for protracted periods, and would therefore be impracticable.

With proper training a substantial part of the effective strength of any police department can be fitted for mutual aid duty. Thereafter such number may be furnished as is mutually agreed upon.[3]

---

[1] Office of the Secretary of Defense, *Civil Defense for National Security* (Washington, D. C.: Government Printing Office, 1948), p. 145.

[2] For example, see the Michigan State Civil Defense Act. The California Disaster Act has been ratified by most local governments in the state, and formal agreements are in effect for their police departments.

[3] *Civil Defense for National Security, op. cit.*, pp. 146-47.

In some states, standard procedure provides for calling for aid from a state police organization. In addition state or federal military aid can be provided under certain conditions. In disaster planning it is desirable that key police personnel be familiar with these plans, know the proper channels through which to request assistance, and to understand the working relationship that will exist between the civil and military organizations.

Conclusion

The inherent nature of the police service places upon it a responsibility to develop necessary police plans to meet disaster conditions. In some communities, with the possible exception of the fire service, there may be no real disaster planning for the community unless the police take the leadership. In other communities it is too often true that those charged with disaster planning have no concept of the true police function. It is because of this, in part, that disaster boards established outside the normal framework of city government lack a readiness for action that will be present where the board is designed as the conversion factor of regular municipal functions into the requirements of the disaster emergency. Where the concept of the police function is lacking, or where lay disaster boards have been established, the police have an obligation to counsel those responsible for planning and perhaps more importantly to take a positive position of leadership. Certainly the police service is the agency that will control the conduct of the civil population in times of disaster, and it is a major and vital agency in many other aspects of disaster relief operation.

The Police and Civil Defense

The preceding section has dealt with disaster preparedness with respect to emergencies which may result from peacetime disasters. This section deals with civil defense, which has come to be specifically defined:

Civil defense is the organization of the people to minimize the effects of enemy action. More specifically it is the mobilization, organization and direction of the civilian populace and necessary supporting agencies to minimize the effects of enemy action directed against people, communities, industrial plants, facilities and other installations — and to maintain or restore those facilities essential to civil life and to preserve the maximum civilian support of the war effort.[4]

Development of CD Organization

Just before the United States entered World War II the Office of Civilian Defense was established. At the same time, some state and local governments began independently to develop local civilian defense organizations. With the coming of war, the program was expanded and, under federal guidance, standardized protective services were developed. The program was never tested by enemy attack.

In the postwar years, the civilian defense agency at the federal level underwent several major organizational changes as the apparent CD requirements changed rapidly with developments in military technology and capabilities. Since 1950, particularly, planning for civil defense has been an extensive concern of federal, state, and local governments.

It has become evident that a fully developed civil defense program will include all of the elements of natural disaster preparedness, but attention must be given also to the

----

[4] *Ibid.*, p. 1.

many special and serious problems that will develop in the event of actual enemy action. This leads to the conclusion that there should be a single basic plan for disaster relief and civil defense. It is important that police agencies have basic organization and procedures established to readily adapt to changing needs and concepts. In no phase of police responsibility is there a greater need for built-in flexibility than in the planning for civil defense from military attack.

Federal-State-Local Relationships. Throughout the history of civil defense activity in the United States prior to 1958, responsibility for CD rested primarily in state and local governments. The federal role was one of coordination, guidance, and assistance, the latter including matching funds and surplus equipment programs.

Two major steps were taken in 1958. One was a reorganization which centralized authority for nonmilitary defense in a new agency, the Office of Civil and Defense Mobilization, under the Executive Office of the President. The other was a law which amended the Federal Civil Defense Act of 1950 to permit orderly expansion of Federal assistance in the fields of civil defense. It became declared policy that "the responsibility for civil defense shall be vested jointly in the federal government and the several states and their political subdivisions." [5]

This redistribution of functions, however, does nothing to relieve local police agencies of their responsibilities to cope with civil defense problems should they arise. However, the new law does permit expansion of federal training programs, purchase of radiological equipment to be distributed to the states, and federal financial contributions (at least until mid-1964) for personal equipment for state and local CD personnel and for personnel and administrative expenses. These provisions, of course, depend on the extent to which they are implemented by appropriations by Congress.

Police Preparation for Civil Defense

Police preparation for meeting enemy-caused disasters can best be accomplished by the extension of mobilization and operational plans applicable to peacetime disasters. The simple and direct approach is to think in progressive steps of, first, normal civilian police duty; second, disasters such as conflagrations, earthquakes, storms, tornadoes, floods, explosions, or wrecks of common carriers; and third, enemy-caused disasters in varying degrees of seriousness, which will require civil defense operations.

Organization. A police disaster organization, if it is adequate for a major disaster, can be adapted and expanded to meet civil defense requirements. An enemy attack can be expected to extend over wide areas with no respect for political subdivisions, and to create problems of such magnitude that no one police organization could cope with them by itself. Consequently, the importance of coordination and cooperation with other police organizations cannot be overemphasized. There will be added emphasis on the relationship with civil defense organizations and services, and with other agencies of state and federal government, including military authorities. These relationships should not require any material change in the basic organization.

Personnel. The principles concerning personnel in disasters will apply in civil defense planning and operations, except that there are additional personnel considerations which apply in time of war. In peacetime it is a basic necessity that in the ranks of the police service there be no question concerning loyalty. This need is perhaps more

---

[5] Office of Civil and Defense Mobilization, *Advisory Bulletin No. 226* (Washington, D.C.: O.C.D.M., Revised January 26, 1959).

important in the police service than in any other arm of municipal government. In time of war or in case of threat of war there is even more need for considering the loyalty factor in the recruitment and the employment of regular and auxiliary police. There are other personnel factors in civil defense.

It must be anticipated that in time of war regular police strength will need to be increased in substantial proportion. In all aspects of police planning such increases must be taken into account. The development of personnel with high individual competency is a long, costly, and trying process. The loss of trained personnel in any percentage seriously weakens police organizations. Such an effect is not only felt immediately but in months following the actual separation, because it is conservatively estimated that a minimum of two years on the job is required to train an individual to be a thoroughly competent policeman, providing he is interested, intelligent, and adaptable. In addition to the need for increases in strength, there will be necessity for replacements due to separations. In view of the added duties and responsibilities which will devolve upon the police in civil defense, depletion of police forces through recruitment for or enlistment in the Armed Forces should be kept to a minimum consistent with the national interest.[6]

Civil Defense Operations[7]

For civil defense, as in the case of disasters, certain of the normal police functions are expanded and others are contracted. In addition, however, there are certain civil defense police operations which supplement even the disaster requirements.

Emergency Mobilization and Deployment. Failure of the police services to perform their functions efficiently in an emergency could result in confusion and chaos that might well prove disastrous. Plans should be formulated for mobilization of both the regular and auxiliary or reserve forces. Every member and each auxiliary should know in advance what his assignment is in the event of an alert, whether on-duty or off-duty, so that mobilization to duty posts, assembly areas, or other individual assignments will be automatic, even if communications should become overloaded or inoperative. Assignments of auxiliaries should be as near their homes or places of employment as practical to minimize travel and loss of time in getting to their assignments. Plans should include dispersal of reserve personnel and equipment to assembly areas outside the potential damage area.

Explosive Ordnance Reconnaissance. This is a special civil defense function of the police. They should be prepared to receive reports of unexploded ordnance from the public or from other civil defense services. It would be the function of police, especially trained as explosive ordnance reconnaissance officers, to determine the exact location of the object reported, verify that it is unexploded ordnance, estimate probable danger area, initiate evacuation from the area, establish such safety precautions and traffic control as might be necessary, and record all necessary descriptive data and report facts and descriptive data through established channels to the Armed Forces which are responsible for disarming and disposal of unexploded ordnance.

Radiological Defense. For radiological defense, state and local police organizations must be prepared to make available in each police station a location for a radiological situation plot at the headquarters from which police operations are directed. Locker space must be provided in which to store radiological instruments. Space and facilities

[6] Civil Defense for National Security, op. cit., pp. 138-39.
[7] This section based on Ibid., pp. 136, 145-46, and 148-49; and on Department of Defense and Atomic Energy Commission, Technical Information Bulletin on Atomic Weapon Accident Hazards, Precautions, and Procedures (Washington, D.C.: Department of Defense, 1958).

must also be provided where radiological defense area survey units and radiological defense technical service units may report in and maintain static headquarters.

Police transportation should be provided to transport key radiological personnel to their assigned posts of duty from any police station to which they initially may have reported. Police transportation need not be furnished for other than key personnel.

To the greatest extent practicable police communications should be made available to the radiological defense staff and operational personnel. Police actions in radiological defense will include also the issuing of emergency warnings and instructions to the public by means of police mobile public address systems.

These procedures are necessary because in event of radiological attack, police cannot operate until the perimeter of the contaminated area has been defined. Nor will it be advisable for the police to operate within the contaminated area without the assistance of the technical service units.

<u>Chemical Defense.</u> In the event of a chemical attack the police must be prepared to make their communications facilities available to chemical defense staff and operations personnel. Police should arrange transportation to move chemical detection teams to the site of reported war gas contamination. Police will be expected to assist chemical defense teams in enforcing orders concerning the limits of contaminated areas, evacuation of homes, buildings, and unsatisfactory shelters, evacuee baggage limitations and disposal of contaminated personal belongings.

The police should convey to the public, where necessary, by means of police mobile public address systems, instructions for remaining in structures or shelters, or for moving from such structures or shelters. They must also be prepared to supervise the movement of people from structures or shelters to transportation which will move them to noncontaminated areas.

<u>Special Problems of Police Operation.</u> A special problem of the police involves operating relationships under emergency conditions which the police must maintain with agencies other than units of the civil defense organization. The police carry additional responsibility for cooperating with and assisting the Federal Bureau of Investigation, the Army, Navy, Air Force, and Coast Guard and numerous other investigating agencies. The police share with each of these agencies responsibility for internal security.

The Federal Bureau of Investigation nationally coordinates police action in internal security programs which concern sabotage, espionage, and subversive activities. With respect to the military services the police have the additional duty of cooperating in general law enforcement as it affects members of the military services and of maintaining traffic control and regulation.

Conclusion

Police responsibilities and functions in civil defense are little different from normal handling of emergency situations of various degrees of seriousness. The fundamental difference is that the problems will be multiplied and expanded in proportion to the magnitude and scope of the emergency conditions. The basic function of the police has always been, and in any emergency will continue to be, the broad task of protection of the lives and property of the civilian population. The speed and skill with which police agencies adapt themselves to crises can be major factors in meeting the difficult situations which an enemy attack would create, and might well be critical to the success of the entire civil defense operation.

Police and Labor-Management Disputes

Potentially and often actually the most difficult problem of all in police administration and operations is created when labor-management relations develop into strikes or lockouts. Such situations involve management which has at stake investments in production and sales, and employees who have at stake their jobs. Too, the stoppage of work has an economic effect upon the community. These factors often lead to civil disturbances which result from tactics employed by the principals or by the police themselves, or from tensions which develop.

Fortunately, however, both labor and management have taken more responsible positions in recent years in the handling of labor-management disputes. During this same time, the police service has continued to mature, and the police have developed a more skillful approach to their participation.

In these potential or actual civil disturbances the responsibility of the police is clear. Their function is the preservation of peace and order, the protection of civil rights, and the protection of life and property.

There is no more thankless job than to be a policeman in the center of a labor-management dispute. Management often demands "police protection," and these demands may exceed the legal authority or the ability of the police to act. Labor forces may have demands for protection or for "noninterference" by police in strike tactics. Seldom is the action of the police satisfactory to both labor and management. If the situation involves a union jurisdictional dispute there are three principals instead of two, and the police are in the middle.

Impartiality

The proper attitude and action of the police can be only that of complete impartiality. Certainly the ability of the police to maintain this attitude does vary. These variations depend upon the strength of the police, leadership and training, and the size and nature of the police organization. The ability of the police to act depends too upon effective ordinances and laws and most importantly upon court decisions in inferior and superior courts including decisions of higher state courts and the United States Supreme Court. These decisions vary with the changing philosophy of government. The situations change with changing tactics of both management and labor, many instances of which have been witnessed in the last decade. Despite these complexities, any other police position than that of strict impartiality is indefensible.

Procedure

Involvement in arbitration of issues is not a proper function or responsibility of the police. Some city governments have tried, and sometimes with success, to establish themselves as arbitrators of labor-management disputes. To this end they have held conferences with principals to work out temporary or long-range solutions to basic differences. It is debatable whether this type of arbitration is ever a desirable undertaking for city governments. Whether it is or is not desirable for city government, it is not an activity in which the police should become involved.

The police are in the best position to discharge the duties for which they are organized and equipped if they stay within the field of law enforcement. Aside from tactical operation, many progressive police departments have found that there are certain

procedures which help to prevent or reduce civil disturbances. It has been found sound
police practice to maintain effective working relationships with both management and
labor. The police must know and should have the confidence of responsible management
representatives and labor leaders. The police are in the surest position if these relationships are maintained on the highest possible level with management and with the highest
ranking labor leader available in the situation. Seldom can workable understandings be
firm when attempts are made to deal with picket-line captains, for example.

While the police are not arbitrators of issues, it has proven most desirable in each
situation for the police chief to meet with key management personnel and with union officials. The purpose of such meetings is to determine the background of the dispute so that
an estimate may be made of its probable severity and duration. In such conferences the
principals may be informed or reminded of the general responsibilities and limitations of
the police, applicable laws, and policies the police will pursue. Properly conducted, such
conferences tend to reduce the inevitable frictions which accompany civil disturbances.
In many communities definite commitments made by management representatives or labor
leaders in such conferences may be relied upon.

When management and labor leaders are at such odds that they refuse to meet together with the police administrator, it is incumbent on him to confer separately with
each group. He must not jeopardize the police position or the public peace by allowing
any possible enmity between the factions in dispute to preclude his meeting with each
faction. Effective liaison may be established easily and quickly if attempted before a
crisis emerges.

Tactics

Until recent years there have been many demonstrations of police inability to cope
with civil disturbances. Now, however, some cities and a few states have developed plans,
or manuals, which outline effective police methods. The police department of the city of
New York, for example, has issued a general order specifying in some detail the procedure to be followed in unusual disorders or disturbances. While distribution of such literature is usually limited on a confidential basis, information is available to qualified police
officials from the International Association of Chiefs of Police.

Conclusion

It is neither the duty nor the responsibility of the police to attempt to settle the
basic issues in any labor-management dispute. The police do have, however, a responsibility for predispute planning and conferences to minimize the potential conflict inherent
in the situation. Much can be done to improve police operations in civil disturbances
arising out of such controversies. Above this there is need for both labor and management to work out labor and corporate responsibilities, for clarification of the laws, and
for the development of machinery for the peaceful settling of industrial disputes. Police
interest and the public interest are one during a labor-management dispute and the police
must so identify their position. The police cannot be subservient to any group.

Police and Minority Groups

The absorption of racial and national groups has been accompanied by conflicts during the development of the country. The great movements of population that began during

World War II and the new environments for minority groups which resulted from these migrations brought to many communities tense situations and some actual clashes between members of different national, racial, or religious groups. Competition for job opportunities, housing, educational opportunities, and recreation led to antagonisms. In some instances these antagonisms were and are encouraged by professional agitators who find in them a fertile field for subversive infiltration.

In recent years, particularly, a special problem of the police has been actual or potential conflicts arising out of minority group relationships. Although it is quite clear to the police that subversive elements have, on occasion, been successful in the promotion of intergroup conflict, it must be clearly recognized that large national organizations are aggressively pursuing the resolution of problems of segregation and discrimination on a strictly legal basis. This has resulted in a great number of cases of segregation and discrimination being taken each year to the state supreme courts and to the United States Supreme Court. Problems of discrimination are most clearly shown presently in three principal areas: school segregation, segregation in transportation and places of public gathering, and in the exercise of the voting franchise.

Two basic problems are discrimination and prejudice. Discrimination usually involves violations of the constitution and breaches of the peace. Discrimination has been defined as the differential treatment of persons in a particular social group on the basis of race, religion, or some other common characteristic. Prejudice, on the other hand, and not to be confused with discrimination, is the prejudgment of persons who are members of some such social group. The distrinction between these two terms is of importance to the police administrator who has the responsibility of seeing that his men do their work in a legal and ethical manner and that basic constitutional provisions are not violated. Prejudice, as a largely personal matter and one which is not necessarily translated into overt actions, is of less concern to the police unless it precludes the following of prescribed procedures and practices by individual policemen. It must be a basic tenet of the police that justice, equality, and freedom under the law are the basic right of every person — and can be denied to no one except at peril to the rights of all.

He [the policeman] must perceive the anomaly of prejudice not only of the majority against a minority but that of minority against minority; some who only a short time ago were the victims of prejudice are now indulging in the same practices against the newcomer. He must understand that discrimination in all its hideous aspects — segregation, inequality of opportunity, ghettoes -- is the result of prejudice and that these breed tensions and crime.[8]

Effective Policing

The primary responsibility of the police is to maintain the peace; consequently they cannot avoid censure when large-scale disorders occur. Moreover, the police duty is not discharged merely by meeting violence with violence during a riot. The best opportunity for the police to escape serious criticism is for them to undertake preventive police work in the field of race relations. Due to their constant contacts with all neighborhoods of a city, the police are in an ideal position to maintain constant vigilance over troubled areas and to assume the responsibility for making basic causes of unrest known to agencies or groups that can eliminate or reduce them.

Sound police administration is necessary to prevent violent outbreaks between different groups. Recruitment, training, organization, and distribution of personnel all need

---

[8] From speech of Stephen P. Kennedy, Commissioner, Police Department, New York City, June, 1959.

to be considered in terms of the particular local group tensions and trouble areas. Sound police policy regarding the handling of individual members of such groups also needs to be clearly established and enforced.

The police department of any city is a tremendous force for molding public opinion. The activities and attitudes of individual policemen can influence citizens to respect the rights of others or can give them the impression that they can attack some groups without fear of punishment. The latter attitude is obviously a serious menace to the public peace and to the prestige and effectiveness of the police force itself. If all policemen understand these facts, as well as the causes of friction between different groups, and if they are likewise taught how to behave in various situations involving members of such groups, every man in the department can become a positive force in developing a public attitude favorable to efficient police handling of disturbances.

Recent years have brought unusual problems of minority group relations to many of our cities, particularly the larger ones.

A serious problem for the New York City Police Department has resulted from the influx of hundreds of thousands of Puerto Ricans. The Negro continues to be a minority group but now has had his hard-won position in the community challenged by the Puerto Rican with whom he is in direct competition for opportunities of all kinds. Obviously, peaceful and orderly integration in New York, no longer simply that of the Negro into a white community but now of the Puerto Rican into white and Negro communities, can only be accomplished if the present objective and impartial approach to problems of law enforcement is aggressively maintained. What we are attempting to do in the Police Department, by indoctrination and in-service training of all of our members, is to develop an intelligent understanding of race relations to the end that every policeman will be able to carry out his law enforcement duties with legal effectiveness and thorough impartiality.[9]

Washington, D.C., the picture of American democracy to the world, has a population that is 55 per cent Negro. The public school enrollment is in excess of 70 per cent Negro. Immediately after the United States Supreme Court released its decision, May 17, 1954, on segregation in public schools, the police department began a study of all racial incidents of past years to evaluate their effect and influence on school integration. The study covered the periods of other important and similar Supreme Court decisions: the outlawing of restrictive covenants on real estate in 1948 and the integration of public swimming pools in 1949, playgrounds in 1952, and restaurants, barrooms, and soda fountains in 1953. The study resulted in the publication of a departmental memorandum, titled, "Police Arrangements for the Integration of District of Columbia Schools."

The experience of several cities in the constructive handling of tense interracial situations indicates some lessons that may be useful in similar situations in other cities:[10]

Prevention. Police actions to help prevent racial conflict include the following steps:

1. Refusal of police officials to become panicky over wild rumors.

2. Police trust in the peaceful intentions of reputable groups of Negro citizens, insistence of police officials on upholding the rights of such groups to have public meetings, and furnishing police protection to such functions if necessary.

3. Meeting issues openly and publicly.

4. Special distribution of police when that step seems desirable to prevent the possibility of any disturbance.

---

[9] *Ibid.*

[10] J. E. Weckler and Theo. E. Hall, *The Police and Minority Groups* (Chicago: International City Managers' Association, 1944), pp. 5-6.

5. Enlisting the cooperation of local military authorities when the situation seems to warrant such a step.

6. Careful dispersal of threatening groups, if possible without the use of force.

7. Following up such dispersal by correcting, as far as possible, the cause of the tension, thus preventing it from smouldering and perhaps breaking out again, and at the same time reducing the probability that a similar situation will recur.

8. Special efforts to prevent, minimize, or patch up clashes between school children, thus preventing children's quarrels from spreading to their parents and at the same time helping to develop good attitudes in the children.

9. Cooperation on interracial problems among police, other city officials and departments, unofficial citizens' groups, and state or federal agencies.

Handling a Riot. Some of the lessons police have learned in handling a riot include:

1. Immediate recognition by the police of an unusual and dangerous situation and quick report to headquarters.

2. Speedy mobilization of the police force.

3. Rapid effective steps, planned in advance, to prevent curiosity seekers or potential rioters from entering the trouble area.

4. Special precautions against excessive use of force, insistence on diplomatic and impersonal action, and use of Negro policemen.

5. Large reinforcements held in reserve but quickly available if needed.

6. Cooperation of neighborhood leaders enlisted, both to plan strategy and to appeal directly to rioters. Utilization of civilians as police auxiliaries.

7. Personal appeals to rioters by high officials.

8. High officials in direct command of efforts to restore order, staying on the job until it is finished.

General Principles in Minority Group Relations

Accepted principles of police administration apply in the relationship of police and minority groups. Certain of those principles deserve emphasis, however, in the interest of improved relationships.

Impartiality. A police department is in the best position when it maintains a policy of absolute impartiality and when that policy is carried out in the attitudes, statements, and actions of individual members. A consistent practice of avoiding the conversational use of insulting terms and names is simple to achieve in a police organization. Such a practice is important because the person or group referred to by such expressions considers them to reflect the personal attitude of the speaker and of the police organization to which he belongs. Every person should be impartially viewed as an individual and not as a member of a minority group.

The laws should be enforced against all violators without regard to the race, color, or religion of the violator. The same kind of law enforcement should be applied in a minority group district as elsewhere in a city. Any police or practice showing evidence of partiality exposes a police organization to charges of discrimination.

Employment of Members of Minority Groups. There is a continuing trend to employ qualified members of minority groups in police departments in the United States in all sections of the country. Overcoming prejudice against such employment varies with community attitudes as do the problems incidental to departmental and public acceptance of officers of minority groups. Best practice indicates that no person should be appointed to a police force because he is a member of a minority group. If on his own merit he qualifies for an appointment he is entitled to fair consideration for appointment and is entitled to equal opportunity. For maximum benefit in efficient operation and for improving race relations, officers who are minority group members should be impartially treated concerning assignments and duties.

Contact with Minority Groups. Official and personal contact with minority group leaders and organizations is helpful in gaining confidence and cooperation and overcoming any unfavorable attitude toward the police which may exist. Such associations will develop the opportunity for making constructive suggestions to minority group leaders for the education and guidance of their members. From these contacts there will result suggestions for improvement of law enforcement work among minority groups. Liaison with these groups will be invaluable in dealing with any troublesome situations. Liaison with school authorities in working out programs for reducing racial tensions among youth has been demonstrated to be desirable.

The Press and Minority Groups. Good community relations can be enhanced by a harmonious and reciprocal relationship between the law enforcement agencies and the press. This is particularly true with regard to the minority press, whose publications are often organs of protest. While some of them are inclined to sensationalism, most of them accurately reflect the attitudes and reactions of particular groups to current problems and issues affecting the status of their rights. Occasionally, they may suggest or encourage counteractive measures which may have serious implications for the maintenance of law and order.

It is therefore important that each police department and sheriff's office familiarize itself with the minority press in its community. The most prolific presses, particularly in Southern California, are those aimed at Negro and Jewish readership, together with a few newspapers concerned with Mexican-Americans, Japanese and Chinese. A person-to-person acquaintanceship with the editors and publishers of these organs will go a long way toward providing sources of intelligence for law enforcement officials, and afford a means whereby news regarding incidents involving minority peoples will be handled by the press in a fair and dispassionate manner. This reciprocity is ensured where the minority press has experience and reason to believe that the police department or sheriff's office is treating all classes and groups with strict impartiality. The constructive influence of the minority press in obtaining and maintaining respect for the law and cooperation with law enforcement officers should not be underestimated.[11]

The policy of newspapers in printing news of racial matters or of identifying a suspect or defendant as a member of a minority group may not be a proper concern of the police. Some newspapers have been criticized for their handling of racial news in an inflammatory manner while many others sincerely attempt to constructively assist in this field. Where suggestions to newspapers are acceptable, the police may become an influence to reduce racial tensions. A constructive press policy in cooperating with the police department includes:

1. Unbiased, accurate reporting of all newsworthy events in the interracial field.

2. Elimination of racial identifications in crime stories except where publication of the race of a suspect would be helpful in his apprehension.

[11] Department of Justice, State of California, *Guide to Community Relations for Peace Officers* (Sacramento: State Printing Office, 1958), p. 14.

3. Adequate publicity to constructive programs in race relations, such as programs in the schools and activities of interracial committees.

4. Publication of facts to counteract rumors.

5. Close cooperation between newspapers and police to ensure that the press always promptly receives the full and correct facts of any racial incident.[12]

Public Relations with Minority Groups. Normal public relations methods apply also to relations with minority groups. Press cooperation and contacts with groups are sound elements of a good public relations program. In addition, talks by police officers before service clubs, youth groups, religious, and fraternal organizations are desirable to build public confidence in the police department.

In its public relations activity any police department becomes familiar with the necessity for processing complaints concerning the actions of personnel. In the conduct of its affairs a police department is inherently subject to criticism. In dealing with minority groups, complaints about personnel may carry an additional charge that there was evidence of discrimination. All of these personnel complaints should be courteously received, and if by mail, receipt should be acknowledged pending determination of the facts. The circumstances should be objectively investigated to determine the facts. If the officer has made a deliberate or an accidental error this fact should be frankly acknowledged to the person complaining, and he should be assured that proper action will be taken. Then any necessary or desirable action should be taken. Such a program will, over a period of time, strengthen and not weaken the position of any police department. Where the actions of individual officers need improvement, this procedure will tend to improve them. It will certainly result in a better relationship with minority groups.

Observation of Symptoms of Trouble. Because the police have an inescapable responsibility when trouble does occur, they have a responsibility to be continually alert to symptoms of trouble.

Rumors are both a symptom and a cause of trouble. They have been an important factor in every race riot in this country. Seldom is it practical to trace the source of an inflammatory rumor. The best procedure is to get the facts as promptly as possible and, whenever the situation is sufficiently serious, to publish the facts widely. Cooperative relations with the press will assist in this endeavor. In addition use may be made of the radio, civic organizations, minority group organizations, and other information channels.

Within every police organization, regardless of size, one or more police officers, either full time or part time, should be assigned the responsibility of being informed on facts and trends concerning minority group problems within the community or elsewhere which may affect the community. This responsibility should include not only the collection of necessary information, but also the proper evaluation of that information, and either action or recommendation for action when it is warranted.

Race riots never happen without warning.... They are the product of tensions which accumulate over a fairly long period, sometimes years.... The thing to watch is the change in the existing situation; the growth or decline of tensions. The following are generally accepted as reliable indicators of rising tension:

1. An increasing number of rumors, together with an increase in their sensational character.

2. An increasing number of incidents of violence or threats of violence.

---

[12] Department of Justice, State of California, *A Guide to Race Relations for Police Officers* (Sacramento: State Printing Office, 1946), p. 33. (462 tp.)

3. Increasing activity of race-agitating organizations, including groups seeking to exclude minorities from certain districts.

4. Growing distrust of police by minority groups. An increase in the number of charges and complaints of "police brutality" would be one evidence of this.

5. An increase in labor unrest, such as strikes and threats of strikes.

6. An increase in altercations on street cars and buses.

7. Minority reaction to the increasing tension, as reflected in the minority press.[13]

Dormant or active tensions in minority groups offer an opportunity for subversive elements to enter and produce a destructive influence. Where these subversive elements enter, the underlying motive is never in the ultimate interest of the minority group with which they align themselves, and such activity is a potential threat to government.

Institutes on Police-Community Relations

A significant development was initiation in 1955 of annual institutes on police-community relations at Michigan State University. The institutes have been sponsored by the university, the International Association of Chiefs of Police, the Michigan Association of Chiefs of Police, and the National Conference of Christians and Jews. At the sixth annual institute, in 1960, there were 67 representatives from police departments and 15 others representing a variety of social and governmental agencies concerned with minority group problems. Men and women from 50 cities, 22 states, and Canada were in attendance. Each institute has a full five-day program. Recognition of the value of such institutes was instantaneous and widespread, and similar institutes are now conducted annually for one to five days in many cities in other parts of the country.

The institutes bring together people of different ethnic, religious, national, and racial backgrounds to resolve community problems. The week-long opportunity to work and live together is a stimulating and worthwhile experience to most participants who are able to take back to their departments new philosophies of minority group relations, police responsibility, and police programming to assist in the development of orderly communities.

Philadelphia Program

The Philadelphia Commission on Human Relations has worked closely with the city police department and an advisory committee to develop a human relations training program for policemen. The Commission in 1960 reported that the following objectives should be sought in human relations training:

1. To develop in police officers an appreciation of the civil rights of the public.

2. To develop in police officers the ability to meet, without undue militance, aggressiveness, hostility, or prejudice, police situations involving minority groups.

3. To develop in police officers an adequate social perspective.

4. To develop in police officers an awareness of individual and group differences.

5. To develop an understanding by police officers of how their words and actions may be perceived by the public.

6. To develop in police officers an acceptance of integrated situations.

7. To develop in police officers a knowledge of the fact that their behavior will infuse similar intergroup behaviors and attitudes in other members of the police force.

---

[13] *Ibid.*, p. 37.

8. To develop in police officers a recognition and awareness of the role of associated community relations agencies.

9. To develop in police officers the skills requisite for anticipating and meeting the police — human relations aspects of (a) their work, (b) incidents rooted in factors of race, religion, and national origin, (c) juvenile offenses, (d) civil rights complaints, and (e) community tensions.[14]

Jail Management [15]

Persons taken into custody by the police for crimes committed, offenses against the public order, or for other emergency, legal, or humanitarian reasons are likely to be extremely upset mentally and emotionally. For this reason they should frequently be handled patiently but firmly. Their unfortunate lot may often be relieved by the exercise of understanding, judgment, and sympathy.

It must be recognized, however, that the safety both of inmates and of police personnel is paramount and is a basic responsibility of the police administrator. Adequate physical facilities must be provided, and strict procedural instructions and rules of conduct must be followed in exact detail by police personnel to avoid any untoward incident that would involve their injury or injury to an inmate or visitor.

It must be borne in mind, continually, that jail inmates are in fact prisoners and, as such, must be secured from possible escape. The police are not penal administrators, and their jail facilities should normally be planned to provide reasonable safeguards against jail breaks.

Layout of Jail

In addition to securing the person of the prisoner by careful planning of cell blocks, there are other considerations in planning jail facilities. In order to eliminate the escorting of prisoners from room to room or building to building, which may provide escape opportunities, facilities for fingerprinting and photographing prisoners should be provided within the jail proper or within the area controlled by the security key. Another consideration for locating the jail is its relation to the courtroom. Frequently prisoners have escaped while being transferred from their jail to the courtroom. If the court is located in the same building, the jail should be located immediately above or below it with some sort of connecting stairway, and with a holdover room adjacent to the court room. On escorts to court, prisoners should be secured by cuffs, and the cuffs affixed to a chain. This procedure is used in several California cities, including Berkeley, Los Angeles, and Sacramento. Insofar as it can be determined there are no legal restrictions or case law on this procedure. Care should be taken, nonetheless, to avoid this display of police security measures when the prisoner is actually taken into the court room.

Prisoners should be allowed, always, to have counsel upon demand — their civil rights should be protected at all times and this protection should be a continuing responsibility accepted by the police administrator. Prisoners should be allowed to phone or arrange for bail and to notify their families or employers. Most states clearly spell out

[14] Commission on Human Relations, *Summary of Report of Police Human Relations* (Philadelphia: The Commission, 1960).

[15] For a detailed treatment of jail administration, see Myrl Alexander, *Jail Administration* (Springfield, Illinois: Charles C Thomas, Publisher, 1957).

these rights in codes, and state codes should be checked carefully before jail regulations are established. In several states it is a misdemeanor to deny a prisoner the opportunity of obtaining counsel or of trying to control an attorney's relationship to the prisoner.

The visiting room should be so arranged that the prisoner can be brought to the speaking ports or screen without leaving the security of the jail proper. Visiting facilities for relatives, friends, and others, except attorneys, should have baffled speaking ports to prevent the passing of narcotics or other items from the outside to the prisoner. It has been generally ruled that an attorney and his client may be closeted together without hindrance; therefore, departments should have an attorney's room within the jail area where attorneys and clients may confer.

These criteria for jail facilities are illustrated in Figure 12 on pages 100-101 showing the layout of the police and court building in Kalamazoo, Michigan.

Selective Oversight

A policy of selective oversight of prisoners is essential for best results. All cannot be treated alike if the public good is to be well served.

Mental Cases. One inmate may be suffering from a mental disorder and, although not charged with a criminal offense, may display such violence as to require confinement. Medical attention should be summoned promptly and the inmate removed to an institution designed for the treatment of mental sufferers. Or, the prisoner may be one of the criminally insane, either temporarily or permanently. Transfer to a proper place of confinement and treatment should be arranged forthwith. Facilities for the correct handling of such prisoners cannot be provided in a police station.

Intoxicated Persons. The apparently intoxicated prisoner may present a real problem. It is sometimes difficult to distinguish correctly between a drunken stupor and a serious illness. It is not at all uncommon for the police to arrest a person for intoxication when the symptoms fully indicate this to be the case when the person actually is suffering from a serious disease, perhaps a heart attack. Each person who is unconscious or only semiconscious at the time of being picked up should be examined by a physician. Failure to provide such medical care, even toward society's human derelicts, is inexcusable. Detailed reports should be made whenever an unconscious person is picked up and taken to a hospital or a jail for medical examination.

Cells assigned to intoxicated prisoners should have bunks firmly secured to the walls, not more than 12 inches high, one tier only. The floor should be of mastic material with a corner or center drain. Rules should provide that under no circumstances should a person who is semi- or fully unconscious be locked within a cell without the written approval of an examining physician.

Cases of Attempted Suicide and Self-Abuse. Some prisoners must be protected from themselves. Out of remorse for their misdeeds or shame at their plight, prisoners everywhere are known to take their own lives or inflict bodily harm upon themselves. All shaving should be done under the supervision of a jailer, and razors with semifixed blades used. Group shaving should be prohibited. Mirrors should be of polished metal, not glass. Some of them must be prevented from practicing sexual abuse upon their person or from indulging in sexual intercourse with other prisoners. Any prisoner manifesting sexual problems of any type should be removed from all contact with other prisoners. Many prisoners are addicted to the use of habit-forming drugs which they crave strongly enough to commit crime to obtain them.

Segregation. Men and women prisoners must of course be segregated. Boys, when they must be detained, should never be placed near older prisoners. Repeaters should be kept away from first-timers, whatever the age of either. Women prisoners must likewise be kept separated, the young from the old, and the hardened criminals from the newcomers. Racial, ethnic or national origin should not be a basis for segregation. State law usually defines the means of segregation and should be followed strictly. Careful study of the law should be part of the planning of new or remodeled detention facilities. It is logical and proper to separate persons of unclean habits from those of clean habits. A police matron should be on duty or on call to search, watch over, and care for the needs of women prisoners.

It should not be overlooked that criminals themselves may form strong opinions about the criminal acts of some certain individual. Inmates have been known to murder or commit mayhem upon the person of a prisoner charged with some dastardly crime. Such prisoners must be protected as well from an outraged public which may storm the jail and do bodily harm to the culprit.

Duties of Jailer

Satisfactory jail management involves the assignment of definite responsibilities to specific individuals. The desk sergeant may be placed in charge if he has time, or a patrolman may have to be designated to devote his full time to the assignment. Sometimes the patrol wagon driver is designated; when he is absent from the station on a "run," the desk sergeant may take over his duties. Any busy cell block will require the full-time service of a jailer, however.

The jailer should be provided with detailed written instructions covering every phase of jail operation; the instructions or manual should be reviewed by the city and county attorneys to see that requirements set forth are in harmony with existing laws. Privileges granted prisoners as well as the prohibitions and certain jail rules should be printed on gummed stock and posted within each cell.

Maintaining Register. The jailer may, in very large jails, maintain a chronological register of each person ordered confined in the cells, noting the name, address, charge, date and hour of release, and other appropriate information. The jail list suffices in most departments. Another sheet would provide the names of prisoners who are in jail during each 24-hour period. Except where specifically provided, the jailer should not receive and detain anyone in a cell unless so ordered in writing by a commanding officer, and no one should be released without authority of a written order from a commanding officer on duty at the station.

Custody of Prisoners' Property. A prisoner should be searched and relieved of his property only in the presence of the accompanying officer. A receipt for property and money taken from the prisoner should be given to him immediately. He should be allowed to keep the receipt while in custody. On his release he should check the contents of his property box and acknowledge the return of his property by signing the release portion of the receipt. It is necessary to search the prisoner thoroughly and to remove personal property and things from him with which he might injure himself or others.

Supervision of Visitors. No one should be permitted to interview a detained person without a permit from the commanding officer on duty at the station. This is designed to prevent a certain class of legal talent from drumming up business from prisoners while they are confined and at a psychological disadvantage. The jailer should be supervised to insure that this rule is not violated and that there is no conniving with the prisoners by granting unusual favors or privileges in return for money or valuables. A jail arrangement providing for unsupervised visiting of prisoners is to be recommended. The jailer should be required to visit the prisoners at least every half hour to render all necessary and proper services.

Other Duties. Cell blocks should be kept clean and in such condition as to stand public inspection at all times. No confined person should be permitted to create and continue an unnecessary disturbance which may cause other confined persons to become unmanageable. Meals should be served at regular intervals without waste and should be free of deliberate effort to make them unattractive.

Property and Equipment

Repeated emphasis has been placed upon the importance of careful selection, training and management of personnel. Vital as these considerations are, the organization would still not function properly unless provided with the necessary police property and equipment. And yet the mere fact that policemen possess the proper equipment for their business is no assurance that it will be employed for its most useful and intended purpose. The question of attaining the proper use of equipment and property leads back to the training of personnel and opens the way for comment on the human element in the management of the police department's own property and that of others — both its care and its effective use.

A policeman uses his night stick, or baton, as a weapon because training and experience tell him that under certain circumstances its use is necessary. The physical presence of the officer, his uniform, persuasiveness, commands, the power of his hands — presumably all of these have failed. The baton then becomes an essential and useful tool in permitting the policeman to discharge the duties of his office. Much more effective in some circumstances is a revolver, but a dangerous weapon in any hands. The consequences of its unwise use may be so serious that a revolver is generally regarded among police departments as a weapon of defense rather than of offense.

The police are commonly provided with equipment of a new and novel nature only after the criminal enemies of society have adopted it and found it useful to their own ends. Lawbreakers have the tactical advantage under these circumstances. This superiority of opportunity is immediate and continuous. Only within very recent years have attempts been made toward the systematic study of the mechanical equipment of the police in this country. The weapons were found to be of service to the police only after their use for other purposes, often criminal in nature. This was also the case with the automobile, motorcycle, bicycle, searchlight, shotguns, rifle, machine gun, tear gas, railroad flares, and radio. The best long-run solution for crime may not be dangerous weapons in the hands of the police. However, current practices of criminals necessitate the availability to the police of a series of deadly instruments.

The police should have available for use in connection with their routine and emergency duties such equipment as will fit them to cope — to the satisfaction of the community — with the problems which they face. The kinds and use of essential equipment will vary with the problems of the community. In a large department there should be continuing research to assure that the most modern equipment is placed in the hands of police well-trained in its use.

Personal Equipment

Personal equipment of an officer on uniformed patrol is more nearly similar as between cities than the other police paraphernalia. It consists of the uniform -- cap, blouse, and trousers -- usually but not necessarily of blue color; official badge or star; the cap shield; overcoat; shoes; rain cape; waterproof cap or cap cover; night stick; handcuffs; sidearm and extra ammunition; holster; flashlight; small first-aid kit; street guide and information book (usually); official report forms, memorandum book, watch, and pen and pencil. The whistle is normally included.

Firearms

A firearm allows the officer to protect himself and at the same time extend his usefulness into space as well as his skill and effectiveness of his weapon permit. How wisely this power is used depends upon the officer, his training, and established procedures and policy. The weapon only projects the long arm of the law as it is enforced by individuals.

Sidearms. The .38 special caliber revolver is generally used as a police weapon. While there is much to be said for automatic pistols, they are rarely used in this country although frequently found in other countries and were selected by the armed services of the United States many years ago after careful study. However, there is only one make of automatic pistol generally available of American manufacture, and it has had little change in design in the past 40 years.

Many departments standardize on a certain make and model of revolver. This is a good plan. In the only two makes suitable for police service, the Smith and Wesson and the Colt, the cylinders turn in opposite directions. As a result, if an officer is using an unfamiliar gun he is likely to make a mistake in placing the cylinder if he puts in less than a full load of cartridges. Also, the cylinder locking mechanisms work in opposite directions.

There is little reason to use other than .38 special caliber. This is a very well developed cartridge with a wide variety of loads and bullets commercially available. Sidearms of a heavier load or caliber, such as the .357 magnum, the .44 magnum, or the .45, do not have the power approaching a riot gun with a rifled slug, and, under most conditions, all hand guns are ineffective in stopping an automobile by shooting up the vehicle. The heavier weight of the larger revolvers also is a factor since they are to be carried regularly by an officer. Calibers smaller than .38 are rarely found in police service since they have far too little power, and no advantage is gained by their slightly smaller size. Barrel length is usually 4 inches. The 6-inch barrel was standard for many years, but with the advent of modern powders, this greater length is not necessary and the shorter barrel is much more convenient to carry and to shoot. Officers in plain clothes often carry 2-inch barrel revolvers because of their greater convenience and easier concealment.

Officers should be required to do their practice shooting and shoot for score with the revolvers they carry on duty. There is little value in having an officer practice with a target revolver and then carry a 2-inch barrel on the job because of the great difference between shooting the two guns. Use of the service weapon for practice has the added advantage of making certain that the gun is in good condition since many defects not apparent in a casual inspection will show up on the firing line.

Holsters. A proper holster is very important. It should be designed specifically for the gun and fit so well that the revolver will not fall out if the holster is turned up-side-down but at the same time allow the gun to be drawn freely. The holster should have a strap secured with a snap that will hold the pistol but still allow the strap to swing free with a minimum of delay. The patented holsters with various sorts of locking devices should be carefully studied and tested before their use is approved. Some of these look good but may fail in actual service. The simplest designs are often the best and have proven out over the years. They allow for carrying the revolver in a comfortable yet immediately available position. For this reason, holsters with flaps covering the butt of the revolver are losing popularity. It is impossible to make a rapid draw from them, and instead of protecting the gun they may actually damage it. They will not keep rain or snow out yet at the same time conceal the appearance of the weapon.

Ammunition. Almost any of the standard service loads for .38 special caliber are satisfactory although some departments favor the so-called "metal piercing" bullets or one of the heavier bullets. Most important is the condition of the cartridges. Oil is probably the single greatest factor in limiting cartridge life. A revolver should be oiled very lightly. There should be no excess oil running, and the cylinder and chambers should be free of oil. Extreme moisture and heat may also reduce the life of a cartridge. Under proper conditions, a cartridge will be perfectly safe to use after five years, but when carried in service where it is not practical to give them the highest degree of protection, the cartridges in the gun and carried on the belt in a pouch should be shot up in practice at least every six months or year and replaced with fresh ammunition. Certain types of material used in tanning may result in the cartridges carried in the belt corroding rapidly. They should be inspected at intervals and wiped clean with a dry cloth. Oil should not be used.

Storage of Ammunition. While some savings might be made on the largest departments by purchasing ammunition in large quantities, proper storage is usually not possible. Consequently it is good practice to purchase only about a two-year supply at one time. The storage point should be as fireproof as possible, but there is no great hazard from the explosion of cartridges since the force is not confined as it would be in a gun. Tests made by burning ammunition in a fire show that any fire resistant wall would also contain the explosion.

Rifles and Riot Guns. There may be circumstances where one or two heavy-caliber rifles would be of value against a barricaded criminal and where it would be safe to use them. These situations are rare. This is especially true since models of the riot gun, or sawed-off shotgun, are now available with rifle sights. This weapon firing a rifled slug is accurate up to about 75 yards.

The riot gun is a basic police weapon. It has several distinct advantages. With a little training it is shot by pointing instinctively and without using the sights. As a result, it can be fired accurately at night when a pistol would be useless except at the shortest ranges. Second, it has tremendous fire power. The 12-gauge 00 buck load has nine slugs, each about the weight of a .32 bullet and with more velocity than the usual .38 special pistol loads. There are four or five rounds in the magazine as it is carried and additional rounds can be added without putting the gun out of service as it is fired. Third, the range is limited. While this is a dangerous and highly effective weapon up to 60 yards, velocity falls off rapidly so the range is much less than a pistol and only a fraction of that of a rifle. Richochets are much less dangerous. The pellets are soft lead and deform easily so will not travel far after hitting something. Fourth, training is quite simple. Many policemen hunt with their own shot guns and so need little training. Once the proper methods of firing are learned, little practice is needed to retain the skill. Fifth, there is a definite psychological effect. Most people are afraid of a riot gun. They recognize its potential and know that it is hard to miss with the pattern that scatters out.

The usual load is either 00 buck with nine pellets or 0 buck with 12. Rifled slugs are usually carried separately, or they may be carried as the last two loads in the magazine. Some departments use number 4 shot or BB shot. This is highly effective against a person and has less hazard from richochet.

The riot guns carried in the cars should have the magazine loaded, but for safety there should not be a shell in the chamber. The guns should be unloaded and inspected at weekly intervals. Care should be taken to see that the nose of the shell does not expand over a period of time because of pressure from the magazine spring or from dropping the shell. For this reason, guns kept in the station should not be loaded.

Because of the many advantages of the riot gun, police enforcement automobiles should all carry one. Some departments carry them on three-wheel motorcycles. There are a number of ways to carry riot guns in cars. One common method is a locked holder for the gun above the doors, usually on the right side. The key is kept with the car keys so that it can easily be detached. Another method is a zipper case attached to the front seat cushion so that the gun rides along the front edge of the seat. There are two zippers that meet at the middle of the case so that it can be opened from either end. Here a lock is usually not needed. One large force that had over 100 riot guns not locked in the cars lost guns only in cases where the officer had left the keys in the car and both the car and gun were stolen.

Tear Gas. Tear gas is a valuable police weapon. It has the advantage of rendering a person harmless without hurting him. As a result, it can be used not only in dislodging criminals but in securing mentally ill persons. It is normally used as grenades thrown by hand, or it may be fired from a special gun. Since a considerable amount of gas is needed to be effective, the small amount of gas loaded into .38 cartridges or shot gun shells is of little value.

The only effective tear gas gun is the $1\frac{1}{2}$ rifle. It fires three types of shells. The first is a short-range blast type that shoots no projectile but only a blast of gas for 40 feet. This is particularly effective against mobs and no hazard is involved as long as the gun is fired at the feet. Firing directly into the eyes at short range might do damage. The second type of shell is a medium-range projectile with an extreme range of less than 100 yards but with enough force to break through windows or light material. The third type is a long-range projectile with a range of over 200 yards but with a loss of accuracy at extreme ranges. This shell will penetrate many doors and even the sides of some houses. The latter two projectiles are dangerous only if they hit a person directly. The short range can be richocheted into a mob with little danger, but the long range should never be fired at a person unless the intent is to kill.

If tear gas is to be used, two additional pieces of equipment are essential. Officers should be provided with gas masks if they must go into the area covered by gas. All officers involved in an action against a mob should have masks or they will be in trouble if gas is used. Second, both the grenades and the projectiles get up to a high temperature a few seconds after ignition. This is to prevent them being thrown back at the police or out of a building. As a result, there is a fire hazard and extinguishing equipment should be available. This hazard is not too great, but it should be recognized.

Tear gas is usually kept in the station. In some departments, however, a small supply may be carried by the uniformed investigator or in the field sergeant's car. Kits holding a tear gas rifle, several shells, and grenades are commercially available. These are good for storage but are inconvenient to carry and would be difficult for one man to carry in many situations. So far no one has designed commercially available equipment to carry grenades or shells under emergency situations or during riots. One major department did design canvas bandoliers for both grenades and shells for riot duty. These were very convenient and allowed a man to carry an adequate supply of gas yet have both hands free. Grenades should be armed by screwing the detonator into the cannister as soon as received. This may take several minutes to do and is no job for an emergency.

Tear gas has a limited life and the replacement date is marked on the grenade or shell. Properly stored in a cool, dry place, the gas is dependable for at least a year after this date. Supplies, even though carefully stored, should be checked periodically to make sure they have not deteriorated.

Sickening gas is not recommended for police use. It has no real advantage over tear gas and is dangerous both to the police and the persons it is used against.

Submachine Guns. Aside from the psychological effect, submachine guns are of little value to the police. Each costs as much as four riot guns, training is expensive, and they have too much firepower for use in any congested area. Few departments have bought submachine guns in the last 20 years.

Availability of Weapons and Ammunition. Except for surplus items, weapons and ammunition kept in the station should be placed so that they are immediately available. One department solved this by having a gun locker concealed behind a bulletin board in the lobby of the station. It is all too common to find weapons stored in a vault and the man with the combination off duty. If firearms are needed, it will be in an emergency situation and there will be no time to waste. Ammunition for each weapon should be attached to it. One plan is to have an ammunition belt or a pouch of ammunition attached directly to the gun by a light string. This will save a great deal of time rummaging through miscellaneous boxes of shells looking for the right ones. Weapons using clips should have a loaded clip and a spare clip. The loaded clips should be checked at six-month intervals to make certain that the spring has not deteriorated to the point that it will not allow the gun to function. If this occurs, the spring should be replaced or the clip thrown away.

Care of Firearms. Police weapons must always be in top condition. The best way to determine this is to inspect visually at short intervals and then use the weapons regularly for practice. Many serious defects will not appear until the weapon is fired. For example, a riot gun may be improperly stored with the hammer cocked. This may weaken the spring so much that the gun will not fire although inspection will not show this defect. There should not only be practice with the revolvers, but with all of the weapons the men are expected to use. Many departments have a variety of riot guns and rifles that have never been fired by the present members of the force.

Repairs should be made only by a skilled gunsmith. The men should not be allowed to work on their own guns except to tighten screws or to clean them. Range officer should always be on the alert for condition of weapons, looking out for such things as revolvers that are shaving lead, misfires, difficulty in opening the action, and so on.

Bullet Resisting Shields

Bullet resisting shields of light weight laminated steel, hinged in a manner to permit the three parts to fold into a small space, should be a part of the standard equipment of all police departments. The shield has the advantages that it affords protection against gunfire for the entire body except that portion below the knees; it may be picked up readily (and in the process it automatically unfolds), placed in immediate use, and discarded instantly when no longer needed (and thus does not hamper movement); its appearance of obvious invulnerability has a salutary psychological effect on the criminal, when confronted by an officer protected by it.

Shields should be kept at headquarters, available for use on raids of suspected criminal hide-outs and against barricaded criminals. A shield should also be carried in the cars driven by the special investigators and the patrol sergeants.

Lighting Equipment

Independent unit floodlighting devices, such as searchlights and flares, are essential for emergency night use. Flashlights and draft-proof gasoline lanterns and spotlights are frequently needed reserve equipment. A powerful, controlled focus searchlight is valuable in patrolling waterfronts or other areas where investigation may be made at some distance.

Vehicles

Automobiles. Automobiles for patrol use may be selected from a wide range of those commonly on the market. The standard automobile is usually considered adequate for police use. The car should be a two- or four-door sedan of standard specifications. A car of the so-called low priced group is best suited for patrol because of superior maneuverability, shorter wheel base, cheaper purchase price, and lower maintenance cost. Many departments are now experimenting with the smaller than standard size cars, known as compacts. Sufficient experience has not been gained with these cars to determine their suitability for regular police work.

Certain equipment in addition to the officer's personal equipment should be carried in the automobile. Among equipment considered necessary are the following: flares or some sort of emergency lighting equipment, auxiliary firearms (either riot gun or rifle), small fire extinguishers, emergency first-aid kit, and radio equipment. In addition to this material, other equipment may be provided which will make the patrol work of the officer more agreeable. Included in this type of equipment are car heaters, a suitably located dome light, a built-in rack for jotting down messages from headquarters and other material while driving, built-in racks for various traffic tickets and reports needed in patrol work, and so on.

The use of mobile radio equipment in police cars make some changes in the automobile's electrical system necessary. These alterations are ordinarily listed in the bid specifications and are performed at the factory or by the automobile dealer. Of particular importance, however, is the installation of heavy-duty generator, or an alternator, to take care of the added drain on the automobile's electrical system.

A few departments have greatly reduced both the original and upkeep cost of their motor vehicle equipment by the adoption of a car rental plan. In this they have followed the lead of many automobile fleet operators in private business. By renting their cars, these departments have effected substantial savings, have procured new cars at more frequent intervals, and have rid themselves of the responsibility of motor maintenance which is not a function related to police work or one in which the police department may be expected to be proficient.

Patrol Wagon. The so-called patrol wagon which is used to transport prisoners is usually mounted on an auto truck chassis. Its capacity will be adapted to the needs of the situation. The panel body is usual in order to afford maximum security. A rear entrance may be guarded by a locked door if this is permitted by law; otherwise an officer must ride in the rear. Whether the rear entrance of the patrol wagon is locked or not there should be an escape door through the truck cab which may be secured by a simple latch under the control of the police driver. This will allow the ready release of prisoners or others in the patrol wagon in the event of a rear-end collision or other emergency. Some additional equipment may be carried in the patrol wagon, and in this case it may serve as an emergency vehicle. This equipment may include a respirator, a stretcher, first-aid kit, blankets, ropes, and grappling equipment in addition to flares, flashlights, and lanterns. Dead bodies and injured or sick persons are frequently transported in the patrol wagon in some departments.

Emergency Trucks. Certain large cities have found it desirable to provide one or more emergency trucks for instant service of a varying nature. Equipped with a multitude of tools, devices, and appliances, these trucks are used in speeding to the relief of terrorized persons in a burning building, a threatened suicide, or a drowning person or animal. They are used in rescuing a horse in distress, subduing a mentally ill person, aiding the injured, removing a live wire, or rushing to the relief of any situation which threatens life or property. To name individually the items of equipment carried on such an emergency truck would require too much space to be reproduced here. The ingenuity of the emergency crew can be employed for properly equipping such a vehicle.

Ambulance. A fully equipped ambulance should be available to every police department whether or not it owns and operates one. A medical attendant should be on duty or on call to accompany the ambulance on its run. The police should avoid operating either an emergency truck or an ambulance if private service is available or another city department can provide the service. While these seem like legitimate police services, the difficulty arises from requests of a nonemergency nature. No one has yet worked out a good method of determining whether or not an emergency exists before the equipment is dispatched to the scene, and the case that sounded like a real emergency over the telephone will turn out to be a sprained ankle victim who wants a free ride home or a drunk with no injury at all. One police department that started out with an emergency ambulance service soon found that they were being called to take tonsilectomy patients home from the hospital and were involved in an operation that took many men and a good part of the police budget.

Investigation Car. A car should be equipped to rush to the scenes of crimes and accidents for the purpose of gathering evidence before it is altered or destroyed by untrained employees, a morbid public, or persons interested in suppressing the damaging facts. A complete kit of equipment should be instantly available for this purpose, including fingerprint and general service cameras, fingerprint material, paper, printer's ink, medium-sized rubber roller, plates, small rubber roller for taking fingerprints of dead bodies, fingerprint powders of various compositions, materials for sketching the crime scenes, casting, and other plastic material, preliminary blood test chemicals and aids, filter paper, and blotting paper.

Other equipment should include a magnifying glass, electric light cord extension, flashlights, independent-unit electric floodlight, tripod, steel tape, railroad flares, broom, assortment of bottles and glass stoppers, sealing wax, matches, scissors, and so on.

Service Truck. In the absence of a central municipal garage, the service truck is almost a necessity in a department which has a large number of cars in operation. It will carry spare tires and other parts as are found necessary by experience.

Motorcycles and Bicycles. The question of motorcycles and bicycles and their use has already been discussed in the chapter on patrol. Briefly speaking, the use of these two methods of transportation is quite limited. Only in the larger departments where there is need for this special equipment should they be provided.

Who Should Furnish Equipment?

It is no longer common to find that policemen are required to furnish, at their own expense, the uniform, consisting of cap, blouse, and trousers; overcoat; raincoat; and rain-proof cap cover. Neither are they any longer expected to furnish their own service revolver, holster, or handcuffs.

How much equipment should be furnished the policemen at public expense is influenced by several factors, including community practice in uniforming other employees such as firemen, mechanics, and garage attendants; duty conditions; and the type of assignment and its hazards. The most common answer today for municipal participation in uniform cost is that of a uniform allowance which may vary today up to $125 a year paid monthly, semiannually or annually. It is no longer uncommon for a police department to provide the entire first issue of uniform and equipment to the recruit, without charge, and then on an annual basis to provide him with an allowance.

To require policemen to furnish their own uniforms, revolvers, and other equipment, puts a strain on supervision and may contribute to lowered morale and loss of police prestige. Control can be effected more readily and continuously if the department furnishes all of the officer's initial equipment except his shoes, underwear, and socks. He may then be required to make a presentable appearance at all times. The replacement of uniforms and other items of clothing, on the other hand, may be considered the responsibility of the policeman, since they are his "working clothes." In order to save on the cost of purchase and to insure the presentable appearance of officers the department may procure and issue these replacements and charge the officers what they cost. Replacement of equipment other than clothing, however, should probably be a departmental expense.

An average life of the various articles of clothing can be ascertained for ordinary police duty and a time period established for each clothing item. For unusual types of duty the necessary clothing issues should be by requisition, approved by a designated commanding officer.

Provision should be made for certain articles to be withdrawn from and returned to a storeroom, according to need. This will permit the exercise of responsible custodianship, including the cleaning and repair of appropriate property. All articles of issue remain the property of the municipality of course. Damaged or returned clothing or other articles of issue may often be repaired and restored to use, with resultant economies. Misfits can be avoided, with consequent improvement in the appearance of the force.

Except in most unusual circumstances the police should not be required to furnish their own motorcycles, automobiles, rifles, shotguns, radio equipment, or any of the items not properly included in the list of customary personal articles. Informal arrangements of this sort are frequently made by small communities and may be found quite satisfactory where the demands on the police service are simple. Any larger size police department will do well to provide all police equipment and, in so doing, set up the control measures which will insure a presentable personnel, high morale, and budget economies.

Parking Control

Automobile parking in cities is a major problem. Both the numbers of cars and their use has increased greatly. Every city and town has a "parking problem." There has been so much written on parking, so many discussions, so many surveys, and so much expert opinion that it is not necessary to explore the many ramifications and the possible solutions here. Rather, the police responsibility in relation to parking will be discussed.

The traffic problem is largely a development of this century, and until recent years, a rather gradual development. As it developed, the police were given responsibility for control of all aspects of traffic. They helped establish the laws and ordinances, directed traffic at busy locations, prohibited parking at certain points, and performed many of the duties now the province of the traffic engineer. There was no sound reason to give the police some of these duties, but they were involved through the enforcement of traffic laws, and they became more deeply involved. Traffic engineering has become a highly skilled specialty, and so the duties of traffic engineering have been taken from the police in many cities and given to a traffic engineer. This is a sound move. But the police have still retained functions in relation to traffic that are not a part of the police mission of the protection of the life, property, and rights of citizens and the maintenance of order. For example, many police departments still control the painting of traffic lines on the streets or the work of electricians who maintain traffic signals. These duties clearly are not a police function, and as a result they are rapidly being transferred to a division of the city engaged in maintenance.

But there is another function still generally performed by the police that is in no way a part of the police mission. This is the enforcement of overtime parking regulations. Only the widest stretch of the imagination could consider the length of time a car was parked in a stall, metered or unmetered, a threat to the life, property, or rights of the citizens or likely to result in public disorder. Overtime parking regulations must be enforced of course, but it is not the duty of the police to do this. This enforcement can be accomplished as well, and more economically, by another agency, freeing trained police officers for the duties they are intended to perform. This discussion applies only to the enforcement of overtime parking. Other parking violations, such as in fire zones, across crosswalks, or double parking do constitute enough of a hazard in most circumstances so that they can be considered a police problem and enforced by police officers.

Use of Women

In the last few years, many cities have employed women for enforcing overtime parking regulations. The increase has been so rapid that it is not possible to give an up-to-date total of the numbers employed in this new development. It is apparent that this trend will continue. Experience to date shows these advantages:

1. Trained police officers are released from a mechanical sort of a duty requiring only limited ability so that they may perform in the whole range of police responsibilities.

2. Women assigned to overtime parking control have performed well. They have been conscientious and in general have been more effective in public relations than police officers.

3. Because their duties and the skills involved are limited, and since they work only during the daytime and do not work on Sundays and holidays, they are paid a lower salary than a police officer.

There are two drawbacks:

1. Women seem to be more effected by adverse weather conditions.

2. They are limited in their duties to overtime enforcement, although they can perform such services as giving directions and answering questions.

There has been some concern that women employed to enforce overtime parking will assume the status of police officers and so be given the salary, pension, and other benefits of a regular police officer. If this occurred, of course, it would be disadvantageous. To avoid this, and also because it is sound organization, in some cities these women are not a part of the police department, but work for another branch of the city, usually the traffic engineer. While they wear uniforms, they do not have a police badge or police authority. There is no reason for them to be given police authority. Court cases uniformly have held that issuance of a ticket does not constitute an arrest. Unless there is specific local law governing this, the women do not need status as enforcing officers.

Enforcement of Parking Regulations

A number of parking regulations do fall within the duties of the police. The question then arises as to which division of the department should have this function, traffic or patrol? It has been a rather general policy to assign this function to the traffic division if the department has one.

There may be a unit of the traffic division with a title similar to "downtown traffic" that has the combined duties of parking enforcement and direction of traffic. However, in most cities this type of organization results in unneeded and often harmful specialization. These officers are prone to ignore any but parking violations and suffer from all of the ills of specialization as pointed out in other sections of this book, but they do not enjoy any of the benefits of specialization since the writing of traffic tickets or the directing of traffic is so easily learned that specialization is not required. Therefore, it is sound policy to place these men under the patrol division. As a result, they will have plenty of time to write the needed traffic tickets as they patrol the area assigned. They can do an efficient parking enforcement job without interference with their patrol duties. If it is necessary to stop writing a parking ticket to answer an emergency call, little harm is done.

Because the area where most parking problems occur is usually congested, officers assigned to this area during the times when parking is a problem may be on foot. If they are motorized, they are often on three-wheel motorcycles because it is easy to maneuver and park. With the advent of the compact automobiles, there has been considerable interest in their use for parking enforcement. The compact cars are apparently no more expensive to buy or maintain than three-wheel motorcycles, are safer, protect the officer from the weather, allow him to carry additional equipment, and can safely carry additional officers or prisoners. Compacts are not as maneuverable as a three-wheeler nor can they be parked as easily, but they will doubtless find many useful applications in police work.

Policies in Parking Control

Definite, written policies for enforcing parking regulations should be drafted. It is not enough to tell the officers to go out and enforce the law. Many sorts of parking violations are not that clear-cut, and the interpretation of the law will vary widely from officer to officer. Public acceptance will be difficult to gain because the citizen will find that he is given a ticket in one part of town for the same act that is overlooked in another section patrolled by a different officer. The citizen will not like this, and rightly so. Here are some examples where policies should be established:

1. Double parking: Is it permissible to double park so long as the driver remains in the car? If not, how long can he be stopped before he is given a ticket? Should he be

warned first and then given a ticket only if he has not moved the next time the officer comes around?

2. Parking in prohibited zones: How much of a car can extend into a prohibited zone before a ticket is written? Does this rule vary between a loading zone and a fireplug? Can a car be parked in a prohibited zone if the driver remains in the car?

3. Delivery vehicles: What is a delivery vehicle? Is it enough to have a card on a sun visor of a passenger car identifying it as a delivery vehicle? Can recognized delivery vehicles double park or park in prohibited zones? If so, for how long? If they can park in a prohibited area to make a delivery, can they also park to make collections?

Careful establishment of these sorts of policies will take a lot of the difficulty out of administering a parking control program. There will be fewer complaints if the law is enforced on the basis of a uniform and carefully worked out policy. When there are complaints, they will be easier to answer because the reasons for the policy and the studies made before it was adopted will answer many of these complaints. They will not necessarily satisfy the complainant, because few people are happy unless they can park just where they want to when they want to, but a well-developed policy will at least put the police administrator on firm ground when he explains the police position.

Junior Traffic Police

Heavy demands made on the police for services that draw ever larger quotas from patrol make desirable a thorough analysis to discover ways to meet these demands without excessive patrol depletion or the appointment of additional men. The branch of service that continues year after year to increase its demands for manpower more than any other is the traffic division. Mention has been made previously of the desirability of analyzing intersection and crosswalk assignments to establish the genuineness of the need and also to discover, when possible, some mechanical device, regulation, roadway redesign, or other plan that will eliminate the need for continuous attention by a policeman.

The junior traffic police is an example of a plan that has been used for more than 37 years in some communities to eliminate or reduce the use of policemen at school crossings. Scores of small communities, as well as some with populations in excess of 100,000, are forced to assign all on-duty policemen to school-crossing duty during three periods of each school day, thus leaving the city literally without police protection during approximately three hours of each school day. The desirability of salvaging this manpower for regular police duty, if this can be done without jeopardizing the safety of the children, is readily apparent.

Opposition to the junior traffic police is based on two fallacies: (1) that children cannot provide as high a degree of safety protection as adult crossing guards and consequently to jeopardize in this way the life and safety of school children, and especially of the junior traffic police themselves, is false economy and morally wrong, and (2) that children are sent to school for an education, not to be used as policemen.

The first fallacy grows out of a lack of understanding of the method of operation of a well-organized, trained, and directed junior traffic police and the extent of the safety coverage provided by them. Whereas the prevalent custom is to assign one policeman or adult crossing guard to each school, the junior traffic police may establish control points at each of the four corners of the block containing the school and also have junior traffic policemen, individually or in pairs, assigned to intersections that may be removed from the school as much as three or four blocks, thus providing protection far beyond the capacity of one or two adult crossing guards.

"Although this is done in numerous communities, including Berkeley, California, it is not generally approved by school authorities for two reasons: first, it removes boys from the observation and immediate supervision of school personnel; and, second, going to and from these isolated locations does utilize additional pupil time. This system has worked most satisfactorily in Berkeley and has enabled us to supervise some remote locations that would otherwise be unattended."[16]

The cost of providing an equal safety protection for school children by the use of the least expensive adult crossing guards would prove prohibitive to even the most wealthy community. When properly trained in suitable operating procedures, the hazard to the individual junior traffic policeman, while so operating, is less than though he were an ordinary schoolboy for the reason that his conspicuously colored sweater, cap or yellow rain hat and slicker, and the presence of a number of other boys similarly dressed, some with colored signal staffs or semaphores, calls the attention of motorists to the junior traffic police, thus enhancing the street-crossing safety of all school children. The safety of the junior traffic policeman is also protected by regulations that forbid standing in the path of moving vehicles where he might be in danger.

The second fallacy results from a failure to understand the positive advantages that accrue to school children who participate in the junior traffic police as well as to those who are controlled by it. Junior traffic policemen are trained and disciplined in an important traffic function that promotes safety-mindedness; the performance of their tasks stimulates their sense of civic responsibility which is so essential in the development of good citizenship. Since membership in the junior traffic police is not static, a fair proportion of the schoolboys have an opportunity of profiting by this service.

The experience of other school children in complying with the directions of their playmate traffic officers also constitutes valuable training in the important civic virtues of conforming with regulations and complying with the directions of authority. The experience of children at schools that employ junior traffic police trains them in law observance. This feature is important not only to the police but to the parents and the community as well. Also, the close relationship of the police to the participants has a clearly discernible public-relations value, and the friendliness of the relationship provides some delinquency-prevention benefits.

---

[16]Statement by Addison H. Fording, chief of police, Berkeley, California, 1960.

Chapter 14

THE POLICE AND THE PUBLIC

A person's conduct is determined on the one hand by what he wants to do and on the other by what he is afraid to do. His compliance with law and regulation is obtained either by developing in him a willingness to conform to the desired pattern of behavior or by compelling him to conform by threat of punishment.

The two processes — enforcement and the development of attitudes favorable to law observance — cannot be completely separated, with the police free to choose one and reject the other. Instead, their use is a matter of degree or emphasis. The police in one jurisdiction may attempt to accomplish its purpose by enforcement with indifferent or no attention to winning compliance by other means; in others they will give first attention to winning compliance using minimum enforcement on individuals when other methods fail.

Compliance is won principally by force in totalitarian and police states. In those countries the police are a tool of the central government used to impose its will on the people and to perpetuate its administration. Some American police forces have been used in this manner and for the same purpose. On the other hand, compliance with minimum enforcement is the democratic process; it is a basic characteristic of the best British and American police forces. Their leaders are becoming more and more convinced that no lasting good will come of a control imposed on an unwilling people; that no real progress is made in the development of order and security except as an attitude favorable to law observance is developed in the people.

This does not mean that enforcement should not be used by the police in a democracy. It does mean, however, that it should not be used except as approved by the majority. Compliance won principally by force is a characteristic of police incompetence; it is the hard way to do the job. Compliance won principally by other means is evidence of a high order of police ability; it is the easiest and most desirable method of accomplishing the police purpose.

In this chapter the principle will be developed that sound public relations is basic to the effectiveness of the police. The following chapter deals with the development, organization, and administration of a public relations program.

Policemen Work with People

To the citizen in distress seeking assistance or information, and to the citizen in conflict with the law, the policeman *is* the city government. The public relations not only of the police department but of the city government as a whole rest squarely on the individual officer's contact with citizens. It should also be remembered that the children of today are the citizens of tomorrow. Effective police work with children on the basis of friendliness and help will pay returns to the community in crime reduction and to the police in a body of citizens in sympathy with and helpful toward the achievement of police objectives. Some aspects of these contacts may appear to be minor details. If they are neglected, however, public resentment is likely to overpower good will.

Police Dependence on Citizen Attitudes

Protection of citizens is a primary function of government, and representatives of the people hire police officers to perform this important task. As in any other employment, there must exist a suitable employer-employee relationship. The police must recognize and understand this relationship.

The desired relationship between the police and the public is impossible to attain unless both have suitable attitudes. The actions and conduct of each are determined by their own attitudes, which in turn influence the attitudes and conduct of the other. The attitude of the public is molded and built by the police themselves; it reflects the police attitude.

While the police themselves are the most important influence on public attitudes, others are in constant play. The press and motion pictures exert a powerful influence in shaping public opinion, and through misrepresentation they may create an attitude which is unfriendly and unfair to the police. Strong personalities within a community, if not converted to the police point of view, may likewise do much to destroy public confidence in the police, to build resentment, and to prevent the creation of a desirable harmony between police and public. The police, however, may favorably influence these factors by proper attitudes of their own.

The city council and city administration have an important effect on public attitudes toward the police. Unless they have a proper appreciation of police problems, they may embarrass the police by enacting and insisting on the enforcement of ill-advised laws. The police must then bear the brunt of public reaction; this results in reduced efficiency and lowered morale.

The Police Point of View. Since a person's actions are determined by his frame of mind, policemen should scrutinize their own points of view. Their attitudes will be determined by their concept of the police function — of their duty toward the public. They should recognize the line of demarcation between the police function and the judicial function. They should realize that the essence of a proper police attitude is a willingness to serve. They should distinguish between service and servility, courtesy and softness. They must be firm, but at the same time courteous; they must avoid an appearance of rudeness. They should develop a friendly, impersonal, and unbiased manner, pleasant and personal in all nonrestrictive situations but firm and impersonal on occasions calling for regulation and control. They should understand that the primary police purpose is to prevent violations — not to arrest offenders.

Police attitudes influence the public in proportion to the frequency of contact. Since the police make more public contacts in controlling traffic than in any other activity, it is especially important that continuous attention be paid to police attitudes in dealing with traffic offenders if increased respect and improved relations are to be obtained.

Public Attitudes. Generally speaking, police effort to control the public meets with resistance. Americans resist regulation; they resent being told what to do and what not to do. Rebellion against control is sometimes more than ordinary "sales resistance." It is equivalent to the resistance met by salesmen for products of poor quality or for products manufactured or distributed by an organization with a reputation for inferior service. A police department that has been guilty of bad practices toward its citizens may meet a resistance which appears to be impenetrable. The stronger the resistance, the more important it is to break it down and establish a spirit of friendly cooperation. The best way to do it is to develop a strong public relations program.

The police gain distinct advantages by maintaining a spirit of friendly cooperation with the public. There is an interacting relationship between high standards of police conduct and the public support on which those standards depend. Increased support of the police program is fostered by effective public relations which lay the foundation for higher standards of police work and form the basis for renewed public support. The police then find themselves in a favored position. Commendation and praise build morale. This leads to increased police efforts which bring improved police services. With strong support from the community at large, it is possible to carry out difficult programs. Progressive programs and a general increase in police efficiency result in still greater appreciation of police efforts.

A cooperative public renders assistance to the police in many ways. A public that observes laws and complies with regulations relieves the police of a large share of their normal burden. Because people want public esteem, the public's intolerance toward violations favorably influences law observance by individuals. The cooperation of the public is necessary in the enforcement of major laws as well as of minor regulations. It is necessary to the successful administration of any police department.

Fortunate are the police who have the support and cooperation of the public. Without it arrests are made more difficult and convictions are sometimes impossible. Unjust charges are frequently made against the police when their public relations are unsatisfactory. They are ridiculed, criticized, buffeted about, and censured at every move. Their sound and progressive programs may be impeded, and they may find themselves in a mental state that causes them to be fearful of doing anything constructive because of possible criticism.

The police are inclined to assume that unfriendly citizens are their natural enemies and that all citizens are unfriendly. Unfortunately the police frequently act accordingly. Neutral and even friendly citizens, when treated in an unfriendly manner, soon become unfriendly also.

Police morale is jeopardized, and the development of *esprit de corps* is difficult in an unfriendly community. Such a state is disadvantageous to the police. An unfriendly public overlooks no opportunity to make the police task more onerous and working conditions less desirable. In an attempt to appease a dissatisfied public, the administration may take from the police many of their recently gained advantages of salary increases, shorter work week, improved sick relief, insurance provisions, pensions, and other security benefits for members of the department.

A public that cooperates with the police, that supports them in their efforts, and that observes laws and regulations has a proper attitude toward the police and law enforcement. The police administrator is confronted with the important task of creating this greatly-to-be-desired attitude.

Police dependence on citizen attitudes is so important that it is, in one sense, the subject of the rest of this chapter. A favorable public attitude must be earned by the police, but the rewards are great in both public respect and self-respect. This attitude toward the police is influenced greatly by steps toward professionalism, development of police ethics, personal conduct of policemen, personal integrity, and respect for the due process of law.

The Police Profession[1]

Men who have obligations toward mankind in general differ from those who owe their employers only a return for their pay. Those with higher obligations, rooted in religious or ethical philosophy, are the professionals. They violate oath, belief, and purpose if the size of their fees affects their skill in practice. This is an ideal, of course. Quacks, shysters, and racketeering evangelists bear little resemblance to the professional ideal. However, this does not erase the fact that each profession has its hard core of practical idealists who make professionalism a reality.

Professionalism

More specifically, what are the characteristics of a profession? The following definition is taken from a combination of observations: (1) the recorded opinions of professional men both living and deceased; (2) the oaths, canons, and ethical codes of professional societies; and (3) popularly accepted principles of western religion and western philosophy.

Basic Obligations. A profession is that occupational group which practices its skills with the following basic obligations:

1. A duty to serve mankind generally rather than self, individuals, or groups.

2. A duty to prepare as fully as practicable for service before entering active practice.

3. A duty to work continually to improve skills by all means available and to freely communicate professional information gained.

4. A duty to employ full skill at all times regardless of considerations of personal gain, comfort, or safety, and at all times to assist fellow professionals upon demand.

5. A duty to regulate practice by the franchising of practitioners, setting the highest practicable intellectual and technical minimums; to accept and upgrade fellow professionals solely upon considerations of merit; and to be constantly alert to protect society from fraudulent, substandard, or unethical practice through ready and swift disfranchisement.

6. A duty to zealously guard the honor of the profession by living exemplary lives publicly and privately, recognizing that injury to a group serving society injures society.

7. A duty to give constant attention to the improvement of self-discipline, recognizing that the individual must be the master of himself to be the servant of others.

By these standards it is clear that police work is not a profession. While tremendous strides have been made in late years toward improving its technology and further strides may develop a science of law enforcement, it must be borne in mind that the terms "science" and "profession" are not synonymous. For example, the fact that a science of medicine exists does not guarantee professional application of its principles. Professionalism is a subjective concept, concerned with the philosophy that directs the application of the body of knowledge. For this reason practical policemen must recognize that philosophy is a practical thing, not the exclusive possession of dreamers and theorists. If professionalism is to be achieved, policemen must concern themselves as much with police philosophy as with police techniques.

---

[1]This section is based on E. W. Roddenberry, "Achieving Professionalism," *Journal of Criminal Law, Criminology, and Police Science*, May-June, 1953, pp. 111-15.

At least one question remains: should police work be a profession? A report from the National Occupation Council states: "The entire governmental structure is built upon a foundation of law and order, which, in turn, is entirely dependent upon efficient and honest police administration." In other words, order is dependent upon law, and law is dependent upon enforcement. If this is true, police work has deep significance.

Woodrow Wilson, commenting upon the place of policemen in society, characterized their obligations as "sacred and direct." The policeman shirks fundamental obligations if he considers himself mere contracted labor with freedom to prefer private advantage to public welfare.

Few will disagree that society needs honest and efficient law enforcement of the highest type. Few will disagree that police work could attain a position equal with the most respected occupations if sincere and devoted effort were directed toward that goal. It is possible that this can be accomplished if the policeman feels pride in his place in the scheme of things.

Basic Characteristics. It is a natural inclination for homogeneous groups to desire "professional" status — acceptance by others of their occupation as one with social standing. But professionalism carries with it certain characteristics as well as responsibilities. Some distinguishing characteristics of a professional group are: (1) a common fund of knowledge; (2) certain standards or qualifications based on character, training, and competency required for admission to the profession; (3) certain standards of conduct required with respect to relations with others in the profession and with the public, based upon courtesy, honor, and ethics; (4) constructive interest in the selection, training, and apprenticeship of candidates for the profession; and (5) an organization, formal or informal, based primarily on common interest and public duty.

Organizations. A number of organizations growing up within the police field have achieved professional status or are tending toward it. It is good policy for police officials and others in municipal government to support these organizations not only by according them recognition and encouraging their activities, but also by helping them to recognize and accept the responsibilities of professionalism. Although there are upward of one-half million law enforcement officers in this country, there is no one group that brings them all together as in England. Instead, there are numerous separate bodies, each devoted to a single segment of the police field. Among these are the International Association of Chiefs of Police, the International Association for Identification, and the Associated Police Communications Officers. In addition some state groups such as the Women Peace Officers Association of California are considered professional groups.

The objects of the International Association of Chiefs of Police are to advance the science and art of police administration and crime prevention, to develop and disseminate improved administrative and technical practices and promote their use in police work, to foster police cooperation and exchange of information and experience among police administrators throughout the world, to bring about enlistment and training in the police profession of qualified persons, and to encourage adherence of all police officers to high professional standards of conduct. Membership is open to national, state, provincial, county, and municipal police officials with command responsibilities. Associate membership is open for persons qualified by training and experience in police, or other law enforcement activity, or by other professional attainments in police science or administration. The association serves as a clearinghouse of information relating to police administration and current activities in the field, publishes a monthly journal *(The Police Chief)*, the *Police Yearbook*, bulletins on police subjects, and a directory of law enforcement officers. It also conducts an annual conference.

The International Association for Identification has a membership of police officials in charge of fingerprint and identification bureaus — specialists in fingerprints, ballistics, toxicology, microscopy, handwriting, and other phases of the science of identification. It cooperates with the Federal Bureau of Investigation, the International Association of Chiefs of Police, and state bureaus of identification. A newsletter is issued monthly, and a year book also is published.

The purpose of the Associated Police Communications Officers is to foster the development and progress of the art of police communication and intercommunication and to promote, through example and active effort, greater cooperation in the correlation of the work and activities of town, city, county, state, and federal law enforcement agencies.

Police Ethics [2]

The good reputation that police service bears with the public is built on favorable public relationships and is expressed by public confidence in the continued constructive accomplishments of the service. Consistent progress in police service is possible only when the internal strength of the organization is assured. There must be high morale among the members of the service reflected in their *esprit de corps* and springing from their genuine loyalty and faith in the policies and objectives of their organization. There must be a conscious effort on the part of each and every member of the service to so conduct both his official and private life that he will inspire the confidence and trust of the public.

The public demands of its servants more exacting and exemplary conduct than it expects of private citizens. It is an inescapable fact that a public official has little private life; as soon as he enters public service and so long as he remains therein his conduct, whether on or off duty, will be subjected to the unrelenting scrutiny and critical analysis of the public he serves. The agents of law enforcement by reason of their specific responsibilities are bound to a more exacting code than any other public servant. Delinquencies may pass unchallenged when committed by other public officials. Certain conduct of citizens is accepted as commonplace. But such delinquencies and conduct are adjudged reprehensible when committed by policemen.

The honored professions long ago recognized the importance of maintaining public confidence in their endeavors and accordingly enacted exacting rules for their membership. Policemen have long been clamoring for public recognition as a professional service, yet for many years little was done to set standards of official conduct for their members. They relied upon departmental rules and regulations to set the pattern for their public relationships. Some law enforcement agencies put great reliance upon the solemnity of the oath of office or departmental pledge to impel men to exemplary conduct. But the rules and regulations of most police departments relate more to specific techniques and procedures than to the official conduct of officers in their public relationships, and when regulations relating to conduct are found they are usually so specific in character that they lose their influence in shaping general official conduct. Oaths of office and departmental pledges are of necessity brief and are usually too general in substance to serve as a guide to the policeman in shaping his daily relationships with the citizenry.

Code of Professional Ethics. The void resulting from the lack of a clear-cut guide for police conduct was substantially filled in 1956 when a code of ethics was adopted by

---

[2]This section is based on Dan L. Kooken, "Police Ethics" *Journal of Criminal Law, Criminology, and Police Science*, May-June and July-August, 1947, pp. 62-65 and 173-77.

several police organizations. The code was drafted by a committee of the Peace Officers Research Association of California, edited by a committee of the California Peace Officers Association, and was adopted by both organizations. The code reads as follows:

> As a Law Enforcement Officer, my fundamental duty is to serve mankind; to safeguard lives and property; to protect the innocent against deception, the weak against oppression or intimidation, and the peaceful against violence or disorder; and to respect the Constitutional rights of all men to liberty, equality, and justice.

> I will keep my private life unsullied as an example to all; maintain courageous calm in the face of danger, scorn, or ridicule; develop self-restraint; and be constantly mindful of the welfare of others. Honest in thought and deed in both my personal and official life, I will be exemplary in obeying the laws of the land and the regulations of my department. Whatever I see or hear of a confidential nature or that is confided to me in my official capacity will be kept ever secret unless revelation is necessary in the performance of duty.

> I will never act officiously or permit personal feelings, prejudices, animosities, or friendships to influence my decisions. With no compromise for crime and with relentless prosecution of criminals, I will enforce the law courteously and appropriately without fear or favor, malice, or ill will, never employing unnecessary force or violence and never accepting gratuities.

> I recognize the badge of my office as a symbol of public faith, and I accept it as a public trust to be held so long as I am true to the ethics of police service. I will constantly strive to achieve these objectives and ideals, dedicating myself before God to my chosen profession... law enforcement.

Meeting the Public

A policeman's duty is to regulate the conduct of and minister to the needs of people of all walks of life. The rich and the poor, the old and the young, the firm and the infirm, the learned and the illiterate are equally entitled to the protection of the law. The public contacts of policemen are principally with persons who, at the time, are under stress or excitement. They are citizens who, in trouble or difficulty, turn to the policeman for assistance and protection. Their problems are most important to them, though they may seem insignificant to the policeman who is accustomed to deal daily with sordid and distressing situations. It is imperative that matters of such vital personal importance be approached with understanding, compassion, and magnanimity.

Personal Conduct

The relationships between individuals are affected by the impact of their personalities one upon the other. Every characteristic in the personality of one person becomes an important factor in the reaction or behavior of the other. A policeman may develop a favorable personality if he recognizes and cultivates the characteristics or traits that are known to produce favorable reactions in others and suppresses the ones that are responsible for unfavorable reactions. The development of personality, however, involves a sincere acceptance of the fact that, in order to make the proper adjustments and corrections, the policeman must institute disciplinary checks. It is imperative that he develop good habits and eliminate bad habits.

Importance of Good Habits. Habits of politeness are formed in the everyday life of the policeman. These habits may stem from the practice of courtesy in the home as evoked by parental discipline. But among fellow workers courtesy is an official subject; it is compelled by disciplinary measures provided for in the regulations of the organization. The finest example of official courtesy is found in military organizations, where exacting codes of official conduct are enforced by disciplinary authority.

Before policemen can fully appreciate the rights and privileges of citizens, they must first have learned to respect the rights and privileges of their comrades. They will not recognize the importance of their fellow citizens until they have formed the habit of being considerate of their colleagues. If policemen cannot subscribe to the rules of propriety in the intimate relationships with their comrades, then they have not captured the spirit of amenity and cannot sincerely practice courtesy in the less intimate relationships with the public.

Is Courtesy a Sign of Weakness? Numerous contacts with antisocial persons are likely to cause policemen to assume a veneer of hardness. They often entertain an erroneous belief that courteous treatment of law violators is an indication of weakness, of cringing, or of servility. They will say that criminals are not entitled to the treatment accorded gentlemen. Propriety in the treatment of law breakers in no way indicates weakness. Policemen may be firm and exacting in the enforcement of the law; they may be strict and relentless in their relationships with the offenders that come under their control yet remain helpful and gentlemanly in their bearing. The fact that a criminal, by reason of his depravity or because of his antisocial habits, has not earned the respect of his fellow man has no bearing upon the conduct of the policeman with whom he is brought into contact. When officers of the law resort to ungentlemanly treatment of criminals, they do not alter the status of the criminals in the least. They only lower their own social status to the same level occupied by criminals.

Acts of courtesy are disciplinary reminders of the importance of helpful conduct and are important measures in the development of personality. Courtesy is the essence of good manners. It is a manifestation of sportsmanship, and an exposition of gentility and culture. The rules of etiquette that prescribe the common acts of courtesy were established by years of custom and usage, and their performance is a public acknowledgement of understanding and of a sincere acceptance of the rules of gentlemanly demeanor. Strict adherence to the standards of proper behavior curbs undesirable characteristics, thus breaking up and destroying bad habits; at the same time, it strengthens the influence of the favorable characteristics of personality.

Use of Authority. Citizens look upon policemen as representatives of the authority of law. It is obvious therefore that the influence of policemen over citizens is increased by reason of the authority they represent. People under stress or under the influence of excitement are more susceptible to the influence of external stimuli than they would be under normal circumstances. They are likely to be more readily influenced by the actions of those with whom they come into contact. Policemen must be very careful that the influence of their authority does not become oppressive in their relationship with the public, particularly in situations of stress and excitement.

Being courteous involves much more than friendliness. To appreciate and to sincerely and habitually perform acts of courtesy requires cultivation of appearance, voice, manner, intelligence, humor, temperament, and unselfishness. All of these factors comingle in the production of a gentleman in principle and in conduct. Being a gentleman is not a part-time occupation; neither are there varying gradations of politeness in human relationships. One cannot be a gentleman in public and a cad in private; neither can one be a gentleman for a part of the time or only under certain circumstances or only with certain persons.

Courtesy must spring from the heart; it must originate in a sincere desire to be right, to be respected and honored. Sincere courtesy requires one to be friendly without becoming familiar; dignified without being aloof; compassionate but firm and earnestly interested without being over-solicitous. Policemen must continually practice courtesy;

they must not make exceptions. Disagreeable duties must be performed willingly and unpleasant orders obeyed cheerfully. Flares of temper, sarcasm, and periods of moodiness have no place in the conduct of a good police officer.

Police officers must be exceptionally careful not to say or do anything that might be construed as critical or disparaging of any race, creed, or class of people. They must avoid abruptness in answering queries, and they must particularly refrain from harsh or insolent language whether on duty or off duty.

Departmental rules and regulations cannot anticipate all situations that might arise involving courteous behavior. Policemen frequently find many occasions where they are compelled to go beyond the limitations of the rule in their determinations of the courteous courses to follow.

Responsibility of a Policeman

The responsibilities of policemen in providing for the safety and convenience of the public are analogous to those of the doctor. The doctor protects life by combating disease and promoting public health through preventive measures. The policeman insures public safety by the elimination of the hazards of accident and in guarding the citizen against the attacks of the antisocial. However, the policeman has a collateral responsibility to protect life and property — a responsibility that is fundamental to every duty he performs, a grave obligation to preserve to the citizens the constitutional guarantees of liberty and the pursuit of happiness.

A Conspicious Failure. Policemen generally have willingly accepted their responsibility to protect life and property and have made considerable progress despite the many obstacles and inadequacies that beset their paths. Innumerable instances are on record where policemen have bravely given their lives in faithfully discharging their duty. But in the preservation of the constitutional guarantees of civil liberty, the police service has most certainly failed.

False imprisonment, illegal search, "the third degree," special privilege, and denial of due process of law are not the exception but are commonplace in many police organizations. Although these malpractices are rarely openly defended, they are condoned by far too many police administrators, and often it is these same administrators who clamor for elevation of the standards of police service.

When public indignation is aroused by reason of violations of civil liberties by policemen, the responsible administrators usually are quick to place the blame upon political interference, inadequate wages, weaknesses of the law, or lack of public support, instead of accepting the fact that they, the administrators, have failed to discharge their basic responsibility to the public. Political intervention, low wages, weak laws, public apathy, and many other similar factors do contribute difficulties to the effective administration of police service, but their elimination will never occur so long as police administrators use such excuses to cover their own ignorance or deliberate disregard of the fundamental responsibilities of administration. Those police heads who have used every political influence and power at their command to secure an appointment are the first to clamor for protection from political removal.

Elimination of the many bars to effective police functions is a responsibility of the police service — a responsibility that rests squarely upon the shoulders of the profession itself. Although the retarding influences may be directly attributed to politics, public apathy, or other influences from the outside, they will cease only when the police service recognizes its professional responsibility to clean its own house.

The police service will not achieve the goal of professionalism as long as police administrators are unwilling to subordinate their selfish ambitions and sincerely and enthusiastically accept the obligations of their office. One of the basic characteristics of a good administrator is the courage to accept his responsibilities and to deny himself the support of an alibi.

Dependability. The public has a right to demand the same guarantees in the manner of its safety as it exacts in the protection of its health. Public safety is concerned with emergencies, with situations that require immediate attention and effective treatment. Police service, if it is to be of any value, must be dependable. Dependability arises from full appreciation and acceptance of the responsibilities of the service. Policemen must be punctual, attentive, accurate, and unselfish if they are to be depended upon. They must promptly carry out every assigned duty. They must accept the fact that punctuality involves more than reporting to work on time. It involves every detail of the policeman's daily activity.

The practice of being at the right place at the right time must become a fixed habit. All the skill and ability that a man may possess is of little value unless he can be depended upon to apply his skills at the proper time. Punctuality is not only important in relationships with the public but also essential in routine activities. The rendition of reports, appearances in court, and cooperation with colleagues and other law enforcement agencies are dependable duties only if promptly dispatched.

Attention to Duty. Attention is another important factor contributing to the dependability of public service. The majority of contacts of the police with citizens involve interchange of information, information involving the safety or convenience of the public, information that is given in sincere confidence and with the expectation of aid or assistance. Obviously then, the situations demand the undivided attention of the policeman. Only with complete attention can he render dependable service.

Attention to duty must be a habit; it is just as true here as it is of all the other factors that enter into the state of being dependable. Habits can best be developed in everyday associations with fellow workers. Attention to orders, concentration upon the objectives of the service, appreciation of the importance of command, and interest in an analysis of and an understanding of the policies of administration, all are factors requiring the close attention of dependable officers.

Accuracy. Police work is a continuous investigation, a close observation of facts, an exhaustive search of causation involving countless comparisons and numerous experiments. It involves analytical examinations of complaints, information, conditions, operation beliefs, and appearances, all to the end that the truth shall be made clear. Obviously then, policemen cannot be content with hearsay or mere suspicions. They must be accurate in every detail of their work, as exact in their work as a scientist. Though police work has generally been looked upon as an art, modern policing in many of its phases demands this degree of scientific accuracy. The high degree of perfection attained by the sciences today has been due primarily to meticulous accuracy. The brilliant and fruitful ideas of the scientist which are so astonishing in public announcement are not the product of "hunches" or "lucky breaks." They are the culmination of years of exacting research.

Since accuracy is so essential to scientific research, and effective research is vitally important to efficient police service, then accuracy must be maintained in all phases of police service. The complexity of the criminal law hides many pitfalls and hazards in its accurate administration. Nowhere else is it easier to err; nowhere else is a mistake more fatal and dangerous than when the question involves the life or liberty of a human being; and nowhere is it so necessary or appropriate to acknowledge an error, as soon as possible after its commission, as in the service of public safety.

Professional Jealousy. The United States Supreme Court in a decision some years ago severely condemned the methods employed by the police in an investigation of a criminal offense. The court characterized the conduct of the police officers in this instance as "so inherently coercive that its very existence is irreconcilable with the mental freedom of a lone suspect." The foregoing is but one of many official disclosures of instances where law enforcement officers have exceeded the scope of their authority, and there are innumerable instances equally as reprehensible that have gone unchallenged. These questionable practices are the result of faulty techniques, and the predominant factor has been professional jealousy with an accompanying desire for publicity. Officers who are jealous of their professional reputation divide their interest and attention between the tasks at hand and with selfish concern over credit for their work. In their intense desire for self-glorification they are subject to fears and delusions of loss of credit or notoriety, all of which leads to preconceived theories, false arrest, third degree, and other condemned practices.

Nothing will destroy public confidence in a public servant quicker or more surely than to find him basking in the light of his own notoriety. Dependability is the end product of respect, and it is predicated upon how well the person has recognized his responsibilities and how well he has discharged his responsibilities in the performance of his duties.

Due Process of Law

The responsibility of policemen in the proper administration of criminal law is not to procure the conviction of one whom they suspect of a criminal offense. It is rather to gather all of the facts pertaining to the incident, and to present the facts fairly and impartially to the proper court in order that justice may be done. This is true whether the policemen are in favor of or against any suspected person. In the investigation of criminal offenses police officers are in some respects officers of the court, and though they exercise no judicial function they must never forget that the whole scheme of American justice is founded upon the principles of fairness, reason, and impartiality in its administration.

Responsibility To Protect Rights. It is just as much the duty of policemen to see that persons suspected of criminal offenses are not deprived of their statutory or constitutional rights as it is to aid in their conviction of the crimes of which they may be suspected. It is difficult for policemen to appreciate this responsibility. Recognition and practice of this self-evident duty constitute the exceptions rather than the rule. It is regrettable indeed that so many policemen, in their zeal to secure the conviction of a suspect, lose all perspective of fundamental responsibility. In their enthusiasm to add one more conviction to their record, they are heedless of the importance of their obligation as guardians of personal liberty. Probably it is true that bank robbers, kidnappers, and other criminals have forfeited, by reason of their vicious antisocial behavior, all personal right to the respect of decent people, but when, in the enforcement of law, the police fail to extend to them the rights of due process they set precedents that are not restricted to the vicious alone.

Zeal on the part of policemen engaged in criminal investigations is to be commended, but if they allow themselves to be led by their enthusiasm into practices that are not only illegal but seriously endanger the basic principles of American freedom, then they most certainly are to be censured. Grave danger lies in the fact when policemen insist upon the right to decide when and under what circumstances the constitutional rights of liberty are to be applied. They are assuming authority they never had and never were intended to possess. If allowed to go unchallenged it is but a short step to a condition that exists in some jurisdictions where liberty is but an empty gesture.

In the majority of cases where policemen and prosecutors neglect or ignore the protection of inherent rights of the citizen, the case at hand is not strengthened. On the contrary, it is in most instances seriously weakened if not hopelessly lost. When policemen disregard the constitutional provisions of civil liberty in the treatment of a criminal they create a strange paradox. Their relationship with the accused becomes analogous to that of the accessory after the fact. In their zeal to convict, their denial of due process of law adds materially to the legal defense of the accused.

Snap Judgments. Policemen also are negligent in allowing their own personal opinions, often arrived at prematurely and without foundation in fact, to so influence their investigation that many miscarriages of justice have resulted therefrom. Officers who have formed definite opinions as to guilt or circumstances may innocently exert a strong influence on the statements of witnesses whom they interrogate. Furthermore, when investigators allow theories to form before sufficient facts are disclosed, they are likely to find their subsequent investigation restricted to a search for facts to lend support to the ill-conceived theory. Once an investigation has shifted from an open-minded investigation, even though the preconceived theory has been completely abandoned, the influence of the theory will remain long after its abandonment. The search for new suspects tends to be made with only a passive interest in new and additional facts.

Many hazards instantly appear when a criminal investigation centers upon certain suspects because of premature theories. The most troublesome of these hazards is that of premature arrest. Arrests of this character are not likely to be made by reason of a logical analysis of supporting facts, but they occur by reason of the influence of the preconceived theory, strengthened in part by other conjecture such as the probability of the suspect escaping the immediate jurisdiction or the hope that by severe grilling the suspect may be brought to the point of confessing his crime.

In every instance of premature arrest it eventually becomes apparent that there is not sufficient real evidence to support a specific charge. This condition leads to further compromising situations, and the effect of the troublesome factors are forestalled or delayed by resorting to other questionable practices, thus setting off a chain of illegal action that may run the gamut of condemned practices: filing unjustified vagrancy charges with exorbitant bail, incommunicado confinement to escape writ of habeus corpus, coercive grilling in the hope of securing a confession, third degreeing when coercion fails, and even on up to actual "framing" which has too frequently occurred.

Government Functions Are Separate. Policemen, in their eagerness to detect crime and to apprehend and bring criminals to justice, are inclined to overlook the importance of separation of governmental functions as a safeguard of personal liberty. They are wont to usurp the prerogatives of the judiciary in fixing the guilt or innocence of the accused. Eager to assert this pseudo authority, they will resort to practices that are questionable if not actually illegal.

Unfortunately, policemen's efforts to apprehend wanted criminals are often thwarted or hindered by the very laws deigned to protect the law abiding citizen. This situation has undoubtedly encouraged officers to resort to questionable procedures, especially where little hope is held for a solution through the use of approved methods. Thus, the policeman falls into irregular practices for the sake of convenience and to get the job done, practices that are most certain to lead to trouble.

This condition has prevailed since the inception of police service in the United States. Court records show many instances where law enforcement officers have exceeded their authority. Many civil actions have been instituted, seeking redress for wrongs suffered at the hands of overzealous policemen, and innumerable instances have gone unchallenged.

The public in the past has naively avoided consideration of the fact that the principal difference between a democracy and a totalitarian form of government is not so much in the laws under which they operate as it is in the method of their administration. The public is gradually awakening from its passivity toward the principles of personal liberty. Illegal invasions of the sanctity of private homes, unreasonable detention of persons suspected of crime, and withholding from the innocent and guilty alike the right of due process of law, is bringing increased criticism of enforcement officers both from the public and the courts.

The time is near when police administrators, who attempt to protect their agents from false imprisonment suits by pressing vagrancy charges against the individuals illegally detained, will find such ill-considered subterfuge a boomerang.

Temptations

Policemen are in a position of constant temptation to use their real or pseudo authority to their own personal advantage. To succumb to the temptation is a reprehensible breach of public trust. There are innumerable instances where by reason of the subtlety of the temptation, policemen who are innocent of ulterior motive find themselves in most embarrassing or compromising positions. The American people are an appreciative and generous people. They like to demonstrate their appreciation in a substantial and public fashion. It obviously follows that when policemen in the performance of their duties, render valuable services to citizens, it is only natural that the citizens will attempt to reward the policeman in some manner.

Commendation, recognition, and reward have definite value as morale incentives, but policemen are duty bound to render services daily that represent dictinct value to specific citizens. It is not difficult to perceive the implications if policemen are permitted to accept material tokens of appreciation from the public in recognition of duties well performed over a period of time. The next step is for policemen to expect extra remuneration for the normal performance of duty.

A Free Ride. Most policemen recognize no wrong in accepting free admissions to public entertainment, discounts on their purchases, special favors and considerations from persons of influence, or tips and gratuities for services performed in the line of their regular duty. They choose to look upon these incidents as being strictly personal matters between themselves and the donors and are unwilling to recognize the fact that moral obligations are involved. They are naive indeed to believe that their authority was not an influencing factor in the matter.

No matter how much effort is expended to minimize the derogatory effect of the acceptance of gratuities and favors by law enforcement officers, the practice has become so prevalent that the public generally concedes that policemen are the world's greatest "moochers." Aside from the question of the effect of the practice upon the officer's effectiveness in enforcing the law, it is a certainty that a reputation for "mooching" does not elevate the standards of the profession in the public's mind.

Many police administrators see no harm in permitting policemen to accept gratuities and favors, but in localities where this practice has been condoned over long periods of time policemen have not been content with accepting gratuities and favors but actively solicit them. It is but a short step then to the use of their authority to expedite compliance with their solicitations. In many jurisdictions "mooching" has become a lucrative "racket," an activity that is equally as vicious and as costly to the public as the well-organized racketeering activities of the criminal bands. In the one instance the citizen is forced into compliance with the racketeer's demand by reason of the threat of physical violence at the hands of the criminals; in the other instance, if he fails to comply, he is faced with the prospect of prosecution on trumped-up charges of violation of obscure laws or ordinances.

Publication Rackets. One form of police racketeering that is particularly objectionable is the sale of advertising in "police annuals." Many police departments officially permit annuals to be published with the provision that the proceeds from their publication accrue to the police pension fund. The major objection to this practice is that some of the advertising is solicited from persons who are engaged in activities of a questionable nature or that are subject to considerable police supervision. While the cost of the advertisements obstensibly represents a contribution to an honorable and charitable cause, the rates are entirely out of line with any real advertising value. As a result the contribution in fact implies a purchase of protection for questionable practices.

Other variations of the racket are found in police benefit balls and other police-sponsored gatherings, where admission charges are involved and where the charitable disposition of proceeds are alleged. The usual practice is to sell tickets far in excess of the actual accommodations of the gathering by the simple expedient of delivering books of 10, 20, or even larger numbers of tickets to all the persons engaged in questionable activities with the statement, "Here is your share of the tickets for this event." This technique is identical to methods perfected by Al Capone in the distribution of bootleg liquor stocks.

Police Collection of Funds. In some communities, police collect or sponsor the collection of funds to support youth recreation programs. When police collect and handle such funds, public misunderstanding is certain to arise. Police are able to collect money from private sources when other privately sponsored recreation fails. The plain fact is that many people will not refuse a policeman. Even though no one intends extortion, the objective manifestations are identical. The worthiness of the cause of no excuse. *Police should not collect money for any purpose, from anyone, under any circumstances.*[3]

Innocent Beginnings. The corruption of policemen often begins with obligations that are innocently acquired; involvements that have come upon them subtly. Clever criminals are fully aware of the weaknesses of man. They recognize that the most powerful motive of human behaviour is the desire to be of importance. They know too that men will vigorously defend themselves against loss of face. Crooks will use the techniques developed in confidence games to play upon the vanity of policemen whom they hope to corrupt. Working subtly and by the most indirect routes the policeman is maneuvered into a position where he will accept a gift or favor without knowing the real identity of the donor at the time. Once the initial step is taken the policeman rapidly

---

[3] This paragraph is from Jane E. Rinck, "Supervising the Juvenile Delinquent," *The Annals*, January, 1954, p. 84. Italics added.

becomes more seriously involved. It is but a short step until he is faced with the choice of corrupting his office to the benefit of the criminal or publicly accept responsibility for his past indiscretions.

The prevailing habit of policemen seizing upon every opportunity to use their official positions for mercenary gains leads them into practices that are even more discreditable than their "mooching" proclivities. Included in this category of irregularities are many instances where police officers who investigate traffic accidents involving commercial vehicles appropriate to their personal use merchandise salvaged from the wreck. In many instances officers serving search warrants upon illegally operated establishments will carry away and convert to their own use personal property that is not included in the contraband listed in the search warrant.

Abuses of authority are not confined to the official activities of policemen but are often detected in private undertakings. Outside businesses or occupations of policemen often influence or limit their effectiveness in the discharge of their public obligations. Instances are on record where policemen have used their official positions to the direct benefit of private business or undertakings in which they may be interested.

The Importance of Character

The importance of character as a factor in the consideration of police ethics cannot be fully appreciated unless the significance of leadership in police service is understood. The leadership exercised by policemen in the routine discharge of their duties is of an impersonal type. It is leadership of a regulatory nature that is predicated upon the authority that the policeman represents, rather than the leadership of cooperation as exercised by a person in a supervising position. Obedience to the will of a policeman does not necessarily imply deference to the officer's personality.

Leadership. The willingness of citizens to submit to the commands of policemen is motivated to a great degree by appreciation of the importance of public safety, respect, and confidence in the public service. A powerful influence in securing the public's confidence in a police department is found in personalities of the members of the department, the effect that their personalities have upon the citizens with whom they come into contact. If in the aggregate these contacts are favorable, public respect and confidence are assured. This personal type of leadership, which is much less tangible than the leadership of authority, deserves careful consideration in the evaluation of character.

True leadership is personal; it is the psychological effect that a well-integrated personality will have upon those who come under its influence. It is difficult to enumerate specific characteristics that combine in the personality of a true leader because individuals differ in their viewpoints and reactions. The American public is a willing body of people who ask little more of a leader than those qualities that will command their respect, loyalty, and obedience. The qualities that seem most common to persons who command public respect and confidence are those that rate highly as influences in shaping strength of character. Among the most important of these traits or qualities are: self-confidence, self-sacrifice, paternalism, fairness, initiative and decision, dignity, courage, and moral ascendancy. Each needs further comment.

1. Self confidence is faith in oneself. It is predicated upon knowledge, skill in applying knowledge, and in the ability and willingness to pass one's knowledge on to the benefit of others. Self-confidence is in fact a state of mental satisfaction that arises from being able to put the possession of knowledge to constructive use.

2. _Self-sacrifice is fundamental to true leadership._ It is an inescapable fact that to contemplate a situation without bias requires first a complete subordination of self. Effective police work requires the utmost in self-sacrifice. Policemen who are selfishly impressed with their authority cannot succeed as leaders. Obsessed with fears of the loss of power or authority, they are in a defensive position which seriously affects their efficiency and eventually destroys public confidence in their integrity.

3. _Paternalism is a quality found in men who are mindful of the welfare of others._ It is basic to police leadership because public welfare is a primary responsibility of police service. Harmonious relationships between police service and the public depends, to a great degree, upon the paternalistic influence that enters into the shaping of public policies.

4. _Fairness and honesty are qualities that have universal appeal._ Nowhere is there greater opportunity or greater need to display these qualities than in the police service. A preponderance of public criticism of law enforcement agencies is occasioned by reason of partiality or unfairness in exercising the police function. Impartial application of laws and regulations and fairness and honesty in exercising the authority of office are powerful forces in insuring continued public respect of police service.

5. _Initiative and decision stem from self-confidence._ These are traits of men who act correctly and at the proper time. The ability to act decisively and correctly is a manifestation of preparedness and an interest in and an appreciation of the task at hand. Knowledge, mental alertness, and judgment all enter into the development of this very desirable trait. The ability of policemen to meet emergencies with propriety and decision has a profound effect upon shaping favorable public opinion.

6. _Dignity is a powerful factor in creating public respect._ It is indicative of a policeman's appreciation of the honor of his position. It is an excellent manifestation of his _esprit de corps._ Policemen who are paternalistic in their concern for public welfare, sympathetic in caring for citizens in distress, calm in the face of danger, firm in the enforcement of law, and dignified in their public relationships may be assured that they will be held in high esteem by the citizens they serve.

7. _Courage is expected of policemen._ The mere fact that they are in the uniform of law enforcement officers implies that they have courage, yet true courage is not thoroughly understood by most people. It is a common misapprehension to consider reckless disregard of danger as a manifestation of courage or bravery. True courage is that state of devotion to duty that will give men the moral stamina impelling them to the performance of duty even in the face of full knowledge of the dangers involved. There is still another type of courage that is demanded of policemen — a kind of courage that is of even greater importance than physical courage. It is moral courage, the particular kind of courage that enables men to take it on the chin, to assume the responsibilities of their office without quibbling, and to bravely stand up for their convictions without attempting to shift blame or evade personal criticism. Moral courage is synonymous with integrity.

8. _Moral ascendancy grows out of exemplary character._ It is the influence that one person exercises over a group of persons. It arises out of the practice of self-control, of the ability to withstand the hardships and vicissitudes of the work, and of a sincerity of purpose that is manifest in willingness to personally adhere, without equivocation, to the same standards of conduct that are enforced upon others. Policemen are particularly vulnerable to public criticism for lack of this quality. They must be able to control their emotions, tempers, and likes and dislikes. They must be patient in times of stress, calm in the fact of danger, physically able to withstand hardships without

complaint, and able to effectively conceal their worries. The final measure of moral ascendancy is found in the true character of the individual, by the example he sets in his own living.

Moral ascendancy is most important in evaluating the effectiveness of commanding officers in the police service. The moral force or lack of it in commanding officers is reflected in the character of the men under their control and obviously becomes an important influence in the public's appraisal of police service. Commanding officers cannot maintain leadership over their men if at any time they are placed in positions of moral embarrassment. Questionable character of leaders in public service reflects upon all members of the group.

Summary

The International Association of Chiefs of Police and the American Bar Association frequently have stated that police service should be professionalized. But police service as it is now conducted does not meet all the requirements of a professional service. There are no serious bars to professionalism of the service though full attainment of this aim may still seem to remain in the distant future. The greatest obstacle to achievement of professionalism seems to rest with the police themselves. The police must recognize that their goal cannot be reached by the simple expedient of pronouncement or proclamation. The elevation of the standards of police service to professional acceptance must arise from a firm foundation of basic principles.

Some of these principles have been accepted, others have not. Probably the most important principle still waiting acceptance and its proper place in the complete structure is the one that is concerned with rules of official conduct. For only through ethical consideration of police service can full appreciation be gained that no greater power nor higher honor can be bestowed upon any man than the duty of upholding and defending the principles of the American way of life.

Chapter 15

POLICE PUBLIC RELATIONS PROGRAMS

Many definitions of "public relations" have been advanced. One strongly implies that an organization has public relations whether or not it has a public relations program. Public relations according to this definition is the sum total of all the impressions created by an organization's contacts with the public. Of all municipal organizations, police departments give this definition its greatest validity.

The policeman's business is people. While this is essentially true of every local government employee, it is the policeman who most comes into continual contact with the public. Many of these contacts are direct contacts, in the sense that the policeman meets the citizen face to face. Only a comparatively few direct contacts involve violations, but the policeman continually is called upon to provide information and otherwise assist people where no law has been broken.[1]

Indirect contacts between policemen and the public also are frequent. Perhaps the most common are press reports of police activities. Police "news" is probably the most thoroughly covered aspect of modern life. As one police chief has noted, "Police work and human interest stories are synonymous. Both, therefore, are good copy."[2]

Indirect contacts often have great impact on the public. A news story of sloppy investigation by the department, for example, will certainly have its effect on public relations.[3] But word-of-mouth transmission of the results of direct contacts (as when a motorist tells his friends about a surly traffic cop) can be almost as damaging. It is true, to cite another example, that when policemen are "on the take" their department earns a widespread reputation among the people long before any scandal gets into print.

From these direct and indirect contacts the people gain impressions of their policemen and their police department. It is readily apparent that the policeman and the department have within their capacity to contribute to the improvement or deterioration of the circumstances in which the contacts occur. Therefore, they can have a positive or negative effect on the resulting impressions. The development of policies and practices aimed at improving circumstances of the contact and at achieving a positive impression is a *public relations program*.

Much has been written and said about public relations; most of it is confusing, some

---

[1] G. Douglas Gourley. *Public Relations and the Police* (Springfield, Illinois: Charles C Thomas, Publisher, 1953), p. 4. Referring to a report of the Detroit Police Department, the author observes, "It has been estimated that 90 per cent of all police business is not of a strictly criminal nature."

[2] John M. Gleason. "Policing the Smaller Cities," *The Annals of the American Academy of Political and Social Science,* January, 1954, pp. 16-17.

[3] The public's acceptance of scientific police work carries heavy public relations responsibilities for those engaged in it. In one case, local police turned over to a state crime laboratory the clothes of a murder victim. When they got the clothes back they found the victim's rings stuffed in a finger of one glove. The laboratory's failure to find the rings came under heavy fire from newspapers which earlier had reported that the rings, believed to be stolen by the killer, were the police's major clue. The laboratory's director resigned shortly afterwards.

pure bunk. There is an undeserved aura of mystery surrounding public relations. Anyone can learn to apply the basic elements of a sound public relations program. It is the police administrator's task to make sure that all departmental representatives are adequately trained in sound public relations practices and to maintain the controls necessary to see that the training is put into practice. Further, the administrator is likely to take on greater personal responsibility in those activities which one commonly thinks of when he hears the words "public relations" — such things as talks before citizen groups, preparation of reports for the public, and direct contact with press representatives.

People have many attitudes regarding their police department and the men composing it. To oversimplify a great deal in order to point up the contrast, compare one person who respects the policeman for the necessary work he does with another who believes the policeman to be an unimaginative, civil service-protected beat walker whose most important job is to make sure the downtown businessman hasn't forgotten to lock his door. To the first citizen, a policeman is a courteous and reasonable officer who uses tact and discretion when enforcing traffic laws; to the second he is a grumpy, overbearing, ticket-happy cop "making his quota." The first when called upon to assist a police investigation is self-initiating in volunteering information; the second is reticent and close-mouthed, fearful of "getting involved."

A public relations program can also be considered as a series of contacts with the public in which circumstances are administratively influenced for beneficial results. This need not carry a connotation of manipulation and phony image-building. There are proven and respectable techniques which any administrator, given the inclination and desire, can learn to use with good effect. These techniques are the subject of this chapter.

Background for Public Relations

The starting point in development of a public relations program should be an appraisal of the community's sentiments about policemen and the police department. Probably the most effective way to gauge such sentiments is by means of a public opinion poll, but only one city (Los Angeles) has done any extensive research of this kind.

Most veteran observers of police agencies start with the assumption that police public relations have built-in handicaps not of the individual policeman's making. The rise of professionalism in the police service, most writers in the field of police public relations contend, has not entirely overcome the policeman's unhappy heritage.

A Question of Attitudes

The overwhelming tendency of writers in the field of police work is to accept the premises: (1) that policemen once were men of low reputation and this affects public attitudes today, and (2) that since policemen tend to meet people under conditions where the citizen is under a certain amount of tension, the contacts can very easily result in negative impressions that reinforce these old attitudes. How valid are these premises?

Because they are the opinions of many veteran officers there is little reason to throw them aside. Yet the fact remains that there is "very little factual information about attitudes of the people upon which to build an adequate public relations program."[4] In any

[4] Gourley, *op. cit.*, p. 3.

given city, other than the smallest, it is impossible to say just how important these latent hostilities and negative attitudes are.

The Los Angeles Poll.　The only real attempt at relatively precise measurement of public attitudes toward the police was undertaken by G. Douglas Gourley of the Los Angeles Police Department. [5]　The results were published in 1953.　More than 3,100 persons were interviewed, and the results were machine tabulated from punched cards.　The results in some ways were surprising.　For example, it was found that transportation workers consistently rated their police higher than other groups did, even though they had more contact with them.　"Contrary to many popular beliefs unskilled laborers are most favorably inclined, followed closely by skilled laborers.... Among the lowest votes of confidence were those by professional groups."[6]

A survey such as that conducted in Los Angeles is probably the best way to gather factual data.　However, taking a poll involves many technical points necessary to ensure its validity.　Furthermore, it should be repeated at intervals to measure the effectiveness of the department's public relations program.　For most police departments this is not practical, so those responsible for planned public relations activities have to do what most officers do — guess.　It may be of value, however, to examine the reasoning on which most guesses are made today.

The Policeman's Heritage

Much of today's attitudes about police and police work are influenced by three factors, according to writers in the field:

1.　American hostility toward government.

2.　Low esteem earned by the corrupt police departments which affects all police departments.

3.　Expanding nature of police work.

Hostility toward Government.　The American people have always been wary of government.　When this country was predominately rural, police existed to deal with the clear-cut "outlaw" and to "preserve the peace."　This restricted role was indicative of the fact that local government generally had few functions to perform.

But with industrial growth and a rapid change from a rural to an urban society, local government activities became more numerous.　Nowhere, perhaps, was the impact of the new urban society more evident than on the police service.　It is almost axiomatic that people living in close proximity require more laws to govern their conduct than the same number do when widely dispersed.　Many cities which doubled their population found they had to triple or quadruple their police forces.

Yet the public's attitude toward government and the police has not changed as rapidly as urban growth has expanded the police function.　On the one hand a citizen seeks protection from the law breaker; on the other he retains some of the cultural hostility toward authority as symbolized by the policeman.　He also may be personally hostile toward the laws the policeman enforces.　Chief William H. Parker of Los Angeles has observed:

---

[5] Gourley, in *Public Relations and the Police,* provides information on how the poll was conducted.　A summary of the findings are also contained in Gourley, "Police Public Relations," *The Annals of the American Academy of Political and Social Science,* January, 1954, pp. 135-42.
[6] Gourley, "Police Public Relations," *ibid.,* p. 141.

"It is probable that no man exists who agrees with all the statutes. This creates a remarkable paradox. Law exists, not because we do agree on what is right or wrong, but because we do not agree. A universally accepted standard of ethics does not exist. To prevent anarchy, it is necessary to impose this artificial standard based on majority agreement." [7]

A result of these attitudes is the citizen's deprecation of police activity unless he believes his safety or property is threatened or that he has particular need for a law.

The Policeman Is a Symbol. As a highly visible symbol of authority, the policeman receives more than his share of the public's hostility toward authority. This is perhaps one of the most demoralizing aspects of police work — public failure to recognize the value and competency of police work. As William S. Gilbert wrote in *The Pirates of Penzance* more than a half-century ago:

When constabulary duty's to be done,
The policeman's lot is not a happy one.

Yet, most observers feel, the public's attitude today cannot fully be explained simply in terms of hostility to authority. It is influenced also by the reputation gained by policemen and police departments in the past. The operation of departments under spoils systems, the influences of corrupt politicians in police work, the debasement of policemen by bribery and connivance with criminals, the manifest inadequacy of untrained, unimaginative policemen to meet urban police problems — all combined to give the policeman a bad name. Unfortunately, police scandals in the decade of the 1950's in many places overshadowed the constructive and accelerated steps taken toward professionalism of the police service. Indeed such professionalism is a relatively new concept, and the general public is not aware of the trend.

Thus the stereotype of the policemen — the image held by many people — is complicated. It contains elements of corruption, inefficiency, and brutality. From Sherlock Holmes to today's paperbacks, the literature touching on police tends to show policemen with one or more of these three characteristics. While television, in recent years, has tried to alter the stereotype by showing the intricacies and skills of police work (as in the "Dragnet" series), the viewer is just as likely to see an old film on the late show portraying the detective as a dull fellow who never takes his hat off indoors.

Expanding Police Activities. While still required to "maintain the peace," the policeman's job has expanded. Widespread use of the automobile and adoption of detailed and complex traffic laws have resulted in an entirely new relationship between the police and the public. Not only are a majority of people potential violators, they are actual violators. It is almost impossible to drive without breaking the precise letter of the law. Police, on their part, are not numerous enough to witness every violation; enforcement is random or selective. The motorist, on being caught, is not nearly so likely to feel guilty as unlucky.

Police work has expanded in other directions. Policemen working with various groups to prevent juvenile delinquency, promote safety education, and the like are not uncommon. The prevention of crime is considered to be the policeman's job, yet historically this was not the case. Some police administrators state that these new tasks have been given them without public backing for the necessary supporting manpower, money, or equipment. Thus they cut into the abilities of a department to perform its traditional functions.

---

[7] O. W. Wilson, *Parker on Police* (Springfield, Illinois: Charles C Thomas, Publisher, 1957), p. 13.

Many professional policemen, looking at all these factors, have come to a conclusion about general public attitudes toward policemen and police departments. In summary, it is this: There is a combination of: (1) hostility toward authority; (2) suspicion of policemen and police methods; and (3) disrespect for policemen's abilities and integrity. This is why the public, in general, tends to be sympathetic to anyone apprehended by the police, with the possible exception of those charged with the most heinous crimes. Public hostility is an unhappy heritage for today's police departments, the good ones as much as the bad. One of the barriers to improved police units has been low public expectations, in terms of integrity and ability, from their policemen. This expectation is reinforced each time there is a public relations failure by the policeman or his department.

While undoubtedly true that a ground swell of public reaction to police department corruption or scandal can make its weight felt, the Los Angeles poll indicates that public attitudes cannot be safely assumed to be one way or the other. There is a real need for further data on this point. However, until someone does the research, public relations programs probably will continue to be built upon an assumption that the public holds negative and hostile attitudes. This carries with it a danger that police public relations programs will be defensive, even though there may be many people in the community who have no deep-rooted hostility to their police department or to the policemen in it.

The Public Relations Program

Public relations should be a conscious activity guided by administrative policies. These policies, taken together, constitute the department's public relations program.

Goals of a Public Relations Program

The objective of a public relations program is not simply to have people like their policemen. No one can have all the people liking them all the time. The nature of police work is such that this is inherently impossible. However, there is no minimizing the importance of having a majority of the public actively support the police department.

The goals of a public relations program, in general, are:

Public Understanding. This is primarily an educational goal. It presupposes that an informed citizenry is basic to effective law enforcement.

Public Confidence. This is primarily a psychological goal. It involves the building of citizen trust and respect for the policemen and police department.

Public Support. Such support may take many forms such as compliance with the law, assistance in police investigations, and backing of measures to improve the police service.

Elements of a Public Relations Program

To achieve these goals, the public relations program must have at least two major emphases. One concentrates on the circumstances of the direct personal contact between the policeman and the citizen. The other is directed to the flow of information *between* the police department and the public. The first involves primary attention to human relations; the second, to communications. The first seeks the satisfied individual citizen; the second, an informed citizenry.

There is some overlapping here. For example, the policeman who addresses a meeting of citizens has an opportunity to make a favorable personal impression as well as to impart information to his listeners.

Performance — Basic to a Public Relations Program. The earlier chapters in this book dealt with administrative techniques designed to improve departmental performance. The quality of this performance is a basic factor in public relations. Good public relations requires good policemen in a good department.

For example, if it takes 20 minutes for a patrol car to answer a complainant's call, that person's attitude toward the department will not be favorable. For him it has been an anxious 20 minutes, and seems like a much longer period. He is likely to remember his anxiety when he thinks about policemen. This provides another good definition of public relations: Public relations is doing a good job and letting the public know about it. Stated more briefly, public relations is performance plus communication. All the communication in the world, all the publicity releases and newspaper articles, and all the public speeches are not going to counteract a continual failure to do good police work. Good performance and good public relations are possible; good performance and bad public relations are possible; but bad performance and good public relations are impossible.

Organization for Public Relations. By its very nature, a public relations program cannot be an entity unto itself, a responsibility clearly assigned to but one person or to a section. Every policeman has public relations responsibilities. From an administrative standpoint, however, public relations organization is a staff function closely related to the police chief. On a smaller force, the chief will handle major public relations activities himself. A larger force may have one man assigned to plan and coordinate public relations activities; in a big city there may be a public relations unit.

What is the public relations officer's job? First is planning for public relations. This would cover the training of policemen in public relations practices. It would cover the development of policies governing contacts with the newspaper. It would involve planning special activities, either on a one-shot or a continuing basis.

The job of public relations officer involves organization: development of means to prepare press releases, scheduling assignments to special activities, and institution of controls and follow-up to insure that planning and organization are not nullified by indifference on the part of the policemen who must carry out the program.

Special attention should be given to establishing channels of communication, both within the department and between the department and outsiders. These must be two-way channels so that those who plan and organize will have the benefit of "feedback" — that is, information about the impact of the program on the policemen and on the public. This is an important element of a public relations program which is frequently overlooked. The effectiveness of a program cannot be measured by the column inches of newspaper space allocated by a sympathetic editor. There should be a way to evaluate feedback. This would measure such things as fluctuation in the number and nature of complaints about the department, changes in the level of public cooperation, difficulty in obtaining support for new activities, public response in given situations such as educational campaigns, and increase or decrease in praise (as in newspaper editorials). The public relations program should be broad enough to permit gathering this kind of data which is an indispensable aid to public relations planning.

The Program Itself. The public relations program includes internal and external phases.

1. Internal Phases. These are the policies or administrative actions whose

primary effects are internal. They include employee relations as they effect public relations and preparation of police for personal contacts with the public.

2. <u>External Phases</u>. These are those policies or administrative actions which primarily involve people outside the department. These include press relations, exhibits and demonstrations, preparation of printed reports, speeches, and so on. These internal and external phases will be discussed in greater detail later in this chapter.

The Police Department's "Publics"

A concept very valuable in developing a public relations program is that of "publics." This concept distinguishes between *the* public (just about everybody) and *a* public (a group of people with some common characteristic which binds them together as a group). In devising a public relations program it is helpful to identify those publics which are concerned and which can be contacted successfully on the basis of their unifying characteristics. For example, a program aimed at improving relations between the department and the downtown merchant would be diffused if it becomes concerned with general public attitudes. It is far better to define the merchant group and aim for that group. Another example might be the problem of reducing pedestrian accidents. An information program may be aimed at motorists ("Watch out for Pedestrians") but the activity might be better directed with less effort at the two smaller publics most frequently involved in pedestrian accidents: school children and elderly adults.

In many cases, this definition of the public to aim at will also indicate the methods and media to be used. As an example, take the problem of educating the public about the steps which might be taken to prevent burglary. Immediately it becomes apparent that there are two publics deeply concerned: the home owner and the merchant. The home owner might be educated successfully by means of newspaper stories or feature articles. The merchant public might better be approached by means of personal visits by detectives who would also leave a pamphlet especially designed for the merchant. It is apparent that the merchant's problems, and the steps he must take, are somewhat different from those of the home owner. Because the business establishment is more attractive to burglars, the special effort necessary to reach the merchant may obtain beneficial results while a personal visit to every home owner would tie up a disproportionate amount of manpower.

The police department, of course, comes into contact with many publics. Identifying the publics and aiming specific phases of a public relations program at them is the best way to get more mileage from public relations efforts. Each public brings a different approach to his contacts with policemen. The habitual law violator is likely to be excessively hostile, the young school child exceedingly cooperative. It is not likely that the habitual criminal will ever be educated to the purpose of police work. Obviously, in the case of the young school child, the public relations opportunities are substantial. This is one reason why police time spent with young people usually is time well spent.

But public relations must not be concerned only with friends. A police public relations program must be organized so that it can make positive and continuing contacts with those groups of citizens who: (1) must support police work if it is to be effective, such as community, social, business, and political leaders; (2) are most likely to be hostile to police, as in the case of minority groups under certain circumstances; and (3) those which have no strong feelings either way but whose attitudes are likely to be important at some future time, such as young people and taxpayers.

Some of the more important publics with which the police department is concerned are listed below. It is by no means an all-inclusive list, but it does serve to point out the importance of "hitting the target" with public relations activities.

The Driving Public. Specific campaigns are needed to handle specific problems. The introduction of new traffic regulations, for example, involves an educational program before the change, periods of oral and written warnings, then strict enforcement. The use of new equipment and enforcement technique such as radar could be announced with stories emphasizing speed as a major cause of accidents, radar as an impartial measuring device of speed, and the efficiency of the device. This would be followed with information on how it works, a break-in warning period, and evaluation of radar's accuracy when compared with previously used methods.

Store Owners. Store owners might be the objective of specific campaigns aimed at reducing burglaries, holdups, and bad-check acceptances. Store employees would be instructed on what to do in any of these cases. Obtaining data for the store report (Figure 33, page 395) provides an opportunity for direct contact with this public as well as to obtain information necessary to the department.

New Residents. It is possible, in small communities, for the police to make direct contact with the new resident. This would perhaps be a visit by a policeman but might also be a mailed leaflet listing police services, telephone numbers, headquarters location, and similar information.

Labor and Management. The police role in labor-management disputes frequently has been difficult. The police attitude should be that the force exists not to take sides, but to protect life and property and to maintain the peace. A public relations program should make sure that the contacts between the police and the disputing groups are made before trouble develops.

Minority Groups. Advance contacts are important, too, in potential conflicts involving minority groups. Some of these groups have known only totalitarian police conduct. Others have little sympathy for existing (and, they feel, oppressive) laws. In some cases, such as lottery operations, enforcement of the law is sometimes seen as an attack on the group. A good police force will learn what the problems are and where the trouble is likely to start. (This is feedback.) Then they can step in long before the danger point is reached. They can head off trouble by using such media as foreign language or neighborhood newspapers and meetings of social and church groups to build good public relations. The community relations program of the Los Angeles Police Department has been particularly successful. That city has many of the ingredients of an explosive situation, yet it has never had a race riot.

Parents of Young Children. Parents can be reached by news stories, through PTA organizations, by leaflets distributed through the schools, and other material given to teachers. The subject matter may vary according to the problem, from how children can be taught to avoid sex offenders to pedestrian and bicycle safety.

Groups Likely To Be Victimized. Some people seem particularly vulnerable to particular crimes. For example, there are: (1) check writers who specialize in passing paper to particular kinds of businesses, such as sporting goods stores; and (2) swindlers who seek out the elderly to victimize them (itinerant painters and repairmen are frequent operators of this racket). Direct campaigning aimed at the potential victims can be used. This would probably mean visits by policemen and, where the potential racket victims are numerous, news stories warning that the racketeers are working the area. In some cases local groups such as chambers of commerce and contractor organizations will lend support and help to distribute information and warnings.

Automobile Owners. A "protect your car campaign" may be used. This would stress the need to lock cars and to mark the parts of the car, such as hubcaps, which are often stolen and rarely recovered.

Other City Departments. Cooperation of other departments cannot be forced. The police department needs to maintain good public relations with them. Cooperation procedures should be worked out at the upper levels. For example, the public works department is a source of barricades, flares, and other equipment used in emergencies. The police-fire relationship should be especially close. However, there are many policy determinations, such as who will conduct rescue operations at a nonfire scene, which must be made by the top city administrator. It is vital that these relations be in working order at a time when the departments must work together.

Relations with Elected and Appointed Officials. Many relationships are involved in the work of the police department, the city manager, and mayor and city council. In some cases these can be planned and prepared for by the police department. Probably the best example is the annual budget. A department which asks for an amount in excess of usual requirements will have to justify its request. Its chances of obtaining the request will be better if, in addition to being a sound request, its presentation is supported by charts and graphs which are easily and quickly understood. The department must be able to prove its needs. For example, a police chief asks his men to work overtime in order to give a selected area the police coverage he would like to have. He then is able to compare crime rates before and after and make a strong case for the same type of coverage throughout the community.

Other Law Enforcement Agencies. A good relationship here is essential. It is not enough to just talk about cooperation. Ways that this can be done are:

1. Give other law enforcement agencies accurate, rapid, and complete answers to their inquiries.

2. Cooperate fully in helping locate wanted or missing persons.

3. Send them copies of annual reports and other publications of interest.

4. Join law enforcement organizations and attend meetings so that policemen can get to know them personally.

Efficient Public Relations

Public relations activity can be time-consuming. Therefore priority should be given to any phase of the program on the basis of its return in better public relations.

Time and Resources. Any evaluation of possible public relations activities will fall into one of four categories:

1. Those which can be done with little trouble. This would include training of policemen in their public contacts and their telephone manners. The results of such training are obvious. It would also include attention to the public relations phases of those things which must be done anyway.

2. Those which the public expects. Examples of this are press relations policies and educational campaigns relating to new laws or increases in specific crimes.

3. Those which are desirable, if possible. These would be those programs which have a second priority, depending on local manpower and resources. A printed annual departmental report for the public is an example.

4. Those usually not desirable. These are the activities which, while worth while, do not logically belong within the sphere of police activity or which would be excessively time-consuming in relation to their contributions to the department's primary mission. Safety education and juvenile delinquency case work are examples.

Setting Priorities. The selection of any activity and the priority it receives should be based on some standards. Several standards are listed below:

1. Urgency. There are times when the public must be informed of police matters quickly. A paralyzing storm can well tax the operations of a police department. It is at just such a time that people will want to know what to do. A public relation-conscious department will immediately make use of radio and television to spread necessary information. A public relations program which is planned and has set priorities will be more adaptable to meet surprise situations.

2. Timing. This is an exceedingly important aspect of public relations. The up-state New York police chief who declared he needed more men looked good because he made the statement on the day before a bank across the street from headquarters was held up. A day too late he would have been merely stating the obvious. In terms of timing, it is probably better to concentrate on a narrow problem (such as burglary prevention) than on a general program. It is best to plan to make use of current public interest, as in announcing in June a house check service for vacationing families. Such effort might show little return in November.

3. Expense. No department will have a great deal of money to throw around, and the assignment of a man to talk to or work with a group constitutes an expense. It is not particularly wise to use men where other less costly means might do the job better. There is a temptation to do this, however, because the man has to be paid anyway and there is no public relations money in the budget to be used for such things as printed materials. An allocation for public relations activities, justified by sound planning of course, will help make the program more effective.

4. Suitability. Should the policemen and the department be engaged in this activity? This is a question that should be answered at the outset.

Don't Go Overboard. Just because an activity may be a good public relations device it does not necessarily follow that it is an activity for the police. The primary duty of the police is to protect life and property and to keep the public peace. The first concern is the victim or potential victim of a criminal. While programs aimed at preventing juvenile delinquency are fine things beyond question, it doesn't follow that the police should form boys' clubs. Police bands can win public praise, but they do little to advance the primary purposes of the department. The same may be said for many other activities. Each must be examined in light of the duties of the police department. It must be certain that the department is making the most efficient use of police time and money.

This warning must not be considered a mandate to "sit tight" and do nothing about public relations. As has been pointed out, the department has public relations whether it wants to or not. An effective program is the only way to insure that a maximum, positive return, in terms of the public relations goals outlined above, is obtained from the policeman's contacts with the people in the community.

Internal Policies

Public relations, like charity, begins at home. It is essential that the policemen themselves understand, respect, and believe in the department and its work. Outsiders won't if the policeman doesn't. If the patrolman is dissatisfied, if the morale of the force is low, then the department's direct contacts with the public will reflect this dissatisfaction and low morale. Policemen are likely to be discourteous if they feel they are subject to unfair treatment by their superiors. Their hostility to their superiors is likely to be transferred to the public. It cannot be said too often: *The personal attitude of the police-man is the greatest influence on the department's public relations.*

Employee Relations

Employee policies which contribute to a favorable personal attitude should be in force in every police department.

Basic Employee Programs. Fair selection, promotion, and disciplinary and com-mendatory procedures, as outlined in Chapter 4, are essential elements for creating high morale among policemen. Selection of men for appointment or promotion on the basis of "politics" and personal preferences of those in authority are damaging to any department. The policeman who finds himself in a "dead end" situation may look forward only to re-tirement. His efficiency as a police officer, particularly in his public relations responsi-bilities, is sure to deteriorate.

Media of Communication. People appreciate knowing about things that affect them. This holds true for policemen. There must be a medium by which the lower ranks are kept informed of departmental activities and practices. Policemen need to be kept in-formed as to what is happening on policy, budget, and changes in operations or organiza-tion. It is not just enough for them to read these things in the newspaper. They should learn them first, because they are directly concerned.

A number of methods of communication are available. In some cases, a formal staff meeting may be necessary. This provides the lower rank personnel an opportunity to ask questions to clarify the meaning of new policies or program changes. Informal meetings may be used also, but they tend to be less effective than formal meetings held periodically and on those special occasions involving major changes.

Departmental bulletins and "house organs" may be used at other times with good effect. Bulletins tend to be formal and concise and are best prepared so that the police-men may refer to them if necessary. House organs or newsletters are less formal, as a rule, and also provide information not of an official nature. These bulletins and house organs need not be elaborate. A simple mimeographed page may suffice, although in large departments they are printed and carry illustrations.

Standard Operating Procedures. Those rules and guides which are permanent should be readily accessible to policemen. These should be compiled in the form of a manual. A good police manual will thoroughly cover two general topics:

1. The responsibilities of the policeman, including what is expected of the patrol-man, how he is to do it, what he must not do, and what will happen if he does.

2. The rights of the policeman, including vacations, sick leave, appeals in the case of discipline, retirement, and so on.

Operating Methods and the Public

Several aspects of police operating methods have an important impact on the public, and deserve careful attention.

Importance of Appearance

A police department should not only maintain a high standard of efficiency, but it also should give an appearance of efficiency. This is created by a businesslike attitude and conduct on the part of the personnel at headquarters and the patrolman on the street.

The Headquarters Building. The appearance of police quarters influences the attitude of both the police and the public. The public does not react favorably to an ill-smelling, dark, poorly kept, and unclean police station; neither do the police officers themselves. While the police may have little choice in the location and arrangement of their quarters, they do have the opportunity and the responsibility to maintain them in a clean and presentable condition.

Once the quarters are made presentable, constant attention is needed to maintain them in good condition. Regular janitor service will prevent the accumulation of scraps of paper and other trash in corridors and offices open to the public. The offices should give a businesslike appearance in their furnishings and in their freedom from trash and miscellaneous unsightly articles. There should be a place for everything, and everything should be kept in its place when not in actual use. The tops of desks and filing cabinets should be kept free of papers and boxes. Storeroom space should be provided so that no material, in boxes or otherwise, need be stored on the floors in the corners of offices.

The offices should be numbered, and a conveniently located directory should be posted near the entrance to assist citizens in finding offices without inquiry. Posting the name of the officer on duty on his desk is another public convenience.

Keep Busy. The clerical force should always be at work. Officers should not rough-house, visit, crack jokes, or otherwise amuse themselves in the public view; they should restrict these activities to the assembly room or to those sections of the building reserved for their recreation. Otherwise the public will conclude that they are loafing on city time. Officers should not indulge in loud, boisterous talk that can be heard by the public. They should not put their feet on desks or other office furniture. They should avoid an appearance of idleness.

On Patrol. The officer on the street should give conscientious attention to his duties. When on foot, he should neither talk unnecessarily to passers-by, nor stand for a long time in one location. An officer on regular patrol duty in a car should not sit in his parked automobile but should stand on the curb or patrol the immediate vicinity within call of his radio. This is especially necessary in the almost completely motorized departments if the patrolman in a car is to serve successfully as the eyes and ears of the department. While he should be pleasant in his relations with the complainant or any other persons he may talk to, he should avoid "wisecracking" lest he be misunderstood. He should impress those with whom he comes in contact with his ability, his knowledge of what he is doing, and the fact that he knows exactly how to proceed in an investigation.

Handling Offenders. In dealing with an offender, the officer finds himself in a difficult position. He must handle the situation so diplomatically that the offender is not unduly embarrassed, yet so firmly as to leave no doubt of his meaning in the mind of the violator. To accomplish this most effectively, he should adopt a proper attitude — one that is positive and pleasant, yet impersonal. The officer must understand that he is not to penalize, embarrass, irritate, lecture, or scold the offender. His duty consists simply of doing one of three things: inform the violator of his offense (this amounts to a warning), give him a citation, or place him under arrest.

Three Common Problems

Traffic control, selective enforcement, and ticket-fixing are three common problems which develop out of police work.

Traffic Control. Suitable public relations is essential to the accomplishment of the police purpose in all fields of police service. Since traffic control involves the regulation of all citizens — those who walk as well as those who drive — this police activity affects public relations more completely than any other.

Before the advent of the automobile, the police clientele was almost exclusively criminal; now the control of the best and most influential citizens has been added to their responsibilities. The most respected citizens are sometimes guilty of bad driving and walking practices, and the police cannot deal with them as though they were criminals or vagabonds.

This new situation not only makes the public relations problem more difficult, but it also increases its importance. The police and the public alike must recognize that people cannot be made "good" by laws, whether "being good" is interpreted as a moral state or as a pattern of behavior that will contribute to the convenience and safety of all. The desired behavior cannot be permanently induced by a rigid enforcement of prohibitory regulations — it must result from suitable attitudes developed by educational means. Only after the majority has adopted satisfactory practices is society justified in applying punitive pressure to the few who refuse to comply with the accepted procedure.

Selective Enforcement. The public resents an unselective program of enforcement, and rightly so. Such a program not only fails to accomplish its purpose but also results in unjust treatment of a large number of people. The enforcement program must be directed at the locations and during the hours of greatest accident frequency, and against the persistent violators and accident-prone drivers. It must also be directed at the most serious violations.

At the start of any new program of enforcement, the police should first tackle the relatively easy problems, leaving the more difficult ones until later. For example, a department confronted by a double-parking problem that has existed for years should not make its elimination their first point of attack in launching an extensive enforcement program. The resentment aroused by police action against double-parking might be so great, combined with the resentment which usually results from an extensive enforcement program, that the entire plan would need to be abandoned. If the police start their program by directing enforcement against more spectacular and serious violations, they are more likely to succeed. The public will support a campaign against them, especially when several serious accidents have occurred. Once the program is started and public support enlisted, a public tolerance may be developed that will make it possible to tackle the double-parking problem.

Ticket-Fixing. Any police department which attempts to establish an efficient traffic enforcement program will come face to face with the question of ticket-fixing. There is only one acceptable attitude for the police to adopt and that is to oppose any irregular handling of traffic tickets. Many departments dismiss a great many traffic cases because they think that this procedure will gain the friendship and good will of the public. This belief is erroneous. Anyone would resent having to pay a fine on a traffic ticket if he felt that a substantial percentage of tickets (or even a few) were being "fixed." He would feel as though he were being "played for a sucker" if he were required to pay a fine when so many others were getting off without a penalty. He is right in this contention. But if he is convinced that traffic tickets are absolutely "unfixable," then he will more willingly pay his fine and less willingly violate traffic rules. Police departments that have succeeded in eliminating the "fix" are surprised at the ease with which the situation is cleared up. The police should install traffic ticket systems which will prevent this evil.

Preventive and Non-Arrest Work

The motorist appreciates being given a sporting chance on the road and resents being "slipped up" on. "In-the-hole" enforcement creates resentment which must be avoided if good will is to be maintained. The frequent sight of police cars induces a willing compliance with regulations. Since violations cause accidents, such patrol is preventive work of the first importance. It is most effectively accomplished by conspicuous and frequent patrol. The public also appreciates and is entitled to a warning of impending enforcement campaigns directed at new regulations or at old ones that have not been rigorously enforced.

The Warning. The written warning, even though it is not as effective as a citation, has a place in all enforcement programs. The written warning has a more permanent and satisfactory effect on the motorist than an oral warning because: (1) its presentation to the motorist is more impressive; (2) the offender has a reminder of the occasion on his person in the form of the ticket; (3) the knowledge that the warning is filed and will be produced in court in the event of future violations has a salutary effect on his driving habits; (4) it provides a record for the files, ready-made if the warning ticket is 3 by 5 inches (and in duplicate); and (5) it provides a measure of the activity of individual officers. A requirement that the motorist sign the warning provides a more wholesome effect on the violator and a more positive identification in the event the offender at some later date should deny having received it.

As a general rule, the warning should be used in cases of inadvertent violation rather than the citation or arrest. The citizen is impressed with the fairness of the police when they warn him for the violation of a regulation regarding which he was in ignorance. The warning is especially suited to the average motorist whose intentions are good, who has no deliberate intention to flagrantly violate regulations, and who has a decent regard for the right of others.

The warning is not effective unless it is backed up by actual arrests. The flagrant violator must be summoned into court; the persistent violator who receives warning after warning must pay a penalty for his indifference. The driving record of the offender, showing the warnings he has received as well as all other traffic incidents in which he has been involved, will then permit the court to deal wisely with the recalcitrant motorist.

In some departments written notice of defect is issued to the driver of an automobile with improper or defective lights or other equipment. These notices require that the defect be corrected and the notice returned to an officer within a stated period of time. When the citizen returns the notice to any chance police officer for final inspection and approval of the repair, this officer has a further opportunity to make a friend for the department.

Notices To Appear. These notices are used instead of arrest for most traffic violators. The use of these notices should be extended to violations outside the traffic field also. They are less offensive to the public than arrest and therefore are to be favored as an economical means of dealing with noncriminal offenders. They serve the needs of the police department without arousing the indignation of the minor offender.

Personal Contacts with Citizens

Policemen must avoid behavior that may cause resentment among the persons they come in contact with. Sometimes this is impossible, but, even when circumstances are most difficult, it is possible with self control to minimize adverse effects. It is the administrator's job to see that men are properly trained to exercise this kind of control and to make sure that the training is put into practice. Police administrators at the sergeant and lieutenant levels also have frequent contact with citizens and thus have opportunities to have a personal impact on the department's public relations.

Helpful Habits

In this section major points relating to an officer's personal contacts are discussed.

Courtesy. Police work can become so commonplace and arresting violators can become so routine that officers are prone to carry over their gruff mannerisms into those frequent contacts which do not involve punitive action. There are numerous opportunities, during the policeman's work day, to exercise simple courtesy, and the department is better off if the most is made of them.

A simple "You're welcome" when a person thanks you makes a deep impression, particularly on those who approach a policeman with some reluctance. Simple courtesy also can take some of the edge off a difficult situation. For example, if a traffic officer issues a summons in an aggressive manner, the offender is not likely to recognize that the policeman is "just doing his job." Rather, the motorist is likely to believe that the policeman finds pleasure in the opportunity to berate him for what he believes to be an unavoidable infraction.

When so much police work involves contact with persons merely seeking information, the matter of courtesy becomes especially important. Policemen should be ready to assist the public in every way possible, since citizens invariably turn to the police for information. The headquarters staff and all other members of the department should know the geography of the city and surrounding area, the principal highways, the direction and distance to nearby towns, the location of prominent buildings, parks, and schools, and the schedules and routes of the transportation system. Every officer should carry a street guide and directory that contains information likely to be requested by the public.

When information is requested, the officer should ascertain what is wanted; to give a suitable reply he must understand the question. A few cities have set up procedures to handle inquiries from persons who do not speak English. Miami has trained some of its policemen to speak Spanish, and to wear special badges. Several cities have lists of municipal employees who speak other languages and use them as interpreters when necessary.

The policeman should answer the question briefly and concisely in a clear tone of voice. If it is a question of direction, he should make certain that the location is clearly fixed in the citizen's mind. If the route is complicated, he should write the directions on a sheet from his notebook and give it to his questioner.

Of course, this kind of courtesy should not be shown only to the visitor. Giving information builds public good will when it is done cheerfully and willingly. The reaction is negative when the officer scowls, is impatient with the citizen's slowness in understanding, or acts as though the question bothers him.

Courtesy is especially important when women are involved. The average woman expects more courtesy than the average man, and is highly sensitive to an officer's failure to do such things as wipe his feet before entering the home. Further, a woman is likely to be timid when approaching a policeman for help or information. Courteous treatment will help to overcome her shyness. Even where the character of the woman is questionable, the policeman is wise to avoid becoming familiar with her. If an arrest is necessary, he should do it quickly with as little difficulty as possible. The way he arrests a woman is likely to be closely observed by others.

Personal Appearance. Each officer should be aware that persons with whom he comes in contact will judge the police department by their reaction to him as an individual. Consequently he should give careful attention to his personal appearance. His bearing and carriage will influence the citizen's opinion of him as a man and of the department that he represents. By inspection, the administrator can make sure that minimum appearance standards are maintained.

Dress deficiencies should be corrected. A satisfactory uniform, comfortable for the officer and pleasant to the eye, is important. An attractive, snappy uniform influences the morale of the man who wears it. It should be kept in a neat condition of repair and cleanliness and not be permitted to become wrinkled or stained. Personal cleanliness is equally important; not only must the clothes be kept in suitable condition, but so also must the body. Officers should be required to shave daily, and to have their hair cut regularly, to say nothing of frequent baths and clean fingernails. They should be in good physical condition. The best uniform will not improve the appearance of an excessively overweight officer.

It is these factors of personal appearance and their effect on the public that justify periodic inspections of the force. It will aid the effectiveness of these inspections if they are called at rather short notice and not regularly scheduled. The inspections will have more beneficial results if the commanding officer makes it clear to the rank and file that they are not just semimilitary rigmarole but are an aid to the force in maintaining those relations with the public which are so essential to effective police work.

Attitude of the Officer. The attitude of the officer is quite as important as his physical condition and appearance because it determines his conduct and his reaction to the general public. His attitude is reflected in his facial expression, voice, words used, and actions. It must be friendly and show a willingness to serve. He must not forget that he is a public servant, appointed for the sole purpose of serving the public. He must not give an impression of haughtiness, aloofness, officiousness, or condescension. He must refrain from sarcasm and flippancy. He must develop pride in his organization.

In his conversation the officer must avoid subjects of a smutty or questionable nature. He must establish habits of conversation which are pleasing to the listener and avoid giving offense either by the subject matter or the method of presentation. Language itself is important. He must watch his diction and his English, lest he fall into sloppy habits of speech. Although these items may seem of little consequence, and perhaps in a more fundamental analysis may be relatively unimportant, most people are judged by their language and conversation. Therefore the officer who uses poor English or engages in questionable conversations will never gain the respect of some citizens.

Personal Habits. The personal habits of individual officers also strongly influence the attitude of the public toward the police. The officer should avoid restless habits such as tapping his finger or foot, whistling, or other evidences of nervousness. He should not permit himself to develop such unpleasant personal habits as hawking and spitting, tobacco chewing, and smoking while on duty in a public place. Tobacco habits that are offensive to the public should not be permitted. Whether on the street or at headquarters, officers should not smoke while speaking to a citizen. An officer at the complaint desk who puffs a smelly pipe while receiving a complaint from a citizen is indulging in an undesirable practice.

Officers should also avoid those unpleasant personal habits considered by some people to be essential to good fellowship. Back slapping, poking the forefinger into the chest while talking, leaning on the shoulder of someone in a group, constant handshaking, and loud, rough, boisterous talk and conduct are examples. Above all else, officers should avoid standing too close to the man to whom they are speaking. This is sometimes done to appear friendly and confidential. People find it disagreeable to have the person to whom they are talking breathe into their faces. The officer must respect the sacredness of the person of the other man. Some people become extremely irritated when another person touches them.

Private Life of the Policeman. The public expects the officer to practice what he preaches. The police should set an example for others. It is necessary therefore that the officer give strict attention to his reputation and conduct, off duty as well as on. He must lead an exemplary life, for the public is hypercritical. Having taken the oath of office, he waives many of the privileges of a citizen. No longer is he entitled to conduct his life freely and according to his own whims, to indulge in the doubtful pleasures of anger.

Putting Good Habits To Work

The good habits acquired by individual policemen must be applied in their contacts with the public. This section deals with important opportunities to put them into practice.

Assisting the Public

While the police are employed primarily to assure order and security, the heads of some cities give to the police odd jobs that are not precisely related to the duties of other departments. The 24-hour, jurisdiction-wide service provided by the police enables them to perform many tasks more readily than other departments and brings them in touch with many citizens. When the plumbing breaks and they cannot shut off the water, or when they are unable to unlock their doors or suddenly remember, when they are 20 miles from home on a trip, that they have left on the iron or left something cooking on the stove, or when they are distressed in any other manner, citizens usually turn to the police for help.

Officers have an opportunity to create good will by assisting motorists with stalled cars. The officer should not shove the automobile to a service station, but he can take the driver to a telephone or to a point where service may be obtained, or he may send assistance.

At the scene of an accident, officers find an opportunity to serve the public by assisting in clearing the wreckage. The officer who calls at the hospital to obtain additional information from the victim of accidents can build good will by his solicitous treatment of the victim and by his consideration in notifying relatives and friends. After relatives have been notified, there is usually an opportunity for the officer to be of assistance in finding lost property or in attending to other matters that arise when a person is injured.

All policemen should receive first-aid training, and those in cities with lakes or streams should be trained also in water-safety. Officers find many occasions to serve citizens by applying this knowledge. Fainting spells, epileptic attacks, falls, fires, explosions, and industrial, traffic, and water accidents offer opportunities for the police to render important public services. Citizens are favorably impressed by the officer who demonstrates his skill in handling difficult situations, whereas they look askance at a policeman who, by his indecision, reveals his lack of training.

From an administrative standpoint, providing assistance in the home and on the street is not good; the increasing burden of tasks unrelated to primary police functions is a serious one. Yet, the public relations value of successful contacts with citizens in minor distress is not inconsiderable. How is this conflict to be resolved?

First, the department must set policies as to what the policeman can and should do toward aiding persons needing help. These policies should be formulated with the advice of administrative heads of local government and with members of the city council. They should be formulated so that they are put into practice over a period of time, with the interim used to educate the public as to the need for the reduction in assistance and to the specific services to be reduced.

Telephone Contacts. The police should follow the example set by progressive business houses; they give special attention to their public contacts. They train their employees in routine procedures and thereby eliminate many small irritations that bulk so large in the aggregate. Business houses frequently require their telephone operators to prefix the identity of the firm by a cheery "Good Morning" or "Good Afternoon." They give attention to the speaking voices of the operators; they know that an unpleasant voice drives business away. Although the nature of police services obliges the elimination of unnecessary formalities, the quality of the voice and the courtesy of the operator are points the police also should consider.

Telephone calls to the police department are important. A person's life may be at stake. Since the telephone operator is the first contact (and sometimes the only one) with the police department, it is important that this contact be as pleasant and satisfactory as possible. Incoming calls at police headquarters deserve a prompt and courteous reply. Promptness is most important. Persons who telephone the police department usually do so to register a complaint. All too frequently their nerves are on edge; they are emotionally upset and easily annoyed. If, under these conditions, they wait for a protracted time before receiving a response to their call, they become justifiably disgruntled. Telephone calls to headquarters should receive immediate response. When the peak load becomes too great for the regular operator, some calls may be transferred to record clerks; otherwise a sufficient number of well-trained operators must be provided. An adequate number of trunk lines must also be installed to avoid a busy signal.

Frequently the failure to reply to a police call does not arise from too much business but merely from indifference on the part of the operator, who fails to appreciate the importance of the job. Commanding officers should check the time taken to respond to telephone calls in order to curb lackadaisical tendencies on the part of the operators. By counting the rings that are given, the supervising officer may conveniently and accurately measure the elapsed time.

It is important, too, that the operator give attention to his manner in speaking over the telephone. His greeting should be crisp and businesslike, to indicate alertness and willingness to serve, rather than slow and indifferent. The immediate greeting, "Police Department," is most satisfactory for the officer at the complaint desk who also operates the switchboard. Some departments require the officer to follow this greeting with a statement of his name. This practice is not desirable; most persons who telephone the police are not interested in personalities but only in service. As a general rule they are in a hurry; they want service at once, with the least possible delay.

The efficient use of the telephone requires good enunciation. Officers should be instructed to speak with deliberate care and clearness into the transmitter. Special attention should be given to diction, use of the English language, and expressions of courtesy.

The complaint clerk should not be in too great a hurry to dispose of the complainant.

However, when the rush of business demands his attention, he should transfer the call to a clerk with time to deal satisfactorily with the complainant. On the other hand, the complaint clerk should not permit deliberateness to develop into indifference. He should manifest an active interest in the case, yet direct the conversation so as to be able to cut it off at an opportune time without giving offense.

Cutting Red Tape. One of the most common criticisms of governmental departments is that their procedures involve too much "red tape." Much of this criticism is unfair, but the fact remains that cumbersome procedures create public resentment. Every effort should be made, therefore, to simplify those procedures which directly affect citizens.

In some cases, the procedures governing police departments are prescribed by law, and not only become a nuisance to the public but a time-consuming problem for policemen. For example, one state requires that charges be filed before the closest magistrate. A patrolman may have to appear before several magistrates during one day's duty tour. While the department can do little about the law, there are many administrative procedures that can be simplified. The department must be fair. Its policemen should not get a reputation for seeking out "cooperative" magistrates where they have a choice.

For example, some state laws require a driver to file an accident report form. It would be helpful to the citizen if the local department prepared a sheet of instructions to help him. Another example is specific instructions printed on the back of a ticket. Not just "Bring this to city hall," but rather, "Bring this ticket to Room 108, City Hall, 12th and Grand Streets, between 8 a.m. and 5 p.m. except on Sundays and Holidays."

Receiving Case Reports from the Public

When a citizen calls at police headquarters or approaches an officer on the street to make a case report,[8] he should be accorded a suitable reception. The officer must adopt an attractive manner, his attitude alert and his face and voice pleasant. Timid citizens often have a dread of police officers. This dislike and distrust must be dispelled, and the officer should make great effort to place the citizen at ease.

The person at the desk should be alert to avoid ignoring a timid citizen. As soon as he sees a person approach, unless he is busy with another citizen, he should immediately offer his services. When making this offer, he should not give an appearance of distraction but should focus his attention on the person he is addressing in order to demonstrate his sincerity. If possible, there should also be a woman at the desk to handle case reports from women who may be timid about approaching a male officer. This employee need not be a policewoman; a clerical employee may be stationed at the complaint desk for this purpose. She should be selected on the basis of her ability to deal with the public.

A person who approaches a policeman for assistance should be given ample opportunity to tell his story. The citizen gains the impression that the police are not interested in his report when the officer's attention appears to be diverted to other matters. Even though the subject is of little or no importance to the police, the officer should treat it with respect and consideration because it is of concern to the citizen. Should the subject matter require the attention of some other division of the department, the citizen should be referred to that office, but in such a manner as to avoid any doubt as to the officer's interest in the citizen and his report.

---

[8] The term "case report" is used here to cover inquiries, service requests, and complaints registered personally by citizens. In many police departments these are grouped together as "service requests" or "complaints." The term "complaint" should be limited to actual complaints about police conduct and actions.

On receiving a case report from a citizen, the operator, information clerk, or other officer should thank the person for his courtesy in directing the attention of the department to the matter, even though the report may appear to be trivial or even frivolous. This practice should also be followed in dealing with unreasonable citizens whose reports may be the product of their imaginations.

However, police administrators are often recipients of inquiries which touch upon the law. Policemen at all levels should guard against the temptation to be drawn into disputes. Some information can be supplied by a policeman, but it must deal only with his own functions in a given situation. In other cases the proper advice is, "Perhaps you had better talk to your lawyer."

Complaint Procedures. Good complaint procedure may be divided into four principle stages:

1. Receiving the complaint.

2. Assignment of responsibility for an investigation to correct.

3. Follow-up.

4. Notification of correction.

Municipal officials with long experience in handling complaints have found these guideposts to be effective:

1. Listen attentively.

2. Don't interrupt. Give the person a chance to finish his story. Don't give him the impression he is not worth listening to. If the report cannot be handled immediately the complainant should receive a definite statement as to when action will be taken.

3. Thank the person for giving the information.

4. Get the person's name early in the conversation. Get it right and address him by name. Everyone appreciates being called by his name.

Anonymous Case Reports. In some cases the complainant wishes to remain anonymous. The question of whether such a request can be honored may depend on the nature of the complaint being exposed, the seriousness of the infraction contained in the complaint, and the source of the complaint. Generally a legitimate complaint should be handled expeditiously, and the source of the complaint should be kept anonymous. However, in all situations this is not possible. If the complaint is in regard to a matter on which the city can readily obtain facts, there is no need for the course of the complaint to be reported. On the other hand, if a complaint is received that requires the complainant to come forward as a witness, then a request for anonymity cannot be granted. In such instances it is wise to require a signed complaint since the only evidence of guilt is the word of the complainant.

Complaints About the Police

Complaints about departmental activity and individual policemen as distinguished from complaints leading to the arrest of someone, are another matter. Complaints are the warning signals which call official attention to errors or omissions in the police department program. If ignored, a bad situation may become worse. If they are given prompt and careful attention the city may be able to render even better service to the public.

Citizens sometimes complain to patrolmen regarding departmental policies and programs over which patrolmen exercise no control. The unfairness of making such criticisms to a patrolman is quite apparent; they are usually made for the effect they have on the officer who receives them rather than in the expectation of corrective action. Such complainants should be referred to the proper authorities for an audience, or, if permitted, the officer may conduct the complainant immediately to his superior officer. When the citizen offers the complaint in the sincere hope of corrective action, the officer should report the matter to his superior. Sincere citizens sometimes make earnest efforts to offer information and suggestions of value to the police. These should be accepted in the spirit in which they are offered, with graciousness and appreciation, even though the subject matter may gall.

Casual Criticisms. A patrolman also sometimes overhears uncomplimentary conversations about the department, which may or may not be intended for his ears. In such a situation, the officer should hold his own counsel. If he is in a group where the conversation turns to criticism of the police administration, police policies, individual members of the force, or of the police generally, the officer should attempt to change the subject of the conversation. He should not be drawn into a heated argument; he is justified in discussing the matter only when the criticism is based on erroneous information that he can easily correct. Such incidents should be reported in detail to his superior.

Difficult Situations. Commanding officers are the recipients of more legitimate complaints, frequently against members of the force. They sometimes find themselves in situations where skill, tact, patience, and sound judgment are needed to dispose of the matter to the satisfaction of the complaining citizen. Although the commanding officer may feel that the complaint is without foundation, he should not permit a shadow of doubt to cross his face. He must maintain a friendly attitude toward the citizen at all times. The complainant is usually under tension and is likely to be emotionally upset. It is well, therefore, to place him at his ease and to allow him to "get it off his chest" as soon as possible. The relief thus afforded him helps the citizen to forget the incident, especially when the officer is sympathetic and friendly. If the citizen is not permitted to unburden himself and if he is treated coldly and without consideration of his rights, the incident is likely to assume exaggerated proportions and to induce resentment and distrust.

When the citizen is extremely upset or especially unreasonable in his attitude, the commanding officer may provide time for him to cool off by tactfully arranging for him to return the following day. An investigation of the incident serves as a logical excuse for postponing the interview; it also affords the commanding officer an opportunity to learn the police side of the story.

In all except the most trivial cases it is wise to prepare a written record of each complaint. A special form containing the name of the complainant, date, nature of the complaint, department responsible for correction, and the nature and date of correction or investigation is used in a number of cities. Complaints on a prenumbered form will facilitate follow-up.

If a complaint is important enough to be recorded it is deserving of a prompt and thorough investigation, then adjustment. As soon as the complaint is received it should be referred to the appropriate officer or agency, and the responsibility should be clearly fixed. If a careful investigation reveals that the complaint is unfounded or that the cause cannot be corrected, a report of these findings should be made. Otherwise prompt action should be taken. A complaint that is promptly corrected may prove to be a public relations asset, but delay will only further aggravate the citizen's sense of injury.

It is not ordinarily good practice to confront the citizen with the officer he is complaining against.

Clear lines of authority and appeal in complaint matters should be established. Although most complaints may be handled at lower levels, some require a higher decision, and many persons will insist on taking their disagreements directly to the police chief. Every effort should be made to reduce the number of such cases, but no citizen should ever feel that he has been denied the right to be heard.

Press Relations

Every police department's activities are covered by reporters for daily, weekly, and semiweekly newspapers in their communities. In some cities, television and radio newsmen also seek information. It is the rare police department which is not the major source of local news in its city.

One would expect that, since reporters have been visiting police stations for so many years, an effective working relationship between the press and the police would have developed. This is not always the case. For some departments press relations present serious problems.

Heart of the Problem

The most pressing police-press problems arise out of a lack of appreciation on both sides for the responsibilities of the other. Indeed, there is much in the nature of police work and press reporting that leaves both the patrolman and the reporter somewhat cynical. Intent upon doing his police job, the policeman may easily regard the job of meeting the needs of the press as an extra chore that adds nothing to his paycheck. The reporter, intent upon his job, may easily become irritated because the information he wants is not at his fingertips; highly suspicious, he brings a negative attitude to his contacts with policemen.

Goals of Police Press Relations. Policemen, particularly those who come into repeated contacts with the press, need to have a proper understanding of the role of the press in society. Because the public is so very much interested in police department activities, it is not likely that a department which fails to provide complete information will achieve good public relations. A police department cannot operate apart from the public's view. The public looks to the press to provide the information. Thus, in order to fulfill its role in the community, the police department must have a positive goal in its press relations.

That goal is a maximum flow of information to the public through the press with a minimum disruption of the department's primary mission. This goal is easier stated than accomplished. The police-press relationship is a highly unstable one. It is not sufficient for the two merely to "understand" each other. There must be sound, workable policies which, when effectively carried out, reduce the areas of conflict to livable dimensions.

Basis for Good Press Relations. The press traditionally has represented the public in gathering information about their government. Some administrators knock themselves out to provide information to citizens who walk into headquarters off the street. Yet they fail to make the most of their opportunities to make contact with thousands of people through the mass media. Why? Because they fail to recognize and respect the traditional press function. The desk sergeant who thinks of himself as providing information to the public, rather than to the reporter, will probably come to the conclusion that the effort involved in press relations is worth while. Such an attitude, in any case, is a prerequisite to good press relations.

This attitude, of course, must be backed up by sound policies. These policies must deal with these questions:

1. Who is to release information? Who is to speak for the department?

2. What information is to be released and under what circumstances?

3. What rules are to govern the conduct of policemen and reporters in their relations?

Because press relations practices already exist in most communities, changes should be made only after an intensive examination has revealed where improvements can be made and the cooperation and agreement of the news media have been obtained.

Meeting the Press. Sound policies must be based on a recognition of the desires of the local news media for what they want as news. Policies should also take into consideration such things as newspaper deadlines and mechanical limitations. The only way for police administrators to get a proper perspective on these influences is to make it a habit to talk with reporters and editors about the problems that crop up from time to time. Major policies should be formulated only after extensive consultation with those who have to make the policies work, both policemen and newsmen. Not only will such conferences permit the development of acceptable policies, but they will also permit a full explanation of why, under the circumstances, a particular press request cannot be accommodated.

Who Releases Information?

As a general rule, information should be made public at the lowest administrative level possible. In most cases, the brunt of releasing information would fall upon the man, a sergeant or a lieutenant, in charge of the blotter. However, where there are other units such as a detective division or traffic division, the men in charge of these units should be free to turn over to the press the information as to violations, crimes reported, arrests made, and, where possible, the disposition of the case.

The sources of departmental information available to the press should be standardized and reduced to the minimum. This will not only relieve other officers of interruptions and permit better control of news releases, but it will also simplify the task of the reporter who need not waste time in covering a number of possible sources. For most news items the desk sergeant is the logical point of contact, although this will depend on the organization of the department.

There may be circumstances in which it is necessary to call a press conference by the chief or one of his assistants. Press conferences should be avoided unless they are absolutely necessary. In any case reporters should have direct access to the men in charge of the department.

Emergency Rules. In most cities it is wise to set up procedures to handle emergency situations, those in which the press would have a high demand for information. In a big city, this might be a major disaster. In a small city, it might be a murder. It is hard to list all of such occurrences, but their common characteristic is that they are important enough to bring out a senior officer to handle the investigation or operation.[9] And in such cases, the publication of news should come through him. This serves two purposes: (1) it tends to cut down on rumors; and (2) it permits the dissemination of news to all reporters at the same time. (It is important that the department does not favor representatives of one newspaper over another or favor one medium over another.) The following example will suffice:

A suspected killer has been traced to a particular neighborhood. It is better to set up the press information activity at the command post for the search. The desk sergeant in charge of all the routine activities should be divorced from handling the burden of supplying this information. It is not likely that the desk sergeant could perform his own routine activity and provide the reporters with their information. From the newspaper's viewpoint it is essential that the ranking police officer be authorized to speak.

Direct Access to Policemen. While it is necessary to have a spokesman for the department in charge of releasing information, it is often necessary that the patrolman talk to reporters. The desk sergeant cannot provide the color which the newspapermen seek. Only the participating officer can say the words which, when quoted, give color to a story of a dramatic event. Therefore, as part of a press policy, attention should be given to the necessity for policemen to describe events to reporters.

In some large cities on events of secondary importance, this may present some problems. It is probably best to have the policeman available at the end of the tour of duty, and the press should understand that its police reporter should be at headquarters or precinct station at the change of shifts. While it may be inconvenient for the policeman to stay around a few minutes to talk to reporters, it is probably better to handle it this way than to have the policeman called at home for the same information.

Routine News. Reports of traffic accidents can be simplified. Many New Jersey State Police barracks have used a system which ensures that complete information is available to the news media on traffic accidents. The trooper, at the end of his tour of duty, files each of his reports with an extra carbon copy which is attached to a special clip board. A reporter visiting headquarters may then go right to the clip board and get all the information needed. Further, the man in charge of the desk may also refer to it when he receives telephone inquiries. Similar duplicate reports were made available on criminal investigations.

In lieu of such special efforts, the desk sergeant should make sure that the blotter contains all the information the newspapers want. The newspaper may be particularly sensitive to the identification of people mentioned in police reports. Perhaps the most common gripes that newsmen have about police records are failure to identify a woman as "Miss" or "Mrs.", failure to provide middle initials, and failure to record the ages of those arrested.

There may be times when the routine channels of releasing information can be circumvented with no great disruption. For example, if a reporter is sent to the scene of an accident, the investigating officer should be able to tell the reporter the information he has obtained from the drivers; that is, however, only the information which appears

---

[9]What may well be a classic case pointing up the need for preparation to meet the public relations aspects of emergencies is that of the hunt for mass killer Charles Starkweather in Lincoln, Nebraska, several years ago. A tense citizenry was confused by reports that armed volunteers were being organized to hunt for Starkweather when they could see uniformed and armed policemen continuing to perform their routine duties such as traffic control.

on his report. For example, if the officer plans to give a drunkometer test to one of the drivers, he should not gratuitously say, "I think he's drunk." If, however, the driver admits drinking before the accident, and signs a statement to that effect, then this information may be turned over to the press.

Telephone Requests. One problem that has frequently caused difficulty is that of whether the police department should give out information to reporters over the phone. There is no easy answer to this question. Particularly plagued by this problem are police departments in suburban areas which are called by central city newspapers. It is likely that many of the difficulties can be straightened out in talks with newspaper executives. It is probable that the newspaper would want items involving major accidents and the more serious crimes. If the full information would tie up the policeman too long, the officer can give the bare facts as to what happened. This would permit the newspaper editors to decide whether to send a reporter to the suburb for additional information. In such talks it should be made clear that while the department wishes to cooperate, it is placing a great deal of responsibility on the policeman's judgment of the importance of these cases on the borderline between routine and major news stories.

What Information Is To Be Released?

Administrative officers and patrolmen who talk to newsmen should be careful to confine their information to only those matters which are a matter of public record and about which they have personal knowledge. The man who speaks for the department — that is, on matters of policy — is always the chief or his delegated spokesman.

This should not inhibit casual conversation between policemen and reporters, but policemen should be certain to make clear the difference between privileged and unprivileged information. The reporter is free to transmit the contents of public records into public print. Comments of police officers, under certain circumstances, are privileged too. But others, based more on suspicion than actual proof, are not. The newspaper which prints them is in trouble. It is important that policemen do not misrepresent the information they give, even unintentionally and with good motives.

Off the Record. Policemen, like all city officials, should keep their "off-the-record" statements to a minimum. In some situations it is necessary for a police official to give background on a matter not necessarily within his jurisdiction. In addition, there are many circumstances which arise in which a policeman is not free to speak because it might hamper an investigation then under way. Most reporters recognize the need for "strings" on some information. However, the person making such statements should release the newsmen from the restriction as soon as possible and should never use the "off-the-record" device to tie up a story that the reporter might get elsewhere.

"A Nose for News." Police officials responsible for contacts with the press should be encouraged to develop a "nose for news," for if reporters are supplied with a reasonable number of legitimate stories or leads they will not be compelled to rely on less reliable sources. If the police department maintains an adequate system of records and reports (as outlined in Chapter 12) it should have little difficulty in producing a steady flow of good news stories.

Monthly and annual reports abound with information that the public would like to have, provided it is translated into terms they can understand. Police officials should interpret records and statistics and call the attention of the reporter to the significant items in these reports. Reporters, in turn, will exercise their talents and use this information in stories that will attract public interest. In special cases it may be well to prepare special releases or formal written statements, but these should be confined to policy matters where misconceptions or misquotes might result. Newspapers as a rule prefer to write their stories in their own way, and if proper relations between the department and the press have been established, police officials will be able to explain most stories clearly without the use of written statements.

Policemen should alert newspapers to those odd police tasks which make interesting reading. For example, there was the police department which was called upon to help get a lion out of a boarding house basement. The landlady took the animal in payment for a board bill but finally had to sell it to a circus. The press should be told of events such as this so that photographers and reporters may be on hand when the event takes place.

Security. "Tips" should never be permitted to hamper police work. An extreme example is the case of the newspaper story which told of a police trap at a telegraph office. The criminal, reading the story, never showed up. Police raids on suspected gambling houses or other places can be wasted effort if there are security leaks. In cases like this it may be possible to tell the newspaper that a reporter and photographer should be at police headquarters at a certain time, with no other information supplied. Most newspaper editors would take the risk in order to achieve a good story. However, only where the department is sure of its security can this device be used.

Kidnapping is one problem area of police security versus the newspaper's quest for news. San Francisco newspapers some years ago cooperated with police and did not publish stories, even though the kidnapping was common knowledge throughout a large part of the community. It is essential, if there is to be such cooperation, that the police establish personal relations with the editors so that they can call them immediately and ask for help. It is essential of course that this avenue of access be opened to all news media, for they must all agree if the effort is to be successful.

One prerequisite to such cooperation is a police force with a reputation for providing complete information. Another is the assurance that the conditions under which the press will be free from its commitment not to publish are understood by all parties. A third is that the press will have access to all information, as it develops, even though it will not be published immediately.

Except in extreme and highly unusual situations, newspapers should not be asked to withhold information. Policemen should recognize that failure to print what is common knowledge to a large number of people is embarrassing to the press. Holding back on information is not a function of the press.

Physical Facilities. In the larger cities it is standard practice to have space set aside for reporters to work in. A press room is not necessary in most communities.

Some attention must be given to the facilities available to the press, however. The reporters should have access to a telephone that they can use at least in semiprivacy. This phone should not be one which would tie up incoming calls from the public. It is probably wise to work out a procedure under which the newspaper office could call the reporter through the police switchboard.

Rules of Conduct

All policemen should be familiar with policies governing their personal conduct in relationship with the press. In many cases, these policies are not specifically related to the news media but certainly have an effect on news coverage.

Access to Records. The policeman should never take it upon himself to decide what records reporters may see. In many cases it has not been determined clearly what records are "public" and thus open to anyone. (Controversy over what is or is not a public record is a sure sign of a breakdown in press relations.) The police blotter probably contains most information that the reporter seeks. In some cases, the press is not permitted to look at the book itself. It is often permissible for the desk sergeant to go over the book and provide the reporter with information, but there must be clear-cut guides for the desk sergeant as to what may or may not be released. One of the frequent sources of irritation between the police officials and the reporters is the practice of some police officials giving limited information one time, complete information a second time, and no information a third. The policeman who regularly deals with the press must never take it upon himself to set policy as to what kinds of information are to be reported.

Important Policies. Specific policies must be devised in handling certain types of crimes. In some cases, as in the giving of names of juvenile offenders, state law will apply. In other cases, policies of the news media not to use the names will be in force. Other common policies of this kind would include the names of rape victims, acts of mentally ill persons, and suicide attempts.

Photographs. Departmental policies should cover the circumstances under which photographs of prisoners are taken. However, it must be recognized that it is only within the jail or police headquarters that these policies can apply. The photographer who takes a picture outside of prison is not under police jurisdiction. It should be departmental policy not to allow photos of prisoners in jail showing cell bars or the arrested person wearing handcuffs, at least before conviction. The decorum of policemen appearing in such pictures is important too. Police in general got a black eye when the killer John Dillinger was photographed with a smiling group of sheriff's deputies. The picture, still reprinted occasionally, shows Dillinger with his arm around one of the men in the group.

Interviews with Prisoners. Whether reporters should be allowed to interview prisoners is still an unresolved question. In some cities, arrested persons are repeatedly shown on television confessing their crimes. In one recent case this backfired when it was later proved that a confessed killer was elsewhere at the time of the crime, and another man confessed later. It is conceivable that police sanction of such interviews may someday be called into question in the courts, particularly where the prisoner has had no legal advice prior to his questioning before cameras.

Special Treatment. Prisoners should receive equal treatment in relation to news media. Police often will cooperate with newspapers by supplying "mug" shots of prisoners. Unless the department is willing to do this in all cases, it should do it in none. It is impossible to list all of the circumstances which could cause friction on this point, but several can be suggested. For example, if it is common practice for the department to take a prisoner to an arraignment by a certain route, newsmen will protest when another route is selected in order that the prisoner may avoid photographers. Violations by public officials or prominent persons must be handled routinely, lest it appear that the police defer to them and not to average citizens.

Policemen in Trouble. A policeman who breaks departmental rules presents a problem. One police chief in a city of 50,000 persons has pointed out that minor infractions, reported in the press, can be harmful to departmental morale.

These remarks are not to be construed in any way as favoring any suppression of the news on action taken by a disciplinary board or police chief in the matter of any misconduct on the part of any member of his force. But too often bad publicity has been created toward an individual and the department as a whole when only an infraction of the manual of procedure has occurred having no connection with personal honesty, sobriety, or morals.... There is a very fine line at times between what might be termed infraction of rules and a lack of gentlemanly conduct.[10]

This is a problem which should be discussed with editors and reporters. As with all sensitive points it is best done when there is no specific case in which the issues can be entangled with the personality of the policemen involved.

What About the Errors? It is probable that on some occasions the department, because of actions of its men, will look bad. The department should be just as straightforward on these occasions as on any other. Facing up to the situation will dispose of it quickly and with least harmful effects. Many police departments have blown up a situation simply by their efforts to "cover up." A good example is the case of the county prison warden who, when a prisoner committed suicide, quickly called an undertaker. After the body was placed in a hearse at the prison gate, he turned to prison personnel and said: "Don't let the newspapers get hold of this." A police reporter was standing within earshot and the warden's own words cast doubt on the performance of his organization when they appeared in the newspaper.

Other Considerations

Several other points that should be considered by those responsible for press relations.

Police Actions. The training of police recruits in the preservation of evidence should deal in some way with the press. In some cases, usually involving major crimes or killings, the reporters will be at the scene early. Because many newspapers listen to police broadcasts, reporters may arrive at the scene before policemen have been able to isolate the area.

Take, for example, the finding of a body in a wooded area. The first policeman at the scene must make sure that the reporters do not mar any footprints in the area around the body. Photographers should be kept sufficiently far away to protect the physical evidence. As a rule, photographers and reporters should be permitted close access only after the entire area has been examined by departmental specialists. However, a ranking officer when he arrives should give some attention to the possibilities of meeting the press's requirements while not damaging the evidence. Most reporters will want to cooperate, but complete exclusion will bring protests.

The New Reporter. The police "beat" has been a traditional breaking-in assignment for young reporters. To an overburdened police administrator his lack of knowledge about police routine, specific laws, and the like can be a trial. Yet most young reporters are willing to learn. A few extra minutes with a new man not only will save time later but also provide an opportunity to establish good relations that will be remembered by the reporter when he moves on to another assignment.

One way that the new man can be helped is for the police administrator to avoid using obscure police jargon. Policemen have given our language many words now used in other walks of life, but there are still some which the public does not comprehend. Few people outside police work know what Part I offenses are, for example.

Some Operating Guides. A police administrator who regularly meets the press should keep in mind a few simple guides. They help to shape a positive attitude toward press relations.

---

[10] Gleason, *op. cit.*, pp. 17-18.

1. <u>Deal fairly with newsmen.</u> If there are competing news media remember to release information on developing stories as soon as possible without regard for which newspaper or radio station will get it first. On the other hand, releases involving matters that have no particular time element (such as announcements of forthcoming events) can be spread around so that all newspapers get first crack now and then.

2. <u>Get to know the reporter and his editors.</u> Make every effort to explain police problems to them. Make your beef to the reporter if you have cause for complaint about what he does, not to his boss. Don't seek retraction on minor points, but of course don't hesitate to seek one if a clarification is imperative.

3. <u>Operate in the open.</u> Secrecy is the prime problem in press relations of governmental units. It is a point on which the news media are extremely sensitive. Administrators should keep their doors open to the press.

4. <u>Don't be irritated by minor criticisms.</u> A quick response to every complaint in the "letters to the editor" column will make the department appear defensive. Where the issue is important, however, a departmental spokesman should answer criticism with fact. The columns of most newspapers are open to such replies.

5. <u>Don't use the news media to send up trial balloons.</u> Unattributed statements appearing in the press should not be used to further personal or factional objectives within the department, or departmental objectives within city government.

6. <u>Let the newsmen judge what is newsworthy.</u> Make suggestions about possible news stories and articles, but don't be irritated when the suggestions are turned down.

Public Reporting

A police department may use talks before citizen groups, exhibits and demonstrations, motion pictures, radio, television, and printed reports to inform and educate the public about police department activities, methods, and objectives. These methods are described briefly in this section. It should be noted that many of the points made about one medium apply equally well to others in this group.

Talks Before Citizen Groups

From a public relations point of view, there are three important considerations in a lecture or a speech to citizen groups: the composition of the group, the material used, and the speaker himself. City officials who have standardized speeches which they give on all occasions contribute little to good public relations. The nature and interests of every audience must be determined, at least to some extent, before the speech is prepared. In addition, consideration must be given to such matters as the age and education of the audience and the number of people in the group. These will have some bearing on the subject of a talk and the manner of its presentation.

A Speakers Bureau. Any size police force can have a speakers bureau. It is a good idea to have a list of specialists and the subjects they can speak on. A policeman appearing before a group of citizens has many advantages over other speakers. Police work is interesting, and a veteran police officer will have many anecdotes which would interest all sorts of groups, from professional men to kindergarten children. Possible topics are many: traffic safety, traffic congestion, parking, juvenile problems, narcotics, crime detection, laboratory methods (such as fingerprinting, ballistics, lie detection) firearms, firearm safety, judo, and operation of the department are but a few. Speakers representing the police department should have some training in speaking. Three other points probably should be kept in mind:

1. A fee should never be charged for a speech before a local group.

2. The talk should be cleared with a commanding officer for policy and information.

3. A planned "plug" for the department should be included. This "plug" should inform the group as to how they can help in a general or specific way. It would be presented along these lines. "Report suspicious persons to us; we want to stop crime before it starts." "We are here to serve you; don't hesitate to call us because the information you give us may be all we need to solve a crime."

Things To Avoid. There may be some tendency on the part of policemen to rely too heavily on statistics in one form or another. This kind of material can be boring unless it is accompanied by illustrative materials. Photographic slides of charts may help make a point.

There may be some tendency to let the higher ranking officers carry the burden of speech making. However, great use can be made of subordinate personnel — particularly departmental specialists — in public speaking engagements. This would supply a wider range of talent and experience.

Exhibits and Demonstrations

The three most common methods of exhibiting department equipment and demonstrating the police methods are the open house, special exhibits, and demonstrations.

Open House. Many police departments hold an annual open house so that citizens may inspect departmental facilities. At such times each bureau or division is encouraged to prepare special charts, exhibits, and working models of equipment. Other features that will attract public interest and help to explain the department's activities may be devised. Policemen should be present to answer questions and explain the exhibits.

Less formal open house activities can be held by those departments that have personnel to take school groups, clubs, and other organizations on guided tours arranged in advance.

Special Exhibits. Temporary or permanent exhibits can be placed on display in police headquarters or in the lobby of city hall. Illustrative exhibits or materials are often highly effective. These might include displays of weapons taken from criminals, safe-cracker tools, and the like. The exhibit can be set up also at fairs, conferences, and similar meetings not directly related to police work. Again, be sure to include a message on what the citizen can do to help.

Demonstration. Demonstrations involve the enactment of a service rendered by the department. Police pistol exhibitions, motorcycle drills, first aid demonstrations, and the like can arouse considerable citizen interest. To be effective, however, the performance of any public demonstration must be carefully planned and thoroughly rehearsed since impromptu efforts which do not come off well serve to reduce public respect for the department.

No matter what is planned, it is essential that the department do a good professional job. Otherwise it is best not done. The allocation of manpower and time to these things are not insignificant.

Motion Pictures

This is perhaps the least-used public relations device. The costs involved are too high for all but the largest cities. Further, it requires technical and aesthetic skills in the preparation of a script and filming. However, with careful preparation, a police department film probably would stand up well over a period of time and might justify the allocation.

Television and Radio

Only a limited amount of time is available on radio and television for public service programming. Generally speaking, this type of program is presented during "off hours." In broadcasting, it is vital that the interest of the audience be captured immediately, so planning the program is of prime importance. Television and radio programs require a great deal of preparation. If time is available, the station personnel probably will provide suggestions as to the content and the format of the program. A number of formats are possible:

Interviews. These are commonly used to deal with a specific situation. It is perhaps better used on radio than on television.

Panel or Discussion Program. This type of program is probably better than an interview for television. The panel should be carefully chosen so that there are real differences of viewpoint.

Spot Announcements. These are short presentations ranging up to one minute in length. They usually make a single point such as "drive safely," "lock your car," or "the city curfew law requires all children under 16 to be off the streets by 10:00 p.m. unless accompanied by an adult."

Dramatization. This is perhaps the most difficult type of program using police personnel, but it is potentially the most effective.

Casual Conversation Show. This is the type of program, usually hosted by a local TV or radio personality, which presents different people taking turns discussing unrelated items. In some cases, stations will welcome the appearance of a police official in connection with a matter of current interest.

Except in cases of regular programs on such matters as traffic safety (which police should avoid becoming deeply involved in), there appears to be little use of the regularly scheduled police radio or television program. Unfortunately, sporadic scheduling is probably least effective. Visual aids can be used on television, but they should not be expected to carry the whole program.

Printed Reports

Printed materials aimed at the general public may be divided into two categories: annual reports and special publications. The method of presenting the material in these publications is of great importance if it is to be read by those for whom it is intended. Photographs and other illustrative devices should be liberally used. Statistical material must be used wisely and sparingly and should be converted to charts or graphs where possible.

Annual Reports. Many departments now prepare two annual reports. One is a popularized version for general distribution, well-illustrated, and with a minimum of statistical material. The second is a statistical report with limited distribution for those interested in details and statistics. Both are useful.

One failure of those preparing annual reports is that they wait too long after the end of the reporting period to issue the report. The older the material is, the less attention it will receive. This difficulty can be eliminated if two things are kept in mind: (1) administrative reporting throughout the period must be in terms that can be readily translated into popular reports; and (2) a definite procedure and schedule must be set up so that the pertinent information will be available when needed. For example, in order to have "before and after" pictures, someone must take the "before" pictures. This means planning a schedule ahead of time. Similarly, in gathering records and data, a system must be worked out and be in operation at the beginning of the reporting period in order to have a summary of information that is truly representative of the whole period.

The ultimate object in the distribution of the annual report should be to place a copy in every home in the city. A good guide is the ratio of one copy for every three persons in the city. This will probably permit one copy for each home plus additional copies for other distribution.

Special Reports. Occasionally, circumstances will arise which call for preparation of a special report dealing with some particular problem or development. Such reports may range from a one-page insert to an elaborate, especially prepared report dealing with some event such as the dedication of a new police headquarters. Small leaflets or inserts can be sent to homes with tax or utility bills. These smaller publications emphasize single subjects at appropriate times and they may be given wider distribution than the annual report. They are relatively inexpensive.

A special report of another type which is gaining favor in some cities is the general newsletter. This is usually a monthly or weekly sheet of information covering city-wide events and plans of interest to all municipal employees. Often items about the police department can get circulation to other employees, city councilmen, and, in many cases, the public.

Reports to the public should be in simple language, free of jargon. They should be attractive enough to win the attention of the people. People must want to read them if they are to be effective.

Other Ways To Build Good Will

Police administrators should be alert to other activities which will have a beneficial public relations result. Every routine activity should be examined, in terms of procedure, to determine if the potential contact with the public results in some improvement in the public attitude toward the police department.

Expanding Public Contacts. Representative citizens who work with the department can take a close look at all the problems of police operation and can be of great assistance in spreading the word about what a good job the force is doing. Formation of police reserve units or auxiliary police is a good way to do this. The major purpose of course is to provide assistance to police in emergency situations, but training of reserve units also is an excellent public relations activity. Police training of student crossing guards is another way of bringing a substantial number of young people into contact with the police.

Activities of Individual Policemen. Policemen, in their off-duty hours, should be a real part of their community. Administrators, particularly, should join community organizations such as service clubs. The chief should join and encourage other officers to do the same. This permits the top-ranking officers to get together informally with business-men and to learn more about their problems. In the same manner businessmen learn of police problems.

Public Recognition. Meritorious service should be recognized. While an officer appreciates a good pat on the back, public recognition will improve not only his morale but also the morale of the entire department. The commendation should be made with appropriate ceremony, with the press notified in advance. There should be something tangible in the award, such as a framed certificate.

Special Efforts To Meet the Public

Business firms frequently spend substantial sums to gain good will. Good will is as essential to successful police operations as it is to successful business enterprises. There are many nonarrest activities which have special value in this connection.

Meeting the Businessman. Pleasant contacts made by police officers with the busi-nessmen on their beats provide opportunities to disseminate information regarding police policies and programs and to explain police problems. Businessmen are thus enabled to become personally acquainted with individual members of the police department, impor-tant because most people judge an organization by the individual members personally known to them. These contacts also enable the officer to extend police service by per-forming small acts of courtesy to the businessman.

The officer should occasionally visit merchants in order to win their support to the police department. To arouse the businessman's interest, the officer should seek his ad-vice and help in the solution of a problem. Businessmen are usually pleased to have po-licemen come to them in this way.

The police officer should watch for opportunities to meet businessmen. The re-sourceful officer will devise legitimate excuses for such contacts, but the department should establish a program to assist its less aggressive members.

Caution must be observed in contacts with businessmen lest more harm is done than good. The officer must not take too much of the businessman's time, and he should bear in mind that an important attribute of the good conversationalist is his ability to lis-ten. There are also dangers arising out of personality complexes. Some people experi-ence difficulty in getting acquainted and make an unfavorable impression at a first, casual meeting. Some also inadvertently offend and irritate others. Although a wise selection of officers lessens this problem, persons with personality difficulties are found in many organizations. Officers found to have unfortunate personalities should be given assign-ments where the disadvantage is least harmful.

The police may provide inspectional services designed primarily as a security measure and secondarily to build good will. Detectives assigned to the robbery detail may inspect banks and other business houses, where large sums of money create special hazards, and review their operating procedures, from the time of the arrival of the first employee in the morning until the last one leaves at night, in order to eliminate practices that offer an opportunity for robbery or theft. The proprietor should be urged to install an effective alarm when such a device is needed. The detective assigned to this work should realize that, while his primary duty is to eliminate hazards, he is also a good will agent. Businessmen appreciate this police interest and usually will follow the sug-gestions offered. Inspection services should also be extended to establishments carrying such stock as furs, jewelry, liquor, and similar articles of small bulk and great value.

Detectives render a greatly appreciated service to retail merchants in eliminating shoplifters and other fraudulent operators. In addition, patrolmen may warn businessmen of the operations of check operators, shoplifters, confidence men, short-change artists, and counterfeiters. As soon as the officer has performed essential police duty arising from the operation of such a criminal, he should inform the merchants on his beat of the danger, give them a description of the offender, and request them to telephone headquarters if a suspect appears. Some departments also provide mimeographed or printed warning bulletins for distribution to the shops, but these should not displace personal notification of the proprietor.

Meeting the Resident. The contacts of the patrolman with the people on his beat also influence public relations. The resident also is an important information source. The old-time patrolman making his rounds on foot in the residence section became intimately acquainted with everyone on his beat. The motorized officer is more derelict in this respect, and procedures should be designed to bring him into useful contact with the residents of his beat.

An effective procedure was established by one department to stimulate patrolmen to make contacts with people on their beat. A weekly circular from the chamber of commerce contained a list of new residents in the city. The names on this list were checked against police records to establish that none was wanted. On a specially prepared leaflet with a word of welcome on the front cover, a record clerk filled in the name and address of the new resident and the name of the appropriate beat officer. The leaflet described briefly the organization and operation of the department and gave instructions on guarding the home and locking the automobile. It contained safety precautions with special reference to school children and instructed the householder on what to do in case of suspicion or trouble.

This leaflet, with a traffic leaflet and a personal property description card, was presented by the officer in the evening. The officers were trained in what to say and how to say it in order to make the acquaintance of the new resident pleasantly. This procedure made it possible for many persons, who would not otherwise have done so, to become personally acquainted with their police officers and to learn something of the police services available to them.

Many departments keep a special watch on vacant homes during the temporary absence of the occupant. This is an excellent way to build good will. This service requires some advertising at the start, but once the people become aware of its existence, the volume will indicate to the police the popularity of the service. The officer should inspect vacant homes on his beat once during each tour of duty, see that the neighbors keep the front porch clear of the usual accumulation of newspapers, advertising circulars, and milk bottles, and otherwise prevent the deserted appearance that indicates the unoccupied dwelling to the house prowler. When an officer calls shortly after the resident returns home, to learn why someone is in the house, the citizen is convinced that he has received a valuable service. Thus the officer establishes a favorable relationship and the department secures a friend.

Study of Traffic Hazards. Another source of good will is found in the study of traffic hazards reported by citizens. All complaints and suggestions should be investigated. A report on the findings and conclusions of the police following a study of the hazard should be given to the citizen who reported it; otherwise he will feel that the suggestion has been ignored. With a suitable study, it is as easy to prove that the suggested regulation is not needed as it is to prove that it is needed when the facts so indicate.

Identification Services. The police are in a strategic position to furnish valuable identification services to the public. Many departments have undertaken extensive campaigns to fingerprint the general public, utilizing the staff at headquarters and sending members with portable fingerprint sets to business houses, clubs, or other organizations on request. Fingerprints so taken are sent to the FBI for inclusion in their noncriminal file.

Some departments distribute to citizens a 3 by 5-inch form for recording the serial numbers of bicycles, watches, guns, motors, or other equipment likely to be lost or stolen. These cards, filed by the police in their alphabetical file, assure ready access to this information when needed.

The Police and Citizen Groups. Groups of citizens interested in special police activities (traffic, delinquency control, commercialized vice, and crimes against retail merchants) appreciate efforts made by the police in the field of their special interest. By giving some attention to these groups, the police build good will and, in return, obtain the support of these groups in solving the problems they have in common.

Those interested in commercialized vice should be urged to organize a local crime commission to fight organized crime. They should be kept informed of department activities against commercialized vice and of obstacles confronted by the police in their efforts to eliminate it.

Employees of retail establishments may be given police lectures and demonstrations, perhaps illustrated by film strips or movies, regarding the operation of criminals. Salespeople trained to observe and informed regarding common methods of shoplifters are better able to safeguard the enterprise. Clerks in banks and other establishments who may be the victims of bandits may be instructed by the police on points to observe to make identification of the criminals more likely.

Summary

The foregoing pages have attempted to outline a program for the average police department to gain public support. The paramount factor in any public relations program is service. Without giving effective service to the citizens no police administrator can hope to succeed with a public relations program. And without any public relations program as such, a police department can gain the support of the public by rendering service alone. A public relations program, in its final analysis, is a program of providing better and more acceptable service.

Many police administrators are handicapped in doing an effective job by politically-minded superiors. In this situation it is the task of the chief to educate his superiors, convincing them of the political benefits of a good police department, selective recruitment, adequate training, and sound administration. There is no simple way to remove the police from politics. The police administrator must realize that the police department cannot be divorced from city, county, or state government if that government is to remain democratic. In the long run the citizens will get the kind of government they want, but a public relations program will keep them informed and will prompt them to demand better government.

Chapter 16

POLICE ADMINISTRATION: THE FUTURE

The first chapter of this book placed police administration in perspective by discussing the general organization of police activities, purposes and goals of police work, and some of the broad problems influencing police performance. The purpose of this last chapter is to sketch, in broad outline, some of the problems and prospects for the future.

Old Problems in New Forms

There was a time, within the memory of most persons, when the portion of the population against which the police took official action was minute. These were vicious, premeditating criminals and others who violated the law for their own gain. The rest of the population tacitly approved police action against them, and there was little serious concern over tactics, methods, and procedures employed by the police in the process. The "product" of police work sold itself.

There are still criminals in the population, of course, and purposeful disturbers of the peace. A look into the future gives little indication that this fact will ever be otherwise. If statistics are not completely misleading, there are not only more criminals and more crimes today, but the rate of increase is climbing. Public support for vigorous action against this element is likely to increase; if anything, there is usually considerable public impatience with the police for not acting more quickly and more vigorously against criminal offenders.

Growth of Offenses

At many points the growth of crime has been documented. The causes are many, but increased mobility of the criminal is perhaps the most telling. Hardly of less importance is the enormous growth of the population and its rapid concentration in urban areas. This development has greatly altered the environment in which crime and criminals operate. While the changes of the next 30 years may not be as great as for the last 30 years, it is certain that the future urban crime pattern will be closely tied to more people, denser concentrations of people, and mobility whether by automobile or airplane.

Crime Patterns. Some policemen contend that many of the old "skills" of the criminal, such as cracking a safe, are falling by the wayside. The expert "soup" man has given way to the thrashing crowbar wielder. But many of the old "bunco" devices such as the "pigeon drop" and "boiler room" sales of worthless stock continue to find their victims, despite widespread publicity given to such schemes.

Syndicated crime shows no signs of a let-up. Such crime, as amply demonstrated in the Kefauver hearings in 1950, is based on vice, especially gambling, narcotics, and prostitution. As profits accrue, they are invested in legitimate business enterprises to provide a front for criminal activities. The interstate pattern of activity in vice operations makes local enforcement much more difficult.

Whatever happens, police administrators will have to be alert to the crimes, old and new, as they take on a pattern. Further improvements in record-keeping and investigation are vital in this regard. Effective use of new scientific techniques and devices is imperative.

The war on organized crime must be relentless. One of the prime problems in police work will be how to increase effective cooperation among local law enforcement agencies. For this reason alone, departments must be upgraded wherever they are weak in their primary pursuit of the callous criminal.

Standards of Law Enforcement

It is presently difficult for citizens and administrative officials alike to evaluate the performance of law enforcement agencies and the administration of justice because of lack of uniformity of policies, methods, and administrative procedures from one jurisdiction to another. Nor is there any yardstick against which the efficiency of a police department or prosecuting agency can be measured with any degree of accuracy. All too often the conclusions of even the most eminent students in this field are largely personal opinions based upon personal experience and the hearsay experiences of others.

With the exception of efforts in the states of New York and California, no two police agencies adhere to the same standards of training; there is no uniformity in the selection of personnel; procedures, reports, and the methods of reporting statistics vary radically. In relations with prosecuting agencies, areas of responsibility which they may share with police agencies are ill defined and subject to change. This does not exhaust the varying factors which add undesirable complexity to the functioning of law enforcement machinery in the state and which obscure the attempts to measure the effectiveness of its parts.

The Responsibility To Account. At this point one encounters a curious anomaly and perhaps one of the principal causes of weakness in our system of administration. Great authority and power have been delegated to law enforcement officials, but no method has been provided for calling them to account. The principle that every delegation of power and authority shall carry with it corresponding responsibility and accountability is traditional in the American system of government. It has been used with great success in almost every branch and department of government except in law enforcement.

Decentralized Police. In all of the states the basic laws prescribing criminal conduct, with few exceptions, are state laws. But their enforcement is entrusted by the state largely to city and county officials. These local officials, who derive all their powers from the state and act in the name of the state, are seldom called to account to the state for their administration of this vitally important public trust. They do not account in any real sense even to their own local government. Such delegations of power without accountability are opposed to traditional principles, and confusion and inefficiency in the administration of justice can well be expected as the price for this deviation. The principle of decentralization is one that frequently is questioned by the public as a result of police failures to do their job. The occasional calls for a federal agency to war on syndicated crime are a case in point.

State Standards. The administration of public justice and the uniform enforcement of the criminal law are matters of general, and not merely local, concern. So is the elimination of organized crime from any community. The state should recognize that it has some responsibility in this matter. The state should require some accounting from those to whom it has delegated extraordinary duties and powers of law enforcement. Such accounting would be easy to institute and at the same time would be far-reaching in its effects. An annual inspection and public report on law enforcement in every county, including the cities of the counties, should be made by some state agency such as the attorney general or, perhaps, some other agency less directly concerned with the administration of justice.

Such an inspection and report should include a physical examination of the personnel and equipment of local law enforcement agencies; an examination into training, morale, and internal discipline; and an inquiry into the extent that effective cooperation with other agencies of government is maintained. It should include an audit of the finances and examination of the crime rate in the community for the preceding year and an appraisal of the general efficiency of law enforcement. If, on inspection, it should be found that minimum standards are not maintained in any respect, details should be pointed out in the report, and, above all, the report should be made public.

This would mean that every public official engaged in law enforcement would know that the spotlight, at least once a year, would be focused on his work and activities and that he would be subject to a searching examination of his affairs. It would mean that the press and every interested citizen would know whether his local law enforcement agencies are up to standard or are substandard, whether they are efficient or inefficient. If they are substandard or inefficient, he would be informed by a responsible source in what respects and who is at fault. This is the kind of solid fact — the data of the social and legal sciences systematically compiled — which could and would form the background for adequate crime reporting, which could and would form the basis for a vitalized public opinion, which would, in turn, influence the progress of law enforcement.

There is in this suggestion no abandonment and no weakening of the fundamental principle of American administration that the police power should be exercised by local officials responsible to local authority. It is not suggested that any state agency should be given any new authority to intervene directly in local law enforcement even when it involves the enforcement of state laws. Such intervention is entirely unnecessary. It is necessary that any agency setting standards and making inspections and reports be a state agency in order to provide standards that are uniform from county to county and city to city, and in order to provide for disinterested inspection.

The obvious effect of the inspection and report is to make local law enforcement officials directly accountable for their conduct in office to their own local citizens. It would make for local responsibility and not for centralization of the police power. It would make law enforcement more responsible to the people and less responsive to improper pressures, political or otherwise. The force of an informed, crystallized public opinion is the only sanction that has ever been needed for the maintenance of honesty, integrity, and decency in government.

The formulation of such standards and their implementation obviously call for long, thoroughgoing study in the field of police administration, personnel training, selection and administration, policy formulation, and the discovery of the means by which any standards agreed upon can be carried out.

The establishment of minimum standards of education, on-the-job training, equipment, and the like, would not prove difficult since there are many police departments at present whose requirements can be taken as models to be adapted for application to all law enforcement agencies. There are undoubtedly many local situations which would require study in order that any set of standards adopted would be sufficiently elastic to permit compliance without causing changes too rapid or too radical for practical accomplishment.

The establishment of minimum state standards of this nature would not, of course, necessarily provide any assurance that law enforcement, in its actual execution, would automatically reach a higher level of accomplishment. Any methods adopted which would seek the uniform level of professional competence for law enforcement personnel, although not the complete answer to good law enforcement, would at least provide the necessary foundation upon which more far-reaching progress must be based and would help to create a positive public opinion.

Public Information and Education

The most important development in the character of American policing in our time is its growing concern with public relations. Today as never before the municipal police department must deal immediately and continually with the entire population. People in urban concentrations are subject to many more regulations than their rural counterparts. As never before, the need for the transmission of information to inform and educate the public as to the purpose of enforcement and the way enforcement is being carried out will be of prime importance to the administrator in the future.

It is generally agreed that public agencies have a responsibility to inform the public. The effectiveness of programs, it has become clear, depends on effective public relations activities.

The need for effective channels of communication between the public and the police will be sharpened in every community of any size. Many notable efforts have been made, particularly in direct personal contacts, to improve public relations. Use of printed materials prepared by the department have suffered from skimpy budgets and an overemphasis on statistics rather than the presentation of important considerations for the public. One cannot see much improvement in police public relations, and therefore in public cooperation, until broad-scale public relations are given higher priority than has been given by most departments.

Policies in the Future

Those who determine policy governing police departments will be especially challenged in the years ahead to provide a better definition of the policeman's role in society. Pressures toward expansion of the policeman's function and activities have been constant. It appears that the police will operate along a much broader front.

What Should Policemen Do?

The expansion of police activity in control of traffic violations has had many side products, plentifully enumerated in this volume. One which is directly related to the future is the great increase in the amount, variety, and character of work the police are called upon to do. In some instances, such as the servicing of emergency needs in connection with traffic and traffic accidents, this increase has been quite logical. In others, such as social services relating to behavior and delinquency problems, the development has gone well beyond logical extensions of essential police functions.

"Call the Police." This enormous new problem has recently seemed to grow at a greater rate. It can be accurately said in many police jurisdictions that today the rule is: "When anything goes wrong, call the police." It has actually been said facetiously that the modern American police department is "a glorified baby-sitting agency." A police officer in a California municipality recently received a phone call from a social affair. The caller had remembered leaving a Siamese cat out in the yard, and his wife had left a pan of beans on the stove. He was asking the police to check this out for him, which they did, finding the situation as described!

The list of services often performed is incredibly varied, including escort duties, handling crowds and traffic at sports events, directing traffic at weddings, providing a community ambulance service, and guarding school crossings. Three police services should be mentioned especially because of the problems they create:

1. Police work with juveniles too often is concerned with welfare-type services such as boys clubs and athletic leagues. Such services are a drain on departmental man-power and, more important, should be provided by social welfare agencies by group work and case work.

2. In medium-sized and smaller cities, a community ambulance service is under-taken for both routine and emergency service. Where possible this should be discouraged in favor of private operation.

3. In some cities police are unfortunately involved in censorship of movies, books, and magazines. Probably no governmental activity is more controversial, and the police should stay out.

What can be done to limit less "reasonable" police duties is not easy to decide. Even if decided, the decision is difficult to carry out. The possibility of refusing to do certain things the police are asked to do, or of refusing to add additional functions to the already existing list, varies greatly from one jurisdiction to another. It depends upon what has "always been done," who asks for it, the strength of police leadership, and many other factors. It also depends upon the character of the community and its institutions and their needs.

Eye on the Goal. The most serious effect of this situation upon police services is not the additional work load as such. It is, rather, the dissipating effect upon the most critical functions of the police — the detection, prevention, and suppression of crime and the protection of the rights of citizens. In respect to these primary functions, the same public which demands all the extraneous services continues to expect complete success by the police.

Today there are good cases being made for complete removal of the "nursemaid services" of the police from their hands and placing them under other auspices. Already many departments are calling a halt to such things as providing forces at sports events or for private escort duty. Some departments are insisting that the transporting of the ill or injured be taken care of entirely by private agencies operating under contract.

Often when a citizen wonders "where the officer is," he is in the emergency room of the local hospital, waiting for an accident victim to be attended to. It is a great tempta-tion to police departments to engage in acts of mercy and otherwise to provide for the comfort and convenience of the people they serve. In many cases this commendable urge must be firmly resisted in the interest of maximum performance of more critical tasks clearly in the area of police responsibility. The loss of effectiveness in this area is too great a price to pay for good-will producing activities, however vital these may be.

Implications for Administrators

The over-all police job is made much more difficult by virtue of the addition of new functions *with no corresponding increase in personnel to carry them out,* or at least no *proportional* increase. Thus, not only must the entire department carry a greater work load, but the work done must suffer in quality. This discrepancy between the size of the force and the increased work load is substantially contributed to by a strange fixation held by many that somehow police departments are sufficient to do whatever they are asked to do. How long this unconscious conviction will continue in the face of the obviously growing gap is a serious question.

Today's police department in a city of substantial size is a "business," in the purest sense, as well as a service agency. Its internal operations are as complex and varied as those of any private business organization, and more so than most. The growing crime situation and the other services performed by police require increasing supporting staff services. Administrative and staff functions outnumber field operational functions. This is not to say, of course, that the field work of a police organization is not extensive and varied. Indeed, it becomes more so all the time. However, it points up the relatively complex array of staff services and personnel required to back up the patrolling and enforcement units operating on the street.

New Practices. Many police departments, beginning with the larger ones, of course, are introducing modern machines and procedures into their staff operations. This is an effective way of increasing productivity without increasing personnel. Fewer personnel engaged in the routines of filing, summarizing, analyzing, and otherwise processing the reports and records of a modern police organization, for example, mean more personnel in the field performing front-line duties. This approach to records processing, making use of up-to-date equipment, must be broadened to other areas of activity and applied in every practical way. Towns and cities not large enough to support the purchase and operation of modern equipment should seek cooperative arrangements with other departments to purchase or rent the equipment. The costs are quickly recoverable through savings in time and better performance.

Other staff services besides records processing are also being strengthened and made more effective by applications of new knowledge and techniques. The need for continuous training of police personnel is at last universally recognized, though it is not universally exploited to full advantage. Research is far behind training, unfortunately, in quantity, acceptance, and application. This is the case in spite of critical need for research in all areas of police activity — operational, technical, and administrative. There is no greater single tool for increasing the effectiveness of manpower and resources than the discovery and application of better techniques and methods which is possible only by means of continuous study and research.

The Central Issue. The "public" of the municipal police department is today much larger than when its principal and almost exclusive contacts were with criminals and criminal suspects. Indeed, it embraces the entire populace. In addition to providing continuous protection and service to many more people, many more *kinds* of protection and service are demanded. This has had the effect of overburdening the available personnel and, at the same time, limiting the quality of services.

Both crime, the traditional responsibility of the police, and the array of nonbasic services have increased, bringing a growing need for large and various staff services within departments. There is great hope for closing or at least narrowing the gap between the growing problem and the resources for dealing with it effectively — in improved staff services, principally training and research. These are constant problems that the administrator must not lose sight of in his day-to-day activity.

Crucial in the future will be the determination of the relative importance of police work to other aspects of local government. It is clear that urban growth has created a new need for expansion of all services, not just police, and the undertaking of entirely new services with a call on municipal revenues. The priority to be given to police needs, among all the demands on municipal resources, will be a central issue that must be faced by departmental and city administrators and the elected representatives of the public.

Police Administration in Metropolitan Areas

The change from a nation largely rural and agricultural to essentially metropolitan complexes and the dispersion of the central city into the suburbs and beyond has been swift and amazingly painless. As a result many urban areas are one community industrially and economically. But politically such areas are still diffuse and decentralized, with political jurisdictions and boundaries unrelated to concentrations of population, production, and wealth.

The most serious consequence of the sudden political derangement resulting from these economic and technological developments is the effect on public services, and most particularly on local governmental services. Actually, the economic development of the country has always been in advance of governmental improvement, but the explosive growth in the last three or four decades has made the gap greater than ever before.

Today, in many areas of the country, principally those characterized by industrial and commercial concentrations, the town and city are being replaced by the metropolitan area. These areas are heterogeneous conglomerations of cities and towns, brought together by economic interests and welded by transportation. Ninety-seven per cent of the population growth in the United States is occurring in metropolitan areas, and the concentration continues. In the words of Wilfred Owen of the Brookings Institution: "Metropolitan areas are rapidly running into one another to form great interstate urban complexes all the way from Portland, Maine, to Washington, D.C., and from the East Coast to Chicago and the Middle West."[1]

Political and governmental organization and jurisdiction everywhere are dragging along behind this revolution. And indeed there seems to be very little desire or inclination on the part of many government agencies to catch up. Within the new metropolitan sprawls there are many long-established small political and governmental jurisdictions in which entrenched dynasties hold the reins of government from generation to generation as firmly as divine-right monarchies. These jurisdictions in many cases have no reason for existing except to perpetuate their own political identity. Such jurisdictions have the effect of dissipating and disrupting the quality of government services.

The consequences of this situation for municipal policing are profound. Professor Gordon E. Misner of San Jose College makes the following observations:

> The total police resources of our metropolitan areas are dissipated by the very nature of their organization! Viewed from a regional point of view, police agencies are seldom based upon administrative needs and convenience. A given governmental area may be quite inadequate as a police administrative area. Territorial expansion — or contraction — may adversely affect the administrative ability of a given police agency. This has been particularly true of many county law enforcement agencies which have continued generally to lose territory to the encroachments of incorporations and annexations.

---

[1]Wilfred Owen, *Cities in the Motor Age* (New York: Viking Press, 1959).

The ability of police agencies in many metropolitan areas to keep pace with the increased demands placed upon them has not entirely been a matter of insufficient money or manpower. Just as important, perhaps, has been the dissipation of police resources by the nature of their metropolitan organization.[2]

The important facts in the municipal police situation of today are: (1) the problem of crime and the preservation of order are following the patterns of growth and development set by the economic growth of the country; (2) in the face of this policing is still operating, for the most part, in the framework of outworn political jurisdictions and hierarchies, enormous numbers of which cannot furnish support for adequate police services and are completely inappropriate for modern development of those services. Therefore there seems little hope of closing the gap between police capacity and the increasing crime rate without some major moves in the direction of governmental reorganization.

Organization in Metropolitan Areas. Many police departments in metropolitan areas are cooperating in a number of ways to improve service, increase efficiency, and reduce costs. This is particularly true for police communications and mutual aid. Technological developments offer great promise for further improvement, especially in police communications.

Organizationally, however, the work is yet to be done in most places. In three different metropolitan areas in the United States police service has been organized in a way that may indicate future patterns.

The city of Atlanta and Fulton County, Georgia, have cooperated for a number of years in the provision of governmental services. As the result of an extensive study in 1950, known as the "Plan of Improvement," the two governments divided certain responsibilities. The county assumed responsibility for public health. Atlanta, in turn, supplies certain services to Fulton County, including police protection. The city by contract furnishes police services to unincorporated areas within the county and charges for all direct costs plus 10 per cent to cover miscellaneous services and supervision.

Los Angeles County, California, provides some 33 services to municipalities by contract or by resolutions of the municipalities. Police service of course is included. A few cities like Lakewood contract for all of their services except central-office supervision and record-keeping.

The charter adopted in 1958 for Dade County (Miami), Florida, provides for a federated structure of government. The county is authorized to " ... set reasonable minimum standards for all governmental units in the county for the performance of any service or function.... If a governmental unit fails to comply with such standards and does not correct such failure after reasonable notice by the Board [of county commissioners], then the Board may take over and perform, regulate or grant franchises to operate any service." Police service is provided by the municipalities in Dade County, but the county also has its own public safety department for traffic and patrol. The county has adopted a metropolitan traffic code with uniform traffic rules throughout the county. It is designed to provide a model, minimum standard for the regulation of all vehicular traffic, and it replaces the 27 different and conflicting traffic laws previously existing. The traffic code is enforced by municipal police officers within the municipalities.

Irrespective of organization it is to be hoped that police departments in both metropolitan and nonmetropolitan areas will show a better record of cooperation, especially in the detection of crime and the apprehension of criminals. All too often interdepartmental

---

[2]Gordon E. Misner, "Recent Developments in Metropolitan Law Enforcement," *Journal of Criminal Law, Criminology, and Police Science*, January-February, 1960, pp. 497-508.

jealousies and feuds stand in the way of good police work. The state police, including the highway patrol, the state bureau of investigation, and other state law enforcement agencies can help by mediating local differences and by providing leadership in establishing forms of interpolice cooperation. There are many opportunities in communications, equipment, records, and training. Such efforts will be particularly fruitful in metropolitan areas.

The Administrator's Role. These are problems, and opportunities, that are not the sole concern of municipal and departmental administrators. They are problems which only the actions of state and local legislatures, acting within the framework of public opinion, can cope with. And it would be unrealistic to expect that suburban governments are going to press for consolidation, in whole or in part, with their larger neighbors. Yet, the day-to-day problems requiring a high degree of coordination between police departments must concern the administrator.

It is likely that programs designed to establish minimum training standards for policemen, such as those in New York and California, will help considerably in achieving cooperation. But whatever success these and similar cooperative efforts (such as those in communications tie-ups) have, the problem of joint police work by separate departments will continue to be one of the most critical ones in the entire field of law enforcement. Short of basic changes in the political character of metropolitan areas, the only hope for effective solution lies in the ability of police administrators in neighboring jurisdictions to work out procedures of cooperation.

The Policeman of the Future

In general, the policeman of the future must be well-trained, be especially conscious of his public relations role, be prepared to specialize, and be sufficiently motivated, with all that implies in terms of pay and working conditions. But at a more important level policemen must be motivated by a desire to take an important and respected place in society. It is difficult to see how such motivation can be accomplished without steady improvement in the caliber of men and the service they perform. In short, there must be further advancements toward professionalization of the police service.

Every activity of police administration will require new ideas effectively put into practice to meet new conditions. This is particularly true within the area of police management. The concepts of seniority in promotion or of civil service as protection (rather than a means of improving the force) will be under strain as the department attempts to make the most valuable use of its fiscal and human resources.

Personnel Standards. It is likely that municipal police departments over the years will set higher personnel standards for all ranks from patrolman through chief. What may be a trend is illustrated by the Berkeley, California, requirement that all entering patrolmen have completed two years of college education. In many other cities, although the educational requirements are not that high, the examinations and investigations have been tightened up in an effort to secure higher caliber personnel. The educational level of the population as a whole is rising, and it follows that police department requirements will rise also.

California and New York have taken notable steps, as described in Chapter 5, to upgrade the knowledge, abilities, and skills of county and municipal policemen. The state-wide opportunities for in-service training are certain to bring more uniformity and a higher level of law enforcement. Many colleges and universities now are providing police training in both technical and administrative fields. This too will have the long-run effect of raising the caliber of police service.

It is to be hoped, although this is not necessarily a forecast, that the term "merit system" will have general applicability to the police service. The merit system stresses a positive program of personnel administration including aggressive recruitment, competitive examinations, in-service training, equitable classification and pay, and other phases of a comprehensive personnel program that meet the needs of modern-day police management. More than the traditional and narrow scope of "civil service," the merit system approach stresses the positive aspects of developing a more competent working force through personnel methods and procedures. In other words, the merit system is concerned not only with careful employee selection and protection of the employee's rights on the job but also with developing a career that provides the incentives for a life-time of satisfying service.

Professionalism. The merit system of personnel administration, when coupled with good government and administration, can help tremendously in developing a professional police service. Another trend bodes well for the police service — elimination of residence restrictions which will increase the mobility of police officers (usually in ranking positions) from one city to another. As Police Chief Bernard L. Garmire of Tucson, Arizona, has noted:

> The idea that police work is professional is comparatively new. But there is no doubt that it is gaining among policemen and the general public as well. And the very term, *professionalism*, connotes nonexistence of residential limitations on practitioners. This is not meant to imply that importation should be the rule. Indeed, many chiefs accept their responsibility to make sure that subordinates are ready to move up when the opportunity occurs. At the same time it is clear that guildism and ingrowth have afflicted many departments.[3]

Professionalism will advance at a rate consistent with the efforts of policemen of every rank to make theirs a job calling for the highest ideals, the highest skills, and the highest proficiency in its practitioners.

Thus far, professionalism within the police service has tended to be concentrated in the subspecialties closely related with scientific investigation. Yet, it is clear, the challenge inherent in professionalism must be squarely faced by those who hold administrative positions. Professional police service depends on professionalization of police administrators.

---

[3] Bernard L. Garmire, "Appointment of Outside Police Chiefs," *Public Management,* August, 1960, p. 170.

SELECTED BIBLIOGRAPHY ON POLICE ADMINISTRATION

PERIODICALS

Journal of Criminal Law, Criminology, and Police Science. (Baltimore: Williams and Wilkins Company.) Bimonthly. $7.50.

Law and Order. (New York: William C. Copp.) Monthly. $3.

Police. (Springfield, Illinois: Charles C Thomas.) Bimonthly. $5.

The Police Chief. (Washington, D. C.: International Association of Chiefs of Police.) Monthly. $5.

The Police Journal. (Brooklyn, New York: Bausino Publishing Company.) Quarterly. $1.50.

GENERAL

Clift, Raymond E. *A Guide to Modern Police Thinking.* (Cincinnati: The W. H. Anderson Co., 1956.) 270pp. $7.50.

International Association of Chiefs of Police. *The Police Yearbook.* (Washington, D. C.: The Association, annual.)

Nolting, Orin F., and David S. Arnold, editors. *The Municipal Year Book.* (Chicago: International City Managers' Association, annual.) Contains for U. S. cities over 10,000 population detailed statistics on number of police employees, salaries, police expenditures, motor equipment, and other data.

Smith, Bruce. *Police Systems in the United States.* (New York: Harper and Brothers, rev. 2nd ed., 1960.) 338pp. $6.

Sutherland, E. H., and Donald R. Cressy. *Principles of Criminology.* (Philadelphia: J. B. Lippincott, 6th ed., 1960.) 646pp. $9.50.

Vedder, Clyde B., and others. *Criminology: A Book of Readings.* (New York: Holt, Rinehart and Winston, 1953.) 714pp. $6.

Wilson, O. W. *Police Administration.* (New York: McGraw-Hill, 1950.) 540pp. $8.50.

Chapter 1

POLICE ADMINISTRATION: PAST AND PRESENT

California Special Crime Study Commission. *Final Report of the Special Crime Study Commission on Criminal Law and Procedure.* (Sacramento: State Printing Office, 1949.) 128pp.

Council of State Governments. *Handbook on Interstate Crime Control.* (Chicago: The Council, 1955.) 152pp. $2.

Federal Bureau of Investigation. *Uniform Crime Reporting Handbook.* (Washington: The Bureau, 1960.) 55pp.

Peterson, Virgil W. *Barbarians in Our Midst: A History of Chicago Crime and Politics*. (Boston: Little, Brown and Company, 1952.) 395pp. (out of print.)

Puttkammer, Ernst W. *Administration of Criminal Law*. (Chicago: University of Chicago Press, 1953.) 249pp. $5.75.

Reckless, Walter C. *The Crime Problem*. (New York: Appleton-Century-Crofts, 3rd ed., 1960.) 537pp. $6.50.

U. S. Congress, Senate Special Committee To Investigate Organized Crime in Interstate Commerce. *Third Interim Report*. 82nd Congress, first session. Senate Report No. 307, 1951. 195pp. 40 cents; *Final Interim Report*. 82nd Congress, first session. Senate Report No. 725, 1951. 104pp. (Washington, D.C.: Government Printing Office, 1951.)

Vollmer, August. *The Police and Modern Society*. (Berkeley: University of California Press, 1936.) 253pp. (out of print.)

Chapter 2

POLICE ORGANIZATION

Gulick, Luther. "Notes on the Theory of Organization," in Luther Gulick and L. Urwick, editors, *Papers on the Science of Administration*. (New York: Institute of Public Administration, 1937.) 196pp. $3.

James, Charles S. *A Frontier of Municipal Safety*. (Chicago: Public Administration Service, 1955.) 169pp. $4.

_____. *Police and Fire Integration in the Small City*. (Chicago: Public Administration Service, 1955.) 144pp. $2.

International City Managers' Association. *The Technique of Municipal Administration*. (Chicago: The Association, 4th ed., 1958.) 441pp. $7.50.

Kenney, John P. *Police Management Planning*. (Springfield, Illinois: Charles C Thomas, 1959.) 149pp. $5.25.

MacNamara, Donal E. J. *A Study and Survey of Municipal Police Departments of the State of New Jersey*. (Trenton: New Jersey Law Enforcement Council, 1958.) 113pp.

Wilson, O. W. *Police Planning*. (Springfield, Illinois: Charles C Thomas, 2nd ed., 1958.) 492pp. $8.75.

Chapter 3

POLICE MANAGEMENT

Brunton, Robert L., and Jeptha J. Carrell. *Management Practices for Smaller Cities*. (Chicago: International City Managers' Association, 1959.) 430pp. $7.50.

Bush, George P., and Lowell H. Hattery, editors. *Scientific Research: Its Administration and Organization*. (Washington, D.C.: University Press of Washington, D.C., 1950.) $3.50.

Forbes, Russell. *Purchasing for Small Cities*. (Chicago: Public Administration Service, 1951.) 23pp. $1.

Griffin, John I. *Statistics Essential for Police Efficiency*. (Springfield, Illinois: Charles C Thomas, 1958.) 229pp. $7.50.

International City Managers' Association. *Municipal Finance Administration*. (Chicago: The Association, 1955.) 461pp. $7.50. Chapters on budgeting.

Sherwood, Frank P., and Wallace H. Best. *Supervisory Methods in Municipal Administration*. (Chicago: International City Managers' Association, 1958.) 302pp. $7.50.

Vogel, Joshua A. *Police Stations: Planning and Specifications*. (Seattle, Washington: Bureau of Governmental Research and Services, University of Washington, 1954.) 75pp. $3.

Wilson, O. W. *Police Planning*. (Springfield, Illinois: Charles C Thomas, 2nd ed., 1958.) 492pp. $8.75.

Chapter 4

PERSONNEL MANAGEMENT

Brunton, Robert L. *A Manual for Municipal In-Service Training*. (Chicago: International City Managers' Association, 1960.) 40pp. $2.

Coppock, Robert W., and Barbara B. Coppock. *How To Recruit and Select Policemen and Firemen*. (Chicago: Public Personnel Association, 1958.) 65pp. $5.

Germann, A. C. *Police Personnel Management*. (Springfield, Illinois: Charles C Thomas, 1958.) 251pp. $6.75.

International Association of Chiefs of Police. *Police Unions*. (Washington, D.C.: The Association, rev. ed., 1958.) 74pp. $1.

International City Managers' Association. *Municipal Personnel Administration*. (Chicago: The Association, 6th ed., 1960.) 414pp. $7.50.

Municipal Finance Officers Association. *Retirement Plans for Public Employees*. (Chicago: The Association, 1958.) 52pp. $2.50.

Stahl, O. Glenn. *Public Personnel Administration*. (New York: Harper and Brothers, 4th ed., 1956.) 628pp. $7.50.

Tead, Ordway. *Art of Leadership*. (New York: McGraw-Hill, 1935.) 308pp. $4.50.

Chapter 5

TRAINING

Cahalane, Cornelius F. *The Policeman's Guide; A Manual of Study and Instruction*. (New York: Harper and Brothers, 1952.) 276pp. (out of print.)

Frost, Thomas M. *A Forward Look in Police Education*. (Springfield, Illinois: Charles C Thomas, 1959.) 290pp. $8.75.

Los Angeles Police Department. *Daily Training Bulletin*. (Springfield, Illinois: Charles C Thomas.) Volume 1, 1954. 284pp. $7.50. Volume 2, 1958. 287pp. $8.50.

Michigan State College, Department of Police Administration. *Command Officers Training, 1951*. (East Lansing, Michigan: The Department, 1951.) Variously paged.

Chapter 6

JUVENILES

American Academy of Political and Social Science. "Prevention of Juvenile Delinquency." *The Annals*, March, 1959. (Philadelphia: The Academy.) 213pp. $2.

Barnes, Harry E., and Negley K. Teeters. *New Horizons in Criminology*. (Englewood Cliffs, New Jersey: Prentice-Hall, 3rd ed., 1959.) 654pp. $7.95.

California Special Crime Study Commission. *Final Report of the Special Crime Study Commission on Juvenile Justice*. (Sacramento: State Printing Office, 1949.) 84pp.

——————————. *Final Report of the Special Crime Study Commission on Social and Economic Causes of Crime and Delinquency*. (Sacramento: State Printing Office, 1949.) 107pp.

California Youth Authority. *A Guide for Juvenile Control by Law Enforcement Agencies*. (Sacramento: The Authority, 1951.) 31pp.

Delinquency Control Institute. *Delinquency Prevention and Control*. (Los Angeles: University of Southern California, 1946.) Six volumes under various titles on this subject, mimeographed.

Ellingston, John R. *Protecting Our Children from Criminal Careers*. (Englewood Cliffs, New Jersey: Prentice-Hall, 1948.) 374pp. $5.

Glueck, Sheldon, and Eleanor Glueck. *Predicting Delinquency and Crime*. (Cambridge, Massachusetts: Harvard University Press, 1959.) 283pp. $6.50.

Levin, J. L. *How Cities Control Juvenile Delinquency*. (Chicago: American Municipal Association, 1957.) 56pp. $2.50.

National Conference on Prevention and Control of Juvenile Delinquency. *Summaries and Recommendations for Action*. (Washington, D.C.: Government Printing Office, 1947.) 136pp. 30 cents. Other reports by this conference are available.

School of Law, Duke University. "Correction of Youthful Offenders." *Law and Contemporary Problems*, Autumn, 1942, entire issue. (Durham, North Carolina: Duke University, 1942.) pp. 579-764. $2.50.

Shaw, Clifford R. *Delinquency Areas*. (Chicago: University of Chicago Press, 1929.) 214pp. (out of print.)

U. S. Children's Bureau. *Police Services for Juveniles*. (Washington, D.C.: Government Printing Office, 1954.) 91pp. 35 cents.

U. S. Federal Security Agency, National Advisory Police Committee on Social Protection. *Techniques in Law Enforcement in the Use of Policewomen with Special Reference to Social Protection*. (Washington, D.C.: The Agency, 1945.) 93pp.

——————————. *Techniques of Law Enforcement in the Treatment of Juveniles and the Prevention of Juvenile Delinquency*. (Washington, D.C.: The Agency, 1944.) 60pp.

Vedder, B. Clyde. *The Juvenile Offender*. (New York: Random House, 1954.) 510pp. $6.

Vollmer, August. *The Criminal*. (New York: Foundation Press, 1949.) 462pp. $4. (out of print.)

Winters, John E. *Crime and Kids*. (Springfield, Illinois: Charles C Thomas, 1959.) 176pp. $5.25.

Chapter 7

THE PATROL FUNCTION

Bristow, Allen P. *Field Interrogation*. (Springfield, Illinois: Charles C Thomas, 1958.) 101pp. $3.75.

Chapman, Samuel G. *Dogs in Police Work: A Summary of Experience in Great Britain and the United States*. (Chicago: Public Administration Service, 1960.) 101pp. $3.

Cahalane, Cornelius F. *Policeman's Guide: A Manual of Study and Instruction*. (New York: Harper and Brothers, 1952.) 276pp. $3.50.

Gilston, David H., and Lawrence Podell. *The Practical Patrolman*. (Springfield, Illinois: Charles C Thomas, 1959.) 255pp. (out of print.)

Gocke, Blye W. *Police Sergeants Manual*. (Los Angeles: Legal Book Store, 4th ed., 1960.) 296pp. $4.50.

Heffron, Floyd N. *Evidence for the Patrolman*. (Springfield, Illinois: Charles C Thomas, 1958.) 216pp. $5.75.

Holcomb, Richard L. *Police Patrol*. (Springfield, Illinois: Charles C Thomas, 1957.) 128pp. $3.

Holmgren, R. Bruce. *Primary Police Functions*. (New York: William C. Copp and Associates, 1960.) 212pp.

Nelson, Alfred T., and Howard E. Smith. *Car Clouting: The Crime, the Criminal, and the Police*. (Springfield, Illinois: Charles C Thomas, 1958.) 156pp. $4.75.

Chapter 8

CRIME INVESTIGATION

Battle, Brendon P., and Paul B. Weston. *Arson — A Handbook of Detection and Investigation*. (New York: Arco, 1959.) 287pp. $3.50.

Bridges, B. C. *Practical Fingerprinting*. (New York: Funk & Wagnalls, 1942.) 374pp. $4.

Dax, Hubert E., and Rooke B. Tibbs. *Arrest, Search and Seizure*. (Milwaukee: Hammer-smith-Kortmeyer, 1946.) 195pp. $3.50.

Dienstein, William. *Technics for the Crime Investigator*. (Springfield, Illinois: Charles C Thomas, 1959.) 248pp. $6.50.

Else, Walter Martyne, and James Main Garrow. *The Detection of Crime*. (London: The Police Journal, 1934.) 195pp. $2.50. Excellent manual on the nature of evidence.

Fitzgerald, Maurice J. *Handbook of Criminal Investigation*. (New York: Arco, 1959.) 238pp. $3.50.

Heffron, Floyd N. *The Officer in the Courtroom*. (Springfield, Illinois: Charles C Thomas, 1955.) 175pp. $4.50.

Hilton, Ordway. *Scientific Examination of Questioned Documents*. (Chicago: Callaghan and Company, 1956.) 342pp. $15.

Houts, Marshall. *From Evidence to Proof: A Searching Analysis of Methods To Establish Fact*. (Springfield, Illinois: Charles C Thomas, 1956.) 416pp. $7.50.

——————. *The Rules of Evidence*. (Springfield, Illinois: Charles C Thomas, 1956.) 126pp. $3.75.

Inbau, Fred E., and John E. Reid. *Lie Detection and Criminal Investigation*. (Baltimore: Williams and Wilkins Company, 3rd ed., 1953.) 242pp. $5.

Jones, Leland V. *Scientific Investigation and Physical Evidence: A Handbook for Investigators*. (Springfield, Illinois: Charles C Thomas, 1959.) 312pp. $8.50.

Kessler, William F., and Paul B. Weston. *Detection of Murder*. (New York: Arco, 1959.) 239pp. $3.50.

Kirk, Paul L. *Crime Investigation*. (New York: Interscience Publishers, 1960.) 784pp. $7.95.

O'Hara, Charles E. *Fundamentals of Criminal Investigation*. (Springfield, Illinois: Charles C Thomas, 1956.) 744pp. $8.50.

——————. *Photography in Law Enforcement*. (Rochester, New York: Eastman Kodak Company, 1959.) 80pp. $1.25.

Soderman, Harry, and John J. O'Connell. *Modern Criminal Investigation*. (New York: Funk and Wagnalls, 4th rev. ed., 1952.) 557pp. $4.75.

Snyder, Lemoyne. *Homicide Investigation*. (Springfield, Illinois: Charles C Thomas, 1959.) 384pp. $8.50.

Chapter 9

VICE CONTROL

American Academy of Political and Social Science. "Gambling," *The Annals*, May, 1950. (Philadelphia: The Academy.) 209pp. $2.

Anslinger, Harry J., and William F. Tompkins. *Traffic in Narcotics*. (New York: Funk and Wagnalls, 1953.) 335pp. $4.95.

California Special Crime Study Commission. *Final Report of the Special Crime Study Commission on Organized Crime*. (Sacramento: State Printing Office, 1953.) 131pp.

Egen, Frederick W. *Plainclothesman: A Handbook of Vice and Gambling Investigation*. (New York: Arco, 1959.) 230pp. $3.50.

Goldin, Hyman E., and others, editors. *Dictionary of American Underworld Lingo*. (New York: Twayne Publishers, 1950.) 327pp. $5.

Harney, Malachi L., and John C. Cross. *The Informer in Law Enforcement*. (Springfield, Illinois: Charles C Thomas, 1959.) 83pp. $4.50.

Maurer, David W., and Victor H. Vogel. *Narcotics and Narcotics Addiction*. (Springfield, Illinois: Charles C Thomas, 1954.) 320pp. $7.50.

Peterson, Virgil W. *Gambling: Should It Be Legalized?* (Springfield, Illinois: Charles C Thomas, 1951.) 128pp. $2.75.

U. S. Attorney General's Conference on Organized Crime, February 15, 1950. *Proceedings*. (Washington, D. C.: U. S. Department of Justice, 1950.) 308pp.

U. S. Bureau of Narcotics. *Comments on Narcotic Drugs*. (Interim Report of the Joint Committee of the American Bar Association and the American Medical Association on Narcotic Drugs by Advisory Committee to the Federal Bureau of Narcotics.) (Washington, D. C.: Government Printing Office, 1959.) 186pp. 60 cents.

U. S. Federal Security Agency, National Advisory Police Committee. *Techniques of Law Enforcement Against Prostitution*. (Washington, D. C.: Government Printing Office, 1943.) 75pp.

Chapter 10

TRAFFIC SUPERVISION

American Bar Association and Traffic Institute of Northwestern University. *Judge and Prosecutor in Traffic Court: A Symposium for Traffic Court Judges and Prosecutors Conferences*. (Evanston, Illinois: The Institute, 1951.) 345pp. (out of print.)

Baker, James Stannard. *Traffic Accident Investigator's Manual for Police*. (Evanston, Illinois: Traffic Institute of Northwestern University, 2nd ed., 1957.) 617pp. $7.50.

Baker, James Stannard, and William R. Stebbins. *Dictionary of Highway Traffic*. (Evanston, Illinois: Traffic Institute of Northwestern University, 1960.) 336pp. $6.

Donigan, Robert L. *Chemical Tests and the Law*. (Evanston, Illinois: Traffic Institute of Northwestern University, 1957.) 257pp. $7.25.

Donigan, Robert L., and Edward C. Fisher. *Know the Law*. (Evanston, Illinois: Traffic Institute of Northwestern University, 1958.) 442pp. $7.

——————. *The Evidence Handbook*. (Evanston, Illinois: Traffic Institute of Northwestern University, 1958.) 205pp. $5.

Evans, Henry K., and Franklin M. Kreml. *Traffic Engineering and the Police*. (Evanston, Illinois: National Conservation Bureau and International Association of Chiefs of Police, 1947.) 103pp. (out of print.)

Fisher, Edward C. *Right of Way in Traffic Law Enforcement*. (St. Louis: Thomas Law Book Company, 1956.) 265pp. $7.50.
——————————. *Traffic Officer in Court*. (Evanston, Illinois: Traffic Institute of Northwestern University, rev. ed., 1960.) 13pp. 35 cents.
International Association of Chiefs of Police. *Definitions and Enforcement Rates*. (Evanston, Illinois: Traffic Institute of Northwestern University, 1950.) 18pp.
Joint Committee of American Association of State Highway Officials, American Public Works Association, and Institute of Traffic Engineers. *Traffic Engineering: Functions and Administration*. (Chicago: Public Administration Service, 1948, reprinted 1953.) 137pp. $2.50.
National Committee on Uniform Traffic Laws and Ordinances. *Model Traffic Ordinance*. (Washington, D.C.: The Committee, 1956.) 61pp.
——————————. *Uniform Vehicle Code*. (Washington, D.C.: The Committee, 1954.) 179pp.
National Conference on Uniform Traffic Accident Statistics. *Uniform Definitions of Motor Vehicle Accidents*. (Washington, D.C.: Government Printing Office, rev. ed., 1954.) 20pp.
Traffic Institute of Northwestern University. *Traffic Law Enforcement Series*. (Evanston, Illinois: The Institute.) In-service training manuals at modest prices. Complete list available from the Traffic Institute, 1804 Hinman Avenue, Evanston.
U. S. President's Highway Safety Conference. *Report of Committee on Enforcement*. (Washington, D.C.: Government Printing Office, 1949.) 53pp. 20 cents.

Chapter 11

COMMUNICATIONS

Associated Police Communications Officers, Inc. *The National Police Communications Network Directory*. (Detroit: The author, 6th ed., 1951.) 284pp. $3.50.
Leonard, V. A. *Police Communications System*. (Berkeley: University of California Press, 1938.) 589pp. $5.
Nolting, Orin F. *Public Emergency Communications Systems*. (Chicago: International City Managers' Association, 1956.) 27pp. $2.

Chapter 12

RECORDS

Griffin, John I. *Statistics Essential for Police Efficiency*. (Springfield, Illinois: Charles C Thomas, 1958.) 229pp. $7.50.
Ridley, Clarence E., and Herbert A. Simon. *Measuring Municipal Activities*. (Chicago: International City Managers' Association, 1943.) Chapter IV. (out of print.)
Federal Bureau of Investigation. *Manual of Police Records*. (Washington: The Bureau, rev. ed., 1953.) 56pp.
——————————. *Uniform Crime Reports*. (Washington, D.C.: The Bureau, annual.)
Wilson, O. W. *Police Records: Their Installation and Use*. (Chicago: Public Administration Service, 1942, reprinted 1955.) 336pp. $6.

Chapter 13

OTHER POLICE PROBLEMS

Alexander, Myrl E. *Jail Administration.* (Springfield, Illinois: Charles C Thomas, 1957.) 326pp. $6.75.

California Department of Justice, Division of Criminal Law and Enforcement. *A Guide to Race Relations for Peace Officers.* (Chicago: American Council on Race Relations, 1958.) 53pp.

Casey, Roy. *The Modern Jail: Design, Equipment, Operation.* (Keene, Texas: Continental Press, 1958.) 89pp. $3.

Davis, John Richelieu. *Industrial Plant Protection.* (Springfield, Illinois: Charles C Thomas, 1957.) 566pp. $12.

Howe, James V. *The Modern Gunsmith.* (New York: Funk and Wagnalls, 1941.) 2 volumes. $15.

International City Managers' Association. *Municipal Public Works Administration.* (Chicago: The Association, 5th ed., 1957.) 449pp. $7.50. Chapters 10, "Equipment Management."

Kephart, William M. *Racial Factors and Urban Law Enforcement.* (Philadelphia: University of Pennsylvania Press, 1957.) 209pp. $5.

King, Everett M. *The Auxiliary Police Unit.* (Springfield, Illinois: Charles C Thomas, 1960.) 215pp. $8.75.

Louisville Division of Police, Committee on Police Training. *Principles of Police Work with Minority Groups.* (Louisville, Kentucky: The Division, 1950.) 129pp.

Millspaugh, Arthur C. *Local Democracy and Crime Control.* (Washington, D.C.: Brookings Institution, 1936.) 263pp. $2.

_____. *Crime Control by the National Government.* (Washington, D.C.: Brookings Institution, 1937.) 303pp. $2.

Sharpe, Philip B. *Complete Guide to Handloading.* (New York: Funk and Wagnalls, rev. 3rd ed., 1952.) 479pp. $10.

Weckler, J. E., and Theo E. Hall. *The Police and Minority Groups.* (Chicago: International City Managers' Association, 1944.) 20pp. (out of print.)

Chapter 14

THE POLICE AND THE PUBLIC

Kooken, Don L. *Ethics in Police Service.* (Springfield, Illinois: Charles C Thomas, 1957.) 80pp. $3.

Wilson, O. W., editor. *Parker on Police.* (Springfield, Illinois: Charles C Thomas, 1956.) 235pp. $4.75.

Chapter 15

POLICE PUBLIC RELATIONS PROGRAMS

Brashear, Ernest. *Municipal Public Relations Techniques.* (Chicago: International City Managers' Association, to be published in 1961.) Approx. 250pp.

Goetz, Rachel. *Visual Aids for the Public Service.* (Chicago: Public Administration Service, 1954.) 89pp. $3.25.

Gourley, C. Douglas. *Public Relations and the Police*. (Springfield, Illinois: Charles C Thomas, 1953.) 123pp. $5.75.

Holcomb, Richard L. *The Police and the Public*. (Springfield, Illinois: Charles C Thomas, 1957.) 36pp. $1.

Hollingsworth, Dan. *Rocks in the Roadway: A Treatise on Police Public Relations*. (Chicago: Stromberg-Allen and Company, 1954.) 51pp. $1.

King, Everett M. *The Officer Speaks in Public*. (Springfield, Illinois: Charles C Thomas, 1958.) 216pp. $5.75.

Ruhl, Eleanor S. *Public Relations for Government Employees: An Action Program*. (Chicago: Public Personnel Association, 1952.) 32pp. $2.

Chapter 16

POLICE ADMINISTRATION: THE FUTURE

American Academy of Political and Social Science. "New Goals in Police Management." *The Annals*, January, 1954. (Philadelphia: The Academy.) 220pp. $2.

Frost, Thomas M. *A Forward Look in Police Education*. (Springfield, Illinois: Charles C Thomas, 1959.) 290pp. $8.75.

Smith, Bruce. *Police Systems in the United States*. (New York: Harper and Brothers, rev. 2nd ed., 1960.) 338pp. $6. See Chapter 11.

INDEX